THE GENESIS

OF THE

UNITED STATES

THE GENESIS

OF THE

UNITED STATES

A NARRATIVE OF THE MOVEMENT IN ENGLAND, 1605–1616, WHICH
RESULTED IN THE PLANTATION OF NORTH AMERICA BY
ENGLISHMEN, DISCLOSING THE CONTEST BETWEEN ENGLAND
AND SPAIN FOR THE POSSESSION OF THE SOIL NOW OCCUPIED
BY THE UNITED STATES OF AMERICA; SET FORTH THROUGH

A Series of Historical Manuscripts now first printed

TOGETHER WITH A REISSUE OF RARE CONTEMPORANEOUS TRACTS,
ACCOMPANIED BY BIBLIOGRAPHICAL MEMORANDA, NOTES, AND

Brief Biographies

COLLECTED, ARRANGED, AND EDITED BY

ALEXANDER BROWN

MEMBER OF THE VIRGINIA HISTORICAL SOCIETY AND OF THE AMERICAN HISTORICAL ASSOCIATION
FELLOW OF THE ROYAL HISTORICAL SOCIETY OF ENGLAND

WITH 100 PORTRAITS, MAPS, AND PLANS

IN TWO VOLUMES
VOL. II.

NEW YORK
RUSSELL & RUSSELL · INC

1964

59791

FIRST PUBLISHED IN 1890

REISSUED, 1964, BY RUSSELL & RUSSELL, INC.

BY ARRANGEMENT WITH HOUGHTON, MIFFLIN AND COMPANY

EDITION LIMITED TO FIVE HUNDRED SETS

L. C. CATALOG CARD NO: 59—6232

PRINTED IN THE UNITED STATES OF AMERICA

PERIOD III. *(concluded.)*

FROM THE RETURN OF THE FLEET IN NOVEMBER, 1609, TO THE RETURN OF ARGALL IN JULY, 1614.

CLXXXV. PHILIP III. TO VELASCO.

GENERAL ARCHIVES OF SIMANCAS. DEPARTMENT OF STATE, PARCEL 2641.

Copy of two extracts from a letter of the King of Spain to Don Alonso de Velasco, dated El Pardo, November 15, 1611.

" For Don Alonso de Velasco.

" A caravela having sailed under orders from the Governor of the Havana in search of a ship, which left the Port of Cartagena of the Indies with some artillery, which there was taken out of a galleon, which stranded on the coast of Buenos Ayres — and having passed along the coast of ' la Florida ' on this errand — and three men, in good faith, going on shore from the same caravela, called Diego de Molino, Marco Antonio Perez and Master Antonio, some Englishmen took them prisoners, who say that under orders from the King of Great Britain they have made a settlement on a part of that coast, which they call Virginia. Of which I have desired to have you informed and instructed, as I do herewith ; that you will inform the said king of my just resentment at this imprisonment of these men, and that it will be best to give orders by the shortest way that from there may be accessible, so that they be set at liberty, without any further injury being done them, in order that they may return and carry out the commission entrusted to them by the Governor of the Havana. You will report to me at once what steps you have taken and what may result from them."

CLXXXVI. PHILIP III. TO VELASCO.

The second extract, in cipher, deciphered.

" For Don Alonso de Velasco : — In another letter which is sent with this you are ordered to take steps with that king as to the liberty of three prisoners, whom Englishmen in Virginia have captured, and here in cipher, and for yourself alone, I have wished to inform you that those aforesaid prisoners are the Alcayde Don Diego do Molino, Ensign Marco Antonio Perez and Francisco Lembri, an English pilot, who by my orders went to reconnoitre those ports ; but you must not give their names otherwise than you were told in said letter, as long as you do not obtain their liberty, which you will exert yourself to the utmost to secure, employing all your skill and dexterity to prevent that king from finding out the purpose for which those three men went there, and you will promptly report to me what may be doing [going on]."

CLXXXVII. MORE TO WINWOOD.

WINWOOD MEMORIALS, III. PAGE 309.

November —, 1611. [Probably about the 20th, as it was " received on the 29th of November, 1611."]

Extract from a letter of John Moore in London to Sir Ralph Winwood at The Haghe. . . .

" There are some fears among the weaker sort, of some foreign attempts on Virginia and Ireland, but the State doth not apprehend it, as appears by Lord Carew's cashiering one half of all the Irish forces. Neither is there care taken to supply Sir Thomas Dale with the 2000 men whom he demandeth. Neither is it likely indeed that the King of Spain will break so profitable a peace for that which may cost him dear the getting, and much dearer the keeping."

This has been printed before in this country in " Collections Mass. Hist. Soc." ix. fourth series, 1871, p. 6, note.

CLXXXVIII. VELASCO TO PHILIP III.

GENERAL ARCHIVES OF SIMANCAS. DEPARTMENT OF STATE,
VOLUME 2588, FOLIO 94.

Copy of an original letter of Don Alonso de Velasco to the
King of Spain, dated London, December 14, 1611.

SIRE.

" On the 15th [5th] of last month I reported to Y. M.
what I had heard by a vessel which came a few days before
from Virginia, touching the Caravela that went there and
the three Spanish sailors that were left there on shore, as
hostage for the pilot, whom they gave them so that he
might guide them to the mouth of the river (*a duplicate of
which accompanies this letter*). Having received your let-
ter of November 15th, I expressed on the 7th of this month
[*i. e.*, November 28, English], to the Council here the resentment which Y. M. ordered me to convey for the reten-
tion of these sailors, and Count Salisbury replied to me,
that they would at once order them to be brought here and
handed over to me, we returning likewise their pilot to them.
Y. M. will be pleased to command what I am to reply to this
and in the meantime I will solicit the bringing over of these
men, lest they should perish in Virginia with the necessities
and the hard work to which those who are there are sub-
jected.

" May our Lord preserve the Catholic Person of Y. M. as
all Christendon requires. London, Decr 14. 1611.

" DON ALONSO DE VELASCO."

CLXXXIX. CHAMBERLAIN TO CARLETON.

*BIRCH'S COURT AND TIMES OF JAMES I. VOLUME I. PAGES
150, 152.*

Chamberlain to Carleton, November 27, 1611.

" The Spanish ambassador went to the king the last
week at Newmarket, without acquainting any of the Council, which is thought somewhat a strange course."

December 4, 1611. " The Earl of Southampton's journey into Spain is laid aside, and the ceremony of condoling [on the death of the Queen of Spain] shall be left to the ambassador resident there," etc.

" The Spanish ambassador was sent for lately before the Council, where it was roundly told him what criminal wrongs and injustice our nation was still offered in Spain, with this conclusion, that if there was not present redress, the king was fully minded to recall his ambassador," etc.

CXC. LAWS FOR VIRGINIA.

" December 13th 1611 entered, at Stationers Hall, for publication, under the handes of Sir Edward Cecill, knight. Articles, Lawes and Orders, dyvyne politique and martiall for the Colonye of Virginia; first established by Sir Thomas Gates, Knight and Leiftenant Generall the *24th of May 1610;* exemplified and approved by the Right Honorable Lord Governor and Captayne General, the *12th of June 1610;* agayne exemplified and enlarged by Sir Thomas Dale, knight and Deputy Governor the *22nd of June 1611."*

These laws were published with the following title-page : —

" FOR / The Colony in Virginea / BRITANNIA. / *Lawes Divine, Morall and / Martiall, &c.*

Alget qui non Ardet.

Res nostræ subinde non sunt, quales quis optaret, sed quales esse possunt.

Printed at London for *Walter Burre.*   1612."

The printed book was probably sent to Virginia by the John and Francis, which sailed February 27, 1612, or by the Treasurer, July 23, 1612.

These laws were reprinted by Peter Force (vol. iii.), Washington, D. C., 1844. The laws in this reprint, pp. 9–28 (CII.), were sent from England by Gates in June, 1609, and those, pp. 28–62 (CLIX.), were sent by Dale in March, 1611; those on pp. 9–28 were first established by

Sir Thomas Gates May 24, 1610, and the rest added by Dale June 22, 1611. The whole body is said to have been sent back to England by William Strachey, who arrived late in October or early in November. They were probably revised by General Cecil before he entered them for publication on December 13, 1611. Gates, Dale, and Cecil had all served long in the Low Countries, and these laws were " cheifely extracted out of the Lawes for governing the armye in the Low Contreyes." They seem terrible to us now; but really they were not much, if any, more severe than the Draconic code, which then obtained in England, in which nearly three hundred crimes, varying from murder to keeping company with a gypsy, were punishable with death.

The author of " The New Life of Virginea " [CCX.] says : " Their first and chiefest care was shewed in settling Lawes divine and morall, for the honour and service of God, for daily frequenting the church, the house of prayer, at the tolling of the bell, for preaching, catechizing, and the religious observation of the Sabbath day, for due reverence to the Ministers of the Word and to all superiours, for peace and love among themselves, and enforcing the idle to paines and honest labours, against blasphemie, contempt and dishonour of God, against breach of the Sabbath by gaming : and otherwise against adulterie, sacriledge and felonie ; and in a word, against all wrongfull dealing amongst themselves, or injurious violence against the Indians. Good are these beginnings, wherein God is thus before, *good are these lawes, and long may they stand in their due execution.*"

Other authorities of the period approved of these laws, and assert that they were justified by the circumstances, etc., but in the bitter dissensions in the company in 1622–1624, Sir Thomas Smith was much abused for having introduced these severe laws, and, in defending himself before the Grievance Committee in Parliament, he asserted that " Lord De la Warre, Sir Thomas Dale, Sir Thomas Gates, and Captain Argall all saw the necessity of such laws, in some cases *ad terrorem*, and in some to be truly executed."

On the 7th of May, 1623, the Sandys party drew up many specific charges against Sir Thomas Smythe; among them: "That there were few orders and lawes made in Sir T. S. tyme for government of the Company and Colony," to which he replied: *" There were lawes for the Company here, And none for the Colony since, but were made then;"* and, "That Sir T. S. suffered a Book of lawes for Government of the Colony cheifely extracted out of the Lawes for governing the armye in the Low Countryes," to which he replied: *" This was answered before the Lords and allowed."*

They also asserted, "That these lawes were printed at home, and with great Honour dedicated to Sir Thomas Smith," etc. Smith does not notice this charge, and Force's tract (reprint) was not dedicated to him. I have never seen an original. I have never even seen one advertised for sale; but there is one in the John Carter-Brown Library. I have no idea what an original would be worth.

William Strachey, who seems to have been the editor, gives a poetical dedication "To The Right Honorable, the Lords of the Councell of Virginia," and a preface in prose, "To the constant, mighty, and worthie friends, the Committies, Assistants unto his Maiesties Councell for the Colonie in Virginea-Britannia."

This severe body of "Lawes" ends very appropriately with a very long "Praier" of nearly 3,000 words, which was to be "duly said Morning and Evening upon the Court of Guard, either by the Captaine of the watch himselfe, or by some one of his principall officers."

CXCI. DIGBY TO SALISBURY.

December 13, 1611. Madrid. Digby to Salisbury.

" The Advertisement I gave your Lordship concerning the Englishman that was brought from Virginia to the

ROBERT HEATH

Chief Justice

Havana is true, and I have spoken with another English-man that sawe him and spake with him there. And the man is himself kept prisoner in one of the Gallions at Lisbone. I humblie beseech your Lordship, that I may receave *directions* in what manner I shall behave myself herein : for that I beleeve this accident of demaundinge his libertie, will sett the mayne question on foote." [1]

CXCII. VELASCO TO PHILIP III.

GENERAL ARCHIVES OF SIMANCAS. DEPARTMENT OF STATE, VOLUME 2588, FOLIO 99.

Copy of an original letter of Don Alonso de Velasco to the King of Spain, dated London, December 24, 1611.

" SIRE —

" Having represented to the Council here the just resentment which Y. M. felt on account of the 3 seamen, whom Englishmen had detained in Virginia, the Earl of Salisbury replied that orders would be issued to bring them quickly here and to hand them over to me, if we would return to them the pilot who guided the ship that left them on shore, as I reported to Y. M. on the 15th inst. Now the king has sent me word through the said Count that with the first ship that should sail for Virginia, he would send orders to the Governor to put them on Spanish soil and leave them entirely free — if in like manner I should use my good offices with Y. M. that you should be pleased to order the liberation of the subjects of this crown, who may be detained on the galleys and in prisons as pirates or for other crimes. That with such an understanding, the King would write to Y. M., moved by the prayers and petitions, which daily reach him from their wives and kinsmen. In case he should write this special letter, Y. M. will be pleased to give orders to inquire into the expediency of granting him this favor, since there may other opportunities present them-

---

[1] *I. e.*, the question of the right of England to form settlement in territory claimed by Spain.

selves here, to return such courtesy and to resort to such pleasant interchange of kindness.

"Our Lord preserve Y. M. in His Catholic Person as the Church needs it.

"London. December 24. 1611.

"Don Alonso de Velasco."

[Mem. — I do not know when Harley and Hobson returned from their voyage to New England, but they "brought away the Salvadges from the river of Canada," which were "showed in London for a wonder" in the spring of 1612.]

CXCIII. CHAMBERLAIN TO CARLETON.

Chamberlain to Carleton, London, December 18, 1611.

. . . "Newport the Admirall of Virginia is newly come home, and brings word of the arrival there of Sir Thomas Gates and his Companie; but his Lady died by the way in some part of the West Indies, he hath sent his daughters back againe, which I doubt is a peece of a prognostication that himself meanes not to tarry long after.

"The Lord Treasurer [Cecil] is well recovered. All business betwixt the king and him in his absence pass by the Earl of Pembroke, who is communis terminus between them."

[Mem. — "In last December, Captaine Newport in the Starre and since that [prior to May, 1612] five other shippes are arived heere from the Colonie," etc., CCX.]

CXCIV. DALE TO THE COUNCIL.

Strachey (CCXVII.) gives the following extract from one of Dale's letters. When this letter was written or received in England I do not know.

"It would easilie raise a well-stayed Judgement into

wonder (as Sir Thomas Dale hath writt sometimes unto his Majesty's Counsell here for Virginia) to behold the goodly vines burthening every neighbour bush, and clymbing the toppes of highest trees, and those full of clusters of the grapes in their kind, however dreeped and shadowed soever from the sun, and though never pruned or manured " [*i. e.*, cultivated].

CXCV. PHILIP III. TO VELASCO.

GENERAL ARCHIVES OF SIMANCAS. DEPARTMENT OF STATE, VOLUME 2571, FOLIO 302.

Copy of an extract from a rough draft of a letter of His Majesty to Don Alonso de Velasco, dated Madrid, January 6, 1612.

" I shall order the Virginia Pilot, who is in the Havannah to be brought here, so that he may be surrendered when they hand over to us the three Spanish sailors, who were kept in Virginia." . . .

CXCVI. BIARD TO THE PROVINCIAL.

January 21. Letter written by Father Pierre Biard to the Right Rev. Provincial at Paris. (Copied from the autograph preserved in the Archives of Jesus at Rome.) Port Royal, January 31, 1612.

. . . "I have made two voyages with M. de Biancourt, one lasting nearly twelve days, the other of a month and a half, and we have examined the whole coast from Port Royal as far as Kinibéqui, West-South-West. We have sailed up the large rivers St. John, the Holy Cross (Saincte Croix), Pentegoet and the above mentioned Kinibéqui. [Kennebec or Sagadahock.] We have visited the French, who have wintered here this year, in two divisions, on the River St. Jean and that of Sainte Croix; the Malouins in the river St. Jean, and Captain Plastrier at Sainte Croix. . . .

" Two main causes induced M. de Biancourt to do this; the first to obtain news about the English and to know if it would be possible to get the better of them; the second to exchange 'Armonchiquoys' wheat so as to preserve us during the winter, and keep us from dying of hunger, in case we should receive no aid from France.   In order to understand the first motive, it ought to be known that shortly before, Captain Platrier of Honfleur, before mentioned, wishing to go to Kinibéqui, was taken prisoner by two English vessels, that were near an island, called Emmetenic, 8 leagues from aforesad Kennebec.   He was released by means of some presents, (this was the way they mildly called it), and the promise he gave to comply with the prohibitions imposed upon him, not to trade along that whole coast.   For the English claim to be masters here, and in support of this they exhibit Patents of their King, which we, however, believe to be false.   Now M. de Biancourt, having heard all this from the lips of Captain Patrier himself, represented very earnestly to these people, how important it was to him, an officer of the Crown and a lieutenant of his father, how important also to every good Frenchman, to go and prevent this usurpation of the English, which was so very contrary to the rights and possessions of his Majesty.

"For, said he, it is well known to all men (not to speak of higher views of the matter) that the great Henry, whom God may save in His mercy, according to rights acquired by him and his predecessors, bestowed upon M. des Monts, in the year 1604, all this country from the 40th degree of latitude to the 46th.   Since this grant the aforesaid Seigneur des Monts, in his own person and through M. de Potrincourt, my most honored Father, his lieutenant, and thro' others, has often taken real possession of the whole country and this three and four years before ever the English had set forth, or any one had ever heard anything of this claim of theirs.   These and several other things the aforesaid Sieur de Biancourt found out and made known, thus encouraging his people.

"I, for my part, had two other motives which urged me to this same voyage : one, to accompany, as a spiritual assistant the aforesaid Sieur de Biancourt, and his people, the other, to find out and to see myself the disposition of these nations to accept the Holy Gospel. These, then, were the motives of our voyage.

"We arrived at Kennebec, 80 leagues from Port Royal, on the 28th October, the day of St. Simon and St. Jude, of the same year 1611. Immediately, our men went on shore, desirous to see the fort of the English; [see LVIII.] for we had heard, on the way, that there was no one there. Now, as at first everything looks fine, they went to work praising and boasting of this enterprise of the English and to enumerate the advantages of the place; everybody praised in it what he valued most. But a few days later they changed their views; for there was seen a fair chance of raising a counter-fort, which would have imprisoned them and cut them off from the river and the sea; item, that even if they had been left there, they would nevertheless not have enjoyed the commodities of the river, since it had several other and finer estuaries, at some distance from there. . . .

"But, since I here have made mention of the English, some one may perchance wish to hear of their adventures, which we were told here. It is, therefore, thus, that in the year 1608 the English, began to settle down at one of the mouths of this river Kennebec; as has been said before. They had then as their head a very honest man, who got along remarkably well with the natives of the country. They say, however, that the Armonché-quois were afraid of such neighbors, and on that account murdered this Captain, of whom I have spoken. These people are accustomed to this business, to kill people by Magic. Now, in the second year, 1609, the English, under another Captain, changed their policy. They repelled the natives most dishonorably, they beat them, and committed excesses of every kind, without much restraint; hence, these poor, ill treated people, impatient with the present, and fearing more from the future, resolved, as the saying is, to kill the whelp before he should have more powerful claws and teeth. The opportunity offered one day, when three sloops had gone to a distant place, in order to fish. My conspirators followed them upon their track, and drawing near with many signs of friendship (for thus they always are most friendly when they are nearest to treachery) they entered and, at a given signal, each chose his man and killed him with his big knife. Thus perished eleven Englishmen. The others, intimidated, abandoned their enterprise that same year, and have not continued it since, being content to come in the summer to fish near this island of Emetenic, which, as we mentioned before, was 8 leagues from the fort they had begun.

"On this account, therefore, the outrage committed in the person of Captain Platrier by said Englishmen, having been perpetrated on this island of Emetenic, M. de Biancourt considered the expediency of going to reconnoitre it and to leave there some token of having re-claimed it. This he did by erecting in the harbour a very fine Cross, with the arms of France. Some of his people suggested to him to burn the sloops which he found there, but as he is gentle and humane, he would not do it, considering that they were not men-of-war but fishing vessels.

"From there since the season pressed us, for it was already November 6th we made sail to return to Port-Royal. Stopping at Pentegoet, as we had promised the Savages. . . .

"From Port-Royal the last of January 1612.

"PIERRE BIARD."

CXCVII. DIGBY TO SALISBURY.

February 2, 1612. Madrid. Sir John Digby to Salisbury.

. . . "Departure of 800 men out of Portugal and the transporting of 3200 more so that the whole number of men to be sent is 4000. All which though I conceive are to be carried into Flanders, yet I am advertized from one that I appointed to be amongst them, that divers of the Masters of the Ships are discontented, and that they suspect they shall be forced to a far longer journey. The which if it be so, I can only suspect some enterprize of theirs against Virginia, the which I do not think likely, but in regard that divers write unto me, though uncertainly, that there is something now in hand against it, I omit not to advertise it unto your Lordship."

CXCVIII. CHAMBERLAIN TO CARLETON.

Chamberlain to Carleton, London, February 12, 1612.

. . . "We heard yesterday of nine ships, with 1500 Spaniards, come into the Downs, and going into the Low Countries to reinforce their garrisons. The Spanish ambassador's sister and daughter-in-law, whom you met upon Barham Downs, went away the last week towards Brussels, without taking leave, or bidding the Queen Farewell. . . . There is a lotterie in hand for the furthering of the Virginia Voiage, and an under-companie erecting for the trade of the Bermudes, which have chaunged theyre name twise within this moneth, beeing first christned Virginiola as a member of that plantation, but now lastly resolved to be called Sommer Iland as well in respect of the continuall temporal ayre, as in remembrance of Sir George Sommers that died there." . . .

CXCIX. PHILIP III. TO VELASCO.

GENERAL ARCHIVES OF SIMANCAS. DEPARTMENT OF STATE, VOLUME 2571, FOLIO 309.

Copy of an extract from a deciphered letter of His Majesty to Don Alonso de Velasco, dated Madrid, February 25, 1612.

"What you report on the subject of Virginia has been received; also what you say of the people they send out

there, the merchandise for which this crowd of men hastens
thither (as you state) — and I shall be pleased if you will
most carefully try to find out whatever else may appear on
that subject, and to report to me the day on which the
ships will sail — on board which those aforesaid people will
sail — and whatever else they carry and whether in any
suitable way some trustworthy person [see CLXIX.] might
be put among them.   This would be very important and
therefore I order you to arrange it so, since this seems to
be the best way to ascertain the nature of that enterprise
— this said person could then return in the ships which
may come back from Virginia to England — also the exchange of prisoners who are still there is to be carried out
as you have been ordered."

[MEM. — February 24, 1612, Master Welby entered at
Stationers' Hall for publication " under the handes of Sir
Thomas Smithe and Mr. Lownes, warden.   A booke or
thinge called the Publicaͨon of the Lottery for Virginia."
No copy of this publication is now known to be in exist-
ence.   CXCVIII. mentions that the " lottery was in hand,"
and the charter (already granted) which passed the seals
March 12, 1612, authorizes these lottery publications.]

CC. LETTER TO THE GOVERNOR AND COMPANY OF
VIRGINIA, FEBRUARY, 1612.

" A Letter to the Governor and Company for Virginia
affaires to suffer *Daniell Tucker* who hath ben a personall
adventurer ever since the first plantation there to pass by
the next Shipp that shall come for England.

"Subscr. and procur. by Mr. May."

The letter referred to in this minute is now missing ; it
was probably sent to Virginia by the John and Francis,
which sailed February 27, 1612.

CCI. DIGBY TO SALISBURY.

March 9, 1612.   Madrid.   Digby to Salisbury.

" My L^d. I am not hasty to advertise anything upon bare rumors, which hath made me hitherto to forbeare to write what I had generally heard, of their intents against Virginia. but now I have been from good P.^{te} advertised that without question they will speedily attempt against our plantation there.   And that it is a thing resolved of, that ye King of Spaine must runne any hazard with England rather than permitt ye English to settle there: for upon Late consultation, I assure your Lordship they apprehend it to be of much more danger to their West Indies than I conceave it. especially for ther returne of ye West Indian Fleete, & therupon (as I am informed) have determined, that since ye buisines of itselfe hath not fallen as they expected, they must with speed prevent ye further growing of it.   Whatsoever is attempted, I conceive will be from ye Havana, where ye rendevous shall be of all those provisions & shipps, which for that effect goe from ye severall ports of Spaine.   In Sevil they prepare shipping, but that is as your Lordship knoweth, under color of ye West Indian Fleete.   In Portugal likewise there is order for ye making ready speedily of two Gallions.   At ye Passo by St. Sebastians in all hast they make ready foure.   And there are two shipps built by ye Marchants of foure or five hundred tun a peece which I heare ye King will likewise buye.   As I shall herein come to ye knowledge of more particulars your Lordship shall receeve advertisement."

CCII. EXTRACT FROM THE TRINITY HOUSE RECORDS.

" March 11th 1611 [O. S.].   Letter from Sir Thomas Smyth to The Trinity House, asking for payment of the second of the three years' subscription to the Virginia Adventure."   Extract.

" March —, 1611 [O. S.].   A bill of adventure issued
to The Trinity House.   Agreement that The Trinity House
shall have rateably according to their adventure for Virginia their full part of all such lands as shall be recovered,
planted and inhabited, and of such mines and minerals of
gold and silver, and other metals or treasure, pearls, precious stones or other kind of wares which shall be obtained
or gotten in the said voyage."

[MEM. — Chamberlain   to Carleton, March 11, 1612.
. . . " There is a little Treatise of the North-West Passage, written by Sir Dudley Digges. . . . Some of his good
friends say he had better have given five hundred pounds
than published such a pamphlet.   But he is wonderfully
possessed with the opinion and hopes of that passage."
The title of Digges' tract I believe was " A Discourse
concerning the circumference of the earth, or a North-West
passage.   1612."]

CCIII. THE THIRD CHARTER.[1]

" A third charter of King James to the Treasurer and
Company for Virginia."
Article I. [Recital of former charters.]
II. [Former boundaries recited.]
" III. Now, forasmuch as we are given to understand,
that in those seas, adjoining to the said coast of
Preamble
Virginia, and without the compass of those two
hundred miles, by us so granted unto the said Treasurer
and Company, as aforesaid, and yet not far distant from the
said colony in Virginia, there are, or may be, divers islands,
lying desolate and uninhabited, some of which are already
made known and discovered, by the industry, travel, and
expences of the said company, and others also are supposed
to be and remain, as yet, unknown and undiscovered, all

[1] This document was drawn up, I   first published by the Rev. William
suppose, by Sir Edwin Sandys ; it was   Stith in 1747. (See Preface, vii.)

PHILIP HERBERT

and every of which it may import the said colony, both in safety and policy of trade, to populate and plant, in regard whereof, as well for the preventing of peril, as for the better commodity and prosperity of the said colony, they have been humble[1] suitors unto us, that we would be pleased to grant unto them an enlargement of our said former letters patents, as well for a more ample extent of their limitts and territories into the seas, adjoining to and upon the coast of Virginia, as also for some other matters and articles, concerning the better government of the said Company and Colony, in which point our said former letters patents do not extend so far, as time and experience hath found to be needful and convenient : — "

IV. [Extension of boundaries, so as to include all the islands lying within three hundred leagues of the continent, "and being within or between the *one and fortieth* and *thirtieth* degrees of northerly latitude," and "provided always, that the said Islands &c, be not actually possessed or inhabited by any other Christian Prince or estate, nor be within the bounds, limits, or territories of the *Northern Colony* heretofore by us granted to be planted by divers of our loving subjects, in the north parts of Virginia," etc.]

" V. And further, our will and pleasure is, and we do, by these presents, grant and confirm, for the good and welfare of the said plantation, and *that posterity may hereafter know who have adventured and not been sparing of their purses* in such a noble and generous action for the general good of their country, and at the request, and with the consent, of the Company aforesaid, that our trusty and well beloved subjects,

Aditional adventurers admitted.

[2] George [Abbot] Lord Archbishop of Canterbury

[1] I have not found this petition. It was presented to the king some time in the year 1611, I suppose. The charter had certainly been granted before February 12, 1612, and possibly a considerable time before, as the outlook was not promising, and there must have been considerable delay in obtaining the additional adventurers, whose names were to be inserted before it was signed and sealed by the king. See CLXXIV.

[2] A complete list of these names has never been published. Stith only

Gilbert [Talbot] Earle of Shrewsbury,
Mary [Cavendish-Talbot] Countesse of Shrewsbury,
Elizabeth [Vere-Stanley] Countesse of Derby,
Margarette [Russell-Clifford] Countesse of Cumberland,
Henry [Hastings] Earle of Huntingdon,
Edward [Russell] Earle of Bedford,
Lucy [Harrington-Russell] Countesse of Bedford,
Mary [Sidney] Countesse of Pembroke,
Richard [Bourke] Earl of Clanricard,
Lady Elizabeth Graie,
William [Cecil] Lord Viscount Cranborne,
William [James] Lord Byshopp of Duresme,
Henry [Parry] Lord Byshopp of Worseter,
John [Bridges] Lord Bishop of Oxenford,
William Lord Pagett,
Dudley Lord North,
Francis Lord Norreis,
William Lord Knollys,
John Lord Harrington,
Robert Lord Spencer,
Edward Lord Denny,
William Lord Cavendishe,
James Lord Hay,
Elianor Lady Carre,
Maistres Elizabeth Scott, widdow,
Edward Sackvill Esqre.
Sir Henry Nevill of Abergavenny, Knight,

gives "George, Lord Archbishop of Canterbury, Henry, Earl of Huntington, Edward, Earl of Bedford, Richard, Earl of Clanrickard," etc.

This charter contains the names of six corporations and 325 persons, of whom about 25 were in the peerage, 111 knights, 10 doctors, ministers, etc., 66 esquires, 30 gentlemen, and 83 citizens and others not classified, but mostly merchants. The trades, etc., predominated in the second char-ter, while three fourths of these belong to the gentry; but the gentry did not pay their subscriptions so well as the merchants. Of the names in this charter about 125 paid £37 10s. or more, about 83 paid less than £37 10., and about 117 paid nothing. About 120 of them served at some time in the House of Commons; of these about 60 were members of the first Parliament of King James I.

Sir Robert Riche,   Knight,
" John Harrington,   "
" Raphe Winwood,   "
" John Graie   "
" Henry Riche   "
" Henry Wotten   "
Peregrine Berty Esqre,
Sir Edward Phellipps, Master of the Rolls,
" Moile ffinch   Knight,
" Thomas Mansell   "
" John St John   "
" Richard Spenser   "
" ffrancis Barrington   "
" George Carie of Devonshire, Knight,
" William Twisden   Knight,
" John Leveson   "
" Thomas Walsingham   "
" Edward Carre   "
" Arthur Manwareing   "
" Thomas Jermyn   "
" Valentine Knightley   "
" John Dodderidge   "
" John Hungerford   "
" John Stradlinge   "
" John Bourchier,   "
" John Bennet,   "
" Samuell Leonard,   "
" ffrauncis Goodwin,   "
" Wareham St Leiger   "
" James Scudamore   "
" Thomas Mildmay   "
" Percivall Willoughby   "
" ffrauncis Leigh   "
" Henry Goodere   "
" John Cutts   "
" James Parrett   "
" William Craven   "

Sir John Sames   Knight,
" Carew Raleigh   "
" William Maynard   "
" Edmund Bowyer   "
" William Cornewallis   "
" Thomas Beomont   "
" Thomas Cunningsby   "
" Henry Beddingfield   "
" David Murray   "
" William Poole   "
" William Throgmorton   "
" Thomas Grantham   "
" Thomas Stewkley   "
" Edward Heron   "
" Raphe Shelton   "
" Lewis Thesam   "
" Walter Aston   "
" Thomas Denton   "
" Ewstace Hart   "
" John Ogle   "
" Thomas Dale   "
" William Boulstrode   "
" William ffleetwood   "
" John Acland   "
" John Hanham   "
" Robert Millor   "
" Thomas Wilford   "
" William Lower   "
" Thomas Leedes   "
" ffrauncis Barneham   "
" Walter Chute   "
" Thomas Tracy   "
" Marmaduke Darrell   "
" William Harrys   "
" Thomas Gerrard   "
" Peter ffreetchville   "
" Richard Trevor   "

Sir Amias Bamfield   Knight,
" William Smyth of Essex   "
" Thomas Hewit   "
" Richard Smith   "
" John Heyward   "
" Christopher Harris   "
" John Pettus   "
" William Strode   "
" Thomas Harfleets,   "
" Walter Vaughan,   "
" William Herrick   "
" Samuell Saltonstall   "
" Richard Cooper   "
" Henry ffane   "
" ffrauncis Egiok   "
" Robert Edolph   "
" Arthur Harris   "
" George Huntley   "
" George Chute   "
" Robert Leigh   "
" Richard Lovelace   "
" William Lovelace   "
" Robert Yaxley   "
" ffrancis Wortly   "
" ffrancis Heiborne   "
" Guy Palme   "
" Richard Bingley   "
" Ambrose Turville   "
" Nicholas Stoddard   "
" William Gee   "
" Walter Coverte   "
" Thomas Eversfeild   "
" Nicholas Parker   "
" Edward Culpeper   "
" William Ayliffe   " and
" John Keile   " .
Doctor George Mountaine, Deane of Westminster,

Lawrence Bohun Docktor in phisick,
Anthony Hinton, Docktor in Phisick.

[Esquires]

John Pawlett,	Arthur Ingram,
Anthony Irby,	John Weld,
John Walter,	John Harris,
Anthony Dyott,	Wm. Ravenscrofte,
Thomas Warre,	William Hackwell,
Lawrence Hide,	Nicholas Hide,
Thomas Stevens,	ffrauncis Tate,
Thomas Coventry,	John Hare,
Robert Askwith,	George Sandys,
Francis Jones,	Thos Wentworth
Henry Cromewell,	John Arundell,
John Culpeper,	John Hoskins,
Walter FitzWilliams,	Walter Kirkham,
William Roscarrock,	Richard Carmerden
Edward Carne,	Thomas Merry
Nicholas Lickfeild,	John Middleton,

John Smith and Thomas Smith the sonnes of Sir Thomas
Smith,

Peter Franke,	George Gerrard,
Gregory Sprinte,	John Drake,
Roger Puleston,	Oliver Nicholas,
Richard Monyngton,	John Vaughan,
John Evelin,	Lamarock Stradling,
John Riddall,	John Kettleby,
Warren Towneshend,	Lionell Cranfeild,
Edward Salter,	William Litton,
Humfrey May,	George Thorpe,

Henry Sandys and Edwin Sandys the sonnes of Sir Edwin
Sandys,

Thomas Conway Captaine,	Owinn Gwin Captaine,
Giles Hawkridge,	Edward Dyer,
Richard Connock,	Benjamin Brand,

Richard Leigh and Thomas Pelham *Esquires*.

Thomas Digges and John Digges *Esquires*, the sonnes of
Sir Dudley Diggs, Knight.

ffrauncis Bradley,   Richard Buck,
ffrauncis Burley,   John Prockter,   [Ministers]

Alexander Whitaker, Thomas ffrake the elder, and Henry
ffreake the elder *Ministers of God's Word.*

The Maior and Cittizens of Chichester,   [Corpora-
The Maior and Jurates of Dover,   tions]
The Bayliffes, Burgesses and Cominalty of Ipswich,
The Maior & Cominalty of Lyme Regis,
The Maior and Cominalty of Sandwich,
The Wardens Assistants and Companie of The Trinity
House.

Thomas Martin,   ffrauncis Smallman,
Augustine Steward,   Richard Tomlins,   [Gentlemen]
Humfrey Jobson,   John Legats,
Robert Barkley,   John Crowe,
Edward Barkley,   William Ffleet,
Henry Wolstenholme,   Edmund Alleyne,
George Tucker,   ffrauncis Glanville,
Thomas Gouge,   John Evelin,
William Hall,   John Smithe,
George Sams,   John Robinson,
William Tucker,   John Wolstenholme *Esquire,*
William Hodges,   Jonathan Nuttall,
Phineas Pett *Captaine,*   John King *Captaine,*
William Beck,   Giles Alington,
ffrauncis Heiton and Samuell Holliland *Gents.*

Richard Chamberlaine,   George Chamberlaine,   [Merchants
Hewett Staper,   Humfrey Handford,   and citizens
Raph ffreeman,   George Swinhoe,   of London]
Richard Piggott,   Elias Roberts,
Roger Harris,   Devereaux Wogan,
Edward Baber,   William Greenewell,
Thomas Shilds,   Nicholas Hooker,
Robert Garsett,   Thomas Cordell,
William Bright,   John Reynolds,
Peter Bartley,   John Willet,
Humfrey Smith,   Roger Dye,

Nicholas Leate,
Lewes Tate,
Robert Peake,
Sebastian Vittars,
Richard Warner,
Warner . . . ,
Andrew Throughton,
Thomas Hodges,
Richard Harper,
William Haselden,
William Burrell,
Richard ffishborne,
Edward Cooke,
Richard Hall *ankersmith*,
Richard ffranckline,
John Britton,
Edmund Pond,
Robert Bell,
William fferrers
Anthony Abdy
Benjamyne Decrowe,
Humfrey Basse,
Richard Moorer,
Richard Pontsonne,
John Beomont, *clothier*,
William ffaldo, *ffishmonger*,
John Jones, *marchant*,
Edward Plomer *marchants*.
John Stoickden,
Peter Erundell,
Thomas Hampton and

Thomas Wale,
Humfrey Merrett,
Powell Isaackson,
Jarvis Mundes,
Gresham Hogan,
Daniell Dernley,
William Barrett,
John Downes,
Thomas ffoxall,
James Harrison,
John Hodsall,
John Miller,
Richard Hall *marchant*,
John Delbridge,
Edmund Scott,
Robert Strutt,
Edward James,
Richard Herne,
William Millet,
Robert Gore,
Henry Timberly,
Abraham Speckart,
William Compton,
William Wolaston,
Alexander Childe,
ffrauncis Baldwine,
Thomas Plomer, and

Robert Tindall,
Ruben Bourne,
ffrauncis Carter

Cittizens of London, who since our said last letters patents are become adventurers, etc. etc.

Additional Councillors.
    "VI. And we are further pleased, and we do, by these presents, grant and confirm, that

[1] Philip [Herbert] Earle of Montgomery,

[1] A complete list of these has not been published. Stith only gives three

William Lord Paget,
Sir John Harrington, Knight,
[1] " William Cavendish, "
" John Sammes, "
" Samuel Sandys, "
" Thomas ffreke, "
" William St John, "
" Richard Grobham, "
" Thomas Dale "
" Cavalliero Maycott, "
Richard Martin, Esquire,
John Bingley, "
Thomas Watson "
and Arthur Ingram "

whom the said Treasurer and Company *have, since the said last letters patents*, nominated and set down as worthy and discreet persons, fit to serve us as Counsellors, to be of our Council for the said plantation, shall be reputed, deemed and taken as persons of our said Council for the said first Colony, in such manner and sort, to all intents and purposes, as those who have been formerly elected and nominated, as our Counsellors for that Colony, and whose names have been or are inserted and expressed in our said former letters patents."

VII. [[2] Courts or meetings of the treasurer and company to assemble " *once every week or oftener*," to be constituted

names, and one of these he gives incorrectly, viz.: " Philip. Earl of Montgomery, William Lord Paget, Sir John Starrington, Knt.," etc. Starrington should be Harrington.

[1] In the copy made for me at the British Museum, the name of " Sir William Cavendish, Knight," does not appear ; but this may be an oversight of the copyist, as the name is found in the list as copied for me from the Kimbolton manuscripts.

[2] The words in [ ] are only intended to convey an idea of the article numbered, as this seems to answer all purposes.

No one was admitted to share in the Virginia colony for a less sum than £12 10s. This amount finally entitled the payer to a share of not less than 100 acres in Virginia. Of those who paid their subscriptions and took therefor bills of adventure, it may be stated, as approximately correct, that about one third came to Virginia themselves and settled on their lands ; about one of not less than *five* members of his majesty's council for the first colony in Virginia (of which the treasurer, or his deputy, to be always one) and not less than fifteen " of the generality of the said Company" shall be a sufficient court for handling casual occurrences, etc.]

VIII. [For matters of greater weight, such as concern the weal publick, etc. Four great and general courts were to be held yearly upon the last Wednesday save one of Hillary (Winter) term, Easter (Spring), Trinity (Summer), and Michaelmas (Fall) terms. These courts had power to regulate the government (appoint or remove officers, make laws, etc.) of the colony in Virginia, to dispatch the affairs of the said company, to expulse from the company all persons who failed to pay their dues as adventurers, subscribers, etc.]

IX. [The judges at Westminster and elsewhere to favor suits brought by the company against non-paying subscribers.]

X. [The treasurer and company may admit new members, etc.]

XI. [May encourage migration. May send things necessary for the plantation free of duty for seven years from 12th March, 1612.]

XII. [The oath of supremacy and allegiance to be administered to every one going to Virginia.]

XIII. [Certain oaths to be administered to the officers of the colony for faithfully discharging the matters committed to them for the good of said colony.]

XIV. [Whereas divers persons, having received wages, etc., from the company, and agreed to serve the colony, have afterwards refused to go thither; and divers others who have been employed in Virginia by the Company, and having there misbehaved themselves by mutinies, sedition, or other notorious misdemeanors, have come back to England

third sent over their agents, or finally their heirs, to occupy theirs; while the remaining third sold their shares to others, who generally settled on the lands. These classes were the landed gentry, and they brought, or sent, over another class as servants, etc.

WILLIAM HERBERT
Third Earl of Pembroke

in some treacherous way, or by stealth, or without licence from the governor of Virginia, or having been sent hither as misdoers and offenders, have shown no respect to the Council of the Company; and others for the colouring of their lewdness and misdemeanors committed in Virginia, have endeavored, by most vile and slanderous reports of the country, of the government and estate of the colony, to bring the plantation into disgrace and contempt, whereby "the utter overthrow and ruin of the said enterprise hath been greatly endangered, which cannot miscarry without some dishonour to us and our kingdom.]

XV. ["Now, forasmuch as it appeareth unto us, that these insolences, misdemeanors, and abuses, not to be tolerated in any civil government, have, for the most part," proceeded from the fact that said council have not had authority to correct and chastise such offenders; we therefore, for the speedy reformation of so great and enormous abuses and misdemeanors heretofore practised and committed, and for the prevention of the like hereafter, do, by these presents, authorize the said Council or any two of them (whereof the Treasurer, or his deputy, to be always one), by warrant under their hands, to cause to be apprehended any person hereafter guilty of said offences, to examine them, and if found guilty upon just proof made by oath, the said Council, or any two of them, shall have full power and authority either here to bind them over with good sureties for their good behavior, and further therein to proceed, to all intents and purposes, as it is used, in other like cases, within our realm of England; or else, at their discretion, to remand and send them back to the said colony in Virginia, there to be proceeded against and punished, as the governor, deputy, or council there shall think meet, etc.]

"XVI. And for the more effectual advancing of the said plantation, we do further, for us, our heirs, and successors, of our especial grace and favour, by virtue of our prerogative royal, and by the assent and consent of the Lords and others of our privy

Lotteries authorized for the benefit of the Colony.

council, give and grant unto the said treasurer and company
full power and authority, free leave, liberty, and licence, to
set forth, erect, and publish, one or more lottery or lotteries,
to have continuance, and to endure and be held, for the
space of one whole year, next after the opening of the same;
and after the end and expiration of the said term, the said
lottery or lotteries to continue and be further kept, during our will and pleasure only, and not otherwise. And
yet nevertheless, we are contented and pleased for the good
and welfare of the said plantation, that the said treasurer
and company shall, for the dispatch and finishing of the said
lottery or lotteries, have six months warning after the said
year ended, before our will and pleasure shall, for and on
that behalf, be construed, deemed and adjudged, to be in
anywise altered and determined.

"XVII. And our further will and pleasure is, that the
Where opened. said lottery and lotteries shall and may be opened
and held, within our city of London, or in any
other city or town or elsewhere, within this our realm of
England, with such prizes, articles, conditions, and limita-
tions, as to them, the said Treasurer and Company, in their
discretion shall seem convenient:

"XVIII. And that it shall and may be lawful, to and
Treasurer and Com- pany may appoint offi- cers to con- duct the Lotteries and administer oaths to them. for the said Treasurer and Company, to elect and
choose receivers, auditors, surveyors, commission-
ers, or any other officers, whatsoever, at their will
and pleasure, for the better marshalling, dispos-
ing, guiding, and governing of the said lottery
and lotteries; and that it shall likewise be lawful,
to and for the said Treasurer and any two of the
said council, to minister to all and every such person so
elected and chosen for officers, as aforesaid, one or more
oaths, for their good behaviour, just and true dealing, in
and about the said lottery or lotteries, to the intent and
purpose, that none of our loving subjects, putting in their
names, or otherwise adventuring in the said general lottery
and lotteries, may be, in any wise, defrauded and deceived

of their said monies, or evil and indirectly dealt withal in their said adventures.

"XIX. And we further grant in manner and form aforesaid, that it shall and may be lawful, to and for the said treasurer and company, under the seal of the said council for the plantation, to publish, *May publish the schemes of their Lotteries.* or to cause and procure to be published, by proclamation or otherwise (the said proclamation, to be made in their name, by virtue of these presents) the said lottery or lotteries in all cities, towns, boroughs, and other places within our said realm of England; and we will and command all mayors, justices of peace, sheriffs, bailiffs, constables, and other officers and loving subjects, whatsoever, that, in no wise, they hinder or delay the progress and proceedings of the said lottery or lotteries, but be therein touching the premises, aiding and assisting, by all honest good and lawful means and endeavours."

XX. [Construction of charters to be made in the most ample and beneficial manner for the company.]

XXI. [Former privileges confirmed, etc.] "In witness whereof we have caused these our letters to be made patents. Witness ourself, at Westminster, the twelfth day of March, in the ninth year of our reign of England, France, and Ireland, and of Scotland the five and fortieth."

CCIV. PHILIP III. TO VELASCO.

GENERAL ARCHIVES OF SIMANCAS. DEPARTMENT OF STATE, VOLUME 2571, FOLIO 312.

Copy of a rough draft of a letter of His Majesty to Don Alonso de Velasco, dated Madrid, April 1, 1612.

"In a letter of February 25th I ordered you to write to me in matters relating to Virginia, what you may have learned, and since afterwards the subject has again been discussed on account of a paper presented by a person zealous to serve me, which treats of the serious troubles likely to arise if the English get a footing in that region, and proposes the way and the means which might be employed in order to drive them out from there.[1]   I order you and charge you to proceed most carefully in ascertaining the precise condition of things there and to report to me — also that the pilot [Clark] who now is in the Havannah comes over promptly for the purposes of the exchange, which you know — and you will act with dispatch in all that concerns this matter."

CCV. VELASCO TO PHILIP III.

GENERAL ARCHIVES OF SIMANCAS. DEPARTMENT OF STATE, VOLUME 2589, FOLIO 25.

Copy of a deciphered letter of Don Alonso de Velasco to the King of Spain, dated London, April 14, 1612.

" SIRE. —

" On the 8th of last month [February 27] two ships[2] sailed from here with the first assistance which I reported to Y. M., was preparing for Virginia, they took not more than 100 men, and the second is understood not to reach 1000, they will sail from here in eight ships in the last days of this month.   It is however, still doubted whether Lord de la Warre, the former Governor there, will go with the expedition as had been reported.   Those who are interested in this Colony show, however, that they wish to push this enterprise very earnestly and the Prince of Wales lends them very warmly his support and assistance towards it.   If a suitable person could be found, he [I] would send him with these vessels to establish friendly relations with all [*i. e.* while really acting the spy] as Y. M. commands me in the letter of February 25 [15].   [CLXIX. and CXCIX.]

" May our Lord " etc.

---

[1] This important paper has not been found.   Was this an Englishman, who was so anxious to serve Philip III. of Spain ?

[2] The John and Francis and the Sarah, I suppose.

CCVI. SANDYS TO THE MAYOR OF SANDWICH.

FROM "VIRGINIA AND VIRGINIOLA," BY REV. E. D. NEILL, 1878, PAGE 44.

" To the Right Worthie, my very loving friends, The Mayor and Jurates of Sandwich : —

" GENTLEMEN. — I am required by his Majesties Counsel for Virginia, to call on you for the twenty five pounds which long since you promised to adventure with them, towards the furthering of that plantation.   And have received from them a Bill of adventure under their seale to be delivered unto you upon paiment of that sum, which Bill I have sent you [1] by Mr Parke to be disposed accordingly.

" I am also in their names very earnestly to pray your furtherance towards the furthering of a Lotterie lately granted to them by his Majestie.   The use and nature thereof you shall perceive by the proclamation concerning it,[2] which I have also sent.   And Mr. Mayor of Sandwick is particularly desired to receive and return such monies as men shall be disposed to adventure in it, according to such instructions as are contained in a book,[3] sent to you for that purpose : presuming greatly of you affectionate rediness to aid and advance *so worthie an enterprise tending so greatly to the enlargement of the Christian truth, the honor of our nation, and benefit of English people, as by God's assistance the sequell in short time will manifest.*   The example also hereof, how beneficiall in your best and most needful occasions, it may prove unto yourselves.   I know in your wisdome you will easily see and consider.   So with my very hartie salutations I commend you to the divine tuition and rest.   Y^r Very loving friend.

" EDWIN SANDYS.

" Northborn, 8 Aprile, 1612."

---

[1] [2] [3] These documents are not now preserved among the muniments of Sandwich.   [2] or [3] was probably the   "Booke or thinge " entered at Stationers' Hall, February 24, 1611.

CCVII. DIGBY TO SALISBURY.

Madrid, April 18, 1612.   Sir John Digby to my Lord
Salisbury.

An extract from a letter indorsed : " Touching our Renouncing the Plantation in Virginia."

" It is thought, he [Don Pedro de Çuñiga[1]] will be
directed, to use many Instances unto his Majesty, for the
Removing of the Plantation in Virginia, and which they
thinke fit first to assay by fayre meanes and Intreaty to his
Majesty, tho' I should be sorry, in the meane tyme, they
should be trusted ; ffor that I know, they have had many
consultations for the supplanting of our men.   But I cannot
learne, that there is any particular Resolution taken therein,
but that in generall it is concluded, that our setling there
is not to be permitted."

[MEM. — The deserters of Captain Hudson, after their
return to England in October, 1611, convinced many that
they had found the long looked for and greatly desired
northwest passage, and in April or May, 1612, an expedition was sent out, consisting of two ships under the command
of Captain Thomas Button, namely, the Resolution, Francis
Nelson, master, and the Discovery, Captain John Ingram,
to explore the said passage and with special instructions to
search for Hudson and his friends.   Robert Byleth, one of
those who had deserted him in the summer of 1611, was
sent along to aid in the search.   Henry, Prince of Wales,
who took especial interest in Hudson's fate, drew up the
instructions for this expedition.]

[1] Zuñiga was sent to England at this
time as ambassador extraordinary, for
special purposes.   Velasco was still
the resident ambassador.   Among
other pieces of diplomacy, Zuñiga
came to offer the hand of Philip III.
himself to the Princess Elizabeth of
England.   See Gardiner's *History of
England*, vol. ii. p. 151.

CCVIII.   MOORE'S COMMISSION.

April 27, 1612.   " A Commission graunted by us the undertakers for the Plantacon of Somer Islands unto our welbeloved frend Mr Richard Moore and the rest of the men and mareniers imployed upon the said voyage whome wee beseeche God to preserve."   Commencing : —

"Imprimis.   1. Whereas, we whose names are hereunder written togeather with divers others have to the glorie of God and good of our Countrye undertaken the Plantacon of Somer Islands (some times called Bermudaes) " etc.

The document is given in Lefroy's " Memorials of the Bermudas," vol i. pp. 58–63.   Moore was to be governor for three years.   Among his assistants were Mr. George Keth, preacher of the word, and Mr. Edwin Kendall.   The ship in which he sailed, the Plough, was commanded by Captain Robert Daviss.   They sailed April 28th.   Their seal was "a Seale Ring with Sir Thomas Smythes Armes engraven."

[MEM. — Howes in his Chronicle says, "In the Spring of 1612 there were sent to Virginia more supplies [by the John and Francis and the Sarah?] besides a particular supply for the English in the Bermodes."]

CCIX.   EXTRACT FROM THE GROCERS' RECORDS.

" Court of Assistants.   Grocers Company.   Tent die Mercurii xxix die Aprilis 1612.

" Present : — Sir Stephen Soame, Sir Thos Middleton *K^{ts}*.

" Mr Nicholas Stile, Mr George Bolles, and Mr Richard Pyott. *Aldermen.*

" Mr Richard Burrell, Mr Robert Morer and M^r Wm. Pennifather, *Wardens.*

Mr Robert Sandy.   Mr George Holman.
" John Newman.   " Hugh Gold.
" Richd Denman.   " Robert Cox.

Mr Humphrey Walcott.	Mr Gyles Parslowe.
" Richd Aldworth.	" Robt Bowyer.
" Richard Cox.	" Thomas Nutt.
" Anthony Soda.	" Roger Gwyn.
" Thomas Longston.	" Thos Westraw.

. . . .

"This day upon the special motion and request of Sir Thomas Smyth Kt it is consented and agreed that this Company will adventure £62, 10. for V¢ lotts in the Lotterye for Virginia, and that the sayd adventure shall be made by Wardens with the Comen Goodes of this House and that the benefitt happening shall be whollye employed to the use of this House & Companye." . . .

[MEM. — May 16, 1612, Master Welby entered for publication at Stationers' Hall, "under the handes of Sir Thomas Smithe, &c. A publication by his Maiesties Councell of Virginea, touchinge the deferringe of the Lotterye."

No copy of this publication is known to be in existence.]

CCX. THE NEW LIFE OF VIRGINIA.

May 1, 1612, Master Welby entered at Stationers' Hall for publication, "under the handes of Sir Thomas Smith, Sir Dudley Digges, Master Robert Johnson and the Wardens. The Lotterys best prize, declaring the former successe and present estate of Viriginia's Plantation." The tract is dedicated "to The Right worshipfull Sir Thomas Smith," by R. I. It was reprinted by Peter Force, at Washington, in 1836 [No. 7 in vol. i.] ; and also in vol. viii. 2d series, Mass. Hist. Collections.

Originals, which are worth about $160 each, are preserved in the Library of Congress, of Harvard College, of John Carter-Brown, and of Mr. Kalbfleisch.

It was published with the following title-page : —

THE
NEW LIFE
of Virginea:
DECLARING THE

FORMER SVCCESSE AND PRE-
fent eftate of that plantation being the fecond
part of *Noua Britannia*.

Publifhed by the authoritie of his Maiefties
Counfell of *Virginea*.

LONDON,
Imprinted by *Felix Kyngston* for *William Welby*, dwelling at the
figne of the Swan in Pauls Churchyard. 1 6 1 2.

CCXI. FROM THE MERCERS' RECORDS.

At a court of the Mercers' Company held on May 20, 1612, it was agreed at the request of Sir Thomas Smith, knight, that the company should adventure £50 in this present lottery for Virginia.

CCXII. PHILIP III. TO VELASCO.

GENERAL ARCHIVES OF SIMANCAS. DEPARTMENT OF STATE, VOLUME 2571, FOLIO 317.

Copy of an extract from a deciphered letter of His Majesty to Don Alonso de Velasco, dated Madrid, June 6, 1612.

" I approve of your plan to send to Virginia in the first vessels that should sail some trustworthy person, who should bring a reliable account of how matters stand there — and as to the matter of Don Roberto Sirley, nothing more is to be done than to report to me whatever else may present itself."

CCXIII. VELASCO TO PHILIP III.

GENERAL ARCHIVES OF SIMANACS. DEPARTMENT OF STATE, VOLUME 2589, FOLIO 50.

Copy of a deciphered letter of Don Alonso de Velasco to the King of Spain, dated London, June 18, 1612.

" SIRE. —

" In order to encourage the settlement of Virginia and to progress there with a more solid foundation they have determined here to send and establish a post in the Bermuda, for which purpose they are preparing 300 men and 60 women, who will sail certainly during the month of July in a ship which will also take out whatever is necessary to erect a fort, where they can secure a better footing and continue more conveniently in their design.

" God grant " etc.

Anno Dom 1628
Ætatis Suæ 66

SIR WILLIAM HERICKE

CCXIV. DIGBY TO CARLETON.

Madrid, June 20, 1612.   Digby to Carleton.

. . . "Thei are very much displeased with our new discoverie of the North-Weste passage ; but more particularly
with our plantation in Virginia.   Which thei stick not now
to say, that yf his Majestie will not cause yt to bee recalled,
this King will bee forced by a strong hande to assay ye
removall of yt.   And I heare that Don Pedro de Cunega
hathe commission to move his Majestie that his subjects may
desiste from any farther proceeding therein.   If hee have,
I doubt not but hee will receive a cold answeare.   And for
their doing anything by ye way of hostilitie, I concive thei
will be very slowe to give England (who is very apte to lay
holde on any occasion) so juste a pretence to bee doing with
them."

CCXV. FROM THE GROCERS' RECORDS.

From Wardens' Accounts, Grocers' Company.   Under
head of " Casual paymentes " in
   " Th' accompte and Reconing of

Richard Burrell,   } Wardens of the Misterie of the
Robert Morer,   } Grocerie of the Cittie of London.
Wᵐ Pennyfather,   }

From 22. July A. D. 1611 to 20 July 1612.

" Paid to Sir Thomas Smyth Kᵗ 23ʳᵈ day of ⎫
June 1612 for the Companys adventure for ⎪
5 lottes in the presente Lottery for Planta- ⎬ LXij. x.
tion in Virginia according to an order of ⎪ [£62 10.]
Court made 24. April 1612, as by acquit-   ⎪
tance may appeare."   ⎭

CCXVI. STRACHEY'S VIRGINIA. — I.

Strachey's "Virginia" — Ashmole MS. 1758.[1]   Collated and extracted by G. Parker, Bodleian Library, August 25, 1885.

[fol. 1.]   The[2] First Booke of the First Decade containing the Historie of Travaile into Virginia Britania, expressing togither with the conditions, manners and Quallities of the Inhabitauntes, The Cosmographie, & commodities of the Country : obtayned and gathered by William Strachey gent. three yeares thether Imployed, Secretarie unto the State, and of Counsell, with the Right Hono:[ble] the Lord La Warre, his Ma:[ties] Lord Governour and Captayne Generall for the Colonie./

"Alget, quj non ardet. / W St : /

[fol. 2.]   [3] "To the right worthie and noble gent. covetous of all knowledge, Sir Allen Apsley Knight Purveyor for His Majesties Navie Royall.

"Worthy Sir.

"It is common, if not naturall to worldlings, where things succeed not according to the heat of their large expectations, not only to fall from their resolutions (in a Busines

---

[1] There are two copies of the MS. of Strachey's *Virginia ;* the one in the Bodleian Library at Oxford which has never been printed — from which I am now giving these extracts ; the other (CCXVII.) in the British Museum, Sloane Collection, No. 1622, which was published by the Hakluyt Society of London, England, in 1849.   At the request of Mr. Kingdon of London, Mr. Parker of the Bodleian Library compared the Ashmole MS. 1758 with the Hakluyt publication for me, and I have given in this document most of the differences of any consequence.   The text in each is nearly identical.   I also had the Sloane MS. 1622 examined at the Museum.

[2] The Sloane (CCXVII.) title-page is somewhat different.

[3] There has been some doubt as to when this treatise was written ; but it seems very evident to me that the original was written between the date of Strachey's return from Virginia and July 23, 1612 (before Captain Argall sailed for Virginia), and that the Ashmolean copy was presented to Sir Allen Apsley before the death of Henry, Prince of Wales (November 6, 1612).   The original Sloane, evidently written about the same time, was afterwards presented to Lord Bacon in 1618 (after July 11), with several alterations in the text, rendered necessary by the lapse of time.   See note 1, page 565.

how well-weyed soever in Counsaile, or full of fame, honour,
or goodnes,) and first grounds ; but to quarrell all meanes
that gave heart (almost connivaunce) to the setting on:
so testy is the insatiate passioun and that ymmeasurable
hope which will needes convert ytselfe into deluding assur-
aune : as low Hillocks, such are such men, covered with
snow, let the least sunn or Wind give them up naked
though no worse thenn they were, yet the mountannous
Imagynatioun not satisfied turnes into such a Laughter as
mad-men take up, an unkindly and bastard Laughter, little different from madnes ytselfe : I confesse I would ever
be free from the fury of such, yet what I can speak of
goodnes I must not be ashamed nor feare, and all good
Angells deceave me, if any Aviso in that, returne the
Reader distraction, or me a chiding : and can my voice be
exalted in any tune more full of pietie and happines then*n*
in the Busines for Virginia ? Which was once a thing so
full of expectaunce (and that not above three years since[1])
as not a yeare of a romain-jubile, no nor the Ethnick-
Queene of Ephesus, can be said to have beene followed
with more heate and zeale ; the discourse and visitatioun of
yt tooke up all meetings, times, termes, all degrees, all
purses, and such throngs and concourse of personall undertakers, as the aire seemed not to have more Lights thenn
that holie Cause inflamed Spiritts to partake with yt, almost
every religious Subject that stood sound indeed at the
coare within to Loialtie and to the professioun of the present
Faith brought his Free-will-offring, and professed thenn to
throw his bread upoun those waters, however, (alas) now in
these tymes the back and worse face of Janus with the repy-
ning eye, and tongue of slaunder, hath bene turned upoun
yt. When yet yt transcends the Reach of such who both
will and doe understand yt, what rubbish Interpositioun
should so straungely chaunge her former conceyved felicity,
or whie the Plenulune and fulnes of her hopes should suffer
under so many petulent new-Feares, and falce Freinds.

[1] This is a reference to the great rush for Virginia in the spring of 1609.

" I will councell no man*n* in the waies of the world, but
where my reasoun may tell me, that I maie advise of proffitt, since interposing hazardes maie meete (there being on
permanent or reall happines under the Sun*n*) and thenn
maie I be well assured of hastie and sinister judgment, censured a *partie* to the least losse though no Competitour in
any gaine : only yet let me dare to publish to any one that
hath adventured in this sprightly and pious actioun, especially [fol. 2ᵇ] to such who have assumed that for their rav-
isht love to faire vertue, that the Former endes and first
motives to the undertaking stand yet. as apparant and profitable as at first, whether be respected a natioun to blesse
with knowledge, a fruictfull and pleasant country to seat
and settle the swarmes of our ranck multitude, who tast in
this *our* owne clyme nothing but of Idlenes, Prophannes,
and waut ; or whither be respected a secure and necessary
Retreyt for our manie shipps, when the insolent Enemy of
those Seas shall at any tyme quarrell us ; or whither be respected, the commodities and materialls for shipping, so
much exhausted, and so dearely obteyned from the easterly
Countries, as Flax for Cordage, Pitch and Tarr, Pine and
Firre for mastage, &c, or whither be respected the hopes
of the upland-country amongest the mountaynes, we conceave of many sorts of mineralls, fynding alreddy in the
surface and upper crust the sparre of good proufe, and
worthie the expence of Triall ; or lastly whither be respected that more thenn likelyhood of the discovery that
waie, westerly the great and hopefull discent into the *mar
del Zur* or South-Sea, of which the late discourse published in print by an able and understanding gentleman*n*
of Qualitie, of the Nor-West passadge,[1] gives so cliere and
undoubted Testimonie.

" But worthie Sʳ I doe forget myself to openn a Book
unto your knowledge which is full of Love and understanding of the true endes of this great action, yet so yt maie be
that these geathered observations thus bungled, bound up,

1 Written by Sir Dudley Digges, see March 11, 1612.

and to *your view alone intended by* me maie fall into such
handes as maie put some doubtes which even this entraunce
may resolve them in, and so begett towards the further
reading hereof a better opinion : Be yt only your honour to
pardoun me the appealing of you from your more serious
affaires to the perusall of these infirme and scatterd collections, since yf I have offended, the noblenes & Bountie of
your faire Disposicioun (expressed evenn in my knowledge
to manie of my best Freindes) makes me presume that I
cannot (in any actioun, which hath relish of virtue and
goodnes) too much challenge or provoak your patience.

" And so not striving to be unnecessarily troublesome I
wish unto you the iust accomplishment of your owne vertuous desires : by him who is truly to you divoted.

" WILLIAM STRACHEY.

"ECCLESIAE, ET REIPUB: [fol. 3.]
Wild as they ar, accept them, so were wee :
To make them civil, will our Honour be :
And if good workes, be the effects of myndes,
That like good-angells be, let our Designes,
   As we ar Angli, make us angells too :
   No better worck, can church, or statesman do.

W. ST.

" We call Cape Henry, in honour of our most [fol. 16.]
royall prince.[1] . . .

" We call Cape Charles in honour of our [fol. 16^b.]
princely Duk of York.[1] . . .

" Yt being the place wherein our aboad and habitatioun
hath now (well neere) six yeares consisted.[1]

---

[1] These passages were originally
written in the same way in the Sloane
MS. ; but before presentation to Bacon it was necessary to correct them,
and they now appear in that MS. as
follows : —
       that our   deceased
" in honour of our most royall prince."

" in honour of our princely Duk of
York."   .   .   .   .   .
" Our aboad & habitation hath now
(well neere) six yeares consisted."
   [" I have copied the foregoing
exactly as they occur in the MS. The
corrections are most certainly in a different handwriting from that of the

[fol. 56.]   " The [1] Second Book of the First decade of
        the Historie of Travaile into Virginia-Britania,
expressing the severall voyages, and Colonies addressed into
these partes of America, now by us intituled Virginia, at
whose Chardges first undertaken, and what Captaines
therein imployed, with what their success, casuallies &
adventures ; gathered by William Strachey gent. / &c. /

" Alget, qui non ardet.[2] /

" Wee seek not yours, but you : Pet. /

" Res nostrae sub inde non sunt quales quis optaret, sed
quales esse possunt.[2] /

                                                " W. St.
[fol. 57.]   " Cap. I. /

" A collection, necessarily gathered, of the most
matteriall perticulers, of every Severall Colonie, & voyage
addressed by the English at any tyme, into these partes of
America which hath gotten the Denomination of Virginia. /

" Whether that ever famous Genoese Christopher Columbus," etc. [about as in the Hakluyt volume ; but with the
marginal note, " Of the first finders out of Virginia, the
Captaynes thether Imployed, & by whom," etc.]

CCXVI. has also the following introduction to the
" Dictionary of the Indian Language," which is not given
in CCXVII. (See Hakluyt Society volume for 1849, pp.
181–196.)

text, and are written by the same person who added the marginal notes ;
but possibly these corrections were
made at a later day by the original
writer of the MS." E. Salmon, Brit.
Mus. April 17, 1884.]

[1] The Sloane title is different
(CCXVII.).

[2] These same mottoes were used by
Strachey on the title-page of *Lawes
Divine, Morall and Martiall*, etc.
(CXC.). The Sloane motto is the
same on both title-pages ; namely :
Psalm cii. ver. 18.

The Præmonition to the reader, of

about 7,000 words, defends the enterprise against the claims of Spain,
etc. The first book, containing about
35,000 words, is mainly descriptive ;
but it also gives something of events
in Virginia from April, 1607, to about
August, 1611. The second book, containing about 14,000 words, goes over
American discoveries, etc., from 1492
to 1606, and then gives an acconut of
the Northern Colony (1607–8) nearly
as in XXXVI. Then there is a *Dic-
tionarie of the Indian Language*. The
second book was published in *Mass.
Hist. Soc. Coll.* 4th series, vol. i. 1852.

" A Short Dictionary, added unto the former Discourses, of the Indian Language, used within the Chessiopioch Bay; more perticulerly about the Tract and amongst the Inhabitaunts of the first River, called by them Powhaton, and by us, the Kings River, wherin as yet our Townes, and Fortes, ar seated. By which, such who shall be Imployed thether may know the readyer how to confer, and how to truck and Trade with the People."

CCXVII. STRACHEY'S VIRGINIA. — II.

The Strachey MS. in the Sloane Collection, No. 1622, already referred to in my notes on CCXVI., was published by the Hakluyt Society of London in 1849, to which publication the reader is referred.

The following are the title-pages of the two books: —

"*The First Booke* of The Historie of Travaile into Virginia Britannia, expressing The Cosmographie and Comodities of The Country, Togither with the Manners And Customes of The People: — Gathered And Observed As Well By Those who went First Thither, As Collected By William Strachey, gent., Three yeares thither Imployed secretarie of State, And of Counsaile with the Right Honorable The Lord La-Warre, His Majesties Lord Governor and Capt. Generall of The Colony. Psalm. CII. Ver. 18. This shalbe written for the generation to come: and The people which shalbe created shall praise the Lord."

" *The Second Book* of The First Decade of The Historie of Travaile into Virginia-Britannia, entreating of the First Discoverie of The Country, and of the first Colonie, Transported by Sir Richard Greenville, Knight, upon the Island of Roanoak, at the Expence and charge of Sir Walter Raleigh, knight.

" As also of the Northern Colonie, seated upon the River of Sachadehoc, Transported Anno 1585, [1607?], at the charge of Sir John Popham, Knight, Late Lord Chiefe Justice of England, gathered by William Strachey, gent.

" Psalm CII, Ver. 18. This shalbe written for the generation to come ; and the people which shalbe created shall praise the Lord."

I think Strachey refers to this compilation in his prose preface to CXC., where he promises in the course of time to submit to the views of " The Committies," etc., " *The full Storie*," both of Virginia and the Bermudas. He evidently planned a large work, but whether his plan was carried out or not is uncertain. Only the manuscript of the first and second books of the first decade has been found. It was evidently a personal venture, and Strachey certainly met with no encouragement in publishing such a work at this time, from The Committies of the Company, and after several trials he failed to find a patron elsewhere. We know but little of Strachey ; his command of language seems to me very striking, and his initials, W. S., are the most interesting of the period.

CCXVIII. FROM STOW'S CHRONICLE.

" The 29. of June 1612 [at the West end of Saint Paules Church] began a great Lottery in London, the greatest Lot or prize was a thousand pound in plate." — Stow's Chronicle abridged by Howes.

The following relates to one of the first lotteries which I have found mentioned in English history : —

" A great Lotterie being holden at London in Paules Church yard, at the West doore was begun to be drawne the 11. of Januarie and continued day and night till the 1st of May 1569, when the said drawing was fully ended. The prizes consisted of plate, and the profits were appropriated to the repair of the sea-ports." The troubles with Spain were then brewing over the **Hawkins** incident at Vera Cruz, etc.

CCXIX. CHAMBERLAIN TO CARLETON.

Chamberlain to Carleton, July 9, 1612.

"My very goode Lorde: the Spanish ambassador, Don Pedro de Cuniga marques de villa Flores had his first audience on Sonday last at Hampton court, wherin he was very short and in a manner did only shew his letters of credence, referring the rest of his message to a more private hearing : which is appointed him tomorrow at Whitehall, whether the K. comes this day for that purpose, having past all this weeke at Windsor and therabout. The K. makes haste to dispatch him, and when he hath heard what he can say, meanes to invite him to Tiballs [Theobalds] and feast him there on Sonday, and so to dismisse him.

"I have yt from a goode hand that besides matter of ceremonie and acquainting the K. with the reasons of these late contracts with Fraunce a principall part of his errand is to cleere himselfe of some imputations laide upon him by the Lord Treasurer [Cecil] about the powder treason, and to have cried quittance with him (yf he had ben alive) in accusing him of some unwarrantable practises. He lies at the Ambassador lidgers[1] house, refusing to be lodged or defrayed by the King because he understoode his entertainment was not like to be aunswerable in every point to that of the D. of Buillon. Yt is generally looked for that he will expostulate about our planting in Virginia, wherin there will need no great contestation, seeing yt is to be feared that that action will fall to the ground of ytself, by the extreem beastly ydlenes of our nation, which (notwithstanding any cost or diligence used to support them) will rather die and starve then be brought to any labor or industrie to maintain themselves. two or three of the last ships that came thence bring nothing but discomfort, and that Sir Thomas Gates and Sir Thomas Dale are quite out of hart, and to mend the matter not past five days since here

---

[1] Velasco.

arrived a ship[1] with ten men, (who being sent foorth to fish for theyre releife and having taken great store) have given them the slip and run away, and fill the towne with yll reports, which will hinder that business more then the Lotterie or any other art they can use for the present will further yt. and yet they have taken goode order to have these runaways apprehended and punished or at least sent backe again. . . .

"From London this 9th of July 1612.

"Your Lordships to command

"JOHN CHAMBERLAINE."

CCXX. THE LOTTERY DRAWING.

"The King's Majestie in special favor for the present
A Lottery.   plantation of English Collonies in Virginia,
granted a liberall Lottery, in which was contained five thousand pound in prizes certayne, besides rewardes of casualtie and began to be drawne, in a
It began the new built house at the West end of Paul's the 29.
29. of June
and ended
the 20. of of June 1612; But of which Lottery, for want
July.   of filling uppe the number of lots, there were then taken out and throwne away three score thousande blanckes, without abating of any one prize; and by the twenteth of July, all was drawne and finished. This Lottery was so plainely carryed and honestly performed that it gave full satisfaction to all persons. Thomas Sharplisse, a Taylor of London, had the chiefe prize, viz; foure thousand crownes in fayre plate, which was sent to his house in very stately manner. during the whole tyme of drawing of

---

[1] The Trial, I suppose, which ship had arrived in Virginia in August, 1611, and probably remained there until Percy returned in her for England, April 22, 1612, and after a long and dangerous voyage "anchored in Dover Roade where we did mete with Sʳ Samuell Argall bownde for New England to displant the French Collonie there, the which as I after heard was Valliantly performed." See "A Trewe Relacyon of the procedeinges and ocurentes of momente which have hapened in Virginia . . . 1609 untill . . . 1612," by George Percy, written about 1625.

SIR HENRY HOBART

Chief Justice

this Lottery, there was alwaies present divers worshipfull Knights and Esquiers accompanied with sundry grave discreet Cittizens." — Howes' Chronicle, edition of 1615. See CCXVIII. also.

"A Lottery granted for the Plantation of Virginia, 1612.

"About this time [June, 1612] the King, in special favour to the present plantation of the English Colonies in Virginia, granted a Lottery, to be held at the West-end of Paul's whereof one Thomas Sharplys a Taylor of London, had the chief prize, which was four thousand crowns in fair plate." — Baker's Chronicles.

> "One byrde in the hande is worth two in the woode
> If we get the great lot, it will do us goode."

July 2, 1612. "Master Welby, entered at Stationer's Hall for publication. Under the hands of Sir Thomas Smithe — A booke called, The Lottery for Virginea opened the xxixth of June 1612, declaringe the names of suche as have prices or rewardes."

July 17. "Master Welbye entred for his copy in full courte holden this day, and under the hand of Sir Thomas Smithe, Knighte.

"The Articles sett downe for the Second Lottery." — From the Register of the Stationers.

No copies of these two publications, I believe, are now known to be in existence.

CCXXI. RECORDS OF ST. MARY, COLECHURCH.

Extract from the vestry minutes of the Church of St. Mary, Colechurch, "which anciently stood on the north side of the Poultry, at the South-West Corner of the Old Jewry, London, England. It was destroyed by the Great Fire, A. D. 1666."

" Att A vestry Houlden the vijth daye of June 1612 it is agreed to adventur sixe pounde of the proffitt of our churche stocke in the lottrey for the plantacion of Vergenya and what benifitt shall hapen thereby shalbe for the good of our church."

After which is written : —

" For this adventure above written our church had *twoe spones* price twentye shillinge as apereth in the accoumpt of Edward Draper then Elder Church Warden."

CCXXII.

Extract from the Churchwarden's book of St. Mary, Woolchurch Hawe, 1612–13 : " Received from the lottery for 50 lotts which was by order of the parish to be drawn in twelve penny lotts. £0. 10s. 0d."

CCXXIII. FLORES (ZUÑIGA) TO PHILIP III.

GENERAL ARCHIVES OF SIMANCAS. DEPARTMENT OF STATE, VOLUME 2589, FOLIO 61.

Copy of a deciphered letter of the Marquess of Flores to the King of Spain, dated London, August 1, 1612. Received August 18 (8).

" SIRE. —

" A ship has arrived here from Viginia, and altho' the well-informed and others think that that business does not grow, but rather continues to diminish ; I have been told by a friend, who tells me the truth, that some of the people who have gone there, think now some of them should marry the women of the savages of that country ; and he tells me that there are already 40 or 50 thus married, and other Englishmen after being put among them have become savages, and that the women whom they took out, have also gone among the savages, and they have received and treated them well — that a zealous minister of their sect was seriously wounded in many places, because he reprehended them.

" They have established a lottery from which they will

obtain sixty thousand ducats, and by these means they will dispatch six ships, with as many people as they can get by such pretexts.

"In this beginning it will be easy to drive those people out from there, and the not punishing hereof is the cause why they so boldly attempt other things, and Y. M. will see this, because already they have houses and begin another Colony in Newfoundland, in those regions where they have their fisheries. Now is a very favorable time for their punishment, because if it is done, they will see that Y. M. will not proceed with them altogether by demands (requests, petition &c) which has only made them more haughty than they could hope, if relying upon their own strength alone.

"God preserve Y. M." etc.

[MEM. — Captain Samuel Argall in the Treasurer was "dispatched with *Commission* to displace the French, who had taken the opportunitie to settle themselves within our limits." . . . See "A Briefe Relation of the Discoverie and Plantation of New-England . . . 1607 . . . to the present year 1622," and Mr. Neill's preface to "Virginia Vetusta," p. x. Argall's commission, I fear, is now lost. He sailed some time before the 23d of July, 1612, on which day "he departed from the coast of England."]

CCXXIV. CHARTER OF THE N. W. P. COMPANY.

SAINSBURY'S CALENDAR OF STATE PAPERS, COLONIAL, EAST INDIES, 1513–1616, NUMBER 616.

Bletsoe, July 26, 1612. Grant incorporating the North West Passage Company.

The grant recites that in Hudson's voyage, April, 1610, to October, 1611, they had found a strait or narrow sea by which they hope and purpose to advance a trade to the great kingdoms of Tartary, China, Japan, Solomon's Islands, Chili, the Philippines, and other countries, for the better accomplishment and discovery of which they have sued for license to be incorporated into a company. "In regard, it is an enterprize tending to so worthy an end, and which now at last after many proofs hath obtained so happy and likely a beginning, we have thought of some extraordinary means to grace and honour the same;" and do constitute "our dear son [Prince Henry] immediately under ourselves (whose protection is universal) supreme protector of the discovery and company," and 22 peers, three sons of peers, 36 knights, one lady, 38 esquires, and 188 merchants, etc., a body corporate and politic by the name of the "Governor and Company of the Merchants of London, discoverers of the North-West Passage." Sir Thomas Smythe, Sir Dudley Diggs, and John Wolstenholme having been the first movers and principal instruments of setting forth ships to sea for accomplishing the discovery. Sir Thomas Smythe is appointed first governor. Sir Robert Mansell, Sir Ja⁵ Lancaster, Sir Dudley Diggs, Wm. Cockayne, Fra⁵ Jones alderman, John Wolstenholme Esq., Wm. Greenwell, John Eldred, Nic Leate, Nic. Salter, Robt. Offley, Hewett Stapers, William Russell, Ric. Wyche, Raphe Freeman, Wm. Stone, Robᵗ Middleton, Wm. Harrison, Morris Abbott, Humfrey Hanforde, Philip Burlamachi, Abrah. Chamberlain, Robᵗ Bell, and Wm. Burrell, merchants, the first twenty-four committees and directors. This Company was "to enjoy forever the whole entire and only trade into the North West passage, and unto the lands, territories, and dominions aforesaid," — i. e., the northern parts of America — and "unto the very territories of Tartaria, China, Japan, Coray, &c." Most of the incorporators of this company were also members of the East India, the Muscovy, and the Virginia companies of London.

CCXXV. FLORES (ZUÑIGA) TO PHILIP III.

GENERAL ARCHIVES OF SIMANCAS. DEPARTMENT OF STATE, VOLUME 2589, FOLIO 67.

Copy of an original letter of the Marquess de Flores to the King of Spain, dated August 16, 1612.

" SIRE. —

" I reported to Y. M. that they have obtained from a lottery sixty thousand ducats for Virginia matters ; now permission has been granted for another lottery worth 120.000 ducats, and they will make great haste to finish it and will send more than two thousand men to that country, because they wish to make another fortification on the river below. In order to get the footing there, which they desire to obtain, they will sell their own children, to put the Colony into the best possible condition, which even the well-informed cannot deny !

" Don Alonso de Velasco has been told that it is an object of ridicule (a laughing stock, a shame), that this business will never come to bear fruit in any way, for this Kingdom. I myself have been assured by friends, that in their opinion, they will very soon open the port and let them go out to sea as pirates.   This is a very shameless (highhanded) matter, as I have already told Y. M. ; and if Y. M. will command them to leave that country at this time, it will appear to them as if it had been most courteously done ; because if they should be broken to pieces, they have no right to complain of it. — the whole thing is building up stones without any foundation [castles in the air]."

" Our Lord preserve the Catholic Person of Y. M. as all Christendom feels the need.   London. Augᵗ 16. 1612.

" THE MARQUES DE FLORES."

CCXXVI. PURCHAS HIS PILGRIMAGE.

August 7, 1612, there was entered at Stationers' Hall, for publication, " Purchas his Pilgrimage, or Relations of The World and the Religions observed in all Ages and places Discovered, from the Creation unto this Present. In Foure Partes. This first contayning a Theologicall and Geographicall Historie of Asia, Africa and *America*, with the Ilands adjacent. Declaring the ancient Religions before the Floud, the Heathenish, Jewish, and Saracenicall in all Ages since, in those parts professed, with their severall opinions, Idols, Oracles, Temples, Priests, Fasts, Feasts, sacrifices, and Rites Religious : Their beginnings, Proceedings, Alterations, Sects, Orders and Successions.

" With briefe Descriptions of The Countries, Nations, States, Discoveries : Private and publike Customs, and the most remarkable Rarities of Nature, or Humane industrie, in the same " . . . " By Samuel Purchas, Minister at Estwood in Essex. Unus Deus, una Veritas. London. Printed by William Stansby for Henrie Fetherstone . . . 1613." Dedicated to George, Archbishop of Canterbury.

The preface is dated November 5, 1612, and the work probably issued from the press soon after. There was a second edition in 1614, a third, " much enlarged with Additions through the whole Worke," in 1617, and a fourth in 1626, which latter edition generally accompanies " Purchas his Pilgrimes " as a fifth volume.

In the edition of 1614, Purchas gives probably 1,000 words regarding the Northern Colony, apparently compiled from the writings of Christopher Fortescue, Thomas Hanham, James Davies, John Eliot, George Popham, " Let[ter] to S[ir] J. Gilbert and E. S[eymour]," Ralegh Gilbert, and Edward Harley.

About 2,500 words regarding the Southern Colony, chiefly compiled from CCXLV., but with several extracts from CLXXI. and CCX. ; and with reference also to XLIX. and CCXXX. He evidently gives us only what met his own approbation and, therefore, only his own opinions. He then gives about 8,000 words describing the country, people, religious rites, etc., the marvelous always preferred.

CCXXVII. DIGBY TO JAMES I.

August 21, 1612. Madrid. Digby to James I.

" I have formerly advertised your Majestie of a report come unto Sevill that three or foure of this Kings Galleons should be cast away upon the Coast of Florida, which went forth with an intent to have attempted somewhat against the English Plantation in Virginea. But though this newes be not absolutely contradicted, yet I can learne so smale grownde for the report therof, that I can conceave it to be likelyer to be untrue then otherwise."

CCXXVIII. DIGBY TO JAMES I.

September 1, 1612. Madrid. Digbye to James I.

. . . " Has endeavoured to inform himself of the reasons for the stay of Don Pedro de Cuñega in England being longer than His Majesty expected. That when he was sent from hence he had *three* businesses in which he was instructed to carry himself according to the state he should find them in at his coming thither. . . . His second business was concerning Virginea; in which he was likewise not to make any proposition unto your Majestie, but upon second directions from hence, when he should have learned and advertised, what Your Majesties inclination was and what your answer was like to be, for that in case he should perceave that your Majestie was not likely to give way to that which by this King should be propounded, he should avoyd the having of a peremptory negative given unto his Master."

[MEM. — A ship which left Virginia after the 28th of July arrived in England some time in September, it seems, bringing Whitaker's letter (CCXXIX.) and book (CCXXX.), and other documents unknown.

No news from Virginia was received in England from the
date of the arrival of this ship (probably the John and
Francis or the Sarah), about September, 1612, until the
arrival of the Elizabeth on the 20th of July, 1613. And
this period was the darkest hour "in all that time of three
years disaster."]

CCXXIX. WHITAKER TO SIR THOMAS SMYTHE.

Neither of the following has ever been published in America, I believe. I can only give extended extracts from
CCXXX., as it is too long to publish entire. The fact that
it was written in Virginia gives it an additional interest. I
quote from the book as published later (CCLVIII.) noting
the page extracted from.

" To the Right Worshipfull Sir Thomas Smith, Knight,
    Treasurer of the English Colonie in Virginia: Grace and
    Peace be multiplied.
    " Right worshipfull, the noblest attemps have alwaies had
the most doubtfull beginnings, most dangerous enemies.
For wheresoever any goodnesse shall begin to bud forth,
the Divell will labour by all meanes to nip it in the head.
Wherefore, I doe not marvell though there have been great
discouragements, and many adversaries of this Plantation.
For the Divell knowing that where Christ wins, he loseth,
doth with all his might and policie hinder the publishing,
and propagation of the Gospell. Such was his practise to
discourage the Israelites from the conquest of Canaan, raising up ten of their owne Princes, that weakened the hand
of their brethren. By his meanes also there stood up some
of the Disciples that spake against Peter, for preaching the
Gospell to the Gentiles. Yea, God himselfe of purpose suffers the divell to rage thus for a while, that those that are
his might bee tried. And this hath been the case hitherto
of this godly Plantation, this the successe. But since the
affairs of this Colony have now taken better footing and are

advanced by the helpes of so many honorable Adventurers, I was greatly emboldened to write these few lines of Exhortation, to encourage the noble Spirits of so many worthy men, to goe forward in Wel-doing, wherefore (honored Sir) since all the dispatches of our affaires passes through your hand, I request of you to accept of my poore endeavours, and to publish it to the view of our Adventurers that the prejudicate opinion of some, and the disheartened mind of others may be reformed. The God of heaven and earth crowne your undanted spirit with his heavenly reward. And Let the beautie of the Lord our God be upon us : and direct thou the workes of our hands upon us, even direct thou our handie workes.

" From Henrico, this 28. of July 1612.

" He that daily prayeth for the prosperitie of this Plantation.   ALEXANDER WHITAKER."

CCXXX. WHITAKER'S GOOD NEWS FROM VIRGINIA.

" Good Newes From Virginia.   [p. 1.]

Text. " Ecclesiastes 11. 1. Cast Thy bread upon the Waters : for after many daies thou shalt finde it.

" Aude hospes contemnere opes & te quoque dignum Finge Deo.

" Be bould my Hearers to contemme riches, and frame yourselves to walke worthie of God ; for none other be worthie of God, but those that lightly esteeme of riches. Nakednesse is the riches of nature ; vertue is the only thing that makes us rich and honourable in the eyes of wise men. Povertie is a thing which most men feare, and covetous men cannot endure to behold : yet povertie with a contented mind is great riches : hee truly is the onely poore man, not that hath little, but which continually desireth more. Riches (as they are esteemed) have no limits, but still crie, *plus ultra*, still more. Neither is any man absolutely rich, but in comparison of a poorer man, of one (I meane) that hath lesse then he : for if he make diligent enquirie, he may finde divers richer then himselfe: if riches of gold and the like, had bin such as the world doth esteeme them, it is not likely that Jesus Christ would have taken so poore a state upon him: when we esteeme them at the best, they are but an heavy burthen to some, an Idoll to others, and profitable to few."

He continues in the same line (pp. 1–4). On the fourth page of his discourse, referring to his text, he says, " The words naturally divide themselves into two principal parts. A Commandment to be Liberall and Charitable: and a promise of reward, which hereafter we shall find. The Commandment also containeth in it five points, touching the doctrine of Liberalitie.

" 1. The dutie to be performed, Cast thy bread: be liberall to all.

" 2. The manner of bestowing our almes, by casting it away.

" 3. What is to be given, Bread; all things needfull, yea, and of the best kind.

" 4. Who may be liberall: even those that have it: Thy bread, it must be thine owne.

" 5. To whom we must be liberall; to all, yea, to the Waters.

" First, we wil briefly speake of the five points of this Commandment as they lie in order; and then directly come unto the Promise more particularly. The enjoyned *dutie* is Liberalitie, which sometimes is termed almes: sometimes is more largely used for all Kind of good workes, and very often is signified by the names of Charitie and Brotherly love," etc.

On pp. 4 to 8, he continues his discourse on the first point, The Duty.

On pp. 8 to 14, on the second point, " the manner." For this he lays down five rules: " First, that we give in faith; " second, " in love; " third, " bountifully and with a cheerfull minde; " fourth, " with discretion," and " the last rule of giving is, that we give in Justice."

On pp. 14 to 17 he discourses on " thirdly what is to be given " . . . " according to the several necessities of those

HENRY HOWARD
First Earl of Northampton

that want. The wants of men bee divers; some are of the minde, some of the bodie, and some be of the outward goods."

On pp. 17 to 19, on fourthly, " Who may properlie give almes, which may easilie be determined, if we consider the divers kinds of good workes which wee have now lately rehearsed. For hee that is not able to bee liberall in one kinde may be fit for another." . . .

" And remember the poore estate of the igno- [p. 18.] rant inhabitants of Virginia. Cast forth your almes (my brethren of England) and extend your liberality on these charitable workes, which God hath called you to performe. Let not the servants of superstition, that thinke to merit by their good workes (as [p. 19.] they terme them) goe beyond us in well doing; neither let them be able to open their mouths against us, and to condemne the religion of our Protestation, for want of charitable deeds.

" It may bee some men will say the worke is great, I am not able to relieve it; I answer the work is such and such order is now taken, that those that cannot give much, may be liberall in a little. Those that cannot helpe in monies by reason of their poverty, may venture their persons hither, and heere not only serve God, but helpe also these poore Indians, and build a sure foundation for themselves, but if you can do neither of these, then send your earnest prayers to God for the prosperity of this worke."

On pp. 19 to 28 he dwells on the fifth point, " To whome we are to bee liberall." Under this heading he says, on p. 21: " Wherfore, since God hath opened the doore of Virginia, to our Countrey of England, we are to thinke that God hath, as it were, by word of mouth called us in, to bestow our severall charity on them." He then goes on (pp. 21 to 28) to make an earnest appeal in behalf of the enterprise; and the Apostle does not forget to send from Henrico, in Virginia, to the men of means in (pp. 24–28) England, a fervent prayer in behalf of the Indians, " the

naked slaves of the divell." Mr. Neill, in his " Virginia
Company of London," pp. 78–81, has made some extracts
from Whitaker's discourse on the fifth point.

Pages 28 to 44 he devotes to " the promise more particularly " — " For after many days thou shalt find it." — He
prepares the way with a scriptural discourse, and then makes
his point : " Let then your liberall minds (you
[p. 32.] honorable and charitable Adventurers of Virginia)
be stirred up to cast your almes on the waters of
Virginia, without hope of present profit. . . . The husband-
man casting his seed into the earth, waiteth upon God untill
Harvest for a fruitful crop. . . . God will not yet reward
you, that he may make you more famous in the world. . . .
The worke is honourable, and now more then ever, sustained
by most honorable men. O let us not then be weary of
well-doing : fortie yeares were expired, before Israel could
plant in Canaan, and yet God had called them by the word
of his mouth, had led them himselfe by an high
[p. 33.] hand. . . . Shall our Nation, hitherto famous for
noble attempts, and the honorable finishing of
what they have undertaken, be now taxed for inconstancie,
and blamed by the enemies of our protestation, for unchari-
tableness? Yea, shall we be a scorne among Princes, and
a laughing stocke among our neighbour Nations, for basely
leaving what we honorably began ; yea, for beginning a
Discoverie, which riches other men shall gather, so soone as
we have forsaken it ? Awake you true hearted Englishmen,
you servants of Jesus Christ, remember that the Plantation
is Gods, and the reward your countries."

He then goes on to strengthen his position (pp. 34–35)
with scriptural illustrations ; and then tells of the various
rewards of faith, of love, " the [p. 36] meanes to helpe our
soules forward in their passage to heaven," of good works,
etc.

" Thus shall the Lord abundantly reward our soules for
our liberalitie, and many waies more besides if we bee truly
charitable. But the bountie of God would have us to tast

of some temporall blessings besides, and after a [p. 37.]
few daies, if we be cheerefull givers, returne a plen-
tifull reward home unto us.   Wherefore that I might content the longing minds of every man, I thought it fit in
the last place to recite a few commodities which in short
time we may finde here in Virginia, for the charitie bestowed
in this Plantation.

[1] " The whole Continent of Virginia situate within the
degrees of 34. and 47. is a place beautified by God, with all
the ornaments of nature, and enriched with his earthly
treasures : that part of it, which we already possesse, beginning at the Bay of Chesapheac, and stretching itselfe in
Northerly latitude to the degrees of 39. and 40. is interlined
with seven most goodly Rivers, the least whereof is equall
to our River of Thames : " etc.   He describes the location
and convenience of these rivers, etc.

" The River which we inhabit (commonly called [p. 38.]
Powhatans River) ebbeth and floweth 140. miles
into the maine ; at the mouth whereof are the two Forts
of Henrico and Charles : 42 miles upwards is the first and
mother Christian towne seated, called James-Towne, and 70.
miles beyond that upwards is the new towne of Henrico built,
and so named in the memorie of the Noble Prince Henry
of lasting and blessed memorie :[2] tenne miles beyond this
Towne is a place called the Fals, because the River hath
there a great descent falling downe betweene many mineral
Rocks which bee there : twelve miles farther beyond this
place there is a Christall Rocke wherewith the Indians doe
head many of their arrowes : Three dayes journey from
thence there is a rocke or stonie hill [3] found, which is in the

[1] The *Narration of the Present State of that Countrey, and our Colonies there,* mentioned on the published title-page (see CCLVIII.) begins here and con-tinues to the end.

[2] Crashaw evidently revised this before publication, as Whitaker could not have known of the death of Prince Henry when he wrote.

[3] The day's journey is indefinite. The English, probably about fifteen miles, the Indian, much farther.   This mine is said to have been found by a Dutchman.   The locality was in what is now known as the eastern gold belt of Virginia.   We are again giving proper attention to our minerals in Virginia.

top covered all over with a perfect and most rich silver oare. Our men that went to discover those parts had but two iron pickaxes with them, and those so ill tempered that the points of them turned againe and bowed at every stroake, so that wee could not search the entrailes of ye place, yet some triall was made of that oare with good successe, and argument of much hope. Six daies journey beyond this Mine a great ridge of high hils [1] doe runne along the maine land, not farre from whom the Indians report a great Sea doth runne, which we commonly call a South Sea, but in respect of our habitation is a West Sea, for there the sunne setteth from us. The higher ground is much like unto the molde of France, clay and sand being proportionably mixed together at the top; but if we digge any depth (as [p. 39.] wee have done for our bricks) wee finde it to bee redde clay, full of glistering spangles. There bee many rockie places in all quarters; and more than probable likeliehoods of rich Mines of all sorts: though I knew all, yet it were not convenient at this time that I should utter all, neither have we had meanes to search for anything as wee ought, thorough present want of men, and former wants of provision for the belly. As for Iron, steele, Antimonium, and Terra sigillata, they have rather offered themselves to our eyes and hands, then bin sought for of us. The aire of the Countrey (especially about Henrico and upward) is very temperate and agreeth well with our bodies. The extremitie of Sommer is not so hot as Spaine, nor the colde of Winter so sharpe as the frosts of England. The Spring and Harvest are the two longest seasons and most pleasant, the Summer and Winter are both but short: The Winter is for the most part drie and faire, but the Summer watered often with many great and suddaine shewers of raine; whereby the cold of Winter is warmed, and the heate of Summer cooled. . . .

[1] The Appalachian system, in a direct line, is about 100 miles from the falls, westward — 12 miles + 3 days' journey + 6 days' journey = say, 150 miles; but Whitaker's day's journey probably applied to the devious route of the Indians.

"The naturall people of the Land are to be   [p. 40.]
feared of those that come upon them without defensive Armour, but otherwise faint-hearted (if they see their
Arrowes cannot pearce) and easie to be subdued.   Shirts of
Male, or quilted cotton coates are the best defence against
them.   There is but one or two of their pettie Kings, that
for feare of us have desired our friendship. . . . Our eldest
friends bee Pipsco and Choapoke, who are our over thwart
neighbors at James-Towne, and have been friendly to us in
our great want.   The other is the Werewance of Chescheak,
who but lately traded with us peaceably.   If we were once
the masters of their Countrey, and they stood in feare of us
(which might with few hands imployed about nothing else,
be in short time brought to passe) it were an easie matter to
make them willingly to forsake the divell, to embrace the
faith of Jesus Christ, and to be baptized.   Besides, you cannot easilie judge how much they would be availeable to us in
our discoveries of the Countrey, in our buildings and plant-
ings, and quiet provisions for ourselves, when we may peace
ably passe from place to place without neede of armes or
guarde.

"The meanes for our people to live and subsist   [p. 41.]
here of themselves are many and most certaine
both for Beasts, Birds, Fish and Hearbes.   The beasts of
the countrey are for the most part wilde: as Lions, Beares,
Wolves and Deare: Foxes blacke and red, Rakowns, Be-
vers, Possowns, Squerrels, Wilde-Cats, whose skinnes are of
great price, and Muske-Rats which yeelde Muske as the
Muske-Cats doe.   There be two kindes of beasts amongst
these most strange: one of them is the female Possown,
which will let forth her young out of her bellie and take
them up into her bellie againe at her pleasure without hurt
to herselfe, neither think this to be a Travellers tale,[1] but

---

[1] Doubtless the people in England
heard many "a traveler's tale" from
Virginia; but the "Possown" (opos-
sum) *is* a curious animal, one of whose
traits has created in Virginia a new
word, nearly allied to "a traveler's
tale," namely, "possuming," *i. e.*, deceiving.

the very truth; for nature hath framed her fit for that
Service, my eyes have been witnes unto it, and we have sent
of them and their young ones into England.   The other
strange conditioned creature is the flying squirrell, which
through the helpe of certaine broad flaps of skin growing on
each side of her forelegs, will flie from tree to tree 20. or 30.
paces at one flight and more, if we have the benefit of a
small breath of winde.   Besides these, since our coming
hither, wee have brought both Kine, Goats and Hogges,
which prosper well, and would multiplie exceedingly if they
might be provided for.   This countrey besides is replenished
with birds of al sorts which have bin the best sustenance of
flesh, which our men have had since they came; also Eagels,
and Hawkes of all sorts, amongst whom are Ausprech, fishing Hawke, and the Cormorant.   The woods be every where
          ful of wilde Turkies which abound, and will runne
[p. 42.]   as swift as a Grey-hound.   In Winter our fields be
          full of Cranes, Herons, Pigeons, Partridges and
Blackbirds: the rivers and creekes bee over spread everywhere with water-foule of the greatest and least sort, as
Swans, flocks of Geese & Brants, Duck and Mallard, Shel-
drakes, Dyvers, &c. besides many other kinds of rare and
delectable birds, whose names and natures I cannot yet
recite, but we want the means to take them.   The Rivers
abound with Fish both small and great: the sea Fish come
into our Rivers in March and continue untill the end of
September: great sculles of Herings come in first: shads of
a great bignesse, and the Rock-fish follow them.   Trouts,
Base, Flounders, and other daintie fish come in before the
others be gone: then come multitudes of great sturgeons,
whereof we catch many, and should do more; but that we
want good nets answerable to the breadth and deapth of our
Rivers: besides our channels are so foule in the bottom with
great logs and trees, that we often break our nets upon
them: I cannot reckon nor give proper names to the divers
kinds of fresh fish in our rivers; I have caught with mine
angle, Pike, Carpe, Eele, Perches of sixe severall kindes,

Crea-fish and the Torope or little Turtle, besides many
smaller kinds.   Wherefore, since God hath filled the elements of the earth, aire and waters with his creatures, good
for our food and nourishment, let not the feare of starving
hereafter, or any great want, dishearten your valiant minds
from comming to a place of so great plentie : if the Countrey
were ours, and meanes for the taking of them
(which shortly I hope shall bee brought to passe.)   [p. 43.]
then all these shall be ours : we have them now,
but we are fain to fight for them, then should we have them
without that trouble. . . .

   " But these are not all the commodities which we may
finde heere : for the earth will yeelde much more fruit to
our industrial labours, as hath been proved by the Corne and
other things which wee have planted this last yeare.   I have
made proofe of it with the helpe of three more, being a
stranger to that business and having not a bodie inured to
such labour, and set so much corne *horis succisinis unius
septimanæ,* in the idle howers of one weeke, as will suffice
me for bread one quarter of a yeare : and one commoditie
is besides in this corne, that from the time of setting, unto
the time of gathering, five moneths will abundantly suffice :
for we set corne from the beginninge of March, until the
end of May, and reape or gather in Julie, August & September.   Our English seeds thrive very well heere, as Peas,
Onions, Turnips, Cabbages, Coleflowers, Carrets, Time,
Parseley, Hysop, Marjoram, and many other whereof I have
tasted and eaten.

   " What should I name unto you the divers sorts of trees,
sweete woods and Physicall plants : the divers kind of
Oakes and Walnut trees.   The Pines, Pitch-Trees, Soape-
ashes trees, Sassafras, Cedar, Ash, Maple, Cypress,
and many more which I dailie see and admire at   [p. 44.]
the beautie and riches which God hath bestowed,
upon this people, that yet know not how to use them.

   " Wherefore you (right wise and noble Adventurers of
Virginia) whose hearts God hath stirred up to build him a

Temple, to make him an house, to conquer a Kingdome for him heere : be not discouraged with those many lamentable assaults that the divell hath made against us : he now rageth most, because he knoweth this Kingdome is to have a short end.   Goe forward boldly, and remember that you fight under the banner of Jesus Christ, that you plant his Kingdome, who hath already broken the Serpents head : God may deferre his temporall reward for a season, but be assured that in the end you shall find riches and honour in this world, and blessed immortality in the world to come. And you my brethren, my fellow labourers, send up your earnest prayers to God for his church in Virginia, that since his harvest heere is great, but the labourers few, hee would thrust forth labourers into his harvest ; and pray also for me that the ministration of his Gospell may be powerfull and effectuall by me to the salvation of many, and advancement of the Kingdome of Jesus Christ to whom with the Father and the holy Spirit, bee all honour and glorie for evermore, Amen."

CCXXXI. DIGBY TO JAMES I.

September 13, 1612.   Madrid.   Digby to James I.
. . . " It is here held for certayne that this King will not permit Our plantation at Virginea, and the Bermudas, in so much that it is here publiquely and avowedly spoken in the Court, that they will shortly attempt the removing of them.   And I have Letters from some in the Fleete with Don luys de Fajardo, who is now at Cales ready to put to sea, that so soone as he hath conducted home the West Indian Fleet, he shall goe to the Havana and winter there ; and from thence in the beginning of the Spring shall attempt Verginea.   But therunto I give not much credit, for that I am informed here from good part, that there hath beene of late, a consultation and almost a resolution taken, that one Don Diego Brochero, now of the Councell of Warre, and a greate Commander at Sea, shall have the

conducting of this enterprise, and that he shall goe from Portugall, where this King's Navie is commanded to meete, under Cullor and pretence of the King's remayning at Lisbone. But of these things I shall use all the dilligence I may, to attayne unto the truthe."

CCXXXII. NORTHAMPTON TO JAMES I.

The whole letter is published in "The Magazine of American History," vol. viii. pp. 505–507 (1882). It was evidently written after the return of the Plough from the Bermudas early in September, 1612, probably on Sunday, September 14.

"Henry Earl of Northampton to the Kinges (Jame I.) sacred and Royall Maiesty.

"From Greenwich, Sunday at xii.

"Most excellent, most gratiouse, most redoubted and deer soveraine." [Sends three advertisements, which remind him of the roses, violets, and gilly flowers he used to send to his Majesty from thence. The first concerns the archduke; the second, the Muscovy Company, who have prospered strangely, got within nine degrees of the pole, saw 700 whales, and brought home seventeen; the third;] "Another companie are in like sorte advertised of the safe arrivall of their shippes in the Bermudos upon which Iland the Spaniardes affrighted and dismaied with the frequencie of Hurricanes which they ever meete about that place durst not adventur but calle it *Dæmoniorum insulam.* But from this Iland of Devilles our men have sent some amber and some seede perles for an assaie which the Devilles of the Bermudos love not better to retaine then the Angeles of Castile doo to recover. The place aboundes in swine in fowle and fishe, which moves our men to growe more confident in the safe possessione of a place which they have possessed so peaceably." [Wonders the people who thrive so well under his Majesty are not more thankful to him, etc.] "I humbly and affectionately Kisse your M^{tis} faire hande and prayinge for your preservation as for my sowle live and die.

"Your M^{tis} most affectionat humble and loyall servant and subject till death.

"H. NORTHAMPTON."

CCXXXIII. DIGBY TO CARLETON.

September 22. "Sir John Digby to Sr Dudley Carleton. . . . There is nothing so generally spoaken of in this Courte as their intent to remove Our plantation in Virginia. And for myne owne parte, I am of beliefe, that the Spaniards will serve us, as thei did the Frenchmen in Florida, unles wee undertake ye business much more throughly and roundely, then hitherto wee have donne. But heereof, thei have had sufficient warning in England."

CCXXXIV. FROM GROCERS' RECORDS.

As CCXXXIV., CCXXXV., and CCXXXVI. relate to "the same Salt," I have placed them together, regardless of their dates.

Court of Assistants, Grocers' Company.

"Die Martis xxix die Septembris 1612.

"Present:— Mr Giles Parslowe, Mr William Millett, Mr Roger Gwyn, *Wardens.*

Mr John Newman,	Mr Richd Denman,	⎫
" Robert Cocks,	" Robert Morer,	⎬ *Assistants.*
" Wm Pennyfather	" Laurence Greene,	⎭
" Wm Barrett,	" Robert Johnson,	⎫
" Chas Glascock,	" John Farmer,	⎪
" Edwd Jennings,	" Arthur Blakemore,	⎬ *Livery.*
" George Scott,	" Jeffrey Kirby,	⎪
" Thomas Foxall,	" John West, Junior.	⎭

"To day Mr Wardens made knowen to their Brethren as

The rigtte Honourable THOMAS:
HOWARD Earle of Suffolke. Lorde Walden
and Lorde Tresurer of England and one of his
Ma.tie most hon.ble prime Counsell and knight of the
most noble Order of ye Garter.

R. Elstracke sculp:

THOMAS HOWARD

First Earl of Suffolk

well of the Assistants as Livery of this Company here presente in the Hall, of the some of thirteene pounds and ten
shillings that was due to the Companye for theyr adventure
in the late Lottery made for the plantacon in Virginia. In
which Lottery was putt of the Companyes Comen Goodes
of this house Lxij^{li} x^s and asked theyr opinions whether M^r
Wardens should accept of the said xiij^{li} x^s soe due unto
them and to abate after x^{li} per cent. or to accept of a faire
rounde Salt with a cover of Silver all gilt poiz 44^{oz} $\frac{1}{4}$ 1^d at
6^s 7^d per oz amounting to the some xiiij^{li} xix^s vi^d.

" The which Salt they all agreed that Mr. Wardens should
accept both in respect it would not be so much losse to the
Company as to take the xiij^{li} x^s with the sayd abatement,
and alsoe in regard this Company want Salts, and alsoe that
Mr Wardens shall paye the overplus being xxix^s vi^d of the
Comen Goodes of this House in full discharge for the same
Salt."

CCXXXV. FROM GROCERS' RECORDS.

Court of Assistants, Grocers' Company.

" Curia Assisten. tent die veneris xviij die Decembris
1612. 10. James.

" Present : — Sir Stephen Soame and Sir Thomas Middleton. Kt^s

" Mr Nicholas Stile, Mr George Bolles and Mr Richard
Pyott, *Aldermen*.

" Mr Giles Parslowe, Mr William Millett and Mr Roger
Gwyn. *Wardens*.

Mr George Holman,	Mr John Newman,
" Robert Cocks,	" Humfrey Walcott,
" Richard Burrell,	" Wm. Dale,
" Richard Aldworth,	" Robert Bowyer,
" Richard Cox,	" Robert Morer,
" Anthony Soday,	" Thomas Longston,
" Thomas Westrowe,	" Laurence Greene,
" Richard Bourne,	" Danyel Wynche.

" To day Mr. Wardens acknowledges the receipt of one

faire rounde Salt and Cover all of silver guilt weighing
xliiij oz one quarter of an oz and a pennyweight to the use
of this Company — which this company hath in regard of
xiij^{li} x^s happening to them in the late Lottery made for
plantacon in Virginia upon their adventure or putting in
lxij ^{li} x^s and for xxix^s vi^d more payd by Mr Wardens for the
same praying allowance thereof whereof this court allowed
accordingly."

CCXXXVI. FROM GROCERS' RECORD.

From Wardens' Account under "Casual payments," July
20, 1612, to July, 1613.

"Item paid to Clement Fryer the some of xxix^s
vi^d which was added to the xiij^{li} x^s happening to this Companye for Lxij^{li} x^s adventured
in ye late Lotterye for plantacon in Virginia
to by a Silver and gilt Salt for this Company   } xxix^s vi^d.
as by order of Courte made the xviijth day of
December 1612 as ꝑ acquittance may appeare."

CCXXXVII. DIGBY TO CARLETON.

October 10, 1612.   Madrid.   Digbye to Carleton.
. . . "Others say, that these forces united in Portugal, shall
under the commaunde of Don Diego Brochero attempte
the removing of our plantation in Virginia. . . . I have
lately received advertisement from Lisborne, that there arrived there a shipp, which coming from the Havana bring-
ethe worde, That there were diverse soldiers there bothe of
those parties and others, which this laste Spring were sente
from hence out of Andalusia, which were ready to goe to
attempte Virginia.   And that to this ende all shipps that
for some monthes before had arrived there were imbargued.
Since, there is newes come from Sevill, that the Spaniards
have overthrowen our men in Virginia.   To which though
I give little beliefe, yet I thought fitt to sende unto ye

Secretarye of State to give him notice of what I heard.
Hee sent me worde, I might fully assure myselfe, that there
was no suche thing hitherto to their knowledge. But that
yt was true indeede, that the King of Spaines people were
muche discontent and muttered, that ye plantation was permitted. And that yt had beene likewise handled in the
Councell of State heere; and that this helde yt very unfitt,
that a Companie of Voluntarye and loose people (as hee
tearmed them) without the commaunde or interposition of
their King, should goe forward with that which mighte in
tyme prove of so muche inconvenience to the King of
Spaine."

CCXXXVIII. PHILIP III. TO VELASCO.

*GENERAL ARCHIVES OF SIMANCAS. DEPARTMENT OF STATE,
VOLUME 2571, FOLIO 328.*

Copy of a deciphered letter of H. M. to Don Alonso de
Velasco, dated Valladolid, November 3, 1612.

" Your letters of June 18th [CCXIII.] informed me of the
martyrdom which two priests underwent there — also of
what you state concerning the affairs of Savoy — and of
the post which it was proposed to take in the Bermuda,
so as to encourage the colonisation of Virginia — and I
thank you much for the zeal which you show in keeping me
informed of what is going on — and I charge you to continue, so that here may be done whatever may appear to be
necessary." . . .

[MEM. — November 5. The prayers of the church for
Prince Henry. November 6. Henry of Wales, the patron
of Virginia, died.]

CCXXXIX. DIGBY TO JAMES I.

November 12, 1612. Madrid. Digbye to James I.
. . . " I got a view of his (Don Pedro de Cuñega) dispatch.
The chief matters were . . . That there was no cause to

apprehend so much danger in Virginea as they did in Spaine, there being only as he certaynly learned, five hundred men, who had of late suffered great extremitie and miserie, and that the first undertakers were growne so weary of supplying the charge, that they were faine to make a generall kynde of begging (for so he tearmed it) by the way of a Lottery for the furnishing out of those shipps and men which were now sent; so that he judged it not fit to make any kynde of mention thereof unto your Majestie, both for that he held it not unlikely that the Business might sinke of itselfe, since it was maynteyned but by these shifts, which could last but for a yeare or two, and likewise for that he was certeynly informed, that yf he should propound the having of the plantation revoked, it would in no kynde be condiscended unto."

[MEM. — The 25th day of November, 1612, the Virginia Company of London sold the Somer Islands, " for £2.000 of lawfull English money," to " Sir William Wade, Sir Dudley Diggs, Sir Baptist Hicks knights, Richarde Martin of the Middle Temple, London Esquier, John Wolstenholme, Esquier, Richard Chamberlaine, Robte Offley, Robte Johnson, Jerome Heydon, George Scott and George Barkeley of London, Merchants."]

CCXL. CHAPMAN'S AN EPICEDE.

By George Chapman.

" An Epicede, or funerall Song, on the most disastrous death of the high borne, Prince of Men, Henry Prince of Wales. with the Funerals and representation of the Herse of the same high and mighty Prince; Prince of Wales, Duke of Cornwaile, and Rothsay, Count Palatine of Chester, Earle of Caricke, and late Knight of the most noble order of the Garter. Which noble Prince deceased at St. James, the sixt day of November, 1612, and was most princely interred the seventh day of December, following within the

Abbey of Westminster, in the eighteenth yere of his age.
London, printed by T. S. for John Budge, and are to bee
sould at his shop at the great south dore of Paules, and at
Brittaines bursse, 1612." "With a large folding plate of
the Hearse and Representation of the Prince by Wm.
Hole." . . . Extract.

[Fever is impersonated instilling her venom into the
prince, and the poet exclaims :]

"Was there a sight so pale, and desperate
  Ever before seene, in a thrust-through state?
  The poore Virginian, miserable sayle

"Description
of the tem-
pest that
cast Sir Th.
Gates on the
Bermudas
and the State
of his ship
and men to
this King-
domes plight
applyed in
the
Princes
Death."

A long-long-Night turn'd Day, that lived in Hell
Never so pourtrayed, where the Billowes strove
(Blackt like so many Devils) which should prove
The dammed Victor, all their furies heighting:
Their Drum the thunder: and their colours lightning:
To drown the waves in noyse: the other spending
His Hel-hot sulphurous flames to drink them dry:
When heaven was lost, when not a teare wracked eye
Could tell in all that dead time, if they wer
Sincking or sayling: till a quickening chere
Gave light to save them by the ruth of Rocks
At the Bermudas: where the tearing shocks
And all the miseries before, more felt
Than here halfe told: all, all this did not melt
Those desperate few, still dying more in tears
Then this Death, all men, to the marrow weares,
All that are men." . . .

CCXLI. EXTRACT FROM THE FRENCH MERCURY.

*EXTRACT FROM THE MERCURE FRANÇOIS, VOLUME III., 1612
TO 1615, PAGE 179.*

Translation. "The English in their voyages to Virginia were badly treated by the Spaniards : for having
wished to settle an Island near Virginia and having commenced to fortify themselves there, the Spaniards, who did
not want neighbours for the West Indies, went with several ships of war to attack them and to bombard them so
vigorously that entering the Island, they (the Spaniards)

put to the edge of the sword all the English. This being reported to the King of Great Britain, and that the English Colony in Virginia is becoming enfeedled, he sent thither a new Governor with men of war, munitions and two hundred women with as many daughters to re-enforce this Colony."

CCXLII. AND CCXLIII. SMITH'S MAP OF VIRGINIA.

A map of Virginia (CCXLII.) " Discovered and Discribed by Captayn John Smith, graven by William Hole."

I do not know exactly when this map was engraved ; but as it is mentioned (in CCXXVI.) as then " printed," it was probably engraved prior to August 7, or quite certainly before November 5, 1612.

The various editions of this map are discussed by Mr. James Lenox and Mr. Charles Deane, in " The Curiosities of American Literature," — " Norton's Literary Gazette," March 15 and May 18, 1854.

It was a part of " The Oxford Tract " (CCXLIV.), and was evidently published under the same auspices, without the authority of the Virginia Council. When Smith was president in Virginia copies of the surveys must have come into his hands, and he probably furnished William Hole with the drawing from which the engraving was made ; but I do not believe that Smith made the drawing himself. He does not always claim to have done so. In CCCLV. he alludes to CCXLIV. and CCXLII. as the " Booke and Map printed in my name." It seems to me certain that this map was engraved from a copy of the Virginia part of CLVIII. Correct maps must be alike ; but when one inaccurate map follows so closely another, as in this case, it furnishes quite conclusive proof that the latter was copied from the former. As a further evidence that Smith did not make the drawing for the map (CCXLII.), it may be noted that the distances given in the text of his work do not always correspond with the distances on the map. I have found no real evidence that Smith could draw a map. In 1618, " to

SMITH'S MAP OF VIRGINIA.

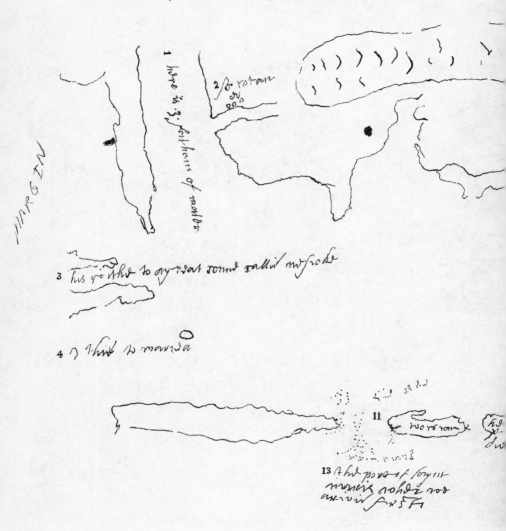

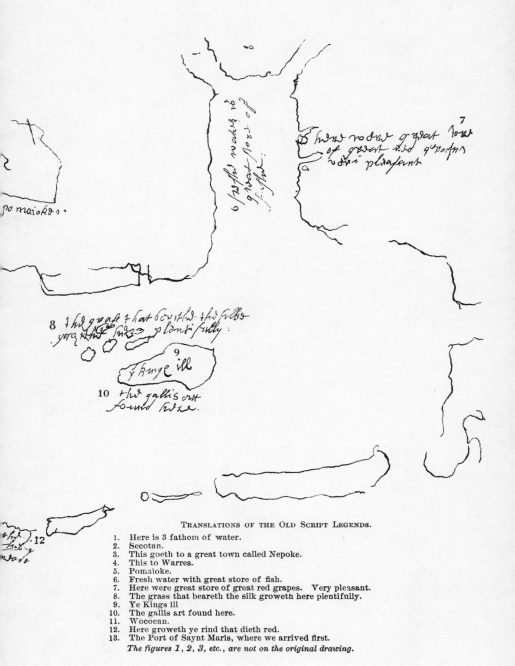

TRANSLATIONS OF THE OLD SCRIPT LEGENDS.

1. Here is 3 fathom of water.
2. Secotan.
3. This goeth to a great town called Nepoke.
4. This to Warrea.
5. Pomaioke.
6. Fresh water with great store of fish.
7. Here were great store of great red grapes.   Very pleasant.
8. The grass that beareth the silk groweth here plentifully.
9. Ye Kings ill
10. The gallis art found here.
11. Wococan.
12. Here groweth ye rind that dieth red.
13. The Port of Saynt Maris, where we arrived first.

The figures 1, 2, 3, etc., are not on the original drawing.

show the difference betwixt Virginia and New England," Smith sent Lord Bacon "maps of them both." The map of New England is missing; I give the map of Virginia (CCXLIII.). I believe it to be an illustration of Smith's capacity as a draughtsman as it is probably an attempt by Smith to copy from some drawing of our present North Carolina coast.

CCXLIV. AND CCLV. "THE OXFORD TRACTS."

CCLIV. and CCXLV. were published at Oxford some time between the 5th of November, 1612, and 25th March, 1613. The exact date is not known. Smith had evidently secured the sympathy and interest of certain clergymen and ladies in England, who thought that he deserved more credit than he had received from the managers of the Virginia enterprise; and as this was the most trying time in the history of the colony, there were very many disappointed adventurers in sympathy with fault-finders. CCXLIV. is chiefly descriptive, and need not be reviewed at length. The avowed object of CCXLV. was to "give satisfaction to all indifferent readers, how the businesse hath beene carried," and "howe it came to passe there was no better speed and successe in those proceedings." It is a eulogy of Smith. It is a partisan criticism of the management of the enterprise; it attempts to prove that the troubles which happened while Smith was in Virginia could not have been prevented, and that the troubles which had happened since he left, had happened because he was not there to prevent them. The Stationers' Company of London was a member of the Virginia Company, and it was evidently against their interest to license the publication of such tracts and maps as these (CCXLII., CCXLIV., and CCXLV.) at that time, and we are probably indebted to the sympathy of Crashaw, Symonds, and Purchas for having them printed by the clerical press at Oxford. If so, the sympathy of these clergymen may speak well for their hearts; but their judgment in this matter was certainly at fault.

I have carefully collated CCXLV. with the same as published by Smith in his "General History," and as published by Purchas in his "Pilgrimes," and also with all the other evidences which I have found in the premises; and without doubt the narrative is inaccurate and unjust. The summing up of the case on the title-pages and in the prefaces is very strong, and of course the evidence is also, if we accept it (as has been done sometimes) without question; but a cross-examination will reveal its inaccuracy and injustice, and sustain the judgment of the managers of the enterprise. For instance, we are lead to believe that the tract was a disinterested compilation by Richard Pots; but as Pots was clerk to Smith while in Virginia, their interests were probably identical. We are assured that the authors were many and that their "particular discourses are signed by their names;" yet the discourse relating to events between September, 1607, and January, 1608 (where we are told that Smith prevented the abandonment of the colony three times, and did other wonderful things), is signed by Thomas Studley, alone, who had died August 28, 1607, before any of these wonderful things happened. Of course Studley's death is not mentioned in the tract, and he is again used as a witness for events as late as June, 1608. Another leading witness was Ananias Todkill, who had been a servant to Captain John Martin, and evidently bore Martin malice; but enough. CCXLV. is embraced in the fourth book of Smith's "General History," where it is somewhat altered and enlarged. It is partisan evidence. It was against the interest of the managers of the enterprise, and of the enterprise itself, that affairs should be made public at this time, and this is the only publication of the period which pretends to give a detailed account of events in Virginia, during the time that Smith was there. The managers had the correct accounts. This account is not correct; but the public had no other. As to the witnesses to this tract then in England, it must be remembered that many of those sent to Virginia by the company had been guilty of a breach of trust by returning to England, and that the company had no adequate law for protection in these premises, until after the passage of the fifteenth article of the third charter. The enterprise was then going through the crucial test, which "enterprizes of this nature, especially in the Infancie thereof, are subject unto" (Kimbolton MSS. No. 344), and doubtless there were many swift witnesses in England among those referred to in the fourteenth article of the third charter (CCIII.).

Although we cannot rely on this tract when it is relating the acts of Smith or criticising the acts of others, it is evidently more trustworthy than the same account as given in the "General History." It is curious to note how Smith continually alters it to his own advantage in the latter work. I will give a single illustration. It is a subject of illustration in Smith's History.

The account of how "Smith taketh the King of Paspaheigh prisoner."

From CCXLV. — "long they[1] struggled in the water, *from whence the King perceiving two of the Poles*,[2] *upon the sandes would have fled; but the President held him by his haire and throat till the Poles came in;* then seeing howe pittifully *the poore Salvage* begged his life, *they conducted* him prisoner to *the fort.*"

From Smith's History. — "long they struggled in the water, *till the President got such a hold on his throat, he neare strangled the King; but having drawn his faucheon to cut off his head* seeing howe pittifully *he* begged his life, *he led* him prisoner to *Jamestowne and put him in chaynes.*"

The following is the title-page of CCXLIV. : —

" A Map of Virginia, with a description of the Countrey, The Commodities, People, Government and Religion. Written by Captaine Smith, sometimes Governour of the Countrey.

---

[1] The president, Captain John Smith, and the Indian king.

[2] Evidently the Poles aided in making the capture, and probably saved Smith's life, as Newport had done; but they get neither acknowledgment nor thanks in Smith's History; nor do they appear in the picture.

" Whereunto is annexed The proceedings of those Colonies, [CCXLV.] since their first departure from England, with the discourses, orations, and relations of the Salvages, and the accidents that befell them in all their Journies and discoveries.

" Taken faithfully as they were written out of the writings of

Doctor Russell.	Richard Wiffin.
Tho. Studley.	Will. Phettiplace.
Anas Todkill.	Nathaniel Powell.
Jeffra Abot.	Richard Pots.

And the relations of divers other diligent observers there present then, and now many of them in England.

" By W. S.

" At Oxford, Printed by Joseph Barnes. 1612."

The larger part of this title really refers to CCXLV. CCXLIV. was, as stated, a description of the country, etc., accompanied with Smith's map (CCXLII.) which had been previously engraved.

These two tracts and the map belong together. Originals are various priced, as to condition, etc. Mr. Quaritch priced a complete and perfect set in 1885 at $650. Originals are preserved in this country in the following libraries : Charles Deane, of Cambridge, Mass. ; of Congress, at Washington ; John Carter-Brown, Providence, R. I. ; Mr. Kalbfleisch, and The Lenox, New York.

CCXLIV. was again printed nearly as in the original in the second book of Smith's " History of Virginia," and in this shape is reprinted in Rice's reprint of Smith's works, Richmond, Virginia, 1819. The next, CCXLV., has been reprinted in England (by Mr. Arber) but not in America, I believe, except as it is in his " General History." It contains about 27,000 words. As in his " General History " (Smith having erased about 3,000 words and then added about 16,000 words) the tract contains about 40,000 words.

The following is the title-page of CCXLV. : —

" The Proceedings of The English Colonie in Virginia
since their first beginning from England in the yeare of
our Lord 1606, till this present 1612, with all their accidents that befell them in their Journies and Discoveries.
Also the Salvages discourses, orations and relations of the
Bordering neighbours, and how they became subject to the
English. Unfolding even the fundamentall causes from
whence have sprung so many miseries to the under-takers,
and scandals to the businesse : taken faithfully as they
were written out of the writings of Thomas Studley the
first provant maister, Anas Todkill, Walter Russell Doctor
of Phisicke, Nathaniell Powell, William Phettyplace, Richard Wyffin, Thomas Abbay, Tho. Hope, Rich : Pots and
the labours of divers other diligent observers, that were
resident in Virginia. And perused and confirmed by
diverse now resident in England that were actors in this
busines. By W. S. At Oxford, printed by Joseph Barnes.
1612."

CCXLIV. is dedicated " To the Hand," and the dedication is signed " T. A." CCXLV. has an introductory
address "To The Reader," signed " T. Abbay." Of course
I cannot be perfectly sure, but it does seem to me that this
dedication and address was written by the same hand,
whosesoever it was, that wrote all of the works known as
Captain John Smith's.

CCXLVI. BIONDI TO CARLETON.

January 7, 1613. London. Giov. Franc. Biondi to
Carleton.

. . . " Much talk about a Spanish Armada which is gathering ; some say it is for Virginia ; some for England ;
some for Ireland. The latter most probable, because of the
intelligence of Spain with Ireland ; but the Hebrides Islands
might afford a counterpoise." . . .

[MEM. — CCLVII. mentions letters from Velasco of January $\frac{12}{22}$ and $\frac{13}{23}$, 1613, which I have not found.]

CCXLVII. VELASCO TO PHILIP III.

GENERAL ARCHIVES OF SIMANCAS. DEPARTMENT OF STATE, VOLUME 2590, FOLIO 92.

Copy of an original letter of Don Alonso de Velasco to the King of Spain, dated London, January 25, 1613.

" SIRE. —

" The Embassador of the King here, who resides at your Court, has informed him, that Y. M. is fitting out a great fleet for this summer, with the intent to send the larger part of it to dismantle the forts of Virginia and of Bermuda. This report has been confirmed to them and thus they are now making ready five ships with fifteen hundred men, much ammunition and two engineers, to reinforce those posts, and they say, these vessels will sail towards the middle of March. They go with the understanding, that if those reports should continue, still larger forces would be sent, altho' they feel very confident, that Y. M's fleet will not be strong enough to drive them out from there. May Our Lord preserve Y. M. as is required by all Christendom.

" London, January 25. 1613.

" DON ALONSO DE VELASCO."

[MEM. — About the last of January, 1613, the companies sent out two ships to the Bermudas, warning the colony there " to prepare with all expedition for their defence against the Spaniards, whom they understood ere long would visit them." These vessels were sent " the speedier, by reason of some distrusts they tooke of the Spaniards soudaine supplantinge of it in its birth (as not likely to endure patiently such a thorne in his West Indies sides)." One of these ships, the Elizabeth, went on to Virginia, reaching there May 14, 1613. The other went only to the Bermudas and returned to England prior to May 20, 1613.   See CCLXVIII.]

CCXLVIII. EDMONDES TO JAMES I.

January 26, 1613.   Paris, France.   Sir Thomas Edmondes[1] to James I.

. . . " Though I make no doubt but that your Majestie is otherwise sufficiently advertised of that which passeth in Spayne ; nevertheless I holde it my duetie to make knowne unto your Majestie that manie advertisements which I have seene both out of Italie and from other partes, doe report, that the intent of the preparations which the King of Spayne maketh by Sea, is certainely to employe the same this Springe for the removing of our plantation in Virginia."

CCXLIX. PHILIP III. TO VELASCO.

GENERAL ARCHIVES OF SIMANCAS.   DEPARTMENT OF STATE, VOLUME 2572, FOLIO 3.

Copy of a rough draft of a letter of H. M. to Don Alonso de Velasco, dated February 13, 1613.

"In a letter dated December 14th of the last year of 1611 [CLXXXVIII.] you wrote me that the Ministers of Great Britain had replied to you, that they would order the three prisoners of ours to be brought to London, whom they held in Virginia, and that they would hand them over to you, whereupon we would restore to them the pilot who was taken from the English on the same occasion — and because this man has already been brought to this court, I charge and command you to complete the exchange of aforesaid prisoners, asking that our men be handed over to you and assuring said King or his ministers that the pilot, for whom they ask, will be given up here to their ambassador, or to any one they may select — and you will promptly inform me of what may be done in this matter."

[1] The English ambassador to France.

CCL. THE MASK AT WHITE HALL.

" The Memorable Maske of the two Honorable Houses or Inns of Court; The Middle Temple and Lyncoln's Inne, as it was performed before the King, at White-Hall on Shrove Munday at night; being the 15th of February 1613. At the Princely celebration of the most Royall Nuptialls of the Palsgrave, and this thrice gratious Princesse Elizabeth. Invented and fashioned with the ground and speciall structure of the whole worke, by our Kingdomes most Artfull and Ingenious Architect *Innigo Jones*. Supplied, Aplied, Digested and Written, by *Geo. Chapman*. London, Printed by G. Eld for George Norton, and are to be sould at his shoppe, neere Temple Bar."

Howes says: " At the Mask of The Middle Temple and Lincolnes Inne came two chariots Triumphat, very pleasant and full of state, wherein rode the choyce musicians of this Kingdome in robes *like to the Virginian priests*, with sundry devises, all pleasant and significant, with two rankes of Torches," etc.

Mr. Neill, in his " Virginia Company of London " (pp. 61, 62), quoting from " Nichols's Progresses, etc., of King James," says: "The chief maskers were in Indian habits, with high spriged feathers on their heads, their vezirds of olive collour, hayre black and lardge waving downe to their shoulders." The musicians were attired like Virginian priests, who were supposed to adore the sun, and therefore called Phœbades. On the stage was the representation of rocks and caves, and Plutus, god of riches, was a principal person in the play. The following speech is made by one named Capriccio: " With this dull deity Riches, a rich island lying in the South Sea called Pœana, being for strength and riches called the navill of that South Sea is by Earth's round motion moved near this Brittan shore, in which island being yet in command of the *Virginian* Continent, a troupe of the noblest *Virginians* inhabiting attended hither the God of Riches all tryumphantly shining in a mine of gould. For hearing of the most royal solemnity of these sacred nuptials, they crost the Ocean in their honour and are here arrived."

In the course of the play Honor and Eunomia allude to the Virginian priests.

> *Honor.* " Plutus, the Princes of the Virgine land
>   Whom I made crosse the Britain Ocean
>   To this most famed ile of all the world
>   To do due homage to the sacred nuptials
>   Of Law and Vertue celebrated here
>   By this howre of the holy eve, I know
>   Are ready to perform the rights they owe."

After the Virginian princes sing they are addressed by

> *Eunomia.* " Virginian Princes, ye must now renounce
>   Your superstitious worship of the Sun,
>   Subject to cloudy darknings and descents ;
>   And of your sweet devotions turne the events
>   To this our Britain Phœbus, whose bright skie
>   Enlighted with a Christian piety
>   Is never subject to black error's night,
>   And hath already offer'd Heaven's true light
>   To your darke region ; which acknowledge now
>   Descend, and to him all your homage vow."

Of this celebrated mask, in which the Virginian idea obtained so largely, John Chamberlain wrote to Mrs. Alice Carleton : " London, 18. Feby 1613. . . . On Monday night, was the Middle Temple and Lincoln's Inn Masque prepared in the hall of Court, whereas the lords was in the banqueting room. It went from the Rolls, all up Fleet street and the Strand, and made such a gallant and glorious show, that it is highly commended. They had forty gentlemen of best choice out of both houses, and the twelve masquers, with their torch-bearers and pages, rode likewise upon horses exceedingly well trapped and furnished, besides a dozen little boys, dressed like baboons, that served for an anti-masque, and, they say, performed it exceedingly well when they came to it ; and three open chariots, drawn with four horses a piece, that carried their musicians and other personages that had parts to speak. All which, together with their trumpeters and other attendants, were so well set out, that it is generally held for the best show that hath been seen many a day. The King stood in the gallery to behold them, and made them ride about the Tilt Yard, and then they were received into St. James's Park, and so out, all along the galleries, into the hall, where themselves and their devices, which they say were excellent, made such a glittering show, that the King and all the company were exceedingly pleased, and especially with their dancing, which was beyond all that hath been seen yet. The King made the Masters kiss his hand on parting, and gave them many thanks, saying, he never saw so many proper men together, and himself accompanied them at the banquet, and took care it should be well ordered, and speaks much of them behind their backs, and strokes the Master of the rolls [Sir Edward Phillips] and Dick Martin, who were chief doers and under-takers."

[MEM. — Frederick Prince Palatyne and the Lady Elizabeth were married on Shrove-Sunday [Saint Valentine's day] the 14th of February, 1613, in his Majesty's Chapell Royall at White Hall, by the Right Reverend father in God, George, Archbishop of Canterbury, assisted by James Montague, Bishop of Bathe and Welles.]

CCLI. DIGBY TO JAMES I.

February 18, 1613. Madrid. Digbye to James I.
. . . "It is true that they do make ready their Fleet at Lisbone. . . . The only action which I conceave possible (and indeed something probable) for them to enter into, is to Essay the removing of the English from their Plantation in Verginea; the which they here generally profess, toucheth this King (both in Honor and likewise in prevention of the inconvenience, which the English setling there may pro-

cure to their West Indies) not to permitt.   And this verie day, they have clapped up into close prison Clarke the English Pilot, whome two yeares since they brought from Virginea, having formerly used him well, and permitted him his libertie, only being attended by a keeper. . . .

" Yf they attempt anything against Verginea it will be the West Indian galleons from the Havana, in the island of Cuba, with the forces of those parts.   I do meane presently to send downe a couple of fitt persons, whome I have provided to enter themselves into this King's service in his Navie, who I hope wilbe able to attaine in some part, to the knowledge of their intents, and to advertise me from time to time, of such things as they shalbe able to learne."

CCLII. LETTER FROM LISBON.

February 11, 1613.   " An abstract out of a letter written from Lisborne bearing date the 21. of februarye 1613.   *stilo novo.*

" Here is upon the suddaine comaundment geven for the preparinge thirteene sayle of shippinge to bee readye to sett sayle by the 25th of march next : — First they are to sayle unto Cadiz there to take in soldiers munition and victuals ; from thence it is divulged amongst the common sort that they are to goe unto the Bermudas there to inhabit, others say playnelye that they goe where the English shall pay for it, which is for Virginia, for that is the marke they shoote at, as theire owne proceedings doe manifest.   For in theire entertainment they receive of all nations that will offer themselves to goe in this service : Almains, Italians, French and Irish ; but neyther English, Scottish nor Dutch will be permitted nor entertayned to goe in the voyadge. To such straungers as will come . . . there shall be geven 9 months pay before hand."

CCLIII. A BROADSIDE BY THE COUNCIL.

Written between February and May, 1613. It is No.
135 in the " Catalogue of Broadsides " in the possession of
the Society of Antiquaries of London, 1866. I know of no
other copy.

" By his Maiesties Councell for Virginia.

" Whereas sundrie the adventurers to Virginia in their
zeale to that memorable worke, the plantation of that country with an English Colonie, for the establishing of the
Gospell there, and the Honour of our King and Country,
have published a little standing Lotterie consisting but of
12 pence for every Lot. And therein have proportioned
to the adventurers more then the one halfe to be repayed in
money, of faire Prizes without any abatement, besides sundry
other Welcomes and Rewards ; hoping that the inhabitants
of this honourable citie adventuring even but small summes
of money, would have soone supplied so little a summe
appointed to so good a worke : Which wee did purpose to
draw out in Candlemas Tearme last ; yet now seeing that the
slow bringing in of their money hath crossed our intents,
either because there was no certaine day nominated for the
drawing thereof, or for some lewd aspertions that no good
successe was likely to ensue to this action.

" Wee doe therefore signifie, that a month past, We sent
away a ship thither with her competent number of good men
and munition, and doe purpose continually to supply them
to the utmost of our meanes. The rather for that wee have
information from them, that they are now able to subsist of
themselves, and want only more able labouring men, and
convenient clothing for them.

" In consideration whereof, We do certifie all men, that
we do purpose (God willing) to begin the drawing of this
Lotterie the 10. day of May next. And that the last day
of bringing in any money shall be the 3. day of the same
moneth. Betwixt which times the books shall be brought
in, and made up, and the Lots written out proportionable
according to the moneys that shall come in.

"Imprinted by Felix Kingston for William Welby, dwelling at the Signe of the Swanne in Pauls Churchyard, 1613."

CCLIV. DIGBY TO JAMES I.

March 5, 1613, Madrid. Digbye to James I.

. . . "I am advertised from Sevill and Lisbone, that they use all possible dilligence for the making ready of the shipping and soldiers . . . so that by the end of Aprill they intend certeynely to put to Sea. Those that I imploye send me word that they every day growe more to doubt, that there wilbe something attempted against the Plantation in Verginea, and they are strengthened in this their beleife, for that though they have so greate want of men, that they have made publique Proclamations, that whosoever will serve in this voyage shall receave nine monethes pay beforehand, yet they refuse to admitt of English, Scottish and Hollanders, but not of Irish. But men of good judgement here in Court (and in whome I have reason to have some confidence) assure me that there is no such intent : But howsoever it wilbe requisite that those of Verginea live in a Continuall expectation of being assailed, for first or last, the Spaniards will certeynely attempt them, for therof they make already publique profession."

CCLV. CHARTER GRANTED TO THE RUSSIA COMPANY.

March 13, 1613. King James granted new letters patents to the Muscovy Company "enlarging their Privileges."

"As the Company had been at vast charges in fitting out great Numbers of ships for the discovery of New Countries, Isles &c. And had discovered several countries, the trade whereof, is of very great advantage to this Nation, viz; Cherry Islands, Greenland, Nova Zembla, Davyes's Streights, Grooneland, Hudson's Bay, New foundland, the North of America : as will at large appear by the Journals kept by their commanders, in the said voyages, and registered in the High Court of Admiralty." — Strype.

This charter excluded all others from the seal and whale fisheries of the northern ocean, Greenland, Spitzbergen, etc. This company was managed by nearly the same officers as the East India and Virginia companies.

CCLVI. CHAMBERLAIN TO CARLETON.

London, March (14–25 ?), 1613.

. . . "The elder Taylor, that was in the Gate-house, hath found the means to escape, so that now they are both gone. The keeper is committed, and a Florentine that served the Lord Vaux, as suspected to be privy to his escape. For my part, I am not sorry to be rid of them; for, though they were notorious rascals, yet I know not what we should have done with them. Yet it was in consultation to send them to *Virginia;* but I see not to what purpose." . . .

CCLVII. PHILIP III. TO VELASCO.

GENERAL ARCHIVES OF SIMANCAS. DEPARTMENT OF STATE, VOLUME 2572, FOLIO 7.

Copy of an extract from a letter of H. M. to Don Alonso de Velasco, dated Madrid, April 1, 1613.

"There has been received what you say in your letters of January 22^d and 23^d as to the subject of the marriage of the Palatine — and as to the preparations made for Virginia — and I am well pleased with the zeal which you show in keeping me informed of all that comes to your knowledge — and I shall be still more so, if you succeed in finding out what really goes on so as to give me an account of it — and if you can find decent and secret means for it, I shall be glad for you to prevent that marriage." [1]

---

[1] The marriage had already taken place, at an earlier day, I take it, than expected. On February 27, John King, bishop of London, wrote to Carleton: "The festivals have passed, not without caution against some prac-

RICHARD HUMBLE, Esquire

[MEM. — "James by his letters patent dated March 29, 1613, in his eleventh year, incorporated the Irish Society, by the name of ' The Governor and Assistants of the New Plantation in Ulster, within the realm of Ireland.' ' A new county was thereby erected, which, uniting the old name of Derry with its new Masters, the Corporations and Companies of London, is now called London-Derry.' This new settlement was mapped and divided by the Irish Society, as nearly as could be, into twelve equal parts; and the twelve companies,[1] who had equally contributed to the raising of the £60,000, drew lots for their several shares." — Herbert's " Hist. of the Twelve Livery Companies of London."]

CCLVIII. CRASHAW'S EPISTLE DEDICATORY.

I do not know the exact date of publication of CCXXIX., CCXXX., and CCLVIII., as it seems they were not entered for publication at Stationers' Hall; but as CCLIX. was probably published in April, 1613, and as CCLVIII., which probably preceded it, was evidently printed after CCXLV. I suppose we may place their publication about February or March, 1613. I have already given Whitaker's letter (CCXXIX.) and extracts from his book (CCXXX.). They were published with the following title : —

" Good Newes from Virginia. Sent to the Councell and Company of Virginia, resident in England. From Alexander Whitaker, The Minister of Henrico in Virginia. Wherein Also is a Narration of the present State of that country, and our Colonies there. Perused and published by direction from that counsell. And a Preface prefixed of

tise so much prognosticated. The King shows his people that he will not be surprised sleeping. Rome would be mistress of the Church, and Spain of Nations."

[1] Very many merchants of London as individuals continued their interest in the American enterprise ; but these companies, as corporate bodies, soon transferred their interest in the far distant Virginia plantations, and devoted themselves to their lands in Ireland, nearer at hand.

some matters touching that Plantation very requisite to be
made knowne.   At London.   Imprinted by Felix Kyngston
for William Welby, and are to be sold at his shop in Paul's
Churchyard at the signe of the Swanne.   1613."

The " Preface prefixed " is really W. Crashaw's " Epistle
Dedicatorie " (CCLVIII.).

Originals, worth over $500 each, are preserved in the
libraries of Congress, Carter-Brown, and Mr. Kalbfleisch.

I have never seen a complete reprint.   Some extracts are
given by Mr. Neill in his " Virginia Company," and by
Professor Tyler in his " History of American Literature."

Crashaw had a wonderful command of language and used
a great many words in expressing his ideas.   His " Epistle
Dedicatorie " contains over 7,000 words.   I cannot give
the whole of it; but as it has never been printed in this
country I will give enough of it to show its character, and
then make some extracts from the remainder.

I quote from the book as printed, noting the pages extracted from.

[p. ii.]   " To The Right Honorable, My very Good Lord,
            Raph Lord Uere, Lord President of Wales : Con-
tinuance and encrease of all Honor and happinesse, from
Christ Jesus.

" Right Honorable, amongst the many discouragements
that have attended this glorious businesse of the Virginian
plantation : none hath been so frequent, and so forcible, as
the calumnies and slanders, raised upon our Colonies, and
the Countrey it selfe.   These being devised by the Divell
and set abroach by idle and base companions, are blowen
abroad by Papists, Players and such like, till they have
filled the vulgar eares : . And having once entred, then
they run (like wilde fire) from man to man : for as wilde
fire, hardly findes a house which is not matter combus-
tible ; so these idles tales hardly meete a man who gives
not (passage at the least, if not) credit to them : where-

upon the Divell and his associates (of all sorts) [p. iii.]
hold and practise this rule, as a sure Maxime,
speake anything, some will beleeve it : be it never so
false, some will entertaine it, Truth and Inno-   *Calumniare*
cencie shall never so wipe it off, but some thing   *audacter,*
will stick behind.   Our onely Comforts is (next   *aliquid*
bæret.
to the assurance of God's acceptation of the worke) that men
of honourable minds, and ingenuous dispositions, and all
that are godly-wise, will check and controule these idle and
slanderous surmises, as they meet with them : and for their
better assistance, encouragement and direction in so doing,
our Counsell and Governours hold it needfull to make
knowne to the world, such relations and informations as we
receive from thence, from men of judgement and experience,
and of approved faithfulnesse and integritie.   And therefore though this ensuing Treatise (written by Master
Whitaker, one of our Ministers in Virginia) was spoken
there, and sent hither rather for the private use and encouragement of such, whose purses heere, or persons there,
were engaged in the action, then with any intent to make
it publike : yet for the reasons aforesaid, it was held fit
after mature consideration to divulge it, that so the naked
and plaine truth, may give a just affront to the cunning and
coloured falsehoods devised by the enemies of this Plantation.   And because the man was once so well knowne to
me (as he is still, and ever shall be beloved of me) I was
desired by them, that may command mee, to peruse the
originall itselfe, and for that I had (as they probably thought)
some knowledge of his hand, to consider whether
truly or suspiciously it bore his name.   And if [p. iv.]
I found cause of the least suspicion, to reject it :
but if, by true and infallible tokens, to be his hand, then
to give some testimony to the world of a truth so evident?

"Two points therefore I perceive needfull to bee made
knowne, which I desire all men to take notice of, from mee,
who have peculiar reason to know them both, so well, as

few or no other can : first, who the Author is; and then,
whether this come undoubtedly from him or no.
"The Author is Master Alexander Whitaker,
Preacher to the Colonie at Henrico, under the
government of the valorous and worthy Knight
Sir Thomas Dale, with whom also he went: he was sonne
to that reverend renowned Doctor Whitaker : a Master of
Arts of five or six yeares standing in Cambridge ; was
seated in the North-Countrey, where he was well approved
by the greatest, and beloved of his people, and had competent allowance to his good liking, and was in a good pos-
sibility of better living, as any of his time : he had also
some meanes of his owne left him by his parents : all
which notwithstanding, he meerely of himselfe, for ought I
know, entertained a purpose of going to Virginia, to assist
that Christian plantation in the function of a Preacher of
the Gospell.   And having after many distractions and com-
bates with himselfe (as he told me) settled his resolution,
that God called him thither, and therefore he would goe :
He accordingly made it good notwithstanding the earnest,
diswasions of many his nearest friends, and the great discouragements which he daily heard of, touch-
ing the businesse and Countrey itselfe : and arrived there with Sir Thomas Dale, by a very
speedy and safe passage (scarce of eight weekes long) in May
1611. from whence he hath since then written many comfortable letters, both to the Counsell and Committies, and
his private friends : and of late (after he had beene there a
yeare and more) hath sent us this little Treatise, which as I
know assuredly to come from him, and to be a
great part of it written, and all of it subscribed
with his owne hand.   So I dare say if he had
thought wee would have published it, he would
otherwise have adorned it : for I know (and so
do others that know him) hee is able to have written it in
Latine or in Greeke, and so to have decked it both for
phrase and stile, and other ornaments of learning and lan-

Marginal notes:

The first point — who Master Whitaker is that wrote this Treatise.

[p. v.]

The Second point : That it is assuredly his, and written with his owne hand.

guage, as might shew him no unworthye sonne of so worthy a father : And I dare say, if he live (be it in England or Virginia) he will in due time manifest to the world by true and good evidence, that God hath made him heire, as of divers of the holy vertues, so of a good part of the learning of his renowned father. And the more liberall am I in giving him his due, the further he is off mee, and by that meanes can be the lesse sensible of it.

" Nor speake I this so much for his sake (though I love him above many, and know it above any other) whose owne deeds will sufficiently approve him. As for the truth which is so much suppressed, and that Christian plantation so much disparaged in this base world : for are they not so impudent as to say ; who go thither but base and bankerupt persons, and who have no meanes [p. vi.] of their owne ? or else such as are perswaded and wrought upon to go ? And when they come there, are they not starved, and do they not die like dogges ? But how false this is in respect of the Countrey, the narration interlaced in this discourse from him that lives there, will declare : and how slanderous the other is to the persons, I shall in some sort make it appeare.

" I therefore hereby let all men know (and malice itselfe shall never disprove it) that a Schollar, a Graduate, a Preacher, well borne, and friended in England, not in debt nor disgrace, but competently provided for, and liked, and beloved where he lived, not in want, (but for a scholler, and as these days be) rich in possession, and more in possibilitie, of himselfe without any perswasion (but Gods, and his owne heart) did voluntarily leave his warme nest, and to the wonder of his kindred, and amazement of them that knew him, undertooke this hard, but in my Judgement, heroicall resolution to go to Virginia, and helpe to beare the name of God unto the Gentiles. Men may muse at it ; some may laugh, and others wonder at it. But will you know the reason ? God will be glorified in his owne workes, and what he hath determined to do, hee will find

meanes to bring to passe, for the perfecting therefore, of
this blessed worke; he hath stirred up able and worthie
men to undertake the manning and managing of it: Magis-
tracie and Ministery are the strength and sinewes; nay the
very life and being of a Christian body politique. Therefore seeing without these all emptying of purses heere,
and ventering of persons thither, is to no pur-
[p. vii.] pose. God in his wisdome provided, and in his
mercie provoked, godly and able men to furnish
both these functions: and such as might at home have
lived in place of honour and command, or in fashion competent and convenient to their conditions.

" And this, Right Honorable, is one of the foure Arguments, and as it were plaine demonstrations, that have convinced mee to beleeve that assuredly God himselfe is the
founder, and favourer of this Plantation. And I will crave
leave of your Lordship to put them downe, because I am of
minde, that the want either of knowledge, or consideration
hereof, hath beene, and is the cause of the error and mis-
prision of the world, touching this busines; and do thinke
that if men did ruminate, and advisedly consider of these
particulars, they would reprove themselves for their former
thoughts, and say plainly, Digitus Dei est hic.

" 1. The marvellous and indeed miraculous deliverance
of our worthy Governours, Sir Thomas Gates, Liefetenant
generall, and Sir George Somers, Admirall, with all their
Company, of some hundred and fiftie persons, upon the
feared and abhorred Ilands of the Barmudaes, without
losse of one person, when the same houre nothing was
before their eyes, but imminent and inevitable death; as
never ship came there that perished not, so never was it
heard of, that any ship wrackt there, but with the death of
all or most of the people, save onely this of ours. Oh how
the world should have rung of it ere this, if a
[p. viii.] farre lesse deliverance had happened to any of
the Jesuiticall plantations: and surely the Counsell of Virginia doe wrong themselves and the businesse:

nay they must give me leave to tell them they obscure the glorie of God, if they take not order, that a full compleate and *plaine* narration of that whole action, both danger and deliverance be published to the world. [See CCLIX.]

" 2. The full discoverie (by meanes of their former deliverance) of those Barmuda Ilands, which hitherto have beene held in the world, as inaccessible . . . and [Extracts given up to the divels power . . . are found a begin.] habitation of such safetie and securitie (having no enemie within nor any to be feared without, because the entrance is so difficult :) and of such plentie of all things for life. . . . as for the present they bee even as a new life [CCX.] and a seminarie to Virginia. . . . [p. ix.]

" 3. The speciall and most fatherly providence of God over this action, in upholding it when man had forsaken it, and giving it life againe when man had left it for dead : for had not Sir Thomas Gates and Sir George Somers come into Virginia from the Barmudaes even when they did, the poore Colonie (which during that year of their absence, by enduring the miserie of mis-government,[1] had fallen into all extremitie of distresse) had been gone away, and our Plantation possessed by the Savages : and (which was much more miraculous) when they being come in, and in all about 240. persons, and in such extreame miserie and faminine, as the Honorable Commander was even forced to yeeld to that which others moved (but himselfe had rather have died then done) namely to put themselves to the Sea to come for England, and quit the countrey : and when this (full sore against his heart) was put in execution, and every man aboord, their Ordenance and Armour buried, and not an English soule left in James Towne, and giving

---

[1] The disasters of this time made "varnished reports," as the managers of the enterprise called them, necessary, and the truth was not then known to Crashaw or generally in England. Some years after, Sir Thomas Smythe was taken to task for stating the fact that the trouble was really " *the sickness* " and *not* " *misgovernment.*" As a further proof of this fact, when De la Warr left Virginia in March, 1611, he made especial selection of Captain George Percy, in approval of his government of 1609–1610.

by their peale of shot, their last and wofull farewell to that
pleasant land, were now with sorrowfull hearts going downe
the River : Behold the hand of heaven from above, at the
very instant, sent in the Right Honorable La-War to meet
them even at the rivers mouth, with provisions and comforts of all kind : Who, if hee had staied but two
[p. x.]   Tydes longer had come into Virginia, and not
found one Englishman : whereupon they all with
as much joy returned, as with sorrow they had come away,
and making as it were a new entrie and possession, tooke
up their Ordnance and their Armour and the next day
received their Honorable Lord Generall, with all joy and
applause, and from that day by Gods blessing they never
wanting government, they never wanted bread, for him
that would take paines and do his dutie.   If ever the hand
of God appeered in action of man, it was heere most evident : for when man had forsaken this businesse, God tooke
it in hand ; and when men said, now hath all the earth cast
off the care of this Plantation, the hand of heaven hath
taken hold of it : God therefore bee glorified in his owne
worke."

Crashaw then goes on to give his version of the cause why
the colony "should fall in such extremities of want."
[p. xi.]   " When the two forenamed Commanders, in the
great shippe (called the Sea-Venture) were lost,
and yet saved upon the Barmudaes, their Fleet consisting of sixe or seven ships more, and fraught with almost
foure hundred men landed (after a long and terrible tempest) in Virginia, where so many men wanting their Governors, and being too many to be commanded by the Colony they found there before them, fell first into factions,
and at last into plaine distractions : and so one yeare of
misgovernment overthrew that body, which till then had
prospered, and by good government was brought to so
good a state, as at their landing they had corne sufficient in
store,[1] a harvest in the ground, good store of living cattell,

---

[1] This statement is not sustained by the facts.

and had the Savages in good correspondencie : but this one, yea our want of government (the most disasterous accident that ever befell that businesse) brought all to nothing, for it hindered the building of houses, and planting of corne, nay it burnt up the houses, and consumed the provisions; so that of good store of poultrie, it left not one alive, and of six hundred living Swine, not three : and which was worse, consumed our men, and which was worst of all, it lost us the Savages, which since has cost many a man his blood, and to this day is not recovered.

" All this while were the Commanders, and their Company in the Barmudas," etc.

"My fourth and last Argument [that the planta- [p. xiii.] tion was God's work] is, the stirring up of so many Honorable and worthy persons of all conditions, to disburse so freely and so willingly, such faire summes of money, and some of them even a good part of their estate, and that without any certaine or apparent hope of speedie profit," etc.

On p. xv. he gives a sketch of Mr. Glover, who " went away with Sir Thomas Gates in June, 1611." On p. xvi., of Master Whitaker, and on p. xvii., of Master Bucke, who went to Virginia " with the commendation of a right reverned Prelate. Doctor Ravis, Lord Bishop of London." " And thus (Right Honorable) you [p. xviii.] have the reason that have satisfied my conscience, that this worke is of God, and will therefore stand, though man should unfaithfully forsake it," etc.

In conclusion he writes : " It may hereby appeare they have God their friend and pro- [p. xxiii.] tector, they have honorable and worthie Governours, godly and painefull Preachers, a goodly Countrie and no want of necessaries, since they had government, they onely want the hands and helpe of men willing and able to do such duties of men, as be requisite in a Plantation, and the expence that principally and almost onely now lyes upon us, is the charge of sending away, a competent number of men, the charge whereof will be about 20. pound a

man. If this were done, it would soone appeare, that our
cares and costs were at an end, and that a glorious and
Comfortable Issue is shortly to bee looked for; which howsoever it may be deferred, through the backwardnesse of
some, back sliding of others, and coldnesse of all: yet that
it will come assuredly in the end, the goodnesse, riches, and
excellency of the Countrey, doth undoubtedly promise us,
as may appeare (beside others) in the booke lately put out,
[CCXLIV.] of Captaine Smithes [1] who was there divers
yeares, (and whose paines and service there, deserves in my
judgement high commendations,) and by this exhortation
and narration of Master Whitaker, who now is there." The
editor has placed in a side - note, opposite the reference to
Captain Smithes book: " See the booke called, The New
life of Virginia." [CCX.]

Crashaw ends with a courteous address to the Lord
        Eure : —

[p. xxiv.]   " And these true and welcome newes from
        Virginia, as they go out to the world ushered,
and attended with this my poore preface, So I send them
first to Your Lordship, as having a peculiar interest both in
them and me : . . .

" Your Lordships devoted in Christ.

                        " W. CRASHAWE."

CCLIX. A PLAIN DESCRIPTION OF BERMUDA.

" A plaine Description of the Barmudas, now called Sommer Ilands. With the manner of their discoverie Anno
1609. by the shipwrack and admirable deliverance of Sir
Thomas Gates, and Sir George Sommers, wherein are truly
set forth the commodities and profits of that Rich, Pleasant
and Healthfull countrie. With an Addition, or more ample
relation of divers other remarkable matters concerning those

[1] This shows from what source Crashaw obtained his incorrect ideas expressed on p. xi.

Crashaw evidently thought Smith
deserved more commendation than he
had received.

IN UTRUMQUE **PARATUS**

BARO DE GRAYES et **HONORATISS: D⁹**

VICECOMES WALLIN **VICECOMES WALLIN** **WILHEL KNOLLIS**

The righte Honourable WILLIAM KNOLLIS
Vicount Wallingford: Baron of Grayes Mr.
of the Courte of Wardes. And one of his Ma.ties
most honble privie Counsell. and knight of the Garter

WILLIAM KNOLLYS

First Earl of Banbury

Ilands since then experienced, lately sent from thence by one of the Colonie now there resident.

" Ecclesiastes iii. 11.   God hath made everything beauti-full in his time.

" London : Printed by W. Stansby, for W. Welby. 1613."

This tract was reprinted by Peter Force, in 1844, in vol. iii. It consists of " The Epistle-Dedicatorie " (to Sir Thomas Smith, " Treasurer for the Colonies and Companies of Virginia. and Governour of Muscovia, East India, North-west Passage and Sommer Ilands Companies ") which was written just before the Martha sailed (in April, 1613 ?), and signed "your servant in Christ Jesus. W. C." (the initials of the Rev. Wm. Crashaw).   Then Jourdan's relation (CXXXVII.) followed by " An addition sent home by the last ships from our Colonie in the Barmudas."   April to August, 1612.

Originals, worth about $150 each, are preserved in the John Carter-Brown Library, and in the library of Mr. Kalb-fleisch.

CCLX.   REPORT OF THE SPANISH COUNCIL.

April 20, 1613.   " Madrid, Spain.   Advertisements sent from Don Alonso de Velasco, Ambassador in England, with the Councils opinion of them and the King's direction. April 30ᵗʰ 1613:

" Three matters of great consideration in the despatches of Don Velasco. . . .

" The Thirde, for exchange of the Prisoners, it is good to procure that, that may take effect which hath byne agreed upon, and that perfect and true information be procured of the estate of Virginia, which yf the Ambassador alreadie have not hee must procure speedilie, and accordinglie the fittinge remedie must bee ordayned, and in case ytt doe certainelie appeare to bee a matter of Consequence, provi-sion must bee made to remoove the English from thence.

"The Marques of Velado agreeth with Don Juan de Idiaques and holdeth itt convenient that this matter of Virginia bee lookt unto with much care, for that yf itt shoulde bee soe prejudiciall for the Indies (as some doe saye) a remedie may bee provided speedilie.

"The Duke de Infantado agreeth with Don Juan de Idiaques, and addeth concerning the Prisoners, that the change of them was longe since agreed uppon and to this effect. The Spaniards shoulde bee sent into England and the Englishman to this Courte, and for which Don Alonso de Velasco ought so have laboured itt more earnestlie, and that ytt may bee written unto him, hee loose not time in procuringe performance of the agreement, and that hee hath understoode yt this Pylote, all whoe will, may see him, wherby hee judged the Spanish Prisoners to bee alreadie in England, hee holds itt meete this Englishman be restrained, and kept with more strictness ; because this care appearinge, they in Englande may esteeme him the more, and seek to procure him Release.

"The Marques de Villa Franca and the Marques de la Laguna agreeth. . . .

"The Kinges decree was that order shoulde bee given in all the particulars accordinge to the opinion of the Lordes."

CCLXI.   EDMONDES TO JAMES I.

April 24, 1613. Paris, France.   Sir Thomas Edmondes to James I.

"Word brought to him that Monsr de Hauterive a nephew of Mons^{sr} de Villeroy's, who is newely arrived out of Spayne, is certainly informed that the fleete which is there preparing for the West Indies is intended to be employed for the removing of our Plantation in Virginia."

CCLXII. EDMONDES TO JAMES I.

April 28, 1613. Paris, France. Sir Thomas Edmondes to James I.

. . . "I have againe understood that parte of the forces which are prepared in Spayne are certainely intended to remove our plantation in Virginia." . . .

CCLXIII. BROOKE TO ELLESMERE.

The following is one of the documents preserved by Mr. John Smith of Nibley. A copy was presented to me by Mr. Kalbfleisch of New York. It has never been printed.

April 28, 1613. Clapham. "To the Right Honourable Thomas Lord Ellesmere Lord Chauncellor of England.

"Evelyn p. def.

"Complaynynge shewen unto your Lordshippe your dayly oratours the Treasurer and Company of Adventurers and Planters of the cytty of London for the first Colony in Virginia That whereas diverse of his Majesties subjects in the tyme of the late Queene Elizabeth of happy and famous memory, did discover and finde out that parte of America which was then uppon that first discovery named Virginia in honour of the saide late Queene and is now generallie called and knowne by the same name and did after such discovery made continewe from tyme to tyme to plante and inhabite the saide countrey to theire greate charge and ex-pences untill the tyme of the happy goverment (*sic*) of our gracious soveraigne the Kings Majestie that nowe is Who beinge informed by the said planters and adventurers as well of theire greate charge bestowed in that discovery and plantac̄on, as of the greate comodities and advantages like to arise to his Majestie and this Kingdome by the saide plantac̄on did by his Letters patents under the greate seale of England bearinge date att Westminster the three and

twentith day of May in the seventh yeare of his raigne of
England ffraunce and Ireland and of Scotland the twoe and
ffortith, for the propagacon of Xtian religyon and reclaym-
ynge of people barbarous to civilitie and humanitie, give
and graunte that they the saide planters and Adventurers
and all such and soe many as shoulde from time to tyme
forever after be joyned with them as planters and Adventurers in the saide plantacon and theire successors forever
shoulde bee one bodie politique incorporated. by the name of
the Treasurer and Company of Adventurers and planters of
the cittie of London for the first Colony in Virgynya with
diverse graunts liberties ffranchises preheminences, priviledges, proffitts, benefitts and comodities graunted in and by
the saide Letters patents as by the same more att large ytt
doth and may appeare   And where as allsoe his gracious
Majestie by other his Letters patents under the greate seale
of England bearinge date att Westminster the twelveth day
of March in the ninthe yeare of his raigne of England,
ffraunce and Ireland, and of Scotland the five and ffortithe,
tendringe the good and happy successe of the saide plantacon
both in regard of the generall weale of humane society as in
respecte of the good of his Majesties owne state and Kingdomes and beinge willinge to geve furthrance to all good
meanes that might advance the benefitt of the saide Company and which might secure the safetie of his subjects
planted in the saide Colony under the favour and protection
of God allmightie, and his Majesties royall power and
authoritie, did likewise geve graunte and confirme unto the
saide Treasurer and Company the said Countrey of Virgynya
with further extent of grounde and islands adjacent in the
saide last letters patents mencoued and granted togeather
with such further privyledges as to his gracious Majestie
did seeme convenient for thadvancinge of so noble an
action   And his saide Majestie of his more abundant grace
and favour to the saide plantation did allsoe cause a peculier
and speciall clause to bee incerted in the saide Letters patents
namely that whereas the faylinge and none payment of

such monies as have benne promised in adventure for the
advancement of the saide plantacōn hath benne often by
experience founde to bee dangerous and prejudiciall to the
same and much to have hindered the progresse and pro-
ceedinge of the saide plantacōn And for that ytt seemed
unto his Majestie a thinge reasonable that such persones as
by theire handwritinge have ingaged themselves for the payment of theire Adventures and afterwards neglectinge theire
faithe and promise shoulde be compellable to make good and
keepe the same that therefore his Majesties will and pleasure was that in any suyte or suytes comenced or to bee
comenced in any of his Majesties Courts att Westminster or
elsewhere by the saide Treasurer and Companie or otherwise against any such persones, that his Judges for the tyme
beinge both in the Courte of Chauncerie and att the Comon
Lawe shoulde favor and further the saide suyttes soe farre
fourth as lawe and equitie will in any wise suffer and permitt as in and by the saide last recited letters patents
amongst diverse other favours and pryvyledges therein con-
teyned ytt doth and may more att large appeare And after
the saide first graunte of Incorporacōn soe obteyned the
saide Treasurer and Company did sett fourthe diverse shippes
fraught and furnished with all kinde of necessary provisyon
and munition and well manned with soldiers and persons of
other qualities and conditions fitt for such an enterprise
hopinge and intendinge by that greate charge and prepa-
racōn to have perfected and setled that plantacōn Butt
findinge ytt afterwards to bee a worke of greater difficultie,
and beinge informed by Sᴿ Thomas Gates knight whom
they had imployed there with the charge and title of Generall of that Colony who was newly sent home from Virginia for that purpose, that greater supply of men and
money was requisite and necessary for the accomplishment
of that honourable action and the establishment of the saide
plantacōn the saide Company entred into a newe counsell
and findinge that without a newe aide and supply to bee
sent unto Virginia such as was required by the saide

Sr Thomas Gates in the name of the Lord Governour and Colony there, soe honourable and religious an action must fall to the grounde to the utter overthrowe of the saide Company, the losse of all theire former charges and expences the detriment of Christian religion and greate prejudice unto this Kingdome ytt was finallie concluded and agreed that as well all those who had benne former adventurers in the saide plantaćon and free of the saide Company as those who were to bee received into the freedome, society and ffellowshippe of the saide Company for the tyme to come shold severallie and particulerly adventure and lay downe towards a newe supply to bee sent for the relief of the saide Colony in Virginia the some of three-score and ffifteene pounds att the least for every particuler mans adventure, the saide some to bee paide in three yeares. that is to say the some of five and twentie pounds every yeare and the first payment thereof to begynne and bee at the tyme of such persons underwritinge

" Whereuppon the same beinge made knowne diverse and sundry persons as well of those who were free of the saide company as others that desired to bee free of the saide ffellowshippe and corporaćon in consideraćon of theire ffreedome and for that theire names shoulde bee incerted as freemen and adventurers in the saide second Letters patents and for diverse other good causes and consideraćons them thereunto movinge did promise unto the saide Treasurer and Company that they woulde disburse, pay in and deliver unto the saide Treasurer everie one of them the some of threescore and ffifteene pounds att least and diverse other persons out of theire good affection and inclynation to soe honourable and Christian an action did promise to disburse and pay unto the saide Treasurer greater somes of mony whereof the payments were to bee made in three years proportionably in manner aforesaide

" And thereuppon in the months of November and December in the eight yeare of his Majesties raigne and att diverse tymes scince in a booke and in certeine rolles to that purpose made by generall advise and consent with a title and inscription in the begynnynge of the saide booke and severall rolles conteynynge the purpose and promisses of the saide adventurers every one of the saide adventurers that had soe promised to adventure did write downe his name with the some that he did promise to adventure for the three yeares insuinge thereby testifieenge the saide agreement and promises of purpose more assuredlie to binde themselves to the saide Treasurer and Company for the true performance of theire promised adventures and to geve incouragement and assurance of indempnitie to the saide Treasurer and Company for the disbursinge and layinge out of such greate somes of money as shoulde bee thought requisite and necessary for the relief and supply of the saide Colony And afterwards accordinge to the saide promise agreement and underwritinge many reverend prelates Earles Lords honourable and vertuous ladies knights gentlemen cittizens of good accompt and quallitie and others did pay in unto the Treasurer of the said Company such somes of mony as they had agreed and underwritten to pay — who uppon such payment delivered them billes of receipt and infranchisement sealed with the comon seale of the saide Company After which severall agreements and promises soe made and executed in manner aforesaide the saide Treasurer and Company did undertake to furnish the saide Colony with all things necessary, and did from time to time sende out shippes for the advancement of the saide plantaōon sufficiently furnished with able governours and comaunders both att sea and land with sufficient nombers of men as well saylers soldiers husbandmen ffishermen as artezans of sundry kindes for the necessitie of that busines with all sorts of victualls and severall kinds of cattle with other necessaries and conveniences of severall natures requisite for the setlinge of that plantaōon and for the sustenance and well beinge of the colony to theire greate and excessive charge, which charge amountinge to many thousand poundes more then they had ready meanes to satisfie the saide Treasurer

and Company were inforced to ingage themselves and theire
creditts for very greate somes of money which they the
more readilie and willinglie did adventure to doe for the
generall cause in hope to bee freed and saved harmeles by
the monies to bee received from the saide adventurers, which
they assured themselves everie one as hee was bounde in
honestie and conscience, woulde pay in his due tyme accordinge to that which hee had underwritten But nowe soe
ytt is, may ytt please your good Lordshippe, that many of
the said adventurers out of a carelesse and covetous disposition have not only refused to sende in theire saide adventures att the times due by theire owne agreement and underwritinge but being required and sent unto for the same
monies some of them doe make slight and dilatorie an-
sweares and others doe utterlie deny to pay the same unles
they shalbee hereunto by lawe compelled as namelie S^r
Henry Nevill of   [a blank, *sic*] in the countie of Kent
knight, havinge in November 1610 in and towards the saide
adventure and plantaċon and for the consideraċons aforesaide promised att the tymes and dayes of payment afore-
menċoned to pay in the some of threescore and fifteene
poundes and havinge in November aforesaide underwritten
for the payment of the same hath not paide in the saide
some of threescore and ffifteene pounds nor anye parte
thereof accordinge to his saide promise and underwritinge
and likewise Sr Henrye Carye Sr William Cornewallis S^r
John Cutts the younger Sir George Huntley Sr John Radcliffe Sr Walter Chute Sr Arthur Manwaringe Sr John S^t
John and Sr Thomas ffreake knights John Vaughan Richard Monyngton, John Smithe and Arthur Ingram Esquires
William Hall and Edmond Allen havynge in like manner
about the same time everie one of them the saide Knights
Esquires and others for himselfe severallie and respectivelie
in and towards the saide adventures and plantaċon for the
consideraċons aforesaid promised att the tymes and daies of
payment before menċoned to pay in and deliver everye of
them severallie the some of threescore and ffifteene poundes

a piece which they the aforesaid Sr Henry Carey and the
rest of the aforesaid Knights, esquires and others did every
one of them severally and respectivelie assume and promise
to pay in accordinglie   Yet never the les neither they the
saide parties nor any of them have att all made payment
of the saide some accordinge to theire severall promisses nor
of any parte or parcell thereof   But are all and everye of
them behinde and areare with theire saide severall and respective somes of three score and ffifteene pounds a piece
and with everye parte thereof

" And further Sr Thomas Connyngsby of   [*sic*, a
blank] in the Countie of Heref' knight and Richard Hall
of London marchant havynge likewise about the tyme
aforesaide either of them severallie for himselfe in and
towards the saide adventures and plantacon and for the
consideracons aforesaide promised att the dayes and tymes
before mencōned by equall payments either of them severallie to pay in and deliver the some of ffiftie poundes a
piece   And likewise Sr Willm Boulestrode of   in the
Countie of   [*sic*, blanks] knighte havynge allsoe in
November aforesaide promised and underwritten for the
intent and causes aforesaide to pay in the some of five and
twentie poundes att three severall dayes by equall payments
proportioned and devided   And allsoe Nicholas Wheeler of
        [*sic*, blank] havynge allsoe promised about the tyme
aforesaide to pay in the some of twelve pounds and tenne
shillinges att a day by him agreed and underwritten, they
the saide Sir Thomas Connyngsby Richard Hall Sir Willm
Boulestrode and Nicholas Wheeler nor any of them have
made payment of the saide last mencōned severall somes of
mony nor any parte thereof soe by them severallie promised as aforesaide but are all and everie of them likewise
behinde and areare with theire saide severall and respective
somes and with every parte thereof

" By meanes of all which promisses not only your Lordshippes oratours are like greatly to bee prejudiced in theire
owne estates and utterly overthrowne in theire creditts

and this soe honourable and Christian an action which
was in soe greate forwardnes of prosequuēon utterly relin-
quished and neglected to the greate dishonour and detriment of this Kingdome but allsoe many of his Majesties
subjects in a farre countrey must bee abandoned and lefte
to the danger of famishinge and to the cruell rage of the
barbarous infidels. In tender consideracon whereof and
for the avoidinge of multiplicitie of suytes att the comon
Lawes wherein your Oratours cannot hope for soe certeine
and speedy a remedy as the extremytie of theire case and
the present necessitie and importance of the busines re-
quireth Your Lordshippes Oratours doe in all humblenes
beeseche your Lordshippe accordinge to his Majesties aforesaide direcēon menēoned and recomended unto Your Lordship and other his Judges in the saide last recited letters
patents and of your accustomed goodnes to graunte unto
your saide Orators his Majesties most gracious writte of
sup̄na to bee directed to the said Sʳ Henry Nevill, Sʳ Henry
Carey, Sʳ Willm Cornewallis, Sʳ John Cutts the younger,
Sʳ George Huntley, Sʳ John Radcliffe, Sʳ Walter Chute, Sʳ
Arthur Manwaringe, Sʳ John Sᵗ John, Sʳ Thomas ffreake,
John Vaughan, Richard Monyngton John Smythe Arthur
Ingram, Willm Hall, Sʳ Willm Boulestrode and Nicholas
Wheeler [Edmond Allen, Sir Thomas Connyngsby, and
Richard Hall are not named; but their names have been
probably omitted by an oversight.] comandinge them and
every of them att a certeine day and under a certeine payne
therein to bee lymitted to bee and personallie to appeare
before your Lordshippe in his Majesties highe Courte of
Chauncery then and there to answeare the premisses and
to sett downe uppon theire Corporall oathes wheather they
and every of them have not made such promise or underwritten theire names in such booke or rolles [a word torn
off] aforesaide as adventurers towards the saide plantaēon
or supply of the saide Colony of Virgynya And whether
they or any of them have paide the saide severall somes
which they severally promised as aforesaide and for which

Who wast their Patron (worthy Leate).

Let Armes and Arts thy prayses speake

London may boaſt thy prayſe and magnifie·
Thy Name; whoſe care her Ruynes did repare:
And in Exchange of foule deſormitie;
Hath deckt and grac'd her with Bewties rare:
The fame wherof reſoundeth farr and neare·
Then honour him, who thus hath honour'd theē
And loue his Name, in all poſteritie·

Io·Payne ſculp·

NICHOLAS LEATE

they underwritt or how much thereof they or anie of them have paide and what or how much thereof is behinde and unpaide And to abide such further order and direcĉon herein as to your Lordship etc.

"CHRIS : BROOKE."

[MEM. — On the 26th of April 1613 seven good ships sailed from London and on the 13th of May, set sail from Queenborough — set forth by the Muscovy Company, under their charter of March 13th last to fish for whale, to drive away interlopers and to make further discovery. [See the account of this voyage in " Archæologia Americana," vol. iv. pp. 239–314, and Purchas, vol. iii. pp. 716–720.] They returned to England September 6. See CCLXXXVIII.]

CCLXIV. PHILIP III. TO VELASCO.

GENERAL ARCHIVES OF SIMANCAS. DEPARTMENT OF STATE, VOLUME 2572, FOLIO 10.

Copy of a part of a deciphered letter of H. M. to Don Alonso de Velasco, dated Madrid, May 19, 1613.

" You will make every effort to carry into effect the exchange of the prisoners of Virginia, since it is so long ago now that it was agreed upon and the pilot of the English is detained here all the time to surrender him here as soon as over there they shall surrender to us our men — and you will not take your hand from it till it is accomplished."

CCLXV. PHILIP III. TO VELASCO.

GENERAL ARCHIVES OF SIMANCAS. DEPARTMENT OF STATE, VOLUME 2572, FOLIO 11.

Copy of a deciphered letter of H. M. to Don Alonso de Velasco, dated Madrid, May 23, 1613.

" Although it is understood that for the present the colonization and the fortification of Virginia by the English cannot cause any apprehension, nevertheless I shall be glad to hear all the details that can be ascertained about this matter — and thus I charge and command you to try to find them out by all possible means — also the plans which they now have there, since the death of the Prince of Wales, on the same subject — and you will report to me all about this and about anything else that may present itself."

CCLXVI. DIGBY TO JAMES I.

May 13, 1613.   Madrid.   Digby to James I.

. . . "They have further the last weeke had a Consultation concerninge Virginia, but theire resolution is not to stirre therein untill they shall bee better informed of ye true state thereof.   For that here, by the advertisements that they have had out of Englande, they are yet in a greate hope that the businesse will fall of ittselfe.   Though Don Pedro de Cuñiga att his Laste beeing in England, mooved that the remoovinge of our Plantation might bee noe longer deferred as your Majestie shall see by the Copie of a Letter sent from him in September laste."   [CCLXVII.; but see CCXXIII. of July 22, 1612, which is evidently the same.]

CCLXVII. ZUÑIGA TO PHILIP III.

The following was inclosed in the foregoing letter; it is a contemporary translation.

"A Letter from Don Pedro de Cunega of ye 22. of 7ᵇʳᵉ 1612, concerning Verginia, to the King of Spain.

"Sʳ   There is come hether a shippe from Virginia and although some principall men and others suppose that the Plantation there doth rather diminish then increase, I have understoode by a friende of good Credit, that they treate and have a determination to marrie some of ye People that goe thether with the Virginians; and hee telleth mee that there are fortie or fiftie persons alreadie married there and other English intermingled with them and that the weomen which were sent over live amongst the Virginians and are receaved and used kindelie by them, and that they wonded a certain zealous Minister of their secte for reprehendinge itt. They have made a Lotterie out of which they will raise 20. thousande Ducattes and herewith sende away six shippes with all the People they can procure, uppon this pretext of their turninge Infidels, itt wilbee an easie matter to remove theise People from thence in the beginninge, for the not punishinge hereof is the cawse why they soe boldelie attempt others, as your Majestie may well perceave, for they have alreadie howses and begin another Plantation in Terra Nova, in the partes where the greate fishinges are, and now itt will bee to ye purpose to punish itt, which if itt may bee done they shall perceave that your Majestie will not proceed with them altogether by intreatie, which hath alreadie made them more presumptious, then theire owne forces can promise them.

"London 22. of Septem^r.

"God preserve Your Majestie."

CCLXVIII. VELASCO TO PHILIP III.

GENERAL ARCHIVES OF SIMANCAS. DEPARTMENT OF STATE, VOLUME 2590, FOLIO 66.

Copy of a letter from Don Alonso de Velasco to the King of Spain, dated London, May 30, 1613.

"SIRE. —

"Of the two ships which sailed from here for Bermuda at the end of January [21] of this year, one has returned and the report which it brings, is that the Country is good and healthy, and that all they had planted brought forth much fruit — that on the East and the West side of this island the Coast is steep and and there is no port; but on the North they have found a very good harbour, altho' the entrance to it was very difficult — that there fell also a river, that could be sounded and had good water, into this harbour. They had commenced to settle at this port the people who remained behind, who might be about two hundred and fifty persons. With a view to this, some merchants are now exerting themselves to put two other ships in order, in which every kind of workmen shall go, who will receive a share in the distribution of land. From Virginia no news has been received for several months, and from the straights in which they were according to the last reports from there, great fears are entertained that hunger may have made an end of those people. The Indians were holding them in such strict confinement that they could not leave their forts without running great danger. Thus they are here discouraged about this plan, on account of the heavy expenses they have incurred, and the disappointment, that there is no passage from there to the South Sea, as they had hoped, nor mines of gold or silver.

"May our Lord preserve Y. M. as all christendom needeth.

"London. May 30. 1613.

"DON ALONSO DE VELASCO."

CCLXIX. DIGBY TO CARLETON.

May 22, 1613.   Madrid.   Digbye to Carleton.

. . . "Concerning our plantation of Virginia (which I have often written unto your Lordship is a greate eye-sore unto them) thei have lately had severall consultations about yt. Their resolution is, that yt must bee removed, though thei have thought yt fitt for a while to suspende ye execution, till thei gett perfect information of the state thereof. For that thei are not yet out of hope, that the businesse may fall of ytselfe, since thei see yt not mantayned by the King nor State, but only uphelde by Lotteries, and such like uncertaine shiftes. For our new plantation in ye Bermudos (whereof your Lordship will have formerly heard) yt yet prospereth better then that of Virginia, and giveth greater incouragement to prosecute yt. For that good commodities have allready been brought from thence. And yt is written unto me for certaine, that a poore fellowe by stealth convoyed home into Englande as muche Amber-greece, as was solde in London for six hundred pound starling. The Spaniards had thought to have attempted this yeare the removing of us from thence; and to that ende, the laste summer sent a shipp thither to make discoverye; and to informe them of ye fittest course that was to be helde for the assayling of us. But the sayd shipp is returned without having donne anything. Alleaging, that thei by no meanes could finde the Islande. But by examination yt is probable, that thei were afrayd to come neere yt, bycause of the Englishe. Moste of the men are clapped up in prison at Sevill. And the Captaine and eight more of the cheife of them are brought up to this Towne in cheines, where yt is thought thei will bee proceeded against with muche rigour."

CCLXX. DIGBY TO LAKE.

May 26, 1613. Madrid. Digbye to Sir Thomas Lake.
. . . "They have latelie had here severall Consultations about our Plantation in Virginia, The resolution is — That itt must bee remooved but they thinke itt fitt to suspende the execution of itt 'till they receave perfect information in what state itt nowe is, for that they are in hope that itt will fall of ittselfe. They have geven precise order to theire Ambassadour speedilie to advertise what hee can learne of itt, and that hee use all meanes for the restitution of the Spaniards that were left there. And to this ende have clapt upp Clarke the Englishe Pilote into close Prison, and I heare they meane to sende him to the Galleis, hoping therebie that Clarke's freinds, to redeeme him will labour for the restitution of the other, by whome they hope to discover the true State of Virginia."

CCLXXI. DIGBY TO JAMES I.

June 4, 1613.   Madrid.   Digbye to James I.

. . . " There went from hence ye Spanish Ambassadour[1] in England with directions to this effect : that though yt was conceived by ye King of Spayne that the plantation and fortifications of the Englishe in Virginia neede not (in the case yt now standeth) give muche cause of feare, yet to the ende, that heere may bee taken ye fittest resolutions, hee commaundethe him to procure a true and certaine information of the present estate thereof.   And what the intent of your Majestie and the Englishe is in this pointe.   And whether bussinesses of that nature growe not muche colder since the deathe of the late Prince.   And likewise, that hee informe himself very particularly concerning the Bermudos, and give speedy advertisement hither."

CCLXXII. INSTRUCTIONS TO GONDOMAR.

1613.   " Extract from the Secret Instructions of Don Diego Sarmiento de Acuña, sent by the King of Spain as his Ambassador into England."   (Translation.)

" And itt shalbee fitt for you having perused those copies (of despatches sent heretofore to Don Pedro de Quniga,[2] Marques de Flores et Avila) and informed yourselfe uppon them from the said Marques and Don Alonso de Velasco in what estate these matters (the marriages made with France) stande, as also these others specified in the saide Copies about the League of ye Protestants, the Peopling of Virginia, the suits of ye English, of ye Pyrates, and of ye Consulls and that yowe prosecute al those matters, as yf they were here given yowe in your Instruction, and that yowe advertize mee often of whatsoever shall succeede thereuppon."

---

[1] This was the celebrated Diego Sarmiento de Acuna, Count de Gondo- mar, going to try to suppress English colonization in America.

[2] Zuñiga.

[MEM. — Rev. Thomas Lorkin to Sir Thomas Puckering, Bart.

"London, June 30. 1613. . . . No longer since than yesterday, while Burbage's Company were acting at the Globe the play of Henry VIII., and there shooting off certain chambers in way of triumph, the fire catched and fastened upon the thatch of the house, and there burn so furiously, as it consumed the whole house, all in less than two hours, the people having enough to do to save themselves."

Burbage and Shakespeare had been associated in this house, in which the latter gained his great reputation, and "the play of Henry VIII." was Shakespeare's. Cranmer's prophecy, act v. scene 4, contains these words: —

> "But as when
> The bird of wonder dies, the maiden phœnix,
> Her ashes new create another heir,
> As great in admiration as herself;
> So shall *she* [Queen Elizabeth] leave her blessedness to one,
> (When heaven shall call her from this cloud of darkness.)
> Who, from the sacred ashes of her honour,
> Shall star-like rise, as great in fame as she was,
> And so stand fix'd: Peace, plenty, love, truth, terror,
> That were the servants to this chosen infant,
> Shall then be *his* [King James I.], and like a vine grow to him;
> *Wherever the bright sun of heaven shall shine,*[1]
> His honour and the greatness of his name
> Shall be, and *make new nations:* He shall flourish,
> *And, like a mountain cedar, reach his branches*
> *To all the plains about him:*[2] Our children's children
> Shall see this, and bless heaven."]

[1] We find this idea also in Bacon's *Advertisement touching an Holy War:* "As one saith in a brave kind of expression, the sun never sets in the Spanish dominions, but ever shines upon one part or other of them."

[2] Bacon, in his celebrated speech to the speaker of the House of Commons, January 30, 1621, when enumerating the "benefits, attributes and acts of government " of James I., says, "This kingdom now first in his Majesty's times hath gotten a lot or portion in the New World by the plantation of Virginia and the Summer Islands. And certainly, it is with the kingdoms on earth as it is in the kingdom of heaven; sometimes a grain of mustard-*seed* proves *a great tree.* Who can tell ? "

The Virginia Council, in CXIV., prayed to God "So to nourish this graine of seed, that it may spread till all people of the earth admire the greatnesse, and seek the shades and fruite thereof."

CCLXXIII. VELASCO TO PHILIP III.

GENERAL ARCHIVES OF SIMANCAS. DEPARTMENT OF STATE,
VOLUME 2590, FOLIO 52.

Copy of an original letter from Don Alonso de Velasco to
the King of Spain, dated London, July 12, 1613.

The italicized part is in cipher in the original.

SIRE.

" In a letter of May 23d. [13] which I received two days
ago, Y. M. commands me, without ever taking my hand
from it, to insist with the King here upon granting their
freedom to the prisoners in Virginia, in exchange for the
English pilot who is at your Court.

" I have reported to Y. M. the last effort I made in a
special audience which the King gave me, and how he
ordered that they should at once write to the Governor of
Virginia, that he should send the prisoners here, and how
this order went out in a ship which sailed for Bermuda
about a month after, in order to reinforce the colony which
they have been establishing on a large harbour, which, however, is difficult of access, and which they discovered in the
northern part of the island, because all the rest of the
island is inaccessible.   From there it was to sail from Virginia, but now for more than nine months no news of it
have been received, and according to the last reports it is
believed that the people must have perished, partly from
disease, to which the country is subject and partly from
starvation, with which they were threatened, as the Indians
kept them so closely besieged, that they could not come out
from the fort to search for provisions.   Thus this plantation has lost much ground, as it was sustained by companies
of merchants, who were disappointed at finding no gold,
nor silver mines, nor the passage to the South sea, which
they had hoped for.   They now fix their eyes upon the
colony in Bermuda, partly because of its fertility and being

unoccupied (by savages) so that they will meet with no opposition. *When as it seems to them that in the course of time there must be a rupture with Y. M., they will be able from this island, which lies right in the way of ships returning from the Indies, to take many prizes, especially as there is but one safe harbor in the island, if they have time to fortify that, as they mean to do with great earnestness.* May our Lord preserve Y. M., as Christendom needeth it. London July 12. 1613.

"DON ALONSO DE VELASCO."

[MEM. — The Elizabeth, Captain Adams, left Virginia about June 28, 1613, and arrived in England about July 20, 1613, bringing the following documents: Dale to Sir Thomas Smith (CCLXXIV.), Argall to Hawes (CCLXXV.), Molina to Velasco, May $\frac{18}{28}$ (CCLXXVIII.), Molina to Velasco, June 28 (CCLXXIX.), and probably other documents now lost.

This ship brought the first news from Virginia which had reached England since about September, 1612, " which put some life into that action, that before was almost at the last cast." See CCLXXXI. She also, probably, brought to England Rolfe's crop of tobacco of 1612 ; which is said to have been the first crop cultivated by an Englishman in America, and the first third of " the amber-greece " from the Bermudas.]

CCLXXIV. DALE TO SIR THOMAS SMITH.

Sir Thomas Dale's letter to Sir Thomas Smith, dated June, 1613. An extract only, but all that remains.

" Let me tell you all at home this one thing, and I pray remember it ; if you give over this country and loose it, you, with your wisdoms, will leap such a gudgeon as our state hath not done the like since they lost the Kingdom of France ; be not gulled with the clamorous report of base people ; believe Caleb and Joshua ; if the glory of God

have no power with them and the conversion of these poor
infidels, yet let the rich mammons' desire egge them on to
inhabit these countries. I protest unto you, by the faith of
an honest man, the more I range the country the more I
admire it. I have seen the best countries in Europe; I
protest unto you, before the Living God, put them all together, this country will be equivalent unto them if it be
inhabitant with good people."

See also Stith's " History of Virginia," pp. 132, 287.

CCLXXV. ARGALL TO HAWES.

" A Letter of Sir Samuell Argoll touching his Voyage to
Virginia, and Actions there : Written to Master Nicholas
Hawes. June 1613." [From Purchas, iv. pp. 1764–
1765.]

" Master Hawes, within seven weekes after my departure from the Coast of England, being the three and
twentieth of July, 1612. I fell with the Coast of Virginia,
in the Latitude of fortie degrees, the twelfth of September,
with all my men in good health, the number being sixtie
two, and all my victualls very well conditioned : my course
being fiftie leagues to the Northward of the Azores. The
seventeenth, I arrived at Point Comfort, where by the discreet and provident government of Sir Thomas Gates, and
great paines and hazard of Sir Thomas Dale, I found both
the countrey and people in farre better estate there, then
the report was by such as came home in Sir Robert Mansfield's ship. From my arrivall untill the first of Novem-
The Deliver- ber, I spent my time in helping to repair such
ance. ships and Boats, as I found heere decayed for
lacke of Pitch and Tarre : and in pursuing the Indians with
This was in Sir Thomas Dale, for theire corne, of which we
the river of got some quantitie, which we were like to have
Nansamund. bought very deerely : for by the Providence of
God, Sir Thomas Dale escaped killing very narrowly. Then

RICHARD MARTIN, Esquire

about the beginning of November, by the advice His voyage to Sir T. Smiths Iland. of Sir Thomas Gates, I carried Sir Thomas Dale to Sir Thomas Smiths Island to have his opinion of the inhabiting of it; who, after three dayes march in discovering it, approved very well of the place : and so much the better, because we found abundance of fish there, and very great Cod, which we caught in five fathome water, of which we are in hope to get a great quantitie this Summer, for the reliefe of our men, as also to find safe passage for Boats and Barges thither, by a cut out of the bottome of our Bay, into the De la Warre Bay. For which De la War Bay. fishing and better Discovery, I have my ship readie, with my Company in as good health, as at my arrivall, and as they have continued ever since : for which God be glorified, to whom we give daily thankes, for the continuance of his mercy.

"After my returne from Sir Thomas Smiths Iland, I fitted my ship to fetch corne from Patowomeck, His first voyage to Patowomec and Penbrooke River. by trading with the Indians, and so set sayle from Point Comfort the first of December : and being entred into Penbrooke River, I met with the King of Pastancie a hunting, who went pres- Ayapassus the Weroance of Pastancie. ently aboord with me, seeming to be very glad of my comming, and told me thatt all the Indians there were my very great friends, and that they had good store of corne for mee, which they had provided the yeere before, which we found to be true. Then I carried my ship presently before his Towne, and there built me a stout shallop, to get the corne aboord withall, which being done, and having concluded a peace with divers other Indian Lords, and likewise given and taken * Hostages : * Cap. Web, Ensigne Swift, Rob. Sparkes & two Boyes. I hasted to James Towne, beeing the first [31. ?] of January, and arrived at Point Comfort the first of February.

"In this Voyage I got 1100. bushels of Corne, which I delivered into the severall storehouses, according unto the direction of Sir T. Gates : besides the quantitie of 300.

bushels, reserved for mine Company. As soone I had
unladen this Corne, I set my men to the felling of Timber,
for the building of a Frigat, which I left halfe finished in
The second voyage to Penbrooke River. the hands of the Carpenters at Point Comfort,
the 19. of March : and returned myselfe with the
ship into Pembrook River, and so discovered to
the head of it, which is about 65. leagues into the land,
Note.— and navigable for any ship. And then marching
Great store of Oxen in Penbrooke River. into the Countrie, I found great store of Cattle as
big as Kine [Bison], of which, the Indians that
were my guides, killed a couple which wee found
to be very good and wholesome meate, and are very easie to
be killed in regard they are heavy, slow, and not so wild as
A Myne. other beasts of the wildernesse. In this Journie
A medicinable Earth. I likewise found a Myne, of which I have sent a
triall into England : and likewise a strange kind
of Earth, the vertue whereof I know not ; but the Indians
A water that hath the taste of Allum. eate it for Physicke, alleaging that it cureth the
sicknesse and paine of the belly. I likewise
found a kind of water issuing out of the Earth,
which hath a tart taste much like unto Allum-water, it is
good and wholesome : for my men did drinke much of it,
An Earth like Gumme. and never found it otherwise. I also found an
earth like a Gumme, white and cleere ; another
A red Earth like Terra sigillata. sort red like Terra sigillata ; another very white,
and of so light a substance, that being cast into
the water, it swimmeth.

"Whilst I was in this businesse, I was told by certaine
The great King Patowomeck. Indians, my friends, that the Great Powhatans
Daughter Pokahuntis was with the great King
Patowoneck, whether I presently repaired, resolving to possesse myselfe of her by any stratagem that I could
use, for the ransoming of so many Englishmen as were prisoners with Powhatan ; as also to get such armes and tooles,
as hee, and other Indians had got by murther and stealing
from others of our Nation, with some quantitie of corne,
for the Colonies reliefe. So soone as I came to an anchor

before the Towne, I manned my Boate and sent on shoare, for the King of Pastancy and Ensigne Swift (whom I had left as a pledge of our love and truce, the Voyage before) who presently came and brought my pledge with him: whom after I had received, I brake the matter to this King, and told him, that if he did not betray Pokohuntis into my hands; wee would be no longer brothers nor friends. Hee alleaged, that if hee should undertake this businesse, then Powhatan would make warres upon him and his people; but upon my promise, that I would joyne with him against him, hee repaired presently to his brother, the great King of Patowomeck, who being made acquainted with the matter, called his Counsell together: And after some few houres deliberation, concluded rather to deliver her into my hands, then lose my friendship, so presently, Pocahuntis taken. he betrayed her into my Boat, wherein I carried her aboord my ship. This done, an Indian was dispatched to Powhatan, to let him know, that I had taken his Daughter: and if he would send home the Englishmen (whom he deteined in slaverie, with such armes and tooles, as the Indians had gotten, and stolne) and also a great quantitie of corne, that then he should have his daughter restored, otherwise not. This newes much grieved this great King, yet, without delay, he returned the messenger with this answer. That he desired me to use his Daughter well, and bring my ship into his River, and there he would give mee my demands: which being performed, I should deliver him his Daughter, and we should be friends.

" Having received this answer, I presently departed from Patowomeck, being the 13. of Aprill, and repayred with all speed to Sir T. Gates, to know of him upon what condition he would conclude this peace, and what he would demand: to whom I also delivered my prisoner, towards whose ransome within few dayes, this King sent home seven of our men, who seemed to be very joyfull for that they 7. men freed. were freed from the slavery and feare of cruell murther, which they daily before lived in. They brought also three pieces, one broad Axe, and a long whip-saw, and one canow of Corne. I beeing quit of my prisoner, went forward with the Frigat which I had left at Point Comfort, and finished her.

" Thus having put my ship in hand to be fitted for an intended fishing Voyage, I left that businesse to be followed by my Master with a ginge of men, and my Lieutenant fortified on shoare with another ginge to fell timber, and cleave plankes to build a fishing Boat; my Ensigne with another ginge was imployed in the Frigat, for getting of fish at Cape Charles, and transporting it to Henries Towne for the reliefe of such men as were there : and myselfe with a fourth ginge departed out of the River in my shallop, the His third first of May, for to discover the East side of our Discovery. Bay, which I found to have many small Rivers in it, and very good harbours for Boats and Barges, but not for ships of any great burthen ; and also great store of Inhabitants, who seemed very desirous of our love, and so much the rather, because they had received good reports from the Indians of Pembrock River, of our courteous usage of them, whom I found trading with me for corne, whereof they had great store. We also discovered a multitude of Ilands bearing good Medow ground, and as I thinke, Salt might easily be made there, if there were any Kerned Salt ponds digged, for that I found Salt kerned where found. the water had over-flowne in certain places. Here is also great store of fish, both shel-fish and other. So having discovered along the shore some fortie leagues Northward, I returned againe to my ship, the twelfth May 12. 1613. of May, and hasted forward my businesse left in hand at my departure : and fitted up my ship, and built my fishing Boate, and made readie to take the first opportunitie of the wind for my fishing Voyage, of which I beseech God of his mercy to blesse us."

He was going fishing for Frenchmen.

CCLXXVI. PORTION OF VIRGINIA AND SUMMER ISLAND HISTORY.

KIMBOLTON MS. NUMBER 205.

March 12, 1612–3, to June, 1613. Portion of what appears to have been a history of the Virginian and Summer Islands settlements. The eight pages remaining consist chiefly of an abstract of the "third charter" to the Virginia Company, dated March 12, 9 James I. Mention is made also of the "separation of the Summer Islands from the Virginian body," of Captain Argall's voyage in 1612, and of a letter from him to Mr. Nicholas Hawes in June, 1613, in which he gave a more favorable account of the colonies than had been expected.

CCLXXVII. VELASCO TO PHILIP III.

GENERAL ARCHIVES OF SIMANCAS. DEPARTMENT OF STATE, VOLUME 2590, FOLIO 46.

Copy of a holographic letter of Don Alonso de Velasco to H. M., dated London, August 2, 1613.

SIRE.

"Three days ago, [July 20?] came to this city a vessel from Virginia, after more than nine months, during which no news had reached here from that country, and as this special opportunity offers, I send herewith a letter [CCLXXVIII.] which I have received from Don Diego de Molina, whom I believed to be dead with the others who were with him. The bearer of the letter is sick; as soon as he gets better I shall make him come to me and I will open communications with the others as to what is doing, of which I shall render an account to Your Majesty, ascertaining as positively as it can possibly be done that all I can see so far shows that what I have written to Y. M. about that country, has come true. From the Bermuda this ship

brings a few pearls and some amber, and they are every
day more bent upon aiding that Colony.

" May Ou^r Lord protect Y. M. as is needful.

" From London, August 2^d 1613.

"Don Alonso de Velasco."

CCLXXVIII. MOLINA TO VELASCO.

GENERAL ARCHIVES OF SIMANCAS. DEPARTMENT OF STATE,
VOLUME 2590, FOLIO 47 (CONNECTED WITH FOLIO 46).

Copy of a holographic letter of Don Diego de Molina (it is
not said to whom it is directed), dated Virginia, May 28,
1613. (It must have been addressed to Don Alonso de
Velasco.)

" The person who will hand you this is perfectly trustworthy and you can rely upon all he tells you, and thus I
shall not say much in this letter, but only state what is most
important.

" Altho' my imprisonment followed by such extraordinary
adventures will have opened H. M.'s eyes and led him to see
this new Algiers in America, which is being established here,
I do not marvel that he should not have corrected this evil
in all this long time, since the delivery would require a
voyage — especially as there is wanting all certain knowledge for its carrying out — altho' I believe that with your
own great intelligence and with the going of $\frac{the}{this}$ Caravel to
Spain, H. M. will have been able to decide what is of most
importance, and that this would be to cut short the advance
of a Hydra in its infancy, since the intention is the destruction of the whole West, by sea as well as on land, and I do
not doubt that great results will follow, because the advantages of this place are such as to make it a rendezvous of all
the pirates of Europe, where they will be well received.
This nation has great ideas of a league with them and it will
be very powerful, even by itself alone, because on the day,
when there shall be produced here a sufficiency of grain

and an abundance of cattle, there will not be a man of whatever quality he may be, who will not, alone or in company with others, arm a vessel to come out here and join the others — because as you know, this Kingdom abounds with poor people, who abhor peace, and this is necessarily so because in peace they perish — and the rich are so haughty and so selfish that they even covet the wealth of the Indies, their gold and their silver — altho' this will not be wanting much here, as they have discovered some mines which are considered productive, altho' they have not yet been able to benefit much by them, until they shall be well established here. There are great expectations of what they will find in the mountains in great abundance; so say the Indians and offer to show the places which they know. They say that at the headwaters of the rivers, after they have come forth from the mountains, there is a great quantity of grains of silver and gold; but as they do not attach any value to them, but only to copper which they esteem very highly, they do not collect them. Until now these men have not been able to go out to discover them, however eagerly they may desire it — and to pass beyond towards New Mexico, and from thence to the South Sea, where they think of establishing great colonies, and fit out fleets, with which to make themselves masters of those waters; as of this Sea, by colonizing a few islands of those that lie Easterly of the Bahama Channel, and by conquering others like Portorico, San Domingo and Cuba. Altho' this may be difficult for them at least we have already seen evidences of these purposes in the settlement of Bermuda, where it is said, they have strong fortifications, because the conformation of the land is such that a few can defend themselves against a large number, especially by preventing a landing and disembarking troops. According to what is understood, the depth is not great enough for ships of a hundred tons, but I believe they make it shallower than it is, because I have described that island from the relation of Captain Diego Ramirez, who was stranded there, and it seems to me that other and larger vessels may enter. I do not remember it well, because it is long ago, but the description is in the house of Don Rodrigo de Aguiar, of the India Board, and the [padron?] in Sevilla, in the house of the Licentiate Antonio Moreno, Cosmographer of the same. But above all this Captain will give you a sufficient account of the island, and this is very important on account of the military measures which may hereafter be taken there. Its fertility is great; fish and game abound infinitely, and pork is there as much as they can wish, and thus they are very comfortable in that Colony, because they have little need of England, since they are likewise rich in amber and pearls, of which they say they have in very few months sent to this Kingdom more than fifty thousand ducats in value, counting the ounce at a moderate value. About four days ago there arrived here a vessel which brought them men and supplies, and they do not cease praising the good features of this island and its advantages.

" The soil here is fertile, good for every variety of ^{things} crops, except for such as require very great heat, because it is cold here. There is much hunting and fishing, but as they have not yet had any profit from the mines, — except only in timber which is very good, the merchants have not been able to support this colony with such liberality as is required, and thus they have suffered much want with only a miserable supply of wheat or maiz and dressing wretchedly, so that if to-day three hundred men should come the first year consumes a hundred and fifty of them, and there is no year that half of them do not die. Last year there were seven hundred people here, and only three hundred and fifty remain, because the hard work and the scanty food, on public works kills them, and increases the discontent in which they live, seeing themselves treated like slaves, with great cruelty. Hence a good many have gone to the Indians, of whom, some have died at their hands, and others have gone out to sea, being sent out to fish, and those who remain do so by force and are anxious to see a fleet come from Spain

to release them from this misery, because from the grievance which they suffer they call upon God and appeal to
Your Majesty, in whom they place great hopes.   And thus
let a fleet come and give them a passage to that Kingdom,
not a single person will take up arms.   They will rather
give up all respect and obedience to their rulers, who think
they can keep this up until death, and altho' there it is
understood that the merchants are abandoning this Colony,
it is not so, because this is a stratagem, by which they think
they mislead Y. M., making it look as if this matter were to
finish by itself and that thus there would be no necessity for
going to the expense of fitting out a fleet of any size that
might come with eight hundred or a thousand men and settle the matter with great facility — and even with five hundred, because no succor is expected from England to resist,
and the fortifications which they have are $^{\text{low}}_{\text{level}}$ and so fragile
that a kick would destroy them, and when they are once
supported by walls, those on the outside are better than those
within because their beams and loopholes are common to
both parts, a fortification without skill, and made by people
who do not understand it.   Nor are the men soldiers, altho'
the rulers and Captains make a great profession of them,
because of the great assistance they have rendered in Flanders, in favor of Holland, where some of them have companies and castles.   The men are badly disciplined and not
drilled at all, altho' their hopes are based upon one of two
colonies, which they have established twenty leagues from
here, up the river, in a turn of the river on a peninsula,
which is very rough, with a small harbour for landing, and
they are convinced that there they can defend themselves
against the whole world.   I have not seen it, but I know
that the fortifications are like the others, and that one night
the Indians broke in and took the whole place without resistance being made, shooting arrows in at all the doors, so that
I do not fear any difficulty in taking this place nor Bermuda,
especially if my advice is taken in both cases, as coming
from a person who has resided here two years and who

has examined all most carefully. I am looking for the decision of Y. M, desirous of being of some service, and I lay no stress upon my captivity nor the suffering which I have endured as a prisoner, by hunger, pain and illness, because he who suffers from love, looks upon his afflictions with indifference. The Ensign Marco Antonio Perez died fifteen months ago, more from hunger than from sickness, but certainly with the patience of a Saint and the spirit of a good soldier.

"I have not suffered excessively, altho' considerably, because since I came here I have been acceptable to the people here, and they have sympathised with me, in proportion to their own misery, but with real good will. The sailor, who came with me, is said to be an Englishman and a pilot. He claims to be from Aragon and really no one would take him to be a foreigner.

"This country lies in the midst of thirty-seven degrees and a third, in which lies also the bay which $\frac{we}{they}$ call Santa Maria; five rivers fall into it, very wide and very deep; this one measures at the entrance nine fathoms, and inside from five to six.

"The others measure five, seven, eight and twelve. The bay measures eight at the mouth, but in some parts it is very wide, up to thirty leagues. There is much valuable timber there and material for shipbuilding; trees fit for such purposes as they may desire — very dark walnut wood, which they esteem very highly, together with other kinds of valuable trees.

"The bearer is a gentleman from Venice, very honorable, who, having fallen into certain grave errors, is now restored to his first religion, and says that God has made me His instrument in this change, for which I am deeply grateful. He desires to go to Spain and to make amends for his sins. If I am restored to freedom, I think, I shall assist him as far as I can. I beseech you to do me the favor and to make him some present, since I believe it will be a kindness very acceptable to Our Lord. You see, Sire, that I do not

HENRY MONTAGUE

First Earl of Manchester

believe Charity to be extinct yet in Spain, and think it must
be excited in you by a man who leaves here poor and sick,
who cannot make any use of his good parts, and if I shall
have to remain here long, I shall be no less in need of your
assistance. By the information of this man, who will tell
you what I endure you might assist me with some shipstores,
such as brought here for certain private persons, and especially linen and cloth for clothing ourselves, this man and
myself, since we go naked or so ragged, that it amounts to
the same; not being able to change shirts for a month,
because as the soldiers say, my shirts are odd and do not
amount to three. I trust in God, who will assist me, since
He begins already by giving me health after eleven months,
during which I had none. I have not space enough to
write to His Majesty and you will be able to do it, informing him of all I state.

"May God preserve you, as I desire it. From Virginia,
May 28th (as it is counted in Spain) 1613.

"If you have the Key to my cipher you can write to me
in the same cipher; but this letter goes between the soles of
a shoe, where it is sewed in, and thus I trust to God that I
have not done wrong in writing in this manner. At first
when I came here, I wrote to His Majesty a letter which
required some interpretation and I addressed it, with some
others to you. I do not know if you have received it. I
hoped I would be able to send a description of this country,
but the public nature of my lodging does not permit it;
but the most important feature is the Bay which extends
N. W. – S. E — and at the distance of four leagues from the
mouth is this river in a Southerly direction, with 9 fathoms
depth. At the entrance there is a fort, or, to say more correctly a [flaco de tablas ?] ten hands high, with 25 soldiers
and 4 iron guns. Half a league from here there is another
one, but smaller, with 15 soldiers, without artillery. There is
still another smaller one, all of which are inland, half a league
off, against the Indians; this has 15 soldiers more. Twenty
leagues higher up is this Colony with 150 persons and 6 guns.

Still higher up, twenty leagues off, is another strongly situated settlement, to which all of them will be taken, when the occasion arrives, because there they place their hope. Here there are a hundred persons more and among them as among the people here there are women, boys and field labourers, so that there remain not quite two hundred effective men and they are badly disciplined.

"DON DIEGO DE MOLINO."

CCLXXIX. MOLINA TO VELASCO.

GENERAL ARCHIVES OF SIMANCAS. DEPARTMENT OF STATE, VOLUME 2590, FOLIO 141.

Copy of a holographic letter of Don Diego de Molina to Don Alonso de Velasco, dated Virginia, July 8, 1613.

"When I was captured in this province I wrote to you and to His Majesty, and addressed my letters to the care of the President of the Merchants Board, who have repeatedly assured me that they were handed to you — on which account I am very much astonished, that you have never replied to me, even as a comfort in so long a captivity — and thus I determined not to do it again, but to leave in God's hands as in the hands of a Father of Mercy and Compassion all my affairs. But having asked Mr Thomas Guietz [Gates] the Governor of this country, to send me on board the ship that is now sailing, to that kingdom, he has replied to me and actually ordered me to write to you beseeching you to manage it so that Master Clare [Clark] be restored and I be at once taken to Spain. If it be not for any other reason of yours, I should venture to trust the word of the Board, because the men of this nation, who do not like to bind themselves much, pride themselves much to keep their word, and thus it seems to me that if they offer to send me to Spain as soon as the others (are surrendered) in England this exchange might be made without any difficulty whatever. I understand very well that you will have left no means untried, but one who is suffering, always likes to speak of his own affairs and suggest something that might be of advantage to him. I beseech you to do in this matter all that you can do, since it is a righteous cause. Here they have certainly treated me with great courtesy and Mr. Thomas Guiets has been a father to me, to whom I am greatly indebted, — and everybody here in particular, have shown me such love, that if I had been in need, they would have assisted me with everything that I could have needed — but as all the necessaries of life are provided by the Government and as there are many private persons here, there are given out to them every year provisions and cloth and fine linen for clothes, and I have desired to request that the same be done to me, so that I may not be compelled to weary the Governor and to exhaust the good will which he shows to myself and to the sailor who came with me, and who they say is an Englishman and a pilot — a thing very new to me who have always taken him for a Spaniard of Aragon, as he himself asserts. — and as Marco Antonio Perez the soldier who died here fifteen months ago, told me, has assured him that he came from the same country and on account of their intimacy. asked him to embark and to provide him with something from the Havannah to Spain. His captivity and mine are very free and we go about in the same manner as if we were Englishmen. They are certainly courteous and kindly disposed, Captain Adams, who sails in this vessel and it is understood will soon returne in it, I have asked to speak with you about my business, primary and secondary, about food and wearing apparel, because with that, they say, troubles are less. He will carry everything you may give him, for so he has promised me, and above all I beseech you, write to me, and if you do not do it, upon my word, this is my last, because, although a prisoner, I have my [juntos y collares?]. Pardon me, I pray, my eccentricity, and may Our Lord protect you as I desire, since all my affairs are summed up in this letter, and in my previous letters I gave you an account of

all that I did until I was captured and the manner in which
my misfortune came about.

"From Virginia, July 8ᵗʰ 1613, according to the Grego-
rian Calendar.

"DON DIEGO DE MOLINA."

CCLXXIX. was probably not forwarded to Philip III.;
it was evidently only a blind intended to be shown for the
purpose of deceiving the English.

CCLXXX. PHILIP III. TO GONDOMAR.

GENERAL ARCHIVES OF SIMANCAS. DEPARTMENT OF STATE,
VOLUME 2572, FOLIO 17.

Copy of a draft of a letter of H. M. to Don Diego Sarmiento de Acuña, dated San Lorenzo, August 10, 1613.

" I have these last days, written to the Ambassador Don
Alonso de Velasco in reply to another letter of his what
you will see in the enclosed copy on the subject of the freedom of three sailors from Spain, who had been captured in
Virginia — and since it is not known as yet whether they
have come back to that kingdom, nor what is done in this
special case — I charge and command you to ascertain the
state of this question. You will endeavour with great
energy to secure these three sailors their freedom, taking
for this purpose all such measures as may be most efficient,
in conformity with the contents of the aforesaid copy —
and you will promptly inform me of whatever may . . ."

CCLXXXI. CHAMBERLAIN TO CARLETON.

Chamberlain to Carleton. " From Ware-Parke this first
of August 1613."

. . . " Arthur Ingram for his good service was Knighted
before the Kings going. I heard not long since that the
younge Lady Rich is brought a bed of a daughter at Kensington. The Countesse of Cumberland wife of the now

Earle is lately dead and so is old Simons of Oxfordshire.
. . . There is a ship come from Virginia with newes of
theyre well doing, which puts some life into that action,
that before was almost at the last cast.   They have taken
a daughter of a King that was theyre greatest ennemie, as
she was going a feasting upon a river to visit certain
frends : for whose ransome the father offers whatsoever is
in his power, and to become theyre frend, and to bring
them where they shall meet with gold mines : they propound unto him three conditions, to deliver all the English
fugitives, to render all manner of armes or weapons of
theyrs that are come to his handes and to geve them 300
quarters of corne.   The two first he performed redelie and
promiseth the other at theyre harvest.   Yf his daughter
maybe well used in the meanetime.   But this Ship brought
no commodities from thence but only these fayre tales and
hopes.   Marrie touching at the Bermudaes she hath brought
thence some quantitie of perle, and between 20 and 30
pound weight of ambergreece worth £900. at least; and
by the next that is to come thence they are promised to
have a return of fowre times as much.

"When the business of Virginia was at the highest, in
that heat, many gentlemen and others were drawn by perswasion and importunitie of frends to underwrite theyre
names for adventurers, but when yt came to the payment
(specially the second or third time) theyre handes were not
so redy to go to theyre purses as they were to the paper,
and in the end flatly refused, wherupon they are sued by
the companie in the Chauncerie, where this action findes such
favor that they have redy dispatch, and the underwriters
are forced to make payment, which amounts to a round
summe, between three and fowre thousand pound : among
the rest your cousen Will. Lytton was drawne on by Sir
Walter Cope with perswasion that he shold not neede to
adventure anything unles he list, but only to geve his
name for incouragement to others and for a countenance to
the cause : but now yt comes to the reckening he is faine

to disburse £40. and his frend Sir Walter cannot protect
him, et sic solet *beare* (sic) amicus." . . .

CCLXXXII. DIGBY TO JAMES I.

August 15, 1613.   Madrid.   Digbye to James I.

. . . "Desire of this State to maintain peace : they med-
dle not in slight or uncertain enterprises : if they were fit
for war, and that any occasion of important advantage
were offered, they would not omit to layhold of it ; But
herein I restraine myself to these parts of the world, for
that I knowe they would have attempted the removing of
the English from Verginea, but that they are certeynly
informed ; the Buisines will fall of itself. And within these
two daies I knowe both the Councell of Warr and of State,
have satt about the over throwing of our new plantation in
the Bermudas ; of the resolution taken therin, your Majestie shall, I hope, by my next, be particularly advertised."

[MEM. — "Gondomar (to call him by a title not yet conferred on him as count, though he possessed the name
seignorially) landed at Portsmouth, as Philip the Third's
Ambassador, at the close of July, 1613." — "Life of Ralegh," by Edwards, vol. i. p. 571.

The exact date of his arrival in London I do not know.
In his letter to the king, of September 25 (O. S.),
(CCLXXXVII.), he mentions having previously written
regarding the English-American colonies on the 27th of
August (O. S.) ; but I have not found a copy of this letter,
which was probably his first on the subject. In the same
letter (CCLXXXVII.) he mentions having received from
the king, on August 30 (O. S.), two letters, one CCLXXX.,
and the other of August $\frac{10}{20}$, which has not been found.]

CCLXXXIII. THE HARCOURT COLONY.

August 28, 1613. " Grant to Robert Harcourt, Sir Thomas Challoner and John Rovenson [Robenson], and to the heirs of Harcourt, of all that part of Guiana or continent of America, between the rivers Amazon and Dollesquebe," etc. — Grant Book, Domestic, Jac. I., p. 126.

" A Relation of a Voyage to Guiana, Describing the Climat, Situation &c of that Country. . . . The Pattent for the Plantation of which Country, his Maiestie hath granted to the said Robert Harcourt under the Great Seale. . . . At London Printed by John Beale, for W. Welby. . . . 1613."

Dedicated to Prince Charles. Now worth $125.

CCLXXXIV. DIGBY TO JAMES I.

Madrid, September 3, 1613. Digbye to James I.

. . . " Touching Verginea ; The Spanish Ambassador in England hath receaved Letters from Molina the Spaniard that is there, of the misery and distress in which they live ; So that it is determined by this Councell, not to speake any more in that Buisines, being a thing (they suppose) which will die of itself ; only it is ordered that the Spanish Ambassador shall represent unto your Majestie, the yll usage that the Spaniards have had in Verginea, and that one of them is dead with Hunger, notwithstanding that the English Pilot which was brought from thence and is here, hath beene verie well used."

CCLXXXV. PHILIP III. TO VELASCO.

GENERAL ARCHIVES OF SIMANCAS. DEPARTMENT OF STATE, VOLUME 2572, FOLIO 22.

Copy of a deciphered letter of H. M. to Don Alonso de Velasco, dated San Lorenzo, September 14, 1613.

" I have seen your letter of the 2ᵈ ult. [CCLXXVII.]

and also that which came with it from Virginia from Don
Diego de Molina [CCLXXVIII.], and I am thus made
aware of all that is there said of the state of things in those
countries. It will be well and I charge you, to succour
him in the way which he suggests to you, with all the
stores, cloth and linen he asks for, so that his sufferings
may be somewhat relieved and his captivity eased. I also
charge you to present to your King new and urgent remonstrances, so that they may as promptly as possible bring the
said Don Diego over here, telling him how the Ensign
Marco Antonio has died there (calling him however a
sailor), and how his pilot here is well treated, and that in
justice the treatment ought to be the same, Molina being
treated there as his pilot is treated here — and you will
report to me all that . . ."

[MEM. — The Martha returned from the Bermudas about
the 19th of September, bringing the second third part of
the " amber-greece."]

CCLXXXVI. DIGBY TO JAMES I.

Madrid, September 22, 1613. Digby to James I. (In
cypher-deciphered.)

. . . "Heere is lately arrived a Poste from the newe
Spanish Ambassadour,[1] And I have founde meanes to come
by a sighte of his dispatche.[2] . . .

" Hee (the ambassador) advertizethe further diverse things
concerninge Don Alonso de Velasco's departure and your
Majesties bountie in presenting him : As likewise of ye state
of our people in Virginia. And of ye course which is helde
in ye newe Plantation of ye Vermudos."

---

[1] Gondomar, who has succeeded Velasco.

[2] From this it seems that Gondomar insinuated that the King of England had bribed Velasco. I suppose this is the letter of September 6 / August 27, mentioned in CCLXXXVII., which has not been found.

CCLXXXVII. GONDOMAR TO PHILIP III.

GENERAL ARCHIVES OF SIMANCAS. DEPARTMENT OF STATE,
VOLUME 2590, FOLIOS 118, 119.

Copy of an original letter of Don Diego Sarmiento de Acuña to H. M., dated London, October 5, 1613.

" SIRE.

" Y. M.'s letters of the 10th [1] and 20th [2] August were received by me on the 9th ult : with a copy of what Y. M. ordered to be written to Don Alonso de Velasco, on February 7th of this year,[3] concerning the release of Don Diego de Molina, who is a prisoner in Virginia — in which Y. M. commands me to make every effort that may be necessary, until the desired result be obtained. In compliance with this I have tried to inform myself as to the condition in which this matter is, and I have ascertained that more than a year ago this King here ordered Don Diego de Molina and his companions to be exchanged for the English pilot, who is in Spain and that this order has not been carried out because nothing was known of this pilot until now and because there was no opportunity of getting Don Diego de Molina here. And having renewed now the remonstrances which Don Alonso de Velasco had presented on this subject, I have caused the merchants of the Virginia-Board to be compelled to have Don Diego de Molina and his companions brought over here to be put into my hands, with the first ship that comes, and now Antonio de Acosta, a Portuguese merchant, an honorable man, who resides here, thro' who at the same time the English pilot in Spain will be handed over to the ambassador of this King, with which an order will be dispatched by a vessel [4] which sails within 20 days from here to

---

[1] Philip III.'s letter of July 31/August 10, 1613, CCLXXX.

[2] Philip III.'s letter of August 10/20th, 1613. Not found.

[3] Philip III.'s letter of January 28/February 7th, 1613. Not found.

[4] The Elizabeth, which sailed October 14th, on the nineteenth day thereafter, thus showing that Gondomar was correctly informed on this point. But he is not generally more accurate than the previous ambassadors.

Virginia, that the Governor shall send Diego de Molina to this city, him and his companions by the first opportunity that may offer. By this vessel I shall send him some supplies of cloth and linen and some money, so that he may be able to dress himself more suitably than he says he is now able to do. Y. M. commands me to have him brought over and I hope that within six months this ship will be back here and that these men will come in her.

" Considering that Colony and Bermuda I reported to Y. M. on the 6th ult : [1] as to the state in which they are, and desirous to ascertain the correctness of that information, I have examined several persons of those who have come from Virginiä in the last ship, and they all agree upon this : That there is a good bar and the entry into the harbour is by a river higher up — that upon the river they have erected five fortifications : the first Gomes [James] which is the name of this King here in English ; the second is called ' Henerique ' after the Prince who died ; the third is Charles, *like the one who came to-day ;* [2] Point Comfort the fourth, and Fort Henry the fifth ; and these forts are surrounded with earthworks, on which they plant their artillery. The Commander is now Don Thomas Gates, and Marshall Don Thomas Dale ; there are about three hundred men there more or less ; and the majority sick and badly treated, because they have nothing to eat but bread of maize, with fish ; nor do they drink anything but water — all of which is contrary to the nature of the English — on which account they all wish to return and would have done so if they had been at liberty.

" The cattle which they take with them from here does not produce, nor does it improve, because there is but scanty and bad grazing on the fields.

" The Savages and natives of the Country stand in bad

---

[1] Gondomar's letter to Philip III. of August 27 / September 6 not found. It was received prior to September 22d, when Digby had found out something of the contents. See CCLXXXVI.

[2] That is, the third is called Charles after the present prince.

JAMES MONTAGUE
Bishop of Bath and Wells

relations to them and no Englishman can leave his fort without running great risk of his life. When the General sometimes goes a hunting, he takes a guard with him to protect his person.

" Nothing is brought from Virginia, of any importance, but there is an abundance of good timber for ship building.

" In Bermuda there is as a Captain and Governor, a Master Mour, who was a carpenter in this city. It is about six days that a ship[1] from there arrived here, and it brings sixty-four pounds of Ambergris, which is sold in this city at fourteen ducats an ounce ; it also brings some of the wheat that has been sown there, which, however, I am told, does not produce very well.

" They have erected there a fort which is well intrenched, and with some few pieces of artillery and eighty persons, counting men and women, as I reported to Y. M., in my letter of the 6th ult : and on this subject there is nothing new to be added.

" Don Thomas Esmit [Smith] who is President of the Merchants' Council and Board, who have maintained and still maintain those Colonies at their own expense, has given us to understand that they have spent as much as forty-six thousand pound sterling in this enterprise, which make in our money a hundred and eighty four thousand dollars, counting the dollar at ten reales. All this has been contributed by merchants and has been obtained by some lotteries which they have had here, and without costing the King a single real. But weary of spending so much money without any hope of reaping a profit, because the soil produces nothing, they now think of carrying all the people that are there to Bermuda or to Ireland by the coming Spring.[2] For the ship which they now are dispatching, they have

[1] The Martha.

[2] A great deal of this talk was evidently intended to mislead the Spaniard. From the beginning the enterprise was necessarily carried on with great diplomacy and secrecy. Consequently very few, if any, people outside of the council were correctly informed as to the facts. Thus it happened people were misinformed then, and have been misled since.

found only low and lost people to sail in it, because it has become known that of the thousand persons who last year went there, and of the few who were still there, up to now more than eight hundred have died, so that there remained there only three hundred.

" May God preserve Your Catholic Majesty, as all Christendom needs it !

" London, October 5ᵗʰ 1613.

" DON DIEGO SARMIENTO DE ACUÑA."

CCLXXXVIII. EDMONDES TO JAMES I.

Sir Thomas Edmondes to King James. Paris, France, October 11, 1613.

. . . " I understand, that they are nothing well satisfied here, . . . that the french shippes were hindred this yeare by the English from the making of anie benefitt of the whale fishing at Greenland ; [1] which discontentment is also further aggravated by another advertisement which is come hither that the English shippes at Virginia [1] tooke a french shipe, which was going to make a plantation in those partes, and killed diverse of the men ; but as they here say, used greatest crueltie against certaine Jesuittes which were in the said shippe."

CCLXXXIX. DIGBY TO JAMES I.

Madrid, Spain, October 13, 1613. Sir John Digbye to James I.

In reference to the dispatch of the Spanish ambassador, he says : " It is appointed, That for the business of Vir-

[1] These voyages of Captain Joseph and Captain Argall caused a great commotion at the time. The first will be mentioned several times hereafter in these documents. It only belongs to this work in an illustrative way. The expedition sailed under the char- ter of March 13, 1613 ; accounts of the voyage will be found in Purchas, iii. pp. 716, etc., and *Archæologia Americana*, iv. pp. 239–314. Argall's voyage is of course frequently mentioned hereafter.

ginea and the Bermudos, his advertisements be made known unto the Counsell of the Indies, and that ye Spanish Ambassador bee willed to advertise what hee shall farther heare of them ; and that ye Spanish Ambassador particularly labour to gett the liberty of Don Diego Molina, the Spaniard that was left in Virginea."

[MEM. — On the 14th of October, 1613, the Elizabeth, Captain Adams, sailed from England to Virginia via the Bermudas, taking potatoes to the island and silkworms to Virginia.]

CCXC. PHILIP III. TO GONDOMAR.

GENERAL ARCHIVES OF SIMANCAS. DEPARTMENT OF STATE, VOLUME 2572, FOLIO 27.

Copy of an extract from a deciphered letter of H. M. to Don Diego Sarmiento de Acuña, dated Ventosa, October 24, 1613.

" It was well in you to give me an account of what has become known concerning Bermuda and Virginia, and I shall be pleased if you continue, so that here may be done whatever may be proper — and you will carry out the exchange which has been agreed upon, of Don Diego de Molina and the sailor with him, for the English pilot who is here — remembering that the said Don Diego is likewise called a sailor, which you must use instead of the other name, so as to prevent any difficulty in the exchange — and you will attend to the matter of clothing and provisions as he has requested." [1]

[1] This request was made in CCLXXVIII. The contrast between CCLXXVIII. and CCLXXIX., which were written by the same person, possibly to the same person, but for different purposes, will show very clearly what little reliance there is to be placed in partisan evidence. Gondomar does not urge Philip III. to remove the English from Virginia by force, as Zuñiga did. To the contrary his letters seem to be intended to produce the impression that the colony would be abandoned. He was thus "playing into the hands " of the English ; but whether intentionally, or not, I cannot say.

CCXCI. MONTMORENCY TO JAMES I.

H. de Montmorency, Admiral of France, to King James.

" SIRE.

" I thought it was my duty to accompany the *letters*[1] *which the King* my master wrote you, with some of my own, in order to have the honor to offer to your Majesty my very humble service, and to entreat you to be favorable, (since as Admiral under the authority of the King, I have the charge of the marine affairs of this Kingdom,) that I represent to you the just complaint and the injury which the French have received from some of your subjects who, being in an English ship called the Treasurer, whereof Samuel d'Argail is Captain, went to that country of Canada, called New France, to the harbor of Pentagoet, where they found a small settlement, which was begun by permission of the King with our leave, and at the expense of Madame La Marquis de Guercheville, lady of honor to the Queen, through a good and holy zeal to lead the poor Savages of the said country to a civil conversation, and to preach to them the doctrine of Jesus Christ, and for that purpose, a number of Jesuit fathers were there.

" But your said subjects have ruined this plan ; they have attacked the colony ; they have slain many men, and among others, two of the said Jesuits ; and besides, they carried away two others with them into Virginia, (by what people say) ; and have abandoned the rest of the people to the mercy of the waters, in a small skiff. We know well enough, Sire, the goodness, and the usual clemency with which you are filled, and that you are so far removed from such inhumanity that you will assuredly do justice in this matter, when you are informed of it. Therefore in the name of France, and of the private parties interested in

---

[1] I suppose these were the " French ceedings of the Mass. Hist. Society,
Complaints." (See CCCXVIII.) 1884.
CCXCI. was published in the Pro-

these Countries, I beg your Majesty for three things : —
One, that you will command the two Jesuit fathers to be
returned in safety with the other prisoners ; the other, that
restitution shall be made for so remarkable a robbery,
which costs the said dame Marquise more than a hundred
thousand livres of loss. And the third, that your Council
or the Company of Virginia may be obliged to declare and
explain as far as where they understand to be carried, the
boundaries and confines of the said country of Virginia, in
asmuch as we thought the difficulty might have come on
account of the neighborhood of the two Colonies. But your
Majesty knows that for more than eighty years, the French
have been in possession of it, and have given to it, the name
of New France. The hope that your Majesty will be . . .
how prudently to remedy this, and find it good, if it please
you, that Mons. de Buisseaux, Ambassador may be interested more particularly with it, to give us an answer to it as
favorable as the complaint of it is reasonable, and full of
justice.

" Nevertheless I pray God, Sire, That he may give your
Majesty a very long and very happy life.

" Your very humble Servant,

" H. DE MONTMORENCY.

" At Fontainebleau the xxviij of October. 1613."

Indorsed : To the King of Great Britain : " A letter
from the Admiral of France to his Majestie concerning
Samuel Argall," etc.

CCXCII. CHAMBERLAIN TO CARLETON.

. . . " I have heard underhand that Sig^r Fabritio [Sir
Henry Wotton] is like to be sent into Spaine about some
match, which I beleve the rather for that the Spanish
Ambassador hath ben heard to say that he marvailes we
shold treat or incline to Savoy or Fraunce, wheras his master is able to part with more then they both. Yesterday

here arrived an ambassador from the new elected emperor
of Moscovie, he had a peale of ordinance at his landing at
towre-wharfe, and was receved by a *100* citizens on hors-
back in velvet coates and chaines of gold and most of the
Aldermen in scarlet, with about twenty coaches furnished
with courtiers and gallants : The Spanish, the Archdukes
and Savoy ambassadors stoode in windowes not far asunder
to see him passe. . . . Our Companie of Moscovie have for
these three or foure yeares found out a new and rich trade
of fishing for the whale, about green-land or certain ylands
there along, which yeelds above *cento pro cento*, with a
short return and small charge, they injoyed yt quietly till
this yeare that both Hollanders, French-men and Spaniards
wold have come in for a share, but our men having some
inckling of yt went well appointed with seven goode ships
and so put them by, and sent them away, wherat there is
much murmuring and complaint specially by the Hollanders, who have sent certain deputies hither about yt, but our
men pretend possession, and mean to maintain yt, though
peradventure yt will come to blowes : this yeare they killed
almost fowre-score whales, and almost ten times as many
morses or seahorses, whose oyle, finnes and teeth are a
great commoditie.

" From the Bermudas or Sommer ylands there hath come
great store of amber-greece this yeare, which is the only
commoditie they have thence as yet, but they hope for
more hereafter of many kindes though nothing so rich, and
begin to nestle and plant there very handsomely : wherwith the Spaniard is nothing pleased but threatens the next
yeare to remove them, which advertisement they have by
goode meanes and many wayes, but they seeme nothing
dismayed therewith trusting rather to the difficultie of
accesse, then to any other strength of theyre owne : the
greatest peece of amber in one lumpe that hath ben heard
of was found there this yeare, beeing as bigge as the body
of a giant and aunswerable or resembling almost in all
points saving for the want of the head and one arme : but

they handled the matter so foolishly that they brake yt in peeces, and the biggest they brought home was not above 68 ounces : which sells better by twelve of fifteen shillings in an ounce then that which is smaller. Since Michaelmas we have had fowre ships come from the east Indies well and richly laden, and though they have ben long missing yet this return doth recompence theyre stay. . . . Ned Blunt tells me he hath sent you Sir Fra : Bacons essais and other bookes, which I was willing to have provided according as you gave order in one of your former letters. There went a ship away in my absence, which I could not heare of till yt was gon. For almanachs I will send you one in a letter so soon as they come forth, for I cannot yet meet with any better conveyance. So with all due remembrance to my Lady I commend you to the protection of the Almighty. From London this 27th of October 1613.

" Your Lordships to commaund

" JOHN CHAMBERLAIN."

Addressed : " To the right honorable Sr Dudley Carleton K^t Ld Ambassador for his Matie at Venice."

[MEM. — October 29. The Lord Mayor's pageant " The Triumphs of Truth " (the triumph of England's true policy ?) was emblematical of the new trades, traffics and discoveries.

October 30, 1613. Digby wrote to King James from Madrid : " Concerning the North-West Passage to the East Indies, the Spaniards always conceived that it would never prove matter of any consequence, but they are very glad now to be freed of this care, and that the Spanish Ambassador in England be thanked for his vigilancy therein." This, I suppose, is based on Captain Button's report. He returned to England from Hudson's and Button's Bay early in the autumn of 1613 ; but the exact date of his arrival is not known to me.]

CCXCIII. DIGBY TO CARLETON.

Madrid, Spain, November 3, 1613. Digbye to Carleton. Describes his interview with the Spanish Secretary of State, who " fell soddainelie into a very great complaint of his Majesties proceeding with this King, that hee woulde (as hee sayd) cause so great an Innovation as that the Spaniards, which had for so manie yeares fished in the Northerne-Seas over which hitherto no Prince had challenged any particular Dominion shoulde now by his Majesties Subjects bee prohibited. And yet that his Majestie would give permission to his subjects to plante & inhabite in Virginia, and the Ilandes of ye Bermudos which had for manie yeares byne esteemed & knowne to belong unto the Conquest of Castile. for that hee thought yt strange that his Majestie should att the same tyme suffer his people to possesse themselves of what was rightlie the King of Spaynes and shoulde forbidd the Spaniards from that which they had long used & to which hee knewe not what particular clayme his majestie coulde pretend."

Digbye's reply : " I told him, that first I conceaved hee had byne misenformed, that the Spaniards had divers yeares used to theise parts now spoken of ; which had byne of late discovered & the Spaniards were never there untill the last Summer, when an Englishman lead them thither. — Secondlie, I could no way yeeld unto him that eyther Virginia or ye Bermudos were . . . parts of the conquest of Castile but that the . . . selves the first Possidents. — Soe that I supposed what is sayd of the Whale-fishing was to bee debated & disputed in the same nature the Indies were, which the Crown of Castile without controversie discovered and possessed. And that then hee would see that his Majestie onelie followed theire owne foote steppes. For that there were att the present divers of his Majesties subjects in theire Gallyes for having offred to trade to the Indies beeing onlie taken in the way thither. And that I conceaved the same reason of beeing the first Possident was equallie to holde in both. And that as his Majestie had followed theire example in reserving the trade of his discoveries unto his owne subjects, so hee would willinglie give free accesse unto them, when they should hold yt fitt to permitt the like unto theirs. . . . . And that for the Pope's donation it was grown to be so lightly esteemed, that it was almost left to be alleadged by them."

Digby says there were arguments on both sides; and that he ' desired the Secretary would provide against the English merchants being wronged by way of fact, and that disputes as to title might be decided by fair courses between the two kings.'

CCXCIV[1]. AND CCXCIV[2]. LIMITS OF THE SPANISH POSSESSIONS.

These papers are apparently rough notes for a reply to the Spanish claims to America. They are from the English State Paper Office. — Colonial Papers, vol. i. No. 32. They are filed under 1613; but their date is indicated as questionable thus, " 1613 ? " They were written after December, 1609, and I am inclined to think before 1613; but I place them here about as I find them in the State Paper Office. The name of the author is not given, but the documents were evidently written either by the Rev. Richard Hakluyt, or with his assistance, or were compiled from his works. They contain many of his ideas, expressed almost in the same words as in his publications.

CCXCIV[1].

" The true limites of all the countries & provinces at this present actually possessed by the Spaniards & Portugales in the West Indias.

" All that parte of the West Indias which at this day is inhabited by the Spaniards & Portugales is almost included within the two Tropiques; excepting the two small townes of Sant Augustin & Santa Helena in Florida & the province

of Nuova Biscaia northward, & 5 townes in the river, namely
Buenos Aeres, Santo Spirito, Santa Anna, the city of Ascension, & Santa Fee beyond the Southerne tropique, as also in
the Kingdome of Chili upon the South Sea, the townes of
Coquimbo, Penco, Angol, Sant Jago, La imperial, Villa
rica, and Villa del lago.

" I doe not deny, but that northward & southward they
have discovered much farther : but that they have no farther
actual possession then before is specified, their own later
histories, ruttiers & Journals which We have to shew, &
our Englishmens manifold experience do assure us.

" The most Northerly provinces of Nueva Espanna within
and near the Tropique, are Nueva Galicia upon the South
Sea & Guastecan upon the bay of Mexico.   The most northerly Spanish towne in Culiacan a province of Nueva Galicia is St Michael situate in 24 degrees of North latitude
and the Northernmost Spanish townes in Guastecan are
Tampico, Panuco, Sant Jago de las Valles; as evidently
appeareth by the 8th & 9th mappes seen in the last edition of
Ortelius his Theatrum Orbis, who was the sworne cosmographer of the King of Spaine.

" Southward of these lyeth the Kingdome of Mexico com-
prehending in it the provinces of Yucatan, the Honduras,
Guatimala & Veragua on the east parte, as likewise Mechu-
acan, Colima & Sacatula on the west, & downe more southerly the provinces of Soconusco, Chiapa, Nicaragua & Costa
ricas besides other inferiour provinces ; and it streatcheth to
the townes of Panama and Nombre de dios standing both
upon the Istmus or Neck-land of Darien.

" The second general part of the West Indias called by the
Spaniards Tierra firma beginneth upon the North Sea at the
gulfe of Uraba [Darien] & is inhabited eastward by the
Spaniards both on the sea coast, & within the land as far as
the isle of Trinidad.   Their principal inland townes are
Mompox, Santa Fee, Caly, Ançerma, Popaian, Pasto, Victo-
ria, Carthago, Timana, Meriola, Pamplon, Tunxa, Santa Fe,
Tocayma, St Jago de Leon, &et.   Their chief townes &

GEORGE MONTAIGNE
Archbishop of York

havens on the sea-coast are Cartagena, Santa Marta, Rio de Hacha, Coro, Burburaté, Caracos, Cumana, wherunto may be added the isles of Margarita & Trinidad.

" From the isle of Trinidad standing in 10 & 9 degrees of North latitude all along the coast to the Equinoctial line, & thence forward to Paraiba, Petiguaras, & Fernambuck situate in 7. & 8. degrees of southerly latitude, to the space of 500 leags, there are no Christians at all inhabiting, as we are taught by our owne late & yearly experience.

" From Paraiba in 7 degrees of latitude southward, the Portugales doe inhabite upon the Coste of Brasill the townes of Fernambuc, Baija de todos Santos which is the seat of the vizroy & bishop of Brasil, the towne of Baija das Ilhas, Porto Seguro, Baija del Spirito Santo, with the townes of Santos & Sant Vincente, which towne of Sant Vincente standeth in 24 degrees of south latitude.

" From Sant Vincente to the streights of Magellan all along the sea-coast, for the space of 700 leags ther are no Christian inhabitants : onely the Spanniards have planted 5 inland townes before mentioned upon the river of Plate.

" Within the streights of Magellan they have not anie towne either upon the North or South shore. And as for the townes of Nombre de Jesus, & ciudad del Rey Philippe, they have bin found long since by Mr Candish in both his voiages & by diverse others of our notion, to be utterly ruined and dispeopled.

" Also from the streights of Magellan to the Isle of Santa Maria standing within the South Sea in 37 degrees, to witt, for the space of 300 leags they have no habitation at all.

" From this isle to the Tropique of Capricorne streatcheth the lande of Chili containing the 7 townes before mentioned.

" At this tropique beginneth the province of Peru which extendeth between the sea-coast & the mountaines called Andes somewhat to the northward of the Equinoctial. And here the Spaniards have many townes & cities both upon the coast & also within the country. On the coast they have Arica, Arequipa, Pisca, Lima, the seat of the Vizroy containing 2000 housholds, & the townes of Santos, Truxillo, Cherepe, Paita, & the isle of Puna. The chief places of the inland are Potossi, Charcas, Cusco, & Quito.

" From Quito to Panama the coast lieth in a manner desolate.

" These before mentioned are the principal provinces, cities & townes actually possessed by the Spaniards upon the maine of America.

" The chief islands that they possesse as parte of this new World are St Juan de Puerto rico, Hispaniola, Cuba & Jamaica. As for the great multitude of those other small Isles called Las Antillas adjoining to these 4, they are either utterly desolate, or inhabited by a few Salvages.

" So that besides all those huge coasts & mighty inlandes lying southward of the Tropique of Cancer, which hitherto are quite free from any Spanish government ; all those large & spatious countries on the East parte of America from 32 to 72. degrees of northerly latitude, have not nor never had any one Spanish Colonie planted in them ; but are both by right of first discovery performed by Sebastian Cabota at the cost of King Henry the 7th & also of later actual possession taken in the behalfe & under the sovereign authority of her Majesty, by the several deputies of Sir Walter Ralegh, & by the two English Colonies thither deducted (wherof the later is yet ther remaining) as likewise by Sir Humfry Gilbert, Sir Martin Frobisher, Mr John Davis, & others, most justly & inseparably belonging to the Crowne of England. Which countries being greater then all Europe, & in goodnes of soile nothing inferiour therunto, are by no meanes by us to be given over unto them, who have already a great deal more then they can well wield.

" Lastly on the backside or west of America, beyond Cape California, from 24 degrees of Northerly latitude to 43 degrees (all which coast Sir Francis Drake in his voiage about the world discovered & took possession therof for her Majestie in 38 degrees, calling the country Nova Albion) they have not one foot of actual possession, much lesse more Northerly. And therfore in time to come they shall have no pretense of cavillation against a Northwest passage, if it should please God to lay open the same.

" FINIS."

CCXCIV[2].

" Whither an Englishman may trade into the West Indies, with certain answers to the Popes Bull.[1]

" First it is to be understood that the King of Spaines title to the Indias dependeth upon a guift or bull of Pope Alexander the 6th dated 1493. Against which it may be said that the Pope had no authority to subject temporally the infidels, or to take away their landes without a cause.

" Secondly the consent of the pope if it ever ratified, was only conditional, and is to be understood, that things already safe should be kept. And the very wordes of the Bull be not to grant a conquest or such an absolute power, but a meanes to converte & reduce them to Christianity; although the usage of the Spaniard hath bin otherwise, & so the grante voide. *The Story of Bartholome de las Casas.*

" *Thirdly* the Bull or grante is to be understood in cases lawfull, & not tending to the prejudice of a thirde person.

" All princes & estates had & have by the laws of nations the right of navigation in the sea, & the right of traffique, which the Pope by the fulnes of his authority cannot take from them : & the wordes of the said Bull are express that the Pope did not intende to take from any Christian Prince such right as he had obtained.

" *Fourthly* in case any such guift or inhibition of the Pope were lawfull, & the right were soly in the King of Spaine, as he pretendeth : yet wheras after the date of the same bull his auncesters accorded & covenanted with the King and crowne of England, that the subjects on both

---

[1] This paper is indorsed "Certayne briefe answeres to the Bul of Dona- tion, with reasons why the English may trade into the West Indies."

sides might freely traffique in the Kingdomes & dominions
of both the parties contracting, ther is no doubt but that
Englishmen may lawfully repaire into the West Indias being
parcel of the dominions for trade & traffique of marchandise.
For the wordes of the treaties with King Ferdinand & his
wife Queen Isabell of Castile, & likewise with the Emperor
Charles are general & generally to be understood.   And as
it would be hardly taken, that the King of England contracting of free traffique, & commerce in his kingdomes
& dominions, should (for examples sake) inhibite the Spaniard to come into Irland: so the like reason is, that the
King of Spaine contracting in like sorte should permitt
onely a traffique in Spaine & in no other places.

"Seing therfore, that the Sea & trade are common by
the lawe of nature and of nations, it was not lawfull for
the Pope, nor, is it lawfull for the Spaniard to prohibite
other nations from the *communicatio* & *participatio* of
this lawe.

"And if they do prohibite them from those things which
are allowed by the lawe of nations, that is from marchandise, which also are due by special consideration, every man
may defend himselfe & resist violence by violence.

"And therfore the Spanish lawiers themselves have concluded that the Venetians cannot inhibite that none but
themselves shall navigate and trade within their Gulfe in
the Adriatick Sea: neither can the Spaniards or Portugales
make any such prohibition of their Indies, to prohibite lawfull & orderly traffique ; which right appertaineth unto all
nations, by the lawe of nations, as well as unto them.

"Such were the first navigations of Sir John Hawkins,
Sir Francis Drake, and others.

"And considering that the hostility & injuries offered
unto them traffiquing peaceably & lawfully (which are to
be sett downe) were both against the lawe of nations, and
also special treaties between both nations; they might defend themselves, & lawfully continue traffique with the Indians both subject & not subject to the King of Spaine.

" And so much may be alleaged for the excuse of Sir Francis Drakes first voiages into the West Indias.

" For the maintenance of the justice of his two last voiages thither with some of her Majesties ships, the first to St Domingo & Cartagena & the second (in which he died) to Nombre de Dios being no private but publique actions, another course must be holden. Viz: of injuries & hostilities declared by the open actions of the King of Spaine from time to time against her Majesty & her realme, & this to be deducted particularly & at large.

" Besides the cruel usage of her Majesties subjects lawfully & peaceably traffiquing into Spaine, without offence, by inquisicion against the lawe of nations, & the treaties. And this point is to be amplified by examples : and the evil usage of her subjects traffiquing unto the Indias.

" The preparation of an intended conquest, as appeared afterwards by the fleet sent under the charge of the duke of Medina Sidonia, & such like.

" FINIS."

CCXCV. GONDOMAR TO PHILIP III.

GENERAL ARCHIVES OF SIMANCAS. DEPARTMENT OF STATE, VOLUME 2590, FOLIO 18.

Copy of an original letter of Don Diego Sarmiento de Acuña to the King of Spain, dated London, November 16, 1613.

" SIRE —

" The ship [1] which I reported to Y. M. on the 5th ult: [September 25] as getting ready for Virginia, sailed from here on the 24th [October 14] and carried the supplies of cloth and linen, which Diego de Molino asked for, and some money to treat himself with. I hope that he will come to this country, with the return of this vessel, which from what I hear, will be in four or five months.

[1] The Elizabeth.

" May God protect the Catholic person of Y. M. as Christendom needeth so much.   London, November 16, 1613.
" DON DIEGO SARMIENTO DE ACUÑA."

[MEM. — In November, 1613, the English merchants went " roundly to work and in less than a fortnight subscribed £400,000 [equal to about $10,000,000 present values] to be employed in the trade to East India."

In 1613, Champlain published his journals, maps, etc., of his voyages to America made in 1604–1613. This work gives the result of his surveys along the coast of Massachusetts and Maine, made in the summers of 1604, 1605, and 1606. Purchas had Champlain's works, and gave translations from them. Translations have also been published in this country by the Prince Society of Boston in 1878, 1880, and 1882.

" The Description and use of the Sphære Devided into three principal Partes : . . . By Edward Wright . . . London, Printed for John Tap, dwelling at S. Magnus corner. 1613." I merely call attention to the above work as a sample of sundry books which were appearing from year to year, having an indirect bearing on the enterprises of which we write.]

CCXCVI. ORDER IN THE PRIVY COUNCIL.

From London " Documents relating to the Colonial History of the State of New York," vol. iii. p. 1.   Albany, 1853.

Order in Council respecting certain complaints against Captain Argall, etc.

" At the Court at Whitehall the 2. of January 1613. being Sunday before noone.
                    Present.
[Geo. Abbot] Lo. Archbp. of Cant.   [Wm.] E. of Pembroke.
[Thos. Egerton] Lo. Chancellor.   [Edwd.] Lo. Zouche.

[Robt. Carr] Lo. Privie Seale.   [Wm.] Lo. Knollis.
[Thos. Howard] Lo. Chamberlaine. [John] Lo. Stanhope.
[Edwd. Somerset] E. of Worcester. Sr Jul: Caesar.
        [Sir Edwd. Coke] Lo. Chiefe Justice."

This council sent the following letter to Sir Thomas
Smythe : —

" We have latelie received divers Complaints exhibited by
the French Ambassador on the behalfe of certaine Frenchmen of Rochelle, St. John de Luz, and others, some of
them concerninge outrages committed upon them (as is
alleged) on the coast of Canada by Captain Argall employed for Virginia, others on their fishing voyage towards
Greenlands by one Captain Benjamin Joseph, who commanding a ship of the Moscovie Companie this last summer,
found some of those Frenchmen in those parts and tooke
from them a great quantitie of Traine and whalebones,
wherewith they had laden their shipp, and sent them away
emptie, as appeareth by the memorialls presented by the
French Ambassador, which we send you here withall.

" Forasmuche as it will be expected that His Majestie
should forthwith give some satisfaction to the said Ambassador, touchinge both complaints we have thought good
first to require you to acquainte some of the Councell of
Virginia herewithall, as also some of the Moscovie Companie so far as it concernes eyther of them respectively and
to returne us their severall and particular answers unto
eache of them with all expedition, that the ambassador,
may likewise receive his answer from his Majestie or his
Boord." . . .

CCXCVII. EDMONDES TO JAMES I.

Sir Thomas Edmondes to King James.   Paris, France
January 2, 161$\frac{3}{4}$.
        " SIRE.
. . . " Finding Monsr de Villeroy, that tyme, in a better
moode, then when I formerly debated these matters with
him, I made it appeare unto him by manie instances, that

the interest which they (the French) pretended to have in the discoveries which we had made with great perill and charge (concerning the which he had before spoken to me much out of square) was contrarie to the received custome and practise of all nations, wherewith he was so well satisfied, as he said, that he would no more dispute that matter with me." . . .

CCXCVIII. THE MASK OF FLOWERS.

January 6, 1614. "The Maske of Flowers, presented by the Gentlemen of Graies-Inne, at the Court of White Hall at the Banquetting House, upon Twelfe-Night 1613. Being the last of the Solemnities and Magnificences which were performed at the marriage of the Earle of Somerset and Lady Frances, daughter of the Earl of Suffolke. London. Printed by N. O. for Robert Wilson . . . 1614."

This mask was prepared by Sir Francis Bacon. In it Florida Indians and tobacco are made to play important parts. There is a colloquy between Silenus (in praise of wine), and Kawasha, the god of the Florida Indians (in praise of tobacco) : —

> "*Silenus.* Kawasha comes in majestie,
> Was never such a God as *he:*
> He's come from a farre countrie
> To make our nose a chimney.
> *Kawasha.* The Wine takes the contrary way
> To get into the hood,
> But good Tobacco makes no stay
> But seizeth where it should.
> More incense hath burned at
> Great Kawashae's foote
> Than to Silen and Bacchus both,
> And take in Jove to boote.
> *Silenus.* The Worthies they were nine, 't is true,
> And lately Arthurs' knights I knew,
> But now are come up Worthies new,
> The roaring boys, Kawashae's crew.
> *Kawasha.* Silenus toppes the barrel, but

Tobacco toppes the braine,
And makes the vapours fire and soote,
That man revives againe —
Nothing but fumigation
Doth charm away ill spirites,
Kawasha and his nation
Found out these holy rites."

CCXCIX. ORDER IN THE PRIVY COUNCIL.

From London "Documents relating to the Colonial History of the State of New York," vol. iii. p. 2. Albany, 1853.

"At the Court, Whitehall the 23. of January 1613. being Sonday afternoone.

Present.

Lo. Archb. of Cant.	Lo. Knollys.
Lo. Chancellor.	[Thos.] Lo. Wotton.
Lo. Pr. Seale.	Lo. Stanhope.
Lo. Chamberlaine.	Sr Jul: Caesar.

"The answer of the Lords of His Majesties unto the compleynts exhibited by the Lord Embassador of France touchinge spoyles and other violences supposed to be committed by His Majesties subjects of Great Brittaine upon the subjects of France on the Coast of Greeneland and Cannada. . . . [The part relating to Greenland is omitted.] For the matter of Cannada, their Lordships having required The Treasurer and Councell of Virginia, whom it concernes, to make answer thereunto, they say, that since the month of June, they have not received any shipp or advice from Virginia, whereby they cannot be informed of any such misdemeanors, but upon Captain Argall's returne, which they expect about the beginning of the Spring, or upon any other notice of the fact, (whereof they will seeke to be informed by all the means they may,) they will certifie their Lordships, whereupon such course shall be taken for restitution and punishment of the offenders as shall be to the good satisfaction of the sayd Lord Embassador, and the parties interested."

[MEM. — Court minutes, East India Company. February 26, 1614. " Permission to Sir Thomas Dale, now employed in Virginia, to adventure £100. in the joint stock, at the request of Sir Wm. Throgmorton." March 3. " Lent two culverins to The Virginia Company."

In March the States General grant the Dutch charters, for making discoveries, trading, etc., in America.

Captain Marmaduke Roydon, Captain George Langam, Master John Buley, and Master William Skelton sent two ships from London, under Master Thomas Hunt and Captain John Smith, for our New England coast. They went from the Downes the third of March, 1614, " Set out by certaine Merchants for the love of gaine."

The Somers Islands Company sent out about this time for the Bermudas, the Blessing, the Starr, the Margaret, and two pinnaces, the Thomas and the Edwin.]

CCC. GONDOMAR TO PHILIP III.

GENERAL ARCHIVES OF SIMANCAS. DEPARTMENT OF STATE, VOLUME 2592, FOLIO 44.

Copy of an original letter of Don Diego Sarmiento de Acuña to the King of Spain, dated London, March 17, 1614.

" SIRE.

" Since I have come here I have continued reporting to Y. M. about the condition of the Colonies of Virginia and Bermuda, as far as I have heard. About Virginia they tell me that a resolution has been passed to abandon that colony, and carry the people to Bermuda ; because Virginia does not in any way answer to what had been expected, and is on the contrary very expensive to the company here, which sustains it, and the King gives nothing but Patents and Titles towards the establishment of these Colonies.

SIR HENRY NEVILLE

The members of the Virginia Company have now asked
permission from the King and the Council, to withdraw the
people from there this Spring, before the few survivors
should die.   This permission has not been granted, (has
been refused) with the suggestion that it was well to preserve that place, altho' it be good for nothing more than to
kill people and to afford an outlet to them from here;
since in this Kingdom here, they grow and multiply so as
to be innumerable.   Thus they have gone back and tried a
kind of fortune, which here they call a Lottery, to succor
and maintain that colony of Virginia, which as Y. M. no
doubt has heard had its beginning more than twenty years
ago.   He who first brought the English here was Captain
'Don Guater Rale' [Sir Walter Raleigh] a great favorite
of the Queen Elizabeth, and for her sake he called it Virginia.   We expect Don Diego de Molina very shortly here
and he will surely tell us what there is in all this; but some
of the English themselves who have been over there have
spoken to me about it exactly as I have informed Y. M.

" It is three years since the English have had a footing
in Bermuda, by the accidental loss of a ship on that coast.
It was coming from Virginia; the Captain was called ' Neo-
porte,' a famous sailor; with a part of the timber and the
rigging of the wrecked ship they built themselves on the
island of Bermuda another small vessel, and in this ship
building and in well reconnoitreing the country they spent
ten months.   Here they say that of old that Country was
called the Land of the Devils on account of the dangers of
the Sea, the coast and the harbour; but now this Colony
appears with great power, and here they speak of it with
great consideration.   A company has already been formed
of (citizens?) neighbours of this city, for its benefit, which counts, I am
told, more than four hundred Members, and among them
the Earl of Pembroke of the Council of State, the Earl of
Southampton, Count Montgomery, Baron Walden, eldest
son of the Earl of Suffolk and other great lords and
knights; but the majority are merchants, and great hopes

are entertained from this discovery, if the peace with Spain should ever be broken. The people that were there last year, were one hundred persons men and women. There will probably leave here three hundred persons, two hundred and fifty men, and a few women, most of them lost people, or put in jail as vagabonds, and thus now they send them out to help in Bermuda. These people go out in a ship and in two pinnaces; the ship is called 'The Star,' of two hundred and sixty tons, carries twenty-four pieces of artillery. The pinnaces are of 20 tons each and in each of them go some twenty five men ; they also carry some very small little pieces of artillery. They also send out in this ship some engineers and skilled workmen, who know how to throw up fortifications (earth-works), with some elderly men to be put in charge of these ships and to govern on shore, with a list, and the rank of those who are, each one to succeed others, precisely as if they were dying men and failing ; because he who has so far been the Head of the English in Bermuda, is Master 'Mun' [Moor] a carpenter. They go to this place with the intention of well fortifying that post and to keep putting into it up to a thousand Englishmen, and thus they propose very shortly to send another ship there, which is called 'Mateo' of two hundred and fifty tons, with twenty two pieces of artillery and carrying out a hundred settlers. They say that there is but one single channel by which you can enter the port, that this channel is one 'mile' long in passing, which is the third part of a league. They go to the entrance of this channel intending to erect a fort on each side, and to furnish them with much artillery. They have destroyed and shut up every other landing place in the whole island, so that in no part of it a vessel can come to the shore, unless it be thro' this one channel, the entrance of which is on the Northside, or on the other side, almost directly opposite of it towards the South, which they have not been able to close entirely. Nor do they trouble themselves much about this, because, they say that no large ship can approach it,

but only launches and small boats. It is for this purpose
that they carry the two pinnaces, because it seems to them
that they will be sufficient to prevent any one from entering
that Road and little harbour. Those who are now going
out carry with them power and authority to distribute lands
as heirlooms to private Englishmen, as it may appear best
to them in order that they may work them and reap the
benefit, as if they were their own. They find in this island
of Bermuda such a number of pigs that they need not
much meat; there is also a great abundance of birds and
fishes there. The principal hope of profit which they cher-
ish of this Colony is in the amber, which has been found in
abundance, and in Pearls likewise, because in a very shallow
water and without its being necessary to $\substack{\text{dive} \\ \text{swim}}$ they have
already found a large number, and have brought some
home with them, which have been sold at forty reales each
pearl; while they hope in deeper water they will find more
of them and larger ones. For this purpose they take out
with them some famous divers, and as they have also been
told, that it was on this coast Don Luis de Cordoba was
lost with the four silver-Galleons, they go with the intention of making these swimmers and divers search carefully,
if they may discover some of these ships, which they presume must hold great treasures. In pursuing the pearl
fishery within the sea they meet on the coast of Bermuda
with one great difficulty which has prevented them so far
from fishing except on the coast, and this is a great quantity of certain fishes larger than dogs, which it is said the
English call from their form ' Jarques ' [sharks] and the
latter say that they attack and at once, dispatch any man.
The English, however, are also full of hope, to catch them
and clear the coast of them. This Company continues to
possess much property and thus that Colony will be liberally assisted and helped with everything that may be necessary.

" They tell me that the Embassador of this king here, at
your Court, has written to him that Y. M. was bent upon

destroying this Colony of the English and to drive them out of Bermuda. Now Count Somerset has also thus informed the members of the Bermuda-Company, in order that in conformity with this they may arrange matters, prepare all that may be necessary and send succour promptly. It is this which makes this vessel sail now with the two pinnaces, and the other ship will also sail very shortly. All the Members of this Company, therefore, tell me, that they are filled with anxiety, especially as they have also been told that there are several English pilots in the navy of Y. M., who know that coast perfectly well, as also the harbour, having been there themselves; on this account it is that, altho' they had given orders to these ships who are now carrying these people over there, after having landed them in Bermuda, to go and catch codfish at Newfoundland; they have now, after this warning, changed their plan and ordered those ships to lie by and assist in guarding the island.

" Y. M. will see from all these statements what may be most important to be done for His Royal service, and if it should be necessary for me here to take any special measures, Y. M. will be pleased to command me.

" May God protect the Catholic person of Y. M. etc.

" London March 17. 1614.

" DON DIEGO SARMIENTO DE ACUÑA."

[MEM. — Entered at Stationers' Hall, March 9, 1614, by Felix Kingston — under the handes of Sir Thomas Smithe and Mr Warden Feild. " A declaration of the present estate of the English in Virginia, with the final resolucon of the Great Lotterye intended for their supply."

Copies of this publication seem to have been sent to all the city companies of London; and it has been said that none can now be found; but I am convinced that CCCXLII. was a later issue of the same publication. The reference in CCCXLI. is certainly to CCCXLII., and the reference in CCCI. is certainly to this publication, and I am sure that both references are to the same publication. See, also, the remarks on CCCXLII. and that number itself. The following letter was sent with this Declaration (of March 9, 1614), to the several city companies of London.]

CCCI. PRIVY COUNCIL TO CITY COMPANIES.

" To Our very loving frindes the Master Wardens and Assistants of the Company of . . .

" After our harty commendations, wee send you herewith a true declaration of the present estate of the English Colony planted in Virginia together with a project by help of a lottery to bring at length that work to the successe desired. Wee shall not need to commend unto you that worthy and Christian enterprize full of honour and profitt to His Majestie and the whole realme, yf the endes in the sayd declaration expressed may in processe of tyme be attained unto, whereof the hopes (as you may perceave) nowe are great for advancing and bringing whereof to some good perfection, we hartily pray you to employ your good endeavours amongst the Brethren of your Company to adventure in the sayd Lottery destined to soe good a purpose such reasonable sumes of money as each of them may conveniently and can willingly spare, nothing doubting but that excited by your good example and persuasion they will shew themselves forward to adventure in soe faire a Lottery wherein hapily they may be gainers, and what soever any shall loose shall be bestowed on soe good a worke and so behovefull to the whole realme.

" You shall alsoe receave herewith from the Treasurer and Councell of Virginia such Bookes as are requisite for the registring of the sayd sumes adventured which we pray you with as much expedition as may be (in regarde of their present wants to sett forth a shippe thither this Springe) to return with the money gathered to the sayd Treasurer, from whom wee will take notice of your proceedings herein that we may accordingly give you deferred thanks for the same. And so we bid you hartily farewell.

" From the Court of Whitehall this first of April 1614.
" Your loving friends.

G. CANT,	Exeter,
LENOX,	PEMBROKE,
T. SUFFOLKE.	W. KNOLLYS,
E. WORCESTER.	J. STANHOPE.

JUL. CÆSAR."

[MEM. — " Chamberlain to Carleton, London, 7. April, 1614. . . . On Tuesday the 5th of this present, the King, Prince and Lords, rode in their robes to the Parliament . . . The King made a long and excellent speech, consisting of three principal parts wherein all his care lay — to continue to his subjects *bona animi, bona corporis, et bona fortunæ,* by maintaining religion, preserving of peace, and seeking their prosperity, by *increasing of trades and traffics.*"

In the spring of 1614 Captain William Gibbons, who had been with Button the previous year, sailed on a voyage for the discovery of the northwest passage; but took shelter in " Gibbons his hole " on the coast of Labrador, and returned to England in the autumn.]

CCCII. EXTRACT FROM GROCERS' RECORDS.

Court of Assistants — Grocers' Company.
" Curia Assist: die veneris scilt. 15. die Aprilis 1614 anno . . . xij. . . . Jacobi aug.
" Present : —
    Sir Thomas Middleton K[t] Lo[d] Mayor.
    Sir Robert Napier K[t] & Baronet.
M[r] Nicholas Stile and M[r] George Bolles, *Aldermen.*
M[r] Wm. Dale, M[r] Tho[s] Longston and M[r] Tho[s] Westrow. *Wardens.*

Mr John Newman,

" Robert Cox,

" Richard Burrell,

" Anthony Soday,

" Robert Bowyer,

" Roger Gwyn,

" Richard Bourne,

" Thomas Moulson,

" Robert Johnson,

" Wm. Barrett,

Mr Richard Denman,

" Humphrey Walcott,

" Richard Aldworth,

" Edmond Westall,

" Wm Pennyfather,

" Laurence Grene,

" Danyel Wynche,

" Humfrey Robinson,

" Robert Mildmay.

. . . .

" This day alsoe were read openly to the generallitye of the Company here assembled the letters of the right Honourable the lordes and others [CCCI.] of his Majesties most Honourable privy Counsaile directed to Mr Wardens for adventures in Lottery by the several Brothers of this Company for supporting the plantation in Virginia which letters are dated primo Aprilis 1614. The tenour whereof ensueth in these wordes vizt. [See CCCI.]

" Alsoe was then publickly read to the whole Assembly a declaration printed of the present estate of the English Colony planted in Virginia with a finall resolution of the great Lottery entended for their supply sett forth by his Majesties Councell for Virginia [see 9th March, 1614]. Together with a Lottery Booke with certen directions sent to Mr. Wardens and Assistants of this Company by the Treasurer and Counsell of Virginia for Registring the names of the adventurers with their several somes of money to be adventured therein.

" And thereupon Mr. Warden Dale with many forcible reasons for the general advancement of Christianity and good of the common-wealth moved and persuaded the whole assembly then present to write perticulerly with their owne handes how much every of them would willingly sett-downe severally to adventure in the sayd Lottery entended to soe good a purpose.

" Whereupon it then pleased the Right Honourable Sir

Thomas Middleton, K[t] Lord Mayor of this city and many other Brethren of this Company with their several handes to write in the sayd booke howe muche they woulde therein voluntary adventure as by the sayd booke may appear."

[There are no more entries in minute books nor wardens' accounts of the Virginia Company after this. The book mentioned is not now among the muniments of the Grocers' Company. It is presumed that whatever was done after this was by Grocers in their individual and not in their corporate capacity. The Irish plantation is mentioned at nearly every court for some years following this date as a serious business of the company as a body; not so the Virginia plantation. — J. A. Kingdon, 1885.]

CCCIII. THE LORD MAYOR TO CITY COMPANIES.

A letter from Sir Thomas Middleton, Lord Mayor, directed to the master and wardens of the city companies.

" After my hearty Comendaçons.

" These are to lett you understand that I am required by the Lords of his Majesties most honorable privy Counsell to recommend unto your care the effecting of their Lordships desires for the furtherance of the Virginia plantaçon, as by their Lordshipps letters [CCCI.] herewithall sent may appeare.

" Wherefore I pray and require you forthwith to call a Courte and to use your best endeavours to accomplishe their Lordshipps pleasures in regard it is for soe charitable and Christian a worke, and by which meanes wee maybe disburthened of many idle and vagrant persons which otherwise are, and wilbe more and more, chargeable, dangerous, and troublesome unto the state.

" And soe I bid you hartely farwell.   xx[th] of April, 1614.

" Your Loving ffreind.   THO : MIDLETON, Maior."

[MEM. — The Elizabeth, Captain Adams, which sailed from England October 14, 1613 (see CCXCV.), taking the first potatoes to the Bermudas, reached Virginia, bringing silkworms, etc., in the winter of 1613–14. She sailed from Virginia in March following, having on board Sir Thomas Gates, the Sieur de la Motte, etc.

Gates carried to England the official accounts of " Argall's Voyages to the Northward," and other documents now unknown. He certainly reached England some time before the 12th of May, and I am inclined to think before the 20th of April, 1614. Howes says: " This yeere 1614. Sir Th: Gates came from Virginia into England, using his best meanes for more supplies to continue their plantation, having left behind him not full 400. men of all that were sent thither, over whom Sir Th : Dale, Knight, a valiant souldier and discreet Governour had the full charge and rule."]

CCCIV.   EXTRACT FROM COMMONS JOURNAL.

The Muscovy Company was now upon the question, with Spain, France, and Holland. The English-American enterprise was " between two fires," France and Spain. The colony was in jeopardy, and the company wished to yield up their patent, and have the colony attached more directly to the crown. Among the " Bills to be drawn by his Majesties most gracious direction for the good and comfort of his people upon certain of the propositions exhibited to his Majesty [about February, 161¾], and to be offered to the [next] Parliament," was " An act for the better plantation of Virginia and supply thereof." — See Bacon's " Letters and Life by Spedding," vol. v. p. 17.

Mr. Neill in his " Virginia Company of London," pp. 67, 68, says: " Sir Thomas Smith, a member of the House of Commons, in a debate on the 20th of April, said that if he as the Governor of the Company could influence the members, the patent should be brought in. Sergeant Montague declared that the patent was against law, and a member by the name of Middleton said, ' That the Company were willing to yield up their patent, that it had not been their intention to use it otherwise than for the good of all parties, and confessed that there had been some miscarriages. The shopkeepers of London sent over all kinds of goods, for which they received tobacco instead of coin, infinitely to the prejudice of the Commonwealth. Many of the divines now smell of tobacco, and poor men spend 4d. of their day's wages at night in smoke, and wished that this patent may be damned, and an act of Parliament passed for the government of the Colony by a Company.'

" After considerable discussion it was ordered by the House of Commons that the patent should be brought the next day."

CCCV. EXTRACT FROM MERCHANT TAYLORS' RECORDS.

From the minutes of a court of assistants of the Merchant Taylors' Company, held May 6, 1614.

" At this Courte was openly read a letter receaved from the Lords of his Majesties most honorable privy Counsell, the words whereof are these, viz : [See CCCI.]

" Alsoe another letter from the right honorable the Lord Maior directed to the Master and Wardens in these words, vizt : [See CCCIII.]

" Alsoe a paper booke under the hand of Sir Thomas Smyth Knight, and the Virginia Companyes Seale, for such as shalbe disposed to make any Adventure in the Lottery to sett their hands to such somes of money as they purpose to putt into the Lottery.

" And lastly there was alsoe presented to this Courte a true declaration in print of the present estate of the English Colony planted in Virginia. [See March 9, 1614.]

" All which letters and printed declaration being openly read and duely considered of — It is ordered and agreed at this Court as well in respect of the Counsells letters, as in regard of the future good that may come thereby. That

SIR JOHN OGLE

the some of ffifty pounds shalbe putt into the Lottery, out of the stock of this howse, and what prizes or other proffitt soever may growe or come thereby to be truely aunswered agayne to the use of the howse, Our Master to pay the same, and have it allowed in his Accompt. And soe many of the assistants as please in particular to make any adventure in the said Lottery to sett their hands and somes to the said booke. And after the assistants have done, It is ordered that our Mr. and Wardens shall cause the whole Livery and all of the Batchellers Company to be sommoned unto the Hall, and there to lett them understand, what the Counsells pleasure is, and what hath bin done by the assistants, that as many as have any desire to further, this worke intended, may sett their hands and somes to the booke before mentioned."

CCCVI. CHAMBERLAIN TO CARLETON.

John Chamberlain to the right honorable Sir Dudley Carleton, Knight, Lord Ambassador for his Majestie at Venice.

. . . "Sir Thomas Gates is come from Virginia and brings word that that plantation will fall to the ground yf yt be not presently supplied. He speakes of wonderfull commodities that are to be had there, yf we could have the patience and would be at the cost to bring them to perfection. . . .
"From London May 12th 1614."

There was so much diplomacy in the management of the enterprise, and in the various reports given out — so many "stratagems," as Molina calls them, — that it is really impossible to know exactly how much reliance to place in the various contemporary letters, reports, publications, etc.

CCCVII. EXTRACT FROM COMMONS JOURNAL.

Mr. Neill in his "Virginia Company of London," on p. 68, gives the following. [See CCCIV.]

"On the 12ᵗʰ of May the Council for Virginia presented a petition for aid, which was read, and the next Monday [16th], at nine o'clock in the morning, was designated as the time to hear the case; but on the 16ᵗʰ Mʳ Brooke moved that the Virginia business should be taken up the next day at seven o'clock.

"On the 17ᵗʰ of May it was ordered that Lords Southampton, Sheffield, and others, should come in to hear the discussion of Virginia affairs, and shall sit with uncovered heads until otherwise requested by the Speaker. It was further ordered that any member that stood in the entry should pay a fine of 12d. to the Sergeant-at-arms, and that there should be great silence while the Lords were present." [See CCCVIII.]

CCCVIII. EXTRACT FROM COMMONS JOURNAL.

COMMONS JOURNAL, VOLUME I. PAGES 487–489.

I give CCCVIII.; and CCCIX. as they are in the Commons Journal, in "the short hand" of the period, without attempting to fill them out. The report is a mere outline; but it probably affords a fair idea of the debate.

"Martis.   17ᵗʰ Maii. 12.ᵈ Jacobi. A. 1614. . . .

"Mr. Martyn of Counsel with the Company cometh in before the Lords — The Bar, first down taken up at the Lords coming in. The Lords stood bare, till after Mʳ Martyn had begun. Then Mʳ Speaker spake to him to stay; And then, in the name of the House, spake to them, signifying to them the pleasure of the House, that they should sit down, and be covered.

[Mr. Martyn continuing.]   "Queen Eliz. of ever-growing memory, compared by the King to Augustus. That the

Lady of the Seas, whole fleet stooping — the Red Cross in one of her Ships. The discovery by her subjects, of all the Seas about the world.

"Amadis. And after, Whyte, Employed by Sir W. Raleighe, in those Discoveries. He termed a subject of Envy, in his Greatness; now a Mirror of the Vanity of all Earthly things.

"This Plantation began 1606. Religion. Captain Newport. Sir Tho. Gates. Virginia, a Bridle for the Neopolitane Courser, if our Youth of England able to sit him; for which they will give them golden spurs.

"L. d' la Warre.

"That now a settled Plantation : all things necessary for food.

"That this conquest just. The Spanyards course in the Indyes — Don John D'Aquyla in Ireland. Our usage of the Indyes merciful & respective — That this country never yet felt the yoke of the plow.

"1. Objection, that, if this undertaken by this House, and King, this might prove to a War.

"Ans. That this no just cause of offence. The name given by the Queen. The Spanyards defend the West Indyes; the Por'. the East; the French the River of . . . The Hollander their forts in the Moluccos.

"That the Spanyard, by our Forces, drawn to that extremity, that they would —

"That this city hath not three Armourers —

"This time of Relief for the King —

"That they require, is but a few honest Labourers, burthened with children.

"Moveth, a committee may consider of the means for this, for seven years; at which some of their Company may be present.

"Columbus his offer to H. VII. neglected, because no prement Profit.

"That this Country giveth Hope of all those commodities which a Southern Country can promise." . . .

[Old Fuller, says of Martin, "He is eminent, as for many speeches, so especially for that he made in parliament in the tenth [twelfth?] year of King James, when account was taken of forty gentlemen in the house which were not twenty, and some of them not sixteen, years of age. '*Formerly*,' said this Recorder Martyn, 'it was the custom of old men to make laws for young ones; but now nature is invaded and inverted, seeing young men enact laws to govern their fathers.' "]

When Martin concluded.

"*Sir Roger Owen*. [Moved.] That the Treasurer of Virginia, and those that be of that Company, shall withdraw themselves, 'till the matter be debated.

"*Mr. Brooke*, contra: For, if a Bill here that concerneth Yorke, he not to be withdrawn; for that it concerneth the Commonwealth.

"*Mr. Edw. Montague*: That the Speech of Mr. Martyn the most unfitting that ever was spoken in this House."

[Here follows a debate on the unfitness of Mr Martyn's speech.]

"*Sir E. Hoby* was for calling him to the bar.

"*Mr. Duncombe* said he patronized as a schoolmaster-teaching his scholars.

"*Sir R. Phillips*. while admitting that he had made a great mistake, spoke in the defensive.

"*Sir G. Moore*. said it was an extraordinary step to admit counsel in the House upon the hearing of a petition, and that the speech was still more strange." . . .

It was finally.

"Ordered. He (Martyn) shall come to the Bar to-morrow, standing (not kneeling).

"Mr. Speaker to charge him: He to make his submission."

CCCIX. EXTRACT FROM COMMONS JOURNAL.

" Mercurii. 18° Maii 12° Jacobi. . . . He offered to kneel.

[Sir Randolph Crewe.] "*Mr Speaker.* That he had done himself much Right in the Beginning. Petition of Virginia. Order for the Counsel. That he then for Counsel appeared, with divers Lords. That at first prepared to hear him with all Respect and Love. The remembrances of the Plantation well accepted, and looked upon with eyes of our love.

"That after unfortunately digressed to matters of much weight, impertinent. That took upon him to censure somethings and advise.

"That the House took this for a great Presumption, and did disdain and contemn it. That the House, zealous of the honour of the House, hath thought fit to convene him to the Place, where his offence, to receive satisfaction from him. That hath many Friends here; yet now all look upon him with Eyes as Judges, not as private Friends.

"*Mr Martyn:* That all mens actions subject to Error; his more, because so weak. Yet not in Love with Error, and is willing, as any man, to be divorced from it. Confesseth, he hath digressed from order and from his own Purpose.

"This occasioned by the Presense of the Lords, he not well instructed in the Business. That when he came, like to a ship, that cutteth the Cable, and putteth to Sea — So he, to cut his memory and trust to his Invention.

"That never knew of the Lords Presence.

"When here, the zeal of this House eat up his judgment. That he forgat himselfe — Acknowledge his Error, not for Fear of Punishment.

"Glad, be Example to all others.

"Submitteth himself to their censure.

"Doth it not with dejected countenance; for cannot but receive Comfort in acknowleging of his error."

[Here follows short debate.]

"*Sir Wm. Maynard.* Glad the House yesterday inclined to mercy — Commended the carriage and answer.

"*Sir Ro. Phillippes.* . . . . moveth, he may now be called

for, and the Pleasure of the House signified to him. That
the House taketh his offence great, and of a high Pitch :
That they have likewise inclined to the Height of Mercy ;
respecting his Person, good affections, and former service
here. They, upon his acknowledgement here really made,
are pleased to be remitted, presuming, he will sin no more
in the like.

"*Mr. Martin.* That this Doom sheweth, they not persuaded he came to offend with a high Hand. Thanks for
their Favour. Petitioneth, that, to fill up the Measure of
their Grace, they would be pleased to appoint a Committee,
to consider of the Virginia Business."

This Parliament did not take the Virginia business in
hand. It is known in history as the "Addled Parliament,"
from the circumstance that it never passed a single measure.
It will be noted that the Lords are mentioned in the trouble with Martin. The Parliament was dissolved June 7th
following, in consequence of the quarrel with the House of
Lords arising out of the question of the legality of certain
impositions or exactions, which the Commons insisted should
be removed before supplies were voted.

CCCX. CHAMBERLAIN TO CARLETON.

. . . "On tewsday Dick Martin came to the Parliament
house as a Counsaillor to plead for some course to be held
for the upholding of Virginia, and to countenance the cause
the Earle of Southampton, the Lord Sheffield and the Lord
De la Ware, came with him and were admitted to be present :
but after a while having spoken but little in the cause he
came for, he fell to ripping up what had passed since theyre
sitting, taxing them for theyre slow proceeding, for theyre
disorderly cariage, and schooling them what they shold do,
with divers odde glaunces, wherwith he so discontented
them that after he was gon there was much arguing what
course they shold take with him, and in the end yt was

agreed he shold be called to the barre and aunswer his mis-
demeanure: so yesterday he appeared there and with much
shew of humilitie and submission did so insinuate himself
into them that after a while they remitted his kneeling, and
in respect of his goode service heretofore in that house did
after some admonition cleerly release him: but the Lords
that accompanied him are more angry with him then all
the rest, and will not be satisfied. Thus you see though
he abstained from beeing of the parlement for feare of
being transported and doing himself harme, yet yt was *in
fatis* that he should shame himself in that house. . . .

"Sir John Digby carries himself high and lookes after
great matters, sayeing he hath ben in the greatest employment the King hath except the Deputiship of Ireland, and
yet his allowance exceeds that: yt seemes he can stoope no
lower from his cloth of state that he used in Spaine, as likewise his Lady, but I know not *per quam regulare:* he de-
maunds a £1.000 for his transportation or *ayúdas de costa*
for his comming home, but he is like to get yt at leasure.
So with all due remembrance to my Lady, I commend you
to the protection of the Almighty. From London this 19th
of May 1614.

"Your Lordship's to commaund.

"JOHN CHAMBERLAIN."

Addressed: "To the right honorable Sr Dudley Carleton,
Kt Ld Ambassador for his Matie at Venice."

CCCXI. LORKIN TO PUCKERING.

Rev. Thomas Lorkin to Sir Thomas Puckering, Bart., at
Madrid. [From London, May 28, 1614.]

. . . "Not many days since, Mr. Martin, the lawyer, presuming to tax the House, incurred the danger of a severe
censure, if many friends, accompanied by an humble submission of his own, had not the more powerfully mediated for
him. He was no member of the House; but entertained by
the Virginia Company to recommend unto the House a

favourable consideration of something that imported that
adventure.   Coming therefore to speak, he left his theme
which was appointed him, and began to reprove the House
for wasting so much time, to so little purpose; and then, as
if had had more brain than all, undertook to become their
pedagogue, and to instruct them (chiefly the younger sort,
whereof there is some number) in what steps they ought to
tread, and in what order they are to proceed.   The next
day he was called to the bar, and there arraigned for his
presumption; where, upon the earnest mediation of many
friends, and his own submissive acknowledgment upon his
knees, he was pardoned his offence; the House contenting
themselves to have remonstrated unto him his temerity and
arrogance, without inflicting further punishment." . . .

CCCXII.   EXTRACT FROM CARAYON.

Extract from " Primière Mission des Jésuites au Canada,"
page 1, note 1.   See CLXVIII. and CXCVI.

" We shall add to the letters of our first missionaries in
Canada a fragment of a memoir, entitled : *Monumenta
Novæ Franciæ, ab anno* 1607, *ad annum* 1737.   *Insulæ
Martinicæ, ab anno* 1678.   *Insulæ Cayennensis, ab anno*
1668.

" The translation of the second chapter of this MS., preserved in our Archives at Rome, will give a collection of
facts concerning New France, which is not found in the letters which we publish. . . .

" The year following their arrival, two more of our Society [Jesuits] went to join them : they were Father Quentin
and the Brother-Coadjutor Gilbert du Thet.

" Two years spent at Port-Royal convinced our Fathers
that it was impossible to make this the centre of their mission, partly because of the difficulty to draw to that place a
great concourse of Savages, partly because of the trouble
caused by those who were in command.

" They transferred the seat of their mission to another

point of the same Coast, under the 45th degree 30 minutes of Latitude, and this upon a Command of the King. This establishment took the name of Saint Sauveur.

"They had been but recently established there, when the English, coming upon them unexpectedly, took possession of the French vessel, seized the Commander's Letters Patent, and by signal wickedness, treated him as a pirate. At the time of the attack several Frenchmen were killed, and among them Brother Gilbert du Thet, a man remarkable for his courage and his piety.

"The triumphant English, after having leisurely plundered everybody, abandoned a portion of the French in a wretched bark, and carried the Fathers Biard and Quentin with them to Virginia. Our two prisoners expected to be condemned to death, especially, when, upon being brought back to Port Royal, they refused to betray the retreat of those Frenchmen, who kept themselves concealed in the neighborhood. Sent back once more to Virginia, they would there probably have met their death, if Divine Providence had not defeated all efforts made by the English sailors to effect a landing. The violence of the storm driving them back upon the Azores, which belong to the Portuguese, and where, in spite of them, they were compelled to go ashore.

"The English themselves were compelled to admire the loyalty and the charity of our Fathers, who, by simply showing themselves to the Portuguese, might have brought about the seizure of the ship and the condemnation to death of the English, by being declared pirates. Before entering the harbor, they had exacted from their prisoners the promise that they would not denounce them, and would keep themselves in concealment during the whole time of their stay at the Azores. During the visit which the Portuguese paid to the ship the Fathers remained down in the hold, where they escaped all curious eyes. This generosity and this faithfulness in keeping the promise they had made, surprised the English so greatly, that they immediately changed their behavior towards their prisoners and carried them directly to England, where they praised them aloud.

" The French Ambassador, when he heard of their arrival, hastened to reclaim them officially, and caused them to be honorably carried back to their native land in the month of May, 1614." . . .

CCCXIII. BIARD TO ACQUAVIVA.

From Carayon's " Première Mission," etc., pages 106–116.   (See CLXVIII.)

" Letter written by Father Pierre Biard, to the very Revd Father Claude Acquaviva, General of the Society of Jesus."

Translated from the Latin original preserved in the Archives of Jesus at Rome.

" Amiens, May $\frac{16}{26}$, 1614.

" My Very Reverend Father !

" Pax Christi !

" Since thanks to a special blessing of God and to the prayers of your Fatherhood, we have quite recently escaped from various most serious dangers, both gratitude and duty compel me this day to throw myself, as fully as I can at the feet of your Fatherhood, filled with most lively thankfulness and most earnestly, in order to present to you my regard and to prove to you my affection.   I must, in fact, look upon myself as chosen by the Lord Himself, both to repent and to show the triumph of Grace, so very great are the dangers from which I now see myself delivered, to my great joy and surprise — but this is scarcely the time to mention all the events in detail ; and I think your Fatherhood must have heard many things already from Father Ennemond Masse ; leaving other things aside, I shall be content to tell you to-day, how, after our capture by the English in New France, we were dragged from place to place and finally restored to our own Country.

" During the last year, 1613, we were in all, as your Fatherhood knows, four (Fathers Biard, Masse, Quentin

CAPTAIN GEORGE PERCY

and Brother du Thet) members of the Society in New France. At that time, we laid at last at a suitable place, the foundations for a new establishment, and for a new Colony.

"Just then, all of a sudden, I know not by what fortuitous chance (for certainly it was not a premeditated plan) the English of Virginia throw themselves upon our coast, take possession, with great fury, of our ship, whilst almost all our defenders were busy on shore. After some resistance, we were compelled to surrender; two Frenchmen were killed in the fight and four wounded, without counting our brother Gilbert du Thet, who was mortally wounded. He died piously in my arms on the next day.

"When the vessel was taken and everything else stolen, they did us, priests and Jesuits, a great favor by not taking our lives! However, under such circumstances, life is something more cruel even than any kind of death. Stripped of everything and in want of everything what could we have done at this place so completely deserted and unculti-vated? The Savages, to be sure, came to see us secretly at night. They grieved over our misfortune, and promised most heartily and sincerely, that they would do for us all they could do, but such was the state of things and the nature of the place that we saw nothing but Death around us, or a wretchedness worse even than death. We were thirty people, suffering the same anguish. What made our Englishmen less cruel, was that one of our boats, evading their vigilance, had escaped. They saw themselves com-pelled to spare us, because they knew very well, that there were witnesses now abroad who could testify to the violence they had done us. They feared the *lex talionis* and the vengeance that our King might take. They told us at last (a noble favor indeed!) that for us thirty who remained, they would leave at our disposal a boat, in which we might sail along the coast and try to meet some French vessel, that could take us back to our own country. They were shown that this boat could not hold more than 15 persons, but they would not grant us any more, not even one of our own vessels.

"There was no time to lose. In this perplexity, each one did what he could for his safety. Father Ennemond Masse got with 14 others into the boat, of which we have spoken, and God has protected him, as your Fatherhood has already heard.

"I went to see the English Commander ; and obtained for myself and Father Jacques Quentin, my companion, as well as for Jean Dixon, who had been admitted into the Society, and for one servant, that we should be carried to some island near by, where the English are in the habit of fishing, and that we should be recommended to these fisher-ermen in order that they might carry us to England, from whence we could easily return to France. I obtained this, I say, as a promise, but they did not keep their word. In fact, we and the other Frenchmen who remained, fifteen in number, were taken straight to Virginia,[1] nearly 250 post-leagues from where we had been taken prisoners. There, new dangers ! The Governor of this fort wanted to hang us all, but especially the Jesuits. The Captain who had taken us prisoners opposed this, pleading the promise he had given. This pledge or the fear of the King finally pre-vailed.

"This Captain was afterwards ordered to return to that part of New France where he had plundered us, to destroy all French vessels that he might find there, and to burn all forts and all houses.

"In fact, the French had there still two settlements, that of Saint Croix, and that of Port Royal, where I had lived two years. They fitted out three ships for this expedition, two of them had been taken from us ; the third, larger and fitted out for war, was that which had made us prisoners.

---

[1] The situation at Jamestown in August, 1613, was very interesting. There were fifteen Frenchmen, includ-ing two Jesuit fathers, naval officers and others ; a Spaniard of distinction (Molina), a renegade Englishman who pretended to be a Spaniard (Lymbry), and the Indian maiden Pocahontas, all prisoners there.

They allowed only eight Frenchmen to get on board these vessels; with the intention of availing themselves of the first opportunity to send us back to our native land. These ships sailed first to the place where we had been made prisoners, and the English destroyed the crosses which we had erected, but the punishment was not long delayed; before we left one of them, convicted I know not of what crime, was hanged at the very same place. A Cross avenged the Crosses! We found here also new dangers. The English, as I said above, wanted to sail to the settlement of Sainte-Croix, altho' there was then nobody there; but they had left there a supply of salt. I was the only one who knew the way, and the English knew that I had lived there formerly. They ask me to show them the way. I do all I can to invent pretexts and to escape from their demands. But I achieved nothing. Seeing clearly that I would not conduct them there, the Captain broke out into great wrath, and the danger became more imminent for me, when they unexpectedly discovered the place without me. They plundered it and reduced everything to ashes. Besides, they succeeded on this occasion in catching a Savage who led them to Port Royal. If this accident relieved me of a great danger, it exposed me likewise to another, that was still greater. In fact, after they had plundered and burnt Port-Royal, which they found, I do not know why, abandoned by the French, one of the very men who had left this post brought a charge against me. He said I was a true and pure Spaniard and did not dare return to France, because of certain crimes which I had committed there. The Captain, already inimical, seized this new pretext to rage, and asked his companions what they thought of it? Did it not seem just to them, that I should be cast on shore and there be abandoned? The opinion of the majority prevailed: They wanted me to be carried back to Virginia, and that there. in due form, and according to law, I should be restored to the gallows from which I had escaped. Thus I was saved for the time at least; we resumed at once our voyage to

Virginia; but two days later we were assailed by such a
tempest that our ships were dispersed. We do not know
what has become of the others.

"After having battled with the storm for three weeks, the
Captain [William Turner] of our ship, seeing how many
things were wanting, especially water, and that there was
no hope of our reaching Virginia soon, determined to take
refuge at the Portuguese islands called the Azores. This
decision once formed, I, who thought I had escaped the
rope that was prepared for me, fell once more into still
greater and very much greater peril, since now I had companions who shared it with me. In fact, the English as
they came near these islands, began to reflect that they
were lost, if we were discovered, we, priests and Jesuits;
that we would be set free by the Catholic Portuguese and
that they, on the contrary, would be punished as pirates
and persecutors of priests. This anxiety troubled us much.
What were we going to do? Would they throw us into
the water? Would it be enough to hide us? In the midst
of this anguish and these hesitations the Captain sent for
me and explained the matter to me. I replied, that for myself the greatest misfortune in my death was, that I should
become the occasion of a crime for others. I promised him,
that, if he wished to conceal us, I would further his wishes
in all sincerity.

"What thoughts did the Lord instill in his mind, that he
should trust my words? I really do not know, but what I
do know, is that if he had foreseen the dangers which he
had to face thereafter, he would not have listened to me.

"He conceals us therefore in the depth of the hold. For
three weeks we did not see daylight; but in the harbor of
the island of Fayal there arose so many difficulties and the
ship was so often examined, that it is astonishing we should
not have been discovered; the Lord permitted it for the
greater Glory of our Society. The English themselves saw
clearly, that if we had desired to show ourselves and to
denounce them, we had frequent opportunities to do so.

They subsequently, in England and even in the presence of their ministers, praised our loyalty in keeping our word, to the great surprise of the enemies of the Faith.

" The English, after their escape from this danger, decided to sail for England rather than for Virginia, which was much farther off. They were in want of all that was most necessary for such a voyage.

" We steer therefore in the direction of England. The voyage was long and unpleasant. Fogs and darkness made us lose the right way, and we were driven to Wales, not far from Ireland. Our Captain had gone on shore in the little town of Pembroke, in order to procure provisions, when certain appearances made him to be looked upon as a pirate and he was thrown into prison : in order to clear himself he protested that he was no pirate, and in support of his innocence, he appealed to the two Jesuits who were on board his ship, saying that if they were questioned, they would make known the truth. What goodness of Divine Providence ! We were in the middle of winter and everything was wanting on board. If we had not received some assistance, we should have perished from cold and suffering. What happened ? They immediately sent for the Jesuits and brought them into town, to the great astonishment of everybody. They questioned us as witnesses ; we depose what we knew, that is to say, that the Captain was a King's officer and not a pirate, and that his conduct towards us was an act of obedience and not the result of his own will.

" Our Captain was thus restored to liberty, and we with him. They kept us in town with great consideration, until an answer should come from London. We had long to wait. During this time we have had frequent controversies with the ministers, but more frequently still with simple protestants. Everybody was at liberty to call on us, altho' we were not allowed to leave the house. In everything else we were well treated, as I have said before.

" At last we receive order to embark for London. It was a long voyage, and there occurred several very provoking delays.   Not to enumerate all these details, let it suffice to say that the King of England sent us to the town of Dover and made us cross from there to Calais, in France.   The Governor of the town of Calais and the Mayor received us very kindly and kept us three days, to recover from our fatigues. We reached afterwards Amiens, where we now are.

" We have thus been prisoners for nine and a half months, always on board ship, with the exception, as I said, of the days we spent at Pembroke.   For three months we received daily only two ounces of bread and a small piece of salt-fish, and water which was almost always brackish.   Hence we were surprised not to be taken sick, while the majority of the English were sick and some of them even succumbed. Surely, the Lord has kept us, thanks to the prayers of your Fatherhood and of those of our Society.   May Heaven in His goodness turn all this to His greater glory, to the improvement of my life, and to my salvation !   I hope for that, assisted by the prayers and the blessing of your Fatherhood, which I implore most humbly and on my knees, and with all the fervor of which I am capable.

" May the Lord Jesus always protect Your Fatherhood and deign to grant you His Mercy, my Very Reverend and very kind Father !

" Your Fatherhood's obedient son and unworthy servant.

" PIERRE BIARD.

" Amiens, May 26ᵗʰ 1614."

CCCXIV.   BIARD TO LOUIS XIII.

Documents CCCXIV. and CCCXV. were probably not written until 1615 ; but as CCCXII. to CCCXVI., inclusive, are illustrative of each other, I have determined to disregard the dates at which they were written, and to place them all together as being the most convenient arrangement.   Biard's Tract, " Relation de la Nouvelle-France ; de ses Terres, Naturel du Pays, et de ses Habitans, item du Voyage des Peres Jesuites aux dictes contrées, et de ce qu' ils y ont faict jusques à leur prinse par les Anglois. Faicte par le P. Pierre Biard, grenoblois, de la Cie Cy-dessus," was published at Lyons, France, in 1616, under the following privilege: " Michel Coyssard, Vice-Provincial of the society of Jesus in the Province of Lyons (under the Privilege granted by the most christian kings to the said society) authorizes Louis Muguet, to print and to sell the Relation, for the term of four years. Done at Lyons the 23rd of January 1616 " [*i. e.* 13th January, English style]. This tract was reprinted, under the auspices of the Canadian government, at Quebec, in 1858, from a copy of the original edition, preserved in the Imperial Library, Paris, France. In 1871 Dr. O'Callaghan had printed at Albany, N. Y., twenty-five copies in fac-simile, from a copy owned by Rufus King, of Jamaica, L. I.

Originals are very rare. I have never seen mention of the sale of a perfect copy; but I suppose one would be worth $250 or more.

The tract contains thirty-seven chapters and an index of the most remarkable things, the whole being about 50,000 words. Much of it does not come within the scope of my work. I will only give the part that does. The tract has been used by several American historians, who have published extracts therefrom; but we have no English translation of the whole, as far as I know.

Letter Dedicatory of Father Peter Biard of Grenoble of the S. of J.

" To the King [1] [of France].

" SIRE,

" If I present to your Majesty this relation of your New France, the description of the country, and a recital of the manners and strange customs of the savage life of the Canadians, I am bound to do so by many kinds of duty. Your express order, added to that of your Most Honored Mother,[2] then Regent of France, have carried me there, with a few

---

[1] Louis XIII.

[2] Mary de Medici was regent from May 14, 1610, to October 2, 1614.

companions, more effectively than the winds and the tides.
Your Royal liberality has maintained me there for several
years, and your powerful authority has rescued me from the
hands of certain English pirates, who being enemies of our
Faith (some seeds of which we cast upon these new Lands in
the hope of reaping an abundant harvest, the sole motive of
our going and of your command, Sire) caused us to leave
the place to our great regret, who have kept us prisoners
for several months in their vessel, and a hundred times prepared the rope and the gallows to deprive us of life, the
respect for Your Majesty alone keeping them from carrying
out their wicked designs, especially against my person, whom
perhaps divine providence wished to preserve by your interposition, to be commanded to sail once more for these same
regions and to continue the civilisation of this savage race.

"Having thus escaped from this danger, and still wet
from having been shipwrecked in this port of your France,
I present on my knees these few sheets as a token of most
humble gratitude, for, if I live, if I write, this is (next to
God) due to your aid and favor. And having this signal
obligation ever before my eyes, I shall unceasingly pray
God, with all my brethren of the robe, that your Majesty,
increasing in years and in piety, may one day see the Banner
of the Cross, with your own Royal Lilies, wave over the most
distant lands of the heathen, whilst the great King of Kings
prepares for you in heaven a crown of everlasting honor and
glory, which I desire for you, after having born your earthly
crown long and happily, with the same heart and affection,
with which I am,

"Your Majesty's very humble and very obedient subject
and servant

"PIERRE BIARD."

CCCXV. BIARD'S RELATION.

CHAPTER XXV. — Our Capture by the English.

" Virginia is that Continent which the Ancients called Morosa, between Florida and New France under the 36. 37 and 38 degrees N. L. This land had been first discovered and taken possession of by Jean Verazan, in the name of Francis I., as has been stated before; but the English having afterwards explored it in 1593 and 1594,[1] have finally come to inhabit it. Their principal settlement, which they call Jemton, is in a direct line about 250 leagues distant from St. Sauveur, where we were staying. See now, if there was any reason for quarelling with us.

" Now these Virginians are in the habit of coming every year to the Pencoit islands, which lie 25 leagues from St. Sauveur, to provide themselves with food (fish) for their winters. Travelling thither[2] in the summer of the year of which we are speaking, 1613, according to their habit, it happened that while at sea they were overtaken by fogs and mists, which, as has been stated, often spread in summer over these lands and seas. As they continued for several days, the current drove them insensibly much farther N. E. than they thought, for they were perhaps 20 leagues farther into New France than they thought in the neighborhood of our harbor, but did not recognise the place. Unfortunately some savages passed by there and went to meet them, thinking that they were Frenchmen in search of ourselves. The English understood nothing of their lan-

---

[1] These dates are not correct.

[2] The English were in this habit of fishing on that coast, and in this way they knew something of the movements of the French in those parts. There was necessity for secrecy and subterfuge in a matter of this kind ; but if we take a full view of the whole case it seems evident that Argall went properly commissioned and properly equipped in every way in a well-armed man-of-war to do exactly what he did do, — rescue the grant of the North Virginia Colony from the encroachment of the French. If this movement of the French had not been stopped in the beginning, it is interesting to think what might have been the history of this country. Even the least little act of the English in America at this time was very instrumental in shaping its future destiny.

guage, but from their gestures they gathered easily, that they were given to understand by signs, that there was a ship in the neighborhood, and that this ship was French, for they heard the word Normandia, by which they call us; and they recognized the ceremonies, which the Savages performed in order to please them, as ceremonies of French politeness and courtesy.   Hence the English, who were in want of victuals and of all things, ragged, half naked and in search of booty, inquired carefully how large our ship was, how many boats we had how many men, and meeting with ample and very satisfactory information, they uttered joyous cries, showing that that was what they were looking for, and that they should be conducted to us as they wished for nothing better ; and thus they did altho' it was not in the way in which the Savages understood it, for the latter took them to be certain good friends of ours, who were anxious about us and who from friendship desired to see us above all things; thus one of them remained in their ship with them to conduct them to us ; and this he did the wind having become favorable.   The English, as soon as they discovered us, began to prepare for battle, and now the poor fellow of a Savage found out that he had been deceived ; upon which he began to weep at his blunder and to curse those who had thus deceived him.   Often since has he wept and asked to be pardoned for his adventure by us and by the other Savages, because the other Savages intended to avenge themselves on him for our misfortune thinking that he had been the malicious cause of it.

" Now we, when we saw this vessel coming from afar off with full sails, did not know what to think of them, whether they were friends or enemies, French or foreigners, and for this reason the pilot went off in advance in a boat to reconnoitre, while the others took up arms.   La Saussaye remained on shore, with the greater part of the men. Lieutenant La Motte, Ensign Ronferé and Sergeant Joubert, and all the more thoughtful went on board the ship. For it was there that the good men among us were to be employed.

THE PRINCESS POCAHONTAS

" The English vessel came on swifter than an arrow, being favored by the wind, the Flag of England displayed, all dressed in red [the red cross of St. George] and three trumpets and two drums making a great noise. Our pilot, who had gone out to discover who they were, did not return to his ship, because, as he said, the English had the wind on him, and hence, in order not to fall into their hands he went to make the circuit around an island; thus it came about that on this occasion the ship was without one half of her crew, and had only ten men to defend herself; moreover not one of them understood naval warfare unless it was Captain Flory, who certainly was not lacking in courage nor skill; but he had neither time enough to prepare, nor men, so that he could not raise anchor to free himself, which is, of course, the first thing to be done before beginning a battle at sea. It would, besides, have been in vain to raise anchor, because all the sails were secured, for this being summer and as the vessel was lying in port, fearing nothing, they had been stretched in the form of an awning from bord to bord, so as to give shade on deck, and thus they could not easily be loosened in so short a time. But this mishap turned out very fortunate, for our people were well sheltered during the fight, so that the English being unable to take aim at them with their fire arms fewer men were killed and wounded.

" As it is usual when vessels approach each other, to summon them to say who they are, our people cried out sailor-fashion O. O! But the English did not reply in the same manner, but far more furiously, with loud discharges of muskets and guns. They had 14 pieces of artillery and 60 musketeers, trained to serve on board ship, who came and charged on deck, on the bowsprit and wherever it was necessary, quite as well as soldiers do on land.

" The first fire of the English was terrible; the whole vessel was on fire and full of smoke. From outside came a cool reply; the artillery was silent. Captain Flory cried in vain: Fire! Fire the gun! the gunner was not there. But

Gilbert du Thet, who in his whole life had never felt fear nor shown himself a coward, when he heard the order and saw that nobody obeyed, took the match and caused us to speak as loud as the enemy; the misfortune was, that he did not take aim, and if he had done so, perhaps something worse might have happened, than the mere noise.

" The Englishman after this first discharge moved his ship aside and held an anchor ready to board us.   Captain Flory very opportunely withdrew his vessel, which stopped the enemy and made him turn aside, for he was afraid that if he persued, he might be drawn upon shoals; then seeing our ship in motion and being thus reassured, he began the attack once more with musketry fire as before.   It was during this second discharge that Father du Thet received a shot that passed thro' his body, and fell backwards on the deck; Captain Flory also was wounded in the foot and three other places, whereupon they made signs and cried out that they surrendered.   Surely the parties were ill matched.   At this cry the English jumped into their boat to reach the ship; our people, mislead by bad advice, also jumped into their boat to reach land, for they were afraid of the coming of the victors.   These, however, were on board our ship before they had gotten away ; so they took to crying out to them, to return, and to enforce the order, they opened fire upon them ; two of our people were so frightened by this, that they threw themselves into the water, as I think, in order to swim to shore; but they were drowned, either because they were already wounded, or, what is more likely, because they were hit and killed in the water.   These were two very promising young companions, one from Dieppe, called Le Moine, the other called Neven, from the town of Beauvais. Their bodies were not recovered till nine days later ; means were found to draw them on land and to bury them decently.

" Such was the capture of our vessel."

" CHAPTER XXVI. — The plundering of our ship and our people, the anguish we endured.

" The victorious English came on shore, where we had our tents and our houses, just begun, and sent out in all directions in search of our Captain, saying that they wanted to see our commissions ; that this land belonged to them, wherefor they had fallen upon us, when they found us here ; but that if we should be able to show that we had acted in good faith, and that we had come there under authority from our sovereign, they would respect that, as they wished in no way to imperil the good understanding between our two kings. The misfortune was that La Saussaye could not be found, whereupon the shrewd and cunning Englishman seized our trunks, broke them open industriously, and having found in them our commissions and Royal Patents, seized them ; then putting everything else back in its place, just as they had found it, they nicely locked the boxes again. When Captain La Saussaye appeared on the day following, the English Captain, who had learnt his lesson well, received him kindly and asked him the first questions with great urbanity, but then coming to the point, he demanded to see his commissions, so that there might be no doubt whatever, when they should really have before them the words and the authority of our Master, the King. La Saussaye replied that the papers were in his boxes. They brought these boxes in and before he opened them with his keys, they warned him to look well if anybody had touched them ; for, they themselves went very simply to work. La Saussaye acknowledged that everything was in perfect order, but he could not find his letters ! Now the English Captain changed his looks and his voice and, becoming very stiff, he said : How is this ? You are an impostor ! You give us to understand that you are commissioned by your king and yet you cannot produce any evidence. You are, all of you, outlaws and pirates. You deserve death ! And thereupon he divided out the booty among his soldiers, consuming the whole afternoon in this business. . . . [Describes the plundering of the English.]

" I have told you that Father Du Thet was pierced by a musket ball during the fight; when the English boarded our ship, they put him, as well as the other wounded, in the hands of their surgeon. This surgeon was a Catholic and known as such; he was a very kind hearted person and rendered us a thousand kind services. . . . [Personal matters,[1] — the brave death of Father Gilbert du Thet; — the Jesuits, their services, etc.]

" Now he [Captain Argall] had a thorn in his side which gave him great trouble : this was that the pilot and the sailors had run away, and he could hear nothing of them. This pilot, called le Bailleur, from the town of Rouen, having gone off to reconnoitre as was stated above. . . . I fancied that this was the reason why the English Captain determined not to treat us worse, altho' he was strongly inclined to do so, as I afterwards concluded from our experience. He was, to be sure, a very clever and cunning captain, but still a gentleman, with truly noble courage; his men also were neither inhuman nor cruel in their treatment of any of us." . . .

" CHAPTER XXVII. — The means discovered to return to France and how thirty of our people reached there after many difficulties.

" The English Captain, called Samuel Argal and his lieutenant, called William Turnel, began to treat with our Captain La Saussaye about our return, as they had promised. The English offered very unfair conditions, but to cut the matter short, the conclusion was that they left us the one sloop which remained of the two we had before, and told us to go wherever God might lead us. The English Captain, a very cautious man, wanted a written acknowlgedment,

---

[1] I have omitted several passages of a personal character, and others of no special interest to us. Some of these things, however, are spoken of in CCCXII. and CCCXIII.

signed by Captain La Saussaye, in which he admitted that this decision had been come to by his own choice. . . . [Father Biard then explains that 30 persons could not sail in so small a vessel.] The English replied that this was not the impression of Captain La Saussaye, but that if we wished to lighten the sloop he would find means to do so, by taking back to Virginia those artisans who were willing, provided that they were not compelled to change their religion and that they were to be sent back to France after a years service. Three accepted this offer.

" The Sieur de la Motte had in like manner consented from the beginning to accompany the English Captain to Virginia, who had fancied him much, because he found him sword in hand, and discovered in him several other good qualities — which was very profitable to our men. He was, moreover, allowed to take with him several other persons who were to enjoy the same favor as he did. Captain Flory finally decided to try his fortune in the same way, as hopes were held out to him that thus he might recover his vessel. Father Biard requested that four of them, viz; two Jesuits and two others, might be taken to Pencoit Island and that there they might be recommended to the English fishermen who are usually there, so that in this way they might be enabled to return to France — a request which the English Captain most readily granted. In this way the sloop was entirely relieved and our own men were divided into three equal parties : fifteen remained with the pilot; fifteen stayed with the English, and fifteen went on board the sloop left to them. Of these fifteen Father Ennemond Masse was one. . . . [Biard then tells of the adventures, the coming together, etc., of the fifteen under La Saussaye and the pilot's party, and of their return to France, where they arrived probably late in September, 1613.]

" CHAPTER XXVIII. — The voyage to Virginia and the return to New France.

" God be blessed. Here were now two thirds of our company safely back in France, among their Friends and their Kindred, who listen to them as they tell their great adventures. Hence you would naturally wish to know what had become of the remaining third who had been left behind in the hands of the English. Certainly a much longer and more varied fate awaits them and they will not escape without serious losses.

" The English had now three vessels ; viz, their own with which they had captured us, of a hundred and thirty tons, ours, which they had taken, of a hundred tons, and a bark of twelve tons, which they had likewise obtained from us and would not let us have again to enable us to return. They filled these three vessels with their own people, and distributed us among them. The Sieur de la Motte, Captain Flory, and one half of the whole remainder, amounting in all to eight persons, remained on board the Capitanesse, and the others, numbering seven, remained on board the captured vessel of which Lieutenant Turnel was made commander.

" Now, as a beginning of our misfortunes, they did not take the Jesuits to the Pencoit Islands, as had been promised, but carried them straight to Virginia, with the rest of the troop, comforting them with pleasant hopes, in as much as, said they, the Marshall of Virginia [Dale] who had full power and authority of jurisdiction, was a great friend of the French, having won all of his principal distinctions by the recommendation of the late Henry the Great, and having been his soldier and his pensioner. This they frequently preached to us. But our preachers did not take their text from the Gospels. For this fine Marshall, who as they said, was such a friend and patron of the French, when he heard an account of us, spoke of nothing but of ropes and gallows and of hanging every one of us. We were frightened terribly and some lost their peace expecting nothing less but that they would have to mount a ladder ignominiously and dangle miserably by a rope. But Captain Argal showed himself generous in our defence ; for he resisted the aforesaid Marshall, insisting upon the pledge he had given, and when he found himself too weak to oppose, he made known publicly our commissions and Royal Patents, which I mentioned to you before, and which he had surreptitiously obtained from La Saussaye's boxes. And this was the way we found out that he had employed such a ruse, for otherwise we should never have heard anything about it.   The Marshall, seeing these Patents of His Most Christian Majesty, and the determination of the Captain, did not dare go any farther; and thus after some days spent in great apprehension, they informed us that their promises should be kept.

" Now, how they would keep them, and what means they would find to send us back to France that was the great question.   The General [Gates], the Marshall [Dale] and all the chief officers of Virginia assembled in Council.   The result thereof and the conclusion to which they came, was to do worse than ever, since they thought they had it in their power; for it was resolved that Captain Argal, should, with his three ships, go back to New France, pillage and raze to the ground all the fortifications and settlements of the French which he might find on the whole way up to Cape Breton, that is to say, as far as the 46½ degree N. L.,[1] as they lay claim to the whole territory; that he should hang La Saussaye and all of his men whom he might find to have remained within these limits; that he should likewise plunder all the vessels he might meet with, allowing, however, such persons as should make no resistance, to return to France; and that we, old prisoners, should be treated in the same way as these people, whose lives were thus to be spared.   Such were their conclusions.   But God was on High; and as you will hear, He decreed it otherwise, with regard to several points.   According to this decision, Argal resumed once more the voyage to New France; but this time stronger than before, in as much as he had three ships,

---

[1] Cape Breton is in about 46° N. L.   Biard stretches his points as a person
They only laid claim as far as 45° N. L.   making a special plea is prone to do.

and greater expectations, because the booty he had obtained from us increased his cupidity and his hopes. But he took only one half of our people with him, I do not know why. On board his ship were Captain Flory and four others; on board Lieutenant Turnels, which was our boat captured by them, were the two Jesuits and a boy.

" The first stopping-place was St. Sauveur, for they expected here to encounter La Saussaye, and a recently arrived ship. They were mistaken, in as much as La Saussaye was in France, as has been said; they burnt our works and cut down our Cross, but erected another as a sign that they had taken possession of the land, as rightful owners.

" This cross had the name of the King of Great Britain carved on it. They also hanged here one of their men, charged with conspiracy, at the very place, at which eight days before they had cut down our first Cross. From St. Sauveur they sailed for St. Croix, a former settlement of the Sieur de Monts. . . . [Argall asked Biard to guide them, and he refused.] Nevertheless Argal searched high and low, and examined all of their places so carefully, that by comparing them with the maps which he had taken from us, he at last discovered the place himself; he carried away from there a good supply of salt, which he found there, burnt the dwelling, and destroyed every token of French names and French claims, as he had been commanded to do.

" CHAPTER XXIX. — The taking and burning of Port Royal.[1] Two great dangers threatening Father Biard.

" Captain Argal had destroyed St. Croix, but did not know how to reach and sail for Port Royal, according to the orders he had received, and this all the more as he feared he might be lost on such a dangerous coast without a pilot. . . . [Knowing it to be useless to ask Biard or any Frenchman, he looks for and finds an Indian Sagamo, and under his guidance he reached Port Royal. See CCCXVI.] When the

---

[1] Now called Annapolis.

English landed they found not a soul in the fort, and shoes and clothing scattered all about.

" Thus they rejoiced doubly at this capture first because they met, contrary to all expectation, with no resistance at all, and secondly because they secured a good deal of booty, which they had not expected. . . . [Personal matters relative to Father Biard. He mentions that it was the end of October[1] when Argall was searching for Port Royal; an English Puritan, the master of the large ship, more malicious than the others all together against the Jesuits; Frenchmen at Port Royal unfriendly to Biard, etc.]

" Now the aforesaid Captain having carried off from Port Royal whatever seemed to him convenient down to the planks, latches, locks, and nails, set fire to it, a very pitiable thing, for thus, in an hour or two were reduced to ashes the work and expenditure of many years and of meritorious persons. Oh that it would please the Lord to let that same fire destroy in like manner all the sins that may have been committed at this place,[2] so that they might never arise again in any other place, nor ever provoke the just and fearful vengeance of our Lord !

" The English, as I have stated elsewhere, destroyed everywhere the monuments and all other evidences of French supremacy; nor did they forget to do so here, going so far as to use pick and chisel in a large, massive stone, on which were engraved the names of the Sieur de Monts with other Captains, and the lilies of France.

" This being done, they raised anchor to leave the place, but they were kept by bad weather for three or four days, at the mouth of the harbour.

" Whilst they were lying here at anchor, a Frenchman belonging to this port . . . [shows his unfriendliness to Biard by telling the English that he was a ' genuine Spaniard ; ' and other personal matters].

[1] Biard's dates are, of course, New Style.

[2] His relations with the officers at Port Royal had not always been pleasant. See CCCXVI.

" CHAPTER XXX. — Departure from Port Royal; divers
adventures of the ships, and how we were compelled to stop
at the Azores.

" On the ninth of November of this year 1613, the English left Port Royal intending to return to their Virginia
and there to enjoy their booty during the coming winter. . . .

" On the second day after our departure on the eve of St.
Martin, so terrible a storm arose, that it scattered our three
vessels in such a way, that they never encountered each
other afterwards, but sailed, every one in a different direction.

" The bark has never been seen since, and no report has
ever reached us from her, so that nobody doubts but she
has gone down, with the six Englishmen, who were on board.

" The new Captainesse, which Argal commanded in spite
of the tempest, safely reached Virginia in three weeks or
thereabouts. The Marshall, of whom we have spoken before,
heard with delight from Captain Argal all that had happened. . . .

" The two Jesuits and a French boy were in the captured
vessel, which had been handed over to Captain Turnel. . . .
[Biard describes the storm; the ship driven by it for sixteen days; then provisions get low; they finally determine to
give up trying to reach Virginia, and to sail directly to the
Azores; kill the horses taken at Port Royal; horseflesh
quite pleasing to the taste of the Jesuits; Captain Turnel
' spoke good French and several other common languages,
besides Greek and Latin which he understood well, being a
man of fine intellect, who had studied well; ' the many good
qualities of Father Biard, etc.]

" CHAPTER XXXI. — How the vessel was visited at the
Azores and the good faith of the Jesuits towards the English.

[This chapter is devoted to showing the faithfulness of
the Jesuits, while the English were at the Azores. It gives
the same story, but much more particularly than in CCCXII.
and CCCXIII.]

JOHN POULETT

First Baron Poulett

" CHAPTER XXXII. — Arrival in England and Liberation of the Jesuits.

" The English were kept busy three whole weeks at this island, which we call Fayal, during which time the poor Jesuits never saw the sun.   Now because the aforesaid English were without money, they could not there reprovision themselves, and this determined them not to try the return to Virginia; but to sail back to England, and this all the more as they now found themselves in this year 1614, which was the term of their service.

" Now when we were thus trying to make for England, the tempest cast us out of La Manche (as it is called), that is out of the channel which is between England and France and compelled us to seek shelter in the harbour of Milfier [Milford], in the Province of Wales.   There once more our provisions gave out, which compelled our Captain to go to Pembroke, the principal city of this district and Vice-Admiralty; but at Pembroke he was arrested falling under the suspicion of piracy.   This suspicion arose from the fact that he and his men were Englishmen, and yet their vessel was built after French models, which made them think he had come from the port of Gryp, on the Larcin Islands beyond Cape Escumant.   The Captain explained as well as he could by simply telling the truth, but they would not believe him, especially because he had no commission, nor could he have any since, being only a lieutenant, he followed his captain and had only by accident been separated from him, by the storm of which you have heard.

" On this account he was finally compelled to produce in evidence of his uprightness the two Jesuits which he had on board his ship, men without reproach, as he said, and as they were.

" Immediately by order of the Magistrate the aforesaid Jesuits were summoned on shore and examined in court with great respect.   They stated the actual facts, and upon the strength of their deposition the Captain was acknowledged to be a gentleman and a man of honour, provided only that

our difficulties concerning New France were to be submitted
to the king. Nevertheless we had to remain a very long
time at this place Pembroke, awaiting answers from London; for it had become necessary to send there partly in
order to obtain money, and partly to report the matter to
the High Admiral and the Company of Merchants, who were
in charge of Virginia.

" And here it is that my admiration is stopped with my
breath and with my steps, to exclaim with the Wise Man :
That the dispensations of Divine Providence are truly made
by compass, counted by Number, measured by weight and
Balance down to the half of a grain. For this call of the
Jesuits was, no doubt, a contrivance of this paternal Providence, which everywhere assisted them ; and this all the more
so as, if they had remained on board ship, being in entire des-
titution in the midst of winter (for this was in February), and
for four weeks uninterruptedly, it is probable they would
have perished with cold and starvation ; but now, by means
of this summons, they became known to the Judge, who
being a very great and honorable personage, having understood how badly they were off on board the ship, gave them
lodgings at the Mayor's house, and paid for them, saying
that they might pay him back, when they had the means to
do so, for otherwise, he said, it would be a great disgrace to
us, if such honest and learned men should not meet common courtesy among us. This good 'Seigneur' is called
Nicholas Adams, vice-Admiral of said Pembroke.

" Now during this detention, all kinds of people came to
call upon them and some from a distance, curious as they
were to see Jesuits in their costume, such as they wore then
and always have worn till their return to France.

"Ministers, magistrates, gentlemen and others came to
confer with them. Even a Lord of the Privy Council
wanted to have the pleasure of seeing them meet four ministers in public disputation : I call them ministers so as to
be understood by the French, for in England they call them
Priests. At the head of the meeting was an Archdeacon,

because the English still retain much of the Catholic Church, as the order of the hierarchy of the Church, Archbishops Bishops, Priests, Archpriests, Archdeacons, Curates, Canons, &c., the Laying on of hands by Bishops in the consecration of priests, and the minor orders, as well as in the confirmation of children, the Holy Oil and ceremonies, the sign of the cross, its image and other images, the singing of psalms and the Litany, the prescribed holidays of male and female saints, Vigils, Fasts, Lent, the abstinence from meat on Fridays and Saturdays, the sacerdotal costumes and consecrated vessels. And those who condemn all these things, as the Calvinists of Scotland and France do, and call them damnable superstitions and inventions of the Antichrist, are by the English called Puritans and detested like an abominable plague.

"When at last a reply came from London it was found that the French Ambassador had been informed of the arrival of the vessel, and was now negotiating the surrender, especially of the Jesuits, as he had been commanded to do by His Most Christian Majesty.

"This was another result of Divine Providence, that by means of our arrest and detention in the province of Wales, it should become known to everybody, for we had very clear indications, of which you will presently see some, that if the merchants in whose hands is the administration of Virginia, had had their way, not one foreigner who had ever been found within the said Virginia, would ever have been allowed to return to his own country.

"To make a quick end to our relation, note that the Jesuits were carried by a long round-about way to the harbour of Sandwich, and from thence, by order of the King, back again to Dover, and from Dover to Calais, where they thanked God for so many signal mercies of His, and for His special providence, having good ground for this, since they had been kept nine months and a half [1] in the hands of the English.

[1] The Jesuits were taken at St. Saviour about the middle of July, 1613;

"The Sieur d'Arquien, governor of this aforesaid Calais, and Monsieur la Boulaye, mayor, gave them a most hearty welcome and furnished them with the means required to enable them to return to their college at Amiens.

"CHAPTER XXXIII. — Return of the Sieur de la Motte [April, 1614], of Captain Flory [July, 1614] and of some others, and the surrender of the vessel.

"Soon after this liberation of the Jesuits, God also rescued in His Mercy almost the whole remaining number of shipwrecked men in this way : —

"The boy that was with the Jesuits, called Guillaume Crito, was taken to London, and from thence sent back to his father at Honfleur.

"At the same time the Sieur de la Motte came also back to England on board a vessel from the Bermudas, which had stopped in Virginia.

"Captain Argal contended most generously with Marshall Thomas Deel (of whose great bitterness of temper you have heard us speak) so as to secure permission for the aforesaid Sieur de la Motte to return likewise and obtained it at last.

"Now the said Sieur de la Motte was very much astonished to find that suddenly from the time of his arrival in England, no one spoke to him any longer, no one came to see him, he was forsaken by everybody, and the worst was that he was taken sick on board the vessel. He at once suspected the danger which threatened him, and from whence it came, namely, from the Virginia Merchants, who

in Virginia in August and September; again on New England coast in October; sailed from Port Royal October 30 ; at Fayal three weeks until January, 1614 ; at Milford Haven in February ; four weeks at Pembroke, awaiting answers from London until March (?). They were taken around to Sandwich about April ; and being released were sent thence (late in April or early in May), by order of King James, to Dover and to Calais, where they probably arrived about the first week in May (O. S.), 1614.

As I have said, it seems that Lieutenant William Turner and the Jesuits, Sir Thomas Gates and the Sieur de la Motte from Virginia, and Captain La Saussaye from France, all reached the neighborhood of London about April 1614, probably, just before the debate in Parliament of April 20, 1614.

would have liked to get rid of him, and did not know how. He tried, therefore, very cunningly, and in the end successfully, to make his condition known to Monsieur de Bisseaux, the very worthy ambassador of his most Christian Majesty, who immediately sent two gentlemen to him, so that he was set free and well treated, as he fully deserved by his courage and his valor.

" At this same time [April, 1614] also Madame de Guercheville sent La Saussaye to London, there to solicit the liberation of the vessel, and compensation for such iniquitous robbery. The vessel has been restored, but nothing else has up to the present moment been received.

" And now at the very moment when our ship, being once more set free, was winging its way towards France, its native land, here comes Captain Flory, [in July, 1614] its Master, as if by special appointment, to take charge of it and to assume command. Captain Argal, had once more freed it from the hands of the Marshall, coming back to England with him (Flory) and two other Frenchmen. Certainly this said Argal has shown himself such that we desire him to have an opportunity of serving a better cause, and one in which his true nobility of heart may show itself, not in the ruin but in the support of honorable men.

" Out of our whole number three died in Virginia, and four are there still, everything being done that can be done towards their liberation also. May God in His mercy give them patience and let them derive from our affliction all the good that His providence and loving kindness may intend. Amen ! "

CCCXVI. BIENCOURT'S COMPLAINT.

July 8, (O. S.) 1614. An extract from the " History of New France" by Marc Lescarbot. Paris, 1618, 8vo, pp. 686–690.

. . . " Now, if in justice, the first plaintiff and informer is accepted to the prejudice of him, who comes recrim-

Defence of
the Jesuits. inating, the Sieur de Poutrincourt will beyond doubt have the question decided in his favor. For the apology of Father Biart dates only from the year sixteen hundred and sixteen,[1] and the complaint of the aforesaid 'Sieur' presented to the Judge of the Admiralty of 'Guyenne au siege de la Rochelle,' is dated the eighteenth of July sixteen hundred and fourteen, of which these are the contents : —

"'Messire Jean de Biencourt, Knight Lord of Poutrincourt, Baron of Saint Just, lord of Port-Royal and the adjacent lands in New-France, reports to you that on the last day of the month of December last he left this city and sent out of this port and harbour a vessel of sixty-two tons, or there abouts, called 'La prime de la tremblade,' to sail and to go straightways in the direction of Port Royal, where it arrived on the seventeenth of last March, and being there, he found out by the report of Charles de Biencourt, his eldest son, vice-Admiral and Lieutenant-General in the lands, Countries and Seas of all New France, that the commander of some Englishmen being in Virginia, distant one hundred and twenty leagues, or thereabouts, from aforesaid harbour, sent by persuasion of Pierre Biart, a Jesuit, to said port one large vessel, of two to three hundred tons, another of one hundred tons or thereabouts, and one large bark, with a number of men, who on the day of the feast of Allsaints last, landed there, and guided by the said Biart, went to where the said Sieur de Poutrincourt made his habitation,

[1] CCCXVI., I believe, is only to be found in the 1618 edition of Lescarbot. CCCXIII., CCCXV., and CCCXVI. strongly illustrate the uncertainty of data where there is any controversy, and the necessity of having all the evidence before us when we attempt to pass a just verdict; and even then, when the controversy is decidedly partisan, we can scarcely ever decide with any certainty. The account of Father Biard's conduct at Port Royal in October, 1613, as given in CCCXVI., is very different from his own account given in CCCXIII. and CCCXV.

Of course there are other illustrative materials for Argall's voyages in Champlain's and other works ; but I am only attempting to give data written before 1617 ; and only such as has a special bearing on the English in America.

and for the convenience of the latter, and of the French dwellers there, had built a small, square fort, which had been left without protection, the said Sieur de Biencourt having gone along the coast to visit his people, with the greater part of his men, in order to keep them in amity and good will; besides that at this place there was no reason to fear anything, since there was no war against any one, and hence there was no probability that at that very time any foreign vessels should come to this said port and settlement: and as for all his other men, they were two leagues from there, cultivating the ground. And upon this encounter the said English plundered all that there was in this said settlement, took all the ammunition that was there, and all the provisions, merchandise and other articles, demolished and took to pieces the timber for building and for carpenter's work which they thought might be useful to them and carried them to their ships. This being done, they moreover set fire to the place. And not content with this (impelled and led by the said Biart) they destroyed, with a sledge-hammer, the King's Coat of Arms, engraved on a rock, together with the arms of the said Sieur de Poutrincourt, and those of the Sieur de Monts. Then, they went to a distant wood, a league off, from said settlement and took a number of swine, which had been driven there, to pasture and to eat the mast, and beyond that, to a meadow, where they kept the horses, mares and foals and took all. Then under the guidance of said Biard they, went to the place where the farm work was going on, to seize those who were there, whose sloop they took and not being able to take them (because they retired under a hill side) The said Biart left the English and went to this same hill, to induce those who were there to abandon the said de Biancourt, and to go with him and the aforesaid English, to that before mentioned place of Virginia. To which they not being willing to agree, he withdrew with the said English, and embarked in one of the aforesaid vessels. But before they sailed, the said de Biencourt arrived there; who,

seeing what had happened, took himself to a wood, and sent
for the Captain of said English, pretending that he wished
to treat with him, so as to be able to surround him, and to
try by these means to gain some advantage for the evil he
had done. But he conceived some mistrust and was not
willing to come on shore. When the said Sieur de Biencourt saw this, he showed himself, and then when the said
Captain said that he wished to speak to him, he replied to
him, that, if he would come on shore, he would not repent
of it. Thereupon, after they had mutually pledged their
word and promised not to act nor to speak treacherously,
the said Captain came on shore, with one companion, and
remained for nearly two hours with the said de Biencourt,
to whom, the same Captain explained the artifices which the
said Biart employed in order to induce the Commander of
said Englishmen to go to that afore mentioned place.
Where said de Biencourt remained with his men from the
day and feast of All Saints to the twenty-seventh of March [1]
(when the said Sieur de Poutrincourt, his father, went there)
without any provisions, compelled to eat roots, herbs and the
buds of trees. And when the ground was frozen and they
could find neither herbs, nor roots, nor go through the for-
ests, they were forced to go among the rocks in search of the
herbs growing on them, by which means some and these
among the most robust, not being able to support themselves,
had died of starvation, and the others had been very sick,
and would have likewise died, without the assistance they
received upon the arrival of said Sieur de Poutrincourt, to
whom all the above has been represented on several and various occasions by his said son and others, who were with him,
in the presence of those of the crew of said vessel, called La
Prime, which he had taken there from this town, in which he
arrived on the . . . day of this month [July, 1614]. And
altho.' he and his said son, having formally deposed all the
above — to whom credit is due — in consideration of their

---

1 October 22 / November 1, 1613, to March 17/27, 1614.

rank, nevertheless desire to submit them to His Majesty, and to Monseigneur the Admiral, whose lieutenant the said de Biencourt is in those countries, so as to testify to the whole of it, as may be needed, in order that their truthfulness may be the less doubted. And for this end the said Sieur de Poutrincourt would like to have the aforesaid crew examined and questioned on these above-mentioned facts and on the condition in which he found the place, where that said settlement, called Port-Royal, was, according to the deposition which he caused to have drawn up about this matter. In consideration of this &c. Let it be communicated to the King's Attorney General &c. July 18th 1614.

"'Signed.   P. Guillaudeau.'"

[MEM. — I have found no very clear account of the voyages of the Harlies and Hobson to our New England coast; but I believe there were two, one in 1611 by Captain Edward Harlie and Captain Nicholas Hobson, and another, which sailed in June, 1614, under Captain Henrie Harlie (or Hawley) and Captain Nicholas Hobson. The exact date of the return is not known to me.]

PERIOD IV.

FROM THE RETURN OF ARGALL IN JULY, 1614, TO THE RETURN OF DALE IN JULY, 1616.

FROM the beginning the existence of the colony had really depended on the managers of the enterprise in England; but during this period it became evident that the colony would finally be more than self-sustaining. Day was breaking. Spain saw that England would never give up her hold on America, and the destiny of this continent was firmly vested in the hands of the Anglo-Saxon.

[MEM. — The Treasurer, Captain Argall, sailed from Virginia about the 18th of June, 1614, and arrived in England in July following, bringing Ralph Hamor, the author of CCCXXVII., Rolfe's letter to Dale (CCCXXVIII.), Dale to Rev. D. M. (CCCXXIX.), Whitaker to Master G. (CCCXXX.), Molina's letter of April $\frac{20}{30}$ (CCCXXV.), Molina's letter of June $\frac{4}{14}$ CCCXXVI.); the depositions of the French in Virginia, and other documents now unknown; also Captain Flory and two other Frenchmen.]

CCCXVII. VIRGINIA COUNCIL TO PRIVY COUNCIL.

Soon after Argall returned, to the letter of the Privy Council (CCXCVI.), the Council of Virginia sent the following reply.

The reply of the Virginia Council, 1614, in defense of Argall. [Cotton MSS. Otho E. 829.] From the "Boston Daily Advertiser" of August 31, 1870, and the "Proceedings of the Mass. Hist. Society," 1884.

. . . "To the substance of the first complaint: That it

SIR WALTER RALEGH

is true Captain Argall did take a French ship within the limits of our Colony, who went about to plant contrary to the extent and privilege of his Majesty's letters patent to us granted. That he did it by the command of the governor of our Colony by his commission to him given under the seal of the Colony, and by virtue of such authority as is to him derived from his Majesty's great seal of England.

"That whereas it is said, it was 200 leagues from our plantation, intimating thereby that it was out of our limits, we say the coast lying next E. N. E. and W. S. W. many more hundred leagues will not deliver them without our borders, we having granted unto us from 34 to 45 degrees of north latitude; and from E. to W. from one sea to another, with a certain clause that if any other nations should get land to the north of 45 degrees, and by any river or lake, or by land travel should come to the southwards, to plant behind our backs, that it should be lawful for our governor to resist, displant, and take by force any that should make such attempt.

"And we do further avow that the said ship was taken between 43 and 44 degrees, which in express limitation is within his Majesty's grant and is annexed to his royal crown. And that this is proved by the several confessions of divers of the French examined by Sir Thomas Dale, and certified accordingly unto us by him. And that the said Captain Argall, besides his several commissions for his justification to us showed, hath further produced unto [us] a testimonial or certificate under the seal of our Colony, that he hath in these his voyages no way exceeded the commissions to him given . . . that upon the cross-examination . . . certified the said ship and other . . . Letters Patents, and that therefore we suppose [he should] be wholly for the fact excusable.

"Concerning the aggravation of circumstances. We [reply] Argall had not above 60. men in his ship. That the [French] first shot at him; and that all the victuals, munition, utensils for plantation, besides the ship and her

app[urtenances], which was redelivered at the request of
the French A[mbassador], was not to the value of £200.
sterling, as we are [able to] prove by the several inventories
delivered by the F[rench to] the Marshall of Virginia, and
together with their [examinations] unto us certified.

" Secondly, to the imputation of inhumanity used by him
[to his] prisoners, we say it is wholly false.   That neither
Monsieur Saussaye nor any other were detained as prisoners, but that he went and returned from ship to shore at
pleasure.   That Captain Argall did propound to them three
offers, —

" 1. First, to give them a small pinnace, with sufficient
victuals [to] carry them all into France.

" 2. Secondly, to give them passage from thence to the
bank, 120 leagues from Cape Brittayne, there to meet certayne French shipping.

" 3. Thirdly, to give Monsieur Saussy, their Captain, a
shallop, and as [many] of his men as he would choose, with
sufficient provision to their own wage, and to carry the residue [with him] into Virginia.   [And] that condition was
chosen by the Captain, and accordingly performed.

" These offers are proved by the confession of Monsieur
Saussay, his two Jesuits, the Master, and at least ten other
of the Company, which are ready to be shown, with many
attestations of great humanity and . . . courtesy showed to
them. . . .

" And that these our reasonable answers considered, the
King of France is neither in his Homs' [Honours?] nor
title any way injured by the just defense of our own, and
maintenance of those limits and extent of territory given
unto us by his Majesty's Letters Patents many years before
the French had any footing to the south of Canada.

" Neither hath Madame de Guercheville any reason to
expect reparation having entered without our leave, within
our limits and dominion, by force to plant or trade, contrary to the good correspondence and league of these two
most royal Kings.   And that if any particular be hereof

doubted or replied unto, we will be ready to give testimony and further answer thereunto."

CCCXVIII. REPLY OF THE PRIVY COUNCIL.

After receiving CCCXVII., the Privy Council made the following reply to the French complaints.

Published in the " Proceedings of the Mass. Hist. Society," 1884. My copy was made for me (in the original French) at the British Museum in 1883, and translated for me by Professor Schele De Vere of the University of Virginia. This translation is a little different from that published by the Massachusetts Historical Society.

" Reply to the complaints presented to the King by the Sieur de Bisseaux, resident Ambassador to the King. From the most Christian King. [See note to CCXCI.]

" *First* as to the complaint concerning Newfoundland."

The reply to this complaint reviews the history of Newfoundland from the year 1496, when " Robert Thorne and Hugh Eliot, merchants of the city of Bristow, sent to sea certain ships for discovery under the conduct of Sebastian Cabot," to the year 1614.

" The reply to the third complaint concerning the whale fishery." See CCLXXXVIII. and CCXCVI.

" Reply to the fourth complaint concerning Virginia.

" Captain Argol admits that he has taken the French ship in question, within the limits of our Colony on account of this, that contrary to the privileges granted the said Company by Letters Patent from the King, it attempted to intrude and establish itself there by force, and that what he has done in this matter, has been done by virtue of the commission, which had been granted to him under the seal of the said Company for that very purpose. which authority is derived from the special powers granted by His Majesty to said Colony under his Great Seal, and that nevertheless the said vessel has been returned at the request of the

Ambassador.   Notwithstanding which reply His Majesty wishing to show the Ambassador the wish he cherishes to give him all the contentment and satisfaction possible, has caused orders to be issued, that the said Captain Argol shall be produced to account for what he has done, at any time and whenever the Ambassador shall desire it.   And that Turner, his lieutenant, shall in like manner be produced as soon as he can be apprehended." . . .

"The Reply to the *sixth* complaint was touching the arrest and seizure of vessels," and "the Reply to the *eighth* complaint was touching The Marchioness de Guercheville:—As to Madame the Marchioness of Guercheville, she has no reason to complain; nor to hope for any reparation; seeing that her ship entered by force the territory of the said Colony to settle there, and to trade without their permission, to the prejudice of our treaties and of the good understanding there is between our kings." . . .

Indorsed : " D[elivere]d ye Fr[ench] Amb[assador by] Mons‍ʳ Edmo[ndes].¹   1614.   Answer to the French Complayntes."

CCCXIX. LORKIN TO PUCKERING.

Rev. Thomas Lorkin to Sir Thomas Puckering, Bart., July 21, 1614.

. . . "From the Bermudas news is freshly arrived,² that there have been there lately two Spanish ships, with a little frigate sounding the way before them.   Upon the first discovery of them, the Governor of the island sent forth a small vessel towards them, to learn what they were, who, perceiving them to be Spaniards, presently returned and advertised the Governor thereof, who presently saluting them with a friendly shot of artillery, they rendered him his salute, and instantly retired." — From Birch's " Court and Times of James I." vol. i. p. 337.

¹ Sir Thomas Edmonds, ambassador of the king of England, resident in France, embarked for France in the ship Answer, on the 25th July, 1614. — 3d Rept. MS. Com. p. 292b.

² This news probably "arrived" on the vessel which brought Captain Daniel Elfrith.

[MEM. — "July 29th. Court Minutes of the East India Company. Sale by the Candle of Calicoes, Silks, &c; also of two boxes of ambergris, belonging to the Virginia Company, at £3. 1ˢ and £3. 2ˢ an oz."]

CCCXX. JAMES I. TO STATES GENERAL.

From London " Documents relating to the Colonial History of New York," Albany, 1853, vol. iii. p. 9.

" HIGH AND MIGHTY LORDS, OUR GOOD FRIENDS AND ALLIES !

" We cannot but acknowledge the favor, which through regard for us, you have done to Sir Thomas Dale, Marshall of Virginia, by permitting him to absent himself for some time from your service, to which he should have already returned, had not all of that Colony, where he has right worthily comported himself, perceiving the necessity of his remaining among them, to settle and give stability to that enterprize, supplicated Us to interpose again with you, and to request you to permit his absence for two or three years more, in order that he may complete the work, so well begun; which, by his recal, cannot but run great risk of miscarriage. This We have right willingly undertaken for so good an object, and doubt not but you will consent with like promptness, not only in this case, but in all that depends on you for the advancement of so laudable an undertaking; the success of which, as in all probability it will be productive of advantage to our Realms, will, in like manner, not fail to communicate the like to your Provinces.

" Therefore We remain Your very affectionate Friend.

" JAMES R.

" From our Court at Leicester, the 19th of Augt 1614."

Addressed : " To the High and Mighty Lords, The States General of the United Netherland Provinces."

Mem. : " Date 19 August (O. S.) }
Received 30 Septr (N. S.) } 1614."

[MEM. — Captain John Smith sailed from our New England coast on the 18th of July and arrived in England the latter end of August, 1614.

Lorkin to Puckering, London, September 11, 1614. . . . "The present affords no news at all, more than that two or three days since, wee were put into an alarm by the discovery of a fleet upon our coasts, of three score sail, which at the first were feared to be Spaniards, destined for England; but since prove either to be Easterlings, or, if Spaniards, destined for Embden. The council upon this bruit despatched commissioners into all parts of England, to muster the train-soldiers, and to command them to be in a readiness, which whether it shall go forward or not I cannot affirm, that other fear being cleared." — From Birch's "Court and Times of James I." vol. i. p. 347.]

CCCXXI. LETTER TO SIR THOMAS DALE.

September 20, 1614. "Letter to Sir Thos Dale, Marshall of the Colony in Virginia, To send home by the next ship Eliezer Hopkins." — Docquet, Domestic, James I.

The whole of this letter has not been found.

CCCXXII. EXTRACT FROM PRESENT STATE OF IRELAND.

Extract from "A Discourse of the present estate of Ireland," by George Lord Carew. Written in 1614.

. . . "The Spanish king can never want pretences to blind the world for the defence of the breach of his league, which by the Catholics will be applauded; and if no other shift were to be found to preserve his honour, the plantations in the Bermudas and in Virginia, or his obedience to the church (being incited to a war by the Pope) will be enforced as sufficient." — From "Carew Papers," Lambeth.

CCCXXIII. RESOLUTION OF THE STATES GENERAL.

From London " Documents relating to the Colonial History of the State of New York," Albany, 1853, vol. iii. p. 9.

Resolution of the States General on CCCXX.

" Tuesday the last of September, 1614.

" Received and read a Letter from the King of Great Britain, dated at Leicester the 19th of August Old Style, in favor of Captain Sir Thomas Dale, Marshall of Virginia, to the effect that their High Mightinesses would please to give leave of Absence to the said Captain for two or three years more, in order that he may continue his residence in Virginia meanwhile, to bring affairs there into thorough security, for which he has laid good foundation, and commencement. After deliberation, and on the aforesaid high recommendation by his Majesty and the aforesaid Ambassador, their High Mightinesses have agreed and consented that the said Captain may continue his residence in Virginia, on the previous footing, until it shall be otherwise ordered by their High Mightinesses."

CCCXXIV. GONDOMAR TO PHILIP III.

GENERAL ARCHIVES OF SIMANCAS. DEPARTMENT OF STATE, VOLUME 2591, FOLIO 115.

Copy of a deciphered letter from Don Diego Sarmiento y Acuña to the King of Spain, dated London, October 17, 1614.

" SIRE —

" The ship in which they offered me that Don Diego de Molino should be brought in, has returned without him. Two Englishmen, who were in the same vessel and whom I had charged, without the one knowing of the other, to bring me a very detailed account of the state in which matters were over there — to see if it agreed with what I have been

told by others — and likewise informing me of all that had
occurred there, why Don Diego de Molino did not come, or
whether he had died. I had charged them moreover, that
without making themselves known to Don Diego, or to the
other sailor whom they took with them, and who is called
Antonio Perez, they should find out how they were and should
comfort and assist them, both for the purpose of bringing
them over and in any other way that they might be able.
They have returned and brought me letters from Don Diego,
which one had sewed between the soles of his shoes, while
the other had them in a coil of rope, as I herewith send it to
Y. M. ; because they knew that they would be searched and
carefully examined, and if they found that they carried letters from Don Diego, they would hang them, without saying
a word, and besides would learn what Don Diego had written.
Don Diego is well but they keep him with great precautions,
not letting him speak to any one, altho' he is permitted to
go out and fish on the shore with four or five men who are
always with him on guard.   Don Diego, however, had persuaded them to escape with him, if there should turn up any
boat or any way to do it, (by water) ; because some who
have attempted to go by land towards 'la Florida,' so 'tis
said, were killed by the Indians ; whilst on the other hand
this is said to be a report manufactured by the English, in
order to create a terror so as to prevent others from making
the like attempt ; and for those who have gone towards 'la
Florida,' they lay the blame upon Don Diego de Molino.

"I have taken here special pains to find out why they
should have returned without bringing Don Diego, and I
have found out, as a great secret, that notwithstanding the
orders which were given, the Englishman has been permitted
to die in Spain, and resenting this, they keep Don Diego de
Molino in Virginia ; that having requested (as they tell me)
Y. M. in the name of the King here, to hand over the Englishman to their Embassador, since he had come over first
and was already in Madrid, and that the King here gave his
word to send for Don Diego, and to hand him over here, to

Y. M.'s Embassador; and that, seeing Y. M. had not been willing to trust this king in this, and knowing likewise very well, that the persons were very different persons, Don Diego being a gentleman, as here everybody knows full well, better than I myself, the Council has resolved to let the thing have its way and interpose delays and postponements without doing anything. My knowing this so perfectly has been of importance in getting it mended; and thus I have already in my possession a special order of the King in which he commands that without another word, he shall be sent in any [a?] vessel that may [will probably] sail from here within 8 days to Virginia,[1] and return within five or six months; the Captain of which ship has assured me that he will bring him without fail. I, also, endeavour to have the sailor brought. But here they know that he is an Englishman, where he was born and raised: besides, a Member of the Council has told me that at the request of the Embassador of the King here, Y. M. ordered him years ago to be imprisoned for improper words which he had used against the King here. I therefore proceed cautiously 'till we shall see Don Diego de Molino restored to freedom, and after that it seems to me it will be very right to ask for, that other man's liberty as a favor or in whatever manner may seem best.

" The condition in which Virginia affairs are just now, is the same as that I reported to Y. M. on the first; those who are there, are so against their free will, which I have been certified by one of those who come from there. Don Diego de Molino also gives me to understand this, adding that they would be very much delighted if Y. M. would send there even the shadow of a fleet, to drive them out of that country; that if some attack was made upon those of the first fort, and then an offer were made to take them all back to England, all the others would surrender without firing a shot, upon the same condition; and here this Colony is in such bad repute that not a human being can be found to go

---

[1] I suppose this has reference to the John and Francis. If so, the vessel probably sailed for Virginia about the middle of October, 1615.

there in any way whatever. So much so that a person who was present, has told me how in a Court of the Mayor — who is the 'Corregidor' of London — when the case of two Moorish [black?] thieves came up, the Mayor told them, impressing upon them their offences, that they ought to be hanged ; but that, taking pity upon them, he wished to pardon them, with this condition, that they should go and serve the King and the Queen in Virginia — and that they replied at once, decidedly and with one accord, that they would much rather die on the gallows here, and quickly, than to die slowly so many deaths as was the case in Virginia. I am told, they will be hanged ; also, that most of those who sail in this ship of to-day, go with the express condition and agreement, that they must return in it again.

"The Colony of Bermuda has a very different and creditable reputation ; and thus is assisted both in men and in money ; they speak very seriously of fortifying it, and sending Colonists there, as I have very much in detail reported to Y. M., whose Catholic Person," etc.

For a more correct view of affairs in Virginia at this time see Hamor's Narration (CCCXXVII.).

CCCXXV. MOLINA TO GONDOMAR.

GENERAL ARCHIVES OF SIMANCAS. DEPARTMENT OF STATE, VOLUME 2591, FOLIO 116 (INCLOSED IN FOLIO 115).

Copy of a holographic letter from Don Diego de Molina to Don Diego Sarmiento de Acuña, dated in Virginia, April 30, 1614. (Inclosed in a letter from said Don Diego Sarmiento to the King of Spain, of October 17, 1614.)

"Your letter, Sir, and the favor which you did me in succouring me, caused me a satisfaction, which I cannot express, since it alone was the means to relieve me of a disease which for seventeen months had afflicted me sadly. For all this fell upon me on account of the wrong which the Gov-

HENRY RICH

First Earl of Holland

ernor[1] did me in not taking me with him to the kingdom where you are, failing thus to comply with the order he had received, which I had so long wished for and solicited from you, and for which I thank you most sincerely. Because, so great a man, only to comply with this wish, without my ever having obliged him by any service of mine, has interested himself so warmly in doing me a favor. I trust however, I shall still be able one of these days to serve you.

"When the Governor left here, he told me he had no orders to take me with him, as he should go in the first vessel — a decision which was not made known to me 'till he was about to embark, so that I might not find means to send a reply to you; because they fancy that every word of mine contains some crafty device; and thus, of whatever trifle I may speak, they call it tale bearing, and interpret it as deceit concealed under falsehood. I beg our Lord He may well rid me of them. The Chief Marshall has told me that I shall go with him; but I rely but little on his good intentions, and therefore I have wished to write this letter, and leave it with a friend of mine who will hand it to you, as they mean to carry me to a new Colony which they have established this Summer fifteen leagues from here, up the river, and I shall not be able to write after that.

"The sailor who came with me has been taken on board a man of war[2] that is here, where they treat him liberally and use much persuasion to make him confess that he is an Englishman. And if this does not succeed they have assured me they think of making him drunk and then to examine him once more (fine Christian principles!). Captain Argol, who commands the ship of which I speak, went last year as high as the 44°, where he found a French ship, which had come there with some French people, to establish a new Colony. After some little fighting he overcame them and captured fifteen persons; the others fled with their governor. After having burnt all their buildings he re-

[1] Sir Thomas Gates, who left Virginia in March, 1614.   [2] The Treasurer.

turned to this river, with his ship and a captured pinnace, with much wheat, clothing, horses, and working tools. After this he made a second voyage reaching 45° and a half, and burnt another small fort twenty leagues from the other settlement. All this you will probably have heard already, because the ship and the pinnace which he took with him, on the second expedition, lost their way in a storm and it is understood, went to your city with a few prisoners, Fathers of the Jesuits. It may be that the Governor has taken over others also. Thus it seems to me, these men will have a new cause of complaint with the King of France. As those who commit the offence think they will never be within his reach, these poor people who suffer from no fault of their own have nothing to rely upon. Thus they commit here shameless actions as if the forces of Rome and Carthage united were here assembled. I say this with much solicitude, for they have also the intention of going to 'la Florida' and doing the same thing there; but their plans are formed recklessly and without sufficient thought, and thus God will finally pay them according to their works. All this I write as I get the opportunity to write without having what I write pryed into. In like manner, to see, as they give me a new opportunity, without noticing what I may see. I have asked the Marshall to leave me here, because I have no desire to see his new colonies, nor his new fortifications and small forts, for if they keep me a prisoner without charge against me, but merely for having seen what they themselves have shown me, I should not wish their mistakes and ignorances to redound to my injury.

"Of myself in special, I have nothing to say, thinking only of the favor which I am anxious you should do me, since I have left all my affairs in the hands of God, I no longer think of brothers, relatives, property, or honours, because all is fleeting and passes away like the wind. I only wish to do the duty of a good Catholic and to be able to do it among Catholics.

"May God enable me to see them thro' His mercy, and I

will serve you as I ought to do — whom may He preserve as I desire.

"From Virginia. April 30. 1614.[1]

"DIEGO DE MOLINO.

"for Señor Don Sarmiento de Acuña."

CCCXXVI. MOLINA TO GONDOMAR.

GENERAL ARCHIVES OF SIMANCAS. DEPARTMENT OF STATE, VOLUME 2591, FOLIOS 112, 113.

Copy of a holographic paper which reads thus: " For Don Diego Sarmiento de Acuña — Virginia — Don Diego de Molina.   June 14th 1614."

" Until now I had hoped to go in this ship of Captain Argol; but now they tell me, it sailed two days ago [2] and I am not going in it because the Marshall General had many times offered to take me.   From this may be seen the want of truthfulness in these men; and that they only mean to deceive us.   I am amazed at what they have done and how little they have attended to the order of the council, unless it is, as they say, the wellknown proverb of the monkey and the cat &c.[3]   I assume it must be so, that all these are stratagems, for which reason I wish you not to trouble yourself any farther doing me favors, for, altho' I am badly treated and endure much suffering, I reflect that my sins have been great and that I have deserved it all.   But as the father of a family, who, while grieving for his own sorrows, suffers those of his children — and considering the intimacy in which I have lived these three years with these poor people, held captives by their masters, I look upon them as my brothers, whose sorrows I feel more than my

[1] This letter was written April 20, 1614 (O. S.), about fifteen days after the marriage of Rolfe and Pocahontas. The Jesuit fathers cannot be placed in the picture, as they had left Jamestown ; but Captain Flory and possibly nine other Frenchmen, Don Diego de Molina, and Lymbry were there, though probably not at the wedding.

[2] The ship really sailed about the 18th of June.

[3] That is, the Spaniards were being made dupes of, — cat's-paws.

own, because living in their midst and seeing their sufferings, they look me in the face and ask: what is the King
of Spain doing? where is his mercy? why does he not show
it to so many unfortunate ones by releasing us from our
chains or by cutting off all our heads — for would it be
more tolerable for us, for every man to take up arms to
defend and maintain our captivity? Certainly not, but to
receive with bright faces such a great benefit with all kinds
of thanks and everlasting gratitude. Now what is there,
Sir, that I can answer? Except that in a most Catholic
manner the King, our Lord, is bound to reply to this petition with a marvellous effect of his Christian mind [?].[1]
There are here three settlements: this in which I have been
three years, altho' now they have ordered us to a prison in
a stockade a mile distant, with orders not to speak to me,
because the Marshall, says, I persuade and have persuaded
Edward 'Colaque' [Coles] that he should flee with five
other persons to Florida, as he put him to work, and I
believe he did go for the good it did him to escape from
here, and he took the complaint of them all, written in his
memory. He is a man who knew how to retain them.
They have now spread a report that the Indians have killed
them so as to terrify the people. The other settlement is
20 leagues up the river, which they made 3 years ago.
They have made still another three leagues higher up this
Spring, where almost all the people are, who altogether,
and in all parts amount to two hundred fifty persons, men,
women and children. Three stockades which they have at
the mouth of the river have been dismantled and thus there
are in them only six or seven men. I take it for granted
that the King, our Master, would do a work worthy of his
greatness, if he were to take these people away from here,

---

[1] The Christian mind of Philip III.
sustained a wonderful amount of very
wonderful special pleading for the
removing of the English in Virginia.
The determination of the English to
hold their grants in America was
probably more evident to his Christian
mind than was the truth of the special
pleas of his servants and agents. He
was probably aware of some things
not yet known to us.

and I am convinced that the Lord brought me hither by such extraordinary and unheard of events in order to become the Moses of these unfortunate people — not, as they say, as a spy, because in Spain little or nothing was known of this country when I was made a prisoner here. Their own rulers have made it notorious in Spain by my imprisonment, and in France by means of the three Forts and settlements which Captain Argol has burnt in two years that he has been here with a man-of-war. They have nothing to complain of, but their own bad government, because if they wish to settle the country, they ought to do no harm to their neighbours. I, sir, cannot write much longer, because with great labor I have written this with a root from the fields.

"I kiss your hands, Sir, for the favor you have done me, All came safe and was a great comfort to me.

"From Virginia. June 14. 1614.

"They have landed the sailor who is here, today, from the vessel on which he has been two months, and they will take him to another stockade, two miles from this.

"May God preserve you, as I desire.

"DON DIEGO DE MOLINA.

"To Señor Don Diego Sarmiento de Acuña."

[MEM. — 'On October 1 [O. S.], 1614, the States General granted a charter to certain Hollanders for the exclusive trade (until January 1, 1618) to that part of America between Virginia and New France, and now called New Netherland, between 40° and 45° north Latitude.' See "Holland Documents relating to the Colonial History of New York," Albany, 1856, vol. i. pp. 10–12, 53, 149. The Dutch claimed that they had been frequenting the region of the South (Delaware) and North (Hudson) rivers since the year 1598.

The map of the sea-coasts of America between New France and Virginia (40° to 45° north latitude), now named New Netherland, which was annexed to the grant of October $\frac{1}{11}$, 1614, is incorrectly placed in the volume between pp. 12 and 13, and given a wrong date.

The grants of March and October, 1614, of the Dutch to New Netherland, seem to have caused the English to enter again in a more determined manner upon advancing and securing their interest in New England, and we find an increasing number of English vessels going each year to those parts.

CCCXXVII. HAMOR'S NARRATION.

October 20, 1614, there was entered at Stationers' Hall for publication, " A booke called an Narracon of the presente State of Virginia by Ralph Hammer." It was published soon after with the following title : " A True Discourse of The Present Estate of Virginia, and the successe of the affaires there till the 18. of June 1614.   Together with a Relation of the Severall English Townes and Fortes, the assured hopes of that countrie and the peace concluded with the Indians.   The christening of Powhatan's daughter and her marriage with an English-man.

" Written by Raphe Hamor the yonger, late Secretarie in that Colony.

" Alget, qui non ardet.

" Printed at London by John Beale for William Welby dwelling at the signe of the Swanne in Pauls church-yard 1615."   [*I. e.*, after September 29, 1614.]

It is dedicated to Sir Thomas Smith.   It was reprinted at Albany, New York, in 1860.

Originals are preserved in the libraries of Mr. Charles Deane, Mr. Kalbfleisch, the Lenox, and the John Carter-Brown.   An original in the Drake sale, March, 1883, fetched $345.   Quaritch prices a copy at $500.

John Rolfe, in CCCLVIII., mentions this tract as having been " faithfully written by a gent. of good merit, Mr. Ralph Hamor," thus indorsing the account of his marriage, and his letter (CCCXXVIII.).

To this publication of Hamor's there was also added the following three letters: —

CCCXXVIII. ROLFE TO DALE.

" The Coppie of the Gentleman's [John Rolfe] letter to Sir Thomas Dale, that after maried Powhatan's daughter, containing the reasons moving him thereunto."

This letter, it seems, was delivered to Dale in March, 1614. It contains about 2,000 words, and has been reprinted several times.

CCCXXIX. DALE TO D. M.

Sir Thomas Dale's letter " To the R. and my most esteemed friend Mr. D. M. at his house at F. Ch. in London." Dated "From Jamestowne in Virginia the 18. of June 1614." It contains about 2,000 words, and was possibly written to *Master Doctor Mocket in Fenchurch Street.

CCCXXX. WHITAKER TO MASTER G.

Rev. Alexander Whitaker's letter " To my verie deere and loving Cosen M.[aster] G.[ouge] Minister of the B.[lack] F[riars] in London." Dated " Virginia June 18th 1614." It contains about 400 words.

The narrative proper (CCCXXVII.) contains about 14,000 words. All of these four numbers have been reprinted together in this country, so I will not give any of them in this collection.

This tract relates to events in Virginia from May, 1611, to June, 1614, having several references, however, to earlier dates. The leading items of the tract (and letters) are the capture of Pocahontas, her marriage, and the negotiations with the Indians. The account of the estate of the colony in the summer of 1614 is important.

[MEM. — November 23, 1614. " Sir Wm. Wade, Sir Dudley Diggs, Sir Baptist Hicks, Richard Martin Esq., John Wolstenholme Esq., Richd Chamberlaine, Robte Offeley, Robte Johnson, Jerome Heydon, George Scott, and George Barkeley of London, Merchants, by and with the full consent and agreement of William Lord Candishe, Sir John Harrington, Sir Walter Cope, Sir Thomas Smythe, Sir Robte Mansell, Sir Edwyn Sandys, knights and diverse other persons therein interested, resigned The Somers Islands to the Crown " [King James].

These individuals were influenced in thus resigning their plantation to the crown by fear of the Spaniards. A company was afterwards incorporated and a royal charter was granted to them on June 29, 1615. See CCCXLIX.]

CCCXXXI. HOWES' CHRONICLES.

" The Annales or Generall Chronicle of England, begun first by Maister John Stow, and after him continued and augmented with matters forreyne and domestique, auncient and moderne, unto the ende of this present yeere 1614, by Edmond Howes, gentleman. Londini Impensis Thomae Adams 1615.

" Imprinted in London at the Three Cranes in the Vintree, by Thomas Dawson, for Thomas Adams Anno. 1615.

" Dedicated to Prince Charles."

A perfect copy of these " Annales " is worth about $50, I suppose. There was another edition of this work published in 1631, but it does not contain a single word of additional matter relating to the colony in America. The latest reference to this colony is of November, 1614. The following extracts contain the references to the English enterprises in America.

[p. 941.]   " Virginia, is a country in America lying betweene the degrees of thirtie foure and forty five of the North Latitude. The bounds whereof on the East side, are the Ocean, on the South lyeth

The originall and plantation of the

Florida, on the North Nova Francia and New English in
Foundland, as for the West thereof the limits are ^{Virginia.}
unknowne,[1] of all this country, my occasion nor purpose is
not to speake, but onely of some parte, whereof the English,
viz, the Londoners and their Adherents, have made plantation : which said Country was first discovered in the yeere
1584, as [p. 942] aforesayd, and Queen Elizabeth called it
Virginia, and assigned the same unto Syr Walter Raleigh,
as being the chiefe discoverer thereof.   And in the yeere
1587. there were sent thither above an hundred men, women and children, and from that time untill the third yeere[2]
of King James, all yeerely sending thither for plantation
ceased: and then uppon more exact discoveries, there were
yeerely supplies of men, women & children, sent thither with
all necessaries, under the conduct of Captaine Newport.

"And about three yeeres after this time, Captaine Samuell Argall, discovered a direct passage through the ocean
to Virginia, and not to goe by the West India, as they did
formerly.   Also in the moneth of May in the yeere last
above sayd, there were sent thither 9. ships with five hundred men, women and children, with all necessarie provision, under commaund of Syr Thomas Gates, Knight, a
grave expert souldier, now appoynted Lieutenant Generall in
Virginia, Sir George Somers, Knight, a man very industrious and forward, was nowe made admirall of Virginia, and
Captaine Newport an excellent Navigator was made Vice-
Admirall : with these at this time went other expert captaines
and very resolute gentlemen, these arrived at Virginia in the
yeere 1609, and likewise at the end of the yeere 1609[3] there
was sent another supplie of 3. ships, with 150 men, being
for the most part Artificers, under commaund of the Lord
De la Ware, who by free election of the Treasurer and Counsell of Virginia & with the full consent of the generalty of

---

[1] Howes quotes several times from   others for many things regarding
Smith's tract (CCXLV.), which for   America.
cogent reasons was already the only   [2] 1606.
available authority to him and to   [3] Lord De la Warr in April, 1610.
                                       The end of the year was March 24.

that Company was constituted and authorized, during his naturall life, to be Lord Governor & Captayne Generall of all the English Collonies planted or to bee planted in Virginia, according to the tenor of his Maiesties letters patents granted that yeere 1609, unto that Company, Captaine Argall conducted the L. de la Ware by sea. The L. De la Ware being arrived in Virginia, ordered all things in the best manner he could, and with his forces marched up into divers parts of ye country, with full purpose to make farther discoveries; build new townes & forts, and to bring the Salvages unto his obedience: and sent Captaine Argall to the Bermodes, & to discover ye north parts of Virginia. The L. De la Ware used his best diligence & industrie & therewithall tooke such extraordinary paines that he fell into extreame sickness, which prevented all his designes, and forced him to goe thence & seeke a bath in ye West Indiaes; but being at Sea, his sickness so encreased, that he was constrayned to bare up for the Isles of Assoris, where he recovered some part of his strength, & so from thence he with Captaine Argall came for England: the next yeere [1] following Sir George Somers went from Virginia to ye Bermodes, to fetch porke, where he dyed of a surfeit in eating of a pig. Captaine Newport seeing the necessary yeerely supplies for this plantation, not to proceed as was requisite for so honorable an action, he left ye service, being chosen one of ye 6. Masters of ye Navy royall, & being imployed by the Company of the East India Marchants: he transported Sir Robert Sherley into Persia.

"And this yeere 1614, Sir Th: Gates came from Virginia into England, using his best meanes for more supplies to continue their plantation, having left behind him not full 400 men of all that were sent thither, over whom Sir Th. Dale Knight, a valiant souldier & discreet Governour had the full charge and rule.

[1] This is an error. It shows how close the affairs of the company were kept, and how little was really known to the public, that a chronicler of events should have made such a mistake. Argall and Somers, we now know, were sent to the Bermudas from Virginia at the same time in June, 1610.

ROBERT RICH
Second Earl of Warwick

"In this Plantation there were builded divers townes & forts, the first was called Jamestowne, builded by Captaine Smith, the 2. other Townes were called Henricus & Charles, which the L. De la Ware builded. At this time their severall discoveries up into the land were no further then to ye fals, a place so called by reason of the fale of waters: of which Captaine Smith, sometime president there, made a map, and wrote a booke of every particular place, & of all that happened there.[1]

"And amongst other of worthy memory in this plantation, you shall understand that Captaine Gosnoll, a brave souldier and very ingenious, spent much money & adventured his person & drew in many others, at the beginning of this plantation. Captaine Argall being an ingenious active, foward, young gentleman, amongst other his discoveries & bringing of victual, from the enemy to the Collony, which at ye time was like to have perished for want of food. he tooke a French ship a pinace which had brought forces to plant within the English limits: he razed their Forts & supplanted them, for their comming was to have supplanted the English Collonie. He also the last yeere tooke the daughter of the great Powhatan prisoner, who being well entreated, became a Christian; and then marryed Ma. Jo. Rolfe an English gentleman in Jamestowne, by meanes whereof Powhatan discharged & sent home all English prisoners in most kind *This Powhatan is as it were an Emperor and commandeth many Kings.* manner, besides the generall peace which ensued upon it. Through the singular industrie & policy of Sir Tho. Dale being marshall of Virginia & principal commander there. And in July this yeere 1614. Captaine Argall brought letters from Sir Tho. Dale & others certifying the Treasurer & whole Company of Virginia, of the present estate of their Collony & that the English were nowe become laborious & industrious & were plenteously stored *In former time the Eng-*

---

[1] That is CCXLV. The disasters which befell the colony and the uncertain state of affairs there for some years evidently strengthened Smith's evidence for a time, especially during 1612–15, "In which time of three years disaster," he is favorably mentioned several times.

lish were extreame sloathfull and would rather perish in idlenesse then prosper by labour.[1] with foode of their owne, & well furnished with good houses in sundry places for their habitation & most juditiously manifested unto the Company the just cause of good hope and great profit to ensue in short time by this plantation, if they would speedily & competently supply the Collony, whereupon there was sent the first week of Nov. this yeere 1614. a ship with 34 men & 11. women, with apparell & other necessaries for the rest of the Collony there resident.

"And thus much at this time & in this place, touching this plantation shall suffice, by reason Maister Hackluit, Captaine Smith, and others, have written sundry ample discourses thereof."

On page 942 Howes writes of Newfoundland.

On page 943 of Guiana and of the Northwest Passage.

On pages 943–945 of "The first plantation of the English in the Barmodes otherwise called the Somer Islands.

"In the yeare 1609 the Adventurers and companie of Virginia sent from London, a fleete of eight shippes with people to supplie and make strong the Collonie in Virginia, Sir Thomas Gates, being generall in a shippe of 300 tun, in this ship was also Sir George Somers, who was Admirall, and Captaine New-porte vice-Admirall, & with them about 160. persons, this ship was Admirall and kept Companie with the rest of the Fleet to the height of 30. degrees & being then assembled to consult touching divers matters, they were surprised with a most extreme violent storme which [p. 944] scattered the whole fleete, yet all the rest of the fleet bent their course for Virginia, where by God's speciall favoure they arived safely, but this great shippe, though new, and farre stronger then any of the rest, fell into a great leake, so as Mariners, and passengers were forced for

---

[1] I do not believe that men who had the courage to cross the Atlantic in the barks of those days were made of such stuff. This charge, and very many others like it, are directly traceable to the "varnishing reports," which the Council of Virginia was obliged to give out in order to smooth over or conceal the real difficulties and dangers by which they were environed, the publicity of which might have been fatal to the enterprise.

three dayes space, to doe their utmost to save themselves, from sudden sinking : but notwithstanding their incessant pumping and casting out of water by Bucketts and all other meanes, yet the water covered all the goods, within the hold, and all men were utterly tired and spent in strength and overcome with laboure and hopelesse of any succoure, most of them were gone to sleepe, yeelding themselves to the mercy of the Sea, being all very desierous to die upon any shoare, wheresoever, Sir George Sommers sitting at the Stearne, seeing the shippe desperat of reliefe looking every minute when the shippe woulde sinke, hee espyed land, which according to his and Captayne Newports oppinion, they judged it should be that dreadfull coast of the Bermodes, which Islande were of all Nations, said and supposed to be inchanted and inhabited with witches, and devills, which grew by reason of accustomed monstrous Thunderstorme and tempest, neere unto those Islands also for that the whole coast is so wunderous daungerous of Rockes, that few can approach them, but with unspeakeable hazard of shippe wrack, Sʳ George Somers, Sir Thomas Gates, Captayne Newport, and the rest, suddainely agreed of two evills to chuse the least, and so in a kinde of desperat res- At these Islolution, directed the shippe maynely for these ands the Sea doth not Eb Islands, which by Gods divine providence, at a and flow full hie water ran right betweene two strong Rockes, foure foote. where it stuck fast without breaking, which gave leasure and good oportunitie, for them to hoyce out their boate, and to land all their people as well saylers, as souldiers, and others in good safety, and beeing come a shoare, they were soone refreshed and cheered, the soyle and aire being most sweet and delicate. The salt water did great spoyle to most of the shippes lading and victuall, yet some meale was well recovered with many perticular thinges for theire common use & they all humbly thanked God for his great mercy, in so preserving them from destruction.

" Then presently they sought farther into the Island for foode, which being never yet inhabited by any people, was overgrowne with woods, and the woods replenished with wilde swine, which swine as it is very probable swom thither, out of some shippe wracke, they found also great multitude of fowle of sundry kindes, being then in a manner very tame, they found some fruite, as mulberies, peares, and Palmytoes, with stately Ceader Trees, & in the Sea, and in the Rockes, great plenty of most pleasant and holsome fish.

" Here of necessity they were constrayned to stay, almost ten moneths, in which space by the speciall Mercy, and divine providence of almighty God, to make good the discovery of these Islands unto them, that they by diligence and Industry, saved so much of the timber, tacling, and other things out of their great shippe which lay wrackt, and stuck fast betweene two Rockes, as there withall, and with such supply of stuffe as they found in those Islandes, they builded there two vessels, the lesser [1] whereof so soone as it was finished, it was manned and sent to goe to the Collony in Virginia, to signifie unto them how all thinges had happened with their commaunders, and their Company, and that they would shortly set sayle for Virginia, but what became of this shippe & men was never yet knowne, and when the bigger vessel was finished, and victualed with swines flesh, and with what else that place would afford them, these Commaunders, with all their Company imbarked themselves, and by Gods great mercy, arived safely at Virginia, when all Englishmen deemed them to be utterly cast away.

" When these three worthy commaunders, had setled the Collony, then Sir George Somers returned againe to the Bermodies, where he dyed of a surfeit, viz, eating Porke: his ship returned, having left three men there to keepe possession of those Islands.

" These Islands are within the limits of Virginia, and the Company finding land enough to plant uppon the maine in Virginia, soulde these Islands of the Bermodyes unto 120

---

[1] An error. This reference is to the long boat which was sent "as a Barke of Aviso for Virginia," soon after the shipwreck. Both of the vessels built on the island went to Virginia in May, 1610.

persons[1] of the same Companie, who since that time they obtayned a Charter,[2] and so they now hold those Islands from his Maiestie. And in April 1612. the sayd newe Company sent thither a ship with 60. persons, who arryved and remained there very safely.

" And when the said new Company was truly informed of the wholesomnesse of the Ayre and pleasantnesse of the soyle, and the aptnesse thereof, of itselfe in all respects to maintaine a Collony, the ground being so fertile that it will yeeld two harvests in one yeere : great plentie of woods and loftie Cedars : wellstored with fowle and great plenty of good fish ; and that besides the fertilitie of the soyle, which they had tryed, would beare with great encrease, all kind of English grayne, fruites, trees, beaches, and vines besides the great store of Ambergreece, and some pearle, which is found there : they sent yeerely supplies thither of men and some women, with all things necessarie for so worthy a plantation, so as at this time there are sixe hundred persons well fortified, with plentie of great ordinance, being nowe verie well able to resist a proud daring adversarie, by reason there are but two Inlets, and they both so narrow, as but one ship can come in at once into the harbour, and the Islands are invironed with Rockes unaccessable, and within there is a most excellent harbour, for a Navie of great Ships.

" The great Island is divided into eight Cantons, or Tribes, bearing the name of eight of the chiefe Planters, viz. The Earle of Northampton's Tribe, The Earle of Pembrookes Tribe, The Lord Paget, The Lord Candish [p. 944 (? 945)], Lord Harrington, Syr Thomas Smith, Syr Robert Mansell and Syr Edwin

The Bermodoes are about 500 [300 ?] leagues from Virginia.

---

[1] See under November 25, 1612.

[2] Their charter passed the seals June 29, 1615. It was probably understood that a charter would be granted at the time of the surrender to the crown on November 23, 1614. But Howes' account is confusing ; he seems to place the granting of this charter before April, 1612, and I suppose has gotten it confused with the Virginia charter of March, 1612. Howes probably did his best ; but he certainly makes several errors. Reliable evidence was evidently not obtainable at that time, nor afterwards ; but by collating together all the evidence now obtainable, I believe correct ideas may be arrived at.

Sands Tribe. Some of the lesser Isles are one mile and some 2. and 3. miles of ground, in which if they digge, they find good fresh water. The Company hath by this time spent twentie thousand pounds in this plantation and purchase.

" The Company named these Islands by the name of the Somer Islands: they lie in 32. degrees of the North Latitude:

" Richard Moore was sent thither as Deputie Governor there for the Company [?]. Syr Thomas Smith, Knight was then [?] Governor, and Master William Caning the deputie governor of this Company."

On page 945, Howes says: " Amongst the manifoulde Tokens and Signes of the infinite Blessings of Almightie God bestowed uppon this kingdome, by the wondrous and mercifull establishing of peace within ourselves, and the full benefitte of Concord with all Christian nations, and others, of all which graces let no man dare to presume he can speake too much, whereof in truth there can never be enough said." Among the fruits of the peace he mentions, " The universall increase of commerce, and trafique throughout the kingdome, great building or royall ships by private merchants, the repeopling of citties, Townes & Villages, besides the undiscernable and sudden encrease of fayre and costly buildings, as well within the citty of London, as in the suburbs thereof: . . . as also the Plantation of English in Ireland, Virginia, and Newfound Lande, and in the Bermodes, the discovery of the North West passage," etc.

Howes published, about May, 1618, " The Abridgement of the English Chronicle, First collected by M. John Stow, and after him augmented with very many memorable Antiquities, and continued with matters forreine and domesticall, unto the beginning of the yeare, 1618. . . . Imprinted at London for the Company of Stationers, 1618." I have given the references to the Virginia enterprises in this work under the various dates referred to. See extracts from Howes' Chronicles, abridged.

CCCXXXII. EDMONDES TO WINWOOD.

Sir Thomas Edmondes to Secretary Sir Ralph Winwood. Paris, France, December 12, 1614.

[Account of his conference with Mons. de Villeroy and audience of the King and Queen of France, in reference to sundry complaints of the French against His Majesty's subjects.]

. . . " Whereunto she [the Queen] made me no other answeere then that the complaints were great which she received of the spoyles which were committed upon the ffrench by his Majesties subjects, as she was forced to make an extraordinarie instance for the redresse of the same." — English State Paper Office.

CCCXXXIII. EXTRACT FROM STATIONERS' RECORDS.

" A further sum of £45. was subscribed to the Virginia enterprise, from the trading stock of The Stationers in 1614 [exact date not given]; but no return appears to have been received."

Extract from a letter from the clerk of the company.

CCCXXXIV. EDMONDES TO WINWOOD.

Sir Thomas Edmondes to Secretary Sir Ralph Winwood. Paris, France, December 30, 1614.

" I send your Honour herewith a Copie of the Memoriall which I have exhibited to Monsieur de Villeroy, of as many both generall and particular Complaintes, as I could call to remembrance."

CCCXXXV. COMPLAINTS AGAINST THE FRENCH.

[Inclosure.] " Memorial of Complaints concerning the subjects of the King of Great Britain, which his Majesties Ambassador presents to their Majesties [of France] and the

Lords of the Council, in order that it may please them to give orders to have said complaints redressed and prevented in future."

This is a document in French, of twenty-one pages, some of the complaints dating back twenty-five years. They include the following, namely : —

"In the year 1606 Sir Ferdinando Gorge (sic) Governor of the city of Plimuth (sic) and some others having equipped and put to sea a vessel of the said town called The Richard, under the command of one called Captain Chalonour to trade and obtain a footing on the coast of Virginia, this vessel, sailing on the high seas, was met with and taken with all the merchandise and provisions that were on boord, amounting to the value of 14.000 or 15.000 francs, by another vessel, belonging to two merchants from St Malo, called Louis and Servant Graves, being commanded by one called Alphonse Camache, who took the foresaid vessel as a prize, to Bordeaux, where as soon as the men of the crew of the former saw themselves at liberty, one of them, called Tucker, proceeded against the said Camache before the Parliament of that place, so as to obtain justice against him. But after having continued his lawsuit there for the space of two years, he was non-suited by sentence of the 20th February 1609, because he had not been able to furnish security of such an amount and within such a time as was asked of him, notwithstanding that he offered shortly after sufficient security." — English State Paper Office.

CCCXXXVI. EXTRACT FROM ALEXANDER'S DOOMSDAY.

Extract from Sir William Alexander's poem called " Doomsday," probably written in 1614 : —

> " In this last age, Time doth new worlds display,
> That Christ a church, o'er all the Earth may have,
> His righteousness shall barbarous realms away,
> If their first love, more civil lands will leave,
> America to Europe may succeed,
> God may of stones raise up to Abram, seed."

CCCXXXVII. EXTRACT FROM COOKE'S TUQUOQUE.

Extract from " Greenes Tuquoque, or The Cittie Gallant. As it hath beene divers times acted by the Queenes
Maiesties Servants. Written by John Cooke, gent. [the
actor] Printed at London . . . 1614."

One of the characters says: " I dare not walk abroad to
see my friends, for fear the sergeants should take acquaintance of me; my refuge is Ireland or Virginia."

[MEM. — The Margaret and other vessels returned from
the Bermudas in the summer, fall, and winter of 1614 ;
bringing back Master George Berkeley, Captain Daniel
Elfrith, and others.]

CCCXXXVIII. GONDOMAR TO PHILIP III.

*GENERAL ARCHIVES OF SIMANCAS. DEPARTMENT OF STATE,
VOLUME 2593, FOLIO 23.*

Copy of an extract from a deciphered letter of Don Diego
Sarmiento de Acuña to the King of Spain, dated London, February 10, 1615.

" SIRE.

. . . " We expect Don Diego de Molino with the first
ship coming from Virginia. That Colony continues daily
losing more of its credit, and I am told that even the
energy with which the Colony of Bermuda began is no
longer as great, because they do not find there the advantages which they expected." . . .

CCCXXXIX. LETTER FROM LEWIS HUGHES.

" A Letter sent into England from the Summer Islands
written by Mr Lewis Hughes, Preacher of God's Word
there, 1615. Printed at London by J. B. for William
Welby, and are to be sold at his shop at the signe of the

Swanne in Paules Church Yard 1615." The letter is dated December 21, 1614, and extracts from it are given in Lefroy's "Memorials of the Bermudas," vol. ii. pp. 577–580.

[MEM. — Captain Argall in the Treasurer sailed for Virginia about February, 1615.]

CCCXL. MINUTE OF THE PRIVY COUNCIL.

On February 19, 161$\frac{4}{5}$, the Privy Council made the following minute : —

" Whereas it pleased their Lordships some moneths past[1] at the humble suite of the Colony of Virginia to gyve order for the writing of certaine letters unto the several cittyes and Townes of the Kingdome inviting and persuading the Inhabitants thereof to adventure in a certeyne Lotterye, such somes of moneye as they should think fitting according to the rules enclosed in the sayd Letters, thereby the better to enable ye sayd Companye to proceede in that Plantation of Virginia : —

" And forasmuch as upon further consideration it was commanded by the Boarde, that staye should be made of the sayd Letters, until further order might be given on that behalfe. It was this day (upon the humble suite of Sir Thomas Smith, with the rest of the Company of Virginia) thought fitting, and so accordingly ordered, that the sayd letters should forthwith be delivered unto Sir Thomas Smith, to the end they might be sent, and dispersed according to their several directions." — From Neill's " Virginia Vetusta," p. 199.

CCCXLI. PRIVY COUNCIL TO CANTERBURY.

FROM GREEN'S AND SAINSBURY'S CALENDARS OF STATE PAPERS.

White Hall, February 22, 1615.

" The Privy Council to the Mayor and Aldermen of Canterbury."

----

[1] See CCCI.

A Declaration for the certaine time of drawing the great standing Lottery.

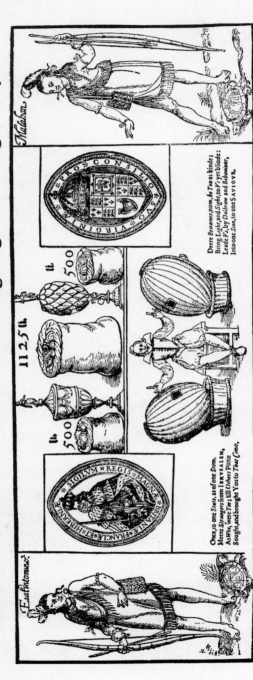

It is apparent to the World, by how many former Publications we manifested our intents to have drawne out the Great standing Lotterie long before this day: Which not falling out as ourselves desired and others expected, whose moneyes are already adventured therein, We thought good therefore for avoiding all unjust and sinister constructions to resolve the doubts of al indifferent minded in three special points for their better satisfaction. The first is, for as much as the adventures came in so slackly with such poore and barren receits of moneys at the Lottery house for this twelve moneth past, that without too much prejudice to ourselves and the adventurers in lessening the blankes & prizes, We found

Welcomes.

To him that first shall bee drawne out with a Blanke }	100. crownes.
To the second	50. crownes.
To the third	25. crownes.
To him that every day during the drawing of this Lottery shall bee first drawne out with a Blanke }	10. crownes.

Prizes.

1. Great Prize of . . .	4.500. crownes.
2. Great Prizes, each of .	2.000. crownes.
4. Great Prizes, each of .	1.000. crownes.
6. Great Prizes, each of .	500. crownes.
10. Prizes, each of . . .	300. crownes.
20. Prizes, each of . . .	200. crownes.

please to leave & remit his Prizes and Rewards, bee they more or lesse, the Lottery being drawne out, he shall have a bill of Adventure to Virginia, for the like sum he adventured, & shall be free of that Company, & have his part in all Lands, & all other profits hereafter arising thence according to his adventure of twelve pounds ten shillings or upwards.

Whosoever is behinde with the payment of any sum of money, promised heretofore to be adventured to Virginia, if hee adventure in this Lotterie the double of that sum & make payment thereof in ready money to Sir Thomas Smith Knight, Treasurer for Virginia, he shall be discharged of the foresaid summe so promised to have been adventured to Virginia, which otherwise we should not in any reasonable time have effected.

The second poynt for satisfaction to all honest and wel affected minds, is, that notwithstanding this our meanes of Lottery, answered not our hopes, yet have we not failed in that Christian care of the Colony in Virginia, to whom wee have lately made two sundry supplies of men and provisions. Where wee doubt not but they are all in health and in so good a way with corne and cattell to subsist of themselves, that were they now but a while supplied with more hands and materials, we should the sooner resolve upon a division of the Countrey by lot, and so lessen the Generall charge, by leaving each severall tribe or family to husband and manure his owne.

The third and last is our constant resolution, that seeing our credits are now so farre engaged to the Honourable Lords & to the Whole State for the drawing and accomplishment of this great standing Lotterie, Which we intend shall be our last of all standing Lotteries for this Plantation, that our time fixed and determined for accomplishing thereof, shall be, if God permit, without longer delay, the 26. of June next, being in Trinity tearme, desiring all such as have undertaken with bookes to solicite their friends, and all such as intend the prosperity of that worthie Plantation, that they will not withhold their monies till the last weeke or moneth be expired, lest we be unwillingly forced to proportion a lesse value and number of our blankes and prizes which hereafter follow.

And whosoever under one name or posie shall adventure twelve pounds ten shillings or upward, if he

Rewards.

To him that shall bee last drawne out with a Blanke } 25. crownes.
To him that putteth in the greatest number of Lots under one name or Posie. } 400. crownes.
To him that putteth in the second greatest number . } 300. crownes.
To him that putteth in the third greatest number . . } 200. crownes.
To him that putteth in the fourth greatest number . . } 100. crownes.

—If divers bee of equall number then these Rewards are to be divided proportionably.—

Addition of new Rewards.

The Blanke that shall bee drawne out next before the Greatest Prize, shal have . } 25. crownes.
The Blanke that shall bee drawne out next after the said Great Prize, shall have } 25. crownes.
The Blankes that shall be drawne out immediately before the 2. next Greatest Prizes, shall have each of them . . . } 20. crownes.
The severall Blankes next after them shall have also each of them . . . } 20. crownes.
The severall Blankes next before the foure Great Prizes, shall have each of them } 15. crownes.
The severall Blankes next after them shall have also each of them . . } 15. crownes.
The severall Blankes next before the six Great Prizes, shall have each of them. } 10. crownes.
The severall Blankes next after them shall have also each of them . . . . } 10. crownes.

And if upon too much delay of the adventurers to furnish this Lottery, We be driven to draw the same before it be full, then we purpose to shorten both blanks and Prizes in an equall proportion, according to that wherein wee shall come short, bee it more or lesse, that neither the Adventurers may bee defrauded nor ourselves, as in the former, any way wronged.

The Prizes, Welcomes & Rewards shall be paid in ready Money, Plate, or other goods reasonably rated. If any dislike of the said Plate or other Goods, he shall have ready money for the same, abating onely a tenth part; except in small Prizes of tenne Crownes or under, wherein nothing shall be abated them.

The money for Adventurers is to be paid to Sir Thomas Smith Knight Treasurer for Virginia at his house in Philpot lane; or to such officers as shall be appointed to attend for that purpose at the Lottery house: or to such other as shall elsewhere, for the ease of the Countrey, be authorized under the Seale of the Company, for receipt thereof.

The Prizes, Welcomes & Rewards being drawne, they shall be paid by the Treasurer for Virginia, without delay, whensoever they shall be demanded.

And for the better expedition to make our sum compleat, as wel to hasten the drawing of our Lottery, as chiefly to inable us the sooner to make good supplies to the Colonie in Virginia: Whosoever under one name or posie shall bring in ready money three pounds, either to the Lottery house, or to any Collector, the same party receiving their money, for every three pounds so received shall render them presently a silver spoone of 6. shillings, 8. pence price, or 6. shillings 8. pence in money.

Imprinted at London, by Felix Kyngston, for William Welby, the 22. of Februarie. 1615.

Abstract: ' Send a True declaration of the state of the English Colony in Virginia,[1] together with a project by help of a lottery, to bring that work to the success desired.

' Commend that worthy and Christian enterprise to their care, and require that they will employ their best endeavors to persuade persons of ability to adventure in the lottery. Inclose from the Treasurer and Council of Virginia, books requisite for registering the sums adventured, which it is requested may be returned with the money collected.'

CCCXLII. A DECLARATION FOR THE LOTTERY.

I am convinced that this was first entered for publication March 9, 1614 (see under that date), and was soon after distributed among the London companies. It was probably again printed February 22, 1615 (with the needed changes in date, etc., I suppose), for distribution among the various cities, towns, etc.

" A Declaration for the certaine time of drawing the great standing Lottery. — [With an engraved heading of Eiatintomino and Matahan, the Council Seal and symbols of the lottery.]

> " Once, in one State, as of one Stem,
> Meere Strangers from Jerusalem,
> As Wee, were Yee ; till Others Pittie
> Sought, and brought You to That Cittie.

> " Deere Britaines, now, be You as kinde ;
> Bring Light, and Sight, to Us yet blinde :
> Lead Us, by Doctrine and Behaviour,
> Into one Sion, to one Saviour.

" It is apparent to the World, by how many former Publications we manifested our intents to have drawne out the Great standing Lotterie long before this day : Which not falling out as ourselves desired and others expected, whose moneyes are already adventured therein, We thought good therefore for avoiding all unjust and sinister constructions

[1] CCCXLII. see also CCCI.

to resolve the doubts of al indifferent minded in three speciall points for their better satisfaction.   The first is, for as much as the adventures came in so slackly with such poore and barren receits of moneys at the Lottery house for this twelve moneth past, that without too much prejudice to ourselves and the adventurers in lessening the blankes & prizes, We found no meanes nor ability to proceed in any competent proportion, but of necessity are driven to the Honourable Lords by petition, Who out of their Noble care and disposition to further that publike plantation of Virginia, have recommended their letters to the Counties, cities and good Townes in England.   Which we hope by sending in their Voluntarie adventurers, will sufficiently make that supply of helpe, which otherwise we should not in any reasonable time have effected.

" The second poynt for satisfaction to all honest and wel affected minds, is, that notwithstanding this our meanes of Lottery, answered not our hopes, yet have we not failed in that Christian care of the Colony in Virginia, to whom wee have lately made two sundry supplies of men and provisions.   Where wee doubt not but they are all in health and in so good a way with corne and cattell to subsist of themselves, that were they now but a while supplied with more hands and materials, we should the sooner resolve upon a division of the country by lot, and so lessen the Generall charge, by leaving each several tribe or family to husband and manure his owne.

" The third and last is our constant resolution, that seeing our credits are now so farre engaged to the Honourable Lords & to the whole State for the drawing and accomplishment of this great standing Lotterie, Which we intend shall be our last of all standing Lotteries for this Plantation, that our time fixed and determined for accomplishing thereof, shall be, if God permit, without longer delay, the 26. of June next, being in Trinity tearme, desiring all such as have undertaken with bookes to solicite their friends, and all such as intend the prosperity of that worthie Plantation,

that they will not withhold their monies till the last weeke
or moneth be expired, lest we be unwillingly forced to proportion a lesse value and number of our blankes and prizes
which hereafter follow.

" And whosoever under one name or posie shall adventure
twelve pounds ten shillings or upward, if he please to leave
& remit his Prizes and Rewards, bee they more or lesse,
the Lottery being drawne out, he shall have a bill of Adventure to Virginia, for the like sum he adventured, & shall
be free of that Company, & have his part in all Lands, &
all other profits hereafter arising thence according to his
adventure of twelve pounds ten shillings or upwards.

" Whosoever is behinde with the payment of any sum of
money promised heretofore to be adventured to Virginia,
if hee adventure in this Lotterie the double of that sum &
make payment thereof in ready money to Sir Thomas Smith,
Knight, Treasurer, for Virginia, he shall be discharged of
the foresaid summe so promised to have been adventured
to Virginia, and of all actions and damages therefrom arising, and have also the benefit of all Prizes and Rewards
whatsoever in this Lottery, due by reason of the like sum
which he shall bring in, and yet notwithstandinge, if after
the Lottery drawne, he list to remit all his said Prizes and
Rewards, he shall have a bill of Adventure to Virginia, for
the said entire summe according to the last preceding Article.

" And if upon too much delay of the adventurers to furnish this Lottery, We be driven to draw the same before it
be full, then we purpose to shorten both blanks and Prizes
in an equall proportion, according to that wherein we shall
come short, bee it more or lesse, that neither the Adventurers may be defrauded nor ourselves as in the former, any-
way wronged.

" The Prizes, Welcomes & Rewards shall be paid in ready
money, Plate, or other goods reasonably rated. If any dislike of the said Plate or other Goods, he shall have ready
money for the same, abating onely a tenth part; except in

small Prizes of tenne Crownes or under, wherein nothing shall be abated them.

" The money for Adventures is to be paid to Sir Thomas Smith, Knight, Treasurer for Virginia at his house in Philpot lane; or to such officers as shall be appointed to attend for that purpose at the Lottery house : or to such other as shall elsewhere, for the ease of the countrey, be authorized under the seale of the company, for receipt thereof.

" The Prizes, Welcomes & Rewards being drawne they shall be paid by The Treasurer for Virginia, without delay, whensoever they shall be demanded.

" And for the better expedition to make our sum compleat, as wel to hasten the drawing of our Lottery, as chiefly to inable us the sooner to make good supplies to the Colonie in Virginia : Whosoever under one name or posie shall bring in ready money three pounds, either to the Lottery house, or to any Collector, the same party receiving their money, for every three pounds so received, shall render them presently a silver spoone of 6. shillings, 8 pence price, or 6. shillings 8. pence in money.

WELCOMES.

To him that first shall bee drawne out with a Blanke	100. crownes.
To the second	50. crownes.
To the third	25. crownes.
To him that every day during the drawing of this Lottery shall be first drawne out with a Blanke	10. crownes.

PRIZES.

1. Great Prize of	4.500. crownes.
2. Great Prizes, each of	2.000. crownes.
4. Great Prizes, each of	1.000. crownes.
6. Great Prizes, each of	500. crownes.
10. Prizes, each of	300. crownes.
20. Prizes, each of	200. crownes.
100. Prizes, each of	100. crownes.
200. Prizes, each of	50. crownes.
400. Prizes, each of	20. crownes.
1,000. Prizes, each of	10. crownes.
1,000. Prizes, each of	8. crownes.

1,000. Prizes, each of	6. crownes.
4,000. Prizes, each of	4. crownes.
1,000. Prizes, each of	3. crownes.
1,000. Prizes, each of	2. crownes.

REWARDS.

To him that shall bee last drawne out with a Blanke	25. crownes.
To him that putteth in the greatest number of Lots under one name or Posie	400. crownes.
To him that putteth in the second greatest number	300. crownes.
To him that putteth in the third greatest number	200. crownes.
To him that putteth in the fourth greatest number	100. crownes.

If divers bee of equall number, then these Rewards are to be divided proportionably.

ADDITION OF NEW REWARDS.

The Blanke that shall bee drawne out next before the greatest Prize, shal have	25. crownes.
The Blanke that shall bee drawne out next after the said great Prize, shall have	25. crownes.
The Blankes that shall be drawne out immediately before the 2. next greatest Prizes, shall have each of them	20. crownes.
The severall Blankes next after them shall have also each of them	20. crownes.
The severall Blankes next before the foure Great Prizes, shall have each of them	15. crownes.
The severall Blankes next after them shall have also each of them	15. crownes.
The severall Blankes next before the six great Prizes, shall have each of them	10. crownes.
The severall Blankes next after them shall also have each of them	10. crownes.

" Imprinted at London by Felix Kyngston, for William Welby, the 22. of Februarie, 1615."

Smith extracts from CCCXLII. in his " Generall History," pp. 117–119. This lottery was drawn November 17, 1615, and was really the Second Great Lottery; the First Great Virginian Lottery, as we have seen, was drawn in June and July, 1612.

CCCXLII. is No. 151, Broadside of the Society of Antiquaries of London; I know of no other original. It has been wrongly catalogued under 1616. (See my remarks on CXIV.) The year is not Old Style ; it would have borne the date 1615, if printed in London between September 29, 1614, and September 29, 1615.

CCCXLIII. EXTRACT FROM THE TRADE'S INCREASE.

Some time prior to February 22, 1615, there issued from the press a tract called " The Trades Increase. Printed by Nicholas Okes, and are to be sold by Walter Burre." The preface is signed with the initials I. R. It was written against the East India Company. It contains the following references to Virginia, viz. : —

On page 26. " I cannot finde any other worthy place of forren anchorage. For the Bermudas, We know not yet what they will doe ; and for Virginia we know not well what to do with it : The present profit of those two Colonies not employing any store of shipping. The great expence that the nobility and gentry have been at in planting Virginia is no way recompensed by the poor returns from thence."

On page 53. " The Virginia Company pretend almost all that Maine twixt it and New-found-land to bee their Fee-Simple, whereby many honest and able mindes, disposed to adventure, are hindred and stopped from repairing to those places, that they either know or would discover, even for fishing."

February 22, 1615. Extract from the Court Minutes of the East India Company.

" Report of Mr Leate and Mr Bell that Mr. Attorney and another lawyer find some points in the book, called the Trades Increase, very near to treason and all the rest very dangerous. The opinion of Mr Solicitor desired ; Sir Dudley Diggs of opinion that a book should be set forth in defence of the East India trade."

CCCXLIV. EXTRACT FROM THE DEFENSE OF TRADE.

Soon after this, there appeared " The Defence of Trade. In a Letter to Sir Thomas Smith, Knight, Governour of the East India Companie &c. From one of that Societie. Vexat censura Columbas. London, Printed by William Stansby for John Barnes, and are to be sold at his shop over against Saint Sepulchres Church without Newgate. 1615." (Signed at the end of pamphlet, Dudley Digges. In the tract he speaks of Sir Thomas Smythe as his kinsman.) The tract is a defense of the merchant companies. On page 30, Diggs, replying to the reflection on Virginia, says : —

" This ready Companie (of Muscovie) to doe him service, and to good their Countrie, May perhaps finde meanes, to save home-store, by trying a conclusion in Virginia, which this worthy author thinkes, men know not what to doe withall."

[MEM. — In March, 1615, Byleth and Baffin sailed on their voyage for Discoverie of Seas, Lands and Ilands to the North-Westwards, etc.

The Welcome sailed for the Bermudas probably about the same time.]

CCCXLV. EXTRACT FROM BRITAIN'S BUSS.

Extract from " Britain's Buss, or A computation as well of the charge of a Buss or Herring Fishing ship ; as also of the Gain and Profit thereby. By E. S. London. Printed by William Jaggard for Nicholas Bourne. and are to be sold at his shop at the south entry of the Royal Exchange. 1615." . . .

" *Timber and Plank.* And for all the great and pitiful waste of our English woods ; yet will England afford timber and plank enough for many Busses : but, to spare England awhile, Ireland will yield us Busses enough, besides many other good ships, if need be ; and Scotland will help us with masts.   But if we would spare so near home, we may help ourselves out of Virginia and Sommer Islands." . . .

As this tract mentions the "Trade's Increase," as "now newly come abroad," I suppose it was written early in 1615, soon after the "Trade's Increase."

CCCXLVI. CAREW TO ROE.

See "The Letters of Carew to Roe," printed for the Camden Society of England in 1860, pp. 6, 7, and also pp. 53, 54.

April, 1615.   "The Frenche, who were planted in an Iland in the mouthe of the river Maraynor, are displanted by the Portugals.   There whole number were 400 Frenchmen, but 100 of them unserviceable by reason of sickness. None were spared, but all of them, allmost to a man, put to the sword, and the women and children found no mercye. The Portugal commander thatt tryumphes with this victorie is the governor of Brasil, who surprised them thatt were over negligent; his forces consisted of 800 Portugals and 800 Indians.   The French fort, which was well fortified, is rased to the ground.   I pray God thatt Virginia may not drinke of the same cuppe ! "

CCCXLVII. EXTRACT FROM RECORDS OF DOVER.

From "Liber Vocatus A."   Commencing 19th Elizabeth, September 15, 1577.   Containing the Common Assembly Minutes of this Borough of Dover.

"*8th May 1615.*   A Letter read from the Lords of the Council to adventure in the Lottery for the Lottery for the Plantation of Virginia.   £5. adventured out of the Towns Yr. [Treasury ?] by 20 Lots to be made in the name of the town of Dover. Mr Mayor to send the same according to direction. If any profit be had to be the corporations."

"*11th July 1615*. The £5. adventure paid in London by 20 Lotts and a receipt of the same and N° of the Lots produced."

CCCXLVIII. EXTRACTS FROM THE RECORDS OF WYCOMBE.

FROM FIFTH REPT. ROYAL HIST. COM. PAGE 559.

From Records of the Borough of High Wycombe. Folio 146b.

Under date May 27, 1615, a list is given " of the names of the adventurers for Virginia," *i. e.* of persons who ventured sums of money in the Lottery made on the new settlement there; the largest venture being that of Robert Kempe, gent., who subscribes 40 shillings ; the smallest sums subscribed being 5 shillings. The common clerk probably made the entry, and does not appear to have very favorably regarded the speculation, as he ends the list with " *Possibilia spes comitatur.*" After which is entered, " Memorandum that it is agreed amongst the said Adventurers that Roberte Gray, seargeant, and Edward Randall, Parishe Clarke, shall have eyther of them, the benefitt of a lott of 5.s., for there paines in collecting of the abovesaid somys of money, as well and fully as though they had adventured there lottes." Many children's names having been entered, each for a lot, the following is added : " It is agreed the parents of the said children shall have and take Sommes due to the children, and discharge the towne."

[MEM. — Four ships were sent out by the Londoners to the New England coast in January, 1615. Returning, one loaded with dry fish sailed for Spain, and was taken by the Turks. One went to Virginia to relieve that colony, " and two came for England with the greene fish, treine oyle and furres, within sixe moneths." Captain John Smith sailed

from Plymouth in March with two ships, on his so-called
"second voyage to New England;" he soon returned with
the large ship, but Master Dermer made the voyage safely
in the small bark. Smith again sailed (on his so-called
"third voyage") June 24, following; but fell into the
hands of "Pyrats."

CCCXLIX. THE SOMERS ISLANDS CHARTER.

COLONIAL ENTRY BOOK, VOLUME XVII. PAGES 1-46.

On the 29th June, 1615, King James granted to Henry
Earl of Southampton, Lucy Countess of Bedford, William
Earl of Pembroke, William Lord Paget, William Lord Cav-
endish, Sir Ralph Winwood, Sir Robert Rich, Sir Thomas
Smith, Sir Robert Maunsell, Sir Edwyn Sandys, Sir Dudley
Diggs, Sir John Watts, Sir Anthony Archer, Sir Samuel
Sandys, Sir John Merrick, Sir Richard Smith, Sir Thomas
Howgan, Sir Lyonel Cranfeild, Sir John Heyward, Sir
Richard Grubham, Sir Lawrence Hyde, *Knights.* John
Walter, Richard Martin, John Wroth, John Walstenholme,
Richard Chamberlaine, Nicholas Hyde, William Garraway,
George Thorpe, Jerom Heydon *Esquires.* George Cham-
berlane, Wm Caninge, *Merchants.* Anthony Hinton *Doc-
tor in Physic,* Richard Tomlins *Esquire,* John Hayward
clerk, William Payne *Esquire,* Morris Abbot *merchant,*
Charles Anthony *Goldsmith,* Anthony Abdey, William
Aderley, Arthur Bromfeild, George Barkley *merchants,*
John Banks *mercer,* Christopher Baron, Edward Bishop,
Jo. Britton, Nicholas Benson, Thomas Church, Thomas
Covel, Abram Cartwright, Allen Cotton, Christopher Clith-
ere, Richard Caswell, Abram Chamberloin, Edw. Ditch-
feild *Salter,* Abram Dawes, Jo: Dike, John Delbridge,
George Etheridge, Nicholas Exton, Richard Edwards,
Nicholas Ferrer *merchant,* John Ferne, Giles Francis,
William Felgate, Edward Fawcet, Jo. Fletcher, William
Greenwell *merchant-tayler,* Robert Gore *merchant-tayler,*

SIR THOMAS ROE

Jo: Gearing Ralph Hamer *merchant-tayler*, George Holman, Leonard Harwood, John Hodges, Robert Johnson *grocer*, Thomas Jadwin, Thomas Johnson, Phil. Jacobson. Ralph King, Jo. Kirrell, Thomas Lever, Edward Lukin, Richard Maplesden, Richard Morer, Thomas Noringcot, William Nichols, Robert Offley *mercht*, William Palmer, Richard Paulson, Heildebrand Pruson, William Quick, Richard Rogers, Elias Roberts *merchant-taylor*, George Robins, George Scot, Edmund Scot, George Swinhoe, Abram Speckard, Cleophas Smith, Robert Smith, Mat. Sheppard, George Smith grocer, John Barnard, Henry Timberlake, William Welby *Stationer*, Thomas Wale, Richard Webb *haberdasher*, Thomas Welles, Thomas Wheatley, John West *grocer*, Jo. Weld, John Wooddall, William Webster, Gideon Delaun, John Osborne, Warren Smith and Robert Philips, a charter of incorporation, by the name of the Governor and Company of the City of London for the plantation of the Somers Islands, with sole government and power to make laws, conformable to the Laws of England, etc.

[MEM. — Richard Hawkins sailed on his voyage for New England in October, 1615.

Court Minutes of the East India Company, September 12, 1615, mentions the " Benefit of the Trade to the East Indies to the King — and His Majesty's gracious inclination and favour towards the Company," etc. " The Royal customs for the *two last ships* returned was about £14.000. while in the Queen's time Mr. Customer Smythe farmed *all* of the Royal customs at £12,000." November 3, 1615. " The East India Company desires the discovery of things yet unknown or uncertain for the future good of Posteritye."]

CCCL. TOBACCO MEMORANDA.

Among the manuscripts of the Right Honorable the Earl De la Warr at Knowle Park, County Kent, are the following, relating to tobacco : —

" *March 22ⁿᵈ 1613–4.*   W. Shipman to Sir John Ferne : He says there was spent yearly in this kingdom £200.000 or more on tobacco.   He offers £5.000 a year as a present to a nobleman of the court for an exclusive patent."

" *Sept. 30. 1615.*   Certificate of the quantity of Tobacco in Portsmouth in *The Flying Horse of Flushing,* from Virginia, 30ᵗʰ Sept. 1615 ; From W. Budd, one great roll containing 105 lbs of Midding Tobacco."   There is also another certificate of February 10, 1616, which gives the number of pounds as 104, showing the loss of weight with time, which those who deal in tobacco have long been familiar with.

There was also published this year : " An advice how to plant Tobacco in England : and How to bring it to colour and perfection ; to whom it may be profitable, and to whom harmfull.   The vertues of the Hearbe in generall, as well in the outward application as taken in Fume.   With the danger of the Spanish Tobacco.   Written by C. T.   London, Printed by Nicholas Okes, and are to be sold by Walter Burre.   1615."

There had been many tracts issued in England, on the tobacco question (*pro* and *con.*) ; in one of them we are told that it was

"Better to be chokt with English hemp,
Then poisoned with Indian Tabacco."

Several historians of Virginia, who seem to me to be ever prone to go even out of their way to give King James a rap, have insinuated that " A Counterblast to Tobacco," by that king, was written against Virginia tobacco ; but this tract was published in 1604, even before any colony was planted in Virginia.

[MEM. — " November 17th 1615, began the drawing of the second great Lottery for Virginia, at the West end of Saint Paules church." — Howes' Abridgement.]

CCCLI. EAST INDIA COMPANY TO THE LORD MAYOR.

From Remembrancia, City of London (1579–1664), Analytical Index, pp. 290, 291.

" A Letter from the Governor and Assistants of the East India Company to the Lord Mayor of London, stating that the Court of Aldermen had been pleased, in the 27. Elizabeth, to bestow upon Captain John Martyn the next office or place that might fall void; since which the office of Judge of the sheriffs' Court, becoming void by the surrender of Mr. Morgan, had been given, during Captain Martyn's absence in Virginia, to Sir Edward Mosely, Knight, who held the next reversion. They prayed the Court to restore him [Martyn] to his ancient right according to his grant. [The names of the Governor and eight Assistants are appended.] " 11th December, 1615."

CCCLII. CAREW TO ROE.

LETTERS FROM CAREW TO ROE. CAMDEN SOCIETY, 1860, PAGE 27.

" There is nothinge this last sommer performed either by the Norwest or Northeast for the discoverye of the passage to the East Indies; I pray God that this next yere may have better successe. The plantation att Virginia and Bermuda sleepes, frome whence I can send your Lordship no relation. I thanke you for your letter from the Cape of Good Hope, and as you may, I pray you to lett me understand of your proceedinges in that eastern world. . . .

" Savoy, 24 Januarye 1615 " [O. S.].

[MEM. — Captain Daniel Tucker's commission as gov-

ernor of the Bermudas is dated February 15, 1616. See
the "Memorials of the Bermudas," by Lefroy.

March 6. " A Bill of Adventure of £12 10ˢ granted to
Mʳ Simon Codrington, being one share of land in Virginia."
— From the Records of the Virginia Company. This is the
first entry of the kind which I have found. In 1617, and
after, these shares began to acquire a value, and were frequently bought and sold.

March 19. " Sir Walter Raleghe is enlardged out of
the Tower, and is to go his journey to Guiana; but re-
maynes unpardoned untill his retourne; he left his mansion in the Tower the 19ᵗʰ day of this monethe " [March,
1616]. — Carew to Roe.]

CCCLIII. A BRIEF DECLARATION.

In 1885, while hunting for the tract, " State of the Colony and affaires in Virginia. London, 1616," which is
mentioned in the Ternaux Compans Catalogue, I received
the following note from a friend in England, which explains
itself : —

BRITISH MUSEUM, July 17, 1885.

. . . " With regard to the entry in the Ternaux Compans Catalogue, I have found in the Grenville Collection a
small tract of 8 pages; but the said tract is without title-
page.   There is a date of ' April 1616,' written upon page 1,
and the Museum authorities have queried the date [1616 ?].

" I believe this to be the work mentioned in the Ternaux
Catalogue.   Yours obediently,

" R. ENGLISH."

As it refers to " Nova Britannia " [LXVIII.] as having
been written " about seaven yeares before," and then speaks
of June 25 as in the future, I suppose it was written between February and June, 1616, probably in " April 1616."
Possibly the writer of this date got it from the title-page,
now lost.   The original in the Museum is the only one that
I know of.   It is a valuable official document.

" By His Maiesties Counseil for Virginia.

" A Briefe Declaration of the present state of things in
Virginia, and of a Division to be now made, of some part of
those Lands in our actuall possession, as well to all such as
have adventured their moneyes, as also to those that are
Planters there.

" When first it pleased God to move his Maiesties minde,
at the humble suit of sundry his loving subjects, to yeeld
unto them his gracious Priviledge for the Virginia Plantation, it was a thing seeming strange and doubtfull in the
eye of the World, that such and so few Vnder-takers should
enterprise a charge of that waight, as rather beseemed a
whole State and Commonwealth to take in hand. But such
was the successe of their sundry attempts, in the happy dis-
coverey of so goodly a Land, the Description of which, for
the excellencie of the climate and fertilitie thereof, had soone
obtayned to lay such an assured ground of future hope, in
the sence and understanding of all men rightly weighing it,
that not long after, their new Letters Patents, with more
ample priviledges granted by his Maiestie, were almost filled
with many hundred Names, both Honourable, and others of
all sorts, that gave their hands and consent to further and
uphold that honourable action.

" Vpon which encouragement of so many worthy Patrons,
the Companie very deeply engaged themselves, in sending
Men and Ships, Cattle, and all kinde of provisions, with
Governours and Captaines for peace and war, insomuch as
no earthly meanes seemed then wanting for the speedy reducing of that barbarous Nation, and savage people, to a
quiet Christian Common-wealth.

" But such was the will of Almighty God, as the world
well knoweth, that this great hope and preparation, by
many disasters on Sea and Land, too long to be here recited,
was in a manner cleane defeated, and there onely remained
a poore remnant of those Men and Women, Cattle and provisions, that escaped the danger and which are now remayning there to rayse and build up that intended Colonie.

" Which when those Gentlemen th' adventurers here saw, and that the expectance of so great a preparation brought nothing home but adverse successe and bad reports, they for the most part withdrew themselves, in despaire of the enterprize, and so gave it over, not enduring to repayre the ruines, nor to supply what themselves had underwritten, to discharge the deepe engagement, whereinto the Company was drawne by their encouragement.

" By whose Vnconstancie and irresolution, the hope of that Plantation, together with the lives of our people there, had then utterly perished, had not God's secret purpose beene more strongly fixed to uphold the same, by stirring up the mindes and undaunted spirits of a very small remnant of constant Adventurers, that with Sir Thomas Smith (their Treasurer and Governor from the beginning) in all that time of three yeares disaster, were never discouraged, nor withdrew themselves from weekly Courts and meetings, yeelding their purses, credit and Counseil, from time to time, to make new supplies, even beyond their proportion, to uphold the Plantation.

" Insomuch as by the favourable assistance of God, who in his owne wisdome doth oftentimes effect the greatest ends by weakest means, it is now come to passe, that our English Colonie there, subsisteth in a very good and prosperous condition : They sow and reape their Corne in sufficient proportion, without want or impeachment ; their Kine multiply already to some hundreds, their Swine to many thousands, their Goates and Poultry in great numbers, every man hath house and ground to his owne use, and now being able to maintaine themselves with food, they are also prepared and ready, once having the meanes, to set upon the Minerals, whereof there are many sorts ; as also to plant and how such severall Kindes of Seeds and Fruits, as may best befit the Soyle and Climate, to make the Land profitable to themselves and th' Adventurers.

" This being a true Relation of the present state and hope of things in Virginia, wee thought good in this short manner to mention it by the way, as well to give those worthy Governors in Virginia their deserved praise, for the unspeakable paines and hazzard which they have endured there, in framing the people and Plantation to so happy a forme, as also to withdraw the despayring thoughts of such old retyred Adventurers, that make no other reckoning, but whatsoever hath beene spent upon the name of Virginia to be lost and cast away; the special purpose of this our Publication, being to another end, which for the further satisfying of all reasonable minded, wee will now in few words deliver.

" It was published to the world, about seaven years since,[1] and the time is now expired, wherein wee promised to cause a Divident to be made of the Lands in Virginia, as well to every mans person that went himselfe to the Plantation, as to every particular man that had adventured his money.

" And in as much as we are now by the Natives liking and consent, in actuall possession of a great part of the Country, the other part not as yet freed from encumber of woods and trees, nor thoroughly survayed,[2] whereby to make a Divident of the whole: yet of that part which is now fit for Plantation, we intend, God willing to beginne a present Division by Lot to every man that hath already adventured his money or person, for every single share of twelve pounds tenne shillings, fifty Acres of Land, till further opportunitie will afford to divide the rest, which we doubt not will bring at least two hundred Acres to every single share.

" This Division is intended to be done by a new Governor with Commissioners and surveyers to be sent from hence to ioyne with others that are there already,[2] to give every man his Lot in due proportion, according to such indifferent [3] Directions as shall be given them in charge.

---

[1] This evidently refers to LXVIII., "Nova Britannia," February 18, 1609.

[2] The council evidently had surveys of the rivers and adjacent lands.

It was afterwards determined to send Captain Argall as the new governor.

[3] That is, impartial.

Charles Campbell, in his *History of Virginia* (edition 1860, p. 116), referring to Chalmers' *Introduction*, vol. i. p. 10, says : " The year of 1615 is remarkable in Virginia history for the first establishment of a fixed property

" And for as much as this course of sending a Governor with Commissioners and a Survayor, with Men, Ships, and sundry provisions, for fortifications and other occasions; as all men may conceive, cannot bee effected without great charge and expence to the Company; it is therefore thought requisite, and determined, that so many Adventurers as will partake of this first Divident, shall present their Names, with their number of shares, into a Booke remayning at Sir Thomas Smith's for that purpose, before the 25. of June next.

" And they shall also promise under their handes, to contribute to the said charge, the summe of twelve pounds ten shillings to be paid within one Moneth after subscription, whether his shares be more or lesse, except any man shall be pleased to adventure more, and for which twelve pound ten shillings (or more if hee will) he shall also have a further Divident of land in proportion, as for all other his monies formerly adventured.   But for such as are not able to lay downe present monie, if they shall desire favour, it is agreed for them, that the Treasurer may receive the one halfe of their said adventure in present money, after their underwriting, to furnish out the ships, and the other halfe at six moneths after that.

" And that no man may hereafter excuse himselfe by ignorance, nor taxe the Company for concealing their purpose, we declare to all men, that this present Division is to be onely in the Lands lying along the Kings River on both sides, and all about the new Townes erected; in which so many as shall give in their names as aforesaid, may have their parts, and those that will not, may at their pleasure forbeare till hereafter, to take their Lot upon the same tearmes in places more remote.

" The Names of all such as will partake of this Divident, shall be given in writing to the Commissioners before they

in the soil, fifty acres of land being granted by the company to every freeman in absolute right.   This salutary reform was brought about mainly by the influence of Sir Thomas Dale, one of the best of the early governors."

goe hence, at whose returne they shall bring with them a perfect Map and Description of the said lands and ground divided, that every man may see and know in what condition and where his land lyeth, that accordingly he may dispose thereof at his pleasure, eyther by going himselfe in person to possesse it, or by sending families to manure it for yearely rent, or for halfe the cleare profits as many others doe.

" And furthermore, every man's portion allotted to him, shall be confirmed as state of inheritance to him and his heyers for ever, with bounds and limits under the Companies Seale, to be holden of his Maiestie, as of his Manour of East Greenwich, in Socage Tenure, and not in Capite, according to his Maiesties gracious Letters Patents already granted to the Virginia Company in that behalfe.

" And notwithstanding, as we hope, the chiefe brunt and doubt of that Plantation is now overpast, whereof to their great charge and hazzard the old Adventurers have endured the most difficult part, and might therefore iustly appropriate this present Divident to themselves, yet at the motion and desire of many Gentlemen and others intending to be new-adventurers, it is resolved and granted by the Company, that all new-Adventurers, subscribing and performing the conditions before mentioned, for twelve pounds tenne shillings, or more, shall, partake in proportion as freely in this present Divident, and in any other priviledge and freedome in Virginia, as if with the Old Adventurers they had been partakers from the beginning.

" FINIS."

[MEM. — March 26, 1616. Robert Bileth, master, and William Baffin, pilot, sailed on Baffin's fifth voyage for the discovery of a passage to the Northwest. Eight ships sailed to the New England coast in the first half of 1616. Richard Vines was probably in command of one of these vessels. I believe that ships were sent to this coast from England each year during 1607–16, either by the Lon-

don Company of Virginia, Sir Francis Popham, Sir Ferdinando Gorges, the merchants of London or Bristol, or by
other Englishmen ; but the masters of these ships were generally not " given to writing," and the records of their
voyages are chiefly wanting.

CCCLIV. SMITH'S MAP OF NEW ENGLAND.

This map of New England, " observed and described by
Captayne John Smith," drawn by Robert Clerke, engraved
by Simon Pass and printed by George Low, was first issued,
I believe, with CCCLV. It was reviewed in its different
conditions by Mr. James Lenox and Mr. Charles Deane in
" Curiosities of American Literature," in " Norton's Literary
Gazette," March 15 and May 1, 1854.

I doubt if it was drawn from Smith's surveys (although
he says so). It does not retain any of the original names
given by the English, French, or Dutch discoverers, and I
believe that these old landmarks of Gosnold, Weymouth,
and others were suppressed by him, as their presence would
have invalidated his claim that the map was engraved from
an original survey made by himself in 1614, and that previous maps of the coast were of no value. I think it will
be readily seen that CLVIII. is equally as valuable as
CCCLIV., if not more so, for this region.

The maps with Smith's works, for cogent reasons, were
the only maps of the colonies engraved in England, thus
becoming public property, and the only authority in the
premises accessible to the public. The more valuable original maps, retaining the names given by the original discoverers, remained in manuscript in the hands of the lawful
guardians, and have never been accessible to the public.
Only three of these have been found, and they are now
given to the public for the first time. XLVI., LVII., and
CLVIII. will give an idea of the capacity of the surveyors,
and LVIII. will serve as an illustration of the capacity of
the draughtsmen employed by the managers of the American enterprises.

CCCLV. SMITH'S DESCRIPTION OF NEW ENGLAND.

" A Description of New England : Or the Observations, and discoveries, of Captain John Smith (Admirall of that Country) in the North of America, in the year of our Lord 1614 : with the successe of sixe ships that went the next yeare 1615 ; and the accidents befell him among the French men of warre : With the proofe of the present benefit this Countrey affords, whither this present yeare, 1616, eight voluntary ships are gone to make farther tryall.   At London Printed by Humfrey Lownes, for Robert Clerke ; and are to be sould at his house called the Lodge, in Chancery lane, over against Lincolnes Inne, 1616."

This tract was entered at Stationers' Hall for publication June 3, 1616, by Robert Clerke under the hands of Master Sanford and Master Lownes Warden.   At the end of the tract is printed : " At London printed the 18. of June, in the yeere of our Lord 1616."

An original of this tract is worth, in perfect condition, about $300.   It was reprinted by the Massachusetts Historical Society in 1837 ; by Peter Force, at Washington, in 1838, and it was again reprinted at Boston in 1865.   The tract is dedicated " to the High Hopeful Charles, Prince of Great Britaine," and there is a flavor of fun in the dressing somewhat similar to that which obtained with Coryat's crudities, brought out in 1611 under the patronage of Prince Henry, with panegyric poetry and high-flying dedications. Smith gravely tells Prince Charles, " In my discovery of Virginia, I presumed to call two nameless Headlands after my Soveraignes heires, Cape Henry and Cape Charles," when, in fact, Smith was a prisoner at that time.   He tells the Adventurers for New England, as to his being taken prisoner at sea in 1615, " that foure men of Warre, provided as they were had been sufficient to have taken Sampson, Hercules and Alexander the Great, no other way furnisht then I was."   But this peer of " Sampson, Hercules and Alexander the Great" overlooks the fact that his ship escaped, while he alone was taken. After this incident he seems to have been dubbed "Admiral" by the North Virginia Company; but they trusted him with no more ships.

The dedications offer his services to many people to do many things. The poetry lauds him to the skies, and yet it all results in nothing; no one employs him to do any of these things, and I think that his patrons were catering to his vanity, as was the case with the Coryat book.

[MEM. — Sir Thomas Dale sailed from Virginia on the Treasurer, and reached Plymouth on the last day of May, 1616. He reached London some time in June. What documents, letters, etc., were brought I do not know; but he brought a very interesting party of people, including our old friend Molina, Pocahontas, Rolfe, and others; he started with Lymbry, also, but had executed him on the way. Dale's time in Virginia is a wonderfully interesting period of our history.

There had been sent to Virginia from England about 1,650 persons. Dale left 205 officers and laborers, 81 farmers, and 65 women and children, "which in all amounteth to three hundred and fifty-one persons — a small number to advance so great a worke," says Rolfe. Probably about three hundred had returned to England at different times, and about 1,000 had died on the voyage or in Virginia. When Dale left, Captain Smaley was in command at Henrico, and Mr. William Wickham was minister there. Captain Yeardley at Bermuda Nether Hundred, and Mr. Alexander Whitaker, minister; Captain Madison at West and Sherley Hundred; Lieutenant Sharpe at Jamestown, and Mr. Richard Buck, minister; Captain George Webb at Kequoughtan, and Mr. William Mease (or Mays), minister there; and Lieutenant Cradock at Dale's Gift.

Dale sent the following letter from Plymouth, soon after he arrived there.]

CCCLVI[1]. DALE TO WINWOOD.

FROM STATE PAPER OFFICE, LONDON, ENGLAND.

Sir Thomas Dale to Sir Ralfe Wynwood.

" RYGHT HONOURABLE — having bin much bound unto you for many favours as yet not deserved by me because the occatyone hath not bin presented, wherby I myght testyfye my thankfullnes unto your honour, I shoud accont myself happye to embrase som subject to demonstrat my fayghtfull love & servyse unto you.

" May it please your honor to understand that I am by the myghtye power of the Allmyghty God, saufly retourned from the hardest taske that ever I undertooke & by the blessinge of God have with pour means left the Collonye in great prosperytye & pease contrarye to manye mens Exspectatyon. This ship hath brought hom exceedinge good tobaco, sasafrix pych, potashes Sturgyon & cavyarye & other such lyk commodytyes as yet that countrye yeldes. I shall with the greatest speed the Wynd wyll suffer me present myself unto you and gyve you full satysfactyon of thos parts. how benyfycyall this admyralble (*sic*) countrye wyll be for oure State I know you are not Ignorant of, both for the emtyinge of our full bodye & the mayntenance of our shipinge (all thinges nessysarye ther unto, beinge ther to be had) & that countrye being Inhabyted by his Majestyes subjects wyll put such a byt Into our ainchent enymyes [1] mouth as wyll curbe his hautynes of monarchie. I shall gyve your honor great encouragements that this Vergynia affords (at my aryvall) to spure us forwards to Inhabyt there If his Majestye wishes to posses one of the goodlyest & rychest kingdoms of the world, & Indeed so fytt for no state as ours. If yt shall please you honerable fathers of our State to thinke seryouslye one yt & his Majestye thorowly to undertake yt — The which I becheth the lord to grant of his Infynyt mersye & so I humblye commend my dutye &

---

[1] The Spaniard.

servyse unto your honour, from plemoth this 3. of June 1616.

"Youre honners to commaund.

"THOMAS DALE."

Indorsed: "To the right Ho^{ble} Sr Ralfe Wynwood K^t Principall Secretary to his Matie.

"Plymouth, 3° Junij 1616, from Sr Tho: Dale."

CCCLVI². CAPTAIN JOHN SMITH TO QUEEN ANNE.

The following letter was first published, I believe, in Smith's " General History " (pp. 121, 122), without date; but with these prefatory lines: —

" And before she [Pocahontas] arrived at London, Captaine Smith to deserve her former courtesies, made her qualities knowne to the Queene's most excellent Majestie and her Court, and writ a little booke to this effect to the Queene: An abstract whereof followeth."

It appears from the above that the " little booke " was sent to the Queen early in June, 1616; but the sending of it has been doubted. It stands on Smith's assertion very much as LXIV. does; neither were published by Purchas, and neither by Smith until 1624. Both are untrustworthy; but they are fair samples of Smith's " General History."

" To the most high and vertuous Princess, Queene Anne of Great Brittaine.

" Most admired Queene,

" The love I beare my God, my King and Countrie, hath so oft emboldened mee in the worst of extreme dangers, that now honestie doth constraine mee presume thus farre beyond myself, to present your Maiestie this short discourse: if ingratitude be a deadly poyson to all honest vertues, I must bee guiltie of that crime if I should omit any meanes to bee thankfull.

" So it is, That some ten yeares [1] agoe being in Virginia, and taken prisoner by the power of Powhatan [2] their chiefe King, I received from this great Salvage exceeding great courtesie, especially from his sonne Nantaquaus, the most manliest, comeliest, boldest spirit, I ever saw in a Salvage, and his sister Pocahontas, the Kings most deare and well-beloved daughter, being but a childe of twelve or thirteene yeeres [3] of age, whose compassionate pitifull heart, of my desperate estate, gave me much cause to respect her : I being the first christian this proud King and his grim attendants ever saw : and thus inthralled in their barbarous power, I cannot say I felt the least occasion of want that was in the power of those my mortall foes to prevent, notwithstanding al their threats.   After some six weeks [4] fatting amongst those Salvage Courtiers, at the minute of my execution, she hazarded the beating out of her owne braines [5] to save mine ; and not onely that, but so

A relation to Queene Anne, of Pocahontas.

---

[1] As Smith was taken prisoner in December, 1607, we would infer from this sentence that this letter was written about December, 1617, or nearly a year after the death of Pocahontas. I can readily understand why Smith's vanity made him "apropriate many deserts to himself which he never performed," and why his envy made him " stuff his relacyons with so many falseties and malycyous detractyons " of others ; but why he is nearly always inaccurate in his dates and periods of time has puzzled me greatly.   Correct dates are essential to history.

[2] He was taken by Opechancanough, chief of the Pamaunkeys.

[3] The time here referred to is December, 1607.   Smith has told us in LIV. that she was ten years old in May, 1608.

[4] This sentence is not trustworthy ; it begins with an untruth.   He was certainly not a prisoner over three weeks in all.

[5] This incident has been fully dis-

cussed.   It is one of the afterthoughts of Smith's *General History*.   Smith was a negative hero.   He praises himself and abuses his peers, which heroes are not wont to do.   He does not save women as heroes usually do ; but women save him, in every quarter of the globe, save Africa — Turk, Tartar, and Indian.   Why did he slight the negro ? He was as much a character of his time as Thomas Coryat and Artherus Severus Nonesuch O'Toole, and evidently afforded as much amusement to the poets and wits of the day.   His women incidents are thus taken off by Richard Brathwait : —

" Two greatest Shires of England did thee beare,
  Renowned Yorkshire, Gaunt-stild Lancashire ;
  But what 's all this ? even Earth, Sea, Heaven above,
Tragabigzanda, Callamata's love,
Deare Pocahontas, Madam Shanoi's too,
Who did what love with modesty could doe :
Record thy worth, thy birth, which as I live,
Even in thy reading such choice solace give,
As I could wish (such wishes would doe well)
Many such Smith's in this our Israel."

Brathwait was quite a famous poet.

prevailed with her father, that I was safely conducted to Jamestowne : where I found about eight and thirtie miserable poore and sicke creatures, to keepe possession of all those large territories of Virginia ;[1] such was the weaknesse of this poore commonwealth, as had the Salvages not fed us, we directly had starved. And this reliefe, most gracious Queene, was commonly brought us by this Lady Pocahontas.

"Notwithstanding all these passages, when inconstant Fortune turned our peace to warre, this tender Virgin would still not spare to dare to visit us, and by her our jarres have beene oft appeased, and our wants still supplyed; were it the policie of her father thus to imploy her, or the ordinance of God thus to make her his instrument, or her extraordi-narie affection to our Nation, I know not : but of this I am sure; when her father with the utmost of his policie and power, sought to surprize mee, having but eighteene[2] with mee, the darke night could not affright her from comming through the irkesome woods, and with watered eies gave me intelligence,[3] with her best advice to escape his furie; which had hee knowne, hee had surely slaine her.

He wrote *Drunken Barnaby's Four Journeys to the North of England,"* in which occur the often quoted lines : —

"To Banbury came I, O profane One!
Where I saw a puritane one
Hanging of his cat on Monday
For killing of a mouse on Sunday."

[1] It is true there were only from thirty-eight to forty-five Englishmen at Jamestown on the morning of January 2, 160⅞, when Smith returned ; but Ratcliffe, and not Smith, was in authority at the time. The account of this time in the *General History* is very misleading. Smith evidently feels the great weakness of his case, and sees the necessity of strengthening his position. He reached Jamestown in the morning, was arrested, tried and convicted, and his execution was only prevented by the arrival of Newport, with provisions, on the evening of the same day. Yet in his story he asserts that on his return he, "with the hazard of his life, with sakre falcon and musket shot" prevented the abandonment of the country; that he "layd those by the heeles" who brought charges against him ; that he had but thirty-eight men to keep that great country ; that once in every four or five days Pocahontas saved their lives by bringing in provisions, and that finally Newport arrived. The condemned prisoner of a single day presents himself to us as the Lord and Master of a week or more.

[2] There were thirty-eight English and four Dutchmen present. This Pocahontas incident is another afterthought of the *General History.* It is not in the account of this voyage in CCXLV.

[3] Another Pocahontas afterthought. Her name does not occur in the narrative of this event in CCXLV.

"James towne with her wild traine she as freely frequented, as her fathers habitation; and during the time of two or three yeeres, she next under God, was still the instrument to preserve this Colonie from death, famine and utter confusion; which if in those times, had once beene dissolved, Virginia might have line as it was at our first arrivall to this day.[1]

"Since then, this businesse having beene turned and varied by many accidents from that I left it at: it is most certaine, after a long and troublesome warre after my departure, betwixt her father and our Colonie; all which time shee was not heard of.

"About two yeeres after[2] shee herselfe was taken prisoner, being so detained neere two yeeres longer, the Colonie by that meanes was relieved, peace concluded; and at last rejecting her barbarous condition, was maried to an English gentleman, with whom at this present she is in England; the first Christian[3] ever of that Nation, the first Virginian ever spake English, or had a childe[4] in mariage by an Englishman; a matter surely, if my meaning bee truly considered and well understood, worthy a Princes understanding.

"Thus, most gracious Lady, I have related to your Maiestie, what at your best leasure our approved Histories will account you at large,[5] and done in the time of your Maiesties life; and however this might bee presented you from a

---

[1] The success of the movement for establishing English colonies in America never depended on John Smith or Pocahontas; but it seems evident that the managers of the enterprise valued the services of Pocahontas much more highly than they did those of Smith; and Smith himself was probably fully aware of this fact.

[2] Smith was sent from Virginia as a prisoner early in October, 1609. Pocahontas was taken in April, 1613; was converted, and afterwards married in April, 1614, one year after her capture.

[3] This may not have been very welcome news to Queen Anne; in fact the letter does not seem very appropriate to her, as her sympathies are said to have been with the Roman Catholics at this time.

[4] It has been asserted, on what authority, I know not, that the child was born in England. It was evidently born before this letter was written.

[5] The account at large referred to is in CCCXXVII.

more worthy pen, it cannot from a more honest heart, as yet
I never begged anything of the state, or any : [1] and it is my
want of abilitie and her exceeding desert; your birth, meanes
and authoritie; hir birth, vertue, want and simplicitie, doth
make mee thus bold, humbly to beseech your Maiestie to
take this knowledge of her, though it be from one so unworthy to be the reporter, as myselfe, her husbands estate
not being able to make her fit to attend your Maiestie.[2] The
most and least I can doe, is to tell you this, because none so
oft hath tried it as myselfe, and the rather being of so great
a spirit, however her stature : if she should not be well received, seeing this Kingdome may rightly have a Kingdome
by her meanes; her present love to us and christianitie
might turne to such scorne and furie, as to divert all this
good to the worst of evill : where finding so great a Queene
should doe her some honour more than she can imagine, for
being so kinde to your servants and subjects, would so rav-
ish her with content, as endeare her dearest bloud to effect
that, your Majestie and all the Kings honest subjects most
earnestly desire.

"And so I humbly kisse your gracious hands."

[1] Wingfield says he was an un-
licensed beggar in Ireland before he
went to Virginia, and evidently during
the last fifteen or twenty years of his
life, "he worked his self-asserted services in America for all that they were
worth," and not without some success.

[2] Her husband, John Rolfe, was of
a good family ; she was brought over
by, and was an object of great interest to, people of far greater influence
than Smith. The letter was superflu-
ous so far as the interests of Pocahontas were concerned, and the writer
seems to be well aware of this fact,
for although it is written ostensibly in
her interest, it does not lose sight of
the interest of Smith for a moment.
Charles Dudley Warner well says,
"Fortunate is the hero who links his
name romantically with that of a
woman." And this was Smith's forte ;
according to his account, "he was rescued and protected and felt reliefe
from that sex in his greatest dangers"
in nearly every quarter of the globe.

CCCLVII. CAREW TO ROE, JUNE, 1616.

FROM CAREW TO ROE, CAMDEN SOC. PUB. 1860, PAGE 36.

" Sir Thomas Dale retourned frome Virginia : he hathe brought divers men and women of that countrye to be educated here, and one Rolfe, who maried a daughter of Pohetan (the barbarous prince) called Pocahuntus, hathe brought his wife withe him into England. The worst of that plantation is past, for our men are well victualled by there owne industrie, but yett no proffit is retourned. In the Bermudas little good is to be expected ; they make some tobacco, but of other industrie, I heare nothinge. Since our plantation there the ratts are so multiplied, whereof that island was free, as that they destroyed whatsoever is planted."

CCCLVIII. CHAMBERLAIN TO CARLETON, JUNE 22, 1616.

FROM ENGLISH STATE PAPER OFFICE.

" Sir Frauncis Bacon has been sworn of the Counsaile and was in election by every man's account to be presently Lord Keeper ; but that rumor is since reasonablie cooled, and yt is saide he must tarrie the time till he may be Lord Chauncellor, for (as a Lady told the King) yt is to be doubted he will never be a goode keeper. . . .

" Sir Thomas Dale is arrived from Virginia and brought with him some ten or twelve old and younge of that Countrie, among whom the most remarquable person is Pocahuntas (daughter to Powatan a Kinge or cacique of that Countrie) married to one Rolfe an Englishman : I heare not of any other riches or matter of worth, but only some quantitie of Sassafras, tobacco, pitch and clapboord, things of no great value unles there were more plentie and neerer hand. All I can learne of yt is that the countrie is goode to live in yf yt were stored with people and might in time become commodious, but there is no present profit to be expected : but you may understand more by himself [Sir Thomas Dale] when he comes into those parts, which he pretends to do within a moneth or little more." . . .

CCCLIX. ROLFE'S RELATION TO JAMES I.

KIMBOLTON MANUSCRIPTS, NO. 208.

" A true relation of the State of Virginia at the time when Sir Thomas Dale left it in May, 1616." It is in the form of a letter from John Rolf to Sir Robert Rich. This is the same document which Rolf also sent " to the King's most Sacred Majestie." " It was carefully transcribed from the Royall MSS.," and was published in the " Southern Literary Messenger " for June, 1839 (vol. v. p. 401), from which it was copied into Maxwell's " Virginia Historical Register " for July, 1848, vol. i. No. iii. pp. 101–113. It is catalogued at the British Museum as " Royal MS. 18. A. XI. John Rolf's Relation."

It gives a brief review of the colony from the beginning, but is mainly devoted to giving the state of the colony in the spring of 1616.

[MEM. — Soon after the return of Dale in the summer of 1616, the company sent out " the first Magazin " in a small ship called the Susan.]

CCCLX. ABBOT'S GEOGRAPHY.

George Abbot, afterwards Archbishop of Canterbury, while master of University College, Oxford, wrote for his pupils, " A Briefe Description of the whole world," generally known as " Abbot's Geography." The first edition was published in 1599 ; the following is extracted from the fifth edition, 1620 (I have no other), but the matter was evidently written in 1616 or before, probably for the fourth edition, which issued, I believe in 1617. The second edition is dated 1600, and the third, 1608. The J. Carter-Brown

MARGARET RUSSELL-CLIFFORD
Countess of Cumberland

Library has a copy of the third edition. The book contains 172 unnumbered pages of nearly 350 words each. Numerous editions have been printed, and it is not a high-priced book.

It has never been reprinted in this country so far as I know. It is interesting, as showing what was taught in the schools of those days about the New World.

"A Briefe Description of the whole world. Wherein is particularly described all the Monarchies, Empires and Kingdomes of the same, with their Academies. Newly augmented and enlarged ; with their severall Titles and scituations thereunto adjoyning.

"At London, Printed for John Marriot, and are to be sold at his shop in Saint Dunston's Church Yard in Fleet-street. 1620." [Title page.]

From the chapter "Of America, or the new World."

· · · "Among other strange opinions, which they conceived of the Spaniards, this was one, that they were the sons of some God, and not borne of mortall seed, but sent downe from Heaven unto them ; and this conceit was the stronger in them, because at the first, in such conflicts as they had with them, they could kill few or none of them ; the reason whereof was, partly the Armour of the Spaniards, and partly the want of Iron and steele upon the Arrowes which the Americans did shoote : but they were not very long of that opinion, that they were immortal, but reformed their errour, both by seeing the dead corses of some of the Christians, and by trying an experiment upon some of them also : for they tooke of them, and put their heads under the water, and held them till they were choaked ; by which they knew them to be of the same nature as other men.

"Among other points which did shew the great ignorance and unlettered stupiditie of these Indians, this was one, that they could not conceive the force of writing of Letters ; in so much that when one Spaniard would send unto another, being distant in place, in India, with any pro-

vision, and would write a Letter by him, what the fellow
had received from him : The poore Indian would marvaile
how it should be possible that he to whom he came should
be able to know all things, which either himselfe brought,
or the sender directed : And thereupon divers of them did
thinke, that there was some kinde of Spirit in the Paper,
and marveilously stood in feare of such a thing as a Letter
was.

" This country yeeldeth great aboundance of strange
Hearbes, the like whereof are not to be found in other
parts of the world : as also some very rare Beasts." . . .

From the chapter " Of the parts of America towards the
North."

. . . " The French had built in Florida upon the river of
Mayo, where they were visited by our Sir John Hawkins, a
fort, which they called fort Carolin, and had reasonably
assured themselves for their defence against the natives :
but some malicious spirits amongst them fled to the Spaniards, with whom they returned againe into Florida to the
murther and overthrow of their owne countrimen. . . .

" After this departure of the Spaniards out of Florida,
brought thither by Ferdinando de Soto, who died in the
Country ; after the defeat of the French, and their revenge
againe taken on the Spaniards, the King of Spaine sent
thither some small forces to take possession of the Country,
and set downe there ; for no other end as it is thought, but
to keepe out other nations from entring there ; the one
halfe whereof set downe on the River of Saint Augustine,
and the other halfe a dozen leagues from thence to the
Northward, at a place by them called Saint Helena.

" In the yeare 1586, as Sir Francis Drake came coasting
along from Carthagena, a citie in the maine land, to which
he put over, and tooke it after he departed from Sancto
Domingo, when the mortality that was amongst our English
had made them to give over their enterprise, to goe with
Nombre de Dios, and so overland to Pannania, there to
have stricken the stroake for the treasure ; as he was on

the coost of Florida, in the height of 30. our men described on the shore a place built like a Beacon, which was made for men to discover to Seaward : so comming to the shore, they marched along the Rivers side, till they came to a fort built all of whole trees, which the Spaniards called the Fort of Saint John, where the King entertained halfe his forces that he then had in that Country, which were an hundred and fiftie souldiers : the like number being at Saint Helena, all of them under the Government of Petro Melendez, Nephew to the Admirall Melendez, that a fifteene or sixteene yeares before had beene to-bring with our English in the bay of Mexico;[1] this fort our English tooke, and not farre from thence the Towne also of Saint Augustine upon the same river, where resolving to undertake also the enterprise of Saint Helena; when they came to the havens mouth where they should enter, they durst not for the dangerous shols : wherefore they forsooke the place, coasting along to Virginia, where they tooke in Mr. Ralphe Lane and his Company, and so came into England, as you shall heare when we speake of Virginia.

" In these Northerne parts of America, but especially within the maine Continent, some have written (but how truely I cannot tell) that there is a Sea, which hath no entercourse at all with the Ocean : so that if there be any third place beside the Mare Caspium, and the Mare Mortuum in Palestina, which retaineth in itselfe great saltnesse and yet mingleth not with the other seas, it is in these Countries. . . .

" The Englishmen also, desirous by Navigation to adde something unto their owne Country, as before time they had travailed toward the farthest North-part of America; so lately finding that part which lieth betweene Florida and Nova Francia was not inhabited by any Christians, and was

[1] Was Admiral Pedro Menendez de Avilés in command of the Spanish fleet which made the attack on Captain John Hawkins in the Bay of Vera Cruz near the end of September, 1568 ? The reference must be to this event.

a Land fruitfull and fit to plant in : they sent thither two severall times, two severall Companies, as Colonies, to inhabit that part, which in remembrance of the Virginity of their Queene, they called Virginia.   But this voyage being enterprised upon by private men, and being not throughly followed by the State, the possession of this Virginia, for that time was discontinued, and the Country left to the old inhabitants.

"There were some English people, who after they had understood the calmnes of the Climate, and goodnes of the Soyle, did upon the instigation of some Gentlemen of England, voluntarily offer themselves, even with their wives and children, to goe into those parts to inhabite ; but when the most of them came there (upon some occasions) they returned home againe the first time, which caused that the second yeare, there was a great company transported thither, who were provided of many necessaries, and continued there over a whole winter, under the guiding of M. Lane : but not finding any sustenance in the Country (which could well brooke with their nature, and being too meanely provided of Corne and victuals from England) they had like to have perished with famine ; and therefore thought themselves happy when Sir Francis Drake, comming that way from the Westerne Indies, would take them into his ships, and bring them home into their native Country.   Yet some there were of those English, which being left behinde, ranged up & down the Country (and hovering about the Sea Coast) made meanes at last (after their enduring much misery) by some Christian ships to be brought back againe into England.

"While they were there inhabiting there were some children borne, and baptized in those parts, and they might well have endured the Country, if they might have had such strength as to keepe off the inhabitants from troubling them in tilling the ground, and reaping such corne as they would have sowed.

"Againe in the daies of our now raigning soveraigne,

in the yeare of our Lord 1606. the English planted themselves in Virginia, under the degrees 37. 38. 39. where they
doe to this day continue, and have built three Townes and
forts, as namely James-towne and Henrico; fort Henricke,
and fort Charles, with others, which they hold and inhabite;
sure retreats for them against the force of the natives, and
reasonable secured places against any power that may come
against them by Sea.

"In the same height, but a good distance from the coast
of Virginia, lyeth the Iland called by the Spaniards, La
Bermuda, but by our English the Summer Ilands, which of
late is inhabited also by our Countrimen.

"North-ward from them on the Sea Coast, lieth Norumbega, which is the South part of that which the Frenchmen
did, without disturbance of any Christian, for a time possesse. For the French-men did discover a large part of
America, toward the circle Articke, and did build there
some Townes, & named it of their own country Nova Francia." . . .

Abbot then refers to the voyages of Frobisher to the
Northwest, to Newfoundland fish, Sir Francis Drake in Nova
Albion, etc. The two chapters on America, from which I
have made the foregoing extracts, contain a total of 9,000
words.

[MEM. — There are some remarks on "Foreign Plantations and Colonies" in Bacon's Advice to Viscount Villiers,
which was probably first written in the summer of 1616, but
I do not think it necessary to give them herein, as they have
been frequently printed, and as Bacon's ideas in the premises will be found given at greater length in CCCLXIII.]

ILLUSTRATIVE DOCUMENTS.

THE following documents (CCCLXI. to CCCLXV.) were written after the special period of which we treat; but they are given for several special reasons.

CCCLXI. HIS MAJESTY'S COUNCIL FOR THE VIRGINIA COMPANY.

FROM DUKE OF MANCHESTER RECORDS. KIMBOLTON MANU-SCRIPTS, NO. 288.

A part of this document really belongs to this period, and a part to a little later time; but it seems best to give the whole of it, rather than an extract; especially as the men were members of the company before 1617.

The names from the Earl of Bath to George Thorpe were probably added to the council during 1613–16; from Tufton to Greenewell, during 1617–18; and the remainder were probably appointed under the Warwick-Sandys agreement in the spring of 1619.

" The names of such as have bin chosen to be of his Majesties Councell for Virginia since the date of the third Pattent —

William [Bourchier] Earle of Bathe.
Sir Robert Phillips, Knight.
Sir John Davers, Knight.
Sir Lionell Cranfield Knight.
Sir Anthoine Aucher.
John Wroth Esquier.
Richard Chamberlaine, merchant.
Robert Johnson, merchant.
George Thorpe.
Sir Nicholas Tufton, Knight.

James [Hay] Lord Viscount Doncaster.
Sir Henry Rainsford.
Sir Francis Egioke.
Captaine George Yardely.
Mr. Morris Abbot, merchant.
Mr. Robert Offley, merchant.
Sir Edward Harwood.
Mr. William Greenewell merchant.
Robert [Rich] Earle of Warwicke.
Sir Thomas Cheeke.
Sir Nathaniel Rich.
John Farrar, merchant.
Captaine Nathaniel Butler.
Robert Heath, Esquier, Recorder of the Citie of London.
Thomas Gibbe Esquier."

CCCLXII. BROADSIDE BY THE VIRGINIA COUNCIL.

This is one of the documents preserved by Mr. John Smith of Nibley. Mr. Charles H. Kalbfleisch of New York has an original, and I know of no other.

Its exact date is uncertain; but it was written some time in the winter of 1616–17 probably, after the period we are specially treating; but as it has never been printed in this country, and as it is really illustrative of Dale's government, I have concluded to give it.

" By his Majesties Councell for Virginia.

" Whereas upon the returne of Sir *Thomas Dale* Knight, (Marshall of *Virginia*) the Treasurer, Councell and Company of the same, have beene throughly informed and assured of the good estat of that Colony, and how by the blessing of God and good government, there is great plentie and increase of Corne, Cattell, Goates, Swine, and such other provisions, necessary for the life and sustenance of man ; And that there wants nothing for the setling of that Christian Plantation, but more hands to gather and returne those commodities which may bring profit to the Adventurers, and encouragement to others : And whereas thereupon the Company hath given a commission to Captaine *Samuel Argol* to be the present Governour of that Colonie, who hath undertaken to transport and carry thither a certain number of men, upon his owne charge, and the charge of other his friends[1] that joyne with him in that Voyage; in which divers men of good qualitie have resolved to adventure, and to goe thither themselves in person, and to carry with them their wives, their children and their families, whereby in short time (by the favour and assistance of Almighty God) that good worke may be brought to good perfection, by the division and setting out of lands to every particular person, the setling of trade, and returne of Commodities to the contentment and satisfaction of all Well affected Subjects, which eyther love the advancement of Religion, or the honour and welfare of this kingdome: *Wee* his Majesties Treasurer, Councell and Company for the same Plantation, have thought good to declare and make knowne to all men by these presents, that wee have resolved to give free leave and license to any who are now remaining in *Virginia*, at his will and pleasure to returne home into *England*, which liberty wee doe likewise grant and confirme unto all those which hereafter from time to time shall goe thither in person, without any other restraint, then to aske leave of the Governour (for the time being) to depart. *And* therefore if any man be disposed to send any supply to his friends there, or to send for any of his friends from thence, he may hereby take notice, that he hath full power and meanes to doe eyther of them at his good descretion.

" God save the King."

---

[1] Among these was his brother, John Argall, Esq. See sketches of Sir William Lovelace and of Captain Raphe Hamor.

CCCLXIII. BACON'S ESSAY OF PLANTATIONS.

This essay bears internal evidence of having been revised for publication between 1620 and 1624; but I believe it to have been first written at an earlier date.

I give it as an illustrative document, and because I think it will be interesting to compare Lord Bacon's essay with the Broadsides of His Majesty's Council for the Virginia Company, of which Lord Bacon was a member.

" Of Plantations.

" Plantations are amongst ancient, primitive, and heroical works. When the World was young it begat more children; but now it is old, it begets fewer, for I may justly account new plantations to be the children of former kingdoms. I like a plantation in a pure soil; that is, where people are not displanted, to the end to plant in others; for else it is rather an extirpation than a plantation. Planting of countries is like planting of Woods; for you must make account to lose almost twenty years' profit, and expect your recompense in the end: for the principal thing that hath been the destruction of most plantations, has been the base and hasty drawing of profit in the first years. It is true, speedy profit is not to be neglected, as far as may stand with the good of the plantation, but no farther. It is a shameful and unblessed thing to take the scum of people and wicked and condemned men, to be the people with whom you plant; and not only so, but it spoileth the plantation; for they will ever live like rogues, and not fall to work, but be lazy, and do mischief, and spend victuals, and be quickly weary, and then certify over to their country to the discredit of the plantation. The people wherewith you plant ought to be gardeners, ploughmen, laborers, smiths, carpenters, joiners, fishermen, fowlers, with some few apothecaries, surgeons, cooks and bakers. In a country of plantation first look about what kind of victual the country yields of itself to hand: as chesnuts, walnuts, pine-apples, olives, dates, plums cherries, wild honey, and the like; and make use of them. Then consider what victual, or esculent things there are, which grow speedily, and within the year; as parsnips, carrots, turnips, onions, radish, artichokes of Jerusalem, maize and the like: for wheat, barley, and oats, they ask to much labor; but with peas and beans you may begin, both because they ask less labor, and because they serve for meat as well as for bread; and of rice likewise cometh a great increase, and it is a kind of meat. Above all there ought to be brought store of biscuit, oatmeal, flour, meal, and the like, in the beginning, till bread may be had. For beasts or birds, take chiefly such as are least subject to diseases and multiply fastest; as swine, goats, cocks, hens, turkeys, geese, house-dogs, and the like. The victual in plantation ought to be expended almost as in a besieged town; that is with certain allowance; and let the main part of the ground employed to gardens or corn, be to a common stock; and to be laid in, and stored up, and then delivered out in proportion; besides some spots of ground that any particular person will manure for his own private use. Consider, likewise, what commodities the soil where the plantation is doth naturally yield, that they may some way help to defray the charge of the plantation; so it be not, as was said, to the untimely prejudice of the main business as it hath fared with tobacco in Virginia. Wood commonly aboundeth but too much; and therefore timber is fit to be one. If there be iron ore, and streams whereupon to set the mills, iron is a brave commodity where wood aboundeth. Making of bay-salt, if the climate be proper for it, would be put in experience: growing silk, likewise, if any be, is a likely commodity: pitch and tar, where store of firs and pines are, will not fail; so drugs and sweet woods, where they are, cannot but yield great profit: soap-ashes, likewise, and other things that may be thought of; but moil not too much under ground, for the hope of mines is very uncertain, and useth to make the planters lazy in other things.

EDWARD SACKVILLE

Fourth Earl of Dorset

" For government, let it be in the hands of one, assisted with some counsel; and let them have commission to exercise martial laws, with some limitation; and above all, let men make that profit of being in the wilderness, as they have God always and his service before their eyes: let not the government of the plantation depend upon too many counsellers and undertakers in the country that planteth, but upon a temperate number: and let those be rather noblemen and gentlemen, than merchants; for they look ever to the present gain.

" Let there be freedoms from custom, till the plantation be of strength: and not only freedom from custom, but freedom to carry their commodities where they make their best of them except there be some special cause of caution. Cram not in people, by sending too fast company after company; but rather hearken how they waste, and send supplies proportionably; but so as the number may live well in the plantation, and not by surcharge be in penury. It hath been a great endangering to the health of some plantations, that they have built along the sea and rivers, in marish and unwholesome grounds: therefore though you begin there, to avoid carriage and other like discommodities, yet built still rather upwards from the streams, than along. It concerneth likewise the health of the plantation, that they have good store of salt with them, that they may use it in their victuals when it shall be necessary. If you plant where savages are, do not only entertain them with trifles and gingles, but use them justly and graciously, with sufficient guard nevertheless; and do not win their favor by helping them to invade their enemies, but for their defense it is not amiss; and send oft of them over to the country that plants, that they may see a better condition than their own, and commend it when they return.

" When the plantation grows to strength, then it is time to plant with women as well as with men; that the plantation may spread into generations, and not be ever pieced from without.

" It is the sinfullest thing in the world to forsake or destitute a plantation once in forwardness; for, besides the dishonor, it is the guiltiness of blood of many commiserable persons."

CCCLXIV. MEMBERS OF PARLIAMENT IN VIRGINIA COMPANY.

KIMBOLTON MANUSCRIPTS, NO. 371.

Indorsed: " The names of such as are of the Comons house free of the Virginia Company, by Mr Farrar."

In the Duke of Manchester Records, Kimbolton MSS., the following is placed under the questioned or uncertain date, " [May 1623 ?]." The members all belong to the Parliament (February 12, 1624 – March 27, 1625), and the list was probably compiled in April, 1624, when " the Virginia question" was before the House. The list contains forty-nine names. All of them are not in the second and third charters; but *they were all either members of the Company before 1616, or were the heirs of members.* (About 150 persons joined the company between March, 1612, and July, 1616, who are not named in the foregoing documents.) I can identify seventy-five members of the Parliament of 1624–25, as being members, also, of the Virginia Company; but probably there were others.

This list will give an approximate idea as to the position held by the M. P.'s in the disputes of 1623–24 in the Virginia Company.

" The names of divers Knights, Cittizens and Burgesses of the Lower house of Commons that are Adventurers and free of the Virginia Company and yet have not had nor followde the buissiness for Sundry yeares.

Sir William Fleetwood.	Sir Jhon Stradlyng.
Sir Thomas Denton.	Sir Baptist Hicks.
Sir Charles Barkly.	Sir Arthur Ingram.
Mr James Bag.	M^r [Richard] Leveson.
Sir Jhon Walter.	Mr Thomas Bonde.

Sir George Moore.
Sir Jhon Cutts.
Sir Edmond Bowyer.
Sir Henry Fane.
Mr Delbridge.
Sir Thomas Jermin.
Sir James Perrott.
Mr John Drake.
Mr [Richard] Dyott.
Sir Oliver Cromwell.
Mr [Richard] Knightly.
Sir Robert Cotton.
Mr [John] Selden.
Sir George Calvert.
Sir Edward Conway.
Sir Edward Cecill.
Sir Robert Heath.
Mr Jhon Arundell.
Sir Nicholas Tufton.
Sir George Goring.

Mr Robert Bateman.
Mr Martyn Bonde.
Sir Thomas Midleton.
Sir Robert Mansfeild.
Sir Dudley Digges.
Sir Humfry May.
Sir Jhon Ratcliffe.
Mr George Garrett.
Sir Henadge Fynch.
Mr Edward Spencer.
Sir Phillip Cary.
[James] Lord Wriothsly.
Mr Jhon Moore.
Mr Morrice Abbott.
Sir Jhon Scudamor.
Sir Arthur Mannering.
Sir Jhon Saint Jhon.
Mr [Thomas] Sherwell.
Sir Thomas Grantharm.

" With divers others which wee cannot uppon a sudden sett downe."

CCCLXV. LIST OF ADDITIONAL MEMBERS OF THE VIRGINIA COMPANIES.

I am anxious to give as complete a list as possible of the leading men who were interested in the American enterprise during 1606–16, and to those mentioned in the foregoing documents I am enabled to add from various sources of a later date the following : —

John Argall, Esq.
Richard Ashcroft.
Ambrose Austen.
Thomas Baker.
Richard Ball.
John Bland.
Capt. George Bargrave or Bargar.
Capt. John Bargrave.
Charles Becke.
Charles Berkeley.
Richard Berkeley, Esq.
Wm. Bing.
Richard Blackmore.
Edward Blunt.
Richard Blunt.

Thomas Bond, Esq.
Henry Briggs.
Richard Briggs.
Capt. John Brough.
Matthew Brownrig.
Minion Burrell.
Sir Richard Bulkeley.
Abraham Carpenter.
Sir Henry Cary, Captaine.
Sir Philip Cary.
Robert Chamberlaine.
Dr. Laurence Chatterton or Chaderton.
Wm. Chester.
Simon Codrington.
Edmond Colby.

Thomas Colthurst.
Sir Robert Cotton.
Robert Creswell.
Wm. Crowe.
George Chudley or Chudleigh.
Abraham Cullimore Colmer or Culliner.
James Cullimore.
Rowley (Ralegh ?) Dausey or Dawsey.
Clement Daubney or Dabney.
Richard Dichfield.
Sara Draper.
Wm. Essington.
John Exton.
John Farrar or Ferrer.
John Fenner.
Sir Heneadge Finch or Fynch.
David Floyd or Lloyd.
Thomas Francis.
Nicholas Fuller.
Richard Gardiner.
Sir Edward Giles.
Edward, Lord Gorges.
Sir Ferdinando Gorges.
Ralph Gore.
Sir George Goring.
Dr. Theodore Goulston, or Gulston.
Thomas Hackshawe.
John Haiward.
George Hanger.
Robert Harley.
Sir Percival Hart.
George Harrison.
John Harrison, gent.
Peter Heightley.
Edward Herbert, Esq.
Gregory Herst.
William Hicks.
William Holland.
William Houlden.
Thomas Howard, Earl of Arundell.
George Isham.
Gabriel Jacques.
James Jewell.
Walter Jobson.
William Jobson.
Edward Johnson.
Samuel Jordan.
Henry Kent.
John Landman.

Wm. Laurence.
Francis Lodge.
Peter Lodge.
Thomas Maddox.
Sir Henry Mannering or Manwaring.
Christopher Martin.
George Mason.
Francis Middleton.
Sir Henry Mildmay.
Capt. Henry Moles or Meoles.
Philip Molex or Mutes.
Nicholas Moone.
Thomas Norton.
Francis Oliver.
John Payne.
Abraham Peirsey or Percy.
Allen Percy.
Thomas Philips.
Henry Philpot.
Sir Francis Popham.
Robert Pory.
Nicholas Purefoy.
Nicholas Rainton.
Humfrey Reynell.
Richard Robins.
Henry Rolfe.
Edward Rotheram.
Stephen Sad.
Sir John Scudamore.
Walter Shelley.
Nicholas Sherwell.
Thomas Sherwell.
Jonathan Smith.
Sir Wm. Smith of London.
Edward Spencer.
Thomas Stacy.
Thomas Stokes.
George Stone.
Sir Martin Stuteville.
William Tracy.
John Tradescant.
Peter Van Lore.
Capt. Alphonsus Van Medkerke.
Edward Waters.
William Ward.
John West, Esq.
Nathaniel West, Esq.
Capt. William West.
Garret Weston.
Capt. Richard Whitbourne.

John White, Esq.   Sir Richard Worsley.
David Wiffin.   Samuel Wrote, Esq.
Wm. Willet.   Sir Thomas Wroth.
Wm. Williamson.   John Zouch, Esq.
Dr. Thomas Winston.   Sir Edward Zouch, Kn't Marshall.

I have not attempted to give the names of those who were employed in the service on wages, unless they were employed in positions of responsibility. Many were sent as sailors, soldiers, servants, and some as planters, whose names are not given. I have a great many of these names, and I know something of interest regarding some of them; but the great mass of the names not given in this work are of those of whom we have now no means of ascertaining anything, — the great unknown.

Virginia was now regarded as a settled plantation; England had placed a check on " Phillipps ambitious growinge;" she had put " a byt into her ainchent enymyes mouth;" she had secured a firm hold on the strategical position afforded by James River, " which in the time of a warre with Spaine would be a commoditie to our Realme, and a great annoyance to our enemies;" Englishmen were already looking for a good place in which to plant another colony on this continent; the destiny of North America was in the hands of the Anglo-Saxon. So let it be.

BRIEF BIOGRAPHIES

OF

PERSONS CONNECTED WITH THE FOUNDING OF VIRGINIA.

BIOGRAPHY throws so much light on History, that I doubt if any history can be clearly understood without a fair knowledge of the biography of the makers of that history. When we know something of the lives, characters, social position, and public surroundings of those engaged in an enterprise, we are then prepared to form a more correct idea of the character of the enterprise itself. Therefore I have made special effort to compile brief biographies of those who were especially interested in the movement for planting English colonies in America, and to illustrate the biography with a portrait; since "it is impossible for me to conceive a work which ought to be more interesting to the present age than that which exhibits before our eyes our fathers as they lived, accompanied with such memorials of their lives and characters as enable us to compare their persons and countenances with their sentiments and actions." [1]

While I have been unable to give sketches and portraits of many, I believe that I have identified a sufficient number to illustrate the character of the whole body.

The leading agents in the grand movement, which resulted in our present existence, were among the most prominent actors in one of the most interesting and remarkable transition periods in British history — the time of the translation of the Bible; the time of Shakespeare, Lord Bacon, Cecil, Ralegh, Ben Jonson, and their contemporaries. It was at this time that the contest between the people, through their representatives, and the Crown began; and it is interesting to note what a large number of members of the House of Commons were interested in the American enterprises. The founders of Virginia were the architects of Great Britain's greatness in colonies and commerce. Their records of

[1] Sir Walter Scott to the Publisher of Lodge's Portraits.

their actions, necessarily kept private at that time, are now nearly all missing; but, even if all were lost, knowing so many of those engaged therein as we now do, we would be prepared to form a tolerably correct opinion of the movement.

I have not found a list of the members of the North Virginia Company; but, after the failure to establish their colony in 1608, the Southern Company made an appeal to them to join that company and aid in taking hold of the remarkable strategic position afforded by James River, in the milder climate of Southern Virginia, and many of those named — especially those from the west and southwest parts of England — were certainly members of the Northern company. And after the colony in South Virginia was established many of the members of that company turned their attention to the northward. Of the forty-three first members of His Majesty's Council for New England, at least thirty had been instrumental in founding the colony on James River.

The special object of the biographies is to give information not found in the history, and therefore it frequently happens that the part taken by the subjects in the founding of Virginia — the most interesting part to us — is not mentioned at all in this portion of my work. These most interesting items will generally be found in the foregoing history, and the General Index will enable the reader to refer to them easily.

The biographies have been compiled from above five hundred volumes, and from a great number of manuscripts. In dealing with so many sources of information, of so varied a character, mistakes have been made sometimes no doubt; yet I have been as careful as possible. I have given nothing that is not based on what I believe to be trustworthy authority. I have tested every statement, and every date, that could be tested. I have not followed my authorities blindly. Of some, I have given about all that I know. Of others, volumes could be written.

Many of those named in the biographies, and entered in the index, are the originators of families, who are to-day largely represented in the United States, and our patriotic citizens should take as much pride in being " *of Founders' Kin,*" as is taken by Englishmen in tracing from *the Roll of Battle Abbey.*

DURATION OF PARLIAMENTS.

THE sittings of Parliament are sometimes given in my authorities under old style, and sometimes under new style dates, and are thus confusing. I have tried to give uniformly the new style year; but the following table will enable the reader to make the necessary correction, whenever I may have neglected doing so.

Elizabeth.		New Style.	Old Style.
1st.	23 January, 1559, to 8 May, 1559	[1559]	1558–9.
2d.	11 January, 1563, to 2 January, 1567	[1563–7]	1562–6.
3d.	2 April, 1571, to 29 May, 1571	[1571]	1571.
4th.	8 May, 1572, to 19 April, 1583	[1572–83]	1572–83.
5th.	23 November, 1584, to 14 September, 1585 . .	[1584–5]	1584–5.
6th.	15 October, 1586, to 23 March, 1587	[1586–7]	1586.
7th.	12 November, 1588, to 29 March, 1589 . . .	[1588–9]	1588–9.
8th.	19 February, 1593, to 10 April, 1593	[1593]	1592–3.
9th.	24 October, 1597, to 9 February, 1598 . . .	[1597–8]	1597.
10th.	27 October, 1601, to 19 December, 1601 . . .	[1601]	1601.
James.			
1st.	19 March, 1604, to 9 February, 1611	[1604–11]	1603–10.
2d.	5 April, 1614, to 7 June, 1614	[1614]	1614.
3d.	30 January, 1621, to 8 February, 1622 . . .	[1621–2]	1620–1.
4th.	12 February, 1624, to 27 March, 1625	[1624–5]	1623–5.
Charles.			
1st.	17 May, 1625, to 12 August, 1625	[1625]	1625.
2d.	6 February, 1626, to 15 June, 1626	[1626]	1625–6.
3d.	17 March, 1628, to 10 March, 1629	[1628–9]	1627–8.
4th.	13 April, 1640, to 5 May, 1640	[1640]	1640.
5th.	3 November, 1640, to 20 April, 1653 . . .	[1640–53]	1640–53.
	"The Long Parliament."		

EXPLANATIONS AND ABBREVIATIONS.

THERE was no fixed way for spelling many names at that time, and it is frequently impossible to give the correct spelling; but I sometimes give several of the different modes.

I have generally attempted to give the new style year, while the day of the month remains as I find it in the old records.

I have the list of paid-up Adventurers as published by the Sandys Administration in 1620, and also a manuscript copy of this list as prepared at that time by the Smythe Party. These generally agree; but whenever they differ, I have given the person the benefit of the doubt, and credited the largest amount. Where the original subscribers died before 1620, the payments must sometimes stand in the names of their heirs or assigns; and when this is the case, the heirs, etc., cannot always be identified by me. As I have only fragments of the subscription list, I am frequently unable to give the amount subscribed.

The figures, 1, 2, and 3, immediately after a name, indicate that the person was an incorporator of the 1st, 2d, or 3d Virginia Charter.

Sub. = subscribed, and is followed by the amount, whenever I have it.

Pd. = paid, followed by amount, when known.

£1 then = from $20 to $25 now.

E. I. Co. = East India Company.

Rus. Co. = Russia or Muscovy Company.

S. I. or B. I. Co. = Somers Islands or Bermudas Company.

N. W. P. Co. = North West Passage Company.

N. Fld. Co. = Newfoundland Company.

N. E. Co. = New England Company.

Va. Co. = Virginia Company.

M. C. for Va. = Member of His Majesty's Council for Virginia (34° to 45°).

M. C. for Va. Co. = Member of His Majesties' Council for Virginia Company of London.

M. P. = Member of Parliament.

Firſt Lord then EARLE (by BLOOD not by CREATION
Of BUCKHURST DORSET whiles heere on EARTHE belowe
From EARTHE to HEAUEN hath nowe remoud his ſtation
Where hee a peerleſſe Glorious SAINT doth ſhine
This was his SHADOWE will you his SUBSTANCE ſee,
YOU THEN muſt Paſſe the CLOWDES for there is hee.
are to be ſould by John Hind

RICHARD SACKVILLE
Third Earl of Dorset

BRIEF BIOGRAPHIES.

Abbay, Thomas. I find no trace of him save in CCXLIV. and CCXLV. He was not a member of the Va. Co. Was sent to Virginia by the company in September, 1608. If he was living in England in 1612, he may have returned without proper consent.

Abbot, George, 3. Sub. ——; pd. £75. Son of Maurice Abbot, clothworker of Guildford in Surrey, was born October 29, 1562 ; educated at the grammar school of Guildford ; entered Baliol College, 1578 ; B. A., 1582 ; M. A., 1585 : B. D., 1593 ; D. D., 1597, and the same year chosen Master of University College ; chaplain to Thomas Sackville, Lord Buckhurst; made Dean of Winchester, March 6, 1600 ; Vice-chancellor of the University of Oxford in 1600, in 1603, and in 1608 ; one of the first appointed translators of the New Testament in 1604 ; employed at the suggestion of George Hume, Earl of Dunbar, to negotiate a union between the churches of England and Scotland in 1608 ; wrote the Preface to Sir William Hart's " Examination, etc., of George Sprot " ; was appointed Dean of Glocester, 1609 ; Bishop of Coventry and Lichfield, December 3, 1609 ; Bishop of London, February 12, 1610, and Archbishop of Canterbury, March 4, 1611. Member of the N. W. P. Co., 1612. He kept an eye on Zuñiga when he was in England ; sat on Ralegh's trial, 1618 ; accidentally killed Lord Zouche's park-keeper July 24, 1621, for which he was tried by a commission of bishops and other lords, acquitted, pardoned November 22, 1621. " He was accused of Puritanism, but the favor and good opinion of King James was never withdrawn from him. He attended the king on his death-bed, and placed the crown on the head of his successor." (Lodge.)

As a result of his differences with Laud, he withdrew to Guildford in 1630 ; and afterwards to Croydon House, where he died August 4, 1633. His last words were, " In te speravi ; non confundebor in eterno." [In thee have I trusted ; I shall never be confounded.]

He founded an hospital in his native town and endowed it richly, and his monument is still preserved in Guildford Church. " His religious views had led him to form a definite foreign policy, of which the one aim was to crush Spain and to be wary of France." (S. L. Lee.)

Abbot, Morris, draper. Sub. £37 10s. ; pd. £50. Fifth son of Maurice Abbot of Guildford, in Surrey, and brother to George, Archbishop of Canterbury, and Robert, Bishop of Salisbury; was baptized at Trinity Church, Guildford, November 2, 1565. An incorporator of the E. I. Co. in 1600, and afterwards one of the directors of that company. An incorporator and director of the N. W. P. Co. in 1612 ; on the commission " to treat with the Hollanders concerning differences in the East Indies, and the fishery in Greenland," December 29, 1614 ; a member of the B. I. Co. in 1615 ; elected deputy governor of the E. I. Co., July 5, 1615, and again chosen to that office frequently thereafter. He was added to His Majesty's Council for the Va. Co. about 1618. Again on the commission to treat with the Hollanders, January 8, 1619. He was recommended by King James to the Va. Co. as a fit person for their treasurer in 1620, and again in 1622 ; M. P. for Hull in 1621–22 ; was one of the farmers of the customs ; elected governor of the E. I. Co., March 23, 1624 ; M. P. for Hull, 1624–25. On the commission for winding up the affairs of the Va. Co., July 15, 1624 ; was the first person knighted by King Charles at Whitehall, April 12, 1625 ; M. P. for Hull in 1625, and for London in 1626 ; was long an alderman of London from Bridge Without, and after from Coleman Street ward ; sheriff of London, 1627–28 ; M. P. for Hull, 1628–29 ; Lord Mayor of London, 1638. Died January 10, 1642. He was one of the leading men of affairs in his day, yet Mr. Stith, in his "History of Virginia," says, "As to Mr. Abbot, little is known of him, only that he was a merchant, and may seem from some obscure circumstances to have been of kin to his grace, Dr. George Abbott, then Archbishop of Canterbury."

He was a leading member of the Levant; Italian, French, Muscovy, East India, Northwest Passage, Somers Islands, and. Virginia companies. The English merchant service was largely under his control, and he was a constant advancer of English colonization and commerce. Sir Maurice Abbot married, first, Joan, daughter of George Austen, of Shalford, near Guildford, by whom he had five children. She died in the autumn of 1597, and he married, secondly, in the spring of 1598, Margaret, daughter of Bartholomew Barnes, an alderman of London. She died September 5, 1630.

Abdy, Anthony, clothworker, 3. Sub. ——; pd. £37 10s. "A lineal descendant of the Yorkshire House, entered into commercial pursuits, establishing himself in London." As he was an apprentice to Nicholas Pearde, clothworker, he must have been a member of that guild. He was the third son of Roger Abdy, citizen and merchant tailor of London, by his wife Mary, daughter of Richard White. Of the E. I. Co., 1609 ; of the B. I. Co., 1615 ; a director of the E. I. Co. from 1619; recommended by King James to the Va. Co. for treasurer in May, 1622 ; on the commission for the Va. Co.'s affairs, July 15, 1624 ; sheriff of London, 1630 ; alderman of London from Bridge Without ward from December, 1631 ; on the commission concerning tobacco, June 19, 1634. He died in September, 1640, and lies buried in St. Andrew Undershaft, Eald-

gate ward, London. By his wife Abigail, daughter of Sir Thomas Campbell, he had three sons, all of whom were created baronets.

Abergavenny, Lord. — Henry Neville.

Abot, Jeffra. Arrived in Virginia in January, 1608 ; he was executed by Sir Thomas Gates for mutiny in 1612.

Acland, Sir John, 3. Sub. £37 10s. ; pd. £12 10s. Of Columb-John in Broad Clyst, Devon ; M. P. for Saltash, 1586–87 ; knighted at the Tower, March 14, 1604 ; M. P. for Devon, 1607–11. Died in 1613 ; a benefactor of Exeter College, Oxford.

Acquaviva, Rev. Father Claude. Born at Atri, September 14, 1543 ; entered Society of Jesus, 1567 ; General of the Jesuits, 1581. Died January 31, 1615.

Acuña. See Gondomar.

Adams, Captain. Made a voyage to Virginia, June to November, 1609 ; a second voyage, April to September, 1610 ; a third, December, 1610, to July, 1611 ; a fourth, December, 1612, to July, 1613 ; and a fifth, October, 1613, to April, 1614. We ought to know more of him than we do, as he made so many of the early voyages. He was evidently a noted and well-known seaman in his own day, and this fact makes it the more difficult to identify him, as he is always spoken of simply as "Captain Adams ;" his first name is not given in the Virginia records. It is probable, however, that he is the Captain Robert Adams who entered the service of the E. I. Co. in 1616, and made several voyages to the East Indies.

Adams, Mr. Thomas, stationer ; pd. £10. Son of Thomas Adams, yeoman, of Neen Savage, Shropshire ; first apprenticed to Oliver Wilkes, stationer, on September 29, 1582, for seven years, and turned over to George Bishop on October 14, 1583, for the same period ; admitted a freeman of the Stationers' Company October 15, 1590, and came upon the livery July 1, 1598 ; younger warden in 1611 ; became warden in 1614, and died about 1620. A benefactor to his company.

Albert, Archduke. See Archduke.

Aldworth, Thomas, merchant of Bristol. Interested in Frobisher's voyages, 1576–78 ; mayor of Bristol in 1583. He was still living in October, 1593, when he gave Charles Lord Howard information regarding a " Carvell," called " The Tobacco Pipe."

Alexander VI. (Borgia.) Pope, August 11, 1492, to August, 1503.

Alexander, Sir William. Of Menstrie ; a celebrated poet ; had a grant of Nova Scotia, September 10, 1621 ; charter of the Lordship of Canada in America, February 2, 1628 ; Viscount Stirling, September 4, 1630 ; Earl of Stirling, Viscount Canada, and Lord Alexander of Tullibody, June 14, 1633. Died in 1640. (See the " House of Alexander," by C. Rogers, LL. D.)

Aliffe, Ayliffe, Ayloffe, Sir William, 3. Sub. —— ; pd. £50. Of Braxsted, Essex ; knighted at Charterhouse, May 11, 1603 ; created a baronet, November 25, 1612 ; M. P. Stockbridge, 1621–22. Title extinct.

Allde, Edward, stationer. Son of John Allde (" who was the first person on the registers to take up the freedom of the Stationers' Company, when in January, 1555, he paid the modest sum of 6s. 8d. for the customary breakfast to the brotherhood." H. R. Tedder) ; made free of the Company of Stationers by patrimony, February 18, 1583¾ ; chosen to go to " my lord Maiour's dynner," in 1611. Probably died in 1634.

Allen, Alleine, Alleyne, Edmund, gent., 3. Sub. £75 ; pd. £25. Of Hatfield, Peverill, Essex. Died in 1616.

Allen, Edward, fishmonger, 2. Sub. £37 10s. ; pd. £100. Also of East India and Northwest Passage companies. He contributed £62 10s. to the first voyages, and afterwards subscribed and paid £37 10s. more ; elected sheriff of London, July 3, 1620 ; chosen alderman of Breadstreet ward, November 7, 1620. Died in 1626.

Allen, John, fishmonger, 2. Sub. —— ; pd. £12 10s.

Allen, Thomas, grocer, 2. Sub. —— ; pd. £12 10s. Probably three of the name were members of the Grocers' Company at this time. One

was sworn to freedom in 1589 ; another in 1592, and a third in 1596.

Allington, Giles, gent., 3. Sub. —— ; pd. £25. Second son of Sir Giles Allington, by his wife Dorothy, daughter of Thomas Cecil, first Earl of Exeter. His elder brother died young, and Giles became his father's heir, and it is said, " was soon after knighted." " The prospects of this gentleman," says Lodge, in his " Life of Sir Julius Cæsar," " were clouded, and his revenues embarrassed, by an unfortunate marriage. . . . April 14, 1631, he was censured and fined in the Star Chamber Court £32,000, only for marrying the daughter of his sister by the half blood. . . . William, his only son, was on July 28, 1642, . . . created Baron Allington, of Killard, in Ireland." Sir Giles Allington is mentioned in the Fifth Report of Hist. MS. Com., as being alive in 1640 ; but the date of his death is not known to me. His marriage caused much of his family history to be excluded from the official pedigrees of the family, and therefore the data regarding him is meagre ; but I believe this identification to be correct. However, this may be the Lieutenant Giles Allington who patented lands in Virginia in 1624.

Amidas, Philip. Said to have been born at Hull, England, in 1550. Probably related to the Hawkins family. (See pedigree.) Owned lands in, and I think it probable that he was from, Cornwall. " Some time after 1586 he had charge of an expedition to Newfoundland." Early in 1609 a warrant was granted to John Shelbury for certain lands in Cornwall, purchased by Sir Walter Ralegh from Philip Amidas, and by Ralegh's attainder devolved to the crown. Amidas, or Amadas, died in 1618.

Andrews, John, the elder, Doctor of Cambridge, 2. Sub. —— ; pd. £25.

Andrews, John, the younger, of Cambridge, 2. Sub. —— ; pd. £25.

Andrews, Nicholas, " citizen and salter," 2. Sub. £37 10s. ; pd. £62 10s. Afterwards of Little Lever, County Lancaster ; married Heth, daughter of Thomas Lever, esquire. Their son, John Andrews, was a captain in Cromwell's army.

Anne of Denmark. — Anne Stuart.

Anthony, Charles, goldsmith, 2. Sub. £37 10s. ; pd. £137 10s. Also of N. W. P. Co. Second son of Derick Anthony, " chief graver of the mynt and seales to King Edward VI., Queen Mary, and Queen Elizabeth," by his wife Elizabeth, daughter of Richard Erley. He was the engraver for King James, Prince Henry, for the Mint, etc. He engraved the stamps for the East India moneys, and I am quite sure, engraved the seals for the Virginia companies. The celebrated Dr. Francis Anthony (1550–1623), who joined the Va. Co. in May, 1617, was, I believe, his elder brother. His sister Elizabeth married Richard Yardley, of London, fishmonger.

Apsley, Sir Allen. Born about 1569 : at Cadiz, 1596 ; knighted at Dublin, June 5, 1605 ; victualer to the navy about 1610 ; Lieutenant of the Tower, March 3, 1617 ; Member of the Council for New England in 1620. Died May 24, 1630.

Aquila, Don Juan de. Commander of the Spaniards at Kinsale, Ireland, 1601.

Archduke, The. Albert, Archduke of Austria, Cardinal and Archbishop of Toledo ; born 1559 ; sovereign of the Netherlands, May 6, 1598. Died July 13, 1621.

Archer (see Aucher), Captain Gabriel, 2. Sub. —— ; pd. ——. Of Mountnessing, Essex ; admitted to Gray's Inn as a student, March 15, 1593 ; but does not seem to have been called to the Bar. Recorder of Gosnold's voyage to our New England coast, 1602 ; first secretary or recorder of the first Colony of Virginia, where he died in the memorable winter of 1609–10. As his brother John was afterwards admitted into the Va. Co., and given a share of land in Virginia as his heir, it seems evident that Captain Gabriel left no children. Archer's Hope, on James River, was named for him, and he has the honor of having been much abused by Captain John Smith. He gave his life to the enterprise, and no one could do more. He was one of the first lawyers in Virginia.

Argall Pedigree. Thomas [1] Argall, of St. Faith-the-Virgin, London, esquire, to whom the Manor of Walthamstow (see Robert Thorne)

was granted in 1553, was an officer of court in 1559. He died in 1563. By his wife Margaret, daughter of John Tallakarne, of Cornwall (who remarried in June, 1564, Sir Giles Allington, of Horseheath, Cambridgeshire), he had five sons and one daughter, namely : Richard [2] (see hereafter), Lawrence,[2] John,[2] Rowland,[2] Gaberell,[2] and Anne.[2]

Anne [2] Argall married, first, Thomas Sisley, of Essex ; secondly, Augustine Steward, of London, esquire.

Richard [2] Argall, the eldest son, of East Sutton in County Kent, esquire, married twice ; the name of his first wife is not known to me. His second wife was Mary, daughter of Sir Reginald Scott (see Scott pedigree). He died in 1588, leaving five sons and six daughters living, by his second wife, namely : —

i. Thomas [3] Argall, who, with his brother Reginald,[3] were the witnesses to the challenge sent by Sir John Scott to Lord Willoughby, in April, 1590 ; which Thomas died in 1605, s. p.

ii. Reginald [3] Argall, of Lincoln's Inn, Middlesex, gent., married in 1599 Anne, widow of William Rowe (uncle to Sir Thomas Roe), of Walthamstow, County Essex, esquire, and daughter of John Cheney, esquire, of Chesham Boys in Buckinghamshire. This Reginald [3] was knighted at Hampton Court, August 17, 1606, and died prior to 1612, s. p.

iii. John [3] Argall, of Colchester.

iv. Richard [3] Argall. (i take this to be the person of the name "noted in the reign of James I. for an excellent divine poet.")

v. Samuel [3] Argall.

i. Elizabeth [3] Argall married Sir Edward Filmore, of East Sutton in Kent, knight.

ii. Margarett [3] Argall married Edmond Randolfe, of Aylesford in Kent, esquire.

iii. Mary [3] Argall married Raynold Kempe, of Wye in Kent, esquire.

iv. Catherine [3] Argall married Randolfe Bathurst, of Horton in Kent, esquire.

v. Jane [3] Argall married Paul

Flettewood, of Roshall in Lancashire, esquire.

vi. Sara[3] Argall, sixth daughter.

After the death of Richard[2] Argall in 1588, his widow (Sir Samuel
Argall's mother) married Laurence
Washington, of Maidstone, Kent,
esquire (his second wife), and died
in 1605. Mr. Washington, who
survived her, dying in 1619, was
register of the High Court of Chancery. He was the great uncle of the
Rev. Laurence Washington, whose
son John was the emigrant ancestor
of "the Father of his country."

The following monumental inscriptions from East Sutton Church are
illustrative of the foregoing pedigree.

" Richard Argall of East Sutton in
the County of Kent Esq., deceased
anno Dm[ni], 1588, leaving 5 sons and
6 daughters living. Mary his second
wife one of the daughters of Sir Reginald Scott of Scot's Hall, married the
second time to Laurence Washington
Esq., died in anno 1605. Thomas Argall eldest son of the said Richard and
Mary, died in anno 1605, whose souls,"
etc.

" Under this rest, in certain hope of
the resurrection of the bodies, Sir Edward Filmer and Dame Elizabeth his
wife, daughter of Richard Argall
Esq. They lived together 44 years
and had issue 18 children 9 sons and
9 daughters. He departed this life 2.
Nov. 1629. She the 9. Aug[t] 1638."

Their eldest son, Sir Robert Filmer, was a strong royalist, and a political writer of some note.

Argall, John, esquire. Of Colchester, Essex. (See pedigree.) He
was interested in Virginia prior to
1617 ; held four shares in Captain
Argall's plantation ; was M. C. for N.
E., November 3, 1620. He married
Sara, daughter of the celebrated scholar, Edward Grant, D. D., master of
Westminster School. At the visitation of 1634 he had four sons and two
daughters, was living at Much Bad-
dow, in Essex, and was one of the justices of the peace for the county.

Argall, Captain Samuel. (See
pedigree.) Was probably born about
1580–85. He was a young man in
1609 ; but, as he was selected to discover a shorter way to Virginia, he
must have been regarded as a mariner

of experience and ability, and I suppose that he had been to America before. He left England May 5, and
returned late in October, 1609, having made the discovery of a direct
way ; thus proving that the reliance
in his ability was not misplaced ; conducted Lord de la Warr to Virginia,
March, 1610 ; made a voyage to our
New England coast ; surveyed the
coast from Cape Cod to Virginia,
June 19 to September, 1610 (CXLI.)
(the beginning of the fishing voyages
sent to the northward from Virginia
every summer). Explored the Chesapeake Bay and the waters thereof
during the autumn and winter, and
sailed from Virginia with Lord de la
Warr March 28, reaching England in
June, 1611.

The Grace of God, with Father
Biard on board, on the way to Port
Royal in New France, was at Newport, Isle of Wight, in February, 1611.
(CLXVIII.) Louis XIII. of France
granted to Madame de Guercheville,
the Protectress of the Jesuit Missions,
all the territory of North America
from the St. Lawrence to Florida,
and she was sending her missionaries
to this region. The account of the
Spaniards in Virginia reached England late in October, 1611. Argall
sailed from England, July 23, 1612,
on the Treasurer, a well equipped
vessel, with a commission to remain in
Virginia, and to drive out foreign in-
truders from the country granted to
Englishmen, by the three patents of
James I. He was employed in the
various waters of Virginia from
September, 1612, to June, 1613.
(CCLXXV.) Soon after June 28,
1613, he sailed from Virginia on " his
fishing voyage, which I beseech God
of his mercy to blesse us," in a well-
armed English man-of-war ; destroyed
the colony of the Jesuits on Mount
Desert, within the bounds of Virginia ;
returned to Jamestown late in July, or
early in August, and was sent back
by Gates in about thirty days, with
orders to destroy the buildings and
fortifications at Mount Desert, St.
Croix, and Port Royal, which he did,
and got back to Jamestown about the
first of December, 1613. He is said
to have visited, while on this voyage,
the Dutch settlement on the Hudson,

and to have compelled the governor, Hendrick Christiansen, to submit to the crown of Great Britain. New England was reserved for the English by Argall's decisive action. The Bay of Fundy was sometime known as Argall's Bay. He was variously employed in Virginia from December, 1613, to June 18, 1614, when he sailed for England, arriving there in July. In November, 1614, he proposed to enter the service of the E. I. Co., but was retained by the Va. Co., and again sent to Virginia in February, 1615 ; returning with Dale in May, 1616.

Early in 1617 he was appointed deputy governor and admiral of Virginia, and soon after granted patents for a plantation. [See Sir William Lovelace.] Sailed for Virginia about the last of March, 1617, and returned to England in May, 1619. Certain charges were brought against him in August, 1618, and some time after this he was "vehemently complayned against" by Padre Maestro and Sanchez [see Gondomar] for piracy committed by the Treasurer on the King of Spain's subjects in the West Indies." On his return from Virginia in May, 1619, he answered these charges satisfactorily to some of the officers of the company ; but not so to others. From October, 1620, to the summer of 1621, he commanded the Golden Phenix, in the fleet under Sir Robert Mansell, in the Mediterranean Sea. About 1621 he proposed a settlement in that part of America called New Netherlands ; a member of His Majesty's Council for New England, probably before May, 1622. In the distribution of "the land of New England by lotts, Cape Cod, and into the Maine," fell to his lot ; knighted at Rochester, June 26, 1622 ; voted to surrender the Virginia charter, October 20, 1623. In April, 1624, he was proposed for governor of Virginia, but was defeated by Sir Francis Wyatt ; one of the commissioners for the Va. Co., July 15, 1624 ; on September 6, 1625, he sailed from Plymouth as admiral of twenty-four English and four Dutch ships ; and during the cruise took seven vessels, valued at £100,000 ; October to December, 1625, he commanded the flagship during the attack on Cadiz.

In 1633, Anne, daughter of Sir Samuel Argall, of Walthamstow in County Essex, was the wife of Alexander Bolling of London, scrivener, a grandson of Thomas Bolling, of Bolling Hall in Yorkshire. From the Visitation of London it seems that Sir Samuel was then alive ; and he probably died that year, as Strype says he was a benefactor of "The Trinity House, London," in 1633. However, he certainly died before June, 1641. His daughter Anne (widow of Bolling, who died in March, 1641), and her second husband, Samuel Percevall, on June 25, 1641, petitioned the House of Commons, complaining that they had been defrauded by John Woodhall of property in Virginia, left to petitioner Anne by her *late* father, Sir Samuel Argall, sometime governor of Virginia, etc.

Arundell, John, esquire, 3. Sub. £37 10s. ; pd. £25. "Jack for the King," grandson of Henry VIII.'s "Jack of Tilbury," and son of John Arundell, of Trerice. Born in 1576 ; M. P. for St. Michaels, 1597–98 ; for Cornwall, 1601, 1621–22 ; for St. Mawes, 1624–25 ; for Tregony, 1628–29, and 1640 ; appointed governor of Pendennis Castle about 1643. Clarendon tells the story of its five months' siege in 1646, and the gallant defense of old Sir John. The fall of Pendennis and the defeat of the king ruined his estates. He died between 1654 and 1656, and was buried at Duloe in Cornwall.

Arundell. The Lord of Wardour. Of N. W. P. Co. Sir Thomas Arundell of Wardour (1560–1640) was the son and heir of old Sir Matthew Arundell (on whose fringed cloak it once pleased Queen Elizabeth to spit), and the grandson of Sir John Arundell, the friend of Father Cornelius.

Elizabeth gave him an autograph Latin letter, said to be still preserved at Wardour Castle, recommending him to the service of the Emperor Rudolph II. as a brave knight and her kinsman. Serving with distinction as a volunteer in the imperial army in

Hungary, he took the standard of the Turks with his own hand, in an engagement at Gran or Estergom ; for which heroic achievement he was created by Rudolph II. a count of the Sacred Roman Empire. The patent of creation is dated at Prague, December 14, 1595. "March 13, 1596, Elizabeth wrote to Rudolph II., complaining of his having created Thomas Arundel a count of the Empire, and she has forbidden him to use the title." "She liked not for her sheep to wear a stranger's mark, nor to dance after a foreigner's whistle." "Augt. 15, 1596. The Emperor replies that he is surprised at the Queen's displeasure at his creating Thomas Arundel a count, and requests her to restore him to favor."

In March, 1605, his brother-in-law, Henry Wriothesley, Earl of Southampton, Sir Ferdinando Gorges, himself, and others sent out the expedition under Captain George Waymouth. Created Baron Arundell of Wardour, May 4, 1605. In the summer of 1605 he was levying a body of men in England for the service of the Archduke Albert, a younger brother of his old friend Rudolph II. Catesby, the gunpowder conspirator, "contrived that several of the officers should be appointed from amongst his friends, and entered into an understanding with them that they should be ready to return to England whenever .the Catholic cause required their assistance." "After the discovery of the Gunpowder Plot, all chance of a close alliance between England and Spain was for the present at an end. The knowledge that the English troops [under Arundell] in the service of the archduke had been intended by the conspirators to coöperate with them by invading England, induced James to refuse to allow any further levies to be made," (Gardiner's "Hist. of England.")

Lord Arundell married, first, Lady Maria Wriothesley, sister of Henry, Earl of Southampton. She is known as "our sweet Lady Arundell." He married, secondly, Anne, daughter of Miles Phillipson, Esq., and his daughter Anne (by the second marriage) married Cecil Calvert, second Baron Baltimore, the founder of Maryland.

Bishop Goodman says "the first Lord Baltimore was converted to the Church of Rome by Gondomar and Count Arundel."

Lord Arundell died in 1639-40.

Arundell, Earl of. — Thomas Howard.

Ashcroft, Richard, merchant. Sub. —— ; pd. £25. A friend of Dr. Poe, he was admitted into the E. I. Co. February 26, 1614. On the special commission concerning tobacco, April 7, 1620.

Ashley, Sir Anthony, 2. Sub. £37 10s. ; pd. £62 10s. Son of Anthony Ashley, of Damerham in the county of Wilts, by his wife Dorothy, daughter of John Lyte, of Lytes Carey in Somersetshire, born about 1551 ; entered the public services, it seems, about 1572-73, and became clerk of the council. He is said to have been "highly distinguished by the favor of Queen Elizabeth." In 1584 Lucas Janz Waghenaer published at Leyden in Holland the first known collection of sea charts for sailors. In 1585 Lord Charles Howard drew the attention of the Privy Council to the work, and they "esteemed it worthy to be translated and printed into a language familiar to all nations." The task was given to Anthony Ashley, and his translation appeared in 1588 as "The Mariner's Mirrour." I think it highly probable that he was aided in this translation by his brother, Robert Ashley (1565-1641), who was a translator of note.

Anthony Ashley was M. P. for Tavistock, November 12, 1588, to March 29, 1589. In 1589 he served in the Norris-Drake expedition. M. A., Oxford, September 27, 1592. 1596, secretary for war in the famous voyage to Cadiz, where he was knighted, and brought over the first account of the capture of Cadiz to her majesty. He had been pensioned by Queen Elizabeth, and in 1605 King James also pensioned him "in consideration of 33 years services." Created a baronet, July 3, 1622. Died January 13, 1628, and was buried at Wimborne, St. Giles, Dorset. He married twice ; first, Jane, relict of Thomas Cokaine, Esq., and daughter of Philip Okeover, Esq., by whom his only child, Anne Ashley, who married Sir John Cooper and became the mother of Sir Anthony Ashley Cooper, Earl of Shaftesbury, the celebrated statesman, a lord proprietor of Carolina, and one of the first governors of the Hudson Bay Company.

Sir Anthony Ashley married, secondly, in 1621–22 Philippa Sheldon (aged 19), a kinswoman to George Villiers, Duke of Buckingham. She married, secondly, Carew, only surviving son of Sir Walter Ralegh.

Ashley, Captain John, 5. Sub. ——; pd. ——. Probably the Captain Ashley who was at the taking of Saint Vincent and Puerto Bello near Panama, February 7, 1602.

Askew — Ascough — Ayscough, James, 2. Sub. £37 10s ; paid £37 10s. Married a daughter of Roger Clarke, alderman of London ; was admitted into the E. I. Co. in 1609.

Askwith, Robert, 3. Sub. £37 10s. ; pd. £37 10s. Alderman of York. Lord Mayor of York in 1617. Knighted at York, April 13, 1617. M. P. for York, 1576–83, 1604–11, 1614, and 1621–22.

Aspley, William, stationer. He dealt largely in plays, Shakespeare's, and others. Died August 18, 1640.

Asten — Aston — Austin, Ambrose. Paid £12 10s. Transferred his share in Virginia to Dr. Anthony, July 18, 1620.

Aston — Ashton, Sir Roger, 2. Pd. £10. A servant to King James, to his father, and grandfather ; for many years the messenger between Queen Elizabeth and King James. From 1587 he was gentleman of the bed-chamber to the king, the letters patent for which office were inclosed with him in his tomb. " He was dispatched to London after the queen's death to concert measures with the council for the reception of King James, and being asked by the lords how he did, replied, ' Even, my Lords, like a poor man who, having wandered above forty years in a wilderness and barren soil, is now arrived at the land of promise.' " Knighted at Grimston, April 18, 1603; made master of the great wardrobe in 1608 ; M. P. for Cheshire in 1610–11 ; died May 23, 1612. His first wife, Mary, daughter of Andrew Stewart, master of Ochiltree, was related to King James. She died in 1606. His second wife was Cordelia, daugh-

ter of Sir John Stanhope. His daughter Elizabeth married Sir Robert Wingfield, who was a member of the Va. Co. in 1619.

Aston — Ashton, Sir Walter, 3. Sub. ——; pd.——. Grandson of Sir Thomas Lucy, " Justice Shallow." Of Texall, Stafford ; born July 9, 1584. His father died in 1597, and he was placed under the wardship of Sir Edward Coke. Created a baronet, 1611 ; ambassador to Spain, 1620–25 ; created Lord Aston of Forfar in the Scottish peerage, November 28, 1627 ; ambassador to Spain, 1635–38 ; died August 13, 1639. (His cousin, Walter Aston, came to Virginia in 1628, and died there in 1656. His tomb is at Westover.)

Atkinson, Richard, clerk of Va. Co. in 1609. Son of Richard Atkinson, descended out of the North of England. His mother married, secondly, William Towerson, of London, merchant. He was for a long time cashier of the E. I. Co.

Atkinson, William, 2. Sub. ——; pd. £37 10s. " Counsellor of the Lawe dwelling sometime in ffoster lane London " ; great uncle of the above Richard. He was especially instrumental in arresting and prosecuting Papists, recusants, etc.

Aucher — Archer, Anthony, esquire, 2. Sub. —— ; pd.——. Sir Anthony Aucher, knight, of Otterden, *temp.* Henry VIII., had issue four sons, among whom John of Otterden (whose daughter married Sir Humphrey Gilbert), and Edward, who married Mabel, daughter of Sir Thomas Wrothe, and had Anthony (of whom I write), and Elizabeth who married Sir William Lovelace. Anthony Aucher, Esq., of Bishopsbourne, married two wives, but had issue only by the second, Margaret, daughter of Edwin Sandys, Archbishop of York (see pedigree). He died January 13, 1609–10, and was succeeded by his son (next).

Aucher — Archer, Sir Anthony, 2. Sub. —— ; pd. £12 10s. Son of preceding ; knighted at Chatham, July 4, 1604 ; sheriff of Kent, 1614 ; M. C. for Va. Co. ; of the S. I. Co., 1615 ; interested in Argall's plantation, and was allowed a bill of adventure of £50 for sending four persons to Virginia at his own charge, February 12, 1617 ;

sent Carleton " a relation from Guiana by a worthy friend," February 23, 1618; married Hester, daughter of Peter Collet, Esq.; buried at Bourne, July 24, 1637. His son, Sir Anthony Aucher, was created a baronet, July 4, 1666. (This name was also spelled Ager and Auger.)

Austen. See Asten.

Avila. See Zuñiga.

Aylmer, John, Bishop of London. Of Aylmer Hall, Norfolk. Domestic chaplain to Henry Grey, Marquis of Dorset, father of Lady Jane Grey to whom he was also tutor. During Queen Mary's reign he resided at Strasburg, and afterwards at Zurich, where he assisted Fox in his compilation of his " Book of Martyrs." On the accession of Elizabeth he returned to England. He died June 3, 1594, and was buried in St. Paul's.

Ayloffe. See Aliffe.

Bache, George, fishmonger, 2. Sub. ——; pd. £12 10s.

Bacon, Sir Francis, 2. Sub. ——; pd. ——. " The younger of the two sons of Sir Nicholas Bacon, Keeper of the Great Seal under Queen Elizabeth, by his second wife, Anne, second daughter of Sir Anthony Cooke, of Gideon Hall in Essex, and sister to the wife of the Lord Treasurer Burghley. Was born at York House, in the Strand, London, January 22, 1561. In April, 1573, he entered Trinity College, Cambridge, and was educated there under the care of Whitgift, afterwards primate. March, 1575, left college; while there he is said to have entered his protest against the philosophy of Aristotle. In June, 1575, he was admitted to Gray's Inn, and became ancient there November 21, 1576. Soon after was attached to the embassy of Sir Amias Paulet to France, and lived in the house with that minister during his embassy, on the affairs of which, he was at least once dispatched to communicate personally with the queen. His father died while he was abroad, February 20, 1579, " leaving him but a small fortune." While in France he wrote his discourse on " The State of Europe." His father's death compelled him to return to England and engage in some

profitable occupation. He solicited his uncle, Lord Burghley, to procure for him such a provision from government as might allow him to devote his time to literature and philosophy; but " he, who desired to live only in order to study," was even now " forced to study how to live." " He devoted himself to the study of the law, and on June 27, 1582, was admitted utter barrister." November 23, 1584, to September 14, 1585, M. P. for Melcombe Regis. Wrote his " Letter of Advice to Queen Elizabeth " in 1584–85. " In 1586 he became a bencher of Gray's Inn, and in the parliament, 15th October, 1586, to 23 March, 1587, he sat for Taunton." Lent reader of Gray's Inn, 1588. He was one of those who aided T. Hughes in the composition of " Certaine Devises and shewes presented to her Maiestie at her Highnesse Court in Greenewich, the 28th day of Februarie in the thirtieth yeare of her Maiesties most happy Raigne." M. P. for Liverpool, November 12, 1588, to March 29, 1589. In 1590, queen's counsel extraordinary ; about 1591 became acquainted with Essex. M. P. for Middlesex, February 19 to April 10, 1593, and incurred Elizabeth's displeasure by speaking on the side of the people. " Elizabeth dismissed this parliament in person, on the 10th of April, 1593, in a speech which the boldest man of the Plantagenet line of monarchs would scarcely have ventured to utter." On January 25, 1594, Bacon held his first brief. M. A., Cambridge, July 27, 1594. He failed to obtain the attorney-generalship in 1594, and the solicitor-generalship in 1595. On the 17th November, 1595, Twickenham Park was leased to Francis Bacon, Esq., and John Hibbard for twenty-one years. This lease is said to have been a present from the Earl of Essex. In May, 1596, Essex recommended him for the mastership of the rolls, without success ; and in the spring of 1597 Essex aided him in vain in pressing his suit with Lady Hatton (the widow of Sir William Newport, and afterwards wife of Chief Justice Coke). The first edition of his Essays was dedicated to his brother Anthony, " 30 Jan'y, 1597." In 1597 he was returned by both Southampton and Ipswich as an M. P., — I have been unable to gather for *certain* for which borough he elected to sit, — October 24, 1597, to February 9, 159⅞ ; arrested for debt September 23, 1598. He was duplex reader of Gray's Inn in 1600. The Essex troubles, 1599–1601 ; Bacon conducted the prosecution of Essex, February, 1601. M. P. for Ipswich, October 27 to December 19, 1601 ; knighted by James I., July 23, 1603 ; appointed king's counsel August 25, 1604 ; M. P. for Ipswich, March 19, 1604, to February 9, 1611 ; May 10, 1606, married Alice, daughter of Benedict Barnham, late alderman and sheriff of London ; was actively employed in the various controversies of the time regarding the Spaniards, the Papists, the Puritans, the Union with Scotland, etc. February 17, 160⅚, replying to Nicholas Fuller, in the debate in Parliament on the Union with Scotland, he denied that the Scots would overrun England ; "but if the land was too little, the sea was open. Commerce would give support to thousands. Ireland was waiting for colonists to till it, and the solitude of Virginia was crying aloud for inhabitants." (Gardiner's "History of England.") He was appointed solicitor-general, June 25, 1607 ; register of Star Chamber, July, 1608 ; M. C. for Va. Co., 1609. "He looked upon the Virginian Colony as upon the romantic achievements of Amadis de Gaul ; while he compared the settlement of Ireland by the English with the deeds related in Cæsar's Commentaries." An incorporator of the Newfoundland Company, May 2, 1610 ; joint judge of Knight Marshal's Court, 1611 ; an incorporator of the N. W. P. Co., July 26, 1612.

While Salisbury lived he continued to fawn on him with high-flown compliment ; after he was dead he wrote his essay "On Deformity." Chamberlain wrote to Carleton, December 17, 1612 : "Sir Francis Bacon hath set out new essays, where in a Chapter of *Deformity*, the world takes notice that he paints out his little cousin to the life." He was "the chief contriver of the Masque of Grayes Inne and the Inner Temple," played before the King, the Queen, the Prince Count

Palatine and the Lady Elizabeth, at Whitehall, in February, 1613. Was appointed attorney-general October 27, 1613. His celebrated masque, in honor of the marriage of Lord Rochester with the divorced Countess of Essex, was performed January 6, 1614. M. P. for Cambridge University, April 5 to June 7, 1614. On April 19, 1615, he gave the hand of his niece, Mrs. Anne (Wodehouse) Hungate, at the nuptial ceremony to Sir Julius Cæsar (his third wife). Made a privy councilor, June 9, 1616. Prosecuted Somerset, 1616. Lord keeper of the great seal, March 7, 1617. Prepared instructions for Sir John Digby regarding the projected Spanish match in March, 1617. Strickland says : "Sir Francis Bacon was the person who governed England in the king's absence" in Scotland, May to September, 1617. On May 7, 1617, he rode from Gray's Inn to Westminster, to open the courts in state, in most regal style. Bacon's rise kept pace with Coke's decline. He became lord chancellor, January 4, and was created Lord Verulam, July 12, 1618. Prosecuted Ralegh in 1618. In this year Captain John Smith vainly sought his patronage in a long letter still preserved among the Colonial State Papers in England, and William Strachey presented him with a MS. copy of his "Historie of Travaile into Virginia Britannia," written in 1612 ; but with alterations in the text to make it correspond with the year 1618. In his letter of presentation Strachey says : "Your Lordship ever approving yourself a most noble factor of the Virginian Plantation, being from the beginning (with other lords and earles) of the principall counsell applyed to propogate and guide it." On February 27, 1618, Sir Thomas Smythe, the governor of the E. I. Co., presented his name for membership, and on March 18 next he was admitted a free brother of the E. I. Co. *gratis.* He prosecuted Suffolk in 1619, and Yelverton in 1620.

The year 1621 was a most notable one in the life of Lord Bacon. He celebrated his sixtieth birthday in great style at York House on January 22, when his friend Ben Jonson read a poem in his honor containing these lines : —

GEORGE SANDYS

" Hail, happy genius of this ancient pile !
How comes it all things so about thee smile ?
The fire, the wine, the men, and in the midst
Thou stand'st, as if some mystery thou didst.
. . . .
England's High Chancellor, the destined heir
In his soft cradle, to his father's chair ;
Whose even thread the Fates spin round and full,
Out of their choicest and their whitest wool."

January 27 he was created Viscount
St. Albans ; January 30 Parliament
met ; February 3, Bacon, in his speech
referring to the " benefits, attributes,
and acts of government of King
James," says : " This Kingdom now
first in his Majesty's times hath gotten a lot or portion in the New World
by the plantation of Virginia and the
Summer Islands. *And certainly it is
with the Kingdoms on earth as it is in
the Kingdom of heaven ; sometimes a
grain of mustard-seed proves a great
tree. Who can tell ? "*

On March 14 a cloud appeared on
the horizon, and from that day his
fall began. During the rest of March
and the month of April he was on
trial, and as he expressed it, " in pur-
gatory." On May 1 the Great Seal
was taken from him, and two days
after he was fined and imprisoned
for a few days in the Tower. " Ban-
ished from public life, he had now
ample leisure to attend to his philo-
sophical and literary pursuits." His
severities were thought to prove, by
accident, happy crosses. " Methinks
they are resembled by those of Sir
George Sommers, who being bound
by his employment to another coast,
was by *tempest* cast upon the Barmudas. And therefore a ship wrack'd
man made full discovery of a new temperate fruitful Region, which none
had before inhabited ; and which Mariners, who had only seen its rocks,
had esteemed an inaccessible and en-
chanted place."

The Rev. Joseph Mead wrote from
Christ College, April 6, 1622, to Sir
Martin Stuteville : " My Lord Verulam's History of Henry VII. is come
forth. I have not read much of it,
but they say it is a very pretty book
who have read it. The price is six
shillings."

The projected Spanish match failed ;
the Spaniards requiring among other
things that " James I. should surrender, unto the King of Spain, Virginia and the Bermudas, and altogether

quit the West Indies;" and the same
year (1622) Bacon wrote " An Advertisement touching an Holy War, with
Questions about the lawfulness of a
War for the propagation of Religion;"
in 1624 he published his " Consider-
ations touching a War with Spain,"
inscribed to Prince Charles. King
James declared war on Spain, March
10, 1624.

Lord Bacon died in the Earl of
Arundell's House at Highgate, April
9, 1626, expiring in the arms of Sir
Julius Cæsar, who had married his
niece, and was buried in St. Michael's
Church, St. Albans. " That glorious
and melancholy instance of the extent
of human wisdom and weakness, the
Philosopher Bacon, found, after his
disgrace, an asylum in the bosoms of
his nephew and niece; composed many
of his immortal works in an utter re-
tirement in the house of Sir Julius
Cæsar ; became a dependent upon his
beneficence for a becoming support,
and expired in his arms." (Lodge's
" Life of Sir Julius Cæsar.")

The first wife of Sir Julius Cæsar
was a sister of Captain John Martin
of Brandon on the James in Virginia,
and while Bacon was living with, Martin corresponded with, Sir Julius.

In Bacon's Advice to Sir George
Villiers, in the article of " Colonies, or
foreign Plantations," and also, in his
essay " Of Plantations," we find some
of the same sentiments which had been
expressed in the Broadsides of the
Council for Virginia. He may have
taken these ideas from those Broadsides, or he may have been one of the
original authors of them, as he was a
member of that Council. Some of
the sentiments of the essay obtained
in the Virginia Council as early as
1609 ; but the reference to the tobacco
trouble in Virginia indicates that it
was not completed as published until
after 1622. It was probably written
or rewritten especially for his enlarged edition of Essays published in
1625. His reference to merchants
indicates that he was friendly to the
Sandys faction of the Va. Co., and
his statement, that " it is the sinfullest thing in the world to forsake or
destitute a plantation once in forwardness," was probably a rap at Ralegh.

May not Bacon have aided Shakespeare in compiling *some* of his plays ? It was the custom of the time for several writers (taking different series of characters, I suppose) to engage on the same play, and Bacon always had a fancy for such things.

Lord Bacon was first cousin to Sir James Bacon, of Friston Hall, the ancestor of Colonel Nathaniel Bacon of the Virginia Council, of Nathaniel Bacon, the first Virginia rebel, and of Martha Bacon, from whom the present (1890) President of the United States *doubly* descends.

Badger, John, 2. Sub. ——; pd. £12 10s.

Baffin, William, pilot of the Patience in Hall's voyage to Greenland, April to September, 1612 ; chief pilot of the celebrated expedition of Capt. Benjamin Joseph to Spitzbergen, April to September, 1613 ; went the next year on the same voyage ; but with Master Thomas Sherwin and Robert Fotherbie went out on a discovery, also, April to October, 1614. (This Robert Fotherbie, I suppose, was related to Henry Fotherbie, sometime secretary of the Virginia Company, and afterwards, possibly clerk of the New England Company. Robert Fotherbie made a voyage to the Northeast himself, May to September, 1615, and was afterwards in the employ of the E. I. Co. at Deptford from October, 1615, to 1621.) Baffin was the pilot of Byleth's voyage to the Northwest, March to September, 1615, and again, March to August, 1616. He was master's mate on a voyage to the East Indies, March 5, 1617, to September, 1619 ; master on a second voyage to the East Indies from early in 1620 to January 23, 1622, on which day he was killed " whilst taking the angles of the Castle Wall " at the siege of Kishm in the Persian Gulf. " He was one of the first to endeavor to determine longitude at sea by astronomical observations."

Bagge, James, of Plymouth, merchant. Son of George Bagge, of Weymouth. M. P. for Plymouth, 1601 and 1604–11 ; M. C. for Va. Co., 1606 ; comptroller of the customs at Plymouth and Fowey ; deputy mayor of Plymouth in 1623. He married Margaret, daughter of John Slone,

Esq. ; was buried at St. Andrew's Church, Plymouth, April 6, 1624. His eldest son bore his name, and it is sometimes hard to distinguish between father and son. One or the other of them was an agent for the E. I. Co. at Plymouth in 1619, etc., and " June 28, 1620, the Virginia Company gave Mr. James Bagge *five* shares " of land in Virginia.

Bagge, James, son of the above ; M. P. for Bodmin in 1621–22 ; West Looe, 1624–25 ; East Looe, 1625–26, and Plympton, 1628–29 ; knighted at Saltcombe, Devon, September 19, 1625; governor of Plymouth Castle ; *member of "ye Councell for New England,"* June 26, 1632 ; voted to resign the N. E. charter, April 25, 1635. In November, 1635, he was before the Star Chamber. " He was the creature of Buckingham, and the *'bottomless bagge'* of the patriot Eliot."

Baker, John, 2. Sub. ——; pd. £25. Probably the father of Sir Richard Baker.

Baker, Sir Richard. Historian ; born about 1568; died in Fleet prison, February 18, 1645. He was first cousin to Sir John Scott.

Baker, Thomas. Sub. ——; pd. £100. (Attorney, Guildhall ; died October 6, 1633 ?).

Baldwin, Francis, 3. Sub. ——; pd. £12 10s.

Ball, Richard, an eminent London merchant ; of the E. I. and N. W. P. Cos. In 1618 he is mentioned as having fitted out two ships for the discovery of an island in the West Indies. He died after 1624. His brother, George Ball, a factor for the E. I. Co. at Bantam, was recalled because of his notorious abuses. Richard was a leading opponent of the Smythe party in the Va. Co. during 1622–24. His name has generally been transcribed from the records as Bull ; but Ball is correct.

Baltimore, Lord.—George Calvert.

Bamfield — Bampfield, Sir Amias, 3. Sub. ——; pd. £12 10s. The Bampfyelds have been settled at Poltimore, Devonshire, since the reign of Edward I. Sir Amias was M. P. for Devon, 1597–98; knighted at Windsor, July 9, 1603 ; died February 9, 1626, and was buried at North Mollon, Devon. Ancestor of Lords Poltimore.

Banbury, Earl of. —William Knollys.

Bancroft, Richard, Bishop of London, etc. Was born in 1544 ; educated at Jesus College, Cambridge; under the patronage of Sir Christopher Hatton about 1585 ; made Bishop of London, 1597 ; Archbishop of Canterbury, 1604 ; Chancellor of the University of Oxford, 1608. Died November 2, 1610, and was interred in Lambeth Church.

In my remarks on XLIX., I have stated my belief that *this first draft* was given by Wingfield to Bancroft, and by Bancroft to the Lambeth Library. It seems natural that Wingfield should do this, as in his defense of himself from the charge of atheism, etc., he makes the following direct appeal to Bancroft : —

" For my first worke (which was to make a right choice of a spirituall pastor), I appeale to the remembraunce of my *Lo. of Caunt: his grace,* who gave me very gracious audience in my request. And the World knoweth whome I took with me : truly, in my opinion, a man not any waie to be touched with the rebellious humors of a popish spirit, nor blemished with ye least suspition of a factius scismatick, whereof I had a special care." (See Rev. Robert Hunt.)

If Bancroft placed Wingfield's appeal (as I think) on record in Lambeth Library, it would seem to be an indorsation by him of the correctness of that appeal.

Capt. John Smith, writing in 1630, in that prevaricating and misleading style which developed with his age, says : " But Jamestowne was 500 pounds a yeare, as they say, appointed by the Councell here, allowed by the Councell there, and confirmed by the Archbishop of Canterbury his Grace, Primate and Metropolitan of all England, An. 1605 to Master Richard Hacluit Prebend of Westminster : who by his authority sent Master Robert Hunt an honest, religious and courageous Divine." A tangle of truth and falsehood. The charter was not sealed until April, 1606, and poor Hunt's salary was certainly less than £50. " 500 pounds a yeare " would be equivalent to over $10,000 per annum, present values.

Banister. See Bannister.

Banks, John, mercer, 2. Sub.——; pd. £112 10s. Born about 1571 ; apprenticed to Baptist Hicks; admitted a member of the Mercers' Company in 1599 ; of the E. I. Co. in 1607 ; N. W. P. Co., 1612 ; B. I. Co., 1615. Was master of the Mercers when he died, September 9, 1630. There is " a faire monument to him in the Parish Church of St. Michael the Quern, in the North Ile, mentioning his many acts of charity " : —

" Much was to him committed much he gave,
Entering his treasure there where all shall have
Return with use. What to the poor is given
Claims a just promise of reward in heaven."

His only daughter and heir, Anne, married, July 5, 1631, Edmond Waller (the poet), of Berkensfield in Buckinghamshire. She died *after* December, 1631, and her husband probably inherited her interests in Virginia and the Bermudas. Capt. Henry Waller of the Massachusetts Company, and a relative of the poet's, aided him in securing his bride, whom he stole from her guardians.

Banks, Miles, cutler, 2. Sub.——; pd. £50.

Bannister, Richard, merchant, 2. Sub. —— ; pd. £50. " Licensed to make cloths and beaver for twentyone years, March 24, 1618."

Barber, Edward. See Barkham.

Barber, Thomas, merchant, 2. Sub. —— ; pd. £62 10s. of the E. I. and N. W. P. Cos.

Bargrave (Bargar), Capt. George. Sub. —— ; pd. ——. Robert Bargrave, of Bridge in Kent, had by his wife Joanna, daughter of John Gilbert, of Sandwich, three daughters and six sons. One of the daughters, Ingle or Angel Bargrave, married, October 4, 1604, Rev. John Boys (1571–1625), afterwards Dean of Canterbury. The sons were: Rev. Thomas (who came to Virginia about 1619, and died there in 1621, leaving his library, valued at 100 marks, to the college at Henrico), Richard, Capt. John, Robert, Capt. George, and Rev. Isaac Bargrave (1586–1643), afterwards Dean of Canterbury. Capt. George Bargrave was born about 1584. He was captain of the Edwin in 1618 and 1619, and I suppose, before and after those dates. The Edwin was sent to the Bermudas in March, 1614 ; remained there some time, and returned to England in the winter of 1614–15. She made another voyage to the S. I. in 1615 ; and sailed from England on a third voyage in February, 161$\frac{5}{6}$; soon after her arrival in the S. I, "being a barke of very good sayle," she was sent to the West Indies, from whence she returned late in the summer of 1616, loaded with lignum vitæ, certain plants and fruits, and " *a Negroe the first thes Islands ever had.*" From the Bermudas, the Edwin returned to England, arriving there some time before March 5, 161$\frac{6}{7}$, on which day the Va. Co. allowed Capt. George Bargrave five shares for services rendered. He made a fourth voyage (probably to Virginia) in 1617–18, about which there was some trouble on his return in the spring of 1618. His fifth voyage, in 1619, was certainly to Virginia, where he arrived in the spring of 1619. He married Dorcas, daughter of John Martin. (I am very sure this was our Capt. John Martin.) See also the next.

Bargrave, Capt. John. Sub. ——; pd. —— ; of Patricksborne in Kent, born about 1578. He tells us that, " after 10 yeares service in the warres in the summer tyme and at my study in the wynter," he became interested in the Virginia Colony, and claimed to be " the first person who established a private plantation in Virginia," I infer, about the year 1618. His brother George was captain ; James Bret, master; and he was part owner of the Edwin. He claimed to have " a patent of free trade from the Va. Co.," and prior to 1619 " had bought and set out divers ships." On the return of the Edwin from the S. I., probably *via* Virginia, the company allowed him fifteen shares of land in Virginia for his services, on March 5, 161$\frac{6}{7}$, and on her return in 1618 he gave Lord Zouch an indemnifying bond May 4, and the Edwin was allowed to pass up to London on May 13. There was a long dispute between Sir Thomas Smythe and Capt. John Bargrave in regard to his trade to Virginia and the S. I., which began prior to 1619, and continued as long as Smythe lived. There were claims on both sides. Smythe sued him for

£500 due the Va. Co., and he claimed heavy damages for being debarred certain privileges of free trade, and of his private plantation. All of his claims were denied by the officials of the company prior to 1619. Early in 1620 he was granted a patent for lands in Virginia by the Sandys administration, and soon after transferred ten shares to sundry persons. In February, 162$\frac{0}{1}$, he presents his " learned treatise upon the government of Virginia, by a gentleman refusing to be named," — who signs as " Ignotus," — to the Va. Co., and it is considered by a committee in February, April, and June, 1621, and is continually referred to by Bargrave in his petitions, etc., until October, 1624. Bargrave's brother Isaac was one of the actors in George Ruggle's Latin comedy of " Ignoramus," and it is thought that Ruggle aided him in his treatise signed " Ignotus." He married, prior to 1600, Jane, daughter of Giles Crouch, of London, and at the visitation of Kent in 1619 had two sons and two daughters living. It is frequently hard to distinguish the captains Bargrave. Capt. George certainly made several voyages to Virginia. Capt. John " sent servants and shipping thither ; " but I doubt if he ever went there himself.

Barker, Robert, cordwainer, 2. Sub. —— ; pd. £25.

Barker, Mr. (Robert), stationer. Pd. £5. The son of Christopher Barker, " The Queen's [Elizabeth] Printer." He was " The King's [James I.] Printer ; " made free of the Stationers' Company, *per patrimonium*, June 25, 1589, and was admitted to the livery, July 1, 1592. With George Bishop and Ralfe Newberie, he printed Hakluyt's " Principal Navigations " in 1598. He was the printer and patentee of the new translation (1611) of the Bible. Died January 10, 164$\frac{4}{5}$, while a prisoner in the King's Bench for debt.

Barkham, Edward, draper, 3. Sub. £37 10s ; pd. £12 10s. Stith gives this name as Barber, the Kimbolton MS. as Barker, and Strype also gives it as Barker, in his list of the lord mayors ; but the correct name is Barkham. He was the son of Edward Barkham by his second wife, Elizabeth Rolfe, of Norfolk ; was a member of the E. I. Co. ; alderman of London, successively, of Farringdon and Cheap wards ; sheriff in 1611 ; lord mayor 1621–22 ; knighted June 16, 1622 ; readmitted into the Va. Co., July 3, 1622 ; will dated January 15, 1632. Died January 15, 1633/4. His son Edward's (created a baronet in 1623 ; M. P. for Boston in 1625 and 1626) daughter Margaret married Sir Edmund Jennings, of Ripon, and was the mother of Edmund Jennings (acting governor of Virginia, 1710), an ancestor of Gen. R. E. Lee, and of very many other distinguished Americans.

Sir Edward Barkham's (the lord mayor) daughter Jane married Sir Charles Cæsar (master of the rolls), the nephew of Capt. John Martin ; another daughter Margaret was the wife of Sir Anthony Irby.

Barneham, Sir Francis, 3. Sub. ——— ; pd. ———. Of Boughton Monchelsea ; knighted, with his father, July 23, 1603 ; M. P. Grampound, 1604–11 ; Maidstone, 1614, 1621–22, 1624–25, 1625-26, 1628–29, 1640, and 1640 till decease about 1645. He was first cousin to Sir Francis Bacon's wife.

Barners — Berners, Anthony, esquire, 2. Sub. £37 10s ; pd. £100.

Barnes, alias **Baron, Edward**, mercer, 2. Sub. £37 10s. ; pd. £62 10s. Son of Richard Baron by his second wife, Margaret Morton ; admitted into the Mercers' Company by patrimony in 1586 ; warden in 1601 and 1610 ; master in 1615. His father and himself were both benefactors of the Mercers.

Barnes, Sir George, the elder, haberdasher. "Dwelled in Bartholomew Lane." Sheriff of London, 1545–46 ; the first merchant adventurer to Barbary, Russia, and Genoa ; an incorporator of the first organized English company for discovery, etc., 1551 ; lord mayor, and knighted, 1552–53 ; "a principall doer" in sending Sir Hugh Willoughby to the N. E. in 1553 ; one of "the first four Consuls" of the Merchant Adventurers, February 6, 1553. He is mentioned most kindly in the farewell letter of Bishop Ridley (the martyr), October, 1555. Died February 8, 1558, and was buried in the Church of St. Bar-

tholomew the Little. He married Alice, daughter of Mr. Brooke, of Shropshire. She died in 1559, leaving two sons and two daughters, George (of whom hereafter), John, Anne, and Elizabeth. John married Jane Langton ;. left two daughters. Anne married, first, Alexander Carliell, of London, leaving at least one son and one daughter : namely, Captain Christopher Carliell, and Alice, who married Christopher Hudson.

Anne Barnes-Carliell married, secondly, Sir Francis Walsingham, but left no issue by him. Elizabeth Barnes married Sir John Rivers, Lord Mayor of London, in 1573. He died in 1584, leaving six sons and three daughters. Captain John Rivers was the second son.

Barnes, Sir George, the younger, haberdasher. Eldest son of Sir George, the elder aforesaid ; was a leading merchant adventurer ; alderman of London, 1574 ; sheriff, 1576 ; interested in Fenton's voyage, 1582–83, and in Davis's voyages to the N. W., 1585–87 ; Lord Mayor of London, and knight, 1586–87. John Stow dedicated the 1587 edition of "The Chronicles of England" to him. President of St. Thomas's Hospital, 1591. Died February 8, 1592. "He dwelled in Lombard Street, over against the George, in the house which was Sir William Chester's, and was buried in the Church of St. Edmond the King, hard by." He married Anne, daughter of Sir William Gerrard, and had issue by her one daughter and eight sons. The daughter, Anne Barnes, married Walter Marler, and the eldest son, William Barnes, married Anne, sister of Sir Edwin Sandys.

Barnes, William, 2. Sub. £37 10s. ; pd. £37 10s. Son of Sir George, the younger (the preceding); married Anne Sandys.

Barnevelt. See Olden Barnevelt.

Baron, Christopher, clothworker, 2. Sub. ——— ; pd. £62 10s.

Barrett, William, "king's grocer," 3. Sub. £37 10s. ; pd. £25. Of the E. I. Co.

Barrington, Sir Francis, 3. Sub. £37 10s. ; pd. £37 10s. Great-great-grandson of George, Duke of Clarence, brother to Edward IV. ; was M. P. for Essex, 1601 ; knighted at

Theobald's, May 7, 1603 ; M. P. Essex, 1604–11 ; created a baronet, June 29, 1611 ; M. P. Essex, 1621–22, 1624–25, 1625, 1626, and 1627–28. Died July 3, 1628. He married Joan, daughter of Sir Henry Cromwell, and aunt of the Protector Cromwell. Their daughter Joan married Sir Richard Everard, and Bishop William Meade of Virginia was a descendant of theirs. Lady Joan Barrington survived her husband. See the letters written to her by Rev. Roger Williams, in 1629, published in "N. E. Register," July, 1889, pp. 316, 320.

Barros, John. Joan de Barros, "the Portuguese Livy." He died in 1571. Gilbert refers to him in his Discourse of the N. W. P.

Bartle, Barklet, Bartley, Peter, 3. Sub. £37 10s. ; pd. £37 10s. On November 15, 1619, he sold his three shares in Virginia to Dr. Theodore Gulston.

Barton, Captain George. A soldier in the Low Country wars.

Baskerville, Sir Thomas. Greatly distinguished himself as a captain in the Low Country wars. The Duke of Parma said of him at Sluys, in 1587 : "There serves no prince in Europe a braver man than this Englishman." Knighted by Lord Willoughby, at Bergen, in November, 1588 ; went to France with Willoughby in 1589 ; commanded the garrison at the Rammekens in 1592 ; commanded troops sent to Brittany, 1594 ; appointed colonel general of the soldiers in the fleet of Drake and Hawkins, June 21, 1595 ; commanded troops in Picardy in 1596, where he died of a fever, June 4, 1597. He married Mary, daughter of Sir Thomas Throckmorton (see pedigree).

Basse, Humphrey, 3. Sub. —— ; pd. £37 10s. Of the E. I. and N. W. P. Cos.

Bateman, Robert, 2. Sub. —— ; pd. £25. "A member of the Skinners' Company ; was joined in commercial matters with Nicholas Ferrar the elder, and others." He was the second son of Richard Bateman, of Hartington, County Derby ; baptized there September 8, 1561 ; an incorporator of the E. I. Co., 1600 ; of the N. W. P. Co., 1612 ; he served on the committee, and was an auditor and

solicitor to the E. I. Co. ; M. P. for Weymouth, 1614 ; deputy governor of the company for bringing a new river to London, 1619 ; one of the treasurers of the E. I. Co., 1620 ; M. P. for London, 1621–22 ; recommended to the Va. Co. by King James as a fit person for their deputy treasurer in May, 1622; M P. for London, 1624–25 ; member of the royal commission for winding up the Va. Co., July 15, 1624. I think he was a member of the Company of Massachusetts Bay in New England, 1629. Was chamberlain of the City of London. Died December 11, 1644 ; will dated August 3, 1641; proved August 2, 1645. He founded and endowed the divinity lectureship of Ashbourne, County Derby, and was a benefactor to the Skinners' Company. He was married twice, and left four sons: first, Robert, of Rotterdam, Holland ; second, Sir William; third, Sir Anthony, lord mayor in 1664 ; and fourth, Sir Thomas, created a baronet in 1664. The last three were aldermen of London and suffered great losses by the fire of 1666.

Bathe, Earl of. — William Bourchier.

Bathurst, Timothy, grocer, 2. Sub. —— ; pd. £25. Having served his apprenticeship to Launcelot Bathurst, was admitted to the freedom of the Grocers' Company, January 14, 1577 ; to the livery, May 24, 1596; paid £15 as his share of the £20,000 levied on the city by Queen Elizabeth in 1598 ; junior warden of the Grocers in 1609 ; became insolvent during his wardenship, and was found to be a defaulter at the expiring of his term to the extent of £368, which the senior warden, Edmond Peshall, was required by the court (of the company) to pay, because he knew of Warden Bathurst's insolvency. (Launcelot Bathurst, alderman, was ancestor of the present Earl Bathurst.)

[signature]

Bayley, Thomas, vintner, 2. Sub. —— ; pd. £25.

Beadle — Bedell, Gabriel, 2. Sub. —— ; pd. £12 10s.

Beadle — Bedell, John, 2. Sub. — ; £12 10s.

Beale, Edward, grocer, 2. Sub. — ; pd. —. Admitted to freedom, 1594 ; to livery, 1609 ; to the Court of Assistants, March 14, 1621.

Beale, Robert (1541–1601). Diplomatist and antiquary.

Beaumont, John, clothworker, 3. Sub. — ; pd. £12 10s.

Beaumont, Sir Thomas, the elder, 3. Sub. £37 10s. ; pd. £25. Knighted April 23, 1603 ; M. P. Tamworth, 1605–11. Died November 27, 1614.

Beck, Charles. Pd. £25.

Beck, William, gent., 3. Sub. — ; pd. £25.

Bedford, Countess of. — Lucy Harrington.

Bedford, Earl of. — Edward Russell.

Bedingfield, Sir Henry, 3. Sub. — ; pd. £37 10s. Of Oxburgh Hall, Norfolk ; knighted at Whitehall, July 21, 1604 ; M. P. for Norfolk, 1614 ; fought under the royal standard in the civil war. Died November 22, 1656. In 1607 George Wilson dedicated to him " The Commendation of Cock-Fighting. Wherein is shewed that cock-fighting was before the coming of Christ."

Bell, Robert, merchant, 3. Sub. — ; pd. £37 10s. Of the N. W. P. Co., and one of the directors of the E. I. Co. ; on the Virginia Commission of July 15, 1624. He married Alice, daughter of Ralphe Colston, of Essex ; was deputy alderman of Lime Street ward, London, in 1633, and was living in 1634.

Bennet, George, 2. Sub. — ; pd. —. Also of E. I. and N. W. P. companies.

Bennet, Sir John, 3. Sub. £37 10s. ; pd. £37 10s. Judge of High Court of Admiralty, and of the Prerogative Court of Canterbury ; M. P. Ripon, 1597–98 ; York, 1601 ; knighted at Whitehall, July 23, 1603 ; M. P. Ripon, 1604–11, Oxford University, 1614 and 1621, until expelled. Died in 1627. His grandson, Henry Bennet, was created Earl of Arlington.

Bennet, William, fishmonger, 2. Sub. — ; pd. £25. One of the six wardens of the Fishmongers in 1605.

Benson, Nicholas, 2. Sub. £37 10s. ; pd. £75. " He was the sixth son of Richard Benson, of the North parts of England, nigh Kendall, in Heram parish."

Benson, Peter, 2. Sub. — ; pd. £25. Of Knaresborough ; a friend of Sir William Craven's. He became interested in the plantation of Ulster, Ireland.

Berkeley — Berkley — Barkley, etc. Berkeley, Sir Charles. Eldest son of Sir Maurice Berkeley, of Bruton, County Somerset. Born about 1597 ; M. P. for Somerset from March, 1621, to February, 1622 ; for Bodmin, 1624–25 ; Heytesbury, 1625, 1626, and 1628–29 ; for Bath in 1640, and again in 1661, until void ; knighted at Bewley, August 26, 1623. Father of Charles, created Viscount Fitzhardinge, in Ireland, March 17, 1664, and Earl of Falmouth, in England, whom he succeeded in the Irish Viscountcy of Fitzhardinge, June 3, 1665, and died June 12, 1668. He was the oldest brother of Sir William Berkeley, the governor of Virginia.

Berkeley, Edward, gent., 3. Sub. — ; pd. £12 10s. He came to Virginia, and was living on Hog Island in 1625.

Berkeley, George, merchant, 2. Sub. £37 10s. ; pd. £12 10s. " Being a childe, he was transported into the East Countries." Purchas, vol. iii. pp. 625–631, gives the narrative of his travels in Europe, Asia, Africa, and America. He went twice to the Bermudas. Smith calls him " Master Bartlet." In 1615 he went out to the East Indies as factor for the company, and died there in 1618.

Berkley, Sir Maurice, 2. Sub. £75 ; pd. £80. Sir Richard Berkeley, knight, of Stoke Gifford in Gloucester, died in 1514, leaving by Elizabeth his wife, daughter of Sir Humphrey Coningsby, two sons, namely, Sir John Berkeley (ancestor of Norborne Berkeley, Baron de Botetourt, governor of Virginia, 1768–70), and Sir Maurice Berkeley, Knight of the Bath, of Bruton in Somersetshire, standard-bearer to Henry VIII., Edward VI., and Queen Elizabeth ; who, by his first wife, Catherine, daughter of William Blount, Lord Montjoy, and his wife, Alice Kebel (Cabell), had a son, Sir Henry Berkeley, who was the father of Sir Maurice Berkeley, of Bruton, Somerset, of whom I write; which Sir Maurice was knighted by Essex for gallantry at Cadiz, in 1596 ; M. P. for Truro, 1597–98 ; for Somerset, 1601, and for Minehead, 1604–11 ; M. C. for Va., March 9, 1607 ; M. C. for Va. Co., May 23, 1609 ; about 1610 he was an undertaker for 2,000 acres of land in Ulster, Ireland; M. P. for Somerset in 1614. He married Elizabeth, daughter of Sir William, and sister of Sir Robert Killigrew, of Hanworth, Middlesex, and died prior to May 10, 1617. George Lord Carew, writing to Sir Thomas Roe (who was in East India) under May, 1617, says, "Sir Maurice Berkeley is lately dead, who was a gentleman, as you know, of many good parts." He left five sons, *all* of whom were knights, and two daughters, namely, 1. Sir Charles (whom see) ; 2. Sir Henry, baptized December 8, 1600 ; 3. Sir Maurice, baptized April 24, 1603 ; 4. Sir John, baptized February, 1606–07 (the first Baron Berkeley, of Stratton, and a proprietor of Carolina) ; 5. Sir William, baptized July 16, 1608 (governor of Virginia, 1641, etc.) ; 1. Margaret, and 2. Jane, daughters.

On the 12th of April, 1621, Lady Berkeley (widow of Sir Maurice) was admitted into the Va. Co. of London for one share, and February 13, 1622, five and a half more shares were allowed her.

Berkeley, Richard, esquire. Of Stoke ; son of Henry Berkeley and his wife Muriel, daughter of Thomas Throckmorton, of Warwick ; was born in 1578 ; married in February, 159⅞, Mary, daughter of Robert Roe, Esq., and sister to Sir Thomas Roe. Richard Berkeley was first cousin to the wife of Sir Thomas Dale and to Sir William Throckmorton (see Throckmorton pedigree), with whom, together with George Thorpe and John Smythe of Nibley, he entered into an agreement to form a plantation in Virginia, on February 3, 161⅝ ; which plantation was afterwards named for him, "the towne and hundred of Berkley." He was probably retaining his interest in this plantation as late as August, 1633 ; but what disposition he finally made of it I do not know. He died May

12, 1661. He had issue five sons and five daughters. His eldest son, Sir Maurice Berkeley, knighted September 11, 1661, died in 1654, was father of Richard, the father of John Syms, the father of Norborne Berkeley, Baron de Botetourt, who was governor of Virginia, 1768–70.

Berkley, Robert, gent., 3. Sub. —— ; pd. ——. Of Spetchley, County Worcester. Born 1584 ; entered Middle Temple, 1600 ; called to bar, May 6, 1608 ; sheriff of Worcester, 1613 ; sergeant at law, 1627 ; knighted in 1632 ; justice of King's Bench, October 11, 1632 ; removed, 1640. Died August 5, 1656 ; buried at Spetchley. Probably M. P. for Worcester, 1621–22 and 1623–24.

Berkeley, William, 2. Sub. —— ; pd. £12 10s.

Berkshire, Earl of. — Francis Lord Norris.

Bernard, Captain John. S. I. Co. Governor of Bermudas. Son of Thomas Barnard, of Elsingham in Essex.

Berresford, Robert (Rowland), grocer, 2. Sub. —— ; pd. —— ; sworn to the freedom, January 27, 1607.

Berty — Bertie, Peregrine, esquire, 3. Sub. —— ; pd. ——. Second son of Peregrine Bertie, Baron Willoughby de Eresby. Capt. John Smith's master, with whom he went to France in 1599. He died in 1640.

Biancourt. See Poutrincourt.

Biard, Father Peter. Born at Grenoble, France in 1565 ; died in France, 1622.

Biggs, Captain Walter. The chronicler of the voyage, died shortly after leaving Cartagena.

Bill, Mr. ——, stationer. Pd. £3. John Bill, king's printer. Died in 1630, aged fifty-six ; buried under a fair monument in Black Friar's Church.

Bing, W. Probably Mr. Byng of Grantchester, counselor, of Gray's Inn, whose servant got into such serious trouble in January, 1622, by saying a good word for Sir Edward Coke.

Lord Coventry, in explaining why Bing was not placed on the Virginia Commission of July, 1624, wrote that he was " a mere good fellow, of no estate, who, for offensive behavior to

Lord Southampton, had been committed to the Marshalsea."

Bingley, John, esquire, 2. Sub. £75 ; pd. £125. "August 2, 1604, grant in reversion to him, of the office of writing tallies in the receipt of the Exchequer," i. e., teller of the exchequer. He afterwards became remembrancer of the exchequer ; M. C. for Va. Co., 1612.

July 22, 1617, George Gerrard wrote to Carleton : " Mr. Bingley of the Exchequer has married Sir John Grey's widow, the mother of Lord Grey." (Elizabeth, daughter of Edward Nevil, Lord Abergavenny, widow of the Hon. Sir John Grey, and mother of Henry, second Lord Grey of Groby, who married the Lady Anne Cecil, and was created Earl of Stamford, March 26, 1628.) He must have married twice, as he is said to have " married a daughter of Thomas Henshaw, silk-man, and servant to King James." He was knighted at Theobald's, January 10, 1618. In October, 1619, he was tried, with the Earl of Suffolk and his countess, and the Lord Keeper Bacon, in his speech against the delinquents, compared the countess to an exchange woman who kept her shop, while Sir John Bingley, pimping for her, cried, " *What d' ye lack ?* " In November he was committed to the Fleet and fined £2,000 ; afterwards released on his resigning his office, and on November 21, 1622, he obtained a pardon of his sentence and fine. He was still living in 1629. The date of his death is not known to me.

Bingley, Sir Richard, 3. Sub. —— ; pd. ——. Knighted at Otelands in 1611 ; he was a member of the African Company in 1618 ; convoyed a Dunkirk privateer to Mardike in September, 1623.

Biondi, Francesco. Born in Liesena, an island of Dalmatia, in the Gulf of Venice, in 1572 ; was introduced by Sir Henry Wotton, to the notice of King James, who sent him with secret commission to the Duke of Savoy, and afterwards made him a gentleman of the bed-chamber. He was knighted at Windsor, September, 6, 1622. He wrote a " History of the Civil Wars betwixt the Houses of York and Lancaster," " The Banish'd Vir-

gin," etc. He died in 1644. His wife, Mary, was sister to Theodore de Mayerne, the king's physician.

Bishop, Edward, stationer, 2. Sub. £37; pd. £75.

Bishop, George, stationer. Pd. £10. Master of the company in 1609 ; " gave ten poundes a yeare forever to be given unto such unbeneficed preachers as shall preach at Paules Crosse." One of the printers of the works of Hakluyt, Brereton, Rosier, and Pory ; an alderman of London. He died in 1610.

Blakemore, Richard. Pd. £25.

Bland, Gregory, merchant-tailor. Pd. £25. Son of Adam Bland, and brother to John Bland. His daughter Jane married her first cousin, Edward Bland, and emigrated to Virginia.

Bland, John [1], grocer. Of Syth Lane, London, in the parish of St. Antholin's, and of Plaistow in Essex ; tenth son of Adam Bland descended of the house of Gibord in Westmoreland ; born in 1573 ; interested in the Colony of Virginia. Mr. David Waterhouse transferred four shares of land there to him, September 16, 1618. He was a leading member of Sir Edwin Sandys' party during 1620–24, and was chosen to be of the Council for Va. Co., June 25, 1623. He was made free of the Grocers' Company in 1626, and was also free of the Merchant Adventurers. He died suddenly, April 20, 1632, leaving a very large family and a very great personal estate, and was buried in his vault at St. Antholin's.

Four of his sons emigrated to Virginia, namely, 1. Adam, 2. John [2], 3. Edward, and 4. Theodorick.

1. Adam died on the way there in 164–.

2. John [2], a merchant, trading to Virginia and the West Indies, probably made his first voyage in 1635. On March 20, 167$\frac{4}{5}$, his nephew Edward, son of his brother Edward, conveyed to him by deed 8,000 acres of land called Kymages in the Parish of Westover, Charles City County, Virginia. His son, Giles Bland, settled on this land, was collector of lower James River, took part in Bacon's Rebellion, and was hanged under the decree of Berkeley's court-martial in 1676. John [2] Bland died in 1680,

leaving Kymages to his wife and Thomas Povey, whose daughter Frances was the widow of his son Giles, aforesaid. This branch is now extinct.

3. Edward married his cousin Jane, daughter of Gregory Bland ; came to Virginia before 1650 and on the 27th August in that year "set out with Abraham Wood, Sackford Brewster and Elias Pennant from Fort Henry at the head of Appamattuck River in Virginia, and made a discovery to the Fals of Bland, to the Southwestward, in a first River in New Brittaine *which runneth West.*" In 1652 he published an account of this discovery which he dedicated to Sir John Danvers. He died in 1653, leaving an only son, Edward, and was buried at Kymages. His only grandson, John, never married. The News and Hortons descend from his only granddaughter, Sarah Bland, who married, first, Edward New, and, secondly, Alexander Horton.

4. Theodorick, the fourth son of John [1] Bland the elder to come to Virginia, was his fifteenth child ; baptized at St. Antholin's, January 16, 16$\frac{29}{30}$; was first a merchant with his brother Edward at St. Luca in Spain ; then in the Canary Islands, and shortly after his brother's death in 1653, he came to Virginia. Purchased "Berkeley" and "Westover ;" was speaker of the House of Burgesses ; member of the council, "and was both in fortune and in understanding inferior to no person of his time in the country." He lies buried at Westover. His descendants have been numerous, and many of them distinguished, both in the male and female lines.

Bludder, Sir Thomas, 2. Sub. ——; pd. £25. Of Sir Thomas Bludder and Company, merchants of London, patentees for the preëmption and exportation of tin ; victualers of the navy ; farmers of the imposition for sea-coals, etc. He was knighted at Chatham, July 4, 1604, as of Essex ; died in 1618 ; buried at Ryegate in Surrey.

Blunt — Blount, John, grocer. Sub. ——; pd. £25. Sworn to freedom, August 13, 1606 ; still found on the books as paying brotherhood money in 1612.

Blunt, Ned (Edward). Sub. ——; Pd. £12 10s. I suppose this was Ed-

ward Blunt, the stationer and translator ; admitted a freeman of the Stationers' Company, June 25, 1588. In 1623 he was one of the printers of the great First Folio of Shakespeare ; married, before December, 1623, Elizabeth, widow of Richard Bankworth ; died after 1632.

Blunt, Richard. Pd. £12 10s.

Bohun — Boone, Dr. Lawrence, 3. Sub.——; pd. ——. "Docktor in phisick." "A long time brought up amongst the most learned Surgeons and Physitions in the Netherlands ;" came to Virginia with Lord De la Warr in 1610. June 7, 1619, he consigned to Richard Boothby, Dr. Thomas Winston, Hugh Windham, John Tucker, and John Strange, one share each in Virginia. Prior to February 2, 1620, "Doctor Bohnne, James Swifte and their Associates, were granted patents" for the transportation of 300 persons to Virginia. He was one of the "ancient adventurers" who petitioned "to have some man of qualitye sent governor unto Virginia." December 13, 1620, he was appointed a "Phisition Generall for the Colony, unto which place they had allotted five hundred acres of Land and twenty Tenants to be placed theruppon att the Companies' charge." And soon after he sailed from England in the Margaret and John, Captain Chester. In the latter part of March, 1621, this vessel had a severe battle with two Spanish men-of-war in the West Indies, in which action Dr. Bohnn was killed. Seeing that he was mortally wounded, Captain Chester embraced him, "and thus recomforted him, saying, *O Doctor Bohnne what a disaster is this ;* the Noble Doctor no whit exanimated replyed, *Fight it out, brave man, the cause is good, and Lord receive my soule.*"

The Spaniards had been constantly on the lookout, in the West Indies, for the vessels of the Virginian adventurers ; but after the taking of the first vessel (Captain Challings), the English captains in some way eluded them. The sea-fight of the Margaret and John caused much excitement, and two accounts were published, one at Amsterdam, the other at London. The following is the title of the latter : "A True Relation of a

SIR JOHN SCOTT

Wonderfull Sea Fight betweene two great and well appointed Spanish Ships or Men of Warre. And A small and not very well provided English Ship, . . . The Margaret and John, or The Black Hodge. London, Printed for N. B. 1621." Smith's History, pp. 128–130, and Purchas, iv. p. 1780, give abstracts from this Relation.

Bolls — Booles — Bolles — Bowles, George, esquire, grocer, 2. Sub.——; pd. £37 10s. Born about 1538; is found on the Grocers' books as paying brotherhood money in 1577; was a " retailing grocer " ; a member of the Rus. Co. ; was admitted on the Court of Assistants of the Grocers, and assessed at £30 as his share of £1,700 contributed by the Grocers to the loan levied on the city by Queen Elizabeth in 1598 ; was junior warden of the Grocers and an adventurer in the East India voyage in 1599 ; an incorporator of the E. I. Co. in 1600. In 1603 he was executor of the last will and testament of the Right Worshipful Sir John Hart, whose eldest daughter, Joan Hart, he had married in 1590 ; senior warden of the Grocers in 1606 ; sheriff of London in 1608 ; was long an alderman from Walbrooke ward ; an incorporator of the N. W. P. Co. in 1612 ; Lord Mayor of London, 1617–18 ; knighted at Greenwich, May 31, 1618 ; died September 1, 1621, and was buried in the family vault in St. Swithin's, London.

" His Charity was better felt than knowne,
For when he gave, there was no Trumpet blowne.
What more can be compriz'd in one Man's Fame,
To crown a soule, and leave a living Name ? "

Bond, Martin, haberdasher, 2. Sub.——; pd. £12 10s. Son of William Bond, " the flower of the merchants," an alderman of London, and merchant adventurer, most famous in his age for his great adventures both by sea and land. Martin Bond was born in 1558 ; captain of the Train Band of London at Tilbury Camp, 1588 ; M. P. for London, 1624–25, and 1625 ; buried May 11, 1643, in St. Helen's Church, Bishopsgate. He was treasurer of St. Bartholomew's Hospital, 1619–1636, and his portrait is still preserved in the hospital ; a merchant adventurer; a benefactor of the Haberdashers' Company, and the chief captain of the trained bands of London from 1588 to his death ; also in the artillery.

Bond, Thomas, esquire. Sub.——; pd. £37 10s. Son of William Bond, Esq., of Holwood in Cornwall ; was M. P. for Launceston, 1521–22, for Southampton, 1624–25, and for Bossiney, 1640, till unseated on petition.

Bond, Sir William, of Highgate, Middlesex. Knighted July 23, 1603 ; son of Sir George Bond, Lord Mayor, 1587.

Bonham, William, vintner, 2. Sub. £37 10s. ; pd. £120. Son of Thomas Bonham, of Stanway Hall in Essex ; a prominent citizen of London ; a member of the N. W. P. Co. and a director of the E. I. Co.

Borlace (Burlacie, etc.), Sir John, 2. Sub.——; pd.——. " Bred a soldier in the wars of the Low Countries, where he served with distinction before the truce of 1608 ; " knighted at Greenwich, June 19, 1606 ; an officer of the Tower ; married, October 1, 1610, Alice Ravis, widow (probably of Thomas Ravis, Bishop of London, who died in 1609) ; served in Sir Horace Vere's expedition to the Palatinate in 1620, and was one of the commanders of the 6,000 who were serving in the United Provinces in 1626. He was master of the ordnance in Ireland, 1634–49 ; lord justice, Ireland, 1640–44 ; died early in 1649. He was the father of Dr. Edmund Borlase, the historian.

Borough — Burroughs — Burrowes — Borowgh — Brough — Burgh. Burgh, Sir John. The third son of William, fourth Lord Burgh. He was born in 1562 ; went to the Netherlands with Leicester in 1585 ; was governor of Doesburg ; knighted by Leicester in 1586, and by Henry IV. of France on the field of Ivry in 1589 ; " admiral of England, renowned for his exploits by sea and land ; " killed in a duel, it seems, with John Gilbert, March 7, 1593–94, and was buried in Westminster Abbey.

Burroughs, William, " navigator and author." Born in 1536 ; a younger brother of Stephen Borowgh, with whom he sailed in the voyages to Russia of 1553, 1556, and 1557. He continued to make these voyages for many years after ; made a map of Russia, 1574–75; published his "Discourse of the Variation of the Compass" in 1581; was comptroller of the navy, 1583; commanded the fleet which took the Earl of Leicester to Flushing in 1585; with Drake in the expedition to Cadiz, 1587; commanded a ship in the Armada fight, 1588; died in 1599.

Boteler. See Butler.

Boulstrode — Bulstrode, Sir William, 3. Sub. £25 ; pd. ——. Knighted at Dublin in 1599; M. P. for Rutland, 1604–11, 1621–22, 1624–25, 1625, 1626, and 1628–29.

Bourchier, Sir John, 3. Sub. £37 10s.; pd. £37 10s. Knighted at Whitehall, June 2, 1609, as of York. "In 1619 Capt. Nath¹ Butler brought Sʳ John Bourchier a letter from his daughter Mrs. Whittakers in Virginia, which letter was said to have been a forgery." (See "Discourse of the Old Company of Virginia," 1625.) He was of the King's Council for New England in 1620; patented lands in Virginia in 1621; M. P. for Hull, 1614. Entered Gray's Inn, 1584. Uncle to the regicide of the same name.

Bourchier, William, Earl of Bath. Succeeded on the death of his grandfather in 1560 as fifth baron and third Earl of Bath ; was in the expedition, 1585–86, to the Netherlands in aid of the Dutch, under Robert, Earl of Leicester; M. C. for Va. Co., 1612–20; of the King's Council for the N. E. Co., November 3, 1620 ; died July 12, 1623.

Bourke — Burke, Richard, Earl of Clanricarde, 3. Sub.——; pd. £20. Knighted at Tyrone's overthrow in Kinsale, December 24, 1601, and was surnamed of Kinsale from the valor he had displayed against the rebels there ; succeeded on the death of his father in 1601 as fourth earl; married in 1603 Frances, daughter of Sir Francis Walsingham, and widow of Sir Philip Sydney and of Robert, Earl of Essex ; lord president of Munster, and one of the councilors of state in Ireland ; created an English peer, April 3, 1624, by the titles of Baron Somerhill and Viscount Tunbridge, County Kent, and August 23, 1628,

advanced to the earldom of St. Albans ; died in 1635–36.

Bourne — Borne — Bone, David, 2. Sub.——; pd. £25. Of the E. I. Co.

Bourne, Nicholas, stationer. (See Butter.) May 23, 1622, Nicholas Bourne and Thomas Archer issued the first extant copy of "The Weekly Newes from Italy, Germanie," etc.

Bourne, Reuben, 3. Sub.—— ; pd. £37 10s.

Bowyer, Sir Edmund, 3. Sub. £37 10s.; pd. £37 10s. Knighted at Charterhouse, May 11, 1603; M. P. for Surrey, 1604–11, 1614, and for Gatton, 1624–25. He was of Camberwell, Surrey.

Bowyer, Robert, esquire, 2. Sub. —— ; pd. £25. I think this was the keeper of the records in the Tower ; afterwards clerk of the Parliament. He was M. P. for Steyning, 1601; died in 1634.

Bowyer, Robert, grocer. I hink this was the second son of Francis Bowyer, sheriff of London in 1578, and the Robert Bowyer who died April 2, 1626.

Brackley, Viscount. — Thomas Egerton.

Brand (or Brond) Benjamin, esquire, 3. Sub. —— ; pd. ——. Probably the son of John Brond, of Boxford in Suffolk, by his second wife.

Brathwaite, R., a prolific poet and writer, was of a Westmoreland family; born about 1588; died in 1673. The most famous of his numerous works, "Barnabæ Itinerarium, or Barnabee's Journal," was first published in 1638. "The Smoaking Age, or the Man in the Mist, with the life and death of Tobacco," was first published in 1617.

Brearley — Bryerley, James, fishmonger, 2. Sub. —— ; pd. £87 10s. Of E. I. Co.

Brereton (see Bretton and Britton), **John,** was admitted sizar at Caius College, Cambridge, 1587, and was B. A., 1592–93; went to our New England coast with Gosnold in 1602, and published a "Briefe Relation" of the voyage. The following items may refer to him : "Westminster, July 18, 1611. Grant to John Brereton of Barrow, Co. Chester, of pardon for life only, for manslaughter."

"Sept. 13, 1613. Letter from Sir

Thomas Smythe to Mr Robert Whit-bee, mayor of the city of Chester. In behalf of the letter's bearer, John Brereton, who is desirous to become a citizen in Chester and to keep an Inn there." Symthe commends him to the mayor's kindly consideration.

Bret, Thomas, fishmonger. Pd. £25.

Bretton — Britton — Brereton, John, 3. Sub. —— ; pd. ——. This may be John Brereton, who went to the New England coast in 1602.

Bretton, Thomas, 2. Sub. —— ; pd. £37 10s.

Brewsey. See Prusey.

Brewster, Captain Edward, son of William, 2. Sub. —— ; pd. £30. " Son of William Brewster," in char-ter of May, 1609 ; came to Virginia with Lord De la Warr in 1610 ; had trouble with Governor Argall in 1618, and returned to England ; June 7, 1619, he transferred one share in Vir-ginia to William Cranmer ; Novem-ber 13, 1620, he transferred four shares to Sir Francis Wyatt, and there still remained to his credit on the books of the company the sum of £30. In 1616, and after, there was a printer of the same name in London, but this was not Captain Edward. Did he go to New England ?

Brewster, William, 2. Sub. —— ; pd. £20. Was this the Pilgrim Fa-ther ?

Bridges, John, Lord Bishop of Oxenford, 3. Sub. —— ; pd. ——. The controversialist ; B. A., Cam-bridge, in 1556 ; Dean of Salisbury, 1577 ; Bishop of Oxford, 1604. Died 1618, at a great age.

Briggs, Henry, mathematician. Born at Warley Woods, in the parish of Halifax, Yorkshire, in February, 1561 ; educated at Cambridge ; M. A. in 1585 ; professor of geometry in Gresham College, 1596–1620 ; mem-ber of N. W. P. Co. in 1612 ; he pro-moted the use of logarithms, first ex-plained by Lord Napier in 1614, and made a journey to Edinburgh in 1616, on purpose to confer with the discov-erer. The Earl of Warwick passed a share in Harington Tribe, Bermudas Islands, to him in 1619. He was pro-fessor of astronomy at Oxford from 1619 to his death, I suppose, in 1631. To " A Declaration of the State of the Colony and Affaires in Virginia," published by Edward Waterhouse in 1622, there is " A Treatise annexed, written by that learned mathematician, Mr. Henry Briggs, of the Northwest Passage to the South Sea, through the Continent of Virginia, and by Fretum Hudson." On page 9, Waterhouse, referring to this treatise, says, " which I having happily attained unto, have published for the common good." It occupies pp. 45–50, and is signed " H. B." He was a promoter of the voy-age of N. W. Fox, but did not live to see its departure. He died January 26, 1631. Fox sailed in 1631, and named a group of islands in Hudson's Bay, " Brigges, his Mathematickes."

Bristol, Earl of. — John Digby.

Britton. See Bretton.

Brochero, Don Diego. Of the Spanish " Council of Warre." A cele-brated Spanish admiral.

Brocket, Thomas, gent., 2. Sub. —— ; pd. £25.

Bromfield, Arthur. Sub. —— ; pd. £25. M. P. for Yarmouth, Isle of Wight, 1604–11, 1614, and 1621–22.

Brooke, Lord. — Fulke Greville.

Brooke — Brookes, Sir Calis-thenes, 2. Sub. —— ; pd. ——. Of Kent ; knighted in the Glynes, Ire-land, May 8, 1597 ; he was discharged by Sir Francis Vere, before Ostend, in February, 1601. January 21, 1609, Ann Lady Cobham writes to Salisbury, " soliciting a pension for her son, Calis-thenes Brooke, wounded in serving against the rebels in the Irish wars." Chamberlain to Carleton, from the Hague, October 5, 1611 : " Sir Calli-phenes Brook died here lately, leaving his wife in very poor estate, for they say he was seven or eight hundred pounds worse than naught."

Brooke, Christopher, esquire, 2. Sub. £37 10s. ; pd. £50. A barrister of Lincoln's Inn, and a poet ; was the son of Robert Brooke, alderman, and twice Lord Mayor of York, by Jane, daughter of Christopher Maltby (al-derman of York). " He was the chamber fellow at Lincoln's Inn, and the bosom friend of the celebrated Dr. John Donne, and aided him in 1600, in his clandestine marriage with Anne, daughter of Sir George Moore. The indignant father-in-law is said to have sent the groom and his two friends,

Christopher and Samuel Brook, to prison." M. P. for the City of York in 1604–1611 ; M. C. for Va. Co., May 23, 1609.

In 1613 he published " An Elegy on the Death of Henry, Prince of Wales." He was the author of several " Eglogues, Elegys," etc. ; M. P. for York City in 1614, when the Virginia business came before the House, and took part in the debate thereon ; afterwards consulted as an attorney by the Va. Co. of London ; was one of a committee to represent that company before the king in 1620 ; continued an active member of the company ; M. P. for York City again in 1624–25, 1625, and 1626 ; buried at St. Andrew's, Holborn, February 7, 1627–28. He married, December 18, 1619, Mary Jacob. His wife died before him, leaving an only son, John. (Capt. Christopher Brooks of Virginia was one of the godfathers of George Washington.)

Brooke, Henry, Lord Cobham. Eldest son of William, seventh Lord Cobham, whom he succeeded as eighth lord, March 6, 1597 ; was Lord Warden of the Cinque Ports, and governor of Dover Castle, 1597 ; Knight of the Garter, 1599 ; he was an enemy to Essex, and was one of the objects of the Essex plot of February, 1601 ; a friend of Ralegh's ; aided in sending Gosnold to our New England coast, in the voyage of March 26, to July 23, 1602 ; was implicated in the plot against James I. in 1603 ; a witness against Ralegh ; was condemned to die, but his life was spared. His estates and honors were forfeited, and he remained in the Tower until 1617, when he was allowed to go to Bath for his health. He died January 24, 1619. The king allowed him a pension of about £500 per annum. He was not concerned in " The Bye Plot " of 1603, in behalf of the Catholics, but in " The Main Plot," " to place Arabella Stuart on the throne, and to kill ' the king and his cubs.' "

Brooke, Sir John, 2. Sub. ——; pd. ——. Long interested in foreign commercial affairs. The E. I. Co. thought of sending him to the East Indies in 1614, but decided to send Sir Thomas Roe. Was M. P. for Gatton in 1614 ; one of the King's Council for New England, and a patentee of lands in Virginia in 1620 ; retained his interest in the Va. Co.; M. P. for Bodmin, 1625 ; on the commission for the better plantation of Virginia, and a patron of Luke Fox in his northwest voyage in 1631.

Brooke, Richard 2. Sub. ——; pd. £50. Of the E. I. Co.

Brooker, Hugh, esquire, 2. Sub. ——; pd. £50. Prothonotary of the Common Pleas. " He lyeth buried in Saint Saviour's Church, in the North Ile, by the Quire. He gave unto the Free school £5 per annum forever, and likewise unto the Poor of the same parish £5 per annum forever." (Strype.)

Brough, Captain John. Sub. ——; pd. £25. I believe this to be the Sir John Brough (or Borough) who was killed at the Isle of Ré in 1627, aged forty-one.

Brown, John, merchant - tailor. Pd. £26.

Brown, Richard. " He was slain about 1577, in The Elizabeth of Mr. Cockin's, of London."

Brown, William, cordwayner, 2. Sub. ——; pd. £12 10s.

Brown, Sir William, 2. Sub. ——; pd. ——. Only son of Nicholas Browne by Eleanor, daughter of Ralph Shirley ; was born in 1558 ; one of the Low Country captains ; taken prisoner at Gravelines. " Sir Philip Sydney was his particular friend and patron, and the valiant brethren, Sir Francis and Sir Horace Vere, who had probably been trained to the military profession under his care, always styled him ' Father.' " (Lodge.) Appointed lieutenant-governor of Flushing towards the end of the reign of Elizabeth.

Brownrig, Matthew, skinner. Pd. £66. Of E. I. and N. W. P. companies.

Brundenel, Edmund, 2. Sub. ——; pd. £25. Of Stoke Mandwill, County Bucks ; March 27, 1622, he transferred his two shares in Virginia to his son Francis. In 1623 he was a member of the New England Council.

Brydges, Grey, Lord Chandos, 2. Sub. ——; pd. £50. Born about 1579 ; was the son of William, the fourth lord, by his wife Mary, daughter of Sir Owen Hopton, lieutenant of the Tower; was implicated in the Essex rising of February 8, 1601, and sent to the Fleet prison, but was soon released; he succeeded his father in the barony, November 18, 1602. Chamberlain writes to Carleton on March 30, 1603, that "the Lord Chandos, who had secretly married the Lady Strange, did now publish his marriage, and made no more dainty." The Lady Strange was Anne Stanley, daughter of Ferdinando, fifth Earl of Derby, and great-granddaughter of the Princess Mary Tudor by her husband, Charles Brandon, Duke of Suffolk. He was made a Knight of the Bath at the creation of Charles Duke of York (afterwards King Charles I.), January 6, 1605; M. A., Oxford, August 30, 1605; M. C. for Va. Co., 1609; served at Juliers in 1610; appointed to receive and introduce the Muscovite ambassadors, November 8, 1617. Died at the Spa, August 10, 1621, and was buried at Sudeley. Collins says he had so great an interest in Gloucestershire that he was commonly called "The King of Cotswould."

Buck, Rev. Richard, 3. Sub. ——; pd. ——. Rev. William Crashaw says he was "an able and painfull preacher, of whom I can say the lesse, because he was of Oxford, and unknown to me; but of whom I have heard Sir Thomas Gates give a good and worthie testimonie; and he came to the Counsell and this imployment with the commendation of a Right Reverend Prelate, Dr. Ravis, Lord Bishop of London."

He sailed from England in June, 1609; wrecked on the Bermudas in July; christened John Rolfe's child there, February 11, 1610; reached Virginia in May, 1610; became the minister at Jamestown; married in Virginia; his first child, Mara, born in 1612; married John Rolfe to Pocahontas, at Jamestown, April 5, 1614. In 1616 Rolfe writes that he was "a verie good preacher." In 1616 or 1617 a child was born to him, called Benoni, who was "the first idiot born in that plantation." During Argall's government (1617–19) a new church was built for him at Jamestown, "wholly at the charge of the inhabitants of that cittie, of Timber, being

fifty foote in length and twenty foot in breadth." And in the Quire of this church, the first General Assembly of English Representatives "convented" in America, met on Friday, July 30, 1619. And "forasmuche as men's affaires doe little prosper where God's service is neglected, all the Burgesses stood in their places, untill a prayer was said by Mr. Bucke, that it would please God to guide and sanctifie all our proceedings to his owne glory and to the good of the Plantation."

March 10, 1621, he was one of the witnesses to John Rolfe's will. His wife and himself both died before February, 1624. They left four children in the care of guardians, a certain number of cattle, 750 acres planted, and 100 acres of glebe land, all by patent, and all in the Corporation of James cittie."

Buckhurst, Lord. See Sackville.

Buillon, Duke de. Henri de la Tour d'Auvergne, Duke of Bouillon. Born 1555; declared for King of Navarre, 1576; Marshal of France, 1592; ambassador to England, 1612. Died March 25, 1623.

Buisseaux — Bisseaux, Monsieur de. Ambassador from France to the Court of London. On May 14, 1617, Ralegh wrote from Plymouth to "M. de Bisseaux, member of the Council of State of France."

Bulkeley (Buckley), Sir Richard. Eldest son of Sir Richard Bulkeley, of Cheadle and Beaumaris. Was born in 1533; sheriff of Anglesey, 1570; M. P. for Anglesey, 1571, 1604–11, and 1614; knighted at Whitehall, November 6, 1604. He was of the Council for Wales, 1617; was admitted to the Va. Co. of London, January 29, 1621; but, I am quite sure, had been interested in the colony at a much earlier date. He patented lands in Virginia. "Died on 18 June, 1621, at the advanced age of eighty-eight. Possessing great wealth, he made use of it in the encouragement of foreign commerce," etc. His second son by his second wife, Thomas, afterwards created Viscount Bulkeley, succeeded to his shares in Virginia on the 13th of February, 1622. Sir Richard's youngest daughter, Katherine, married Sir Edwyn Sandys.

Bull. See Ball.

Bullock, John, esquire, 2. Sub. ——; pd. £25. Of Darley and Norton, County Derby, and of the Inner Temple. Born in 1578 ; married in 1608 Katherine, daughter of Thomas Fanshawe, Esq., and his second wife, Joan Smythe (see pedigree).

Burbage, Richard, the actor. Son of James Burbage, actor and theatrical manager, by his wife, Ellen Brayne, was born about 1567 ; died March 13, 1619. In the Visitation of London, 1633, he is styled "the famous actor on the stage." His name was frequently associated with Shakespeare's by writers of their day.

Burghley, Lord. — William Cecil.

Burgoyne, Peter, 2. Sub. ——; pd. £25.

Burgoyne, Robert, 2. Sub. ——; pd. £12 10s.

Burgoyne, Thomas, 2. Sub. ——; pd. £12 10s. Possibly these were descendants of Nicholas de Burgoyne, the Huguenot, who lived some years in Florida, and was carried thence to England by Drake in 1586.

Burley, Rev. Francis, 2. Sub. ——; pd. £25. Doctor of Divinity ; fellow of Chelsea College ; translator of King James' Bible, etc.

Burnham, Samuel, 2. Sub. ——; pd. £12 10s.

Burrell — Burwell, Ninian. Pd. £12 10s. Of Cuckfield, County Sussex.

Burrell — Burwell, William, 3. Sub. £37 10s.; pd. £37 10s. The son of John Burrell, twice master of the Trinity House. He lived at Stepney. In January, 1612, made a proposition to Henry Prince of Wales for building ships in Ireland; a member of the E. I. and N. W. P. companies ; "one of the commissioners for the Navy Royall 15 yeares and dyed 1630 ; " married Mary, daughter of Thomas Andrews, and sister of Dr. Andrews, Bishop of Winchester, and their son, Andrews Burrell, married Alice, daughter of Capt. Martyn Pring.

Burrough. See Borough.

Burton, George, gent., 2. Sub. ——; pd. £12 10s.

Busbridge — Buckeridge, John, 2. Sub. £37 10s.; pd. £37 10s. Of the N. W. P. Co. and one of the directors of the E. I. Co. May 23, 1614, the E. I. Co. voted him "a gratification towards his expenses in passing a bill through Parliament to stop the exportation of ordinance," etc.

Busby, Ralphe, grocer, 2. Sub. ——; pd. ——. "Admitted a freeman of the Grocers' Co. in 1586. In 1605 he was reproved by the court of assistants, and excluded from all office of authority in the company and not allowed to be of the court of assistants, because of unjust conduct to the clerk and defiance of the authority of the court ; admitted to the livery, 22 May, 1613 ; occupied a house in Wood Street in 1614." (Grocers' Records.) Also of the E. I. and N. W. P. companies.

Butler, George, gent., 2. Sub. ——; pd. £25. Probably M. P. for Carlisle in 1614 and 1621–22.

Butler — Boteler, Captain Nathaniel. Sub. ——; pd. ——. He was "the eldest son of John Butler of Tofte in Sharnbooke in County Bedford Esquier per the 2 venter, Mary dau. of James Gedge and wydow to Christopher Harris Esq." Thus Captain Butler was the half brother to Sir Oliver Butler, or Boteler of Teston, and full brother to James Butler (afterwards of the Va. and S. I. companies) and to —— Butler who married John Cornelius of London, merchant.

Captain Butler was a M. C. for Va. Co.; was elected governor of the Bermudas in the spring of 1619, and was on that island from October, 1619, to October, 1622, during which time Sir Thomas Wrothe wrote an epigram "To his worthy friend Captaine Butler, Governour of Bermuda, or the Summer Iland," which was published in "The Destruction of Troy, or The Acts of Æneas," licensed April 4, 1620.

Butler was in Virginia during the winter of 1622–23, and while there Capt. William Powell and himself led forces against the Indians. He returned to England in the spring, and his "Unmasking of Virginia," one of the causes of the serious factions in the Va. Co., appeared early in April, 1623. He was on the Va. Commission of July 25, 1624 ; at Cadiz in 1625, and the Isle of Ré in 1627 ; a captain in the Royal Navy ; was governor and admiral of the Bahamas from 1638 to 1641, and was probably the person who was committed to Newgate by the Council of State of the Commonwealth for dispersing treasonable and scandalous books in June, 1649. The date of his death is not known to me. He was the author of " Six Dialogues about Sea Services between an High Admiral and a Captain at Sea," which remained in manuscript until 1685, when it was published by Moses Pitt.

Butter, Nathaniel, stationer and journalist. Admitted to freedom of the Stationers' Co., February 20, 1604. " A true and tragical discourse of the expedition to Guiana [1605] was issued by him, June 25, 1607. Newes from Lough ffoyle in Ireland, May 19, 1608. Newes from Spain in 1611. Newes from most parts of Christendom, Sept. 25, 1622; this was his first attempt at a Newspaper and its success induced him to make journalism his chief business, in partnership with Nicholas Bourne and others." " Feb. 22, 1664, Nath. Butter, an old stationer [the first English journalist], *died very poor.*"

Button, Captain Thomas, 2. Sub. £37 10s.; pd. £25. Fourth son of Miles Button, of Worlton in Glamorganshire ; entered the naval service of Queen Elizabeth ; distinguished himself at the siege of Kinsale in Ireland in 1601; was thought to have died in the West Indies, but returned safely to England prior to March 25, 1604; of the N. W. P. Co. 1612 ; entered the service of Henry, Prince of Wales, and in 1612–13 made his celebrated voyage to Hudson's Bay, where he wintered, and named New North and New South Wales for his patron ; commanded his majesty's ship Phœnix on the coast of Ireland, 1614–20; knighted by Sir Oliver St. John, lord deputy of Ireland, August 30, 1616; rear-admiral of the fleet under Sir Robert Mansell, 1620–21 ; on the council of war, 1624 ; on naval commission, 1625 ; consulted by Lord Keeper Coventry about the West Indies in 1629, and by Capt. Thomas James about the N. W. P. in 1630. He died of a fever in April, 1634.

Button's Bay was named for him.

Butts, Thomas. Of Great Riburgh, Norfolk, and son of the very celebrated Sir William Butts, physician to Henry VIII., one of the founders of the College of Physicians, etc. (See Shakespeare's Henry VIII., act V. scene 2.) Hakluyt, writing at some date prior to 1600, says that " Thomas Butts was lately living, to whom I rode two hundred miles only to learn the whole truth of this voyage [of 1536] from his own mouth, as being the only man now alive that was in this discovery."

Byleth, Robert. Master's mate in the voyage to Hudson's Bay, April, 1610, to October, 1611 ; member N. W. P. Co., 1612 ; went with Captain Button, April or May, 1612, to about September, 1613 ; was possibly with Gibbons in 1614 ; made a voyage to the Northwest with Baffin, March to September, 1615; and another, March to August, 1616. The name is variously spelled ; but I believe the correct way to be Blythe, and I am inclined to believe him to be the Captaine Blythe who commanded the fleet in the East Indies in 1622 (when Baffin was killed), although this person is alluded to once or twice in the E. I. records as Capt. Richard Blythe or Blieth.

Cabot, John, a Venetian pilot. Was probably employed in Bristol, England, as early as 1472, but continued to make journeys to Venice for some time after.

The following brief account of his connection with American discovery seems to me about as correct as we can now make it ; yet there is still some confusion on several points : —

" About the year 1491 the people of Bristol, England, began sending out every year, light ships under the command of John Cabot in search of the island of Brazil and the Seven Cities."

It seems probable that he *saw land* while on one [1494 ?] of these private voyages, as he petitioned Henry VII. in 1495 to grant unto him and his three sons the royal authority to discover and possess new lands, etc. In answer to which petition letters patent passed the seal on March 5, 1496, and on May 2, 1497, John Cabot sailed from Bristol on his *first royally authorized voyage,* and returning in August, he was for the first time able to proclaim publicly under the protection of

Henry VII., "The certain news that he had found land." The king gave him presents, and in December, 1497, a pension out of the customs of the port of Bristol. The order for this pension passed the seals, January 28, 1498. On the 3d of February, 1498, Henry VII. granted him authority to impress vessels for another voyage, and "In the begynnynge of Somer" John Cabot sailed with five ships from Bristol. "The king furnished one ship, and with this ship went 3 or 4 more out of Bristol." John Cabot seems to disappear in this voyage, and was probably among the "many men lost." Possibly he died on our coast.

As early as December 18, 1497, we are told that John Cabot "had the description of the world in a *chart*, and also in a *globe, which he made,* showing where he landed in the new world," etc. His charts, or copies of them, had reached Spain in 1499, and it seems certain that a large part of our northern coast on the map of the world made by Juan de la Cosa in 1500 was compiled from them.

It seems almost certain that Europeans had discovered America at much earlier dates ; but Cabot furnishes the first definite starting-point for English claims, and Columbus for the Spaniards, though it may be that Americus Vespucius saw the continent before either of them. Columbus never saw any part of the territory of the United States. As a nation we trace back to the discoveries of John Cabot. We do not trace back to Columbus ; the claims of Spain and the Bulls of the Pope were based on his discoveries. Had England continued to acknowledge those claims, this nation would not now be in existence.

Cabot, Sebastian, second son of John Cabot aforesaid, was probably born in Bristol, England. His name appears in the petition to Henry VII. and in the charter, March 5, 1496. He was probably with his father on several of his voyages of discovery, and I am inclined to infer that the voyage of 1498, which sailed under the father's, returned to Bristol under the son's command ; but much of the old "traveler's tale " has been woven into the early life of Sebastian Cabot. He was making a chart of Gascoigne

and Guienne for Henry VIII. early in 1512, but entered the service of Spain in the fall of that year, and, it seems, remained there until toward the end of 1516, when he returned to England, where he probably continued until 1519. He was appointed pilot-major to Charles V. on May 6, 1619, about which time he probably returned to Spain. He was presumably in England again in 1521, when Henry VIII. required the London companies to furnish him with five ships for the discovery of the new found land. The Drapers record that they considered it "a sore adventure to jepard V shipps wth men and goods unto the said island, upon the singular trust of one man, called, as they understood, Sebastyan, who, as they had heard say, was never in that land himself, and made report of many things, only as he had heard his father and other men speke in times past." In 1522 he had an interview with the Venetian ambassador, in which he offers to enter the service of Venice. He attended the congress of pilots at Badajos in 1524, in the interest of Spain; appointed to command an expedition to Brazil in April, 1526, exploring that country four years ; returned to Spain in August, 1530 ; "was imprisoned for nearly a year, and afterwards condemned by the Council of the Indies to two years' banishment to Oran in Africa for mismanagement of the expedition to Brazil. He returned to Seville in June, 1533, and was soon reinstated in his former position." He remained for many years examiner of pilots in the Contractation House at Seville, during which time he made his famous mappe monde, which was first engraved in 1544. "Shortly after the death of Henry VIII. (28 January, 1547), Cabot received tempting offers from friends in England to transfer his services to the country of his birth." He probably arrived in England in the fall of 1547 and remained there to his death. January 6, 1549, Edward VI. granted him a pension of £166 13s. 4d., to date from September 29, 1548, "in consideration of good and acceptable service done and to be done by him ;" January 19, 1550, Charles V., through the Spanish ambassador in England, demanded the return of Cabot to Spain. The English Council replied, through the English Ambassador, in refusal, April 21, 1550. Some accounts state that Edward VI. renewed to Cabot the patent of March 5, 1496, on June 4, 1550. He settled a dispute between the English and German merchants, and for his services in this matter the king granted him, in March, 1551, a reward of £200. Under his leadership "certain grave citizens of London" formed a company, which was incorporated on December 18, 1551, by the name of "The Mysterie and Companie of the Merchant Adventurers for the Discoverie of Regions, Dominions, Islands and Places, unknown." This company (of which Cabot was "governor for life") set forth the expedition to the Northeast, which sailed under Sir Hugh Willoughby in May, 1553. Edward VI. having died, Charles V. again requested the return of Cabot to Spain, September 9, 1553 ; but he did not go. In answer to the humble petition of William Paulet, Marquis of Winchester, Henry Fitz-Alan, Earl of Arundel, John Russell, Earl of Bedford, William Herbert, Earl of Pembroke, William Lord Howard of Effingham, and others, Philip and Mary granted to "the Company of Merchant Adventurers for the Discoverie of Regions . . . unknown," a second charter on February 6, 1555, with Sebastian Cabot as governor, and on November 27 of the same year, Queen Mary renewed to him his pension. On April 13, 1556, he went aboard the Searchthrift at Gravesend before she sailed on her voyage to the Northeast, and "entered into the dance himself." He resigned his pension May 27, 1557, an annuity was granted him two days after, and this is our last record of him alive. He was then an old man, and within a few months he was probably in his grave.

Opinions may differ as to Cabot's early voyages to the "Newfoundland;" but in the matter of organizing the first English company "for the Discoverie of Regions, Dominions, Islands and Places unknown," his service seems to stand on the "firme lande." This company, which still exists, forms a most interesting chain in the history of English discovery, commerce, and colonization. The first recorded voyages to America from England were sent out under the command of John Cabot, whose son Sebastian (also interested in his father's letters patent) was the first governor; among the first four Consuls ("the Council") and their twenty-four assistants ("the directors") we find Sir George Barnes, Sir William Garrett, Thomas Lodge, and Rowland Haiward, as well as Sir Andrew Judde (grandfather of Sir Thomas Smith), Sir John Yorke (Sir Martin Frobisher's uncle), Richard Chamberlaine the elder, Thomas Offley the elder, Henry Hudson, and others, whose heirs were afterwards interested in colonizing America. And at the time of which we write we find Sir Thomas Smythe, the treasurer of the Virginia Company of London, occupying Cabot's old place of governor in this company, and we see their vessels sailing on the Great White Sea of Russia and taking emigrants to Virginia.

There can be no mistake about the service rendered by Cabot, Barnes, and others, in forming this old merchant company, which was so largely instrumental in laying the business foundation of England's future prosperity, in advancing English discovery, commerce, and colonization. (See the Muscovy Company.) The William Worthington who shared Cabot's annuity in 1557, and who fell heir to the maps and papers of Cabot, was of Orsett in County Essex, esquire, "Pentinor to King Henry VIII., King Edward VI., Queen Mary, and Queen Elizabeth." He married Ann, daughter to Sir Robert Tirrell, of Warley in Essex, master of horse to King Henry VIII. His son, Sir William Worthington, of Springfield in Essex, gentleman, porter of the Tower, and " Pentinor to Queen Elizabeth and James I.," married, first, Mary, daughter to Richard Atkins, recorder of London, and, secondly, Margaret, daughter to Christopher Peyton of Bury St. Edmunds, and widow to Richard Eden.

Cæsar, Sir Julius, oldest son of Dr. Cæsar Adelmare (physician to Queens Mary and Elizabeth) by his wife Margaret, daughter of Martin Perin (Pring ?); born at Tottenham in

840 CÆSAR

1558 ; baptized at St. Dunstan's, February 10, 1558, his sponsors in baptism being William Pawlett, Marquis of Winchester, Henry Fitz-Alan, Earl of Arundel, and Queen Elizabeth, represented by the Lady Montacute. Denization was granted to his father, " Cæsar Aldemarius of Venice, Doctor of Medicine, on the 28th of August, 1558." His father, who was probably a Roman Catholic, died in 1569, and his mother afterwards married Michael Locke, a zealous Protestant. The son, who was baptized Julius-Cæsar Adelmare, finally dropping his ancestral name, was educated at Magdalene College, Oxford ; B. A., May 17, 1575 ; M. A., 1578 ; a subscriber to Frobisher's voyages, 1576–78 ; left Oxford for Paris in 1579, " to finish the study of his profession of a civilian ; and on the 15, 18, and 22 April 1581, was admitted there bachelor, licentiate and doctor, of both Laws. On the tenth of the following May, he received the complimentary appointment of advocate in the parliament of Paris, and within a few weeks after returned to England, which he seems never again to have quitted in the course of his long life." (Lodge.) Appointed " justice of the peace in all causes of piracy, and such like, throughout the land," October 9, 1581. " He now laid the surest foundation for his future advantage, by a most prudent match with Dorcas, daughter of Richard Martin, an alderman of London, who was afterwards knighted, and thrice filled the office of lord mayor, and was master of the mint in the reigns of Elizabeth and James the First. To this lady, who, though scarcely twenty years old, was already the widow of Richard Lusher, a student of the Middle Temple, who had died February 18, 1581, at the age of 28, he was married on the 26th of February, 1582." He was a subscriber to Fenton's voyage, and on March 11, 1582, dined with the Rev. Mr. Maddox (who was licensed to preach in all the world) at Sheriff Martin's (his father-in-law's) house.

Counsel for the City of London, June 11, 1583 ; D. C. L., Oxford, March 5, 1584 ; appointed judge of the Admiralty Court, April 30, 1584 ; a subscriber to the voyage of Cavendish round the world ; master in chancery in ordinary, October 9, 1588 ; " M. P. for Reigate in Surrey, 1589; " Subscriber to the second voyage of Cavendish ; master extraordinary of the Court of Requests, January 10, 1591; treasurer of the Inner Temple ; M. P. for Bletchingley, 1593. Dorcas, his first wife, died June 16, 1595, aged 34, and was buried in the Temple Church, London. (Her son, Sir Charles Cæsar, succeeded Sir Dudley Digges as master of the rolls.)

Master of Request, September, 1595. He married, secondly, on April 10, 1596, Alice, daughter of Christopher Grene, gent., and widow of John Dent, of London, merchant, at her house at Mitcham in Surrey. Master of St. Catherine's Hospital by the Tower of London, June 17, 1596. Wrote " The Ancient State, Authoritie and Proceedings of the Court of Requests, 2 October, 1596 ; " published in 1597. M. P. for Windsor, 1597–98 and 1601. He was visited by Queen Elizabeth at Mitcham, September 12 and 13, 1598, and the entertainment of her majesty cost him £700. Eldest master of the Requests, May 10, 1600 ; Knighted at Greenwich by King James, May 20, 1603 ; M. P. for Westminster, 1604. Appointed chancellor and undertreasurer of the Exchequer, April 11, 1606 ; a member of the Privy Council, July 5, 1607 ; member of the N. W. P. Co., July 26, 1612 ; M. P. for Middlesex, 1614. His second wife, Alice, died May 23, 1614, aged 44 years 11 months, and was buried in the Church of St. Helen's. He was master of the rolls, September 13, 1614. Married, thirdly, April 19, 1615, Anne, daughter of Sir Henry Wodehouse, widow of William Hungate, and niece of Sir Francis Bacon (then attorney-general) who gave her away at the altar. Admitted a free brother of the E. I. Co., January 20, 1618. Many of his papers, still preserved, prove his interest in Virginia, and some of Capt. John Martin's (his brother-in-law's) letters to him from Virginia still remain. M. P. for Malden, 1621–22. He was a member of the commission for winding up the affairs of the Va. Co. of London, July 15, 1624. Lord Bacon is said to have died in his arms in April, 1626. A

JOHN SELDEN

commissioner to examine the case between Capt. David Kirke and the French in Canada, March 5, 1630. He died April 18, 1636, in his 79th year, and was buried in the south transept of the Church of Great St. Helen's, in Bishopsgate Street, where his monument (erected by Nicholas Stone at the cost of £110) with its curious device still remains. The device and inscription were designed and written by himself ; his widow had the monument erected. He left a high character for integrity, talent, and charity. It was said of him, that he was kept alive beyond nature's course by the prayers of the many poor whom he daily relieved.

Cage, Edward, grocer, 2. Sub. £37 10s. ; pd. £87 10s. Admitted to the livery of the Grocers' Company in 1586 ; married Judith, daughter of Sir John Hart ; died in 1619, and on November 15 in that year, his son, John Cage, Esq., sold nine shares of land in Virginia, — six to Dr. Theodore Gulston and three to Isaac Seaward.

Callamata, mentioned in "The Epistle Dedicatory" to Smith's "General History" (1624), in Brathwait's verses prefixed to "The True Travels, etc." (1630), and in "The True Travels," on page 32. The same narrative as printed by Purchas in 1621 contains no reference to her.

Calthorpe. See Galthorpe.

Calvert, George, esquire, 2. Sub. ——; pd. £25. Born about 1579-80, at Kipling in Yorkshire ; entered Trinity College, Oxford in 1594 ; A. B., Oxford, February 23, 159⅗ ; afterwards traveled abroad ; entered public life under the patronage of Sir Robert Cecil ; M. P. for Bossiney in Cornwall, October, 1609, to February 9, 1611 ; A. M., Oxford, 1605. Prothonotary and keeper of. the rolls in Connaught, Ireland, 1606 ; member of the E. I. Co.; clerk of the Privy Council in September, 1611. In January, 1612, " he was settled about the king, and wholly employed in reading and writing." One of the executors of Robert, Earl of Salisbury, May, 1612. One of the commissioners for Ireland, August 24, 1613. He adventured £1,600 in the joint stock of the E. I. Co. in 1614 ; knighted at Hampton Court, September 29, 1617 ; in the

proceedings against Ralegh in 1618 ; appointed secretary of state for life in February, 1619 ; purchased a part of Newfoundland from Sir William Vaughan in 1620, and in 1621 sent a body of settlers there. M. P. for County York, January 30, 1621, to February 8, 1622. Admitted into the New England Company July 5, and his bounds in that colony were laid off July 24, 1622. Avalon ("the first fruits of Christianity "), Newfoundland, was granted to him by letters patent of December 31, 1622, March 30 and April 7, 1623. He was granted lands " at the king's service " in Ireland, February 18, 1623 ; M. P. for Oxford University, February 12, 1624, to (the king's death) March 27, 1625 ; member of the commission for winding up the affairs of the Va. Co., July 15, 1624, and afterwards one of the committee of the Council for plantation affairs ; resigned the secretaryship, for a consideration, in favor of Sir Albert Morton, February 9, 1625 ; created Lord Baltimore, February 16, 1625, and a few days after went into the north of England " with Sir Tobie Matthew, which confirms the opinion. that he is a bird of that feather," *i. e.* a Roman Catholic. On March 11, following, the king granted him the Irish lands " in fee simple," and soon after the king's death he went over to his Irish possessions. He visited " Ferryland," his colony in Newfoundland in 1627, and again in 1628 ; remaining there from about April, 1628, to about September, 1629, when, after having spent about £25,000 in advancing that plantation, he seems to have abandoned it. Going to Virginia, " to view those parts," he arrived at Jamestown early in October, 1629, where he seems to have met with but a " cowlde " reception. Yet he was pleased with the climate and the soil, if not with the people. In December, 1630, he was again in England. In February, 1631, he was very near obtaining a charter for land south of James River. Early in 1632 he overcame all obstacles, and the king agreed to grant him lands north and east of the Potomac ; but he died before his charter passed the seals, " in London, April 15, 1632, in the 53rd year of his age, and was buried in the chancel of St. Dunstan's in the West." He married Anne, daughter of George Wynne. " His rights were transmitted to his son and heir, Cecil, second Lord Baltimore, to whom the Maryland charter was finally issued 20 June, 1632."

Cam, Master Thomas. Probably Thomas Canne, who was afterwards knighted by James I. His son William was mayor of Bristol in 1648.

Campbell—Cambell, James, ironmonger, 2. Sub. —— ; pd. £25. Son of Sir Thomas Campbell, Lord Mayor of London in 1609–10 ; born in 1570 ; became a leading merchant of London ; member of the E. I. Co. ; master of the Ironmongers in 1615; sheriff of London, 1619 ; elected alderman of Billingsgate ward, May 24, 1620; removed to Lime Street ward, May 14, 1625, and at his death in 1642 was the senior alderman of London ; a director of the E. I. Co., 1621 ; master of the Ironmongers, 1623 ; on the Va. commission, July 15, 1624; was a member of the French and Eastland companies; Lord Mayor of London, 1629–30 ; knighted at Whitehall, May 23, 1630 ; master of the Ironmongers in 1641. Died January 5, and was buried in St. Olave's, Jewry, London, on the 8th of February, 1642. By will he left to various objects, charities, and persons, £48,967 6s. 8d., besides real and personal estate, which was a vast sum in those times. His servant, Edward Browne, was inclined to " Bookemakeing," and has thus preserved for us much of interest regarding his master.

Campe, Laurence, draper, 2. Sub. £37 10s. ; pd. £100. Founded an almshouse in the parish of Friarn Barnet ; was a donor to the Parish Church of " Alhallowes the Wall," and " from his love to Learning gave £40 towards the maintenance of poor scholars in Cambridge."

Candish. See Cavendish.

Canning, Paul, 2. Sub. —— ; pd. ——. Member of the E. I. Co.; in 1612 he was sent, with letters from King James and orders from the E. I. Co., to the East Indies ; taken by the Portuguese, September, 1612 ; set on shore at Surat in October, 1612, and died at Agra May 29, 1613, having been " poysoned by Jesuits," so it was said.

Canning, William, ironmonger, 2. Sub. £37 10s.; pd. £37 10s. William and Paul were brothers, being sons of Richard Canning, of Foxcote, County Warwick ; another brother, George, was the ancestor of the celebrated George Viscount Canning, orator and statesman.

William was born about 1562 ; was " of · Bashingshaw Blackwell Hall," London ; patented lands in County Derry, Ireland ; member of the E. I. Co. ; deputy governor of the B. I. Co. ; master of the Ironmongers in 1617 ; elected a director of the Va. Co. of London, April 28, 1619 ; voted to surrender the Virginia charter to the crown, October 20, 1623. During the factions of 1623 in the Va. Co., he struck Thomas Keightley in the Exchange, which resulted in a lawsuit and fines. Master of the Ironmongers in 1627, and died during year of office. He married, in 1592, Rachael, daughter of William Ormshawe, of St. Mary-le-Bow, London, grocer.

Cannon, Thomas, gent., 2. Sub. —— ; pd. £12 10s. Probably M. P. for Haverford West, 1625 and 1626, and for Haslemere, 1628–29; knighted at Greenwich, June 30, 1623.

Cantrell, William, gent., 2. Sub. —— ; pd. £12 10s.

Carbery, Earl of. — John Vaughan.

Carew. See Carne.

Carew, George Lord, 2. Sub. —— ; pd. ——.

Edmund Carew, who was knighted on the field of Bosworth, was the father of Katherine Carew, the grandmother of Sir Walter Ralegh, and of George Carew, the very Reverend Dean of Exeter and Windsor, the father of George Lord Carew, of whom I write.

George Lord Carew was born May 29, 1555 ; at Pembroke College, then called Broadgate Hall, Oxford, 1564 to 1573 ; "distinguished by the variety, the rapidity, and the success of his studies ;" suddenly adopted the military profession ; quitted the university without taking his degree, and joined his uncle, James Wingfield (see pedigree), in Ireland, where he had distinguished himself so early as 1579 ; knighted by Lord Deputy Perrott, lord president of Munster, in 1585 ; M. A., Oxford, 1589 ; lieutenant of the ordnance, Tower of London, in 1592, when his cousin, Sir Walter Ralegh, was placed in his custody for marrying against the wishes of the queen, and it was with him that Sir Walter had the memorable fight (so called) for a sight of Elizabeth; accompanied Essex in the expedition to Cadiz in 1596. In 1597 he was lieutenant of the ordnance of the fleet under Essex sent out against the Azores Islands ; M. P. for Queenborough, 1597–98. In June, 1598, Essex too earnestly advocated him for lord deputy of Ireland, for which Elizabeth gave Essex a box on the ear, and bade him "go and be hanged !" Then Essex lost his temper, and called the queen "a king in petticoats."

Sir George Carew was appointed lord president of Munster, 1599, "when, uniting his forces with those of the Earl of Thomond, he reduced several castles and other strong places, obtained many triumphs over the rebels, brought the Earl of Desmond to trial, and gained great honor to himself." One of the lord justices of Ireland, treasurer of the army, etc., 1600–03 ; "he defeated the Spaniards on their landing at Kinsale in 1601, and obliged them to abandon their projects against Ireland." Upon the accession of King James I. he was constituted captain and governor of the Isle of Guernsey, vice-chamberlain to the queen and receiver-general of her revenues ; M. P. for Hastings from 1604, until he was created a peer. Having married Joyce, only daughter and heiress of William Clopton, Esq., of Clopton, County Warwick, he was elevated to the peerage, May 4, 1605, as Baron Carew of Clopton ; M. C. for Va., 1607. July 27, 1608, he was made master of the ordnance for life, and sworn of the

Privy Council. He continued to have a great interest in the advancement of commerce and colonization. M. C. for the Va. Co., May 23, 1609. June 24, 1611, sent as a commissioner to examine into affairs in Ireland. In 1618 he was on his knees before James I., in behalf of Sir Walter Ralegh, without avail. July 22, 1623, one of a committee "To frame such orders as they conceive most fit for regulating the government of Virginia ;" a movement which resulted in the annulling of the old charters. April 22, 1625, the Privy Council to Secretary Conway and Lord Carew, master of the ordnance: "To take into consideration what forts and places of strength are to be erected and maintained in Virginia, and to give an estimate of the present charge and of the annual cost to maintain them." He was created Earl of Totness, February 1, 1625–26. Died March 27, 1629, at the Savoy in the Strand in the suburbs of London, and lies buried at Stratford-upon-Avon.

He was the author of "Pacata Hibernia," and the unique papers relating to Ireland, collected by him, are now preserved in the Lambeth Library. "He was a wise statesman, an eminent commander, and an estimable historian. His niece Anne married, secondly, Sir Allen Apsley.

Carew, Sir George, statesman. Ambassador to King of Poland, 1597 ; to Court of France, 1605–09 ; "Master of the wards, 1612, succeeding the late lord treasurer ;" died in November, 1612. Author of "Relation of the State of France," etc., written in 1609 ; published in 1749.

Carey—Cary, Sir George, of Devonshire, 3. Sub. £45 ; pd. £45. Of Cockington, Devon ; son of Thomas Carey ; was born about 1540 ; active against the Spaniards in 1588 ; a patron of Cavendish, 1591 ; knighted at Whitehall in February, 1597 ; treasurer for Ireland, March, 1599 ; lord deputy of Ireland, 1603–04 ; died in February, 1617 ; was twice married, but left no surviving issue. His widow was Lucy, daughter of Robert Lord Rich and first Earl of Warwick.

Carey (or **Cary**) **Henry,** first Lord Hunsdon. First cousin to Queen Elizabeth ; subscriber to Frobisher's (1576–78) and Fenton's (1582–83) voyages, and patron of Cavendish. He gathered plants from the farthest parts of the world. " Died at Somerset House, 23d July, 1596, aged 72."

Carey (or **Cary**), **Sir Henry, 2.** Sub. £75 ; pd.———. Son of Sir Edward Cary, of Berkhamstead and Aldenham, Hertfordshire (first cousin to the first Lord Hunsdon), by his wife Catherine, daughter of Sir Henry Knevet, master of the jewel office to Queen Elizabeth. He was educated at Exeter College, Oxford, where he acquired distinction by his talents ; knighted at Dublin, July 12, 1599, by the Earl of Essex ; served in France and the Low Countries, where he was taken prisoner by Don Louis de Velasco, at the battle of Mulheim in 1605, a fact referred to in the epigram on Sir Henry Cary by Ben Jonson. On his return to England he was introduced to court, and became one of the gentlemen of the bed-chamber ; one of the masters of the royal jewels, June 21, 1603–18 ; M. C. for Va. Co., May 23, 1609 ; N. W. P. Co., 1612 ; a privy councilor in 1617 ; comptroller of the household in January, 1618 ; on commission for regulating the deputies of the E. I. Co., 1618 ; created Viscount Falkland, November 10, 1620 ; M. P. for Hertfordshire, 1621–22 ; made an earnest attempt to establish a colony in Newfoundland in 1621–22 ; lord deputy of Ireland, September, 1622, to 1629. Old Fuller says, " an unruly colt will fume and chafe (though neither switched nor spurred) merely because *backed.* The rebellious Irish will complain, only because kept in subjection, though with never so much lenity ; the occasion why some hard speeches were passed on his government." He lost his life by an accident in Theobald's Park in September, 1633. He married, about 1609, Elizabeth, only daughter and sole heir of Sir Laurence Tanfield, chief baron of the

Exchequer (she was a grand-niece of old Sir Henry Lee, " the Queen's knight "), by whom he was the father of Lucius, the celebrated Viscount Falkland, who was killed at the battle of Newbury, September 20, 1643.

Carey (or **Cary**), **Sir Henry.** Sub. ——— ; pd. ———. Son of Sir Robert Carey ; born in 1596 ; made a knight at the creation of Charles, Prince of Wales, 1616 ; married Martha, daughter of Lionel Cranfield, Earl of Middlesex ; succeeded his father as second Earl of Monmouth in 1639 ; died June 13, 1661.

As there were two Sir Henry Careys, members of the Va. Co. in 1619–20, when the accounts were audited, I cannot assign the payments with any certainty. The following payments were made to Sir Thomas Smythe : " Sir Henry Carie, £20 ; " " Sir Henry Carie, Captaine, £25 ; and to Sir Baptist Hicks : " Sir Henry Carie, £75."

Carey (or **Cary**), **Sir Philip.** Third son of Sir Edward Cary of Aldenham, and brother of Henry, first Viscount Falkland. M. P. for Woodstock in 1614, 1621–22, 1624–25, and 1625 ; knighted at Greenwich by James I. on March 23, 1605. Buried at Aldenham, June 13, 1631.

Carey, Sir Robert, 2. Sub. ——— ; pd. ———. Seventh and youngest son of Henry Carey, first Lord Hunsdon ; born about 1560 ; with Sir Thomas Layton in the Netherlands, 1577 ; attended in the suite of Duke of Alençon in the Low Countries, 1581 ; went with Walsingham to Scotland, 1583, when King James became interested in him ; M. P. for Morpeth, 1586–87; with the Earl of Cumberland at Sluys, 1587 ; serves against the Armada, 1588 ; M. P. for Morpeth, 1588–89 ; serves at Rouen, 1591 ; M. P. for Morpeth, 1593 ; for Northumberland, 1597–98 and 1601. After the death of Elizabeth, he left London about 9 A. M., March 24, and reached Holyrood late on the 26th, carrying to King James the news of the death of the queen. He was created Baron of Leppington, February 6, 1622, and Earl of Monmouth, February 7, 1626; died April 12, 1639. His memoirs were published in 1759 by the Earl of Cork and Orrery.

**Carleill (Carliell, Carlile, etc.),
Capt. Christopher,** son of Alexander
Carleill by his wife Anne, daughter
of Sir George Barnes the elder (see
Barnes pedigree). He was born about
1551 ; educated in the University of
Cambridge ; went to Flushing in 1572,
and "followed the fortune of the
Warres in Flanders and by desert was
made a great commander in ye States
Campe ; " served the Prince of Condé
at La Rochelle ; took an interest in
American discoveries as early as 1574;
admiral of the English merchants into
Russia, 1582 ; interested in Fenton's
voyage, 1582–83 ; interested in America to the southwest of Cape Breton,
1582–83 ; serving in Ireland, 1584 ; on
the celebrated expedition to America,
September, 1585, to July, 1586 ; again
serving in Ireland in 1588 ; died in
London, November 11, 1593 ; married
Mary, daughter of Sir Francis Walsingham, and sister of Sir Philip Sidney's wife.

He was the author of "A Brief Summary Discourse upon a Voyage intending to the uttermost parts of America"
(given by Hakluyt) and of "A Discourse on the Discovery of the hither-
most parts of America, written by
Captain Carleill to the Citizens of
London," Lansd. MS. 100, art. 14.

Carleton, Sir Dudley, born
March 10, 1573. After a course of
instruction at Westminster school, he
became a student of Christ Church
College, Oxford, about 1591, and had
for his tutor Mr. John King, afterwards Dean of Christ College and
Bishop of London ; B. A., 1595 ;
spent most of the next five years in
improving himself by foreign travel ;
M. A., 1600 ; accompanied Sir Thomas
Parry, ambassador to the Court of
France, as his secretary, in 1602 ; M.
P. for St. Mawes in Cornwall, 1604 ;
some time secretary to the Earl of
Northumberland, and as such was under some suspicion, and placed under
arrest for a time, during the excitement incident to the Gunpowder Plot.
The series of Gazette Letters *from*,
and *to*, him, still preserved, contain a
perfect mine of historical information,
and throw a flood of light on the times
in which he lived. Many of these letters contain references to Virginia.
Knighted in September, 1610, and sent

ambassador to Venice, where he remained until 1615, when he was transferred to Savoy ; ambassador to the
States General in 1616, and continued
chiefly in this employment until 1628,
except that in the year 1625 he was sent
as ambassador extraordinary to the
Court of France. M. P. for Hastings
in 1626 ; created Baron Carleton of
Imbercourt, County Surrey, May 21,
1626, and Viscount Dorchester, July
25, 1628 ; one of the principal secretaries of state, December 14, 1628,
and in this position he evidently took
great interest in the colonies, as papers
still remaining amply prove. Governor Harvey of Virginia constantly
appealed to him. He was a member
of the royal commission for the better
plantation of Virginia, June 27, 1631.
He died February 15, 1632, and was
buried in St. Peter's, Westminster.
"He was an able diplomatist and a
polished statesman ; a master of different languages ; a good ancient and
modern historian ; and was esteemed
a graceful and eloquent speaker."

He married, first, in November, 1607,
Anne, step-daughter of Sir Henry
Saville, and daughter and co-heir of
George Gerard, Esq., second son of
Sir William Gerard, knight of Dorney,
which lady accompanied him in all his
travels, as is expressed in her epitaph
in Westminster Abbey. He married,
secondly, in 1630, Anne, daughter of
Sir Henry Glenham, and widow of
Paul Viscount Bayning, which lady
survived him. He left no surviving
issue by either wife.

Carlisle, Earl of. — James Hay.

Carne, Edward, esquire, 2. Sub.
——; pd. £37 10s. Of Nashe Glamorgan, eldest son of William Carne,
Esq. He was one of the tellers of the
Exchequer.

Caron, Sir Noel de. "He was
leger ambassador from the States of
the Netherlands to the English Court,
for the space of 33 or 34 years, in
which time he performed that place
with much honor and good to his own
country and State here. He died at his
house at Lambeth, December 1, 1624,
and was buried with due solemnity in
the chancel of the church there, January 25, 1625. Archbishop Abbot
preached his funeral sermon." In
1622 he built and endowed, in Lam-

beth parish, seven almshouses for poor women, "and thereby hangs a tale."

Carpenter, Abraham. Pd. £12 10s.

Carpenter, Thomas, 2. Sub.——; pd. £49 3s.

Carpenter, William, 2. Sub.——; pd. £37 10s. Alderman's deputy of the Ward of Portsoken; married Alice, daughter of Thomas Carpenter (probably the above Thomas) of the Home in Pembridge, Com. Hereford.

Carr, Sir Edward, 3. Sub.——; pd. £37 10s. Of Sleaford, County Lincoln; knighted April 23, 1603; created a baronet, 1611; died, 1619.

Carr, Robert, Earl of Somerset. Knighted December 23, 1607; lord treasurer of Scotland, 1610; Viscount Rochester, March 25, 1611; K. G. May, 1611; privy councilor, April, 1612; Earl of Somerset, November 3, 1613; married Countess of Essex, December 26, 1613; condemned to death for murder of Sir Thomas Overbury, 1616; pardoned and released, 1622; died July, 1645. (See Gondomar.)

Carter, Francis, 3. Sub.——; pd. ——. He was an officer of the Va. Co. of London and a very large shareholder in Virginia; in 1621 and 1622 he transferred 86 shares to 39 persons.

Carter, Randall (or Randolph), tallow chandler, 2. Sub. £37 10s.; pd. £100. He died prior to 1620, and his executors also adventured £25 in addition on account of his estate.

Cartwright, Abram, draper, 2. Sub. £37 10s.; pd. £75. Member of the E. I. Co.; on the Virginia Commission of July 15, 1624. His daughter Frances married Samuel Vassall, of London. (See John Vassall.)

Carvil — Kervill, etc., **John,** 2. Sub. £37 10s.; pd. £75. Barrister at law of New Monkton, York, and of the Middle Temple; married, prior to 1600, Dorothy, daughter of Robert Kay, of Woodsome. He was M. P. for Aldborough (York), 1621–22, 1624–25, 1625, and 1626.

Carwarden — Carmarden, Richard, esquire, 3. Sub.——; pd. £25. He was the surveyor of the great customs to King Charles in 1634; his father, Richard Carmarden, of London, was surveyor of the customs to Queen

Elizabeth. Of the same family, I suppose, as Sir Thomas Carwardine, master of the revels to Henry VIII.

Cassen — Cason, John, grocer, 2. Sub. £37 10s.; pd. £50. Married Margaret, sister to Richard Edwards; also of N. W. P. and E. I. companies.

Caswell, Richard, baker, 2. Sub. £37 10s.; pd. £125. Of St. Swithin, London; married, in 1619, Mary, daughter of Richard Slany, Esq.; on the committee of the Va. Co., April 28, 1619; on the committee in charge of the two Virginia Maydes, November 15, 1620; one of the stewards for ordering and preparing the annual supper of the Va. Co., November, 1621 and 1622; treasurer for the magazine of provisions sent to Virginia in July, 1623. He informed the Archbishop of Canterbury of the non-conformity of the officers and others in the Bermudas, for which he was suspended from his place in the court of the S. I. Co., November 27, 1639. He died 1646.

Cater — Catto, William, 2. Sub. ——; pd. ——. A citizen of London, who lent money to the king; member of the E. I. Co.; in 1608 he was on the committee of that company. In 1609 he lent the company £1,000 at 9 per cent. interest, and asked to be allowed to buy carpets in the Indies for his own use; also of N. W. P. Co.

Cavendish-Talbot, "Mary Countess of Shrewsbury," 3. Sub.——; pd. £50. Wife of Gilbert Talbot, and sister of William Lord Cavendish.

Cavendish, Captain Thomas. Of Grimston Hall in the parish of Trimley, St. Martin, Suffolk. He was probably born about 1555; was on the voyage to Roanoke (North Carolina) in 1585. He sailed around the world in 1586–88, and made a second "attempte to do the like" in 1591, but was obliged to alter his course and return for England. He died at sea in the summer of 1592, and was buried in the Atlantic Ocean somewhere near 8° N. Lat.

Cavendish, William Lord, 3. Sub.——; pd. £187 10s. He was the second son of Sir William Cavendish by his third wife, Elizabeth, daughter of John Hardwick, Esq. His mother was a noted woman for nearly a century in the history of

England. "Bess of Hardwick" was born about 1518 ; at the age of fourteen years, she married Robert Barley, Esq., who died without issue, February 2, 153¾. "She lived a widow a considerable time, and then took for her second husband Sir William Cavendish, who died in 1557, having had by her a hopeful number of sons and daughters." She married, thirdly, Sir William St. Loe, and fourthly, George Talbot, Earl of Shrewsbury, who died November 18, 1590 ; but she had issue by her second husband only. She died February 13, 160⅞, immensely rich.

Lodge says, "She was a woman of a masculine understanding and conduct ; . . . a builder, a buyer, and seller of estates, a money-lender, a farmer, and a merchant of lead, coals, and timber. . . . She lived to a great old age, continually flattered, but seldom deceived." Her second son by her second husband, of whom I write, was probably born about 1550. M. P. for Newport in Cornwall, November 12, 1588, to March 29, 1589 ; sheriff of Derbyshire, 1594–95 ; created Baron Cavendish of Hardwick, County Derby, May 4, 1605 ; an incorporator of the N. W. P. Co., July 26, 1612.

Collins says, "His lordship was one of the first adventurers, who settled a colony and plantation in Virginia ; and on the first discovery of the Bermudas Island, had (with the Earl of Northampton, the Earl of Pembroke, the Lord Paget, the Lord Harrington, and others) a grant of them from the king. Whereupon, in April, 1612, they sent a ship thither, with sixty persons, to take possession thereof, who were followed by others, and yearly supplies, which soon made them a flourishing plantation. The great island was divided into eight cantons or provinces, bearing the name of eight of the chief proprietors, whereof one of them still retains the name of Cavendish."

He was one of the incorporators of the Bermudas Company, June 29, 1615. Mr. Henry Cavendish, his elder brother, died in 1616, "without lawfull yssue, whereby his inheritance, which is esteemed to be of better valew then £4,000 by the yere, is fallen upon the Lord Cavendishe ; " "who thus inherited the whole estate, and possessed three of the finest houses in England : Chatsworth, Hardwick, and Oldcotes, all erected by his celebrated mother." "He was declared Earl of Devonshire, on August 2, 1618, in the Bishop's palace at Salisbury ; but the letters patent bear date August 7, 1618." In the disputes of 1623 in the Va. Co. of London, he sided with the Sandys faction, of which his son, the Lord Cavendish, was a leader. He died March 3, 162⅚, and was buried at Endsore, near Chatsworth, where a monument is erected for him. His second son by his first wife (Anne, daughter of Henry Kighley, Esq.) was " Sir William Cavendish Knight."

Cavendish, Sir William. Sub. ——; pd. £25. Son of the foregoing; was born about 1589–90. In 1608 he went on his travels into France and Italy, under the tuition of Mr. Thomas Hobbs, and on his return was knighted at Whitehall, March 7, 160⅚ ; and by the policy of King James was married to Christian, only daughter to his great favorite, Edward Lord Bruce, of Kinlosse in Scotland. The king gave her a fortune of £10,000, and requested "that Sir William might bear up the port of his son; which mediation proved so effectual, that the Lord Cavendish did what the king thought reasonable." "But this addition," says Collins, "though it answered the king's, yet it did not rise up to the generosity of the son's mind, which occasioned his contracting a very great debt, entered into by an excess of gallantry, the vice of that age, which he too much indulged himself in." M. C. for Va. Co. He succeeded his father as Lord Cavendish in August, 1618. M. P. for Derby in 1621; governor of the S. I. Co., 1622–23 ; a leading member of the Sandys faction in 1623, he frequently presented the case of that faction to King James. "On Wednesday (July 16, 1623) at the Bermudas Court, Sir Edwin Sandys fell foul upon the Earl of Warwick. The Lord Cavendish seconded Sandys, and the Earl told the Lord, by his favour, he believed he lied. Hereupon it is said, they rode out yesterday, and, as it is thought, have gone beyond sea to fight." (Letter to Rev. Joseph Mead, July 18.) On the 19th of July the Privy Council ordered that all the ports of the kingdom should be carefully watched so that they might not cross the Channel. July 26, Chamberlain wrote to Carleton : " The last week, the Earl of Warwick and Lord Cavendish fell so foul at a Virginia, or Bermuda's Court, that the lie passed and repassed, and they are got over to try their fortune; yet we do not hear they are met ; so that there is hope they may return safe. In the meantime, their ladies forget not their old familiarity, but meet daily, to lament their misfortune." " In a few days Cavendish was detected and arrested at Shoreham in Essex ; but Warwick, disguising himself as a merchant, reached the opposite shore, where he was taken at Ghent early in August and ordered to return to England."

Lord Cavendish was M. P. for Derby again in 1624, 1625, and 1626.

" In the year 1625 Lord Cavendish and his lady waited on Charles I. to Canterbury, by his royal appointment, to be present at his nuptials with Maria-Henrietta (second daughter to Henry IV. of France), who arrived at Dover on May 13, and came the same night to Canterbury, where the marriage was consummated."

He succeeded his father as Earl of Devonshire, March 3, 1626, and died at his house near Bishopsgate in London on June 20, 1628.

This earl was a great speaker in both houses of Parliament. Mr. Hobbs, who had lived with him for 20 years (1608–28) held him up as a pattern to his son.

His widow, Christian, Countess of Devonshire, who survived him nearly 47 years, dying January 16, 167$\frac{4}{5}$, was a woman of considerable celebrity, the patroness of the wits of that age, and a zealous royalist.

His daughter Anne married Robert, the eldest son of his old opponent, Robert Rich, Earl of Warwick.

Cecil, Sir Edward, 2. Sub. £75; pd. £25. Third son of Thomas Cecil, first Earl of Exeter, by his first wife, Dorothy, daughter of John Neville, " Lord Latymer." He was born February 29, 157$\frac{1}{2}$, and entered service in the Low Country wars in 1599, where

" he passed the degrees of Captaine of foote and horse; Colonell of foote, and served with great distinction as Collonell of the English horse at the battle of Nieuport in Flanders anno 1600." At Ostend in July, 1601 ; knighted by Elizabeth September, 1601 ; M. P. for Aldborough in 1601 ; granted the keepership of Mortlake Park for life in 1603. In active service in the wars in the Low Countries, 1602–05; M. C. for Va. Co., May 23, 1609; March, 1610, appointed by King James to command the English forces employed in the war about the succession to the deceased Duke of Cleves ; served at the siege of Juliers, July $\frac{1}{1}\frac{7}{7}$ to August $\frac{1}{2}\frac{2}{2}$. In 1612 he acted for Henry, Prince of Wales, as sponsor to the child of Count Ernest of Nassau. " He followed the Warres in the Netherlands 35 years." M. P. for Chichester in 1614. In 1620 he was consulted by the Virginia Company regarding the fortifying of Virginia ; M. P. for Chichester in 1621–22, in which Parliament " they say he made a brave speech concerning the defenses of England ; " M. P. for Dover in 1624–25. He was admiral and lord marshal, lieutenant-general and general of the expedition sent by King James and King Charles against the King of Spain and Emperor, which finally sailed for Spain, October 1, 1625 ; created Baron Cecil of Putney, November 9, 1625, and Viscount Wimbledon, July 25, 1626. He was also "a Counsellor of State and Warre, and Lord Lieutenant of the County of Surry, and Captain and Governour of Portsmouth."

In August, 1636, he wrote two letters from Portsmouth to Secretary Windebank, in which " he blames Governor Harvey for his delays in sailing to Virginia." He died at Wimbledon November 16, 1638, and lies buried in the parish church there, under a tomb on which a brief outline of his life is inscribed.

He was one of the most famous generals of his time, though he lost some reputation by the miscarriage of the expedition to Cadiz in 1625, in which he commanded. He wrote a short defense of his conduct on this occasion which was printed in 1627, and two short tracts on military affairs, which remain in MS. in the British Museum.

He was thrice married, but left no male issue. He married, first, Theodosia, a daughter of Sir Andrew Noel; secondly, February 27, 1617, Diana, daughter of Sir William Drury (who "after the death of her brother, Sir Robert Drury," says Chamberlain, "became a good marriage worth £10,-000 or £12,000 ") ; and, thirdly, Sophia, daughter of Sir Edward Zouche.

Cecil, Robert, Earl of Salisbury, 2. Sub. ——— ; pd. £333 6s. 8d.; contributed £333 6s. 8d. ($8,000) to the Va. Co. and was the constant and faithful friend of the Virginia enterprise ; "The little beagle" of James I. He was the son of Lord Treasurer Burghley by his second wife, Mildred, daughter of Sir Anthony Coke, or Cooke, of Gidea Hall in Essex ; born June 1, 1560 ; educated at home and at Cambridge; M. P. for Westminster, 1586–87; served against the Spanish Armada in 1588; knighted in June, 1591; privy councilor, August, 1591; spoke against Ralegh, and in defense of aliens in 1593 ; one of the principal secretaries of state, 1596; chancellor of the Duchy of Lancaster, and keeper of the privy seal, 1597. He was the chief commissioner on the part of England in the treaty between France and Spain, at Vervins in 1598. "He succeeded his father, who died in the autumn of that year, in the post of master of the wards; and in his office of secretary exercised in fact that of prime minister for the remaining five years of the queen's life, with as full a share of her favor and confidence as she had at any time bestowed on his illustrious natural and political predecessor. No one among her ministers but himself could have supplied the loss of Walsingham, who furnished her with the means of controlling foreign powers through intelligence gained in their own courts. Cecil even rivaled him in this dark faculty." (Lodge.) He was the sole secretary of state to James I. from 1603 to his death in 1612 ; created Baron Cecil of Essingden, May 13, 1603 ; Viscount Cranbourne, August 20, 1604 ; Earl of Salisbury, May 4, 1605 ; Chancellor of the University of Oxford ; Knight of the Garter, May, 1606; lord high treasurer, May 4, 1608.

He died of pulmonary consumption at Marlborough, May 24, 1612, and was buried in the parish church of his princely seat of Hatfield in Herts. He married Elizabeth, daughter of William Brook, Lord Cobham, by whom he had one son, William, his successor, lineal ancestor of the present Marquis of Salisbury.

In 1603 Sir Robert Cecil wrote as follows to Sir James Harington : "Good Knight rest content, and give heed to one that hath sorrowed in the bright lustre of a Court and gone heavily on even the best-seeming fair ground. 'Tis a great task to prove one's honesty and yet not mar one's fortune. You have tasted a little thereof in our blessed Queen's time, who was more than a man, and, in truth, sometimes less than a woman. I wish I waited now in your presence-chamber, with ease at my food and rest in my bed. I am pushed from the shore of comfort, and know not where the winds and waves of a court will bear me. I know it bringeth little comfort on Earth; and he is, I reckon, no wise man that looketh this way to heaven."

Thomas Sackville, Earl of Dorset, who died in April, 1608 (who had been long intimate with Cecil), in his last will, solemnly records, "with the utmost warmth of expression," Cecil's many public and private virtues, because as he says, "I am desirous to leave some faithful remembrance in this my last Will and Testament ; that since the living speech of my tongue when I am gone from hence must then cease and speak no more, that yet the living speech of my pen, which never dieth, may herein thus forever truly testify and declare the same."

After Salisbury's death Digby wrote from Madrid to King James : "Velasco . . . writeth, in his Letters of April 14, 1612, that there is arrived a Secretary from Florence who . . . hath made promises of 100,000 crowns to Beltenebras [*i. e.* Salisbury] in case he procure the effecting of the marriage." And again on September 9, 1613, Digby wrote to King James : "I conceive your Majesty will think it strange that your late High Treasurer and Chief Secretary, the Earl of Salisbury (besides the Ayùdas de costa,

as they term them, — which are gifts
extraordinary upon services) should
receive 6,000 crowns yearly pension
from the King of Spain." But when
Digby made these charges Salisbury
was dead, and it may be remembered
that it is said that Digby's own hand
sometimes felt the roughness of a
Spanish dollar. I will not enter into
these controversies. If the accounts
of the time are to be relied on, the
Duke of Lerma made the Court of
Spain a market in which nothing could
be done without the medium of money,
— state affairs were for trade and bar-
ter. Lerma expected to receive money
for himself from others, and was liberal in bestowing the money of Spain;
but it is not in evidence that Spain always received compensation therefor.
(See Gardiner's "Hist. England," i.
pp. 215, 216.)

Cecil, Thomas, Earl of Exeter, 2.
Sub.——; pd. £220. The only son
of the first Lord Burghley by his first
wife Mary, daughter of Peter Cheke,
and sister of the noted Sir John Cheke,
tutor to Edward VI.; born May 5,
1542; traveling in Europe with his
tutor, Thomas Windebank, in 1560–62;
M. P. for Stamford in Lincolnshire in
1563, and also in two other Parliaments of Elizabeth's reign. In 1573
he served with distinction as a volunteer in the expedition into Scotland
under Sir William Drury, in aid of
the Earl of Murray, the regent of the
young King of Scots, when the castle
of Edinburgh was besieged and taken.
In July, 1575, waiting on Queen Elizabeth at Kenilworth Castle in Warwickshire, when she was entertained by the
Earl of Leicester with all princely
pleasures, her majesty at that time
conferred on him the honor of knighthood. In 1581 he was one of those
illustrious gallants who entertained
Francis of Valois, Duke of Alanson,
heir presumptive of France, and brother to the French King, then in England as a suitor to Queen Elizabeth,

and gained honor in the justs, barriers,
and tourney performed on that occasion. He also distinguished himself
in the wars of the Low Countries, and
was, in November, 1585, made governor of the Brielle, one of the cau-
tionary towns which the states of
Holland pledged to Queen Elizabeth.
In September, 1586, he fought as a
volunteer at Doesburg, and resigned
his command of the Brielle late in
1587.

In 1585 he was chosen a member of
Parliament for the county of Lincoln,
and was also in another Parliament for
that county. In 1588 he was a volunteer on board the fleet which for six
days maintained many sharp fights and
fierce assaults with the Spanish Armada, and at length forced them to fly.
M. P. for Northamptonshire in 1593.
In 1598, at the funeral of his father,
the Lord Burleigh, on August 29, he
was chief mourner, and by her majesty's order mourned as an earl, being
at that time in the 57th year of his
age. Warden of Rockingham Forest
and constable of the castle there for
life in 1599; one of the commanders
against Essex in February, 1601.
"He was elected one of the Knights-
Companions of the Most Noble Order
of the Garter, and installed at Windsor, May 26, 1601." (Collins.)

On the accession of King James to
the throne in 1603, he was sworn of
the Privy Council at the Charter-
House, May 10, 1603, the fourth day
after his majesty's arrival in London,
and was constituted lord lieutenant
of the county of Northampton. And
his majesty, in consideration of his
great merits and services, created him
Earl of Exeter, May 4, 1605. M. C.
for Va. Co., May 23, 1609. The meetings of the managers of this company
were sometimes held at his house in
London, facing the Strand. The old
Lord Burleigh died in this house in
1598. He called it Burleigh House,
and when in London resided there,
and was visited there by Queen Elizabeth. Pennant says it was "a noble
pile, built with brick, and adorned
with four square turrets." It was afterwards known as Exeter House, and
was still existing in 1826 as Exeter
'Change Royal Menagerie, and *adorned*
with the sign of "Edward Cross,

The right Honorable Lord EDMOND Baron
Sheffeild: His M.ties Gouernour of y Cittie and Countie of
Yorke: and President of his Counsell establijhed in y North
knight of the Most noble Order of the Garter.

EDMOND SHEFFIELD

First Earl of Mulgrave

Dealer in *Foreign* Birds and Beasts."
It was pulled down in 1830, and the
Lyceum Theatre, Wellington Street,
stands on part of the site.

The Earl of Exeter was now growing old ; but during the remainder of
his life he continued in many noble
employments. In 1617 he was troubled by the disagreement between his
daughter, the Lady Hatton, and her
husband, Lord Chief Justice Coke,
and in 1618 by the scandalous squab-
ble between his grandson, Lord Roos,
and his wife and her father, Sir
Thomas Lake. And he seems, towards the conclusion of his life, to
have taken up an inclination to church-
government, for in 1618 he accepted a
nomination, with others, to proceed
against Jesuits and Seminary priests,
with authority to banish them from the
realm ; and in 1620 was joined with
the Archbishop of Canterbury in a
special ecclesiastical commission for
that province, and towards the end of
the same year, in another for that of
York. He left some proofs too, not
only of a charitable disposition, but
of an affection to learning, for he
founded and endowed a hospital at
Liddington in Rutlandshire for a ward-
en, twelve poor men and two women,
and gave an estate to Clare Hall in
Cambridge for the maintenance of
three fellows and eight scholars.

He died February 7, 1622, in his
80th year, and was buried in the
chapel of St. John the Baptist in
Westminster Abbey, where a magnificent monument remains to his memory.

He married, first, Dorothy, daughter and co-heir of John Lord Latimer,
by whom he had five sons and eight
daughters. Of the sons, William, the
eldest (see hereafter) ; Richard, the
second son, married a daughter of Sir
Anthony Cope, and the present Marquis of Exeter descends from them ;
Edward, the third son, of whom I have
written ; Thomas, the fifth son, married Anne, daughter of Sir Robert Lee,
mayor of London ; Mary, the fourth
daughter, married Edward Lord
Denny; Elizabeth, the sixth daughter,
married, first, Sir William Newport
alias Hatton (heir to Sir Christopher
Hatton), and secondly, Sir Edward
Coke, the lord chief justice. Dorothy,
the seventh daughter, married Sir

Giles Alington, and Frances, the
eighth, married Nicholas Tufton, Earl
of Thanet.

The Earl of Exeter married, secondly, Frances, eldest daughter of
William Brydges, fourth Lord Chandos, and widow of Sir Thomas Smith
of Parson's Green. She was the sister of Grey Brydges, fifth Lord Chandos.

Cecil, Captain William. Eldest
son of Thomas, Earl of Exeter ; with
Drake 1585–86 ; father of William
Lord Roos. At the death of his father
in 1622 he succeeded as second Earl
of Exeter, and died in 1640.

Cecil, William, Lord Burleigh.
He was born at Bourne, Lincolnshire,
September 13, 1520 ; master of requests to the Protector Somerset, 1547;
at the battle of Musselburgh, September 10, 1547 ; secretary of state,
1548 ; committed to the Tower, 1549;
restored to office, October, 1551 ;
knight and member of Privy Council,
1551 ; resigns office, 1553 ; M. P.,
Lincolnshire, 1555 ; secretary of state;
privy councilor, 1558 ; patron of the
trade to Russia ; master of the wards,
1561 ; interested in Capt. John Hawkins's voyages, 1564–68 ; Baron Burleigh, 1571 ; Knight of the Garter,
1572 ; lord high treasurer, July 15,
1572 ; interested in Frobisher's voyages, 1576–78, and Fenton's, 1582–83;
died May 4, 1598.

He was a truly great man. The
church and state of England probably owe as much to him as they do to
any man. His biography would be
almost a history of the time in which
he lived. He patronized all the English voyages for discovery, etc. He
married, first, May 8, 1541, Mary,
daughter of John Cheke, who bore
him an only child, Thomas (whom
see), and died February 22, 154¾. He
married, secondly, December 21, 1545,
Mildred, daughter of Sir Anthony
Cooke. She was the mother of Robert
(whom see).

Cecil, William, Lord Cranborne,
3. Sub. ——; pd. £25. Only son of
Robert, Earl of Salisbury. In 1600
he was at Sherborne, pursuing his
studies under Ralegh's guidance ;
married, in December, 1608, Catherine, youngest daughter of Thomas
Howard, Earl of Suffolk ; aided in

sending out Hudson to the Northwest in 1610 ; succeeded his father as second Earl of Salisbury in 1612. Ralegh dedicated his "Brief History of England" to him ; May 28, 1619, passed to Captain Brett two shares of land in Virginia. One of his Majesty's Council for New England, November 3, 1620; Knight of the Garter, December 21, 1624 ; served King Charles I. as an ambassador extraordinary to the Court of France; sat in the Long Parliament during the interregnum. Died December 3, 1668, and was succeeded by his grandson.

Chaderton (or Chatterton), Dr. Laurence. His wife was aunt to Rev. Alexander Whitaker of Virginia (see under Dr. William Whitaker). He is said to have been born in 1536 ; was master of Emmanuel College, Cambridge, 1584–1622 ; took part in the Hampton Conference, 1604 ; employed on the Authorized Version of the Bible, 1607–1611. He died November 13, 1640, aged 104(?). He is classed among the Puritan divines. He joined the Va. Co. soon after 1612. "On Feb'y 12, 161⅔ renouncing all Prizes by ye Lottery he had a Bill of Adventure of £12 10s. granted him in Virginia." His daughter Elizabeth was the second wife of Abraham Johnson, whose son, Isaac Johnson (by his first wife), went to New England.

Chaloner, Sir Thomas, 2. Sub. ——; pd. ——. "Son of Sir Thomas Chaloner the elder, of Gisborough in Yorkshire and of Steeple Claydon in Bucks, an eminent scholar, poet, and statesman in the reigns of Edward VI., Mary, and Elizabeth; ambassador to Spain in 1561," etc. He was born in 1559 ; educated first at St. Paul's School, and then at Magdalen College, Oxford. About 1584 he addressed " A Shorte Discourse of the most rare and excellent vertue of Nitre : " etc., "from the Isle of Lamby on the East coast of Ireland, to his cousin John Napper, Apothecary, at the sign of the Ewe and Lamb, over against Soper Lane end in cheapside," which was "Imprinted at London by Gerald Dewes in 1584." M. P. for St. Mawes in 1586 ; knighted by Henry IV. in the wars of France in 1591 ; traveling in Italy in

1596 and 1597, "and several of his letters to the Earl of Essex and Mr. Anthony Bacon written at this time may be found in Dr. Birch's Memoirs of Elizabeth." August 9, 1603, he was appointed by James I. to have the charge of the person and household of Prince Henry. On August 17, 1603, he was appointed tutor to the prince, and James I. presented him with £4,000 "as a free gift." His first wife died June 22, 1603, and he afterwards married Judith, daughter of William Blunt, esquire, of London, and sister to Sir Thomas Smith's wife. June 10, 1604, he accompanied Sir Thomas Smith to the Court of James I., when he was about to leave on his embassy to Russia; and, according to some accounts, he went with Smith on that embassy. M. P. for Lostwithiel, 1604–11. He discovered the alum mines in Yorkshire about 1600, for which he was afterwards granted a pension of 40 marks per annum, and brought its manufacture to perfection near Whitby in 1608. M. C. for Va., March 7, 1607 ; M. C. for Va. Co., May 23, 1609. He became chamberlain to Prince Henry when he was created Prince of Wales in 1610 ; July 26, 1612, an incorporator of the N. W. P. Co. ; August 28, 1613, was one of those who received a grant for "all that part of Guiana or continent of America between the rivers Amazon and Dollesquebe." He died November 18, 1615, and is buried in the church at Chiswick in Middlesex. "This able and upright governor of Henry Prince of Wales lay under some suspicion of puritanism."

Chambers, George, fishmonger. Pd. £12 10s.

Chamberlaine, Abraham, merchant, 2. Sub. £37 10s.; pd. £112 10s. He was a Huguenot ; was first cousin to the celebrated Dr. Peter Chamberlayne; married, in 1594, Hester (born in 1576), daughter of Thomas Purpillian (Papillon) of the bedchamber to King Henry IV. of France; aided in sending out Hudson in 1610; was a member of the Va., E. I., N. W. P., S. I., and Providence (Bahamas) Island companies. He died in August, 1651.

Chamberlain, George, ironmonger, 3. Sub. £37 10s.; pd. ——. Of

St. Mary, Aldermanbury, London ; of the E. I., Va., N. W. P., and S. I. companies ; a brother of John Chamberlain (the next). He died in 1616 ; a benefactor of the Ironmongers, and of Christ's, St. Thomas's, and St. Bartholomew's Hospitals. He married, in 1604, Anne, daughter of Laurence Overton, and niece of Sir John Merrick, the ambassador to Muscovy.

Chamberlain, John. Son of Alderman Richard Chamberlain (sheriff of London in 1561) by his first wife, Anne, daughter of Robert and Margery Downes of Yalding in Kent; baptized at St. Olave's in the Old Jewry, January 15, 155¾ ; educated at Cambridge ; made a voyage to Ireland, 1597; a journey to Venice, 1610–1611 ; was of the Court of Wards. The Horace Walpole of his day, wrote many newsy letters *temp.* Elizabeth, James I., and Charles I. He was buried at St. Olave's in the Old Jewry, March 20, 162⅞.

An abstract of his will, written June 18, 1627, is given in the " N. E. Register," January, 1889, pp. 89–91.

He was brother to the foregoing George and to one of the following Richards.

Chamberlain, Richard, ironmonger, 2. Sub. £37 10s. ; pd. £150. M. C. for Va. Co.

Chamberlain, Richard, 3. Sub. ——; pd. ——. (Two of the name were members of the Va. Co. and it is frequently impossible to tell the one from the other.)

Chamberlain, Robert. Sub. ——; pd. £100.

Champion, Richard, merchant, 2. Sub. ——; pd. £37 10s. Of the E. I. and N. W. P. companies.

Ralegh's wife was under his charge for a time in 1618.

Champlaine, Samuel de, 27. Of Brouage; born 1567; died 1635; founder and governor of Quebec; explored our New England coast in 1604–05.

Chandler, George, 2. Sub. ——; pd. ——. Of the E. I. and N. W. P. companies.

Chandos, Lord. — Grey Brydges.

Chanoyes, Shanois. Capt. John Smith writes : " I was more beholden to the French men that escaped drowning in the man of Warre, Madam Chanoyes at Rotchell, and the Lawyers of Burdeaux, then *all the rest of my country-men* I met in France."

Chapman, George, the poet, dramatist, translator. Born 1559 ; died May 12, 1634 ; buried in St. Giles-in-the-Fields, London.

Charatza Tragabigzanda. Smith tells us that when he was taken prisoner, he fell to the share of Bashaw Bogall, who sent him to Constantinople to his fair mistress for a slave, they marched in chains to this great city where he was delivered to the young Charatza Tragabigzanda, who sent him to her brother in Tartary; "there but to sojourne to learn the language, and what it was to be a Turke, till time made her *Master* of herselfe." He had only her love to cheer him in his captivity ; but he finally killed her brother, and escaped, and never saw his young love again. She was not forgotten, however, and he afterwards named a cape on his map of New England for her, which name Prince Charles changed to Cape Ann.

Charles V., emperor. Born at Ghent, February 24, 1500 ; died September 21, 1558.

Charles, Prince. — Charles Stuart.

Cheeke, Sir Hatton, 2. Sub.——; pd. ——. Grandson of the celebrated Sir John Cheeke ; was killed in a duel by Sir Thomas Dalton in 1610.

Cheeke, Sir Thomas. Of Pirgo, Essex ; grandson of the celebrated Sir John Cheeke, tutor to King Edward VI., and eldest son of Henry Cheke by Frances, daughter of Sir Humphrey Ratcliffe. He was knighted May 7, 1603. His first wife, the daughter of Peter Osborne, Esq., died without issue in February, 1615, and he afterwards married Essex, daughter of Robert Rich, first Earl of Warwick ; M. C. for Va. Co., 1612–20 ; M. P. for Harwich, 1621–22 ; for Essex, 1624–25 and 1625 ; for Malden, 1626 ; for Colchester, 1628–29 ; for Harwich, 1640 and 1640–53 ; died March 25, 1659.

Cherry, Sir Francis, merchant and vintner. Of a Huguenot family, the De Cheries of Picardy and Normandy; Queen Elizabeth's ambassador to Russia in 1598; a leading man in the Muscovy and E. I. companies ; knighted at Chatham, July 4, 1604. The date of his death is not known to me. His first wife, Margaret, died "of her twelfth child" in 1595. His second wife, Elizabeth, was a widow in 1613. Of his daughters, Frances married Sir John Merrick, Rebecca married Robert Fenne the younger, and Elizabeth was the first wife of Sir William Russell, whose ships carried the first colony to Virginia.

Chester, Sir William, merchant, draper. Of the Muscovy Company ; M. P.; alderman, 1553 ; sheriff, 1554; knighted, 1556 ; lord mayor, 1560 ; interested in Capt. John Hawkins' voyages, 1564–68. The martyr, Lawrence Saunders, was an apprentice of his.

Chester, William. Pd. £12 10s.

Chicheley, Clement, 2. Sub. ——; pd. £25.

Chichester, Captain Arthur. Born in May, 1563; educated at Oxford ; served against the Armada, 1588 ; in the American voyage, 1595 ; Cadiz, 1596; in Picardy, 1597 ; at Ostend, 1598; in Ireland, 1599, and after, as lord deputy, etc.; created Lord Chichester of Belfast, February 23, 1613; sent to the Palatinate, spring, 1622; member of the English Privy Council, December 31, 1622; of the council of war (on the projected war with Spain), April 21, 1624; on the Virginia Commission, July 15, 1624. Died February 19, 1625, and was buried at Carrickfergus.

Childe, Alexander, 3. Sub. ——; pd. ——. (Capt. Alexander Childe was in the E. I. Co.'s service.)

Chiles, Alexander, 2. Sub. ——; pd. ——. (Sir Josiah Child was one of the most famous merchants of London in the next generation.)

Christian IV., King of Denmark. Brother-in-law to King James of England. Was born in 1577, and died in 1648. King, 1596–1648.

Chudley (or **Chudleigh**), **George.** Of the N. Va. Co. "Son of John Chudleigh, Esq., of Ashton, who aspired to rival the famous actions of Drake and others by sea, but died a young man in the Streights of Magellan, leaving by his wife, daughter of George Speke, Esq., two sons and two daughters." The eldest son, George, was only three or four years of age at the time of his father's decease, but

was thoroughly educated by his trustees at home and abroad. M. P. for East Love, 1614; of the N. E. Council, 1620; M. P. for Lostwithiel, 1621–22; created a baronet, August 1, 1622; M. P. for Tiverton, 1624–25; M. P. for Lostwithiel, 1625; M. P. for ——, 1640. He fought on the side of the Parliament at Stratton, but afterwards took up arms for the king, and published a declaration in 1643, in vindication of his doing so. He married Mary, daughter of Sir William Strode, and died in 1657, leaving issue.

Church, Thomas, draper, 2. Sub. £37 10s.; pd. £62 10s. Of N. W. P. Co. He was a benefactor of St. Bartholomew's, Christ's, St. Thomas's, and Bridewell Hospitals ; was buried in "St. Bartholomew's behind the Exchange," London. "Here lyeth the body of Master Thomas Church, citizen and draper of London. He was helpfull to many, hurtfull to none, and gave every one his due. . . . He departed this life in August the 26 day 1616, being aged 55 yeeres." "A good Life hath the Days numbred, but a good Name endureth forever."

Chute, Sir George, 3. Sub. ——; pd. £12 10s. Knighted by Sir Arthur Chichester, lord deputy in Ireland, at Christ Church, October 14, 1608.

Chute, Sir Walter, 3. Sub. £75 ; pd £25. Served in the expedition of 1597 against the Azores ; knighted at Beaver (Belvoir) Castle, April 23, 1603. He is mentioned (not favorably) in several of Chamberlain's letters of May, 1614, as being "so near the King that he cuts all the meat he eats."

Clanricard, Earl of. — Richard Bourke, Burke, or de Burgh.

Clapham, John, gent., 2. Sub. ——; pd. £25. M. P. Sudbury, 1597–98; one of the controllers of the Hanaper (1605–10), and one of the six clerks of the chancery; died December 6, 1618.

Clare, Earl of. — John Holles.

Clarke, Captain. 2. Sub. ——; pd. ——. (Engineer at the siege of Ostend in 1601 ?)

Clarke, Captain John. "An Englishman by nation, a native of London, and of the same religion as his king." Born about 1576 ; a pilot by profession; was in Malaga in 1609;

sailed from London with Dale for Virginia in March, 1611 ; taken prisoner by the Spaniards at Point Comfort in the summer of 1611; remained a prisoner in the West Indies and in Spain until about 1616, when he was released ; made a voyage to Virginia in 1619 ; was the pilot of the Mayflower in 1620. On the 13th of February, 1622, at a meeting of the Virginia Court, "Mr. Deputy acquainted the court, that one Mr. John Clarke beinge taken from Virginia long since by a Spanish ship that came to discover that plantation ; that forasmuch as he hath since that time done the companie good service *in many* voyages to Virginia, and of late went into Ireland for transportation of cattle to Virginia, he was an humble suitor to this court, that he might be admitted a free brother of the companie, and have some shares of land bestowed upon him." He was admitted and given two shares. He arrived in Virginia, April 10, 1623, with Daniel Gookin's ship, the Providence, and soon after this he died in that colony.

Cleave — Clive, Sir Christopher, 2. Sub. —— ; pd. ——. Of Kent ; was knighted at Greenwich, April 22, 1605.

Cletheroe (Clitherowe, etc.), Christopher, ironmonger, 2. Sub. £37 10s.; pd. £50. Son of Henry Cletherow of London. Was a member of the E. I. Co. in 1601 ; of the Va. Co. of London, 1609 ; of the N. W. P. Co. in 1612 ; of the B. I. Co. in 1615; on the committee of the E. I. Co. from 1614 ; master of the Ironmongers' Company, 1618; nominated for deputy treasurer of the Va. Co. in April, 1619, and recommended to that company by King James as a suitable person for their treasurer in May, 1622 ; master of the Ironmongers' Company again in 1624 ; sheriff of London in 1625 ; M. P. for London, 1628-29. He was an alderman for many years from Billingsgate ward, and governor of the Eastland Company ; Lord Mayor of London, 1635-36 ; knighted at Hampton Court, January 15, 1636 ; governor of the E. I. Co., 1638-41. Died November 11, 1641, and is buried in St. Andrew's Undershaft, London. He was a benefactor of the Ironmongers' Company and of Christ Church

Hospital, of which he was president, " *where there is a good portrait of him.*"

Clifford, George, Earl of Cumberland. Born August 8, 1558; educated at Cambridge and at Oxford, where he studied mathematics and geography ; married Margaret, daughter of Francis Russell, second Earl of Bedford, June 24, 1577; was interested in Frobisher's voyages, 1576-78 ; sent a fleet to the river Plate, South America, 1586-87 ; served against the Armada, 1588 ; his second voyage, 1588 ; his celebrated voyage to the Azores, 1589 ; succeeds old Sir Henry Lee as the queen's knight, November 17, 1590. He continued to make raids on the commerce of Spain, sometimes going in person. He sent out his twelfth voyage in 1598. His name is first on the list of incorporators of the E. I. Co., December 31, 1600. Appointed governor of the Scottish Marches, June 8, 1603. Died at the Savoy in the Strand, October 30, 1605. " He was by nature what the heroes of chivalry were from fashion." His only daughter, Anne, was equally celebrated. She married, first, Richard Sackville, second Earl of Dorset, and secondly, Philip Herbert, Earl of Montgomery. She lived until 1675, and died in her 87th year.

Clifford. See Russell — Clifford.

Clinton, Edward, Earl of Lincoln. Born in 1512 ; was long lord high admiral ; created Earl of Lincoln, May 4, 1572. He was interested in the voyages of Frobisher, 1576-78, and Fenton, 1582-83. Died January 16, 1585, and was succeeded by his eldest son, Henry.

Clinton, Henry, 2. Sub. —— ; pd. £50. Second Earl of Lincoln. The eldest son of Edward, first Earl of Lincoln, by his second wife, Ursula, daughter of William Lord Stourton ; was one of the fifteen knights of the Bath, made September 29, 1553, two days before the coronation of Queen Mary. May 26, in 14 Elizabeth, he accompanied his father, the Earl of Lincoln, in his embassy to the French Court. January 16, 1585, he succeeded his father as Earl of Lincoln. " In 29 Elizabeth he was one of the Peers in commission, for the tryal of Mary, Queen of Scots ; and was also commissioned for the tryal of Secretary Davison." " In 31 Elizabeth, he was one of the Peers on the tryal of Philip Howard, Earl of Arundel, April 14." Ambassador to the Landgrave of Hesse in 1596. "In 1601, he was one of the commanders of the Forces that besieged the Earl of Essex in his house, and obliged him to surrender ; and was afterwards on his tryal, February 10, in Westminster-hall. On the decease of Queen Elizabeth, March 24, 160$\frac{2}{3}$, he was one of the Privy Council that signed the letter at the palace of White-hall on March 28, 1603, to the Lord Eure, and the rest of the commissioners for the treaty of Breame, directing them how to proceed." M. C. for Va., 1608. He died in September, 1615 (not 1616 as generally stated). His daughter Elizabeth married Sir Arthur Gorges. A granddaughter, Lady Frances Fynes, married John, eldest son of Sir Ferdinando Gorges; another granddaughter, Lady Arabella Johnson, came to New England. He was ancestor of Sir Henry Clinton, K. B., a commander-in-chief of his majesty's land forces in America during the Revolution, and of the present Duke of New Castle.

Cobham, Lord. — Henry Brooke.

Cockayne, William, skinner, a great merchant of London, first governor of the Irish Company. He was not a member of the Va. Co. until May 17, 1620 ; knighted in 1616 ; for many years an alderman of London ; was lord mayor in 1619-20 ; died October 20, 1626 ; buried at St. Paul's Cathedral.

Cockes — Cocks — Coxe, Richard, 2. Sub. —— ; pd. £25. Of the E. I. and Rus. companies, and chief of the first English factory in Japan.

Cockes (etc.), **Robert,** grocer, 2. Sub. ——; pd. ——. A member of the Court of Assistants, 1605, and warden of the Grocers, 1609. Died September 20, 1609, aged 47.

Codrington, Simon. Probably son of Simon Codrington by his wife, Mary Kelway (or Callaway), and if so, the grandfather of Christopher Codrington, Esq., who went to the Barbadoes in the time of Charles I., from whom I, and many other Americans, descend.

Coitmore (**Coytmore** — **Cotemore,** etc.), **Rowland,** 2. Sub. ——; pd. ——. Served in the Drake-Haw-

kins voyage to America, 1595. "A Fair Gallery was built on the south side of the Chappel of St. John's at Wappin, with part of the Benevolence that was given for the Use of the Chapel by the Mariners that went to the East Indies in 1616, in the Royal James, under the command of Capt. Martin Pringe, procured by the care of Master Rowland Coetmore then Master of the said ship, and now at the building hereof Warden of the Chapel, 1622." He died in 1626, and was a benefactor of the Trinity House. His widow and children went to New England about 1636. (See "N. E. Reg.," 1880, p. 253, and 1886, p. 160.)

Coke, Sir Edward, "Lo. chief justice." "Born 1552 ; called to the bar, April 20, 1578 ; solicitor-general, June, 1592 ; conducts prosecution of Essex and Southampton, February, 1601 ; knighted May, 1603 ; conducts prosecution of Raleigh, 1603 ; chief justice of the King's Bench, October, 1613 ; privy councilor, November, 1613 ; dismissed from Privy Council, June 30, 1616 ; discharged from office of chief justice, November 15, 1616 ; reinstated as privy councilor, September, 1617 ; one of the managers of the impeachment of Bacon, 1621 ; died at Stoke Pogis, Bucks, September 3, 1633." (Cates.) He was the early friend of Roger Williams, the father of the Baptists in America.

Coke — Cooke, Captain John, 2. Sub. —— ; pd. £25. Was this the secretary of state (born 1563 ; died 1644) ; knighted September 9, 1624, and appointed secretary in 1625 ?

Coke — Cooke, Sir William, 2. Sub. ——; pd. £25. M. P. Helston, 1598-99; Westminster, 1601; Wigan, 1604-11, and Gloucestershire, 1614 ; knighted May 7, 1603 ; was of Higham, County Gloucester ; married Lucy, daughter of Sir Thomas Lucy of Charlecote. Died in 1618.

Colby, Edmund. Pd. £12 10s. Died in Virginia before 1621.

Colepeper. See Culpeper.

Collins, Henry, 2. Sub. ——; pd. £12 10s.

Colthurst, Henry, grocer, 2. Sub. ——; pd. ——. "Admitted to the freedom, 1567 ; to the livery, 1578 ; sealed the oath of allegiance to Queen Elizabeth, November 6, 1584 ; admitted to Court of Assistants, March 18, 1585 ; junior warden, 1587 ; died about 1610, and his son Thomas was admitted by patrimony and sworn to freedom, May 23, 1610." (Grocers' Records.) His son Thomas held two shares in Virginia, possibly by inheritance.

Colthurst, Thomas. Pd. £25.

Columbus, Christopher. Born about 1445 ; saw land in the West Indies, October ½?, 1492 ; died 1506.

Comock — Conook — Camock, etc., **Captain Thomas,** 2. Sub. ——; pd. £25. Son of Thomas Camock, Esq., and his wife, Frances Rich, aunt of Robert Rich, second Earl of Warwick. Capt. Thomas Camock afterwards emigrated to New England, and died there about 1642. He was for a time in the Bermudas.

Companies of London, 1606–1616. — I. THE LOCAL MERCHANT COMPANIES. The first twelve are the chief ; they are styled "the Honorable," and the Lord Mayor of London is chosen annually from one of them. I will give these first companies in the order of their rank. The others will follow in alphabetical order for more convenient reference. See the reports of the City Companies' Commission published in 1884, which gives most ample particulars.

Mercers, 2. Sub. ——; pd. £200. Incorporated in 1393. (See Herbert's "History of the Twelve Livery Companies of London.") The Mercers bear for their arms "a virgin," and the company's song begins : —

" Advance the Virgin, lead the Van,
 Of all that are in London free
 The Mercer is the foremost man
 That founded a society.
CHORUS. Of all the trades that London grace
 We are the first in time and place."

I have identified ten mercers, who contributed about £600 to the American enterprise.

Grocers, 2. Sub. —— ; pd. £487 10s. "The main stock from which the company arose was the Guild of Pepperers ; the earliest notice of which is found in the Pipe Rolls, A. D. 1180, and seem from the first to have had to do with the Great Beam, " *Peso Grosso,*" the merchant's weight of 15 oz. to the pound by which the king's import tax was levied. The word *Grossarius* of Soper Lane is first found 1310. In the year 1328 the Pepperers appear in city records as Grossarii. In 1345 they call themselves in their own Archives " The Fraternity of St. Antony of the Companions of Pepperers of Soper Lane " (the disciples of St. Antony of Egypt who introduced sterling money (1180) and the art of weighing by a fixed standard of value, the sterling penny or pennyweight, A. D. 1266). In 1365 they appear in the city record as " Mestere Grossariorum Pipperariorum et appotecariorium." From the year 1376 this association has been known as " The Grocers of London." The motto of the company is "God grant grace." With the assistance of Mr. Kingdon I have identified seventy grocers as having contributed about £2,500 to the American enterprise.

Drapers, 2. Sub. —— ; pd. £150. Incorporated 1430. Motto : " Unto God only be Honour and Glory." I have identified twenty drapers as having contributed about £800.

Fishmongers, 2. Sub. ——; pd. 150. The salt fishmongers were incorporated in 1433, stock in 1509, and the two united in 1536. Motto : " All worship be to God only." Members of this Guild contributed over £1,000.

Goldsmiths, 2. Sub.——; pd. £200. Incorporated 1327. I have identified twelve goldsmiths, who contributed about £600. Motto : " Justitia, Virtutum Regina."

Skinners, 2. Sub. —— ; pd. ——. Incorporated 1327. They were also called Tanners. Motto : " To God only be all glory." Ten members of this Guild contributed about £700.

Merchant-Taylors, 2. Sub. —— ; pd. £200. Incorporated 1416. Motto : " Concordia parva res crescunt." Twenty members of this Guild contributed about £1,200.

Haberdashers, 2. Sub. —— ; pd. ——. Incorporated 1447. "They were also called Milleners, from the place Milain in Italy, whence the commodities they dealt in chiefly came." Motto : " Serve and obey." Twelve members contributed about £500.

Salters, 2. Sub. —— ; qd. £50. Incorporated 1558. Motto : " Sal Sapit Omnia." Two members contributed £130 15s.

Ironmongers, 2. Sub. —— ; pd.

£133 6d. 8s. Incorporated 1462. Motto : " God is our strength." Ten members paid £625.

Vintners, 2. Sub. —— ; pd. ——. Incorporated in 1436 by the name of the " Wine-Tonners." Four members paid £220.

Cloth-workers, 2. Sub. —— ; pd. £100. Incorporated 1482. Motto : " My trust is in God alone." King James I. was a member of this Guild. Sixteen members paid £1,000.

Armourers (1463), 2. Henry V. was a member. Sub. ——; pd. ——.

Barbers - Surgeons (1308), 2. Sub. ——; pd. £25.

Basket Makers (——), 2. Sub. ——; pd. ——.

Blacksmiths (1577), 2. Sub. —— ; pd. ——.

Bowyers (1623), 2. Sub. ——; pd. ——. " In regard that the use of the Long Bow hath added no mean Honour to this Realm of England, making it famous in far remote Nations ; They may well stand on a great Privilege of Antiquity, yet their incorporating speaks but of the 21st year of the Reign of King James I." (Strype.)

Brewers (1438), 2. Sub. —— ; pd. ——.

Brown Bakers (reincorporated 19 James I.), 2. Sub. —— ; pd. ——.

Butchers (1605), 2. Sub. ——; pd. ——. A very ancient company, but first incorporated 3 James I.

Carpenters (1344), 2. Sub. —— ; pd. ——.

Cooks (1481), 2. Sub. —— ; pd. ——.

Coopers (1501), 2. Sub. —— ; pd. ——.

Cordwayners or *Shoemakers* (1410), 2. Sub. —— ; pd. ——.

Curriers (1605), 2. Sub. —— ; pd. ——.

Cutlers (1417), 2. Sub. —— ; pd. ——.

Dyers (1469), 2. Sub. —— ; pd. £75.

Fletchers (1536), 2. Sub. —— ; pd. £75.

Founders (1614), 2. Sub. ——; pd. ——.

Fruiterers (1604), 2. Sub. ——; pd. ——.

Gardiners (1616), 2. Sub. —— ; pd. ——.

Girdlers (1448), 2. Sub. —— ; pd. £50.

Glaziers (1637), 2. Sub. —— ; pd. ——. It may be noted that all of these companies were certainly in existence May 23, 1609 ; yet several appear not to have been incorporated at that time.

Imbroyderers (1591), 2. Sub. ——; pd. £25.

Innholders (1515), 2. Sub. ——; pd. ——. Their old motto was, " When I was Harbourless, ye lodged me."

Joiners (1564), 2. Sub. ——; pd. ——.

Leathersellers (1442), 2. Sub. ——; pd. £50.

Masons (——), 2. Sub. —— ; pd. ——. " Being otherwise termed Free Masons, of ancient standing and good reckoning, by means of affable and kind Meetings divers times, and as a loving Brotherhood should use to do, did frequent this mutual Assembly in the Time of King Henry IV. in the 12th year of his most gracious Reign." (Strype's Stow.)

Musicians (1604), 2. Sub. —— ; pd. ——.

Paint-stainers or *Painters* (1580), 2. Sub. —— ; pd. ——.

Pewterers (1474), 2. Sub. ——; pd. ——.

Plaisterers (1500), 2. Sub. —— ; pd. ——.

Plumbers (1611), 2. Sub. ——; pd. ——.

Poulterers (1503), 2. Sub. —— ; pd. ——.

Saddlers (1280), 2. Sub. —— ; pd. ——.

Scriveners (1616), 2. Sub. —— ; pd. ——.

Stationers (1557), 2. Sub. ——; pd. £125. " The Company of Stationers of London was of great Antiquity, before the famous Art of Printing was invented or brought to England, as (for the most part) their dwelling in *Pater-noster-Row*, and the adjoining parts, can testify." Perhaps the first work printed in England was " The Game and Playe of Chesse . . . by William Caxton. Fynysshed the last daye of Marche, A. D. 1474." Caxton was free of the Mercers' Company. Stow says, " The first of the Corporation of Stationers, which I have met with, who practised the Art of Printing Books, were Wynkyn de Worde, and one Pynson, who both flourished in the Reign of Henry VII. and in the beginning of the Reign of Henry VIII. And, also, Thomas Godfrey, who printed about the same time." "In 1533 there were within the Realm of England a great Number, cunning and expert in the Science and Craft of Printing." Books and papers were formerly sold only in stalls ; hence the dealers were called stationers. The company received their first charter of incorporation the fourth day of May, 1557. Sir William Cecil, afterwards Lord Burghley, was the great patron of this company. They were " Printers, Booksellers, and such as sell Paper and Parchment, and Blank Books bound up for the use of Tradesmen and merchants." "In 1575 there were 175 Stationers in London, and of these 140 came to their Freedoms in the company since the access of Queen Elizabeth to the crown. So much did Printing and Learning come in request under the Reformation."

The press and the Reformation were the leading factors in laying the foundation of the English colonies in America.

Three of this Guild were adventurers to the amount of £225 ; but at least seventy others contributed in small amounts or in other ways, while the fruit of the press, without doubt, influenced many hundreds to take part in advancing the American enterprises.

Tallow-chandlers (1463), 2. Sub. —— ; pd. ——. Motto: " Delight in God, and he shall give thee thy Heart's desire."

Turners (1604), 2. Sub. —— ; pd. ——.

Tylers and Bricklayers (1568), 2. Sub. —— ; pd. ——.

Upholsters (1627), 2. Sub.——; pd. ——.

Wax-chandlers (1484), 2. Sub. —— ; pd. ——.

Weavers (1184), 2. Sub. —— ; pd. ——. " One of the earliest incorporations whose record has been preserved."

White Bakers, 2. Sub. —— ; pd. £40. They were a company of London in the first year of Edward II., 1308.

Woodmongers or *Fuellers* (1605), 2. Sub. —— ; pd. ——.

Woolmen or *Wool-packers* (——), 2. Sub. —— ; pd. ——.

(All of the foregoing companies are still existing in London, except the Brown Bakers, White Bakers (now united into the Bakers' Company) and Woodmongers, and all of them have halls of their own, save the Blacksmiths, Cooks, Musicians, and Turners, which companies transact their business at Guild Hall.)

II. USING SHIPPING. There were, at least, ten, which may be divided into the following classes, viz. : —

1st. *Strictly Commercial*, three.

1. The Old Merchant Adventurers, trading to the Netherlands and Germany.

2. The Merchants of Elbing or Eastland Company, trading to the Baltic.

3. The Merchants of the Levant, or Turkey Company, trading in the Mediterranean and overland to East India.

2d. *Commerce and Discovery*, three.

4. The Merchant Adventurers for the Discoverie of Regions unknown (1551); afterwards known as the Russia or Muscovy Company. " They were at vast charges in fitting out great Numbers of Ships for the discovery of New Countries and Isles. They discovered (and traded in) the Cherry Islands, Greenland, Nova Zembla, Davyes's Streights, Grooneland, Hudson's Bay, the North of America," etc. One of their ships was the first English vessel (in 1553) to round the North Cape of Europe, and to enter the Great White Sea of Russia. Their ships brought the first colonists to Virginia in 1606–07. (See Sebastian Cabot.)

5. The East India Company, trading to the East Indies, incorporated December 31, 1600.

6. The North West Passage Company, incorporated July 26, 1612, to advance a trade through said supposed passage along the same and with the great kingdoms of Tartary, China, Japan, etc.

3d. *Commerce, Discovery, and Colonization*, three.

7. The Virginia Company of London, 1609.

8. The Newfoundland Company, 1610. (Not so especially a London company.)

9. The Bermudas or Somers Island Company, 1615.

4th. *Commerce and Plantation*, one.

10. The Irish Plantation Society, first known as "The Governor and Assistants of the new Plantation in Ulster, within the realm of Ireland," and afterwards as the "Irish Society." It was incorporated March 29, 1613, but had been under consideration since 1605, and many emigrants from Scotland and England had settled in Ulster before this patent was granted. Although many of those interested in Virginia were also interested in Ireland, yet from the beginning this plantation was a hindering rival to the Virginia enterprises ; as early as October 2, 1605, Chichester wrote to Salisbury, "that it was absurd folly to run over the world in search of colonies in Virginia or Guiana, whilst Ireland was lying desolate," and as soon as the great city companies of London acquired their plantations in Ireland (1613–14), they ceased to take any farther interest in their corporate capacity in Virginia. But they were still, in a certain sense, planting Virginia, for about a century afterwards many of the descendants of the Scotch-English settlers, bred on Irish soil, and known in our annals as Scotch-Irish, emigrated to Pennsylvania, Virginia, and the Carolinas.

Note. — Of these companies 4, 5, 6, 7, and 9 were largely under the management of one man, Sir Thomas Smythe, who was also a leading member of the Turkey Company (3). The motives of these companies were in many respects very similar, and we cannot readily understand perfectly the movements of one unless we have a correct idea of the others. The records of 4 were destroyed in the fire at the Royal Exchange, where it then had its offices in 1666. The records that remain of 5 have been carefully calendared by Mr. Sainsbury, as have also those which remain of Nos. 6, 7, and 9. Many members of the East India Company (5) were also of the Virginia Company (7), and it was this element which was, so naturally, urgently anxious to find some "ready way" through America to East India. Evidently many of the Russia Company (4) were also interested in the American enterprise. In fact, we find the same great leaders in all of these great companies for commerce, discovery, and for colonization.

Compton, William Lord, 2. Sub. ——; pd. £100. Succeeded his father as Baron Compton in 1585 or 1589 ; summoned to Parliament, 1593 ; escorted Queen Anne from Scotland to England, May to June, 1603 ; made a Knight of the Bath, January 6, 1605 ; attended King James to Oxford, and was created a Master of Arts of that university, August 30, 1605 ; Lord President of Wales, November 16, 1617 ; Earl of Northampton, August 2, 1618 ; knight-companion of the most noble order of the Garter, April 11, 1629. Died June 24, 1630, at his lodgings in the Savoy, London, and was buried at Compton with his ancestors. He married Elizabeth, only daughter of the rich Sir John Spencer, Lord Mayor of London, and thereby hangs many and many a tale. Northampton County, Virginia, was probably named for their son Spencer, second Earl of Northampton, who distinguished himself in the royal cause during the civil wars, and fell at Hopton Heath, March 19, 164⅔.

Compton, William, 3. Sub. ——; pd. £25. Also of the E. I. Co.

Conisbie — Connyngsby, Sir Thomas, 3. Sub. £50 ; pd. £50. Was of Hampton Court, County Hereford ; son of Humphrey Coningsby, Esq. ; knighted by the Earl of Essex, October 8, 1591, before Rouen ; M. P. for County Hereford, 1593, 1597, and 1601 ; sheriff, 1598. Died May 30, 1625.

Connock, Richard, esquire, 3. Sub. ——; pd. £20. Of N. W. P. Co. ; auditor to Henry, Prince of Wales.

Conryo (Conry), Florence, an Irish theologian, was born at Galway in 1560 ; implicated in a plot for a revolt in Ireland, 1607 ; became Roman Catholic Archbishop of Tuam in 1609, and died at Madrid, Spain, in 1629.

Conway, Sir Edward, 2. Sub. £75 ; pd. £100. "Son of Sir John Conway, who being a person of great skill in military affairs, was made by Robert, Earl of Leicester, governor of Ostend. His son, Sir Edward Conway,

MARY SIDNEY

Countess of Pembroke

succeeded to his father's martial skill and valor, and twisted therewith peaceable policy in state affairs ; so that the gown and the sword met in him in most eminent proportion." Sir Edward was knighted by Robert, Earl of Essex, at the sacking of Cadiz, where he commanded a regiment in 1596, at which time, Lodge says, " he was a lieutenant-governor of the Brill." He served with distinction in the Netherlands, and was one of the governors of the Brill, 1606–16.

M. P. for Penryn, 1610–11 ; M. C. for Va. Co., 1609. July 3, 1622, his son (Sir Edward Conway, Jr., who married Frances, daughter of Sir Francis Popham) was admitted into the Va. Co. In January, 1623, he was made one of the secretaries of state. " King James recommended him to the lords, for his birth, for his soldiery, for his languages, for his sufficiency, and for his honesty." M. P. for Evesham, 1624–25. One of the principal secretaries of state during the troubles in the Va. Co. of London, 1623–24, he evidently took great interest and care in those affairs ; and from April, 1623, to June, 1624, he wrote over twenty letters regarding them, which are still preserved, and probably many more, which are now lost. He was a member of the royal commission, appointed July 15, 1624, for winding up the Va. Co., and at least fifteen of his letters, written July, 1624, to September, 1625, regarding Virginia affairs, are still preserved.

He was created Baron Conway of Ragley, County Warwick, March 22, 1625 ; captain of the Isle of Wight, December 8, 1625 ; and was continued as a secretary of state by Charles I. " April 22, 1625. The Privy Council instruct Lord Carew and himself to take into consideration what forts and places of strength are to be erected and maintained in Virginia, and to give an estimate of the present charge and the annual cost to maintain them. April 29, 1625. He wrote to Sir Thomas Smythe, ' The committee for the Virginia business having referred to Lord Carew and myself the consideration of the state of that plantation,' ' Smythe is requested to send the names of such persons as may be of use to them in their proceedings, as

also, *the maps, relations,* and *papers* which may be with him.' "

Quere: What has become of these maps, relations, and papers ? I have evidence that many Virginia papers were preserved by Lord Carew ; but I have been unable to find any of them.

Sir Edward was advanced to the Irish Viscountcy of Killultagh, County Antrim, March 15, 1627 ; to the English Viscountcy of Conway of Conway Castle, County Carnarvon, June 6, 1627, and about the same time made president of the Privy Council.

In 1627 and 1628 his wife and himself were interested in the Newfoundland Colony, and some time prior to March 30, 1628, he subscribed £100 to the New England Colony. He died January 3, 1631, in St. Martin's Lane, London.

He married, first, Dorothy (or Anne), daughter of Sir John Tracy, of Tedington, Gloucestershire, and widow of Edmund Bray. She was first cousin to Sir Thomas Dale's wife. She died in February, 1613, and Lord Conway married, secondly, Katharine, daughter of Giles Hambler, of Ghent in Flanders, and widow successively of Richard Fust, Esq., and John West, grocer. She was a member of the Va. Co. of London, and her name appears in the lists of 1620 as " Mistris Kath : West, now Lady Conway." She was also interested in Newfoundland. A letter writer of London in March, 1615, says, " Sir Edward Conway is to marry a grocer's widow in London ; she is lame and in years ; but is worth about £6,000."

Conway, Captain Thomas, esquire, 2. Sub. —— ; pd. ——.

Conway, Captain Thomas, 3. Sub. —— ; pd. ——. The first named was the brother of Sir Edward Conway. The second was Sir Edward's son ; one of them paid £37 10s. They were both knighted on the same day at Theobald's, July 14, 1624. There was a relationship between the Conways and Sir Thomas Dale's wife (see Throckmorton pedigree).

Cooper, John, 2. Sub. —— ; pd. £25.

Cooper, Matthew, 2. Sub. —— ; pd. £25.

Cooper, Richard, 2. Sub. —— ; pd. £25.

Cooper, Sir Richard, 3. Sub. ——; pd. ——. Of Surrey; knighted at Whitehall July 23, 1603.

Cooper, Robert, 2. Sub. ——; pd. £25.

Cope, Sir Anthony, 2. Sub. ——; pd. £40. Of Hanwell, Oxfordshire (grandson of Sir Anthony Cope, vice-chamberlain to Catherine Parr, and one of the most learned men of the era in which he lived), the eldest brother of Sir Walter Cope; was born about 1548. "In 1571 Mr. Anthony Cope, a zealous Puritan, was chosen member of Parliament for Banbury." He also represented Banbury in the six Parliaments, 1572–83, 1586, 1588–89, 1592–93, 1597–98, and 1601; sheriff of the county of Oxford in 1582, in 1591 (in which year he was knighted by Queen Elizabeth), and in 1603; M. P. for Oxfordshire in 1604–11 and 1614; created a baronet June 29, 1611; died in July, 1614, aged 66, and was buried in Hanwell Church. "He was committed to the Tower (February 27 to March 23, 158$\frac{9}{7}$) for presenting to the speaker a Puritan revision of the Common Prayer Book, and a bill abrogating existing ecclesiastical law." ("Dic. Nat. Bio.," Stephen.)

Cope, Sir Walter, 2. Sub. £75; pd. £215. "Grandson of Sir Anthony Cope, knight (see Sir Anthony Cope), and second son of Edward Cope, esquire, of Hanwell, Oxfordshire. Sir Walter was seated at Kensington House, Middlesex. Was member of the Elizabethan Society of Antiquaries; M. P. for Weymouth, 1601; knighted at Worksop, April 21, 1603; M. P. for Westminster, 1604–11; M. C. for Va., November 20, 1606, and for Va. Co., May 23, 1609; one of the chamberlains of the exchequer, 1609; master of the wards, November, 1612. He was one of the leaders of the time, in the efforts to create a foreign commerce for Great Britain, and to establish English colonies in America, a member of the East India, Muscovy, Newfoundland, North West Passage, Somers Island, and Virginia companies. He was buried at Kensington, August 1, 1614.

He was the friend and one of the executors of Robert Cecil, Earl of Salisbury, and seems to have been the only one who took a prominent part in defense of that great statesman against those who had fawned on him while living and abused him when dead.

"Among the faithless, faithful only he;
Among innumerable false, unmov'd,
His loyalty he kept, his love, his zeal."

Sir Walter Cope married Dorothy (born 1562), daughter of Richard Grenville, esquire. He erected the celebrated Holland House (then called "Cope's Castle") at Kensington in 1607, and left it to Henry Rich, Earl of Holland, governor of the company for Providence Islands (Bahamas), etc., who had espoused his daughter, Isabella Cope.

Coppin, Sir George, 2. Sub. £60; pd. £135. "Of Dunwich in Norfolk;" M. P. for New Romney in 1597–98; knighted at Whitehall, July 23, 1603; clerk of the crown in chancery, May 3, 1604; M. C. for Va., March 9, 1607; M. C. for Va. Co., May 23, 1609.

On November 17, 1616, Mr. John Castle wrote to Mr. James Miller, "A thunderbolt hath fallen on the Lord Coke, which hath overthrown him from the very roots. . . . The supersedeas was carried to him the last week by Sir George Coppin, . . . he received it with dejection and tears."

Sir George Coppin was living July 30, 1618; but probably died soon after. "He lies buried in the Church of St. Martin's in the Fields, Westminster, in the South Ile, under a very handsomely wrought and rich monument."

Coppin, Robert, 2. Sub. ——; pd. £12 10s. He was on a voyage to Virginia, and I think he was the gunner of the Mayflower in 1620.

Cordell, Thomas, mercer, 3. Sub. £75; pd. £50. Of the E. I. Co. He was first cousin to William Cordell, of Fulham, master cook to Queen Elizabeth; "apprenticed to Anthony Hickman; admitted 1558; warden, 1582 and 1590; master, 1596, 1605, and 1612, when he died. He was an alderman of London." (From Mercers' Records.)

Cordoba (or Cordova), Don Louis de, related to the Marquis of Guadalcazar, Viceroy of Mexico in 1620.

Cornelius, John, goldsmith, 2. Sub. ——; pd. £62 10s. Of the E. I. Co.

August 13, 1601, his wife was buried in St. Mary, Colechurch. "She lieth before the great Chest next the Jurie." (Parish Register.) He married Elizabeth Butler, full sister to Capt. Nathaniel Butler.

Cornwallis, Sir Charles. Sir Thomas Cornwallis, comptroller of the household of Queen Mary, upon the accession of Elizabeth, being a Roman Catholic, was left out of the Privy Council, and removed from the comptrollership. He married Anne, daughter of Sir John Jerningham, and died December 24, 1604, aged 85, leaving two sons: "Sir William Cornwallis the elder" (of whom hereafter) and Sir Charles Cornwallis, of whom I write, who was knighted at the Charterhouse, May 11, 1603; English ambassador at the Court of Spain, 1605–1609; treasurer of the household of Henry, Prince of Wales, 1610–12; member N. W. P. Co., 1612; wrote "A Discourse of the most Illustrious Prince Henry, Late Prince of Wales" in 1626, which was published in 1641. He died December 21, 1629. He was the father of "Sir William Cornwallis the younger" (whom see).

Cornwallis, Sir William the Elder, son of Sir Thomas, and brother to Sir Charles aforesaid. He lived at Highgate, was a near neighbor to Zuñiga, the Spanish ambassador, and was quite certainly the "William Cornwallis the elder" of the letter. He married, first, Lucy, daughter of John Nevill, Lord Latimer (she was aunt to Capt. George Percy), and secondly, Jane, daughter of Hercules Mewtas, esquire. Frederick Cornwallis, his son by his second wife, was ancestor to Lord Cornwallis of our Revolution. Sir William the elder died November 13, 1611.

Cornwallis, Sir William the Younger, 3. Sub. £75; pd.——. Son of Sir Charles, aforesaid; probably the "William Cornwallis" of the letter. He married, August 26, 1595, Catharine daughter of Sir Philip Parker, of Erwarton, Suffolk, who was probably "Madama Catalina" (Spanish). He was the author and essayist; dedicated his "Discourse upon Seneca, the Tragedian," to Sir John Popham in 1601. The date of his death seems uncertain. Some accounts place

it as late as 1631; but Chamberlain wrote to Carleton on July 7, 1614, of his recent death. His second son, Thomas, was the commissioner of Maryland, 1638–59. I do not know whether it was Sir William the elder or the younger, who subscribed £75 to the Va. enterprise; but I suppose it was the younger, as it is his name in the third charter. One or the other was M. P. for Lostwithiel, 1597–98; knighted at Dublin, August 5, 1599; M. P. for Orford, 1604–11. It was, of course, "the younger" who was M. P. for Orford in 1614.

Coryate, Thomas. Son of the Rev. George Coryate, rector of Odcombe, Somersetshire, was born about 1577; entered at Gloucester Hall in the university of Oxford in 1596; left the university without taking a degree; became one of the household of Henry, Prince of Wales, and "sweetmeats and Coriat made up the last course of all court entertainments." From May 14 to October 3, 1608, he was traveling in France, Savoy, Italy, etc. He wrote an account of these travels, which was published, under the patronage of Prince Henry, by W. S., in 1611, with engravings by W. Hole, and mock commendatory verses by more than sixty writers of the day.

In 1612 he again started on his travels. In 1613, kneeling upon a stone in the midst of the ruins of Troy, he was knighted by the name of the first English knight of Troy.

" Coryate no more, but now a knight of Troy,
Odcombe no more, but henceforth England's Joy.
Brave Brute of our best English wits commended;
True Trojane from Æneas race descended.
Rise top of wit, the honour of our Nation,
And to old Ilium make a new Oration."

And this he proceeded to do, for he was as fond of making orations as was Capt. John Smith.

He continued his travels to the eastward, and in 1616, and after, he was with Sir Thomas Roe in East India. He died at Surat in December, 1617, "leaving enough written to fill the world with new relations and to have made any printer an alderman." Not knowing that he was dead, George Abbot, Archbishop of Canterbury, in his letter to Sir Thomas Roe, of February 19, 1619, "Wishes for Thos. Coryat's return to England, because he would report of the furthest eastern countries in a better fashion than any Englishman hitherto hath been able. Recommends him to get together all the papers which Coryat hath written. The king blames Coryat for writing in his memoirs that he saw men have their eyes pulled out and their tongues cut off, which before an idol were speedily restored again. The king says this cannot be done by the power of Satan, and he is sure it is not by the finger of God." Purchas published some of his writings, and speaks well of him. His narrative is curious and interesting ; but greatly exaggerated. He traveled on foot over a large part of Europe and Asia, and signed his letters, " the Hierosolymit an-Syrian-Mesopotamian-Armenian-Median-Par-thian-Persian-Indian Legge-stretcher of Odcomb in Somerset, Thomas Coryate."

Thomas Coryate and Capt. John Smith were both characters of the time ; both were vain men, and both wrote of countries then unknown to most Englishmen. One wrote of the Old World, the other chiefly of the New ; but Coryate's vanity did no harm. He was proud of his knowledge of Latin, Greek, and the Eastern languages ; he had some right to be ; he was proud of having traveled far on a single pair of shoes, and he ardently wished to walk over the world. He did not come to America ; but would probably have done so, if he could have walked here ; and would have exchanged brave orations with the learned Indians, as well as Smith. Smith's vanity took a more serious turn, and has done great harm. It has for over 200 years destroyed the truth and the true idea of our earliest history. He was not only vain, but envious ; he took to himself the credit which rightly belonged to others. He cast a stigma on the real founders, and conveyed a selfish, narrow-minded idea of the founding of this country.

Coryate wrote of lands and places from personal observation. Smith's descriptions are generally compilations from the writings of others, and frequently relate to countries and places which he never saw. It is his personal narrative, however, which is most objectionable.

Coryate's writings were as well sus-tained as Smith's. Not only Abbot and Purchas thought well of them, but many others. Aubrey goes so far as to say that " he wrote faithfully, matter of fact." Among the sixty writers of verses appended to his " Crudities " were Ben Jonson, Sir John Harrington, John Davis of Hereford, Inigo Jones, Chapman, Donne, Drayton, Lionel Cranfield, Laurence Whitaker, etc., and of the fourteen persons to whom he sent his " dutyful respect " from the " Court of the Great Mogoll," November 8, 1615, the following ten will be found in this Dictionary, namely : Sir Robert Cotton, John Donne, Richard Martin (the lawyer), Christopher Brooke, John Hoskins, George Gerrard, William Hackwell, Ben Jonson, " Master Doctor Mocket," and Samuel Purchas.

Cottington, Sir Francis. A younger son of Philip Cottington, of Godmanston, County Somerset ; born in 1576 ; at an early age received into the household of Sir Edward Stafford as master of the horse. " Stafford recommended him to Sir Robert Cecil, through whose influence he became secretary to Sir Charles Cornwallis in his embassy to Spain in 1605, and on Cornwallis's return in 1609 he was intrusted, until about April, 1611, with the sole management of the affairs of England at that Court." Was appointed a clerk of the Privy Council in 1614. On the recall of Digby, in 1616, he was again dispatched to Madrid to represent England at the Court of Spain, which he continued to do until 1621–22, when be obtained the office of secretary to Charles, Prince of Wales. He was created a baronet February 23, 1623 ; and in that year went with Prince Charles on his noted trip to Madrid, which resulted in a declaration of war (March 10, 1624) with Spain, and a personal feud between Cottington and Buckingham, which lasted so long as Buckingham lived.

Appointed chancellor and under treasurer of the exchequer, April, 18, 1629. Sent to Spain to negotiate a peace in 1629 ; he executed this commission with the greatest credit, and returning to England in the spring of 1631, was on the 10th of July created Baron Cottington of Hanworth. King Charles authorized him to exercise the functions of lord high treasurer during his absence in Scotland, and he was made master of the Court of Wards on the king's return. Appointed one of the commissioners for the plantations in April, 1634. In 1637, as master of the Court of Wards, he had supervision over Benoni Buck, the first idiot born in Virginia.

He was appointed constable of the Tower of London in 1640 ; but in 1641–42 he resigned his offices and retired into private life. In 1644 King Charles made him lord high treasurer, rather an empty honor at that time. His estates were confiscated by Parliament in 1646, and he had fled to Normandy in 1648. Joined Charles II. at The Hague in 1649, where he was sworn of his Privy Council, and sent ambassador to Spain, arriving at Madrid in November, 1649, and was dismissed, after the news of Cromwell's decisive victories in 1650. In 1651, "weary of the world," he joined the Church of Rome, and retired to Valladolid, where he died in 1653, aged 77. (He had been a Catholic at heart for many years.) His nephew and heir, Charles Cottington, Esq., had his remains brought over to England in 1679, and interred in Westminster Abbey, where he erected a stately monument to his memory.

Lord Cottington married Anne, daughter of Sir William Meredith, of London, and widow of Sir Robert Brett, but left no surviving issue. His grandnephews, Thomas and Philip Ludwell, came to Virginia, and were men of distinction there.

Cotton, Alleine, draper. Sub. £37 10s. ; pd. £62 10s. Of E. I. and N. W. P. companies. Alderman of London ; sheriff, 1616 ; lord mayor, 1625–26 ; knighted at Whitehall, June 4, 1626. Died September 24 (or December 25), 1628, aged 70 ; buried under a rich and very beautiful monument in the chancel of St. Martin Orgars, in Candlewick ward, London.

Cotton, Sir Rowland, 2. Sub. ——— ; pd. £25. Of Alkington, Salop ; eldest son of William Cotton, alderman of London ; was knighted November 13, 1608 ; M. P. Newcastle-under-Lyme, 1609–11 ; Salop, 1626 ; New-castle-under-Lyme, 1628–29. Died in

1634. Fuller speaks "of the valor and activity of this most accomplished knight ; so strong, as if he had been nothing but bones ; so nimble, as if he had been nothing but sinews."

Cotton, Sir Robert. Sub. ——— ; pd. £25. Eldest son of Thomas Cotton of Connington, Huntingdonshire, was born January 22, 1571 ; educated at Cambridge ; B. A., 1585 ; began to collect manuscripts, coins, etc., in 1588, a pursuit which he continued to follow throughout his life ; joined the Antiquarian Society in 1590 ; M. P. for Newton (I. W.), 1601 ; knighted at Whitehall, July 23, 1603 ; M. P. for County Huntingdon, 1604–11 ; one of the commissioners on the state of the navy, 1608 ; created a baronet, June 29, 1611 ; induced by Somerset to seek a private interview with Gondomar, 1615 ; he became intimate with that ambassador, and this intimacy resulted in his imprisonment, 1615–16 (see Gondomar) ; but the friendship continued. He was M. P. for Old Sarum, 1624–25 ; for Thetford in 1625, and for Castle Rising in 1627–28. He died at Westminster, May 6, 1631, and was buried at Connington.

(See S. R. Gardiner's "History of England," 1885, vol. ii. pp. 321–347, for an account of Cotton's negotiations with Gondomar.)

Coutts — Cutts, Sir John the Younger, 3. Sub. £75; pd. £75. Of Childerly, Cambridge, son of Sir John Cutts, Sr. ; was knighted at Charterhouse, May 11, 1603 ; N. W. P. Co., 1612. M. P. for County Cambridge, 1604–11, 1614, 1621–22, 1624–25, 1625, 1626, and 1640 ; created a baronet June 21, 1660. Died in 1679, *s. p.*, when he must have been aged.

Covell, Francis, skinner, 2. Sub. £37 10s. ; pd. £112 10s. He was buried in the parish church of Alhallows, Barking ; the inscription on his monument in the south wall gives a brief outline of his life. "In the Ile against this place lyeth the Body of Francis Covell, citizen and Skinner of London. He lived in this Parish 52 years, was married to his wife Margery 42 years, had issue by her, Thomas, his only son [see next]. He had borne office in his Company and this Ward, with good reputation ; was in his life religious, peaceable, and charitable, and at his Death gave Cloathing to the poor of this Parish yearly forever. He lived 69 years and rendered his soul in Peace to God September 7, 1625."

Covell, Thomas. Sub. ——; pd. ——. Son of the foregoing; was a church-warden of Alhallows, Barking; a member of the N. W. P. Co. He still owned lands in Virginia May 12, 1639, and in a petition to the English Privy Council represented "that he had been an adventurer to Virginia for thirty years past."

Coventry, Thomas, esquire, 3. Sub. £37 10s.; pd. £12 10s. Born at Croome d'Abitot, in Worcestershire

[signature]

in 1578; gentleman commoner at Baliol College, 1592–94; entered a member of the Inner Temple, a student in the laws in November, 1594; autumn reader of the Inner Temple, 1616; recorder of London, November 16, 1616; solicitor-general, March 14, and knighted at Theobald's, March 16, 1617; treasurer of the Inner Temple; ordered to execute the office of attorney-general, pending the complaints against Yelverton, June 28, 1620; appointed attorney-general, January 11, 1621. He was consulted by the New England Company in regard to the renewal of their patent in May and July, 1622, and in January, 1623. He had joined the Virginia Company of London about 1610; but having failed to pay his subscription his membership was forfeited; he again joined that company on July 3, 1622; was continually consulted during the factions of 1623–24, both by the king and company. Said to have condemned the charter as "an unlimited, vast patent." Was on the Virginia Commission of July 15, 1624; lord keeper, November 1, 1625; created Lord Coventry of Aylesborough, April 10, 1628. Ordered the Massachusetts charter to issue, 1629; on the commission for plantations, April 28, 1634.

Died at Durham House, Strand, London, January 14, 1640. He married, first, Sarah, daughter of Edward Sebright, Esq., and, secondly, April 10, 1610, Elizabeth, widow of William Pitchford, apothecary, and sister to Samuel Aldersey of the Massachusetts Company.

Covert, Sir Walter, 3. Sub. ——; pd. £12 10s. Knighted 1591; M. P. Sussex, 1586–87; Petersfield, 1593; Sussex, 1614 and 1626.

Coxe. See Cocks.

Coyse, William, esquire, 2. Sub. £37 10s.; pd. £100; of North Okenden, County Essex; son of Roger Coyse, Esq., of London, by Joane, daughter of Robert Warren, of London, gent. He married Mary, daughter of Giles Allen, of Haseleigh, Essex, esquire, and had issue.

Crakenthorpe, Rev. Richard. Born in Westmoreland, 1567; fellow of Queen's College, Oxford, 1598. In 1603 went over champlain to the Lord Eure, sent ambassador to the King of Denmark and Princes of Germany, and here by use he got an easiness in the Latin tongue. Became champlain in ordinary to King James; rector of Black Notley in Essex, etc. Died in 1624.

Cranborne, Viscount. — Robert and William Cecil.

Cranfield, Lionell, esquire, mercer, 3. Sub. ——; pd. £37 10s. Younger son of Thomas Cranfield, mercer, of London, by Martha, daughter of Vincent Randolph; was baptized at St. Michael's Bassishaw, March 13, 1575; bred to mercantile pursuits, was an active and successful man of affairs; appointed receiver of customs of Dorset and Somerset April 1, 1605. Lodge says his verses prefixed to Coryat's "Crudities" of 1611 "entitles him to the reputation of a smooth versifier." Lieutenant of Dover Castle in July, 1613; knighted at Oatlands July 4, 1613, and made surveyor-general of customs July 26; M. C. Va. Co.; master of the Court of Request, November 20, 1616; master of the wardrobe, September 14, 1618; master of the wards, January 15, 1619; chief commissioner of the navy, February 12, 1619; member Privy Council, January 5, 1620; created Baron Cranfield of Cranfield, Bedford, July 9,

1621 ; lord treasurer, October 13, 1621 ; Earl of Middlesex, September 16, 1622. Much abused by the Sandys-Ferrar faction of the Va. Co., 1623–24. Drew the 13th lot in New England, June 29, 1623. Incurred the enmity of the Duke of Buckingham and Prince Charles by murmuring at the expense of their journey to Spain, and the duke proceeded to have him impeached by Parliament. King James protested, told Stenny that he was a fool, and warned Prince Charles that "he would live to have his belly full of Parliament impeachments; and when I shall be dead, you will have too much cause to remember how much you have contributed to the weakening of the crown by the two precedents you are now so fond of ; " but, says Lodge, "the duke's power, supported by the prince's countenance, was grown so great in the two houses, that it was in vain for the king to interpose." The Earl of Middlesex was impeached, and fined £50,000, May 13, 1624 ; but on May 10, 1625, he was released from the fine, and on August 20, 1626, he was granted special pardon. (See Sir Abram Dawes.) He retired to his fine seat of Copt Hall in Essex, where, says Fuller, "he enjoyed himself contentedly, entertained his friends bountifully, his neighbors hospitably, and the poor charitably." He died August 6, 1645, and was buried in Westminster Abbey.

Crashaw, Rawley, 2. Sub.——; pd. £25. He went to Virginia in 1608 ; was a burgess in 1624, when he was living in Elizabeth Cittie and owned 500 acres by patent, between Fox Hill and Pamunkey River.

Crashaw, William, 2. Sub.——; pd. £37 10s. Sometimes classed as a Puritan divine and poet; was baptized at Handsworth, October 26, 1572 ; educated at Cambridge ; prebend in the church of Ripon, 1604; preacher at the Inner Temple, London ; at Church of St. Mary Matfellon, or Whitechapel, London, November 13, 1618; died in 1626. A good scholar, an eloquent preacher and writer, and a strong Protestant. He was the father of Richard Crashaw the poet and Roman Catholic.

Craven, Sir William, merchant-tailor, 3. Sub. £75 ; pd. £75. Of E. I. Co. ; born at Appletreewick in Burnsale, parish Craven, Yorkshire, about 1548 ; went to London seeking his fortune, and found it there; alderman of Bishopsgate ward, April 2, 1600, to May 18, 1602 ; of Cordwainer ward, May 18, 1602, to January 15, 1611; of Lime Street ward, from January 15, 1611, to his death, July 18, 1618 ; sheriff of London, 1601–02 ; knighted at Whitehall, July 26, 1603 ; Lord Mayor of London, 1610–11 ; president of Christ's Hospital, 1610–18 ; died July 18, 1618 ; buried at St. Andrew's Undershaft. (See Strype's Stow for his will and numerous charities.) Craven County, North Carolina, is named for his son, the very celebrated William, Earl of Craven.

Creswell, Robert. Pd. £12 10s.

Crew, Anthony, 2. Sub.—— ; pd. £25.

Crew, Sir Randolph (1558–1646). M. P. for Saltash in Cornwall, when speaker, 1614 ; sergeant at law, July, 1615; chief justice of the King's Bench, January 26, 162⅘.

Crispe, Ellis, salter. Newfoundland Co.; of E. I. and N. W. P. companies ; sheriff of London in 1625. The father of Sir Nicholas Crisp, the African trader.

Croft, Sir Herbert, 2. Sub.—— ; pd.——. Of Croft Castle, Hereford ; "grandson of Sir James Croft, who suffered severely in the reign of Queen Mary ; " educated at Christ Church College in Oxford ; M. P. for Carmarthenshire in 1588–89; for Herefordshire in 1592–93; for Launceston, 1597–98 ; for Herefordshire in 1601 ; knighted by James I. at Theobald's, May 7, 1603; M. P. for Herefordshire, 1604–11 ; M. C. for Va., March 9, 1607 ; M. P. for Herefordshire in 1614. In February, 1617, he became a monk in the College of English Benedictines at Douay. How long he had been a Romanist I do not know.

The letter writers of the period say that " he was ruined by the excesses of his wife," and Wood says, " that at length full weary of the fooleries and vanities of this world, he retired to Douay in Flanders, and was there received into the College of Benedictines, where he spent the remainder of his days in strict devotion and religious exercise. At length, after he had macerated his body with fasting, hardship, and devotion, he surrendered up his pious soul to the Almighty on April 10, 1622, aged 56." He was the father of Dr. Herbert Croft, Bishop of Hereford, a distinguished minister of the Church of England. Froude says his grandfather, Sir James Croft, the controller of the household of Elizabeth, was for a time in the pay of Spain; and it may be that Sir Herbert Croft was an agent for Philip III. in the Virginia Council and Company.

Croftes, Lieutenant, of Captain Bigg's company; probably continued the account of the voyage (1585–86) begun by Biggs.

Cromwell, Henry, 2. Sub.——; pd. £25. Of Upwood, County Hunts, third son of Sir Henry Cromwell, of Hinchinbroke, and brother of Sir Oliver. He was M. P. for Huntingdon, 1604–11; died 1630.

Cromwell, Henry, esquire, 3. Sub. £37 10s.; pd. £37 10s. The eldest son of Sir Oliver. He was the Colonel Henry Cromwell who took a very active part for the king, and had his property sequestered; but the Protector (who in the worst of times was a kind and considerate kinsman) had the sequestration discharged July 9, 1649. Colonel Henry Cromwell died September 18, 1657, and was interred in the chancel of Ramsey Church. (See Burke's " Vicissitudes of Families.")

Cromwell, Sir Oliver, 2. Sub. £75; pd. £75. His grandfather, Sir Richard Williams, eldest son of Morgan Williams by his wife, a sister of Thomas Cromwell, Earl of Essex, assumed, at the desire of Henry VIII., the surname of his uncle Cromwell, and through the influence of that once powerful relative himself and his family obtained great wealth and station. Sir Richard married, in 1518, Frances, daughter of Sir Thomas Murfin (or Myrfin), then Lord Mayor of London (her sister, Alice Murfin, married Sir Andrew Judde, and was the grandmother of Sir Thomas Smythe, the first treasurer of the Virginia Company), by whom he was the father of Sir Henry Cromwell, called " the Golden Knight," one of the wealthiest gentlemen of Huntingdonshire, who married Joan, daughter of Sir Rafe Warren (twice Lord Mayor of London), and had issue, among others, Sir Oliver Cromwell (of whom I write), Henry Cromwell, Robert (the father of the Lord Protector), Elizabeth (the mother of John Hampden, the patriot), Frances (the mother of Edward Whalley, the regicide), and Joan, wife of Sir Francis Barington. Oliver Cromwell, of whom I write, was born about 1562–63 ; M. P. for County of Huntingdon in 1588–89, 1592–93, 1597–98, and 1601. April 29, 1599, he stood godfather for his nephew, afterwards the Protector. He entertained King James, on his progress to London, from the evening of April 27 to the morning of April 29, 1603, most famously, at Hinchinbrooke. " There was such plenty and variety of meats, such diversity of wines, and those not riff-ruff, but ever the best of the kind, and the cellars open at any man's pleasure." " Master Cromwell presented his maiestie with many rich and acceptable gifts, as a very great and faire wrought standing Cup of golde, goodly horses, deepe mouthed houndes, divers Hawkes of excellent wing," etc. He was made a Knight of the Bath at the coronation of King James, July 25, 1603 ; M. P. for Huntingdonshire, 1604–11 ; M. C. for for Va., 1607; M. C. for Va. Co., 1609. He was master of the game to Henry, Prince of Wales ; M. P. for Huntingdonshire in 1614, 1623–24, and 1625. " At the outbreak of the civil war, Sir Oliver remained not an idle spectator, but enrolling himself under the royal banner (against his nephew), raised men, and gave large sums of money to support the king's cause ; " " and when that cause failed he retired to Ramsey Abbey, and died there August 28, 1655, in his 93d year, impoverished and broken-hearted, but still unshaken in his allegiance." He was buried in Ramsey Church. He married, first, Elizabeth, daughter of Sir Thomas Bromley, lord chancellor, and, secondly, Anne, widow of the celebrated Sir Horatio Palavicino, but had issue by the first wife only.

W. Dugdale wrote to John Langley, from London, September 8, 1655 : . . . "Admiral Pen is come back from Jamaica with part of the Navy . . . The Protector hath been very ill the last week, but they say he is now recovered. His uncle, Sir Oliver Cromwell, is very lately dead by an unhappy accident ; for I hear that he was out in the rain, and after his return, sitting by a good fire without any company in the room, by some weakness or swoon fell into the fire, and was so scorched that he died about two days after."

Crosley, or Crosby, William, grocer and apothecary, 2. Sub.——; pd. £75.

Crosse, Capt. Robert. Knighted at Cadiz, 1596; M. P. Minehead, 1586-87; Yarmouth, 1592–93, and Saltash, 1601; died in 1611.

Crowe, John, gent., 3. Sub. £37 10s.; pd. £37 10s. He patented land in Virginia.

Crowe, William. Pd. £12 10s.

Cullimore — Culliner — Colmer, etc., Abraham. Pd. £12 10s.

Cullimore (or Collymore), James. Pd. £25. Of St. Thomas Apostle, London, merchant ; of the E. I. Co. His son, John Collymore, mercer, married, in 1604, Mabel Lovelace, of St. Bride, London, daughter of Sir William Lovelace, of the city of Canterbury. Mabell Lady Cullamore held four shares in Captain Argall's plantation in Virginia, February 12, 161⅚.

Culpeper — Colepepper, Sir Edward, 3. Sub.——; pd. £12 10s. Of Wakehurst ; knighted at Whitehall, July 23, 1603. His second son, William, was created a baronet by Charles I., September 20, 1628.

Culpeper, John, esquire, 2. Sub. £37 10s.; pd. £37 10s. He was afterwards knighted. His grandson, Thomas Lord Colepeper, was governor-general of Virginia.

Culpepper, Thomas, of Wigsel, esquire, 2. Sub.—— ; pd. ——. I suppose this to be the Thomas Colepeper who married a daughter of Sir Stephen Slaney. His daughter, Elizabeth Colepeper, was born at Wigsale,

Surrey, in January, 1601, and married, in 1620, Sir Robert Brooke. Lady Elizabeth Brooke was a religious writer of note.

Cumberland, Countess of. — Margaret Russell.

Cumberland, Earl of. — George Clifford.

Cuñega. See Zuñiga.

Cutler, Thomas, grocer, 2. Sub.——; pd. ——. "Thomas Cutler, son of Thomas Cutler, deceased, admitted and sworn a free Brother by Patrimony, 18 Feb'y, 1604 ; admitted to Livery, 1609." (From Grocers' Records.) He was the father of Sir John Cutler, the celebrated miser, immortalized by Pope, who left his gains to good purposes ; was a benefactor of the Grocers, of the College of Physicians, Gresham College, etc.

Cutts. See Coutts.

Dabney (Daubeny, etc.), Henry, 2. Sub.——; pd. £20. He was probably the brother of Clement Daubigny (the inventor of an engine, to be driven by water, for cutting iron into small bars, licensed December 11, 1618), as the payment to the Va. Co. stands in the names of "Clement and Henry Daubny."

Dabney, Clement. See Henry Dabney.

Dabney (Dawbeney, etc.), Oliver. "Of London, gentleman ; married Elizabeth Drayner, and left issue." He gave Mr. Richard Hakluyt of the Middle Temple an account of the voyage of 1536, who related it to his cousin, the Rev. Richard Hakluyt, of Oxford.

Dale, Sir Thomas, 3. Sub. £75 ; pd. £25. Entered the service of the United States of the Low Countries with Essex about the year 1588. In 1595 he was sent by the Provinces into Scotland, where, it seems, he became one of the retinue of the infant Prince Henry, and remained with him some years, returning to the Netherlands probably in 1603.

"August 1, 1603, Resolution of the States General on the recommendation of the King of France, to commission Captain Dale provisionally as captain of the infantry company of Captain Condegrave."

"March 29, 1604, Cecil wrote to

the English ambassador at The Hague, to inform him of the King's gracious opinion of the merit of Captain Dale, both for having been a valiant and long servitor of Prince Henry's, and for having, for the most part, resided at his own charge." Cecil continues, " His Majesty commanded me to acquaint you so much, to the intent, that in the alterations and removes of places among the companies, where he is one, he may be respected, both for his own merit and his Master's (Prince Henry's) recommendation, who is persuaded of his honesty and sufficiency."

June 19, 1606, while on a visit to England, he was knighted at Richmond by King James as " Sir Thomas Dale of Surrey." In November, 1606, he was stationed in Oudewater, a small city in South Holland, and probably remained in the Low Countries until about the 1st of February, 1611, when he came to England, and entered the service of the Va. Co. of London ; was M. C. for Va. Co., and his acts from that time to June, 1616, belong to the history of that enterprise. On his return, the celebrated John Rolfe wrote both to King James and to Sir Robert Rich, that " Sir Thomas Dale's worth and name in managing the affairs of this Colony, will out *last* the standing of this Plantation." The Rev. Samuel Purchas writes of Dale as " that worthy commander, and best establisher of the Virginian Plantation," and he is highly spoken of in the Broadsides of the Council and Company of Virginia.

Ralph Hamor wrote in the highest terms of praise of him in 1614 ; but Hamor's name is signed to " A Briefe Declaration," etc., of 1624, which is not complimentary.

March 31, 1617, Sir Raphe Winwood wrote from St. Bartholomew's, London, to Sir Dudley Carleton, ambassador in the Netherlands:

" My Lord. Sir Thomas Daale havinge for many yeares together resided in Virginia, as you know, about the service of this kingdome, is now returninge into those Provinces to his charge, from whence, although hee hath been longer absent then hee had licence of the states for his Warrant, yet beeinge a principall man in an em-

ployment of such consequence as that was, I assure myselfe you will labour soe effectually for him there, that he shall bee noe waye prejudiced thereby. If in any other occasions of his, hee shall stand in neede of your Lordship's favour, I pray you afford it him with much readiness, and give him at all times such countenance, and good respect, as you shall thinck fitt for a man of his qualetie and meritt; whereby you shall not onelye engage a weldeservinge gentleman to your service, but purchase the thancks of many others in this state, whoe hold themselves much interested in his future weldoeinge and advancement. Yo[r] Lp[s] to doe you service. RAPHE WINWOOD.

" [P. S.] His licence to goe to Virginia was procured by myselfe at my being there, upon a letter from the late Prince Henry."

The sickness of his wife prevented Dale from going over to the Netherlands at this time, and this letter was not sent until October. On the 30th of September, 1617, Dale was among those applying for the command of the fleet of the English East India Company, and on November 28, 1617, he was chosen at a salary of £480 per annum. While the aforesaid application was pending, the following three letters were written.

Sir Thomas Dale to Sir Dudley Carleton, October 18, 1617 : " Right honorable. My absenc out of those provinces hath left me destytut of acquantce and frends, which makes me loth to truble your lordship with these lyens. So yt is that since 6 yeares has yt pleased the lord treassurer then to Imbark me for the plantation in Vergynia and used both his power and princ Henrys for my leave of the lords the states for 5 years. The which my lords the states granted, but they would deteyne my enterteynment to the tyme of my retorne, promising by their apostyll, If I retorned I should have it. M[r] Secrytarie that now is effected that leave, by order from the prince and the lord Treasurer that then was. At my departure, I marryed a wyfe, expecting my journey shoud not have bin so long as yt happened to be, and sinc my coming home I borrowed 6 months after my travels for her sake, who then was sickly and so

SIR PHILIP SIDNEY

hath contynued, and since 3 months her sicknes hath much encreased and now I am afraid to loose her. This is the reason of my so long stay here after my aryvall, which may passe for currant with good and honest husbands though not with my lords the states in matter of servyse. Now half a year sins I had a dispach from Mr Secrytarie to your honer and expecting every day a fit wynd to have brought me over to have dylyvered the letters myself I was stayed by the hand of God which hath ever syns lade heavye one my wyfe and yet is the occasion I come not now, by reason wherof I mak bould to send these letters unto your honer by my brother this bearer, and with all thes rude lynes to entreat your honors favour and assystance unto my lords the states for excuse of my long absence, for I am gyven to understand that my leftenant (who is not the honestest there) doth make means for my company underhand, aleaging that I will com no more. Yt is true that at my departure my company was much In debt and I am given to understand my leftenant hath not lessened them but rather augmented them, and doth gyve out that the Stattes wyll not pay my Enterteynment for the tyme of my absens, and that the solysiturs have gotten leave of the lords the Stattes to arrest me at my aryvall, which is straing to me. Now I would entreat your lordship in the Interim of my coming (which I hop shall be in 20 days) your honor would be pleased to make the lords the stattes acquaynted with my casse and the state of my bussynes. The Kings Majestye hath promysed me to wryet to your lordship conserning my bussynes to procuer my pay and Mr. Secrytarie wished me to send his first letter over to your lordship, and withall I would entreat your lordship to advyse me of any means I may procuer from this state. Mr Secrytarie tells me yt shall be effected before my going over. If your lordship please to take my bussines into your favorall protextion you shall not only bynd a poore Gentyllman unto you, but many honorable frends of myen wyll gyve your lordship thankes and so I commend my servyce unto your honer and rest.

Your honers to be commaunded.
THOMAS DALE.
"[P. S.] If I myght be so bould with your lordship, I would entreat 2 or 3 words from your lordship for my better adresse in my bussynes."

Sir Thomas Dale to Sir Dudley Carleton, November 6, 1617 : "Right honerable. Syns my last unto your Lordship yt hath pleased God to call Mr. Secrytarye to his mercie, by whos death, my loss is much in pertyculer, but the generall loss to all honest men is much more, by many he is much lamented, and wyll be myst both in our state and ther wher your lordship lyveth, I have syns his death spoken with my Majestye conserning my bussynes in those partes, who hath gyven order to Mr. Secrytarie Lakes to comend my bussynes unto your Lordship, but as yet I have not my dispach. Now yf yt shall pleas you to geve me any advyse for any means els from hens, I know my frends are such as I shall procure yt to second your lordship in my behalf. I must confesse my acquayntance is but smale with your lordship and my desserts lesse, yet yf yt shall please your lordship to favour me and my cause which is just and honest, you shall not only bynd a pour gentleman unto you, but noble frends of myne here wyll gyve your Lordship thankes and so I comend my servyse unto your lordship and rest. Your honers to be commanded. THOMAS DALE."

(The various documents given in this sketch of Dale have never been printed in full in the United States.)

November 11, 1617, King James to Sir Dudley Carleton. James R: "Trusty and welbeloved wee greete you well : Sir Thomas Dale sometime servant to the Prince Henry our sonne deceased, having a company in the Low Countreyes, was by him commanded to attend the plantacion of Virginia, and that he might bee at Liberty so to doe, at the request of our said sonne, the States Generall gave him leave to bee absent, and that notwithstanding his absence, he should enjoy fully his pay, and thereof as he informeth us there is an apostell extant. Having now left that service he returneth to his charge, and because hee is a Gentleman of good meritt, both in that service of Virginia whiles hee attended it, and before in the service of the United Provinces, Wee have thought it reasonable to call upon the States for the performance of that *promise* which in his favor they made to our said sonne. And do therefor do require you to deale therein effectually, both with the Prince Maurice, and with the States Generall, and to procure for his satisfaction the arrearages of the time past, and continuance in the said pay and favor with them, as he was before his going to Virginia. Wherein wee hope the better of successe, because there is so good reason for the ground of our request, as is a promise made to a person of such quality as was the said Prince.

"Given at Our Court at Theobalds the 11th of November in the fifteenth yeare of our raigne of Great Brittaine."

Addressed : "To our trusty and welbeloved Sir Dudley Carleton, Knt., Our Ambassador with the States Generall of the United Provinces."

Dale was securing strong indorsements; he was not only afraid of being arrested for debt, but the States General had sold his company to Captain Willoughby. He wanted his company or his pay, and probably there were other "bones of contention," and Dale evidently wished to be sure of his ground before crossing the narrow seas. On December 4, 1617, Sir Henry Savile wrote by him to Carleton, "recommending to Carleton Sir Thomas Dale, a friend of the Earl of Southampton, who has done good service in the plantation of Virginia." Dale, who went over to the Low Countries himself soon after the date of this letter, also carried letters from the Earl of Southampton (and probably from others) which are now lost, and a long letter from M. Noel de Caron (the Dutch ambassador in England) to the States General, which has been published in the first volume of " Documents relating to the Colonial History of New York." Dale's petition, letters, etc., were presented to the States General by Sir Dudley Carleton January $\frac{16}{26}$, 1618. These, together with the resolutions thereon (January 16 to January 30) are also published in the aforesaid volume. On January 30 the

States General finally resolved to allow Dale his full wages during his absence on condition that he would not claim his company of Captain Willoughby. Sir Dudley Carleton, in his address, presenting Dale's petition to the States General, says, "Captain Thomas Dale . . . for the space of some years having command and authority for planting a colony of the English Nation in the Country of Virginia, whereof he hath acquitted himself with reputation and honor to himself, to his Majesty's satisfaction, and to the publick advantage, inasmuch as by signal patience, diligence, and valor, he overcame divers serious difficulties and dangers and finally established a good and permanent settlement all along a river navigable for seventy leagues into the interior, and by that means hath preserved it to God, by the exercise of Religion which is introduced there, and to man, by the augmentation of commerce.

"Several of the nation, as well Lords as other gentlemen of quality and honor have considerably contributed to this design. But two of our Captains (Sir Thomas Gates and this one of whom I now speak) have promoted it more than any other."

Soon after receiving his full entertainment, £1,000, for the whole time of his seven years absence, Sir Thomas Dale returned to England. While he was absent, on January 16, 1618, King James, to give a more ample authority to the intended voyage to the East Indies, granted a special commission to "Sir Thomas Dale and Capt. William Parker, authorizing the government of that fleet, as well by common as by martial law : also to seize on the ships and merchandize of any others of his subjects who should be found navigating within the company's limits without their licence," etc.

On the 20th of February 161$\frac{7}{8}$, he made his will, leaving all of his estate to his wife Elizabeth, six days after his fleet of six ships was in the Downs on the way to the East Indies. While he is on the voyage, I will mention some reflections which were being cast upon him at home. February 4, 1618, Sir Dudley Carleton wrote to Secretary (Sir Thomas Lake ?) of his success in obtaining Dale's back pay " in contemplation of his Majesties recommendation and of Sir Thomas Dales goode service in Virginia (wherein there is a comon interest)." February 12, Carleton wrote to the Earl of Southampton that "Sir Thomas Dale by whom I received *your letter*, hathe fownde better successe and quicker expedition in his businesse then is ordinarie with his masters (The States) in affaires of that nature ; . . . and though goode and due regard was had herein of his particular merit yet I can assure your Lordship he was not a little assisted by those recommendations wherewith he came accompanied."

March 3, Carleton wrote again from The Hague to Secretary (Lake ?), "Hears that Sir Thomas Dale left the States service the very day of the receipt of his money *sans dire adieu*, it being given out that he is employed into the East Indies by the King's command. Shall gladly receive some civil excuse, the King's name being interested both in Sir Thomas Dale's good treatment by the States, and in his ill manner of leaving their service." March 26, Secretary Lake replied to Carleton : "Your Lordship wrote to me of late of a fault of Sir Thomas Dale, which his Majesty and all men have condemned in him." This was evident diplomacy; the Dutch did not wish to establish a precedent for making such back payments, and King James knew that Dale was going to the East Indies.

To return to Dale's fleet. On June 20, 1618, they entered "The Road of Soldania ;" November 19, arrived at Bantam ; December 23, in conjunction with Capt. Martin Pring, made an attack on the Dutch fleet, near the island of Java ; "a cruel bloody fight," each side, it seems, claiming the victory. March 15, 1619, Dale wrote from Jacatra to the E. I. Co., "should be glad to hear how Virginia prospers and his [Dale's] business goes forward there." July 23, 1619, the E. I. Co. wrote from London to Sir Thomas Dale in the East Indies, "with advertisement of the peace with the Dutch, and directions to him to take the command of the first fleet that shall be jointly set forth by the English and Dutch of sixteen or twenty good ships of war to prosecute trade on the coast of Malabar, and endeavour to open and enlarge trade with the Chinese by the advice of a Council of Defence, himself to be one if not employed at sea," etc.

Sir Thomas Dale, with his fleet, arrived at Masulipatam July 19, and he died there August 9, 1619, "after twenty days of languishing sickness and many testimonies of good Christianity, contempt of death, and singular zeal and affection towards the Company's service, and his body was enclosed and housed in form of a tomb." "Whose valor having shined in the Westerne, was set in the Easterne India."

In November, 1619 (before his death was known in England), Sir Edwin Sandys, at the General Quarter Court of the Va. Co., "recalled to remembrance, how by the admirable care and Diligence of two worthy knights, Sir Thomas Gates and Sir Thomas Dale, the publick Estate and Revenue of the Company had been set forward, in a way to great perfection: . . . that Sir Thomas Dale building upon the Foundation [of Sir Thomas Gates] with great care and constant severity, had reclaimed almost miraculously, those idie and dissolute Persons, and reduced them to Labour and an honest fashion of life : That proceeding with great Zeal for the good of the Company, he had laid off publick lands, to yield them a Standing Revenue, placed servants thereon, as also upon other publick works, for the Company's use; established an annual Rent of Corn from the farmers, and of Tribute from the Barbarians, together with a great stock of Cattle, Goats, and other animals."

Sir Thomas Dale married, in February, 1611, Elizabeth, daughter of Sir Thomas Throckmorton and his wife Elizabeth, daughter of Sir Richard Berkeley. Lady Dale was related to the wife of Sir Walter Ralegh, and also to the Berkeleys ; dying in 1640 without issue, she gave to Mrs. Dorothea Throgmorton her lands in Charles Hundred, Virginia, and to the son of Richard Hanby (Hanbury ?) her lands in Shirley Hundred. One half of her estate in England and Virginia, after the payment of her debts and legacies, she gave to the children of her brother, Sir William Throgmorton, knight and baronet, deceased. She gave her nephew (John) the Lord Viscount Scudamore, a ring, valued at sixty pounds sterling." (See Throckmorton pedigree, and William Dale.)

Dale, William, grocer. Son of Robert Dale, of Wingle in Prestbury in County Chester, and brother to Roger Dale, of the Inner Temple. He was a warden of the Grocers' Company in 1614, and member of the E. I. Co. He married, in May, 1583, Miss Elizabeth Elliott, of St. Mary Magdalen, London, daughter of Thomas Elliott of Surrey, esquire. In 1613 William Dale had a seat at Brigstock in County Northampton. I have reason to believe that he was related to Sir Thomas Dale.

Danvers — Davers, Sir John, 3. Sub, £37 10s. ; pd. £25. He was the third son of Sir John Danvers by his wife Elizabeth, daughter of John Neville, Lord Latimer (she was sister to the wives of Henry, Earl of Northumberland, Thomas, Earl of Exeter, and of Sir William Cornwallis). Born about 1588 ; married, in 1608, Magdalen, daughter of Sir Richard Newport (widow of Richard Herbert, Esq., and mother by him of ten children, including the noted Edward, Baron Herbert of Cherbury, and George Herbert, the poet), when she is said to have been over forty, and young Danvers under twenty. He was knighted at Whitehall, March 5, 1609; M. P. for Arundel, 1610–11; for Oxford University, 1621–22, 1625, 1626, 1628–29, and 1640; for Newport in 1624–25 ; and for Salisbury, 1645–53 ; M. C. for Va. Co., 1612–20. He was one of the Sandys faction in the Va. Co., 1622–24. His first wife died in June, 1627. He married, secondly, in July, 1628, and, thirdly, in January, 1649, in his old age. On the special commission for the better plantation of Virginia, June 27, 1631. One of the judges who passed sentence on Charles I. in January, 1649, for which act he has been especially condemned because

he had served in the household of the king, and had received many favors from him. " The Discovery of New Brittaine . . . in Virginia " by Edward, son of John Bland, was dedicated to him in 1650. He was governor of the Bermudas Islands Company in 1651, in which year " A short collection of the Most Remarkable Passages from the Originall to the dissolution of the Virginia Company " written in his interest, was published. The account in this tract giving to him the credit of having had the copies of the Virginia Records made is certainly inaccurate. The evidence that Nicholas Ferrer the younger had this work done is conclusive. He died in 1655. It is said that he was the first to introduce into England the Italian method of horticulture.

Darell — Darrell. Sir Marmaduke, 3. Sub. £75 ; pd. £50. Knighted in 1603 ; surveyor-general of victuals for the navy, etc. ; built a new church at Fulmere in Buckinghamshire, which was consecrated by Doctor Barlow, Lord Bishop of Lincoln, November 1, 1610.

Darnelly, Daniel, grocer and apothecary, 3. Sub. £37 10s. ; pd. £45. Buried in St. Mary Woolchurch Haw, London, May 24, 1623.

Dausey, Ralegh. Sub. —— ; pd. £25.

Davies — Davis, Captain James, died at the plantation over against James City, Va., in 1624.

Davies. See Dawes.

Davis, John, 2. Sub. —— ; pd. £25. Possibly the poet of Hereford ; writing-master and Roman Catholic.

Davis — Davys, Captain John. The "lovable John Davis " was born at Sandridge, near Dartmouth, not far from the Gilberts and the Raleghs, about 1550 ; he followed the sea from boyhood ; appears to have made voyages with Adrian Gilbert prior to 1579 ; with Gilbert he is in consultation with Dr. Dee in 1579–80 and 1583 ; interested in the Northwest charter of February 6, 1584. Davys made his first voyage June 7 to September 30, 1585 ; his second May 7 to October 6, 1586 ; and his third May 19 to September 15, 1587. He published " A Traverse Booke " prior to March 25, 1588, and probably served against the Armada in that year ; was commanding a ship about the Azores, waiting for Spanish prizes in 1589 ; in the next year, 1590, he captured a Spanish prize, about which there was some contention ; was on the unfortunate voyage of Cavendish from August 26, 1591, to the summer of 1593 ; published his " Seaman's Secrets " in 1594, and " The Worldes Hydrographical Description," in 1595 ; was probably at Cadiz in 1596 and the Azores in 1597, in which last voyage Sir Arthur Gorges refers to him as " one John Davis, a great navigator reputed" (see Purchas, iv. p. 1967) ; became a retainer of the Earl of Essex, and at his suggestion entered the service of the Dutch, and " went as chief pilot to the Zelanders in their voyage to the East Indies," from March 15, 1598, to July 29, 1600 ; chief pilot of the first voyage sent out by the English E. I. Co. from February 13, 1601, to September 11, 1603. He sailed with Sir Edward Michelborne for the East Indies December 5, 1604, and was killed by the Japanese in the Straits of Malacca December 27, 1605.

Davis, Sir John, 2. Sub. —— ; pd. £25. Stith gives the name " Sir Thomas," but the Kimbolton MS. has it " Sir John." I can find no " Sir Thomas " at that time. I think it was Sir John Davies (1569–1626), the poet and attorney-general for Ireland, — the same who had the difficulty with Richard Martin, the lawyer.

Dawes, Abram, skinner, 2. Sub. £37 10s. ; pd. £62 10s. Of the E. I. and N. W. P. companies ; one of the farmers of the customs to Charles I. ; knighted at Whitehall May 8, 1633 (then described as " of Putney "), in which year he was a benefactor of Sion College Library and a commissioner for Va. ; commissioner for Va. tobacco in 1634 ; for the Caribbee Islands in 1635, and still on the Va. Commission in 1638. In August, 1637, at a dinner given at his house, Mr. Burlamachi, Sir John Wolstenholme, and others being present, it was unanimously agreed that no man ever suffered for so little as Lionel Cranfield, Earl of Middlesex. Dawes died about 1640 ; his will is dated in 1639. He founded an almshouse in Putney, dedicated to the Holy Trinity, and was a benefactor of the Skinners' Company.

Dawes, Lancelot, 2. Sub.—— ; pd. £25. (1580–1654) he published several sermons. [This name is given as Davis and Davies ; but I believe him to be the Rev. Lancelot Dawes, D. D.]

Dawkes, Henry, 2. Sub. —— ; pd. £25.

Deane, Richard, skinner, 2. Sub. —— ; pd. £50. Of the E. I. and N. W. P. companies ; son of George Dean, of Muchdunmowe in Essex. He was for many years an alderman of London ; sheriff in 1619 ; lord mayor in 1628–29 ; knighted at Greenwich, May 31, 1629 ; a benefactor of the Church of St. James, Duke's Place ; died in 1635. He was a Puritan, and the uncle or great uncle of Major-General Richard Deane, the regicide.

Decroe — Docwra, Benjamin, 3. Sub. —— ; pd. £37 10s. He was a member of and an agent for the Muscovy Company, also of E. I. and N. W. P. companies. (It was a member of his family, I suppose, who first adjusted the penny post for London and the suburbs.)

Dee, Dr. John. Born July 13, 1627 ; at Cambridge 1542–46. " In May, 1547, he went into the Low Countries to confer with learned men. On his return home he brought with him the first astronomer's staff of brass, devised by Gemma Frisius, the two great globes constructed by Gerard Mercator," etc. ; M. A., Cambridge, 1547 ; on the continent, 1548–50, intimate with Gerard Mercator ; in England, 1551–62 ; imprisoned by Queen Mary, 1554–55 ; taken into the service of Queen Elizabeth, 1558 ; on the continent, 1562–63 ; in England (save brief absences in 1571 and 1578) from 1564 to 1583. His " Perfect Art of Navigation " was published in 1576 ; had a noted consultation with Sir H. Gilbert, November 6, 1577 ; was interested in Frobisher's voyages, 1576–78 ; was constantly consulted about discoveries of unknown things in the heavens above and the earth beneath ; was interested in Adrian Gilbert's and John Davis's N. W. charter February 6, 1584 ; but had left England privately before that date, and was absent on his celebrated European trip from September, 1583, to December, 1589, from which last date he probably remained in England to his death at

Mortlake in December, 1608. One of the most remarkable characters of a very remarkable age.

Delaun, Gideon, apothecary. Pd. £37 10s. Of London, and of Sharsted, Kent, eldest son of William Delaune, a French Protestant pastor and doctor in phisick ; was born at Rheims about 1565 ; accompanied his father to England, and was appointed apothecary to Anne of Denmark, queen of James I.; of the N. W. P. Co. in 1612. "March 7, 1613, grant by Wm. Segar, garter king-at-arms, to Gideon Launey, the king's servant, and his brothers, sons of Dr. Wm. Launey, who died in London in 1610, of the arms of the family of Launey, of Belmesnil, in Normandy, from which they are descended." In 1617 the Apothecaries were first incorporated as a separate and distinct company from the Grocers, it is said, at the special suit of Gideon Delaune, who was a member of the first court of assistants of the company ; junior warden in 1624 ; senior warden in 1627 ; and master of the company in 1637. He may not have been the first pill-maker, but he was the originator of a long famous pill. February 19, 1623, he transferred two shares of his lands in Virginia to his son Abraham. He was also a member of the E. I. and S. I. companies ; died in 1659, aged 94. He married Judith, daughter of Henry Chamberleine, of London, gent., and his son Abraham married Anne, daughter of Sir Richard Sandys, of Northbourne Court, Kent.

De la Warr, Lord. — Thomas West.

Delbridge, John, 3. Sub. ——; pd. £37 10s. Merchant of Barnstaple ; member of the E. I. Co., N. W. P. Co., etc. ; was M. P. for Barnstaple, 1614, 1621–22, 1624–25, 1625, 1626, and 1628–29. We find his ships making trading and fishing voyages to Virginia, the Bermudas, and New England. He was called "The Free Trader." In 1619 he patented lands in Virginia, and petitioned the Virginia Company "that for the defraying somewhat of his charges in settling his plantation, that he might be admitted to fish at Cape Cod," which request was opposed by Sir Ferdinando Gorges, "aleaginge that he always favored Mr. Delbridge,

but in this he thought himself something touched that he should sue to this company, and not rather to him, as prophe belonging to the North Colony," etc. He received a patent for lands in New England November 26, 1632.

Denmark. See Christian IV.

Dennis, Sir Thomas, 2. Sub. ——; pd. £105. Of Bicton and Holcombe, Devon, grandson of Sir Thomas Dennys (M. P. for Devon, 1529, with whom he is often confused); was born about 1559 ; knighted by Robert, Earl of Leicester, in Holland in 1586 ; M. P. for Devon, 1593 ; died in 1613. He married Anne, daughter of William Powlet, Marquis of Winchester, and left two daughters, co-heirs, Anne, who married Sir Henry Rolle, to whom he gave Biston, and Margaret, who married Sir Arthur Manwaring, to whom he gave Holcombe.

Denny, Edward Lord, 3. Sub. ——; pd. £13 6s. 8d. Born August 14, 1569 ; M. P. Liskeard, 1586–87 ; knighted in 1587 ; M. P. for Tregony, 1597–98; sheriff of Hertfordshire, 1603; M. P. Essex, March 19 to October 27, 1604 ; created Baron Denny of Waltham, October 27, 1604 ; Earl of Norwich, October 17, 1626 ; died in 1630 without male issue. He married Mary, daughter of the first Earl of Exeter.

Denton, Sir Thomas, 3. Sub. £75 ; pd. £37 10s. Only son of Alexander Denton, Esq. ; was of Hillersdown or Hillesdon, County Bucks; born about 1556 ; sheriff of Bucks, 1599 ; knighted, 1603 ; M. P. for Buckingham town, 1604–11, 1614, 1621–22, 1624–25, and 1628–29 ; for County Bucks, 1625 ; died in September, 1633.

Dequester — de Quester, Matthew, 2. Sub. £37 10s. ; pd. £87 10s. Born about 1559. "October 29, 1604, grant to Matt. de Quester, on surrender of Silvester Brooke, of the office of one of the King's post, for beyond seas, for life." January 21, 1608, grant to "Matt. de Quester of the office of a Post, for life." There was a long law plea between this postmaster of England for foreign parts and Lord Stanhope, the English chief postmaster, which was settled in 1632. In 1633 Dequester was an esquire to King Charles I., being then aged 74.

Dermer — Darmer — Dormer, Master. Made a voyage to New England in 1615. I think that he was the Capt. Thomas Dormer who was in Newfoundland in 1616, where he probably remained until late in 1618. He was confident that there was a passage to the South Sea through America. In 1619 he made another voyage to the New England coast, and in 1620 he was in Virginia. July 10, 1621, there was read before the Virginia Company of London a relation of "Mr. Dimmer's discoveries from Cape Charles to Cape Cod, up Delaware river and Hudson's river, being but twenty or thirty leagues from our plantation, and within our limits, within which rivers were found divers ships of Amsterdam and Horne," etc.

D'Evereux, Robert, Earl of Essex. Born in November, 1567 ; serving in the Netherlands, 1587 ; in Portugal, 1589 ; with Henry of Navarre, 1591 ; at Cadiz, 1596 ; at the Azores, 1597 ; lord lieutenant of Ireland, 1599; troubles with the queen, 1598–1600 ; "The Rising," February 8, 1601 ; tried 19, and executed February 25, 1601 ; "the incomparable Essex." He was the son of Walter, Earl of Essex, by his wife, Lettice Knolles ; he married, in 1590, Frances, daughter of Walsingham and widow of Sir Philip Sidney.

Devonshire, Earl of. — William Cavendish.

Dexter, Captain, 2. Sub. ——; pd. ——. (Capt. Ralph Dexter, engineer at the Siege of Ostend in 1601 ?)

Dichfield, Edward, salter, 2. Sub. £37 10s.; pd. £68 15s. On the Va. Commission of July 15, 1624 ; in the same year on the commission for searching and sealing tobacco, and also in 1634. He resided in the parish of St. Mary Woolchurch, London, where the births and deaths of his children are registered. His daughter Sara, born April 26, 1612, married Francis Meade, of London, salter.

Dichfield, Richard. Pd. £25.

Digby, Sir John, 2. Sub. ——;

pd. £25. Son of Sir George Digby by his wife, Abigail, daughter of Sir Arthur Henningham, of Ketteringham; was born at Coleshill, Warwickshire, in February, 1580, and entered Oxford University in 1595. "Being sent by the Lord Harrington to intimate to the king the designed insurrection of the gunpowder conspirators, he was admitted a gentleman of the Privy Chamber and one of the king's carvers in 1605." Knighted at Whitehall, May 14, 1606 ; M. P. for Heydon, 1610–11 ; ambassador to the Court of Spain, April, 1611, to January, 1616. (However he was in England January to September, 1614.) While in Spain, he guarded faithfully the interests of the English colonies in America. He was a member of the N. W. P. Co., July 26, 1612, and was admitted free into the E. I. Co. in September, 1614 ; appointed vice-chamberlain of the household, and sworn of the Privy Council, April 3, 1616. Sherborne was bestowed on him about October, 1616. Commissioned to treat of a marriage between Prince Charles and the Infanta Maria of Spain, April 16, 1617 ; went to Spain in July, 1617, and upon his return was created Baron Digby of Sherborne in the county of Dorset, November 25, 1618 ; ambassador to the Archduke Albert in March, 1621, and in May, 1621, to the Emperor Ferdinand, and the Duke of Bavaria on the business of the Palatinate. In March, 1622, he was again sent ambassador extraordinary to Spain to treat of the marriage and an alliance, and on September 15, 1622, was created Earl of Bristol. He finally left the Spanish Court, after the marriage negotiation had come to grief, in January, 1624. His differences with the Duke of Buckingham may be seen in the history of the times. Not summoned to second Parliament of Charles I., February, 1626 ; complained, was summoned, but ordered to keep on his estates, March ; appealed again ; impeached by the king, May 1 ; impeached Buckingham, May ; committed to the Tower, June 15, 1626. One of the commissioners to treat with the Scots, September, 1640; member of the Long Parliament, November, 1640 ; committed to the Tower, March 28, 1642 ; released in a few

days; went to the king at York, April;
attended the king at Edgehill and
Oxford in October, 1642 ; retired to
France at the close of the civil war ;
died at Paris, January 16, 1653–54.
" The Earl of Bristol was one of
the most accomplished ministers, as
well as one of the most estimable
characters of his time. A very handsome man ; of a grave aspect ; of a
presence that drew respect, and of
long experience in affairs of great
importance."
Old Fuller says, " The worst I wish
such who causelessly suspect him of
Popish inclinations is, that I may hear
from them but half so many strong
arguments for the Protestant religion,
as I have heard from him, who was, to
his commendation, a cordial champion
for the Church of England."

Digges, Sir Dudley, 2. Sub. £75;
pd. £37 10s. Son of Thomas Diggs
and his wife, Anne St. Leger (see St.
Leger pedigree) ; born in 1583 ; entered Oxford University in 1598. His
tutor was George Abbot, afterwards
Archbishop of Canterbury. Took his
degree in 1601 ; wrote a treatise " Of
the worthinesse of Warre and war-
riors," published in 1604 ; licensed to
travel for three years, April 6, 1604 ;
knighted at Whitehall, April 29, 1607;
M. C. for Va. Co., May 23, 1609.

He aided in sending Henry Hudson
to the Northwest (April 17, 1610),
and Cape Digges and Digges Iland
were named for him ; was M. P. for
Tewkesbury, 1610–11. On the 4th of
December, 1611, Chamberlain wrote
to Carleton : " Sir Dudley Diggs, a
great undertaker of this new discovery of the North West Passage, thinks
of nothing else : they are preparing
ships against spring as if there were
no doubt nor difficulty in the matter,
and the Prince of Wales is become a
partner and Protector." Chamberlain
again wrote to Carleton, March 11,
1612 : " There is a little treatise of
the North West Passage, written by
Sir Dudley Digges ; but I may say
beatus qui intelligit, especially the first
period, which is but a bad beginning
to stumble at the threshold. Some of
his good friends say he had better have
given five hundred pounds than published such a pamphlet ; but he is
wonderfully possessed with the opinion

and hopes of that passage." Sir Dudley's sons, Thomas and John Digges,
were both members of the Va. Co. of
London in March, 1612. In April,
1612, the ships for the Northwest
discovery sailed under Capt. Thomas
Button, Master Francis Nelson, etc.
July 26, 1612, the North West Passage
Company was incorporated with Sir
Dudley Digges as one of the first directors. He was one of those who
purchased the Bermudas Islands from
the Va. Co., November 25, 1612 ; was
a member of the Rus. or Mus. Co.,
and a leading member of the E. I.
Co. ; was one of those who sent out
Capt. Benjamin Joseph with seven
vessels to Spitzbergen in May, 1613.
Digges his hundred was planted in
Virginia about 1613 ; July 5, 1614,
was one of the nominees for governor
of the E. I. Co., but Sir Thomas
Smythe was elected.

M. P. for Tewkesbury in 1614 ;
joined his copartners in resigning the
Bermudas to the crown, November 23,
1614. Early in 1615 appeared a tract
called " The Trade's Increase," " some
points in which were very near treason and all the rest very dangerous."
February 22, 1615, at a meeting of the
E. I. Co., Sir Dudley said a book should
be set forth in defense of the East
India trade, which had been attacked
in the said tract. And afterwards
Sir Dudley " replied in a masterly
manner, in the same year, in a treatise entitled ' The Defense of Trade,'
inscribed to his kinsman Sir Thomas
Smythe, the governor of the East
India Company." He aided in sending the voyage for the discovery of
the Northwest passage which sailed
in March, 1615. (William Baffin
wrote an account of this voyage.)
Was a member of the Bermudas Company, June 29, 1615. In 1616 he
aided in sending out another voyage
on Northwest discoveries, in which
another cape was named for him in
" Latitude 76 degrees, 35 minutes."
" He acquired the manor and castle
of Chilham in Kent, by marriage and
purchase, where about the year 1616
he erected a magnificent edifice for his
residence." We find him constantly interested in Virginia, willing to advance
the enterprise by lotteries or by religion. He was ambassador to Russia,

April to October, 1618 ; one of the commissioners in settling a treaty between the English and Dutch concerning the trade into the East Indies, January to June, 1619 ; one of the committee of the Va. Co. of London for compiling and reducing the standing rules and orders for the government of the Va. Co. into one entire body, as more especially for constituting laws, etc. (The result of their labor is reprinted in Force, iii.) He was also in 1619 one of the committee "concerning the colledge in Virginia, being a waighty busines, and so greate that an Account of their proceedings therein must be given to the State."

Sir Dudley Carleton, writing to Chamberlain from "The Hague, January 29, 1620," "prays him to show Sir Dudley Diggs the writer's Virginia Papers, then return them to Carleton, letting him know when there is a passage to Virginia, for he has compassion of poor Porie being hungerstarved for news and wishes to send him a letter."

(*Quere:* Where are Carleton's Virginia papers now?)

Sir Dudley Digges patented lands in Virginia in 1620 ; was a M. C. for the N. E. Co., November 3, 1620. He was in Holland with Morris Abbot, settling differences between the English and Dutch East India companies, November, 1620, to February, 1621 ; M. P. for Tewkesbury, 1621–22 ; one of commissioners in Ireland, March to October, 1622. In December, 1622, he was "following the court hard, and was in hope somewhat would fall to his lot ; but for aught we see yet, the poor gentleman seems in the sand." M. P. for Tewkesbury in 1624–25, in 1625, and in 1626 ; one of the commissioners to conduct the impeachment of Buckingham, May 3, 1626 ; was sent to the Tower, May 10 or 11, 1626, but was released within a few days ; was again imprisoned for a few weeks in 1627 ; M. P. for the county of Kent, 1628–29. In 1629 he was mentioned as a " late commissioner for Virginia ;" granted the reversion of master of the rolls, November 17, 1630 ; entered Gray's Inn bencher, 1630 ; master in chancery, January 22, 1631. May 24, 1631, Attorney-general Heath was instructed to pre-

pare a bill appointing many, including Sir Dudley Digges, commissioners for advising upon some course for establishing the advancement of the plantation of Virginia. This bill was prepared, and was signed by King Charles on June 27, 1631.

He was appointed one of the commissioners for Virginia tobacco, June 19, 1634 ; was master of the rolls, April 18, 1636 ; spoken of as one of the committee in organizing the proposed English West India Company in 1637. He died March 18, 1639, and was buried at Chilham near Canterbury.

" An accomplished scholar, traveler, statesman, and author, a patriotic member of Parliament, and a princely merchant ; his understanding few *could* equal ; his virtues fewer *would ;* and the wisest men reckoned his death among the public calamities of those times."

He married Mary, youngest daughter and co-heir of Sir Thomas Kempe of Olantigh, by whom he left eight sons and three daughters. The oldest son, Thomas, succeeded to Chilham, and married Mary, daughter of Sir Maurice Abbot. Edward, another son, settled in Virginia ; was a member of the council ; governor of the colony in 1656 ; died March 15, 1676, and was buried in the old churchyard at Bellfield about eight miles from Williamsburg on James River.

Digges, John, 3. Sub. —— ; pd. ——. Of Faversham, second son of Sir Dudley.

Digges, Thomas, 3. Sub. —— ; pd. ——. Of Chilham Castle, eldest son of Sir Dudley. His son, Sir Maurice, was created a baronet March 6, 1666

Digges, Thomas. The celebrated mathematician ; born in Kent ; entered Cambridge, 1546 ; B. A., 1551 ; M. A., 1557 ; intimate with Dr. John Dee ; M. P. for Wallingford, 1572–83, and for the town of Southampton, 1584–85. Muster-master-general of the English forces in the Netherlands, 1586–94. Interested in Antarctic discoveries about 1590. " Died in London August 24, 1595, and was buried in the chancel of the church of St. Mary, Aldermanbury, where a monument was erected to his memory, with an inscription which describes him as 'a man zealously affected to true religion, wise, discreete, courteous, faithfull to his friends, and of rare knowledge in geometrie, astrologie, and other mathematical sciences.'" He married Anne, daughter of Sir Warham St. Leger (see pedigree), who, surviving him, died in 1636, aged 81. They had issue, two sons and two daughters, namely, Sir Dudley (aforesaid), Leonard (1588–1635), the poet, Margaret, the wife of Sir Anthony Palmer, and Ursula.

Dike. See Dyke.

Dingley, John, grocer, 2. Sub. ——; pd. ——. Died 1626. (See will in "New England Register," January, 1888, p. 73.)

Dobson, William, esquire, 2. Sub. £37 10s.; pd. £37 10s. Born 1572; of St. Andrew, Holborn; married, secondly, in 1605, Alice, daughter of Edward Barnes, mercer, of St. Mary Magdalen, Milk Street, London, He was "Clerk of the Statutes and Recognizances taken before the chief justices, the Mayor of the Staple, and the Recorder of London."

Doderidge, John, esquire, 3. Sub. £37 10s.; pd. £25. An eminent lawyer, a member of the Society of the Middle Temple, author of various professional works, etc. He was probably born at Barnstaple in 1555; entered Exeter College, Oxford, 1572; Bachelor of Arts, February 15, 1577; entered the Middle Temple; member of the Society of Antiquaries; sergeant at law, January, 1604; Prince Henry's sergeant; solicitor-general, October 28, 1604; M. P. for Horsham, Sussex, 1604–11; M. C. for Va., 1606; principal serjeant at law to the king, June, 1607; knighted at Whitehall, July 5, 1607; member of the Newfoundland Company, 1610; justice of the King's Bench, November 25, 1612; Master of Arts, Oxford, February 4, 1614. Died near Egham, Surrey, September 13, 1628, in the seventy-third year of his age, and "was interred under a stately tomb in Our Lady's Chapel in Exeter Cathedral." He was married three times, but left no issue. Among his published works are, "The Compleat Parson," "The Lawyer's Light," "The English Lawyer," "Law of Nobility and Peerage," etc. Fuller says, "he was commonly called, 'the sleeping judge,' because he would sit on the bench with his eyes shut, which was only a posture of attention, to sequester his sight from distracting objects, the better to listen to what was alleged and proved." "His soul consisted of two essentials, ability and integrity, holding the Scale of Justice with so steady an hand, that neither love nor lucre, fear or flattery, could bow him on either side."

Doncaster, Viscount. — James Hay.

Donne, John. Born in 1573; with Essex at Cadiz, 1596, and the Azores, 1597; married Anne, daughter of Sir George More, about Christmas, 1600; persuaded to enter the church by King James in 1614; in February, 1615, Lord Carew writes, "Mr. John Dun is a Minister, the King's Chaplaine, and a Doctor of Divinite." In 1621 dean of St. Paul's; joined the Virginia Company of London May 22, 1622, and preached the sermon before the company on the 13th of November following, on the text, Acts i. 8. He died on March 31, 1631, and was buried in St. Paul's Cathedral. An eminent wit, poet, author, and divine. His son, George Donne, was marshal of Virginia, 1637–40, and wrote "Virginia Reviewed," addressed to King Charles I. He descended from Judge Rastall, whose brother came to America in 1536.

Dorchester, Viscount. — Dudley Carleton.

Dorset, Earl of. — Edward, Richard, and Thomas Sackville.

Downes, John, 3. Sub. ——; pd. £37 10s.

Drake, Sir Bernard. Naval commander; eldest son of John Drake, of Ashe (whose sister Johanna was first wife to Walter Ralegh, of Fardell), by his wife Amy, daughter of Sir Roger Grenville, of Stowe. On his return from Newfoundland, for his services there, he was knighted by Queen Elizabeth January 9, 1586, at Greenwich. While on this voyage he probably visited Monhegan (N. E.). He died April 10, 1586.

Drake, Sir Francis. Probably the son of Robert, third son of the last John Drake of Otterton, by his wife, Agnes Kelloway. The date of his birth is variously given from 1539 to 1545 inclusive. Probably born at Crowndale, near Tavistock, Devonshire;

ROBERT SIDNEY

First Earl of Leicester

named for his godfather, Francis Russell, afterwards second Earl of Bedford. " He took to the sea " at an early age ; " at eighteene yeares of age he was made a pursei of a ship to Biscay ; at twenty yeares of age he went to Guynea ; " made a voyage to the West Indies in 1565 ; with Hawkins in 1567–68. In 1570 he registered as a Plymouth freeman, and made his third voyage to the West Indies ; made his fourth voyage in 1571 ; and his fifth in 1572–73, when he " the first of known Englishmen " saw the great " South Sea." Served in Ireland under Walter, Earl of Essex, 1573–76. Under the patronage of Sir Christopher Hatton ; on his famous voyage around the world, December, 1577–September, 1580 ; knighted by Queen Elizabeth on board his ship the Golden Hind, April 4, 1581 ; mayor of Plymouth, 1582 ; interested in Fenton's voyage, 1582–83 ; M. P. for Bossiney, 1584–85, and served on the committee for confirming Ralegh's patent ; on the celebrated voyage to America, September, 1585, to July, 1586 ; went to the Netherlands in November, 1586 ; on the voyage " to synge the King of Spaine hys beard," April–June, 1587. He was a friend to Rev. John Fox, the martyrologist ; served against the Armada, 1588 ; in the Portugal expedition, 1589 ; brought water to Plymouth from the River Measy, under contract, from December, 1590, to April, 1591 ; builded six mills, 1591 ; M. P. for Plymouth, 1593 ; sailed on his last and fatal voyage to the West Indies, August 27, 1595. Died near Porto Bello, January 28, 1596, " and being coffined was cast into the Sea " (the Gulf of Mexico).

" The Starres above will make thee knowne, if men here silent were,
The Sunne himselfe cannot forget his fellow travailler."

He was twice married, " yet he himself and ten of his brethren died without issue."

" He made his youngest brother, Thomas, his heir, who was with him in most and chiefest of his imployments."

Drake, George. This may be George Drake, of Spratshays in Littleham, Devonshire, whose daughter married Sir John Popham's nephew, Henry Ford, brother to John Ford, the dramatist, and father of Sir Henry Ford.

Drake, John, esquire, 3. Sub.——; pd. £12 10s. Of Mount Drake and Ashe, Devon ; son of Sir Bernard Drake (whom see) ; is thought to be the person of that name who sailed around the world with his kinsman (1577–80), and won the chain of gold for first sighting the " Cacafuego," on March 1, 1579, off Cape Francisco, South America, and who commanded the Francis, in Fenton's voyage of 1582, when the vessel was cast away near the River of Plate, South America ; but he escaped, lived with the Spaniards in those parts, and finally returned to England. No. 724 of the Sale Catalogue of the late James Carson Brevoort is the report of his examination before the tribunal of the Inquisition in Lima, Peru. M. P. Devon, 1614, 1621–22, and 1624–25 ; of the N. E. Council, November 3, 1620; died in 1628.

Drake, Captain Thomas. The only one of Sir Francis Drake's brothers who left issue. He married Elizabeth ——, and died April 4, 1606, leaving a daughter Elizabeth, wife of John Bamfield, Esq., and a son Francis (named for his uncle and godfather), who was created a baronet August 2, 1622.

Draper, Thomas, 2. Sub. £37 10s.; pd. £87 10s. Of Lincoln's Inn, gent.; he died in 1611, and was buried in the old church at Islington. He married Sarah, daughter of Roger James of Holland ; she married, secondly, Sir Nicholas Kempe, and died in 1650.

Draper, Sara. Pd. £12 10s. (See Thomas Draper.)

Drawfield — Drausfield, Avery, grocer, 2. Sub. £37 10s. ; pd. £25. Also of the E. I. and N. W. P. companies. He died in 1614.

Drayton, Michael, 1563–1631. The poet of " The Virginian Voyage " was born within a few miles of William Shakespeare, and buried within fewer paces of Geoffrey Chaucer and Edmund Spenser. His brow is crowned with laurel, " Apollo's sacred tree," in his portrait and on his monument.

Drewry — Drury, Sir Drew, the Elder, 2. Sub.——; pd. £75. Of Riddlesworth, Norfolk ; born about 1532 ; gentleman usher of the privy chamber to Queen Elizabeth ; sheriff of Norfolk in 1576 ; was knighted at Wanstead in Essex in September, 1579. Fuller says, " He was joined in commission with Sir Amias Paulet to keep Mary, Queen of Scots ; and discharged his dangerous trust therein. It moveth me not, that I find both these knights branded for puritans ; being confident that nickname, in relation to them both, was first pronounced through a popish mouth, causelessly offended at their religion." He died in the spring of 1617. He married, first, Elizabeth, daughter of Sir Philip Calthorpe, by Amata Boleyn, his wife, aunt to Queen Anne Boleyn, and, secondly, Catherine, only daughter and heir of William Finch, Esq., of Lynsted in Kent. By the latter he had issue.

Drewry — Drury, Sir Robert, 2. Sub.—— ; pd. £10. Born about 1575 ; knighted at Whitehall, July 23, 1603 ; M. P. for Suffolk, 1604–11. He spent a part of the summer of 1605 in Flanders.

M. C. for Va. Co., 1609. He was a patron of Rev. Joseph Hall, rector of Halstead in Suffolk, in 1607, and also of the celebrated Dr. John Donne, to whom he gave apartments at his own house in Drury Lane. July 2, 1611, he obtained license to travel for three years with his wife and family, and on December 4, 1611, Chamberlain writes, that " they are already settled at Amiens and with them John Donne." At the end of three years he returned to England. Was M. P. for Eye in 1614 ; died April 2, 1615, leaving his three sisters his heirs ; " only he gave away his land in Drury Lane to Sir Henry Drury," etc. His three sisters were, Frances, married, first, Sir Nicholas Clifford, and, secondly, Sir William Wray ; Elizabeth, married William Cecil, son and heir of Thomas, Earl of Exeter (she died February 26, 1654, aged about 80) ; and Diana, who married Sir Edward Cecil, Viscount Wimbledon, etc.

Druerdent — Durdent, Philip, 2. Sub. —— ; pd. £25.

Dudley, Robert, Earl of Leicester, etc. Born in 1532 or 1533 ; married Amy Robsart June 4, 1550 ; proclaimed Lady Jane Grey Queen of England in July, 1553 ; condemned to death as a traitor, January, 1554 ; pardoned, Easter, 1555 ; served at battle of St. Quentin, 1557 ; master of the horse to Queen Elizabeth, 1558 ; Knight of the Garter and sworn of the Privy Council, 1559 ; the great favorite of Queen Elizabeth ; a patron of the trade with Russia ; sudden death of his wife at Cumnor, 1560 ; created Baron Denbigh, Earl of Leicester, and elected a chancellor of Oxford University in 1564 ; interested in the voyages of Capt. John Hawkins, 1564–68 ; secretly married Lady Douglas Howard in 1573 ; received Queen Elizabeth at Kenilworth in July, 1575 ; married Lettice, widow of Walter, Earl of Essex, 1578 ; interested in the voyages of Forbisher, 1576–78, and of Fenton, 1582–83 ; captain - general of the expedition to the Netherlands, December, 1585 ; sent again, 1587 ; generalissimo of army raised against Spaniards, 1588 ; died at Cornbury Park, Oxfordshire, September 4, 1588. He was greatly interested in pushing abroad the commerce of England.

Dudley, Sir Robert, son of the Earl of Leicester, by Lady Douglas Howard, was born in 1573 ; made a voyage to the West Indies, November, 1594, to May, 1595. The voyage of Master Benjamin Wood to the East Indies in 1596 was set forth chiefly at his charges ; knighted by Essex at Cadiz in 1596. Failing to establish his legitimacy he left England in 1605, and "took up his abode in the territories of the Grand Duke of Tuscany," and died near Florence in 1639. His first wife was a sister to Thomas Cavendish, the circumnavigator ; his second, Alice, daughter of Sir Thomas Leigh, Bart., of Stoneleigh. He was " the first of all that taught a dog to sit in order to catch partridges." " He spent forty years of his life, and the treasures of a vast income, upon the accumulation of authentic material for the illustration of his cherished subjects, ' Hydrography and Navigation,' " and at least a part of the fruit of this labor is given in his " Arcano del Mare," first published in 1646.

Dunbar, Earl of. — George Hume.

Duncombe, Mr. (Edward). Of Battlesden, Bedfordshire ; M. P. for Tavistock, 1604–11 and 1614.

Dunn, Sir Daniel, draper, 2. Sub. —— ; pd. ——. Son of Robert Dunne, citizen and draper of London ; was educated at Oxford, where he took the degree of. D. C. L., July 20, 1580 ; M. P. Taunton, 1601 ; knighted July 23, 1603 ; M. P. Oxford University, 1604–11 and 1614 ; was master of the Requests, dean of the Arches, and judge of the Admiralty Court ; died September 15, 1617.

Dunn, William, 2. Sub. —— ; pd. £25. Probably William Dunn, Doctor of Phisick, brother of Sir Daniel.

Duppa, James, brewer, 2. Sub. —— ; pd. ——. " Dwelling in Saint Catharine's, near the Tower of London." He sent out a voyage to Cherry Island in 1607. He married Anne, daughter of Sir Roger Jones, and one of his daughters was named Lucretia.

Duppa, Jeffery, brewer, 2. Sub. £37 10s. ; pd. £50. "The King's Brewer of Holdenby." (The celebrated Bishop Duppa was the son of Jeffery and Lucretia Duppa. Was he a brother to the brewers of the Virginia Company ?)

Durette — Durant, Philip, 2. Sub. —— ; pd. ——. Huguenot ; buried in the Parish of St. Mary Woolchurch Haw, April 15, 1619.

Dye, Roger, haberdasher, 3. Sub. £37 10s. ; pd. £37 10s. Also of the E. I. and N. W. P. companies.

Dyer, Edward. Interested in Frobisher's voyages, 1576–78 ; knighted (1596) and appointed chancellor of the Order of the Garter ; a friend of Essex ; a poet. He was buried at St. Saviour's, Southwark, May 11, 1607.

Dyke — Dike, John, fishmonger, 2. Sub. —— ; pd. £50. Third son of Thomas Dyke, of Yorkshire ; a member of the E. I. Co. ; on the Va. Commission of July 15, 1624.

John Dyke

Dyke, Thomas. Sub. £37 10s. Elder brother of the foregoing John.

He died in 1615, leaving his adventures in the East Indies, Virginia, and Somers Islands to his five sons. In 1620 his sons John and Thomas held £50 and £25, respectively, of paid-up stock in the Virginia Company.

Dyot, Anthony, esquire, 3. Sub. £37 10s. ; pd. £25. Of Lichfield, barrister at law ; recorder of Tamworth ; M. P. Lichfield, 1601 and 1604–11.

Dyot, Richard, esquire, son of the above Anthony ; was born in 1590 ; M. P. Stafford, 1621–22 and 1624–25 ; Lichfield, 1627–28, and 1640 ; recorder of Stafford and of the Privy Council to Charles I. at York ; was knighted at Dublin, September 13, 1635 ; died March 8, 1659, aged 69.

Eden, Richard. Born about 1521 ; at Cambridge, 1535–44 ; was private secretary to Sir William Cecil, 1552 ; published a translation of "Munster's Cosmography " in 1553, "The Decades of the Newe Worlde, or West India," in 1555. He published several other translations of travels, works on navigation, etc.; was on the continent mostly from 1562 to 1573. He died in 1576.

Edgecombe, Piers. " Eldest son of Sir Richard ; was born in 1536 ; sheriff of Devon in 1566 ; M. P. for Cornwall, 1562–63, 1572, 1588, and 1592 ; and for Liskeard borough, 1584 and 1586. He died in 1607." His son, Sir Richard Edgecombe, was a member of the King's Council for New England in 1620. Ancestor of the present Earl of Mount-Edgecumbe.

Edmonds, Sir Thomas. Son of Thomas Edmonds, customer of Plymouth ; born at Plymouth about 1562; envoy to the Court of France, 1588 ; agent for Elizabeth at the Court of France, 1592 ; " Secretary to the Queen for the French tongue," May, 1596 ; envoy to the Archduke at Brussels in December, 1599 ; clerk to the Privy Council in 1600 ; M. P. for Liskeard in Cornwall, 1601 ; knighted May 20, 1603. He is the " little Edmonds " of Sully's " Memoirs ; " M. P. for Wilton, 1604–11; ambassador resident at the Court of Brussels from August, 1604, to August, 1609; ambassador to France, May, 1610, to 1616; sworn a privy councilor and comp-

troller of the household, December
22, 1616. In January, 1617, Winwood
and Edmonds arranged with Scarnafissi for Ralegh to attack Genoa in the
interest of Savoy; and Ralegh afterwards "charged Edmondes and others
with having instigated him to attack
Spain on his last voyage." He was
appointed treasurer of the household,
January, 1618 ; clerk of the crown in
the King's Bench, 1620 ; M. P. for
Bewdley, 1621–22 ; commissioner for
Virginia affairs, July 15, 1624 ; M. P.
Chichester, 1624–25 ; Oxford University, 1625 ; Penryn, 1628–29 ; ambassador to France, June 1629 ; commissioner of plantations, April 1634 ; died
September 20, 1639, aged 77. "He
had been practised in the arts of foreign negotiation, especially in France,
almost from childhood, and was a minister of great abilities and integrity."
It is said that "the enemies of England never concealed their fear of
him." He married, first, Magdalen,
daughter of Sir John Wood ; their
eldest daughter, Isabella, married
Henry, fourth Lord De la Warr, the
eldest son of the first governor-general of Virginia. Edmonds married,
secondly, in 1626, "the Right Honorable Sara Lady Hastings late wife to
Lord Zouch deceased."

Edolph — Edolfe, Sir Robert, 3.
Sub.——; pd. £37 10s. Of Hinxhill,
Kent ; knighted July 23, 1603 ;
sheriff of Kent, 1609 ; married, in
1590, Emeline, daughter of Sir Thomas
Scott (see Scott pedigree).

Edwards, Richard. Of N. W. P.
Co. He afterwards joined the Virginia Company, and was on the commission of July 15, 1624. He was
alderman's deputy for Bishopsgate
ward, married Elizabeth, daughter
of John Still, Bishop of Bath and
Wells. He was also of the E. I. Co.,
and his younger brother, William, was
sometime president for that company
in the East Indies. Mr. Edwards, a
Turkey merchant, i. e. member of the
Turkey Company, is said to have been
the first Englishman to introduce the
use of coffee in England about the
year 1652. The Dutch East India
Company conveyed coffee-trees from
Mocha to Holland in 1616, and the
coffee-berry, I suppose, before that
date. It is highly probable that the

English E. I. Co., brought coffee to
England, about the same time, as a
curiosity possibly, and not for the
trade.

Richard Edwards

Egerton, Sir Thomas, an illegitimate son of Sir Richard Egerton of
Ridley ; was born in Cheshire, 1540;
entered Brasenose College, Oxford,
1556 ; Lincoln's Inn, October 31,
1560 ; called to the bar, February 2,
1572 ; solicitor-general, June 28,
1581 ; Lent reader, 1582 ; attorney-
general, June 2, 1592 ; knighted
1593 ; master of the rolls, April 10,
1594 ; Lord Keeper of the Great
Seal and member of the Privy Council, May 6, 1596. (His son Thomas
was knighted by Essex on the Island
voyage, 1597.) He was charged with
the custody of Essex, 1599 ; Baron of
Ellesmere by James I., July 19, 1603;
lord chancellor, July 24, 1603 ;
Chancellor of Oxford University, November 3, 1610 ; member of the N.
W. P. Co., 1612 ; Viscount Brackley,
November 7, 1616; resigned the Great
Seal, March 3, 1617. Died at York
House, in the Strand, London, on
March 15, 1617, and was buried at
Doddleston, in Cheshire, the place of
his birth. Lodge says, "It may not
be too much to say that for purity of
reputation this great man's character
stands distinguished from those of all
other public ministers of this country
in all ages ; while for wisdom in
council, profound knowledge of the
laws, and general learning, he has seldom been excelled."

Egiock, Sir Francis, 3. Sub.
——; pd. £37 10s. Appointed a teller
of the exchequer for life, May 28,
1603 ; knighted at Whitehall, July
23, 1603 ; M. C. for Va. Co., 1612–20.
He was seated at Egiocke and Sher-
nock, County Worcester ; married
Eleanor, daughter of Francis Dinely,
of Charlton. He died November 21,
1622, and was buried in the Church
of St. Margaret, city of Westminster,
under a fair monument at the upper
end of the chancel.

Eldred, John, merchant. 2. Sub.
£37 10s. ; pd. £137 10s. Was born

in 1552 at New Buckenham in Norfolk; went to London, devoted himself to business, and prospered. He was one of "the honest English merchants" who made the first effort to open an overland trade with East India. They departed out of London upon Shrove Monday, 1583, in the ship called the Tiger, "wherein they went for Tripolis in Syria, and from thence took the way for Aleppo." "Her husband's to Aleppo gone, master of the Tiger." (Shakespeare's "Macbeth," act i. 3.) He remained in the East, the Holy Land, Asiatic Turkey, etc., traveling and trading, about five years, and returning reached London, March 26, 1588, a wealthy man. He bought the manor of Great Saxham in Suffolk in 1597, and built a large house there. He was a member of the Levant Company; adventured £400 in the voyage to East India, September 22, 1599; one of the directors for setting forth a voyage for the discovery of the trade of the East Indies, September 23, 1600; an incorporator of the E. I. Co., December 31, 1600, of which company he was one of the first directors, remaining in that office for many years and adventuring large sums of money in that enterprise for the advancement of English commerce; M. C. for Va., 1606; M. C. for Va. Co., 1609. His name is frequently met with in the state papers in connection with advances of money to Queen Elizabeth and James I. He was a leading business man of the period; an importer of tobacco; a farmer of the preëmption of tin; a contractor for lands; contractor for the customs, etc.; one of those who set forth Henry Hudson in April, 1610, for the discovery of the Northwest passage; an incorporator and director of the N. W. P. Co., July 26, 1612. Purchas, writing about 1621, says, "Master Eldred yet liveth a grave, rich, and principall Citizen." "He died at Great Saxham in 1632, and was buried there in the church on Dec. 8." He married Mary, daughter of Thomas Revett, of Rishangles in Suffolk. His son, Revett Eldred, was created a baronet in 1642.

Eldred, Walter, merchant-tailor. Pd. 2s. 6d. March 18, 1620, Thomas Hodges left by will three shares of land in Virginia to Walter Eldred.

Elfrith — Elfred — Elfree — Elfrey — Elfrye, Captain Daniel. He first appears as an officer serving under Captain Fisher, on board of a ship "sent out upon a discovery into the river of the Amazones," probably under Harcourt's charter of August 28, 1613. "As they went, a Spanish frigate comeinge in their waye their catchinge fingers layd fast hold on her, and this Elfrye (being in good trust with Fisher) was putt into her as master, who takeinge his opportunitie, requited him so well as sone after he gave him the slyp, and then shaped his course to the Bermudas;" where he arrived about February, 1614, and succoured the hungry colony, with his cargo of meal. "Yet with the meal came a number of rats (the first that the islands ever saw), which multiplying themselves by an infinite increase," a few years after placed the colony in jeopardy.

Elfrith went to England, on one of the returning vessels, in the spring of 1614, leaving his Spanish frigate at the Bermudas, and I find nothing more of him until April, 1618, when he sailed from England in command of that celebrated ship, the Treasurer, "licensed by a commission from the Duke of Savoye (obtained by Robert Lord Rich from Count Scarnafissi) to take Spaniards as lawfull prize." He arrived in Virginia late in the summer; where Governor Argall refitted his vessel and "sent him with the same commission to raunge the West Indies." He arrived in the Bermudas in the winter of 1618–19, and after some six weeks' stay, set out on his roving voyage. He returned to Virginia, in consortship with a man-of-war of Flushing, late in the summer of 1619, "with a part of one hundred negroes which he had captured from a Spanish vessel;" leaving some (20?) of these negroes in Virginia, he soon sailed from there, taking the remainder (29) to the Bermudas. The Dutch man-of-war may have had negroes on board, but Captain Elfrith, "under cover of a commission" from Charles Emmanuel I. the Great, Duke of Savoy, is responsible for bringing the first negroes to the colony of Virginia. " The proceeding of the Treasurer was esteemed not only a manifest act of piracy, but also a thing of great danger to the colony, considering its weak condition and the great strength of the Spaniards in the West Indies," and " the evente thereof (we may misdoubte) will prove some attempte of the Spaniard upon us, either by way of revenge, or by way of prevention; least we may in time make this place [Virginia] *sedem belli* against the West Indies." For these reasons the reports of the said proceeding, given out at that time, are incomplete and guarded ; but I have copies of several documents in the premises (which have never been printed) giving ample information. To show how perfect the Spanish system of obtaining news then was, it may be mentioned that Fray Diego de Lafuente (" Padre Mæstro ") Gondomar's confessor in England, knew of the acts of the Treasurer in the West Indies prior to May, 1619. (See Captain Argall.)

Captain Elfrith remained in the Bermudas for nearly ten years ; was for a time a member of the council there, and probably made more than one voyage from there to the West Indies. His daughter married Capt. Philip Bell, governor of the Bermudas, 1626–29, and brother to Sir Robert Bell.

Elfrith sailed for England on the Earl Warwick late in March, 1629, and arrived late in April. He came to reveal to the Earl of Warwick and Sir Nathaniel Rich his discovery (while on one of his roving voyages) of the island of St. Catalina, and he possibly commanded the successful voyage of discovery sent out by those gentlemen in that year to the West Indies.

In 1630 he was appointed by the company to act as governor of Providence Islands (Bahamas) until the arrival of his son-in-law, Capt. Philip Bell, the governor. " He was then to be admiral, and next in precedence to the governor." Bell arrived in 1631, and Admiral Elfrith soon went to roving in the West Indies and to Cape Gracias-á-Dios. May 10, 1632, the company wrote to him " condemning his indiscretion in too freely entertaining a Mulletto, as you call him, in

the island, and in taking a Spanish frigate." July 3, 1633, they conferred upon him the command of the fort at Black-Rock (Nassau ?) as an evidence of " our love and opinion of your fidelity," and March 28, 1636, they wrote him that " they were willing to employ his son in a ship for taking prizes. Having procured liberty to right themselves of the Spaniard."

In 1636 and 1637 there were dissensions among the officers in the Islands, and in July, 1637, he wrote to the company asking liberty to come home, which was granted in March, 1638, and he was allowed to bring his negroes away with him; but he sold them in 1639 to his successor, Capt. Nathaniel Butler, for the company's use. Among the leading members of the company were Henry Rich, Earl of Holland, Robert Rich, Earl of Warwick, William Lord Say and Sele, Robert Lord Brooke, Sir Edward Harwood, Sir Nathaniel Rich, and John Pym.

Soon after Elfrith's return to England, he petitioned the company for satisfaction for his services in the Bahamas, to which they replied May 9, 1640, that " they conceive nothing justly due him." And this is the last entry which I find regarding the man who carried the first rats to the Bermudas and the first negroes to Virginia, — that is, to the English colony; the Spaniards carried negroes there in 1526.

Elizabeth, Princess. — Elizabeth Stuart.

Elizabeth, Queen. See Tudor.

Elkin, John, merchant, 2. Sub. —— ; pd. £75.

Ellesmere, Lord. Thomas Egerton.

Ellis, John, grocer, 2. Sub. —— ; pd. ——. Entered and sworn to freedom in the Grocers' Company August 6, 1606 ; of St. Lawrence, Old Jewry ; married, in 1608, Cecily. daughter of Richard Wood.

Erizo, Captain James. Son of Richard Erisey, of Erisey in Cornwall. He died February 3, 1601, aged 45. (James Erisey, of Erisey in Cornwall, esquire, of the same family as Richard aforesaid had a daughter Honor, who married William Tucker, and their son William is said to have been the William Tucker of the Va. Co.)

Erondelle — Arundell, Peter, 3. Sub. ——— ; pd. ———. " A Declaration and Catholick exhortation to all Christian Princes to succour the Church of of God and Realme of France. Written by Peter Erondelle, natife of Normandie. Faithfully translated out of the French. At London, Imprinted by Edward Aggas, 1586." "The French Garden : for English Ladyes and Gentlewomen to walke in. . . . By Peter Erondel, Professor of the same Language. London, Printed for Edward White. . . . 1605." "The French Schoole-Maister. . . . P. Erondelle, London, 1612." He reassigned to Sir Thomas Roe three shares of land in Virginia, February 16, 16$\frac{1}{2}\frac{9}{0}$. He went to Virginia on the Abigail in 1621, and in February, 162$\frac{3}{4}$, Peter, John, Elizabeth, and Margaret Arundell were living at Buck Roe, Elizabeth City. He was granted, in 1624, 200 acres by patent on Back River in Elizabeth City in right of a bill of adventure of £287 4s. dated in 1617. He died prior to 23 January, 162$\frac{4}{5}$, leaving a son, John (born in 1602), as heir to his rights in Virginia.

Essex, Earl of.—Robert Devereux.

Essington, William, merchant of London. Son of John Essington, of Cowley near Essington, Gloucestershire. He married, first, Martha, daughter of Sir Thomas Hays, lord mayor ; secondly, Hester, daughter of Sir Roger Jones, and niece of Thomas Jones, Archbishop of Dublin and lord chancellor of Ireland. Was of the E. I. Co., and one of the auditors of the Va. Co. of London. He was still living in 1634.

Etheridge (or Etherege), George, gent., 2. Sub. £37 10s.; pd. £62 10s. (Of Maydenhed, in County Berks, whose daughter married William Canning, of Elsenham, Essex, eldest son of William Canning (whom see) ?)

Evans, Hugh, 2. Sub. ——— ; pd. £50.

Evans, Richard, 2. Sub. ——— ; pd. £50.

Evans, William, 2. Sub. £37 10s.; pd. £87 10s.

(They were from Wales, evidently merchants of London, and members of the E. I. Co. At least ten men of the surname Evans emigrated to Virginia before 1625.)

Evelin, ———. Lawyer for the defendant. Probably the following John Evelin, Esq.

Evelin, John, Esquire., 3. Sub. ———; pd. ———. Of Godstone, brother of Robert (see below) ; was born about 1554; married, about 1582, Elizabeth, daughter of William Stevens. Queen Elizabeth visited him in 1590 at Kingston. He died April 17, 1627. He was not a knight.

Evelin, John, 3. Sub. ——— ; pd. ———. Son of the preceding John. He was M. P. for Bletchingley in 1628-29 and 1640 till secluded ; was knighted in 1641 ; died January 18, 1664 ; father of the first baronet.

Evelin, Richard. Father of John Evelyn, Esq., the elegant author, and half brother to the following.

Evelin, Robert, armorer 2. Sub. ——— ; pd. £17.

Extract from the Evelin pedigree : George Evelin, " who first brought the art of making gunpowder to perfection in England," was born in 1526 ; married, first, Rose, daughter of Thomas Williams, brother and heir of Sir John Williams, knight ; she was buried at Long Ditton July 21, 1577. He married, second, Joane Stint, to whom the letter is addressed. He died May 29, 1603. By his two wives he had 24 children, of whom John and Robert were by his first wife, and Richard by the second wife. Robert's brother John, and his (John's) son John were both members of the Va. Co. of London in 1612.

Robert Evelin was probably born at Long Ditton in Surrey about 1570 ; married, October 19, 1590, at St. Peter's, Cornhill, London, Susannah, daughter of Gregory Young. (Her brother, Capt. Thomas Young, came to Virginia, and his son, Capt. Thomas Young, of Chickahominy, was executed in January, 167$\frac{5}{6}$ for taking part in Bacon's rebellion.) Robert Evelyn, his brother John, and others had a license granted to them August 24, 1599, for the sole making of saltpetre and gunpowder for ten years. He was a member of the Va. Co. of London in 1609 ; came to Virginia about 1610. In 1620 there was still to his credit on the Va. Co.'s books the sum of £17. He died before 1639. Two of his sons came to Virginia, viz.: Robert (who died there) and George (see "The Evelyns in America," by G. D. Scull, 1881). Of George (the eldest son) I will add the following : He was born in London January 31, 159$\frac{2}{3}$; married Jane, daughter of Richard Crane of Dorset ; emigrated to Maryland, 1636 ; was governor of Kent Island, Maryland ; returned to England, and died there. At least two of his children settled in Virginia, viz.: Mountjoy and Rebecca. Mountjoy married November 29, 1653, Dorothy, daughter of Obedience Robins, of Northampton County, Virginia (see Edward Waters). Rebecca married, secondly, " ye Honble Daniel Parke, sometime Secretary of the Colony of Virginia," by whom she had an only son, Col. Daniel Parke, who married Lucy Ludwell, and had by her two daughters, Lucy, who married Col. William Byrd, and Frances, who married John Custis, and their son, John Parke Custis, married Martha Dandridge (she married, secondly, Gen. George Washington), and their great granddaughter, Mary Custis, married Gen. Robert E. Lee.

Everard, Capt. Michael, 2. Sub. ——— ; pd. ———. Knighted at Royston, January 18, 1614. Chamberlain to Carleton, May 12, 1614 : "There hath been a brawl fallen out lately at Flushing among our captains, wherein Sir Michael Everard, sergeant-major, struck Sir John Throckmorton, lieutenant-governor, and, being convented, would not come till he was fetched with five hundred men. He married an heir, one Meg Stewart, a fair, ill-favored piece, who is come over to solicit his cause, and finds so great friends that he is like to be delivered and sent for home."

Eversfield, Sir Thomas, 3. Sub. ——— ; pd. £12 10s. Knighted at Sir William Fleetwood's in July, 1603. He was seated at Den in Sussex ; married Christian, daughter of Sir Robert Sandy, *alias* Napier.

Evington, Francis, merchant-tailor. Pd. £1. Of the E. I. and N. W. P. companies.

Ewens, Ralph, esquire, 2. Sub. £37 10s.; pd. £37 10s. Of Gray's Inn ; was born about 1569. Married, in 1603 or 1604, Mrs. Margaret Hotoft, of St. Botolph, Aldersgate, widow.

Auditor of Queen Anne. Died before September, 1611.

Ewre — Eure, Ralph Lord, 2. Sub. ——— ; pd. ———. Succeeded his father in 1594 as third Baron Eure. One of the commissioners at Bremen 1602–03 ; lord president of Wales in 1607. Crashaw dedicated CCXXX. to him in 1613. Died April 1, 1617.

Exeter, Earl of. — Thomas and William Cecil.

Exton, John. Sub. ——— ; pd. £12 10s.

Exton, Nicholas, draper, 2. Sub. £37 10s.; pd. £75. Of St. Mary Abchurch ; married, in 1585, Miss Judith Westwray.

Facet. See Fawcett.

Fajardo — Fazardo, Don luys. Admiral of the Spanish royal navy. Noted for hanging and drowning his prisoners. I suppose Lymbry was his pilot when he was operating against the pirates in the summer of 1609, and that Clark saw him at that time.

Faldoe (Volday ?) William, fishmonger, 3. Sub. ——— ; pd. £12 10s. This may be·the person who came to Virginia in 1608. Smith, who generally gives the wrong name, called him "Volday;" Dale calls him "Faldoe, the Helvetian." (Robert Faldo, Esq., married Sir George Yardley's niece, Anne Palmer.)

Falkland, Viscount. — Henry Carey.

Falmouth, Earl of. — Charles Berkeley.

Fanshawe, Sir Henry, 2. Sub. £60 ; pd. £70. Of Ware Park ; son of Thomas Fanshawe, Esq., remembrancer of the exchequer to Queen Elizabeth, by his first wife, Mary, daughter of Anthony Bourchier, Esq.; was baptized at Christ Church in London, August 13, 1569. M. P. for Westbury, 1588–89 and 1592–93, and for Boroughbridge in 1597–98. His father died in 1601, and he succeeded him as remembrancer of the exchequer; was knighted May 7, 1603 ; M. C. for Va. Co., May 23, 1609. He was an incorporator of the N. W. P. Co., July 26, 1612. He died March 10, 1616, aged 48, and was buried at Ware.

Chamberlain wrote to Carleton, March 27, 1616 : "Since you went, we have lost Sir Henry Fanshawe, who, being at dinner the 9th of this present, at the assizes at Hertford, was suddenly stricken with a dead palsy, that took him away in forty hours. He is much lamented, and so generally well spoken of, as I have not known any man, which is no small comfort to them that loved him, as it was likewise a great happiness to himself that his memory continued till the very end, and his speech did not quite fail him till some three or four hours before his departure. He hath left all in good order, and had made his will above two years agone ; but the reversion of his office was in great hazard by reason of his son lacking almost two years of twenty-one, was said to be unfit or rather incapable to execute it. But by Mr. Secretary's good means, it is now settled in Sir Christopher Hatton and Sir Arthur Harris for his use till he come of age, and they have appointed John West for his deputy."

Sir Henry Fanshawe married Elizabeth Smythe, the youngest sister of Sir Thomas Smythe, the first treasurer of the Va. Co., by whom he was the father of five sons and five daughters. The oldest son, Thomas, who succeeded his father as remembrancer and in the Va. Co., was afterwards created Viscount Fanshawe. The fourth son, Richard Fanshaw, knight and baronet, the celebrated diplomatist, translator, etc., married Anne Harrison, niece of George Harrison, the early Virginia duelist. The second daughter, Mary, married, in 1616, William Newce, of Hadham, possibly the same person, who died in Virginia about December, 1621.

Fanshawe, Lady. Sir Henry's wife (see Smythe pedigree). Her daughter-in-law, Anne, Lady Fanshawe, wrote in terms of the highest praise of her.

Farmer, George, gent., 2. Sub. —— ; pd. £25. Probably George Fermor.

Farmer, John, grocer, 2. Sub. £37 10s. ; pd. £100.

Farrington, Richard, 2. Sub. —— ; pd. £25. His brother George was "a priest ; " sheriff of London, 1608 ; alderman, 1609.

Fawcett — Faucett — Forsett, Edward, 2. Sub. £37 10s. ; pd. £75.

Of Tyburn, Middlesex. " As a justice of peace he showed himself very active in the examination of those concerned in the Gunpowder Plot." An officer of the Tower, " he occasionally took charge during the absence of the lieutenant, Sir William Waad." The manor of Marylebone was granted to him by James in 1611. Of the S. I. Co. He sold three shares in Virginia to Mr. Nicholas Ferrar, February 27, 162½. He died about 1630. The author " of two ably written pamphlets: 1. 'A Comparative Discourse of the Bodies Natural and Politique,' 1606, and 2. 'A Defence of the Right of Kings,' 1624." (See " Dic. of Nat. Bio." vol. xx. p. 10.)

Fearne — Ferne, Sir John. Sub. —— ; pd. £25. With Ralegh in Guiana in 1617.

Fearne — Ferne, John. Sub.—— ; pd. £12 10s. Of the S. I. Co.

Felgate, William, merchant, 2. Sub. £37 10s.; pd. £62 10s. Of the S. I. Co. Patented lands in Virginia, 1622, and on May 20 passed one hundred acres to Capt. Tobias Felgate ; a commissioner for Virginia in 1633. He was still trading with Virginia in 1639.

Fennor, John. Sub.—— ; pd. £50.

Fenner — Fennor — Vennor, Captain Thomas. The four men whom Lord Howard chose as his advisers in the attack on the Armada (1588), and of whom he wrote, " The Worlde dothe judge to be men of the greatest experience that the realme hathe," were Sir Francis Drake, Capt. John Hawkins, Capt. Martin Frobisher, and Capt. Thomas Fenner.

Fenton, Captain Edward. Son of Henry Fenton of Fenton in the parish of Sturton, and "brother to Sir Geoffrey Fenton ; was born in Nottinghamshire ; " served in Ireland under Sir Henry Sidney in 1566 ; an officer in Frobisher's voyages to the Northwest in 1576–78 ; again in Ireland in 1580 ; one of those mentioned by Hakluyt as having written about his travels prior to 1582. The project to attempt a fourth voyage to the East Indies *via* the Northwest finally resulted in Fenton's voyage of 1582. A large stock company was formed, and there was much difference of opinion. The Frobisher party wished to make another attempt by the Northwest; the Carlisle party, it seems, wished to try America to the southwest of Cape Breton, while the Fenton party wished to work the rich fields of the South Sea, which had so recently afforded such a rich harvest to Sir Francis Drake; and this idea prevailed. Frobisher and Carleill declined to go. Fenton sailed for the Moluccas in June, 1582, and returned to England in May, 1583; failed in the object of his voyage, but defeated a Spanish squadron; was a captain in the Armada fight, 1588; was buried in St. Nicholas' Church, Deptford, August 31, 1603, where a monument to his memory relates his achievements. He married Thomazin, daughter of Benjamin Gonson. She married, secondly, Christopher, son of Sir R. Browne, of Deptford. His niece married Richard Boyle, first Earl of Cork, and their son, the Hon. Robert Boyle, was a benefactor of William and Mary College, Virginia. (See Gonson pedigree.)

Ferdinando, Simon. A Portuguese pilot in Walsingham's service; sailed with Drake in 1577 on a vessel which returned; made a voyage to our coast to the southwest of Cape Breton in 1579; a pilot of Fenton's voyage in 1582–83, of Amidas and Barlow in 1584, of Greenville in 1585, and of White in 1587. He was interested in the Roanoke colony, and possibly remained and died there.

Ferne. See Fearne.

Ferrar, Nicholas, Sr., skinner, 2. Sub. £37 10s.; pd. £50. Born about 1546; "brought up in the profession of a Merchant Adventurer, and traded very extensively to the East and West Indies and to all the celebrated seats of commerce;" died in April, 1620, and was buried in the Church of St. Bennet Sherhog, London. He gave by will "£300 to the College in Virginia, to be paid when there shall be ten of the Infidels children placed in it, and in the meane time 24 pounds by the yeare to be disbursed unto three discreete and godly men in the Colonie, which shall honestly bring up three of the Infidels children in Christian Religion, and some good course to live by." (His son Nicholas finally transferred this bequest to the Bermudas, where there were no "Infidels children.") He married Mary, daughter of Laurence Wodenoth, Esq., and had issue: Susanna (married John Collet, of Bourne Bridge in Cambridgeshire), John, Erasmus ("a barrister of law"), Nicholas, William, and Richard (a merchant of London).

Ferrar, John, merchant. Sub. ——; pd. £12 10s. Son of the foregoing. He married, first, Anne, daughter of William Shepherd, Esq., of Great Rowlwright, Oxfordshire. She died, without issue, July 12, 1613, aged about 21, and was buried in St. Bennet Sherhog. (Stow preserves her curious epitaph.) John Ferrar joined the Va. Co. after 1612; was afterwards added to His Majesty's Council for that company, and was the deputy treasurer from April 28, 1619, to May 22, 1622. He was M. P. for Tamworth in 1621–22; wrote the memoirs of his brother Nicholas (published by P. Peckard, D. D., Cambridge, England, 1790), and of his own son Nicholas, who died in 1640. He married, secondly, Bathsheba, daughter of Israel Owen, of London, and had issue by her: Nicholas, John, and Virginia. He was buried at Little Gidding, September 28, 1657.

Ferrar, Nicholas, the Younger. Sub. ——; pd. ——. Son of Nicholas, Sr.; was born February 22, 1593; from his earliest years was regarded by his family as a prodigy indeed; had a revelation when but six years of age, they said; M. A., Cambridge, 1613; traveled on the continent, 1613–18, and when he returned, his brother John said, "His accomplishments surpassed all report and all expectation." He bought two shares in the Va. Co. from Sir William Smith, March 17, 161⅝; M. C. for Va. Co., 1619; deputy treasurer from May 22, 1622, to July, 1624, during which time (from December, 1623, to June, 1624) he was having the copies of the Virginia records made, which are now preserved in the library of Congress; M. P. for Lymington, 1624–25. In 1625 he gave up his attempt to regulate worldly affairs, settled at Little Gidding in Huntingdonshire, and established the Arminan Nunnery there; ordained a deacon by Bishop Laud on Trinity Sunday, 1626; vicar of Little

CAPTAIN JOHN SMITH

Gidding, 1626, to his death, December 2, 1637. He was known as " the Protestant Saint Nicholas," and was sometimes called " the useless enthusiast."

Ferrar, William, 3. Sub. ——; pd. £37 10s. Son of Nicholas, Sr.; born in 1594–95; educated for the law; came to Virginia in the Neptune in 1618; married the widow of Samuel Jordan; M. C. in Virginia from 1625 to 1633. The date of his death is not known to me. His wife was a party to the first breach of promise case in this country. As he was a lawyer, he was probably her legal adviser in the matter. Several interesting particulars of the case have been preserved. Her suitors were a preacher, Rev. Greville Pooley, and a lawyer. The preacher got the start; but the lawyer won.

Fetherstone, Henrie, stationer. In 1625 " Purchas his Pilgrimes in Five Bookes " was " Printed by William Stansby for Henrie Fetherstone, and are to be sold at his shop in Pauls church-yard at the signe of the Rose." Henrie Fetherstone died March 18, 1647.

Field, Mr. Warden (Richard), stationer. Son of Henry Field, of Stratford-upon-Avon, who was one of the assessors of the estate of John Shakespeare, the father of the poet. Richard Field was apprenticed to George Bishop, stationer, of London, in 1579; printed the first edition of Shakespeare's " Venus and Adonis " in 1593, and transferred his copyright to Mr. John Harrison, Sr., July 25, 1594. He died about 1624.

Field, William, merchant-tailor, 2. Sub. ——; pd. £25 5s.

Finch, Sir Moyle, 3. Sub. £75; pd. £50. Of Eastwell, Kent; born about 1553; M. P. Weymouth, 1575–83; knighted at Greenwich, May 7, 1584; M. P. Kent, 1593, and for Winchelsea, 1601; created a baronet, July 29, 1611. Died December 18, 1614. He married Elizabeth, daughter of Sir Thomas Heneage, and had issue seven sons and four daughters.

Sir Moyle's sister Jane married, October 8, 1582, George Wyatt, Esq., of Boxley, brother of Jane Wyatt who married Charles Scott (see Scott pedigree), and his brother, Sir Henry Finch, was the father of Sir John

Finch, one of the counsel for Sir F. Gorges in the dispute over the N. E. charter in 1621, which Sir John was the speaker, who was forced back into the chair by Holles and others on the memorable, February 25, 162⅝.

Finch, Sir Heneage. Of Eastwell, Kent; son of Sir Moyle; was an attorney at law; M. P. for Rye, 1607–11; recorder of London, February 15, 1620, to December 5, 1631; M. P. West Looe, 1621–22; again admitted into the Va. Co. of London, July 3, 1622. (His first cousin, Sir Francis Wyatt, had married the niece of Sir Edwin Sandys.) Knighted at Wanstead, June 22, 1623; created sergeant at law, 1623; M. P. London, 1624–25, 1625, and 1626; speaker of the first House of Commons of Charles I. in 1625. Died December 5, 1631, and was buried at Raunston, Bucks. He was the father of the first Earl of Nottingham.

Fishborne, Richard, mercer, 3. Sub. ——; pd. £37 10s. Old Fuller gives a sketch of him among his Worthies of Huntingdonshire. He began life as apprentice to Sir Baptist Hicks; became a leading Mercer himself, and was a great benefactor to his company and to mankind. Fuller says, " Nor must it be forgotten how this gentleman, lying on his deathbed (when men are presumed to speak with unmasked consciences), did profess that, to his knowledge, he had got no part of his goods unjustly. No man of his quality won more love in health, prayers in sickness, and lamentation at his funeral; dying a single man, and buried in Mercers' Chapel, May 10, 1625." The whole sum of his benefactions amounted to nearly £11,000, equivalent to nearly $275,000 present values.

Fitch, Master Matthew. In the first voyage to Virginia, 1606–07; in the first company to the Falls in May, 1607. Lost at sea in July, 1609.

Fitzhardinge, Viscount.—Charles Berkeley.

Fitzjames, Master John, esquire, etc. Of Leweston, Dorset; born about 1548; knighted at Lullworth, August 15, 1615; died May 16, 1625, and was buried in the chancel aisle of the church at Long Burton, Dorset.

Extract from his will, dated May 3,

1621, and approved July 7, 1625. . . .
"Item. I give to Alfred [or Aldred]
Fitzjames, my son, my bill of adventure of £25 which I delivered in readie
money to Captain Sommers when my
said son Alfred [or Aldred] went into
Virginia with him."

Fitzwilliam, Walter, esquire, 3.
Sub. £37 10s.; pd. ——. M. P.
Peterborough, 1621–22; brother of
first Lord Fitzwilliam; died *s. p.*
He was related to the Mildmays and
Sidneys.

Fleet, William, gent., 3. Sub.
£37 10s.; pd. £37 10s. Of Chart-
ham, Kent; married Deborah Scott,
daughter of Charles Scott of Egerton,
Kent, by his wife, Jane Wyatt (see
Scott pedigree). He had issue: seven
sons and one daughter, viz.: George,
William, Henry, Brian, Edward, Reynold, John, and Catherine. On July
3, 1622, he transferred to his daughter his three shares in Virginia. At
least four of his sons (Henry, Edward,
Reynold, and John) were among the
early emigrants to Virginia and Maryland. All four of them were members of the Maryland legislature of
1638, the first Assembly whose records
have been preserved. Capt. Henry
Fleet was the most noted of this
brotherhood in our annals. He came
to Virginia at an early date; was captured by the Indians on the Potomac
in 1623; remained a captive until
1627; became familiar with the Indian tongue; an interpreter, trader,
and legislator in Maryland; finally
settled at Fleet's Bay in Lancaster
County, Virginia, and represented the
county in the House of Burgesses,
1652. His daughter Sarah married
Edwin Conway of Lancaster County,
Virginia. Capt. Henry Fleet was first
cousin to the noted Dorothy Scott who
married, first, Major Daniel Gotherson
of Cromwell's army, and about 1655
became a Quaker preacher. She married, secondly, Joseph Hogben, and
about 1680 settled on Long Island,
New York.

Fleetwood, Edward, esquire, 2.
Sub. —— ; pd. £62 10s.

Fleetwood, Sir William, 3. Sub.
£37 10s.; pd. £37 10s. Of Missen-
den, Bucks; eldest son of Sir William
Fleetwood, recorder of London. He
was knighted at Charterhouse, May

11, 1603; M. P. for Bucks, 1604–11,
1621–22, 1624–25, and 1628–29. Died
in 1630.

Fletcher, John, fishmonger, 2.
Sub. £75. He paid £62 10s., and
John Fletcher and Company paid £75
= £137 10s. Died in 1635. A benefactor of the Fishmongers; also a member of E. I. and N. W. P. companies.

Flores, Marquis de le. See Zuñiga.

Floyd (or Lloyd), David, £12 10s.

Forest, Sir Anthony, 2. Sub.
——; pd. ——. Of Huntingdonshire;
knighted at Whitehall, August 20,
1604.

Forest, Thomas, 2. Sub. ——; pd.
£50. Came to Virginia in 1608.

Fotherby, Henry, secretary. After of the N. E. Company.

Fox, Thomas, 2. Sub. ——; pd.
——. (Luke Lodge and Thomas Fox
paid £25.) Probably the Thomas Fox
who came to Virginia in 1608. I suppose there was some relationship between Luke Lodge and himself, and
that Captain Luke Fox (Northwest
Fox, 1631) was of the same family,
and possibly related to John Foxe, the
martyrologist.

Foxall, Thomas, grocer, 3. Sub.
——; £37 10s.; pd. £37 10s. Married
Elizabeth, daughter of Sir William
Garaway ("Gargany" on her tomb) of
London. Died in 1647, buried in the
Churchyard at Lee.

Francis, Giles, gent., 2. Sub. ——
£37 10s.; pd. £50.

Francis, Thomas. Pd. £12 10s.

Frank, Peter, esquire, 3. Sub.
——; pd. £12 10s. "Gentleman Usher
and dayly waiter to Queen Anne — the
which Peter dyed the 24. day of October, 1612." (Strype.)

Franklin, John, haberdasher, 2.
Sub. ——; pd. £25. (The Franklins
of the Va. Co. were probably of the
family of that name seated at Willes-
don in Middlesex.)

Freake, Sir Thomas, 2. Sub. ——
£75; pd. £25. "Son of Robert Freke
of Shroton, Dorset, esquire, who was
for many years auditor of the Treas-
ury in the reigns of Henry VIII. and
Queen Elizabeth, and died *worth a
plum*, (£100,000) an immense fortune
in those times. His son Thomas, of
whom I write, of Ewern Courtney in
Dorsetshire, was "a person of consid-

erable note, great trust, and authority in the County of Dorset in the times of Elizabeth and James I." M. P. for Dorchester in 1584–85; knighted at Whitehall July 23, 1603; M. P. for County of Dorset in 1604–11; M. C. for Va., March 9, 1607; M. C. for Va. Co., 1612; M. P. for the County of Dorset in 1614 and also in 1627–28.

Sir Thomas was born in 1563, and died in 1633; married Elizabeth, widow of Francis Smith, Esq., and only daughter and sole heir of John Taylor, alderman of London, by whom he was the father of five or more children.

Freeman, Martin, fishmonger, 2. Sub. £37 10s.; pd. £75. One of the wardens of the Fishmongers in 1606; interested in the Irish plantation; married Elizabeth, daughter of Mathew Laurence, son of Sir Oliver Laurence; she bore in her arms, 2 and 3, the arms of Washington (vide Visitation of London, 1568). He was a member of the E. I. Co.

Freeman, Ralphe, 3. Sub. ——; pd. ——. Son of Martin aforesaid; was baptized as "Randolpe" at St. Mary-at-Hill, London, July 6, 1589; knighted at Windsor September 15, 1617; sworn a master of requests, January 11, 1618. The king's pleasure to grant the Massachusetts charter was signified to the lord keeper by Sir Ralpe, as "Auditor of Imprests" in 1628–29; a commissioner of the Mint to Charles I.; lord of the manor of Beechworth in Surrey; living in 1663. Author of "Imperiale," a tragedy.

Freeman, Ralphe, clothworker, 2. Sub. £37 10s.; pd. £62 10s. Son of William Freeman, of Northampton; born in 1560; member Muscovy, N. W. P., and E. I. companies; master of the Clothworkers in 1620; "farmed the killing of whales in Greenland, etc.; set forth 8 ships in 1621." Sheriff of London, 1622–23; alderman of Bishopsgate ward, 1622–32, and of Cornhill ward, 1632–34; lord mayor in 1633. Died in office, before knighthood, March 16, 1634; was buried in St. Michael's, Cornhill, and afterwards removed to Aspeden, County Herts. He was on the Virginia Commission of July 15, 1624.

Freeman, William. Probably the younger brother of Sir Ralphe aforesaid. "William and Raphe Freeman"

contributed £25 to the American enterprise; but the elder brother of Ralphe the clothworker was also named William.

Fretchville, Sir Peter, 3. Sub. ——; pd. £37 10s. Of Stavely, County Derby; sheriff of Derby, 1601; knighted at Worksop, April 21, 1603; M. P. for Derbyshire in 1601 and 1621–22.

Frith, Richard, gent., 2. Sub. ——; pd. £25. Came to Virginia in 1606–07.

Frobisher, Sir Martin. Son of Bernard Frobisher by his wife Margaret, daughter of Sir Richard Yorke, and sister of Sir John Yorke (a member of the Merchant Adventurers); born at Altofts, Normanton, Yorkshire, about 1535; on a voyage to Guinea, 1554; probably made other voyages there; plundered the Flying Spirit from Andalusia in 1563; probably with Hawkins at Vera Cruz in 1567; served with Gilbert in Ireland; preparing for a Northwest, voyage of discovery, 1574; the voyage "stayed" for lack of money in 1575; made the first voyage in 1576, the second in 1577, and the third in 1578; projected a fourth voyage to the Northwest in 1581, which resulted in Fenton's voyage of 1582–83; with Carleill proposed another voyage to America in April, 1584; vice-admiral of the Drake-Sidney voyage, 1585–86; served against the Armada and knighted in 1588; commanded vessels employed against Spanish commerce, 1589–92. In 1594 he commanded the squadron sent to aid Henry IV. of France; wounded at the attack on Brest, November 7; returned to Plymouth, and died there, where his entrails were interred; his body was sent to London and interred in St. Giles's Church, Cripplegate, in February, 1595. He married twice, but seems to have left no issue. Peter Frobisher, his heir and executor, sold Frobisher Hall to Lionel Lord Cranfield. Frobisher's second wife (whom he married in 1591) was Dorothy, daughter of Thomas, first Lord Wentworth, and widow of Paul Withypoole, Esq.

martin frobisher [signature]

Fuller, Nicholas, esquire. Pd. £20. Barrister, of Gray's Inn; champion for the Puritans; son of Nicholas Fuller, of London, merchant ; born about 1545 ; M. P. for St. Mawe's 1592–93; M. P. for London, 1604–11. Spoke against the union with Scotland, February 14, 160⅖. His argument for his clients, Thomas Lad and Richard Maunsell, was published in 1607. In November, 1607, he was fined £200 by the commissioners for causes ecclesiastical. He paid his fine, but submissions being expected which he could not digest, he was imprisoned; but was released on January 5, 1608. (See "Lord Bacon's Letters and Life," by Spedding, vol. iv. p. 51, note.) M.P. for London, 1614 ; admitted into the E. I. Co. gratis, May 5, 1618 ; died February 23, 1620, aged 76. He married Sarah, daughter of alderman Nicholas Backhouse.

Fulwood, William. (I take this to be the author of "The Castel of Memorie," "The Enimie of Idenesse," etc., who was a merchant and member of the Merchant-Taylors' Company.)

Gallen-Ridgeway, Lord.—Thomas Ridgeway.

Galthrope (Calthrope), Stephen. Probably the head of the "entended and confessed mutiny by Galthropp" at the Canaries, March, 1607, in which mutiny, Capt. John Smith was in some way implicated.

Garaway — Garraway — Garway, William, draper. Sub. £50; pd. £100. Born 1537; married, about 1570, Elizabeth, sister of Sir Henry Anderson, of London, was a leading merchant ; member of the Muscovy, E. I., and N. W. P. companies ; chief treasurer of the customs ; knighted at Theobald's, July 16, 1615; died September 26, 1625, aged 88 ; buried in St. Peter the Poor, London. His son, Sir Henry, was the celebrated Royalist Lord Mayor of London, 1640.

Gardiner, John, merchant 2. Sub. —— ; pd. £75. Of the E. I. Co.

Gardiner, Richard. Sub. —— ; pd. £12 10s.

Garrard. See Gerrard.

Garraway. See Garaway.

Garsett, Robert, 3. Sub. —— ; pd. £12 10s.

Gate, Peter, grocer, 2. Sub. £37 10s.; pd. £12 10s. "Late apprentice to George Bone, sworn to freedom January 16, 1603. Takes Paul Gate as his apprentice March 26, 1604. Still on Books, 1618." He married Mary, daughter of Edward Josslyn, Esq.

Gates, Lady. Died on her way to Virginia in 1611.

Gates, Sir Thomas, 1. Sub.——; pd. £100. Said to have been born at Colyford, in Colyton parish, Devonshire (Worth's " Hist. of Devonshire," p. 70). Saw service in the wars. Was lieutenant of Capt. Christopher Carleill's own company in the celebrated Drake-Sidney voyage to America, 1585–86 ; published the Briggs-Croftes account of this voyage in 1589, which he dedicated to the Earl of Essex ; distinguished himself at the taking of Cadiz, and was knighted by Essex in June, 1596. July 20, 1597, Essex sent him to Sir Robert Cecil with an important message regarding the Island voyage, in which voyage he served, August–October, 1597 ; entered Gray's Inn, March 14, 1598 ; in public service at Plymouth, 1599. Early in the reign of James I. soldiers were being enlisted in England, both to serve the States and the Archduke ; he enlisted with the States, and in July, 1604, Sir Henry Wotton wrote by him to Sir Ralph Winwood, saying, "I entreat you to love him [Gates] and to love me too, and to assure yourself that you cannot love two honester men." One of the first petitioners for royal license to colonize America ; an incorporator of the first charter, April 10, 1606 ; was in the garrison at Oudewater in South Holland with Dale in November, 1606 ; petitioned the States for leave of absence to go to Virginia, which was granted April ¼/2¼, 1608 ; was selected to command the large expedition then being fitted out ; appointed the first *sole* and *absolute governor* of the colony ; added to His Majesty's Council for the Va. Co. ; sailed in June ; wrecked on the Bermudas July 28, 1609, and remained there until May 10, 1610, when he sailed to Virginia, reaching there May 21 ; left Virginia late in July, and reached England early in September, 1610, giving the first news of his own survival of the tempest. Aided in preparing a confutation of the scandalous reports (CXL.). Again sailed for Virginia in May, 1611, taking his wife and daughters ; but his wife dying on the way, he sent his daughters back with Newport in December following. He remained in Virginia nearly three years, and returned to England in April, 1614. He had brought his company from the Netherlands, and had carried it to Virginia with him in 1609, under the command of Capt. George Yeardley ; whether he brought it away from Virginia or not I cannot say; but after aiding in answering the French complaints, he returned to his post in Holland, and was promptly paid all past dues.

During 1619 he was serving on one of the committees of the Va. Co. in London. In November, 1619, Sir Edwin Sandys, in a speech before the Quarter Court of that company, said that " Sir Thomas Gates had the Honour to all Posterity of being the first named in his Majesty's Patent and Grant of Virginia, and was also the first that, by his Wisdom, Industry, and Valour, accompanied with exceeding Pains and Patience, in the Midst of Many Difficulties, had laid the foundation of the present prosperous State of the Colony."

About this time the governor and council in Virginia asked that " Skilful Engineers be sent over to raise fortifications," "and Sir Thomas Gates was entreated by the Company, as well in Regard of his military Skill as of his knowledge of the country, to write them his Private Letters of Advice and Direction." Early in 1620 Gates was one of the " Ancient adventurers," who " peticioned y° Right Honble the Lords and the rest of ye Cownsayle and bodye politique, for ye State of his Majesties Collonye in Virginia to have some man of qualitve sent Governor unto Virginia." They were, quite evidently, unwilling to serve under Gates's old subordinate, Sir George Yeardley. They "humblye besech this Honorable Court to take into consideration this our only Request (who otherwise finding themselves much disparagied and wronged are resolved to abandon, and quitt the Countrye & Action forevar) that some eythar Noble, or little lesse in Honor

or Power may be maturelye advised upon to maintayne and hold up ye dignitye of so Great and Good a Cawse."

From March to June (inclusive), 1620, Gates transferred to sundry persons sixty shares of 100 acres of land each, in Virginia. November 3, 1620, he was appointed by James I. one of " the first moderne and present Councill established at Plymouth, in the County of Devon, for the planting, ruling, ordering, and governing of New England in America." January 13, 1621, Sir Dudley Digges, writing from Amsterdam to Sir Dudley Carleton at the Hague, " sends his love to the honest Sir Thomas Gates," from which it may be inferred that he was then in Holland. April 12, 1621, he is alluded to in the records of the Va. Co. as *then dead*. In 1623 fifty great shares of land were still remaining in his name in Virginia.

He had at least two sons, Thomas and Anthony, and three daughters, Margaret, Mary, and Elizabeth. On April 24, 1626, Edmund Dawber, gentleman, of " East Inynham," in County Norfolk, and Margaret, daughter of Sir Thomas Gates, of " Holdinge " in County Kent, were married in the Church of St. Mildred the Virgin, Poultry, London.

Capt. Thomas Gates, the son of Sir Thomas, served in the expedition of 1626 against Cadiz, and in 1627 at the Isle of Ré and Rochelle, where he was killed by a cannon shot. Anthony, the other son, died before 1637; his widow was then living. In 1637 the daughters, Mary and Elizabeth, petitioned the Privy Council to order payment to them of the arrears due on their brother's (Capt. Thomas Gates's) account ; and the lord treasurer was instructed by order of the council to sign an order to that effect. They alleged that they were " destitute of means to relieve their wants, or to convey themselves to Virginia, where their father, Sir Thomas Gates, governor of that Isle, died, and left his estate in the hands of persons, who had ever since detained the same." It would seem from this that he died in Virginia, and I have found no other evidence of the place of his death. " July 30, 1639. Report of the Sub-

Committee for Foreign Plantations to the Privy Council. ' Upon Petition of Edmund Dawber, administrator of the Estate of Sir Thomas Gates, deceased — that a similar letter to that written to the Earl of Dorset and Danby, bearing date November 30, 1632, be addressed to the Governor and Council of Virginia, on behalf of the petitioner, for the full recovery of the Estate in that Colony, belonging to Sir Thomas Gates, deceased.' ''

I have, as yet, been unable to locate with any certainty the family of Gates ; but as we find him (when he must have been quite a young man) in service with Carleill and Essex, the sons-in-law of Walsingham, I think we may infer that he was not without position and influence. He was probably about 50 years of age when he sailed to Virginia in 1609.

Gee, Sir William, 3. Sub. —— ; pd. £25. Born 1540; an outer-barrister of Lincoln's Inn ; M. P. for Hull, 1588–89 ; Beverley, 1604–11; knighted May 30, 1604 ; secretary to Council of the North.

Geeringe — Gearinge — Greeninge — Geringe, John, grocer, 2. Sub. £37 10s.; pd. £112 10s. Of the E. I. Co. Married Phebe, daughter of Jo. Reeve, of London, goldsmith.

Gerrard — Garrett, George, esquire, 3. Sub. —— ; pd. ——. M. P. for Wigan, 1621–22; Newton (I. W.), 1624–25 ; Preston, 1626 and 1628–29.

Gerrard — Garrard, John. Son of Sir William, whom see. Born 1546; sheriff, 1592 ; lord mayor and knight, 1601–02 ; died May 7, 1625, aged 79. His son, Sir John, was created a baronet February 16, 162½.

Gerrard, Sir Thomas, 3. Sub. —— ; pd. ——. Probably the eldest son of Sir Thomas Gerrard, of Bryn ; M. P. Liverpool, 1597 ; Lancashire, 1614 ; Wigan, 1621 ; created a baronet, May 22, 1611 ; died in 1621.

Gerrard — Garrard, Sir William. Son of John Garrard, citizen and grocer, of London ; born in 1507 ; alderman, April 26, 1547 ; sheriff, August 1, 1552 ; lord mayor, September 29, 1555; knight, 1555. " A grave, sober, wise, and discreet citizen equal with the best and inferior to none of our time." Died September 27, 1571, in the " Parish of St. Christopher, but was buried in the Church of St. Magnus, as the parish where he was born and a faire monument is there raised on him."

He married Isabel, daughter and co-heir of Julius Nethermill, Esq., and had issue : 1. William (Sir) who died in 1607; 2. George, whose daughter married Sir Dudley Carleton ; 3. John (Sir), (whom see); 4. Anne, who married Sir George Barnes.

Gibbs, Thomas, esquire. Sub. —— ; pd. £12 10s. M. C. for Va. Co. prior to 1618. On " May 6, 1618, Sir Eustace Hart surrendered unto him a Bill of Adven. of £25, and for that he paid in £12 10s. more had allowed him 3 shares " in the Va. Co. March 18, 1620, he transferred two shares in Virginia " to his two sonnes Edmond & Thomas Gibbs." He was active in the company affairs, 1620–22; also of the S. I. Co.; on the Virginia Commission, July 15, 1624; one of the Council for Virginia, November 16, 1624, and after ; a commissioner for the advancement of Virginia in 1631. I think he married Isabella, daughter of Rev. William Wilson, D. D.

Gilbert, Adrian. Of Sandridge; son of Otho of Compton ; made a voyage to the Northwest prior to 1583; interested in the Northwest patent of 1584, in the Davis voyages, 1585–87, and in the voyage of Cavendish, 1591 ; was constable of Sherborne Castle, 1596–1603 ; M. P. for Bridport, 1597–98.

(An Adrian Gilbert married Mary Johnson, spinster, at All Hallows' Barking in 1577.)

Gilbert, Bartholomew. Son of Sir Humphrey. On the voyage to our New England coast, March 26 to July 23, 1602 ; sailed on a voyage to the Chesepian Bay, May 10, 1603, and was killed by the Indians on the eastern shore of Virginia in July.

Gilbert, Sir Humphrey. Of Compton ; son of Otho Gilbert and his wife, Katherine Champernoun, was " borne in Devon at his father's house called Greeneway upon Dart river about

1539 ; educated at Eton and Oxford ; destined by his father to the law, but followed his own bent for more active enterprises." Devoted himself to the study of navigation and the art of war ; got his first reputation at Havre in Normandy, where he was wounded in fighting against the French Catholics, September 26, 1563 ; petitioned the queen for privileges for making Northeast discoveries in April, 1566 ; serving as captain under Sir Henry Sidney in Ireland in July, 1566. While in Ireland, Salva-terra tells him of the Northwest passage. Petitioned the queen for the privilege of making Northwest discoveries in November, 1566 ; enlisting soldiers in England for service in Ireland in April, 1567, and soon went over ; returned to England in the summer of 1568, and to Ireland again the next year, where, after defeating the celebrated McCarthy More, he was made governor of Munster in October, 1569; knighted at Drogheda by Sir Henry Sidney, January 1, 1570 ; returned to England in the same year, and married Joan, only daughter and heiress of John Aucher of Otterden (see Anthony Aucher, Esq.) by his wife, Ann, daughter of Sir William Kelleway. (Sir Humphrey afterwards sold the manor of Otterden to William Lewin, LL. D.) He was M. P. for Plymouth in 1571 ; resided at Limehouse, 1571–72 ; commanded the squadron sent to reinforce Flushing in the autumn of 1572 ; returned to England in the fall of 1573 ; living at Limehouse, 1573–78 ; was still desirous of making new discoveries in 1574. Visited by George Gascoigne in the winter of 1574, he showed him "sundry profitable and very commendable exercises which he had perfected plainly with his own pen." One of these exercises was probably "The Erection of (Queen Elizabethe's) Achademy in London" (printed by Dr. Furnivall in London, 1869) ; another was Gilbert's "Discourse of a Discovery for a New Passage to Cataia." Lock says that Gilbert printed a book regarding new discoveries in May, 1575. Gascoigne published, probably without Gilbert's authority, his "Discourse of a Discovery" in April, 1576. Gilbert was interested in Frobisher's voyages of

1576–78 ; consulted Dr. John Dee, November 6, 1577, and the same day proposed to Elizabeth to attack the shipping of Spain under color of a patent for colonization in America ; obtained a patent for planting an English colony in America, June 11, 1578 ; sailed in the fall of that year, but was soon forced to return; prepared to sail in 1579, but was stayed ; returned to Ireland in the summer of 1579 ; sent John Walker to our coast in 1580, and probably made other ventures, but the data for these enterprises from May, 1579, to August, 1582, is very deficient; consulting Dr. Dee in the fall of 1580, and in the same year made an assignment for colonization to Sir Thomas Gerrard and Sir George Peckham ; examined sundry persons regarding America to the southwest of Cape Breton, 1582 ; sailed on his voyage, June 11, 1583 ; landed in Newfoundland, August 4 ; sailed to the southward, August 20 ; went down at sea, September 9–10, 1583. He was the father of one daughter and nine (or five) sons, among whom were John (the eldest), Bartholomew, and Ralegh Gilbert.

Gilbert, John, of Greenway ; eldest son of Otho Gilbert. Knighted by Queen Elizabeth at Westminster, 1571; vice-admiral of Devon, 1585 ; mayor of Plymouth, 1589; married Elizabeth, daughter of Sir Richard Chudleigh, of Ashton, but died without issue. "This eminent and learned man was interred in St. Peter's Cathedral, Exeter, where a sumptuous monument remains to his memory."

Gilbert, Sir John. Eldest son of Sir Humphrey Gilbert ; with Ralegh in Guiana, in 1595 ; knighted by Essex at Cadiz, 1596 ; governor of the fort at Plymouth, 1597. Ralegh was proposing to send an expedition under his command to Guiana in November, 1598. M. C. for Va., March 9, 1607. He was an officer of reputation ; married a daughter of Sir Richard Molyneux, of Sefton, but died without issue, July 5, 1608, of the small-pox, and was buried at Marldon Church.

His brother, Ralegh Gilbert, who was then (July, 1608) in North Virginia, was his heir, and returned to England to take charge of his estate. Several letters from Sir Walter

Ralegh "to my nephew, Sir John Gilbert, knight," are still preserved.

Gilbert, John, 2. Sub. —— ; pd. £62 10s. The inventor of a dredging machine, called a water plough, and a pump for draining mines ; licensed July 16, 1618.

Gilbert, Otes or **Otho.** Of Compton (who was related to Sir Richard Greenville) married Katherine Champernoun (who was first cousin to George Carew, Earl of Totness), and had by her three sons: John Gilbert of Greenway, Humphrey Gilbert of Compton, and Adrian Gilbert of Sandridge. Otho Gilbert died probably before 1550, and his wife married, secondly, Walter Ralegh of Fardell, and bore.him three children, namely, Carew, Walter, and Margaret Ralegh.

Gilbert, Ralegh, 1. Son of Sir Humphrey Gilbert, brother of Sir John Gilbert, aforesaid, and nephew of Sir Walter Ralegh; an incorporator in the first charter, April 10, 1606 ; president of the Council in North Virginia, 1608; married Elizabeth, daughter and heir of John Kelley, Esq., of Devon, and was living in 1620, having then five sons, the eldest of whom was five years old; M. C. for New England in 1620. He died in 1625, leaving seven children. His descendants, many of them, are now living in Cornwall, England.

Giles, Sir Edward. Of the North Virginia Company ; born at Totnes about 1580, one of Prince's worthies, and a prominent Devonian throughout a long career. A soldier in the Low Countries, under Elizabeth ; a courtier, knighted by James I., July 23, 1603 ; constantly chosen M. P. for Totnes during the reigns of James I. and Charles I. ; was a member of the New England Council in 1620 ; was one of the five members called. to court for remonstrating against shipmoney in 1634, but excused himself on the score of ill health. Died in 1637, and was buried in Dean Prior Church. The epitaph on his monument was written by Robert Herrick, who was for many years vicar of Dean. (Worth's " Devonshire.")

Gipps — Gypes, Thomas, clothworker, 2. Sub. —— ; pd. £12 10s. " Son of Thomas Gipps, of St. Edmonds Bury in Com. Suffolke." He was master of the Clothworkers in 1635.

Glanville, Francis, esquire, 3. Sub. —— ; pd. £37 10s. Of Kilworthy, Devon ; eldest son of Sir John Glanville, justice Common Pleas. M. P. for Tavistock, 1614, 1621–22, 1625, and 1628–29 ; knighted at Greenwich, May 16, 1621. Died in 1638. His younger brother, Sir John, was speaker of the Short Parliament of 1640.

Glanville, Richard, 2. Sub. —— ; pd. ——. Probably a party to the celebrated case in chancery, 1616.

Glover, Rev. Mr. "An ancient Master of Arts in Cambridge, an approved Preacher in Bedford and Huntingtonshire, reverenced and respected, and never wanting a competent stipend ; " sailed for Virginia with Sir Thomas Gates in June, 1611, " but being in yeares, and of a weake constitution, and so after zealous and faithful performance of his Ministeriall dutie whilst he was able, he gave his soul to Christ Jesus, not long after reaching Virginia."

Goddard, Richard, 2. Sub. —— ; pd. £25.

Godolfine, Sir William, 2. Sub. —— ; pd. £37 10s. " Eldest son and heir of Sir Francis Godolphin of Godolphin, Cornwall, by his wife, Margaret Killigrew ; was one of those gentlemen of quality who accompanied Robert, Earl of Essex, in his expedition to Ireland against the rebels in 1599 ; and for his valour at Arclo, was knighted by the said Earl on his return to Dublin, July 13, 1599. He set out with great reputation, having, besides a very liberal education, traveled into most parts of Europe, and attained several languages. Mr. Carew makes this honourable mention of him : ' That he had so enriched himself with sufficiency for matters of Policy, by his long travels ; and for martial affairs, by his present carriage in Ireland, that it is better known how far he outgoeth most others in both, than easily to be discerned ; for which he deserveth principal commendation.' He had so far signalized himself by his valour and conduct, that on the Spanish invasion in 1600, he was in such esteem with the Lord Montjoy, Lord Deputy of Ireland, that he intrusted him with the command of his own brigade of horse, in the decisive battle of Kinsale, December 24, 1601, which victory was principally owing to his gallant service, having broke through the whole body of Spaniards, entirely routed them, taking their chief commander prisoner, whereupon the Irish immediately threw away their arms and fled. And when Don John d'Aquila, commander of the Spaniards in the town of Kinsale, offered a parley desiring the lord-deputy to send some gentleman of special trust to confer with him and to receive his proposals, he was employed in the negotiation [related verbatim by Stow in his Annals] which was brought to a conclusion on January 2, 1602, the Spaniards agreeing to quit all places in that kingdom. He afterwards performed divers services against the rebels, and on March 20, 1602, for the great trust reposed in him, he was specially appointed to confer with the Earl of Tyrone and receive (according to his request) his humble submission to her majesty. In the year 1603 he commanded in the Province of Leinster ; and the Irish rebels being subdued, he returned into England soon after the death of Queen Elizabeth, and in the first Parliament called by King James, he was unanimously elected one of the knights for the county of Cornwall."

M. P. for the county of Cornwall, 1605–11 ; M. C. for Va. Co., May 23, 1609. He was buried at Breage, September 5, 1613. His sister, Thomasin, married Sir George Carew, afterwards Earl of Totness. He married Thomasin, daughter and heir of Thomas Sidney, Esq., and had issue : three sons and a daughter, Francis, Sidney, William, and Penelope. The eldest son, Francis, was the father of Sidney, Earl of Godolphin, the celebrated prime minister ; the second son, Sidney, was a poet of some celebrity, and the third son, William, was a colonel of a regiment in the service of Charles I. The daughter, Penelope, married Sir Charles Berkeley, the oldest brother of Sir William Berkeley, so long governor of Virginia.

Gondomar, "Don Diego Sarmiento de Acuña, Count de Gondomar." Spanish ambassador to England. Edward Edwards in his "Life of Ralegh,"

vol. i. pp. 569–572, gives his pedigree, also a biography of him, from which I will extract : "He was born on All Saints' Day in 1567 ; was serving (though not actually in arms) against Francis Drake in 1584. He served against Portugal in 1589. He was made civil and military governor of Tuy in 1596, when the news came to the Escurial of the sailing of the expedition under Essex and Ralegh. In Galicia, he acquitted himself so much to his master's satisfaction, that Philip the Second soon afterwards made him a knight of the order of Calatrava and governor and alcalde of Bayonne; with which he retained his important command at Tuy. He also became corregidor of Valladolid, and, eventually, a member of the Spanish Council of State."

"In the first days of 1613 the English government was in expectation of a Spanish invasion," and on January 10 the Council ordered the sheriffs to search the houses of recusants for arms ; but the Spaniards persuaded themselves that the colony of Virginia, which was the "bone of contention," would certainly die out of itself, and they, resolving to leave the matter to diplomacy rather than to arms, replaced their ambassador in England by one of the ablest diplomatists in their service, Don Diego Sarmiento de Acuña (see Gardiner's "Hist. of England," ii. pp 164, 165). He arrived at Portsmouth late in July, and at London in August, 1613. He found only four survivors of the original pensioners of Spain, "the Earl of Northampton, and Lady Suffolk, Sir William Monson, the admiral of the narrow seas, and Mrs Drummond, the first lady of the bedchamber to the queen." To these Sir Thomas Lake was added within a few years, and Gondomar became very intimate with Sir Robert Cotton.

The following is a copy of one of the last letters that I have from Gondomar relating to the American enterprise : —

General Archives of Simancas. Department of State, vol. 2596, folio 7. November 28, 1616. Copy of an original letter from Don Diego Sarmiento de Acuña to the King of Spain, dated London, December 7, 1616.

"Sire, — I have told Y. M. of the Colonies of Virginia and Bermuda what is found in different dispatches; there is no news of importance, except that here altho' they consider that of Bermuda as of great importance; on the other hand, it is reported that the mice have multiplied to such an extent as to eat their wheat and any other grains which they sow, so that the English who have gone there have endured such suffering that five men took a boat with four oars, with a sack of bisquits and a barrel of water and came to this place. It took them nearly twenty days, having made the voyage in a very short time and meeting no storms, which has excited great admiration at their happy escape, and on this account they have been pardoned. They speak now of sending large supplies of provisions to Bermuda. I have heard that the people on the island have sent some vessels to plunder and provide themselves with victuals in the countries nearest to Y. M.'s subjects.

"In Virginia matters are said to go on better since they have made peace with the Indians; but in spite of all that they complain very much of the misery endured there by the English, who are there, and it must be so, for the President of the Company of these Colonies, having authority here to take for their benefit any prisoners he may choose among those who have been condemned for criminal causes, has had some who have preferred hanging to going to Virginia. A few days ago, when they were about to hang some thieves, three of them, the soundest and strongest, were chosen to go to Virginia; two of them accepted, but the third would not, and seeing the two returning to gaol, he said; Let them go there, and they will remember me! Then he urged the hangman to shorten his work, as if he was thus relieved of a greater evil, and thus it was done. Here, however, they preserve these places very carefully, as it appears to them that they will be very useful to England, if there should be war with Spain. *And I feel sure that for this reason and for honour's sake they will never give them up. May God preserve the Catholic person of Y. M. as Christendom needeth it.* London,

December, 7, 1616. DON DIEGO SARMIENTO DE ACUÑA."

He was created Count of Gondomar in April, 1617; but remained in Eng. until July, 1618. Lorkin to Puckering, from Greenwich, June 16, 1618: "The Spanish ambassador [Gondomar] took his leave here at court on Sunday was sennight" (June 8th). The same letter mentions the arrival in London of Sir Walter Ralegh.

During his absence the Spanish secretary, Julian Sanchez de Ulloa, was the acting Spanish ambassador, and on September 26, 1618, Philip III. wrote to him that "the English king assured Gondomar that he would either punish Raleigh and his associates for the mischief they had done in the Indies, or send them to Spain for punishment." Fray Diego de Lafuente ("Padre Mæstro"), Gondomar's confessor, was also representing Spain in England during the autumn of 1618.

Sanchez wrote to Philip III. from London October $\frac{2}{12}$, 1618 : "The English are very hastily settling and fortifying Bermuda and Virginia, sending every year a number of men there, and this year more than 700 persons have already gone, taking with them samples of various fruits to plant, and a variety of fowls and cattle to raise there, and a supply of artillery, ammunition, and arms, and many tools to erect earthworks and fortifications."

Gondomar returned to England in March, $16\frac{19}{20}$ (Philip III. died March 31, 1621, and was succeeded by Philip IV.). I have a long letter written by Gondomar, on January 23, $162\frac{1}{2}$, to Secretary Juan de Ciriza regarding the taking of the Spanish ship, Sancto Antonio, at the Bermudas; but Virginia is not mentioned. The new Spanish ambassador, Don Carolo de Columbo (Don Carlos Coloma), arrived in England about the last of April, 1622; Gondomar returned to Spain in May, 1622, and was never in England again. He was made a councilor of state at Madrid in March, $162\frac{2}{3}$. The assertion that James I. annulled the Va. charter at the instance of Gondomar is incorrect. When the charter was declared null and void by Chief Justice Lee, Gondomar had been absent from England for more than two years. Spain's de-

SIR THOMAS SMITH

mands were really against the colony, not the company. Spain's strongest point had been that her territory was being settled by a mere company of English adventurers. The annulling of the charter, and taking the colony more immediately and publicly under the protection of the crown of England was the conclusive answer to this point ; and the act was rendered necessary at this time, as well by the war then existing with Spain as by the factions which existed in the Va. Co. In fact, every member of the Council of War (April 21, 1624) was interested in Virginia, namely : Lord Grandison, Lord Carew, Lord Brooke, Lord Chichester, Sir Edward Conway, Sir Edward Cecil, Sir Horace Vere, Sir John Ogle, Sir Robert Mansell, and Sir Thomas Button.

Gondomar died at Bommel in Flanders in 1625. "He told a merry tale; read Shakespeare's plays, subscribed for a First Folio; liked English wines; assured Sir John Digby that he was an Englishman at heart ; was very gallant to the ladies ; " and "became all things to all men." Granger says, "Perhaps there never was a man who had so much art as Gondomar, with so little appearance of it."

Gonson, Benjamin. Of Much Badow in Essex. Treasurer of the marine causes. Elizabeth writes of him as "our well-beloved cousin, Benjamin Gunson, Treasurer of our Admiralty." He married "Ursula, daughter of An. Hussey, judge of the admiralty, and agent at Anvers to Queen Mary," by whom four sons and ten daughters. (See "Visitation of Essex," Harl. Soc. Pub.) Of the daughters, Avice (or Katherine ?) married Sir John Hawkins, and Thomazine married, first, Capt. Edward Fenton, and, secondly, Christopher Browne, of Sayes Court, whose granddaughter, Mary, married John Evelyn (1620–1706), the virtuoso.

Goodere — Goodyear, Sir Henry, 3. Sub. £37 10s.; pd. ——. (There were two knights of this name: one knighted at Dublin August 5, 1599, the other at Lamore in June, 1608.)

Goodwin, Sir Francis, 3. Sub. £37 10s.; pd. £37 10s. Of Upper Winchenden, Bucks. M. P. Bucks

County, 1586–87; Wycombe, 1588–89; Bucks again, 1597–98, and 1604 till he resigned in 1606, when elected for Buckingham town, 1606–11 ; for the county again in 1614, 1625, and 1626.

Gore, Robert, merchant-tailor, 3. Sub. ——; pd. £37 10s. Also of N. W. P. Co. Robert and Ralph Gore were brothers, sons of Gerrard Gore of London, alderman, who died December 11, 1607. Ralph joined the Va. Co. soon after 1612, and was one of the directors of the company in 1618. His brothers William and John were also members prior to 1620, and Thomas Gore, who died in Virginia August 16, 1607, was probably another brother. John Gore was Lord Mayor of London in 1624. The four brothers, Robert, Ralph, William, and John, were also of the E. I. Co.

Extract from the Gorges Pedigree. — Sir Edward Gorges, who died in February, 155⁶⁄₇, married Mary, daughter of Sir Anthony Poyntz, and had by her, with others : (1) Sir William, (2) Sir Thomas, and (3) Edmund.

(1.) Sir William Gorges, who died in 1584, married Winifred Budockshead, first cousin to Sir Walter Ralegh, and they were the parents of Sir Edward Gorges, buried in Westminster Abbey, 1625.

(2.) Sir Thomas Gorges, who died in 1610, married Helena Shackenburg, a Swede (widow of William Parr, Marquis of Northampton), (see West pedigree), and had by her, with others, Edward Lord Gorges, Elizabeth (who married, first, Sir Hugh Smythe, secondly, Sir Ferdinando Gorges), and Bridget, who married Sir Robert Philips of Montacute, Somerset.

(3.) Edmund Gorges, Esq., who died in 1557, was the father of Edward, who married, in 1559, Cicely Lygon, and had by her two sons, Sir Ferdinando and Sir Edward (born 1564, died 1624), who married Dorothy, daughter of Sir G. Speke.

Gorges, Edward. I take this to be either the son of Sir William or the brother of Sir Ferdinando (see pedigree), both of whom were knighted in 1603. (See p. 14.)

Gorges, Edward Lord. Of the North Va. Co. Eldest son and heir of

Sir Thomas Gorges (see pedigree). He was born in 1582 ; knighted April 9, 1603 ; created a baronet of England November 25, 1612, and advanced to the peerage of Ireland July 13, 1620, as Baron Gorges of Dundalk, County Louth. Was a member of the New England Council, November 3, 1620, and continued to take an active interest in that council and colony. He was chosen president of the council, and held that office in April, 1635, at the time of the resignation to the crown of the Great Charter of New England. He was still living and still interested in colonization in November, 1638. The date of his death is not known to me. He was succeeded by his son Richard, second Lord Gorges, who was for a time one of the council for foreign plantations. He died in 1712 in his 93d year. Married Bridget, daughter of Sir R. Kingsmill, but left no surviving issue.

Gorges, Sir Ferdinando. Son of Edward Gorges (1537–68) and his wife, Cicely Lygon, of Madresfield, Worcestershire (see pedigree) ; born about 1566 ; served at Sluys in 1587 ; knighted by Essex before Rouen in October, 1591 ; M. P. for Cardigan, 1592–93 ; " Governor of the Forts of Plimouth " prior to 1597, in which year he was sergeant-major in the fleet sent to the Iles of Azores, under Essex, in which voyage he was very sick ; in some way implicated in the so-called " Rising of the Earl of Essex," February 8, 1601, and was for a time confined as a prisoner in the Gatehouse. He is said to have revealed the plot to Cecil and Ralegh, for which act he is blamed by some and commended by others. It was in connection with this fracas that Ralegh had his quarrels with Gorges and Preston. He was deprived of the command of the New Fort at Plymouth about July, 1603 ; but on " Sept. 15, 1603, he was restored to his former post," etc., and he continued in this office for many years. He aided in sending out the Weymouth expedition of May–July, 1605 ; and continued to take an active and earnest interest in America as long as he lived. He was a member of his Majesty's Council for Virginia from the first. Was a member of Lord Rich's African Com-

pany, November 16, 1618 ; member of the South Va. Co. prior to November 17, 1619. In December, 1619, he had some decided differences with Mr. Delbridge and the Va. Co. of London, regarding the fisheries about Cape Cod, within the bounds of the Northern Company, and on March 3, 1620, the North Colony asked for a separate or special charter with additional privileges, etc., as the South Colony had done eleven years before. March 31, 1620, Sir Ferdinando Gorges was one of the arbitrators chosen by the Earl of Warwick, in settling the differences between the said earl and the E. I. Co., regarding the taking of the Lion, Capt. Thomas Jones (a ship belonging to the earl), in the East Indies; attended the quarter court of South Va. Co., June 28, 1620. The warrant for preparing the new charter for the Northern Company was issued July 23, 1620. The Mayflower, Capt. Thomas Jones, was sent out by the Southern Company in August, 1620, with a patent for lands within the bounds of that colony, which did not extend north of 40° north latitude. The new charter for the North Colony passed the seals and was issued November 3, 1620, granting to that company the lands north of the Southern Colony, that is, from 40° to 48° north latitude. Sir Ferdinando Gorges was a member of His Majesty's first Council for New England, named in the said charter of November 3, 1620. Although the Northern Company had strengthened their rights to the Cape Cod fisheries, by planting a colony as near there as convenient as well as by the new charter, the question was not settled ; but was taken before Parliament in 1621, where the rights of the Northern Company were defended by Gorges. June 1, 1621, he was one of the signers of the first Plymouth patent. July 27, 1621, he requested the E. I. Co. to loan him " certain stores for a ship he is building of a new fashion, such as the East India Company might make use of, and that he hoped to find a way to out-sail the Dutch." " August 29, 1621, the East India Company lent 2,000 trenails to Sir F. Gorges, captain of His Majesties Castle at Plymouth." In this year 1621, Capt. Samuel Argall, Gorges, and others protested against the Dutch settling in certain parts of America.

In 1622 he sent his son Robert, with a large patent for lands, to " Messachuset " in New England.

In June, 1624, he was intending to send his son on an expedition fitted out in New England, to annoy the Spaniards, in their possessions in the West Indies.

He was a regular attendant at the meetings of the Council of New England, serving as governor and as treasurer. In 1624 he answered the French claim to New England.

July 15, 1624, he was one of the commissioners for winding up the Va. Co. of London, and was afterwards a member of the Council for His Majesty's Colony of Virginia.

"In 1625 he commanded a ship-of-war in a squadron under orders from the Duke of Buckingham, which was sent to the assistance of France, under pretense of being employed against the Genoese. But a suspicion having arisen that they were destined to assist Louis against his Protestant subjects at Rochelle, as soon as they were arrived at Dieppe, and found that they had been deceived, Gorges was the first to break his orders, and return with his ship to England. The others followed his example, and their zeal for the Protestant religion was much applauded."

November 17, 1629, the Council for New England granted, by indenture, to Sir Ferdinando Gorges and Capt. John Mason certain lands upon the rivers of the Irroquois, which they intended naming the Province of Laconia.

During 1632 began some differences in the N. E. Council and Colony, which I cannot discuss ; as a final result, on April 25, 1635, the Great Charter was surrendered to the king, and the next day the king appointed Sir Ferdinando Gorges governor of His Majesty's Colony of New England. He was a member of the Church of England, and many leading men in the colony were Puritans ; naturally there were differences of opinion between them, which I cannot attempt to decide.

April 3, 1639, certain lands in New England were granted to Sir Ferdi-

nando, " to be hereafter called the Province of Maine; " and to this province he chiefly devoted his remaining years.

" When the civil dissensions in England broke out into a war, Gorges took the royal side ; and, though then far advanced in years, engaged personally in the service of the crown. He was in Prince Rupert's army at the siege of Bristol in 1643 ; and when that city was retaken in 1645 by the Parliament forces, he was plundered and imprisoned. His political principles rendered him obnoxious to the ruling powers, and, when it was necessary for him to appear before the Commissioners for Foreign Plantations, he was severely frowned upon, and consequently discouraged."

He died at Long Ashton, Somerset, and was buried there, May 14, 1647.

I have only attempted a mere outline of the services of Sir Ferdinando Gorges in the matter of our genesis. He is said to have expended £20,000 ($500,000) in the Northern Colonies, being a principal agent, and chiefly interested in them for forty odd years, and from the beginning.

He married, first, February 24, 1590, Ann, daughter of Edward Bell, of Writtle, Essex. She died August 6, 1620, and was buried in St. Sepulchre's, London. He had issue by her four sons and two daughters. Married, secondly, December 21, 1621, Mary, daughter of Thomas Fulford, Esq.; she died in 1623, without issue. Married, thirdly, December 6, 1627, Elizabeth, daughter of Tristram Gorges, and widow, first, of Edward Courtney, secondly, of William Blythe ; she died in March, 1629, without issue. Married, fourthly, September 23, 1629, " Madame Elizabeth Smyth de Long Ashton." She was the daughter of Sir Thomas Gorges (see pedigree). Sir Ferdinando's fourth " venture " survived him, but had no issue by him. He had children by his first wife only, namely : John, born 1593 ; married, first, Lady Frances Clinton ; secondly, Mary, daughter of Sir John Meade. Robert, sometime governor of New England. Ellen and Honoria. Both daughters died young ; the other two sons, both named George, died young, I believe.

Goring, Sir George, Sub. ——; pd. £25. Knighted at Greenwich, May 29, 1608 ; M. P. Lewes, 1621–22, 1624–25, 1625, 1626, and 1627–28 ; created Baron Goring in 1628, and Earl of Norwich, 1646. Distinguished royalist, and father of the celebrated Gen. George Goring. He married Mary, daughter of Edward Neville, Baron Abergavenney ; died in 1662 or 1663.

Gosnold, Anthony, Sr. (see next), brother of Capt. Bartholomew Gosnold, was drowned in James River, Virginia, in January, 1609.

Gosnold, Anthony, the Younger, 2. Sub. —— ; pd. ——. Son of Anthony, Sr. (Mem. — There was a family of the name at " Swyland in Com. Suffolk." See " Vis. of London," Harl. Soc., 1883, vol. ii. p. 176.) He went to Virginia in 1606 with his uncle and father ; October 30, 1621, the company granted him three shares of land in Virginia for his adventures, and on the same day he transferred one share to Robert Gosnold, and another to Roger Castle. In February, 1601, a Robert Gosnold was implicated in the Essex rising, and confined for a time in the " Marshalsey," the same, probably, who was afterwards captain of St. Andrew's Castle, County Hants.

Gosnold, Captain Bartholomew. He served Sir Walter Ralegh in one or more expeditions to America. In 1602 he made a direct voyage to our New England coast. In December, 1606, he sailed for the South Virginia Colony, where he died August 22, 1607. The solicitor-general in the reign of Edward VI. was a Mr. Gosnold, probably of the same family.

Gouge — Goughe, Thomas, gent., 3. Sub. £37 10s. ; £37 10s.

Gouge, William, D. D., Puritan divine. Born December 25, 1578; educated at King's College in Cambridge ; minister of St. Anne's, Blackfriars, in London, 1608–53; a cousin of Rev. Alexander Whitaker of Virginia; he took an especial interest in, and care of, the Virginia Indians sent to London. He was a member of the celebrated Westminster Assembly of divines, 1643. Died December 12, 1653. " He came to his grave in a full age, like as a shock of corn cometh in his season." (See Dr. William Whitaker.)

Gourges, Dominic de. Died in 1593, on his way to London.

Gower. See Gore.

Grantham, Sir Thomas, 3. Sub. £37 10s. ; pd. £37 10s. Of St. Catherines, Lincolnshire ; knighted April 23, 1603 ; M. P. Lincoln, 1604–11 and 1614 ; Lincolnshire, 1624–25 ; Lincoln again, 1625, 1626, and 1628–29.

Graves, Thomas, gent., 2. Sub. —— ; pd. £25 ; went to Virginia in the Mary and Margaret in 1608 ; a member of the first House of Burgesses in America (for Smythe's Hundred), July 30, 1619 ; living on the Eastern Shore in 1620 ; a burgess for Accowmacke (Northampton) in 1629–32 ; a commissioner in 1621–32 ; and a member of the first regular vestry of the parish, September 14, 1635. He was possibly the father of John Graves, who wrote " A Song of Sion, by a Citizen thereof whose outward habitation is in Virginia. 1652."

Gray — Grey, Lady Elizabeth, 3. Sub. —— ; pd. £25. Second daughter and sole heir of Gilbert, Earl of Shrewsbury, and wife of Henry Grey de Ruthyn, son and successor of Charles, the seventh Earl of Kent. She married, secondly, John Selden.

Gray, Sir John, 3. Sub. £37 10s. ; pd. £12 10s. Knighted by Essex at Cales in 1596 ; M. P. Grampound, 1601, and Aldborough, 1610–11.

Grey, John, 2. Sub. —— ; pd. £25. Transferred his two shares in Virginia to Richard Baynam on June 28, 1620.

Gray, Robert, author. (Probably the author of " An Allarum for England." Licensed to John Budge, January 26, 1609. A person of this name was the schoolmaster at the Charterhouse, 1624–26.)

Greene, Laurence, grocer, 2. Sub. £37 10s. ; pd. £37 10s. " Late apprentice with Mr. Alderman Brooke ; sworn to freedom January 26, 1592 ; admitted to livery, 1601 ; elected on the Court of Assistants July 26, 1611 ; was second warden in 1615." (From Grocers' Records.) Also of E. I. and N. W. P. companies. In October, 1641, Laurence Greene, merchant, petitioned the Privy Council, for a warrant for the transportation of twenty passengers and provisions to Virginia, where he had twenty-four servants; the license was granted October 20, 1641, and the provisions were transported to Virginia in the Mayflower.

Greenville — Grenville — Granville, Bernard, esquire. Eldest son of Sir Richard Greenville, of Stow, who brought the first colony to Roanoke. He was sheriff of Cornwall in 1596; M. P. for Bodmin, 1597-98. January 16, 1598, Ralegh wrote to Lord Burghley, asking to have "Mr. Barnarde Grenville" made one of the deputy levetenantes in Cornwall, saying, "the gentleman is very sufficient, and the rest shall receive great ease thereby; and her Majesties service the better performed." M. C. for Va., March 9, 1607; knighted by Lord Deputy Chichester, in Ireland, November 5, 1608; one of his majesty's tenants in Ireland, 1611, etc.; buried at Kilkhampton, June 26, 1636. He married Elizabeth, daughter of Philip Bevil, Esq., and had issue four sons and two daughters; one of the sons, Sir Bevil Granville, the boldest of the Cavalier leaders, the Bayard of England, was grandfather of the celebrated George Granville, Lord Lansdowne.

Greenville — Greenefield, Captain Edward. Son of Richard Greineville, of Wotton, esquire. He was born July 4, 1561; was first captain of a pinance called the Swallow, and after of a bark called the Thomas, under Sir Francis Drake. He died at Carthagena, South America, unmarried.

Greenville, Sir Richard, son of Sir Roger Granville, an esquire of the body to Henry VIII., and his wife Thomasine, daughter of Thomas Cole, Esq., of Slade in Devon, was born in 1540; at an early age, by permission of Queen Elizabeth, he entered the imperial army in Hungary, and attained high reputation for his achievements against the Turks; M. P. for Cornwall in 1571, and for Launceston, 1572 to 1583; interested in new discoveries, 1574; knighted at "Windesore" in 1577; sheriff of Cornwall, 1578; aided in sending out Amadas and Barlow, 1584; M. P. for Cornwall, 1584–85; and served on the committee for confirming Ralegh's patent; took the first colony to Virginia, April to October, 1585; made a voyage to supply them, April to December, 1586;

took Spanish prizes on each voyage; member of the council of war preparing to meet Spain, 1587; serving against the Armada, 1588. In 1591 he was vice-admiral of the fleet sent under Sir Thomas Howard to intercept the Spanish Plate fleet, and "closed a noble life in the stoutest sea-fight ever waged." He "gave up the ghost with great and stout courage, and no man could perceive any true sign of heaviness in him." He married Mary, daughter and co-heir of Sir John St. Leger, and their eldest son was Bernard Greenville (whom see).

Greenwell, William, merchant-tailor, 3. Sub. £37 10s.; pd. £100. Of the E. I. and N. W. P. companies; contractor to supply cordage to the navy, etc. He was added to the King's Council for the Va. Co.; was a director of the N. W. P. Co., and deputy-governor of the E. I. Co. He died in 1621. Was of St. Gabriel, Fenchurch, London; married, in 1582, Ellen Kettell, spinster.

Gresham, Sir Thomas. Born in London, 1519; king's agent at Antwerp, 1552; knighted by Queen Elizabeth, 1559; Gresham's Exchange, 1569; interested in Frobisher's voyages, 1576–78; planned Gresham's College in 1575; died in London, November 21, 1579. He was one of the greatest merchants of his time. (See his life by Burgon.)

Greville, Sir Fulke. Son of Sir Fulke Greville, Sr., by his wife Anne, daughter of Ralph Neville, Earl of Westmoreland, was born at Alcaster, in Warwickshire, in 1554.

He was a kinsman to Sir Henry Sidney, the father of Sir Philip, and to Sir Francis Walsingham. About 1564 or 1565 he was at school with his cousin Philip Sidney, at Shrewsbury. From thence, it seems, he went to Jesus College in 1568, and not to Trinity College, in Cambridge; thence to his travels on the continent, etc.

One of the sponsors for Penelope West, September 9, 1582; M. P. Heydon, 1584–85. Sidney's scheme for colonizing America; with Sidney about to embark for America in July, 1585.

M. P. for County Warwick in Parliaments of 1592–93, 1597–98, and 1601. Speed says, "He was many times elected knight of the shire, with that thrice worthy and honoured knight, Sir Thomas Lucy. A better choyse the Countie could not make ; for they were learned, wise, and honest." Served Henry IV. in 1591; knighted October, 1597. "Treasurer of Marine Causes for life in 1599, and is said to have accepted about the same time a commission as rear-admiral in the fleet, which was then equipped to resist a second invasion threatened by the Spaniards." He was consulted by Queen Elizabeth before she granted the charter to the E. I. Co. in 1600 ; Knight of the Bath at the coronation of King James, July 25, 1603 ; M. C. for Va., March 9, 1607 ; chancellor and under-treasurer of the exchequer, 1614 to 1621. Admitted into the E. I. Co. in 1615, and into the Va. Co. of London, December 17, 1617.

M. P. for County Warwick, 1620–21, till peer. He was created Baron Brooke of Beauchampe Court, January 19, 1621, and soon after made lord of the bedchamber.

He founded a Professorship of History in Cambridge in 1628. His will is dated February 18, 1628. He never married. Died at Brooke House, Holborn, from a wound received from one of his servants, September 30, 1628, in his seventy-fifth year. "His body was laid in his own vault, in the great church at Warwick, under a monument, which he had erected himself, with this remarkable inscription : —

FULKE GREVILLE.
Servant to Queen Elizabeth,
Councillor to King James,
and Friend to Sir Philip Sidney.
Trophæum Peccati."

"One great argument of his merit was his regard to that of others, desiring to be known to posterity under no other character than that of Shakespeare's and Ben Jonson's Master, Lord Chancellor Egerton's and Bishop Overal's Patron, and Sir Philip Sidney's Friend." (Lloyd.)

His cousin and heir, Robert Greville, second Lord Brooke, was one of the founders of Saybrook in Connecticut.

Grey. — See Gray.

Grobham, Sir Richard. Sub. £75; pd. £50. Of Wishford, County Wilts; the son of Nicholas Grobham, Esq., of Bishop's Lydiard, Somerset ; knighted at Royston, April 1, 1604 ; married Margaret, daughter of William Whitmore, of Buldwas, Shropshire, and London (who married Anne, daughter of Alderman Sir William Bond), and sister of Sir George Whitmore. M. C. for Va. Co., 1612. He died in 1629, without issue. His sister and heir, Jane Grobham, married John Howe, Esq., and was ancestor of the Viscounts Howe.

Gryce, Nicholas, 2. Sub. ——; pd. £25.

Guercheville, Antoinette de Pons, Madame La Marquis de. "Lady of Honor to the Queen of France " (Marie de Médici).

Gulstone — Goulston, Dr. Theodore. A celebrated physician ; born in 1572; educated at Merton College, Oxford, where he took his doctor's degree April 30, 1610 ; after which he became fellow (December 29, 1611) and censor of the College of Physicians, and practiced his profession with great celebrity in London. September 6, 1614, he was sworn a free brother of the E. I. Co., gratis, at the request of Sir Edwin Sandys, whose life he had saved ; and on September 11, 1614, Lorkin wrote to Puckering : "The Archbishop [George Abbot] hath been lately in great danger of death, from a fish's bone, which stuck in his throat as he was one day at dinner, and could not a long time be removed. The doctors gave him over as desperate ; yet, at length, Dr. Gulston found means to relieve him."

"Ultamatamakin (commonly called Tomacomo), one of Pohatans councellours, that came over with Dale, was a frequent guest at Master Doctor Goldstone's in 1616, where he sang and danced his diabolicall measures, and discoursed of his Country and Religion."

June 14, 1619, Dr. Gulstone was appointed on the committee of the Va. Co., concerning the college in Virginia.

December 15, 1619, he bought six shares of land in Virginia from John Cage, Esq., three shares from Peter

Bartle, and one share from John Payne, gent.

In July, 1621, he recommended to the Va. Co. Dr. John Potts for the physician's place in Virginia, vacated by the death of Dr. Lawrence Bohun.

He died May 4, 1632, and left by his will £200 to purchase a rentcharge for the endowment of a pathological lecture, to be delivered yearly in the College of Physicians of London; which lecture now bears his name. He was distinguished as a Latin and Greek scholar; translated several works from the Greek into Latin, two of which he published during his life, and a third was edited, after his death, by his friend the Rev. Thomas Gataker (1574–1654).

He married Helen Sotherton, daughter of George Sotherton, a merchant-tailor and M. P. for London, who died in 1599.

Guy, John. N. Fld. Co.; a merchant of Bristol trading to Newfoundland. He wrote a treatise in 1609, to animate the English to plant in that island; was an incorporator of the company in 1610, and governor of, and living in, Newfoundland, 1610–12. He was an alderman and mayor of Bristol, and M. P. for that city in 1621–22, "when the monies collected in Bristol for the Palatinate were transmitted to John Whitson and himself, to be by them paid to the proper authorities." He was also one of the arbitrators with Whitson in November, 1626, in the Callowhill case.

Gwinn. See Winne.

Gypes. See Gipps.

Hackshawe, Thomas. Sub. ——; pd. £12 10s.

Hackwell. See Hakewell.

Haiward — Hayward — Haward — Heyward, etc., **Sir George,** 2. Sub. ——; pd. £12 10s. Son of Sir Thomas Smythe's sister, Catharine, by her first husband, Sir Rowland Hayward; knighted at Theobald's in 1604. Chamberlain wrote to Mrs. Alice Carleton on February 16, 1614: "Sir George Haywood, the Lady Scott's son by old Rowland, is fallen mad."

Haward, James, merchant, 2. Sub. £37 10s.; pd. £12 10s.

Haiward (Hayward, etc.), **John.** (There were evidently three members

of this name in the Va. Co., namely, (1) John Hayward or Master John Hayward, (2) Rev. John, or John, clerk, or John, minister, and (3) Sir John Haiward, knight. They paid in all £112 10s.)

Hayward, Master John, the historian, was born in Suffolk in 1560; was D. C. L. of Cambridge; pleader in ecclesiastical courts. The first part of his "Life and Raigne of King Henrie the IV." was published in 1599. Elizabeth was displeased with the book, and ordered Bacon to search it for treasons. He reported no treason, but many felonies; for the author "had stolen many of his sentences and conceits out of Cornelius Tacitus." He was historiographer of Chelsea College in 1610; wrote the lives of the three Norman kings (William I. and II. and Henry I.) of England for Prince Henry, which were published in 1613; knighted November 9, 1619; M. P. for Bridgenorth, 1621–22, and for Saltash, 1626; married Jane, daughter of Andrew Paschal, Esq., of Springfield, Essex. He died in London, June 27, 1627, and was buried in Great St. Bartholomew's. His will is dated March 30, 1626, and was proved June 28, 1627. "His Life of Edward VI." was published, after his death, in 1630.

Haiward (etc.), **Rev. John,** 2. Sub. £37 10s. (In Stith's list of members in the second charter he is called "John Howard, clerk;" in the list of subscribers, "John Heyward, mynister;" in the Somers Islands charter, "John Hayward or Heyward, clerk.") Author of "The Strong Helper, 1614," etc.

Haiward, Sir John, 3. Sub. £75. Second son of Sir Rowland Hayward by his second wife, Catharine Smythe; knighted at Windsor, July 23, 1609; high sheriff of Kent in 1624.

Haiward, Roland. See Hayward.

Hakewell, William, esquire, 3. Sub. £37 10s.; pd. £12 10s. Born in Exeter, 1574; barrister of Lincoln's Inn; M. P. Bossiney, 1601, St. Michael's, 1604–11, 1614, Tregony, 1621–22, Amersham, 1624–25 and 1628–29; was master in chancery at decease; died October 31, 1655, aged 81. He married a niece of Lord Bacon's; was queen's solicitor in 1617. His brother,

Dr. George Hakewill, Archdeacon of Surrey, and himself were committed to custody in August, 1621, for presenting to Prince Charles, without the king's knowledge, a discourse against the Spanish match. He was on the Virginia Commission of July 15, 1624. Author "Liberty of the Subject, 1641."

Hakluyt, Richard, the Elder. Of the Middle Temple, a cousin to the Rev. Richard. He was much interested in foreign lands and the advancement of English commerce. Henry Lane, of the Skinners' Company in 1567, wrote to him in behalf of the fur trade of that company. About 1568 he showed his cousin, Richard, "certeine bookes of Cosmographie, with an Universall Mappe," and pointed out to him the various seas, lands, etc., and then turning to the 107th Psalm, directed him to the 23d and 24th verses, where he read "that they which go downe to the sea in ships and occupy by the great waters, they see the works of the Lord and his wonders in the deepe," etc., and his discourse influenced his cousin in prosecuting those studies.

He consulted Dr. Dee, June 30, 1578 ; gave instructions for the Pet and Jackman voyage in May, 1580. Walsingham sent a letter by him to the Bristol merchants, March 11, 1583. Lane wrote a letter to him from Virginia, September 3, 1585.

Hakluyt, Rev. Richard, 1. Sub. ——; pd. £21. Born about 1552 ; "brought up at Westminster school ;" became interested in cosmography ; entered Christ Church College, Oxford, in 1570 ; B. A., February 19, 1573; M. A., June 27, 1577; consulted Ortelius; delivered public lectures on Cosmography, etc. ; dedicated his "Divers Voyages," to Sir Philip Sidney in 1582; letters from Walsingham and Parmenius to him in 1583; chaplain of the English legation at Paris, 1583–88. Letters from Paris, 1584–86. Wrote discourse on "Western Planting" for Ralegh in 1584; caused the journals of Ribault and others to be published, 1586. He published "De Orbe Novo," etc., in Paris about March, 1587, and in London, May 1, 1587, his translation of the journals of Laudonniere, etc. The first edition of his "Principal Navigations," etc., No-

vember 17, 1589. His first wife died about 1597, leaving an only child, Edmond. The second edition in three volumes of his "Principal Navigations," etc. : first volume in 1598, second, 1599, and third in 1600. Published "Galvano's Discoveries of the World" in 1601 ; was interested in Pring's voyage to New England, 1603 ; one of the chaplains of the Savoy ; married, secondly, about March 30, 1604, when about 52 years old, Frances, widow of William Smithe of St. Botolph, Bishopsgate, gent., deceased ; had been prebendary of Bristol Cathedral since 1585 ; in 1605 was appointed a prebendary of Westminster, and rector of Wetheringset in Suffolk. He died at Eaton in Herefordshire in November, 1616. His will, dated August 20, 1612, was proved November 23, 1616. He was buried in Westminster Abbey, November 26, 1616. June 13, 1621, his son Edmond transferred two shares in Virginia to John Moore.

Richard Hakluyt younger

Hall, Richard, grocer, 3. Sub. £50 ; pd. ——. One of the farmers of the impost on tobacco; in February, 1610, he was granted £160 11s. in consideration of his great losses as abatement of his impost on tobacco.

Haman. See Hampton.

Hamer — Hamor, Ralph, the Elder, merchant-tailor, 2. Sub. £37 10s. ; pd. £133 6s. 8d. He was an incorporator, and for a time a director of the E. I. Co. He died in 1615, leaving his widow, Susan, as executrix of his estate. Two of their sons went to Virginia, Raphe in 1609, and Thomas in 1617. Thomas was at Master Harrison's house near Warraskoyack at the time of the massacre, March 22, 1622. On the 24th of January, 1623, George Harrison wrote from Jamestown that "Thomas Hamor was very sick." He probably died before February, 1624.

Hamor, Ralph, the Younger, 2. Sub. ——; pd. £25. Went to Virginia in 1609, and remained there until June 18, 1614. On the 8th of January, 1617, the company gave him eight shares in Virginia, and on the 15th of

January "bills of adventure allowed to Capt. Raphe Hamor and the persons here under named for every man transported at their charge being 16, who were to have noe Bonds, vizth. : one bill of £12 10s. for Mr. Rob. Sturton ; one Bill of £25 for Mr. Christo: Martin ; one Bill of £12 10s. for Mr. John Blackall ; one Bill of £50 for Mr. Tho: Hamor ; one Bill of £62 10s. for Mr. Raphe Hamor ; one Bill of £25 for Mr. William Tucker ; one Bill of £12 10s. for Mr. Elias Roberts." He sailed from England about March, and arrived in Virginia in May, 1617. He was a member of the council in Virginia, 1621 to 1628, and probably after.

Hamersley, Master Hugh, haber-dasher, 2. Sub. ——; pd. £25. " A great and general merchant ;" member of the Rus., E. I., N. W. P., and other companies ; was a director and an auditor of the E. I. Co. ; sheriff of London, 1618–19 ; alderman of Bishopsgate ward, 1619–22, and Aldgate ward, 1622–36 ; " Coronel of London and President of the Honorable Artillery Company ;" lord mayor, 1627–28 ; knighted June 8, 1628 ; president of Christ's Hospital, 1634, till decease. Died October 19, 1636, aged 71, and lies buried under " a great Monument in the North Wall," of the Church of St. Andrew's Undershaft, London. He gave the Haberdashers' Company a silver gilt salt cellar by Cellini.

Hampton, Captain John, of Plymouth. Ralegh referred to him as " a sea captain of the greatest experience in England " in 1595.

Hampton, Thomas, 3. Sub. ——; pd. £25.

Hanbury, John, merchant-tailor. Pd. £1 + £25.

Hancock, William, 2. Sub. ——; pd. £62 10s.

Hanger, George. Pd. £25.

Hanham, Sir John, 3. Sub. £37 10s. ; pd. £37 10s. Of Dean's Court, Winborne, Dorset ; eldest son of Thomas Hanham, sergeant at law, by his wife, Penelope, daughter of Sir John Popham ; M. P. East Looe, 1601; knighted at Charterhouse, May 11, 1603 ; M. P. Weymouth, 1604–11. He was sheriff of Dorset, 12 James I. Died in 16—, without issue, and was succeeded at Dean's Court by his brother Thomas (see Popham pedigree).

Hanham, Thomas, 1. Son of Thomas Hanham and brother of the above Sir John ; was a member of the New England Council, November 3, 1620 ; succeeded his brother, Sir John, at Dean's Court ; left a son, John, whose son, Sir William Hanham, was created a baronet. (It may have been the father, but I think it was this Thomas, who was named in the charter of April 10, 1606, and who went to North Virginia with Pring in that year. See Sir John Popham.)

Hansford, Humfrie, grocer, 3. Sub. £37 10s. ; pd. £50. Son of William Hansford, of London ; was baptized in St. Mary Woolchurch Haw, March 11, 1565 ; was an incorporator of the E. I. Co., 1600 ; churchwarden of St. Mary Woolchurch, 1606–08 ; a director of the E. I. Co. in 1607, and for many years thereafter ; incorporator of the N. W. P. Co., July 26, 1612 ; gave " an elegant cushion for the Pulpitt and a Pulpitt Cloth " to St. Mary Woolchurch in 1613. Lyson says, "The old house at Woodford-row was built in 1617, by Sir Humphrey Handforth, master of the wardrobe to James I., who is said frequently to have dined there, when hunting in the forest." Was a member of the N. Fld. Co.; on the commission to treat with the Hollanders, January 8, 1619 ; recommended by King James for treasurer of the Va. Co. in May, 1622; sheriff of London, 1622–23 ; knighted at Woodford Row, July 14, 1622 ; elected alderman of Castle Baynard ward, August 13, 1622. On February 5, 1623, he transferred one share of his lands in Virginia to Sir Timothy Thornehill. He was on the commission for the Va. Co., July 15, 1624. Died at Woodford Row, and was buried " in his vawte at Wool-church, Nov. 1, 1625."

Hansford, John, merchant-tailor. 2. Sub. ——; pd. £37 10s. Probably the brother of Sir Humfrey who was baptized February 25, 1571. (Colonel Hansford of Bacon's Rebellion, "had the honor of being the first Virginian born that ever was hanged.")

Harcourt, Robert. Eldest son of Sir Walter Harcourt, of Stanton-

Harcourt, by his wife Dorothy, daughter of William Robinson, of Drayton-Bassett in Staffordshire. "His brother Michael and himself were interested with Sir Walter Ralegh in Wiaffero, and Guyana in South America." He was on a voyage to Guiana, March to December, 1609, and his brother, Capt. Michael Harcourt, remained there at "Wiapoco," until 1612. James I. granted to him and others a patent, August 28, 1613. They sent out an expedition under Capt. Edward Harvey in 1616–17, and Collins says that "Robert Harcourt was the most considerable adventurer with Sir Walter Raleigh in his Voyage to Guyana," 1617–18. He married, in 1598, Frances Vere, sister of Sir Horace Vere, and died in 1631, aged fifty-seven years.

Hare, John, esquire, 3. Sub. £37 10s.; pd. £37 10s. Probably the eldest son of Sir Ralph Hare, of Slow Bardolph, Norfolk. M. P. for Aylesbery, 1625, Evesham, 1626, and King's Lynn, 1628–29. Knighted December 4, 1617; married Elizabeth, daughter of Lord Keeper Coventry.

Harfleet, Sir Thomas, 3. Sub. £37 10s.; pd. £12 10s. "Thomas Septuans als Harfleete of Kent" was knighted at Whitehall, July 23, 1603.

Harington. See Harrington.

Hariot, Thomas. An eminent English mathematician; was born at Oxford in 1560, and, having been instructed in Grammar-learning in that city, became a Batler or Commoner of St. Mary's Hall in that University, where he took the degree of Bachelor of Arts, February 12, 1579 [1580], and in the latter end of that year completed it by determination in School Street. Soon after he came to the knowledge of Sir Walter Ralegh on account of his admirable skill in the Mathematics, and was entertained by that gentleman, with the allowance of an annual pension, for instructing him in that science. He was sent by Sir Walter to Virginia in 1585, where he was employed, from June 1585, to June 1586, in the discovery and surveying of the country, observing the manners, customs, etc., of the people. And, upon his return he published the result of his labors in "A Briefe and True Report of the Newfound Land

of Virginia, etc., London, 1588." In 1594 he published a chapter on rhumbs, and in 1596 he framed a chart of Guiana, etc. About this time "Sir Walter got him into the acquaintance of that noble and generous Count Henry Percy, Earl of Northumberland, who finding him a gentleman of an affable and peaceable nature, and well read in the obscure parts of learning, he did allow him a yearly pension of £120." He shared in the troubles of his patrons. At the trial of Ralegh in 1603, Chief Justice Popham referred to the devilish opinions of Hariot, and he was not without suspicion of having some knowledge of the Gunpowder Plot in 1605. When Ralegh and the earl were in the Tower, Hariot, Hues, and Warner were their constant companions, and were usually called the Earl of Northumberland's Three Magi. He made a sun-dial for the earl which is still to be seen on the south face of the Martin Tower. In 1607 Hariot drew up observations on the comet since known as "Halley's Comet," which were published by Professor Rigaud, Oxford, 1832. In 1609 he was in consultation with the Va. Co. of London. In 1610 he is said to have observed the satellites of Jupiter, a few days after Galileo first discovered them, and to have been himself the first to detect the spots on the sun, December 8, 1610. "He was noted for skill in Algebra, his treatise on which, entitled, 'Artis Analyticæ Praxis ad æquationes Algebraicus nova,' etc, edited by his friend, Mr. Walter Warner, was published after his death in 1631." "Hariot . . . was destined," says Hallam, "to make the last great discovery in the pure science of Algebra. . . . He arrived at a complete theory of the genesis of Equations, which Cardan and Vieta had but partially conceived." He lived for some time in Sion College, and died at London "of cancer in the lip" and other troubles, July 2, 1621. His body was interred in St. Christopher's Church in London (the site of this church is now occupied by the Bank of England), where a monument was erected for him by his noble executors, Sir Thomas Aylesbury and Robert Sidney Viscount Lisle, with a Latin

SIR GEORGE SOMERS

inscription which may be thus translated: —

"Stop traveller, tread lightly/just here lies what was mortal/of the celebrated man/Thomas Hariot./He was that most learned Harriot/of Syon near the river Thames,/By birth and education/an Oxonian./He was versed in all sciences./He excelled in all things./Mathematics, Philosophy, Theology,/The most studious explorer of Truth/The most pious cultivator of the Triune God./A sexagenarian or thereabouts,/he bid farewell to mortality; not to life, In the year of our Lord, 1621, on the 2d July."

The following extracts are from "The Accomptes of the Church Wardens of the Paryshe of St. Christofer's in London." From the Introduction by Edwin Freshfield, vice-president of the Society of Antiquaries of London, etc.: "Mr. Harriote was a frequent resident in the parish with his friend Mr. Buckner; indeed he died at his house in 1622 [1621]. . . . He had always kept up his interest in Virginia, and with his friend Mr. Buckner was instrumental in promoting the colonization of that country." From "The Accompt, etc., for Anno 1622" (i. e., from May, 1621, to May, 1622). "Received for the Knell of Mr. Harriote, 6 shillings and 8 pence." "Received of Mr. Thomas Buckner, being the gift of Mr. Harriot, £4." "Paid to the poore by the Gifte of Mr. Harriot — four pounds." From "The Accompt, etc., for Anno 1626" (May, 1625, to May, 1626). "Received of Mr. Thomas Buckner for the Erectinge of Mr. Herriot his monument in the Chauncell the some of one pound."

Harley (etc.), **Captain Edward,** 2. Sub. ——; pd. ——. His name is variously spelled: Harlow, Hawley, Harley, etc. Among the papers in the collection of Lord De L'Isle and Dudley, catalogued in the Third Report of the Royal Hist. Commission, is the following: "Folio paper, 16th Century. Ars Naupegica. Art of Shipbuilding, by Edmund Harlow, Gent." Captain Harlow made the voyage to our New England coast with Popham, May 31, 1607, to December, 1608. He was again on our coast in 1611, "and brought away the salvadges from the river of Canada," which were "showed in London for a wonder," in the spring of 1612. In June, 1614, Capt. Henry (?) Harley was sent to our coast by Sir Ferdinando Gorges and others. He probably returned to England the same year. March 28, 1623, "Edward Hawley, gentleman, was close prisoner in the Gate house at Westminster, by the King's own warrant;" but whether this was our captain or not, I am not able to say. Many of the same family name were afterwards interested in the English colonies in America.

Harley (**Hawley**, etc.), **Captain Henry.** Of the 1614 voyage. Possibly the third son of Jeremy Hawley, Esq., of Boston, near Brentford, Middlesex, England. . He died unmarried, and is classed as a merchant in the family pedigree. His brother, John Hawley, married Amy, daughter of Thomas Studley, who may have been "the first cape merchant in Virginia." His eldest brother, James Hawley, Esq., of Brentford, born in 1558, and still living in 1619, was twice married and had a large family, by his first wife, Susan, daughter of Richard Tothill of Devonshire. He is said to have had seven sons, viz.: (1) Jerome, (2) Capt. Henry, (3) Dr. Richard, (4) James, (5) William, and two others. I think the two others were Gabriel, who died in Virginia, and John, who came to Virginia in 1619. (1) Jerome (born about 1580) was interested in Virginia and Maryland — was a councilor in the first and commissioner of the other. (4) James and (5) William were also interested in these colonies; (2) Capt. Henry Hawley (who may have made the voyage of 1614 when a young man) was long interested in colonization, and became famous as a governor of the Barbadoes (1632–39). The present baronet descends from the third son (3) Dr. Richard Hawley of London.

Harley, Robert. Pd. £12 10s.

Harper, John, fishmonger, 2. Sub. ——; pd. £62 10s. Also a member of the E. I. Co. June 23, 1620, he gave Mr. John Whitcombe, who married his daughter, Anne Harper, a share in Virginia. There is a fair monument to himself and wife on the south side of the parish church of St.

Margaret Moyses, Breadstreet ward, London, with this inscription : "Here lieth the Bodies of John Harper, citizen and fishmonger, Treasurer of Christ's Hospital, and Alderman's Deputy of Breadstreet Ward, London. And Frances his wife, daughter to James Smyth, of Great Lunber, in the County of Lincolne, gentleman. By whom he had issue five children ; but at the time of their Death left only a son, John, and a daughter, Anne, married to John Whitcombe of London. He died the 27 of November, 1632, in the 79th year of his age, and she departed this life the 30 day of October, 1630, being 72 years old." By his will, he gave money to purchase books for Sion College Library.

Harrington, John Lord, 3. Sub. ——; pd. ——. He was the oldest son and successor of Sir James Harrington, Knt., of Exton, by his wife Lucy, daughter of Sir William Sidney of Penshurst; born about 1540; knighted January, 1583; M. P. for Warwickshire, 1586–87; and for Rutlandshire in 1593, 1597–98, and 1601; elevated to the peerage as Baron Harrington of Exton, July 21, 1603. " A sincere Christian and a learned man," he was tutor to the Princess Elizabeth until her marriage with the Electoral-Palatine; and in April, 1613, he attended her royal highness into Germany. He died, on his way back to England, at Worms, on the 24th of August, 1613, at the age of 73. He was first cousin to Sir Philip Sidney, and " a grand benefactor to Sidney College in Cambridge." He married Anne, only daughter and heir of Robert Kelway (Callaway), Esq., surveyor of the Court of Wards, and had, with other issue, John, his successor, and Lucy, who married Edward Russell, third Earl of Bedford.

His stock in the Va. Co., at his death, passed to his son John, I suppose.

Harrington, Sir John, 3. Sub. £150 ; pd. £187 10s. Son of John Lord Harrington; was baptized at Stepney, May 3, 1592; was made a Knight of the Bath at the creation of Charles Duke of York, " Twelfth Day [January 6] 1605 " (O. S.). He returned from his travels abroad in 1609, with learning and experience far beyond his years,

and at once took an active interest in affairs. M. C. for Va. Co., 1612. July 26, 1612, he was one of the incorporators of the N. W. P. Co. Succeeded his father as Lord Harrington, August 24, 1613 ; died of the smallpox on Sunday, February 27, 1614, at Kew, near Richmond, unmarried. The friend and companion of Henry, Prince of Wales, " he was pious, temperate, and chaste without the least tincture of sourness or austerity." " A most bountiful benefactor of Sidney College in Cambridge."

Harrington-Russell, Lucy, Countess of Bedford, 3. Sub. ——; pd. ——. The elder of the two daughters of John, first Lord Harrington of Exton, and sister of Sir John Harrington aforesaid; married at Stepney in Middlesex, on December 12, 1594, to Edward Russell, third Earl of Bedford ; inherited two thirds of her brother's vast estate in 1614. Her husband died on May 1, 1627, and she died thirty days after. She took great interest in rare plants, in the management of her gardens and orchards, and probably obtained many varieties from Virginia and the Bermudas. She was the patroness of Ben Jonson, Dr. Donne, Samuel Daniel, Drayton, and other poets.

Harris, Sir Arthur, 3. Sub. ——; pd. £37 10s. Of Woodham Mortimer, Essex. Son of Sir William Harris ; was born in 1584 ; licensed to travel for three years, May 12, 1604 ; knighted at Otelands, July 15, 1606 ; M. P. for Maldon, 1624–25 ; for Essex, 1625 ; for Maldon again, 1628–29 ; died January 9, 1632. He married, first, in 1606, Anne, daughter of Robert Cranmer, of Chepsted, County Kent, esquire, and, secondly, in 1615, Dame Anne Bowyer, widow of Sir Henry Bowyer, and daughter and sole heir to Sir Nicholas Salter.

Harris, Sir Christopher, 3. Sub. ——; pd. ——. Of Radford, Devon. One of the executors of Sir Francis Drake. M. P. Plymouth, 1584–85 ; knighted June 7, 1609 ; buried January 27, 1625. Ralegh spent nine or ten days at his house in June, 1618.

Harris, John, esquire, 3. Sub. £37 10s.; pd. £37 10s. Son of Sir William Harris. (M. P. West Looe, 1614.)

Harris, Roger, 3. Sub. £37 10s.; pd. £68 15s.

Harris, Thomas, gent., 2. Sub. ——; pd. £25. This may have been the son of Sir William Harris. I think it was the person of the name who went to Virginia with Dale in 1611, and was living at the Neck-of-Land, Charles City, in February, 1625, aged 38, with his wife, aged 23.

Harris, Sir William, 3. Sub. £75; pd. £75. Of Crixith and Woodham Mortimer, Essex. Knighted at Whitehall, July 23, 1603. Died in November, 1616. Himself and wife are buried at Crixith in Essex. He married Alice, daughter of Thomas Smith, of Westonhanger in Kent (see Smythe pedigree), and had by her four sons and four daughters, namely, Sir Arthur, William, of Lincoln's Inn, Thomas, John, Alice, Mary, Frances, and Elizabeth. The daughter, Alice Harris, a niece of Sir Thomas Smythe's, married Sir Henry Mildmay of Graces, who was own cousin to John Winthrop, governor of Massachusetts.

Harrison, Edward, ironmonger, 2. Sub. £37 10s.; pd. £112 10s. An incorporator and leading member of the E. I. Co. November 13, 1620, he transferred 500 acres of land in Virginia to Raphe Fogg.

Harrison, George. The only brother of Sir John Harrison. Came to Virginia in 1618. March 6, 162⁰⁄₁, Sir George Yardley, governor of Virginia, granted to "George Harrison of Charles City, gentleman, who hath abode in the colony three years, 200 acres of land situate on the opposite side of the river over against the Governor's Mansion House, to be doubled by the Virginia Company, when sufficiently planted and peopled." This land was near "Chapokes Creeke," and was still standing in Harrison's name in 1626. He wrote to his brother John from James City in Virginia May 12, 1622 ; another long and interesting letter January 24, 1623. These letters are still preserved among the colonial papers. In the spring of 1624 he had a duel (probably the first in Virginia) with Richard Stephens, somewhere near James City in Virginia, in which he received a small cut in the knee only, but died fourteen days after. The jury at the inquest affirmed that he died of natural disease. He left property in Virginia and "the West Indies" [The Bermudas?].

Harrison, Harmon, gent., 2. Sub. ——; pd. £25. Came to Virginia in 1608. I take this to be the Ensign Harrison who was complained of, together with Captain Martin, before the First Assembly, July 30, 1619 ; massacred by the Indians in March, 1622. There was probably some relationship between Martin and the Harrisons — Brandon finally came into the possession of the latter family.

Harrison, James, gent., 3. Sub. ——; pd. ——. I think this person was the son of William Harrison, of London, merchant, by his second wife, Mary, daughter of John West, grocer.

Harrison, John, merchant-tailor. Pd. £1. The founder of the grammar school at Great Crosby, in the parish of Shelton, in the county of Lancaster, England, in 1620.

Harrison, Mr. (John), the Elder, stationer. Pd. £5. Of St. Michael-ad-Bladum. Master of the Stationers' Company in 1583 ; married, in 1586, Juliana Barnes, widow of Francis Barnes, of St. Magnus, London, haberdasher, deceased. "June 25, 1594, Richard Field assigned over unto Mr. Harrison, Senʳ., in open court holden this day, a book called 'Venus and Adonis.' "

Harrison, John, gent. Son of William Harrison, of Aldcliffe, Com. Lanc., and his wife Margaret, daughter of Christopher Gardiner, of Urswich. Was born about 1589. He married, in August, 1616, Margaret, daughter of Robert Fanshawe, who was brother to Thomas Fanshawe, the husband of Sir Thomas Smythe's sister Joane (see Smythe pedigree). At this time John Harrison was "of St. Olive, Hart Street, gent.," and his bride was a member of the family of Sir John Wolstenholme. On February 13, 162½, Sir John Wolstenholme transferred to Mr. John Harrison three shares of land in Virginia. Possibly governor of the Bermudas early in 1623. September 16, 1623, he sent goods, etc., to his brother George Harrison in Virginia. April 28, 1624, George Menefie wrote to him from James City about his brother's death. August 16, 1624, he gave James Carter, master of the Anne, a power of attorney to manage the estate of his deceased brother in Virginia.

At the Visitation of London, 1633, he had five children : John, William, Abraham, Anne, and Margaret. The eldest son, John, was then married to Jane, daughter of Edmond Chapman, of Greenwich in Kent.

He was one of his majesty's farmers of the custom-house. In December, 1640, he was a member of the House, and advanced £50,000 on the security of the coming subsidies. As a reward for his patriotism he was knighted by the king at Whitehall, January 4, 164⁰/₁.

In May, 1641, "Harrison again came to the aid of Parliament, and offered to lend £150,000 on the security of the customs. At once the question was raised whether Parliament had it in its power to give any such security. The Commons were in instant fear of dissolution. . . . It was at once proposed that a Bill should be brought in, providing that the existing Parliament should not be dissolved without its own consent. The proposal was welcomed with singular unanimity." ("Gardiner's History of England.) This was the beginning of the Long Parliament.

He owned Aldcliffe Hall, Lancaster, and was M. P. for Lancaster in both Parliaments of 1640 ; was imprisoned by order of the Parliament in 1642, and was deprived of his property ; removed from his seat in Parliament, as a royalist, in September, 1643. After the Restoration he was M. P. for Lancaster, May 8, 1661, to his death, September 28, 1669.

His daughter, Anne Harrison, married Sir Richard Fanshawe (nephew of Sir Thomas Smythe), the diplomatist and author (see Sir Henry Fanshawe). Lady Anne Fanshawe became an authoress, and her memoirs are well known.

Harrison, Ralphe, 2. Sub. ——— ; pd. £25. One of this name went to the East Indies prior to 1609. Probably the same person. He went to Virginia, and died at Elizabeth City, some time thereafter, in 1623.

Harrison, William. A leading merchant of London; of the E. I. and N. W. P. companies. His pedigree is

given in the Visitation of London, 1633–34 : Harl. Soc. Pub., vol i. p. 355. His second wife was Mary, daughter of John West, grocer. (See Sir Edward Conway.) He was for a long time treasurer of the E. I. Co. ; died in 1620.

Hart, Sir Eustace, 3. Sub. ——— ; pd. £25. Of All Hallows-in-the-Wall, London ; mentioned in Chamberlain's letter of April 30, 1616, and in the "Calendar of State Papers, Domestic, July 11, 1616 ; " transferred his bill of adventure in Va. of £25 to Mr. Thomas Gibbs, May 6, 1618. He married, first, Mary, relict of Lord Willoughby de Eresby, and, secondly, in 1628, Jane, daughter of John Evelyn, Esq., of Kingston, in Surrey (widow of Sir Anthony Benn, recorder of London.) Sir Eustace Hart died September 18, 1634, and was buried at St. Bennett's, Paul's Wharf, London.

Hart, Sir John, grocer. Elected alderman of Farringdon Without, June 18, 1575 ; chosen sheriff, August 15, 1579 ; lord mayor, 1589 ; M. P. for London, 1592–97 ; president of St. Bartholomew's Hospital, 1593–1603 ; died about February, 1603, and was buried in the Church of St. Swithin, London Stone, the living of which was in his patronage. He married, in 1586, Anne, relict of Anthony Cage, of London, salter. His eldest daughter, Joan, married Sir George Bolles. His second daughter, Anne, married Alderman Humphrey Smith. His daughter Judith married Edward Cage (whom see).

Hart, Sir Percival. Sub. ——— ; pd. £37 10s. Of Lullingstone Castle, Kent, son of Sir George Hart ; knighted June 1, 1601 ; M. P. Lewes, 1601 ; one of the heirs of the patent of Sir Jerome Bowes (his uncle) for the sole importing of Venice glass, in 1616. He married three wives : Anne, daughter of Sir Roger Manwood ; Jane, daughter of Edward Stanhope, Esq., and, April 28, 1623, Mary Harrison, widow.

Harwell — Harewell — Horwell — Howell, Sir Thomas, 2. Sub. ——— ; pd. £37 10s. Of Worcestershire ; knighted at Whitehall, July 23, 1603.

Harwood, Captain Edward, 2 Sub. ——— ; pd. ———. Son of William Harwood, of Thurlby, County Lincoln ; was knighted before December 9, 1618, when the Earl of Bedford assigned to him a bill of adventure in Va. of £50. He was about this time added to His Majesty's Council for the Va. Co., and in 1619 was one of the committee for compiling and reducing the standing " Rules and orders, for the Government of the Virginia Company, into one entire Body of Laws, Form of Government," etc., which have been reprinted by Force, vol. iii. No. 6. He was a captain and afterwards a colonel (as early as 1604) in the Low Countries. In November, 1626, he was ordered to conduct his regiment to assist the King of Denmark. He was an incorporator (December 4, 1630) of the Providence Islands or Bahamas Company ; was slain at the siege of Maastricht, 1632. He is one of Fuller's Worthies of Lincolnshire. " The Advice of that Worthy Commander. Sir Ed : Harwood, Collonell. Written by King Charles his Command upon occasion of the French Kings preparation, and presented (in his life time) by his owne hand, to his Maiestie," etc. ; was printed at London in 1642. His brother, George Harwood, of London, was treasurer of the Massachusetts Company.

Harwood, Leonard, mercer, 2. Sub. —— ; pd. £37 10s.

Haselden (Hazleden), William, 3. Sub. £37 10s. ; pd. £12 10s. Of N. W. P. and E. I. companies.

Hasilrige (Hazlerigg), Francis, gent., 2. Sub. —— ; pd. £12 10s.

Hastings, Henry, Earl of Huntingdon, 3. Sub. —— ; pd. £120. Son of Francis Hastings, by his wife Sarah, daughter to Sir James Harrington ; at the death (in 1605) of his grandfather, George, fourth Earl of Huntingdon, he succeeded as fifth earl ; was lord lieutenant of the counties of Leicester and Rutland, steward of the Duchy of Lancaster, and, in May, 1616, one of the peers for the trial of the Earl and Countess of Somerset. He was a noted patron of the stricter class of divines ; was one of the first that rose for King Charles in Leicestershire. He died November 14, 1643, and was buried at Ashby de la Zouch.

Hatton, Sir Christopher. Born at Holdenby, 1540 ; made a gentle-man pensioner to the queen. June 30, 1554 ; admitted to the Inner Temple, May, 1560 ; introduced at court before June, 1564 ; one of the representatives of Elizabeth at the baptism of James VI. of Scotland, December, 1566 ; M. P. in 1571 and 1572 ; captain of the queen's guard, 1572 ; vice-chamberlain and member of the Privy Council, November, 1577 ; knighted December 1, 1577 ; patron of Drake in his voyage round the world in the Golden Hind, 1577–80 (Hatton's crest was a golden hind) ; interested in Fenton's voyage, 1582–83 ; on the committee for confirming Ralegh's patent in December, 1584. He was the patron of several of the writers on naval affairs, discoveries, etc. ; was on the commission for the trial of Mary Queen of Scots, in October, 1586 ; made lord high chancellor in April, 1587 ; created Knight of the Garter, St. George's Day, 1588 ; Chancellor of the University of Oxford, September 20, 1588 ; died at Ely Place, November 20, 1591, and was buried in St. Paul's. He died a bachelor, but had adopted the son of his sister Dorothy, by her husband, John Newport, Esq., of the same family, possibly, as Capt. Christopher Newport.

Haukinson, George, 2. Sub. ——; pd. £12 10s.

Hawes, Humfrey, clothworker. Sub. —— ; pd. £12 10s. Of the E. I. Co. ; second son of Lawrence Hawes, of London, by his wife Ursula, daughter of John Herrick, of Leicester, and sister to Sir William Herrick.

Hawkins, Charles, 2. Sub. £37 10s. ; pd. £62 10s. Of the E. I. Co. ; son of Capt. William Hawkins the younger, and nephew of the famous Sir John Hawkins.

Hawkins, Sir John. Grandson of John Hawkins, Esq., of Tavistock, Devon, which John married Joan, daughter of William Amydas, Esq., of

Launceston, Cornwall, by whom he was the father of "Capt. William Hawkins, the elder, of Plymouth, who for his 'skill in Sea-causes' was much esteemed by Henry VIII., and was the first Englishman who sailed a ship into the Southern Seas." He made several voyages to the coast of Africa, and thence to Brazil in 1530, and after. He married Joan, daughter of William Trelawney, Esq., of Cornwall, and granddaughter of Sir John Trelawney, a descendant of Edwin, who held the lordship of Trelawney in the time of Edward the Confessor ; by her he had two sons, William (of whom hereafter) and John (of whom I write), who was born about 1532 ; in his youth studied the mathematics ; entered the naval service about 1551, and went divers voyages into Spain, Portugal, and the Islands ; admitted a freeman of Plymouth, 1555–56 ; invented the chain-pump for ships, 1558–59 ; on his first voyage to the West Indies, from October, 1562, to September, 1563 ; on his second voyage there, from the fall of 1564, to September, 1565 ; moved to London, to the Parish of St. Dunstan's in the East, about 1565, where he continued to dwell at least thirty years (1565–1595) ; on his third voyage to the West Indies, October, 1567, to January, 1569. In March, 1569, La Mothe wrote from London : " John Hawkins has undertaken to revenge the injury which the Spaniards did him at Mexico, and intends, next July, laying in wait at the Azores, with a good naval force for the arrival of the Spanish fleet from the West Indies." M. P. for Plymouth, 1571 ; pretended to be a traitor ; deceived the Queen of Scots and Philip ; was made a grandee of Spain in September, 1571, receiving a large sum of money, etc. In the summer of 1572 with 20 ships, equipped with Philip's money, he sailed for the Azores to lie in wait for Philip's Mexican fleet. M. P. for Plymouth, 1572–83 ; appointed treasurer of the navy to succeed his father-in-law, Ben Gonson, deceased, in 1573 ; was interested in Drake's voyage, 1577–80. He proposed to destroy the Spanish fishing fleet at Newfoundland in April, 1585. He was "the man to whom is due all the credit of preparing the royal fleet to meet the Armada." Served against

the Armada, and was knighted on the high seas July 26, 1588. In 1590 he was sent with Frobisher to intercept the Plate fleet, and harass the trade of Spain. Founded and endowed St. John's Hospital at Chatham for decayed mariners and shipwrights of the royal navy, by letters patent, dated August 27, 1594. On August 27, 1595, he sail on his last and fatal voyage to the West Indies ; died at sea, November 12, 1595, "neere the Eastermost end of Saint Juan de Puerto Rico," and " being coffined he was cast into the sea." His widow had a fair monument erected to his memory on the north side of the chancel of St. Dunstan's in the East, London. "He was the first true friend of the British sailor; and not only the ablest captain, but the best shipwright of his time." He was twice married; first to " Dame Katharine " (the Gonson pedigree says Avice), and secondly to " Dame Margaret ;" one of these, probably the first, was a daughter of Ben Gonson, and she, Burke says, was the mother of Richard Hawkins, who was afterwards interested in the Virginia enterprises.

Sir John Hawkins was 63 years old when he died, in 1595. (See London " Notes and Queries," § 6, xi. p. 388.)

Hawkins, John, 2. Sub. ——. pd. £25. Of the E. I. and N. W. P. companies ; son of Capt. William Hawkins, the younger.

Hawkins, Sir Richard. The son of the celebrated Sir John Hawkins (whom see). I do not know the date of his birth ; but he was " of tender yeares " in September, 1570. " In a voyage, under the charge of his uncle, William Hawkins, of Plimouth, esquire, in the West Indies at Porto Rico in 1582 ;" again in the West Indies at the island of Margarita, in 1583. In command of the Duck in the celebrated Drake-Sidney expedition to our coast, September, 1585, to July, 1586. In 1588 he commanded the Swallow in the attack on the Spanish Armada, in which action he greatly distinguished himself. Having determined on a voyage to Japan and the East Indies " in the end of anno 1588," he ordered a ship to be built for that purpose ; in the meantime we find him in command of the

Nonpareil, near the Azores, on the lookout for Spanish ships. In 1593, his ship for the East Indian voyage, being finished, was named by the Lady Hawkins the Repentance ; but Queen Elizabeth, passing by the vessel, commanded her bargemen to row round about her, and viewing her from post to stem, disliking nothing but her name, said that she would christen her anew, and that henceforth she should be called the Daintie ; in which vessel he sailed soon after, passing through the Straits of Magellan early in 1594 ; on the 22d of June, 1594, off Cape San Francisco, Equador, he was forced to surrender to an overwhelming fleet of Spain. In 1595–96 a prisoner in Lima, Peru ; in 1597 "brought out of the Indies (America) in a galeon, which was chased into the rode of Tercera," by the English fleet under the command of Essex. He was for some time a prisoner in "the Terceras" (the Azores Islands), and then in Seville and in Madrid ; sent back to England in the beginning of the reign of James I., by whom he was knighted July 23, 1603 ; M. P. for Plymouth, 1604–11, and vice-admiral of Devon in 1605, etc. ; M. C. for Va., March 9, 1607. In 1614 the E. I. Co. proposed a voyage to the Straits of Magellan, and Sir Richard was "generally held to be of Courage, Art, and Knowledge to attempt such an enterprise ; " but it seems the idea was abandoned.

"In 1615 he undertook, by authority from the council of the second colony of Virginia, to try what service he could do them as president for that year. Having received his commission and instructions, he departed in October, and spent the time of his being in those parts (New England) in searching the country, and finding out the commodities thereof. From thence he passed along the coast to Virginia, and staid there some time." From Virginia he went to Spain to make sale of his fish.

In October, 1616, "seven English ships, which this year fished at Newfoundland, and from thence directing there course for Italy, were within the straits, assailed and taken by 30 Turkish men of war," and Lord Carew, writing to Sir Thomas Roe on the 18th of January, 1617, says, "It is thought that Sir Richard Hawkins of Plimouth was in one of these English ships, for he is not retourned from the fishing upon the Northern English Colony (which Sir John Popham projected), and he intended to make sale of his fishe in Italye." He returned from Virginia before September, 1617, at which date he petitioned to command the fleet of the E. I. Co., but the choice finally fell on Sir Thomas Dale; member African Company, November 16, 1618 ; appointed deputy of Sir Robert Mansell, vice - admiral, for suppression of piracy in the Levant, October 3, 1620. "He was a Vice-Admiral of the fleet which sailed from Plimmouth the twelfth of October in the morning in the yeare 1620," to "attack and destroy the pirates in the Mediterranean Sea."

In the patent of November 3, 1620, he was appointed a member of "the first moderne and present Councill established at Plymouth, in the county of Devon, for the planting, ruling, ordering, and governing of New England in America."

He returned from the expedition against the Levant pirates in 1621–22. Prince says, "After many high-spirited actions, which had they been recorded (as pity it is they were not) would have made a large volume of themselves, he died suddenly in 1622, being seized with apoplexy while at the Privy Council."

There was some trouble growing out of the fact that the fleet against the pirates had been insufficiently provided with provisions, and the men badly paid. April 27, 1622, Chamberlain wrote to Carleton : " Sir Robert Mansell and the rest of the crew are nothing well paid neither ; insomuch that Sir Richard Hawkins, the vice-admiral, finding his reckoning come short of what he expected, of mere grief and discontent, sunk down before the lords, and died the next day."

"The observations of Sir Richard Hawkins, knight, in his voyage into the South Sea, Anno Domini 1593," dedicated to Charles, Prince of Wales, were printed in London in 1622.

His widow, the Lady Judith, survived him seven years. They were ancestors of Sir John Hawkins (1719–

1789), the author of "The Science and Practice of Music."

Hawkins, Captain William, the Younger. Eldest son of Capt. William, the elder, and brother of Sir John Hawkins. "He was the most influential resident of Elizabethan Plymouth ; a merchant and a sailor ; the holder of a commission under the Prince of Condé ; represented Plymouth in Parliament ; mayor of Plymouth in the eventful Armada year, 1588, and was active in fitting out vessels for the fight." He died October 7, 1589, and was buried in the Church of St. Nicholas at Deptford. "A faithful believer in the true religion ; a great benefactor of poor mariners ; a most learned man in naval affairs, he frequently made long voyages. He married two wives ; by one of them he had 4, by the other 7, children." I have mentioned two of his sons (Charles and John). Another son, Capt. William Hawkins, the third, was the founder of the first trading-house at Surat for the E. I. Co. He was in the East Indies from 1607 to 1614, and died on his return in the latter year.

Hawley. See Harley.

Hay, James Lord, 3. Sub. ——; pd. ——. "A gentleman of small means, but of great ability and many personal recommendations, whose greatest fault, so far as I have been able to find out, was being a Scotchman." He was made a Knight of the Bath, June 4, 1610. Having failed to pay his dues to the company, it seems, he probably forfeited his membership under the 3d charter ; but he was again admitted into the company on December 2, 1618, and was some time after added to the King's Council for that company. He had been created Baron Hay of Sanley, County York, June 29, 1615, sworn of the Privy Council, March, 1617, and created Viscount Doncaster, July 5, 1618, and Earl of Carlisle, September 13, 1622 ; was of the Sandys party in the Va. Co. in 1623–24 ; chosen a Knight of the Garter in 1624 ; a councilor for New England ; governor of the Caribbee Islands, etc. He died April 25, 1636. His first wife was Honora, heiress of Edward Lord Denny ; his second (whom he married in 1317)

was the Lady Lucy Percy, youngest daughter of Henry, Earl of Northumberland, and niece of Capt. George Percy, some time governor of Virginia.

Haydon — Heydon, Jerome, ironmonger, 2. Sub. £37 10s. ; pd. £75. Of St. Mary Colechurch, London ; an alderman of London ; master of the Ironmongers in 1611, and a benefactor of that company ; married, in 1599, Agnes, relict of William Wennington, gent. ; died before 1632. I suppose he was the father of Sir John Heydon, some time governor of the Bermudas, as Sir John inherited Jerome's property in that island. Jerome's widow married Francis Morrice, clerk of his majesty's ordinance.

Henry Hexham, who translated the Atlas of Gerard Mercator and Judocus Hondius into English in 1636, was a nephew of this Jerome Heydon.

Hayes, Captain Edward. He had written of his travels prior to 1583 ; was on Gilbert's voyage to our northern coast in 1583, and wrote an account of the voyage. "A Treatise of M. Edward Hayes conteining important inducements for the planting of those parts and finding a passage that way to the South Sea and China " is annexed to the second edition of Brereton, 1602. "September 16, 1603, grant to Captain Edw. Hayes of pension of £100 per annum for life."

Hayward (see **Haiward**), **Sir Rowland,** clothworker. Elected alderman of Farringdon Without, September 19, 1560 ; chosen sheriff, August 1, 1563. He was president of St. Bartholomew's Hospital from 1572 to his death ; lord mayor, 1570–71, and again in 1591. Died December 5, 1593, and was buried in St. Alphage's Church, London Wall, where the monument to his memory, with the effigies of his two wives and sixteen children, is still preserved. By his first wife,

Joan, daughter of William Tilles-worth, he was father of Joan Hay-ward, who married Sir John Thynne, of Longleat (ancestor of the Marquis of Bath). Sir Rowland married, sec-ondly, in December, 1580, Catherine, daughter of Thomas Smythe (see Smythe pedigree), by whom : 1. Sir George Haiward : 2. Sir John Hai-ward ; 3. Alice Haiward ; 4. Cath-erine, who married, first, Richard Scott (see pedigree), secondly, Sir Richard Sondes, of Throwley, Kent, son of Sir Michael Sondes ; 5. Mary Hayward, married Sir Warham St. Leger ; 6. Anne Hayward, married Edward, eld-est son of Sir William Craford. Mrs. Catherine Smythe-Hayward married, secondly, in 1599, Sir John Scott.

Heale (Hele), Sir Warwick, 2. Sub. £37 10s. ; pd. £62 10s. Eldest son of Sir John Hele, the celebrated serjeant at law. M. P. for Plymouth, 1597–98 ; knighted at Greenwich, May 22, 1603 ; M. P. for Plympton, 1614 ; member of the African Company of 1618 ; high sheriff of Devon, 1619 ; member of the New England Council in 1620 ; M. P. for Plymouth, 1621–22 and in 1625. He married, first, Mary, eldest daughter of John Halse, Esq., of Kenidon, in Devon, and relict of William Hawkins, Esq., of Plym-outh (a descendant and heir of the great admiral) ; and, secondly, Mar-garet, daughter of Sir William Court-enay, knight, of Powderham Castle, but died without issue in January, 1626.

Heath, Robert. Born in 1575 ; called to the bar, 1603 ; recorder of London, November 10, 1618, to Janu-ary 22, 1621 ; member of His Maj-esty's Council for the Va. Co. of London ; patented lands in Virginia, 1619–20 ; member of His Majesty's Council for N. E., November 3, 1620 ; solicitor-general, January 22, 1621, to October 31, 1625; knighted at White-hall, January 28, 1621; M. P. for Lon-don, 1621–22; as solicitor-general took part in colonial affairs ; on Va. Com-mission, July 15, 1624 ; M. P. for East Grimstead in 1624–25 and 1625; attor-ney-general, October 31, 1625, to Octo-tober, 1631 ; received a grant of land between 31 and 36 degrees of north latitude in America, called Carolana, in October, 1629 ; proposed to send Huguenots and others there ; created

serjeant, October 24, 1631 ; chief jus-tice of the Common Pleas, October 26, 1631, to September 14, 1634 ; on spe-cial commission for better plantation of Virginia, June 27, 1631.; king's ser-jeant, October 12, 1636; justice of the King's Bench, January 23, 1641, to October 31, 1643 ; master of the Court of Wards and Liveries, May 13, 1641; chief justice, October 31, 1643, till impeached by Parliament, July 24, 1644 ; fled to France, 1646 ; died at Calais, August 30, 1649.

Heiborne (Hepburne, etc.), Fer-dinando, esquire, 3. Sub. £37 10s. ; pd. £37 10s. Gentleman of the privy chamber to Queen Elizabeth and King James. He married, first, Anne Can-dler, great-granddaughter of Sir Wil-liam Lock who died in 1550 ; was knighted December 20, 1611. Anne (Candler) Heyborne was buried at Tottenham, July 11, 1615. Sir Fer-dinando married, secondly, on April 4, 1616, Elizabeth, daughter of Francis More, Esq., of Sussex. Sir Ferdi-nando was buried at Tottenham, July 2, 1618.

Heightley, Peter. Pd. £25.

Henry, Prince of Wales.— Henry Stuart.

Henshaw, Thomas, merchant-tailor, 2. Sub. £37 10s. ; pd. £75. "Silkman and servant to King James I. ;" an incorporator of the E. I. Co. He died January 11, 1612, aged 76 years, and " his body lyeth under a fair stone at the entrance into the Quire of St. Mary Magdalen Church, Cripple-gate ward, London." " He had to wife Flower Gouldesborough, and had issue by her : 9 sons and 4 daughters."

Herbert, Edward, esquire. Sub. —— ; pd. ——. Son of Charles Her-bert by his wife Jane, daughter of Hugh ap Owen. He was a lawyer of the Inner Temple ; an active member of the Va. Co. during 1619–24 ; a first cousin to George Herbert the poet. Lord Bacon, in his will, desired Sir John Constable to consult Mr. Selden and Mr. Herbert, of the Inner Tem-ple, about the publication of his liter-ary remains. Appointed queen's attor-ney-general, 1635 ; solicitor-general, 1640 ; knighted January 28, 1640 ; attorney-general, January 29, 1641 ; entered an accusation against the five members, January 3 ; impeached by the Commons, February 14 or March 8, 164½; sentenced to imprisonment, April 23, 1653; Charles II.'s lord keeper of the Great Seal, 1653; died in Paris, 1657. He married Margaret, daughter of Sir Thomas Smith, clerk of the Privy Council (widow of the Hon. Thomas Carey), and their son, Arthur Herbert, was created Earl of Torrington.

Herbert, Philip, Earl of Montgomery, 2. Sub. ——; pd. £160. Second son of Henry Herbert, second Earl of Pembroke, by his third wife, Mary, daughter of Sir Henry Sydney; was born about 1582; "being a young man scarce of age at the entrance of King James, had the good fortune, by comeliness of his person, his skill and indefatigable industry in hunting, to be the first who drew the king's eyes towards him with affection, which was quickly so far improved, that he had the reputation of a favorite." He was made a Knight of the Bath at the coronation of King James, July 25, 1603. On the 4th of January, 1605, he married Lady Susan Vere, daughter of the Earl of Oxford, and the letter writers of the time gave the most glowing accounts of the ceremonies, etc. "The bride and groom were lodged that night in the council chamber, where the king, the next morning, in his shirt and night-gown, gave them a *reveille matin* before they were up." He was created Baron Herbert of Shurland, isle of Sheppey, County Kent, and Earl of Montgomery, May 4, 1605; Knight of the most noble order of the Garter, May 18, 1608; M. C. for Va. Co., 1612; an incorporator of the N. W. P. Co., July 26, 1612; a member of the E. I. Co. in 1614. The Folio Shakespeare of 1623 was dedicated to him and his brother, the Earl of Pembroke. An incorporator of the Guiana (South America) Company, May 19, 1627. In 1628 the king granted him certain islands in the West Indies lying between 8° and 13° of north latitude, called "Trinidado, Tabago, Barbudos [Barbuda], Fonseca," etc., and in 1629 he had a hot dispute with the Earl of Carlisle, claiming the Barbadoes, which had been previously granted to Carlisle, as being the Barbuda which was granted to him.

His brother William, Earl of Pembroke, dying April 10, 1630, without issue, he succeeded him as heir and earl. "To his second wife," he married, June 3, 1630, the celebrated Anne Clifford, sole daughter and heir to George Clifford, Earl of Cumberland, and widow of Richard Sackville, Earl of Dorset. "His conduct to her became intolerable some time after their marriage. She separated herself from him, and survived him for many years." She was born January 30, 15$\frac{8}{90}$, and died March 22, 167$\frac{5}{6}$, in her 87th year.

He was interested in Newfoundland in 1639. He took sides with the Parliament against the crown; was sent by Parliament to remonstrate with Charles I. at New Market, March 9, 1642; one of the Parliament commissioners for plantations, November 2, 1643; joint commissioner to present propositions of Parliament to Charles I. at New Castle in July, 1646; as joint commissioner of Parliament received the king from the Scots at New Castle, January 30, 1647; from his apartment, saw King Charles walk from St. James to the scaffold.

In the service of the Commons he had divested himself of every dignity of a nobleman, and in April, 1649, sat in the House of Commons as the representative of Berks. He was one of a committee to examine the business of the Bermudas Islands, December 18, 1649. He died January 23, 1650. The cavaliers hated him, and among their many lampoons was the following: "The last Will and Testament of Philip Herbert, Burgesse for Barkshire, vulgarly called Earl of Pembroke and Montgomery, who dyed of Foole-age, Jan. 28, 1650. With his Life and Death, and severall Legacies to the Parliament and Councill of State. Also his Elegy, taken verbatim, in Time of his Sicknesse, and published to prevent false copies by Michael Oldisworth. Nodnol, 1650." It is said to have been written by Samuel Butler. The will begins: "I, Philip, late Earle of Pembroke and Montgomery, now Knight for the County of Berks, being, as I am told, very weak in body, but of perfect memory (for I remember this time five years I gave the casting voyce to

ROBERT SPENCER

First Baron Spencer

dispatch old Canterbury ; and this time two yeares I voted no addresse to my master ; and this time twelve-month saw him brought to the block) yet, because death doth threaten and stare upon me, who have still obeyed all those that threatened me, I now make my last Will and Testament.

"Imprimis, for my soule : I confesse I have heard very much of souls, but what they are, or whom they are for, God knowes I know not. They tell me now of another world, where I never was, nor doe I know one foot of the way thither. While the King stood I was of his religion, made my sonne weare a cassock and thought to make him a Bishop : then came the Scots, and made me a presbiterian; and since Cromwell enter'd I have been an independent. These I believe are the kingdoms' three Estates, and if any of these can save a soule, I may claime one. Therefore if my Executors doe find I have a soule I give it him that gave it me," etc.

Herbert, William, 2. Sub. ——; pd. £400. Third Earl of Pembroke; eldest son of Henry, second Earl of Pembroke, by his wife, Mary Sidney, "Sidney's sister, Pembroke's mother." Was born at Wilton, Wiltshire, February 8, 1580; educated at New College, Oxford, 1593-95. (Was he not the "Lord Herbert" who was knighted by Essex at Cadiz in September, 1596 ?) He was at home in 1597-98 ; in London about the court, 1599-1600 ; succeeded to his father's honors and estate, January 19, 1601. In 1603 he was much interested in securing the pardon of Sir Walter Ralegh. His mother wrote to him, " conjuring him, as he valued her blessing, to employ his own credit, and that of his friends, to insure Sir Walter's pardon." January 18, 1604, he was made steward of the Duchy of Cornwall, and warden of the Stanneries in Devon and Cornwall, and the same day an incorporator of "the Society of London for Mineral and Battery Works." May 8, 1604, made a Knight of the Garter, and May 14, 1604, lieutenant of Cornwall. M. C. for Va. Co., May 23, 1609. October 16, 1609, made keeper and captain of the tower and isle of Portsmouth, constable of Porchester Castle, and lieutenant of Southbear Forest for life.

An incorporator of the N. W. P. Co, July 26, 1612. The Rappahannock River in Virginia was at one time called Pembroke River, being so named for him. He was interested in the E. I. Co. prior to 1614. An incorporator of the B. I. Co., June 29, 1615, and one of the divisions of the island was afterwards named Pembroke Tribe, for him. Lord chamberlain, December 23, 1615, to 1625. He was constantly interested in advancing the interest of the Va. Co., and was a member of the Council for New England, November 3, 1620. In 1620 he patented thirty thousand acres of land in Virginia, and undertook to send over emigrants and cattle. In July, 1621, Mr. Leech went over to view the country and to locate these lands; and the Council in England instructed Governor Wyatt " *To see that the Earl of Pembroke's thirty thousand acres be very good.*" To which the Council in Virginia replied in January, 1622: "It shall comand from us our best endeavors in chusinge out for his Lordship and his Assocyatts the most comodious Seate that maye be." In 1622-24 he was still a member of the New England and Virginia councils, and was taking an active interest in both colonies.

The great Folio Shakespeare of 1623 was dedicated to him and to his brother Philip, Earl of Montgomery. About 1626 he was made Chancellor of the University of Oxford, and steward of the royal household. Broadgate Hall, Oxford, was remodeled, and named for him Pembroke College. Was an incorporator of the Guiana Company, May 19, 1627. Obtained a grant of the Island of Barbadoes, February 25, 1629, which was revoked April 7, 1629 (previously granted to the Earl of Carlisle). He died suddenly at his house, called Baynard's Castle, in the City of London, April 10, 1630, and was buried in the Cathedral of Salisbury. He was succeeded in his titles, etc., by his brother Philip, Earl of Montgomery.

" He was as generally and deservedly esteemed as any nobleman of his time. He was well-bred ; but his breeding and his manners were entirely English. He was generous, open, and sincere ; loyal, and yet a friend to liberty. Few men possessed a greater quickness of apprehension, or a more penetrating judgment; and none could express themselves with more readiness or propriety. He was a man of letters himself, and an eminent patron of learned men; a distinguished favorer of Shakespeare and his works. But he had, with all his excellencies, a strong propensity to pleasure, and frequently abandoned himself to women." "He married Mary, eldest daughter and co-heir of Gilbert, seventh Earl of Shrewsbury, of the Talbots, and had by her two sons, neither of whom survived infancy." His poems, "edited by John Donne, son of the Dean of St. Paul's," were "printed by Matthew Inman," London, 1630 (the first edition).

Herbert, William, Earl of Pembroke. Knight of the Garter, 1548; Earl of Pembroke, October 11, 1551; was interested in the Rus. Co., 1555; in Hawkins's voyages 1564–69; died in 1570. By his first wife, Anne Parr, sister to Henry VIII.'s last wife, he was the father of Henry, second earl, who was, by his third wife, Mary Sidney, the father of William and Philip Herbert, the earls of Pembroke and Montgomery of the Va. Co.

Heron, Sir Edward, 3. Sub. £37 10s.; pd. £25. Of Langtoft and Stamford, County Lincoln. Reader at Gray's Inn, 1587; recorder of Stamford, 1588; serjeant at law, 1600; knighted in 1603; one of the barons the Exchequer, 1607.

Heron (or **Herne**), **Master Richard,** merchant, 3. Sub. ——; pd. £37 10s. Of the E. I. Co. Was sheriff of London, 1618; esquire and alderman; died February 24, 1625. He was the son of Nicholas Herne, of Tibenham in Com. Norfolk. "Lived at the Blew Anchor in Cheapside, at Foster Lane end." Married Alice, daughter of John Pasck, of Cambridge, D. D., and left issue.

Herrick, Sir William, goldsmith, 3. Sub. £37 10s.; pd. £37 10s. A younger son of John Herrick of Leicester. Was born in 1557; apprenticed in London, about 1574, to his elder brother Nicholas, a goldsmith; succeeded his brother in his business in Cheapside; principal jeweler to King James, or teller to the crown, May 2,

1603; knighted for making a hole in the great diamond for the king, April 2, 1605; M. P. for Leicester in 1601, 1606–11, and 1621–22. He was really one of the king's bankers. A retired merchant of great wealth, about the year 1624, he settled down on his fine estate of Beaumanor Park, Leicester, where he continued to live in right royal style until his death, March 2, 1653, at the age of 96; buried at St. Martin's Church, Leicester. He married Joan, daughter of Richard May, Esq., and sister of Sir Humphrey May. She bore him seven sons and five daughters.

Robert Herrick, the celebrated poet, was his nephew, son of his brother Nicholas, who taught him his trade.

Herst, Gregory. Pd. £12 10s.

Hewit, Sir Thomas, clothworker, 3. Sub. £75; pd. £75. Member of the E. I. Co. Was knighted at Theobald's, December 15, 1613; master of the clothworkers in 1619.

Tho. Hensyet [signature]

Heyward. See Haiward.

Hicks, Sir Baptist, mercer, 2. Sub. £75; pd. £150. A younger brother of Sir Michael Hicks; was born about 1551; was admitted to the freedom of the Mercers' Company, as a retail mercer, gratis, in 1577. He afterwards appears to have followed the trade of a silk mercer, keeping a shop in Cheapside, and by successful application to business, and having great dealings with the court, for his rich silks imported from Italy and other foreign parts, thereby amassed a princely fortune. Upon King James coming to the throne, he was sworn his servant in 1603, and soon after knighted at Whitehall, July 23, 1603; lent the king, at various times, vast sums of money; was one of the first citizens who kept shop after being knighted, and in 1607, having some dispute with the court of aldermen about it, he replied to the effect that "he did not intend to live altogether upon interest, as had been the custom after knighthood; but still intended to have a regard for his trade." M. C. for Va. Co., May 23, 1609.

He built Hicks Hall, 1610–12; **was**

elected an Alderman of Bread Street ward, November 12, 1611. Built the celebrated Campden House about 1612. One of those who purchased the Bermudas Islands from the Va. Co., November 25, 1612, and resigned them to the crown, November 23, 1614. He collected a large sum from the Adventurers for the Va. Co. of London; created a baronet July 1, 1620; M. P. for Tavistock in 1621–22, and for Tewkesbury, 1624–25; member of the royal commission for winding up the affairs of the Va. Co., July 15, 1624; M. P. for Tewkesbury in 1625, 1626, and in 1628.

In 1626 he gave the parish church of Chipping Campden, Gloucestershire, "two gilt comunion bolles with their covers," and in acknowledgment the church-wardens sent him " three couple of chickens, which cost them two shillings and three pence." He was created Baron Hicks of Ilmington, in the county of Warwick, and Viscount Campden of Campden in Gloucestershire, May 5, 1628.

He died October 18, 1629, aged 78, and was buried at Campden, where a magnificent monument was erected to his memory by his widow, Lady Campden (Elizabeth, daughter of Richard May, Esq., of London).

" To the memory of her Dearest and Deceased Husband, Baptist Lord Hickes, Viscount Campden ; Born of a worthy Family in the city of London. Who, by the Blessing of God on his ingenuous endeavours, arose to an ample estate and to the foresaid Degrees of Honour. And out of those Blessings, disposed to charitable uses, in his Lifetime, a large Portion, to the Value of £10,000. Who lived religiously, Virtuously, and generously, to the age of seventy-eight years ; and died October the 18th, 1629."

The following title-page will explain itself : " A Defiance to Death, Being the Funebrious Commemoration of the R^t Hon : Baptist Lord Hicks, &c., late deceased. Preached at Camden in Gloucestershire, November 8, 1629, (by John Ganle). London. Printed by Thomas Harper for Robert Allot, &c. 1630."

Hicks, William. Pd. £30.

Hide, John, grocer, 2. Sub. ——; pd. ——. " Son of Mr. John Hide,

grocer, deceased, and Helen his wife, was sworne a free Brother by Patrimony, March 5, 1603. He did business at the sign of The Baskett at Billingsgate in Thames Street, and was still living in 1617." (From Grocers' Records.) Also of E. I. and N. W. P. companies.

Hide (or Hyde), Lawrence, esquire, 3. Sub. £37 10s.; pd. £37 10s. Second son of Lawrence Hide, of West Hache in Wilts (third son of Robert Hide, of Northbury, Cheshire). He was seated at Heale near Salisbury in Wilts; M. P. for Heytesbury, 1584–85; Chippenham, 1586–87 ; Heytesbury again, 1597–98 ; Marlborough, 1601 and 1604–11 ; attorney-general to Anne, queen of James I. ; knighted at Whitehall, November 7, 1614 ; elected to the Council of Virginia on February 5, 1623 ; married Barbara, daughter of John Baptist Castillon, Esq., of Benham, Berks, by whom he left eleven sons. (See Le Neve's "Knights.") (His brother Henry was the father of Edward Lord Clarendon, whose daughter Anne became Duchess of York, and mother of queens Mary the second and Anne, her successor.)

Hide (or Hyde), Nicholas, esquire, 3. Sub. £37 10s. ; pd. £37 10s. Brother of Sir Lawrence, aforesaid, was born about 1572 (?) ; M. P. for Andover, 1601, Christ Church, 1604–11, Bath, 1614, and Bristol, 1626 ; Lent reader at the Middle Temple in 1617 ; prepared defense of Buckingham in 1626 ; knighted at Whitehall January 28, 1627 ; three days after (31st) appointed a sergeant at law, and five days after (February 5), chief justice of the King's Bench ; died at Hinton Lodge, Hampshire, August 25, 1631. His nephew, afterwards the Earl of Clarendon, studied the law under his guidance.

Hill, Robert, 2. Sub. ——; pd. £87 10s. Clerk of assignments.

Hill, Tristram, 2. Sub. ——; pd. £25.

Himes. See Hawes.

Hine. See Hawes.

924 HINSON — HOLECROFT

Hinson, Tobias, grocer, 2. Sub. ——— ; pd. £45. Entered and sworn to freedom in the Grocers' Company, July 6, 1586.

Hinton (Henton, Hunton, etc.), **Dr. Anthony,** 3. Sub. ——— ; pd. £37 10s. " Docktor in Phisick."

Hinton, Griffin, 2. Sub. ——— ; pd. £12 10s.

Hobart, Sir Henry, 2. Sub. ——— ; pd. ———. I find this name frequently spelled Hubard. Granger says, " the name is pronounced Hubbart or Hubbard." " He applied himself to the study of the Laws ; was called to the bar, June 24, 1584 ; having been entered at Lincoln's Inn, attained such knowledge therein, and grew into such esteem, that in 1597 he was elected one of the Governors of that Society." M. P. for Yarmouth in 1597 and in 1601 ; sergeant at law in 45 Elizabeth ; knighted by King James, July 23, 1603 ; M. P. for Norwich, 1604–11 ; attorney for the Court of Wards, November 3, 1605, and king's attorney-general, July 4, 1606 ; M. C. for Va. Co., May 23, 1609. He was appointed one of the governors of the Charterhouse, at the institution of that great charity, June 22, 1611, and created a baronet, November 22, 1611 ; one of the incorporators of N. W. P. Co., July 26, 1612 ; constituted lord chief justice of the Common Pleas, November 26, 1613 ; which post he filled with notable sufficiency to his death ; sworn a free brother of the E. I. Co., December 5, 1617 ; umpire in the case between the Earl of Warwick and the E. I. Co., March–April, 1620 ; contributed £100 towards new building the chapel of Lincoln's Inn, which was finished in 1623 ; died December 26, 1625. " A great loss to the weal public," as Sir Henry Spelman writes. His " Law Reports " were first published in 1641, and have been frequently republished. He married Dorothy, daughter of Sir Robert Bell, of Beaupré Hall, chief baron of the Exchequer, by whom he had a large family, including the following : Sir John, his successor, ancestor of the earls of Buckinghamshire ; Sir Miles, who married Susan, daughter of Sir John Peyton, and " Robert Hubbard, christened at Hackney Church, September 28, 1606," who was probably

the Robert Hubbard living in Virginia about 1650.

Hobson, Captain Nicholas. " A grave gentleman, who was willing to go that voyage, and to adventure £100, himself." (Gorges.)

Hodges, John, grocer. Sub. £37 10s. ; pd. £50. Elected alderman of Cordwainer ward, July 9, 1622 ; sherriff in 1622–23 ; died in 1629 ; he was colonel of the Archers in 1627.

Hodges, Thomas, merchant-tailor, 3. Sub. £37 10s. ; pd. £37 15s. March, 1620, he gave to Walter Eldred, by will, his three shares in Virginia.

Hodges, William, gent., 3. Sub. ——— ; pd. £25. A captain of the Archers in 1627.

Hodgeson. See Hudson.

Hodsale, John, 3. Sub. ——— ; pd. £37 10s.

Hogan, Gresham, esquire, 3. Sub. £37 10s. ; pd. £37 10s. The son of Edmund Hogan, treasurer of the Company of Cathay (1577–79), and one of the friends, factors, and executors of Sir Thomas Gresham ; who sent to Gresham the memorable " payre of long Spanish silke stockings, which he presented to Edward VI., which was a great present, for Edward's father, Henry VIII., did weare onely cloath hose." Gresham Hogan was also a member of the E. I. Co., and from the records of that company we find that he came to " a violent and wilful end," in 1621, leaving issue.

Hole, William. He engraved the pictures in Coryat's " Crudities ; " the title-page and some of the maps in Camden's " Britannia," etc. He was not a member of the Va. Co.

Holecroft, Captain Jeffrey, 2. Sub. ——— ; pd. ———. Son of Thomas Holcroft, of Battersea in Surrey ; was a captain in the Low Countries.

Holecroft, Captain Thomas, 2. Sub. ——— ; pd. ———. Came to Virginia with Lord De la Warr, in 1610 ; afterwards commanded one of the forts at Kicoughtan, and died there. He was the son of Sir Thomas Holecroft (see next) ; was the last known of the Vale royal family ; married Mary, daughter of the Hon. Henry Talbot (son of George, Earl of Shrewsbury). His widow married Sir William Airmyn (Armyne), baronet (M. P.

for Boston in 1621 and 1624). She was a celebrated woman.

Holecroft, Sir Thomas, 2. Sub. ——; pd. £10. Of Vale Royal, Cheshire; son and heir of Sir Thomas Holecroft, knight (receiver of the Duchy of Lancaster to Edward VI.), by Juliana, daughter and heir of Nicholas Jennings, of Poyeton, alderman of London.

When a young man, in some quarrel, he killed Henry, second son of William, fifth Baron Burgh, and brother to Sir John Burgh; knighted at York, April 17, 1603; gentleman of the privy chamber to King James; M. C. for Va., March 9, 1607; died February 26, 1620, on which day Chamberlain writes, "On Saturday last Sir Thomas Holcroft, an old Knight that long since killed the Lord Burgh's brother, fell down a pair of stairs at his lodging in the Strand, and so bruised his skull that he died this morning" He married, first, Elizabeth, daughter of Sir Edward Fellon, of Gawsworth, Cheshire; second, Elizabeth, daughter of Sir William Reyner, of Overton, Hants. By his first wife he had a son, Capt. Thomas Holcroft, aforesaid.

Holeman, George, grocer, 2. Sub. £37 10s.; pd. £100. Admitted to the livery in 1590, and was on the Court of Assistants of the Grocers for many years, up to 1615. He married, at St. Mary Woolchurch Haw, November 14, 1574, Miss Alice Staper; was a leading member of the E. I. and N. W. P. companies, and gave a thousand pounds towards the new erection of the Church of St. Benet Fink, Broadstreet ward, London. George Holeman, Jr., his son, I suppose was admitted to the livery (Grocers) in 1613.

Holland, Earl of. — Henry Rich.

Holland, (Holliland), Samuel, gent., 3. Sub. ——; pd. £37 10s.

Holland, William. Pd. £12 10s.

Holles, Sir John, 2. Sub. £75; pd. £75. Of Houghton, County Northampton; son of Denzell Holles, Esq.; was one of the band of gentlemen pensioners under Queen Elizabeth and King James; knighted in Ireland by Sir William Fitzwilliam, the lord deputy, in January, 1594; served under his cousin, Sir Francis Vere, and

was with him in the Island voyage; comptroller of the household of Henry, Prince of Wales, 1610; member of the N. W. P. Co., 1612; created Baron Houghton of Houghton, July 9, 1616, and Earl of Clare, November 2, 1624. He died October 4, 1637. The celebrated Denzill Hollis (one of the five members) was his second son by his first wife. "The Earl of Clare was one of Ralegh's earliest and latest friends, in association with whom he had served both in court and in camp, and to whom he was attached by reciprocity of sentiments and similarity of pursuits."

Holt, Christopher, 2. Sub. ——; pd.——. His fair marble tomb in the south wall of the Quire of Alhallowe's Stane, or Stayning Church, Langborne ward, London, contained the following lines:—

"Our Holt (alas!) hath stint his hold,
 by Death cal'd hence in haste,
Whose Christen name being Christopher
 with Christ is better plac't.
In Sawton born of gentle race,
 in London spent his days,
A clerke that serv'd in Custom house,
 in credit many wayes.
So that altho' we feele the losse
 of this so deare a Friend,
His life spent well while he was here,
 hath gained a better end."

Holt, John, gent., 2. Sub. ——; pd. £12 10s. Came to Virginia in 1608.

Hood, Thomas. In Drake's voyage round the world, 1577–80; in Fenton's voyage, 1582–83; was reading a lecture within the Leadenhall on Geometry, Astronomy, and Geography about 1583–84; reading the said lecture in the house of Master Thomas Smith in Gracious Street in 1588. One of those to whom Ralegh made an assignment from his charter for colonization, March 7, 1589. "The use of the Celestial Globe in Plan set foorth in Two Hemispheres. . . . Set Foorth by Thomas Hood, Mathematicall Lecturer in the citie of London, sometimes Fellow of Trinitie College in Cambridge. . . . Imprinted . . . 1590," dedicated to John Lord Lumley and Master Thomas Smith. He also published the "Use of the Jacob's Staffe;" a corrected edition of Bourne's "Regiment of the Sea;" a map; "The Marriner's Guide;" and other works in 1590, 1592, and 1596.

"The making and use of the Geometricall Instrument called a Sector.

. . . Written by Thomas Hood, Doctor in Physicke, 1598."

Hooker, George, gent., 2. Sub. ——; pd. £25.

Hooker, Nicholas, 3. Sub. £37 10s.; pd. £37 10s. "Royston, March 3, 1615. Grant to William Jordan and Nicholas Hooker, of London, nominees of Edward Lord Morley of the sole printing of a small book, entitled ' God and the Kinge ; or, a Dialogue, shewing that our Sovereign Lord, King James, being ymediate under God within his Dominions, doth rightfullie claime, whatsoever is required by the Oathe of Allegiance ;' witĥ instructions for the same to be taught in Latin and English, in all schools, as a means to ' season yonge mindes against the pestilent doctrines of the Jesuits.' "

Hope, Thomas, a tailor. Came to Virginia in January, 1608, and probably returned to England.

Hopkins, John, alderman of Bristol, 2. Sub. ——; pd. ——. February 6, 1610, he wrote to Lord Admiral Nottingham about the taking of a Bristol merchant ship by pirates ; of the pirate Eston, etc. (see State Papers).

Hore, Robert. "A man of goodly stature, of great courage, and given to the study of cosmography."

Hortop, Job. "Borne at Bourne in Lincolnshire ; chief gunner of the Jesus of Lubec; set on shore by Hawkins in 1568; after many miseries he reached Mexico; was a prisoner to the Spaniards for 23 years ; namely, two years in Mexico, one year in the contraction-house in Seville, another in the Inquisition house in Triana, twelve years in the galleys, four years (with the cross of St. Andrew on his back) in the Everlasting-Prison, and three years a drudge to Hernando de Soria. The vessel on which he was confined was taken by an English ship, and he was landed at Portsmouth, December 2, 1590." In 1591 he published an account of his "Travailes," which he dedicated to Queen Elizabeth.

Hoskins, John, esquire, 3. Sub. £37 10s. pd. ——. Youngest son of John Hoskins, M. P. for Hereford ; was born about 1566; was of the Middle Temple ; M. P. for Hereford, 1604–11, 1614, and 1628–29. He made a noted speech in the Parliament of 1614, for which he was committed to the Tower on June 8; but was afterwards enlarged ; made a sergeant at law, and one of the judges of Wales. He died August 27, 1638, aged 72.

Houghton, Lord. — John Holles.

Houlden, William. Pd. £12 10s.

Howard, Charles, Lord High Admiral. Son of William Lord Howard and grandson of Thomas, second Duke of Norfolk ; was born in 1536 ; ambassador to France, 1559; in 1569 was general of the horse under the Earl of Warwick in the army sent against "the Rising in the North ; " succeeded his father as Lord Howard of Effingham in 1573 ; subscriber to Frobisher's voyages, 1576–78. Bourne's "Inventions and Devises " and Hellowes's "Art of Navigation," etc., were dedicated to him in 1578. In 1582 he was a subscriber to Fenton's voyage; lord high admiral of England in 1585. Tanners's "Safety for Sayler ," etc., dedicated to him in 1587. Defeated the Spanish Armada in 1588. Anthony Ashley's account of his exploits in 1588. Daunce's Discourse dedicated to him in 1590; commander-in-chief at sea in the expedition against Cadiz in 1596, distinguished himself there, and is advanced to the dignity of Earl of Nottingham. The first volume of Hakluyt's "Principal Navigations " dedicated to him in 1598. Lieutenant-general of England in 1599, in which year Edward Wright's "Haven finding art " was dedicated to him. In 1605 he was sent ambassador to Spain to take the oath of Philip III. to the treaty of August 18, 1604, which was done at Valladolid, June 15, 1605, and Cervantes wrote an account of the festivities on the occasion. Of the N. W. P. Co., 1612. He retired from service in 1618, and died December 14, 1624, aged 88. He married, first, Katherine, daughter of Henry Carey, first Lord Hunsdon, and secondly, Lady Margaret Stewart, daughter of James, Earl of Moray.

Howard, Henry, Earl of Northampton. Second son of Henry Howard, the celebrated Earl of Surrey, beheaded on Tower Hill January 19, 1547. He was born at Shottisham in Norfolk in 1539 ; educated at Cambridge; restored in blood by the first

Parliament of Queen Elizabeth, 1559. In 1583 he printed at the Earl of Arundel's press, "A Defensative against the Poyson of supposed Prophesies, etc," a very large work. Lodge says, " he was all but a declared Papist, and was strongly suspected of favoring the cause of the Queen of Scots." On January 6, 1604, King James made him constable of Dover and warden of the Cinque Ports, and on March 13 following, created him Baron Howard of Marnhill and Earl of Northampton ; a pensioner of Spain ; Knight of the Garter, February 24, 1605 ; lord privy seal, April 28, 1608 ; was Chancellor of the University of Cambridge, and high steward of Oxford. George Abbot, Archbishop of Canterbury, is said to have secured a letter from the earl to Cardinal Bellarmine, in which he declared " that, notwithstanding the temper of the times compelled him to dissemble, and the king himself urged him to turn Protestant, his heart was still with the Catholics, and he should be ready to aid them in any attempt." (Aiken's " Court of James I." vol. i. p. 442.)

Of N. W. P. Co. in 1612. After an illness of about four months, he died at his mansion at Charing Cross, June 15, 1614, and was buried in the church of Dover Castle. He left no children; his nephew, Thomas Howard, Earl of Suffolk, was his heir. He founded three hospitals: at Greenwich, at Clun in Shropshire, and at Castlerising in Norfolk.

Howard, John, clerk. See Haiward.

Howard, Theophilus, Lord Howard of Walden, 2. Sub. ——; pd. £137 10s. Eldest son of Thomas Howard, Earl of Suffolk, by his second wife, Catherine, daughter of Sir Henry Knevet, and widow of the Hon. Richard Rich, eldest son of Lord Rich. He was, in his father's lifetime, summoned to the House of Peers, during the whole reign of James I. (1603–1625) by the title of Lord Howard of Walden.

M. C. for Va. Co., May 23, 1609. He was an officer in the expedition sent under Sir Edward Cecil to the siege of Juliers in 1610, where he had a noted quarrel with the notorious Edward, Lord Herbert of Cherbury.

He was a member of the N. W. P. and E. I. companies ; was made governor of the Isle of Jersey and castle cornet for life in 1621; succeeded his father as Earl of Suffolk, May 28, 1626; installed at Windsor one of the Knights of the Garter September 24, 1628, being then lord warden, chancellor, and admiral of the Cinque Ports, and the members thereof ; constable of Dover Castle ; captain of the Honorable Band of Pensioners, and one of the lords of the Privy Council. He married Elizabeth, daughter of George Hume, Earl of Dunbar. He died June 3, 1640.

Howard, Thomas, Earl of Surrey, *temp.* Henry VIII. Only son of " Jockey of Norfolk." He defeated the Scots at Flodden September 9, 1513; died May 21, 1524. By his second wife he was grandfather of Charles, lord high admiral. By his first wife he was great-grandfather of Henry, Earl of Northampton ; great-great-grandfather of Thomas, Earl of Suffolk; and great-great-great-grandfather of Thomas, Earl of Arundel, and of Theophilus, Lord Howard of Walden.

Howard, Thomas, Earl of Arundel. Sub. ——; pd. ——. (In reading the Virginia Records, Thomas Lord Arundell of Wardour has been sometimes confused with this Earl of Arundel.) Son of Philip, first Earl of Arundel, the half-brother to Thomas Howard, Earl of Suffolk ; was born 1585–86 ; restored in blood by act of Parliament, 1603 ; married Alathea, daughter of Gilbert Talbot, Earl of Shrewsbury; sworn of the Privy Council, 1607; traveled, 1609–11; K. G., May 13, 1611 ; of the N. W. P. Co., 1612; accompanied Elector Palatine to Heidelberg, 1613; visited Italy, 1613–14 ; joined the Church of England, 1614 ; conducted Gondomar to his first public audience ; of the Va. Co. of London, March 2, 1620; of the New England Council, November 3, 1620 ; earl marshal of England, 1621 ; ambassador to States General, 1633 ; to Emperor Ferdinand II., 1636 (his son, Henry, Lord Maltravers, was granted the county of Norfolk, in Virginia, April 11, 1637) ; went abroad, July, 1641 ; created Earl of Norfolk, June, 1644 ; died at Padua, Italy, October 4, 1646, in his 61st year. The celebrated patron of fine arts ; the collector of the Arundel marbles, and other treasures of antiquity.

Howard, Thomas, Earl of Suffolk, 2. Sub. —— ; pd. £200. Son of Thomas Howard, fourth Duke of Norfolk, by his second wife, Margaret, daughter and heir of Thomas, Lord Audley of Walden; was born in 1561. In 1572 his father, the Duke of Norfolk, was beheaded on account of his efforts in behalf of Mary Queen of Scots.

He was restored in blood by act of Parliament in 1585 ; knighted at sea for gallant service against the Spanish Armada by the lord admiral in 1588 ; commanded the fleet cruising near the Azores in 1591, which was attacked by an overwhelming fleet of Spanish ships, when the bravery of Howard and of Sir Richard Grenville was so conspicuously displayed; distinguished himself at the capture of Cadiz in 1596, and on his return to England was summoned to Parliament as Baron Howard of Walden. One of the commanders in the noted voyage to the Azores in 1597; made a Knight of the Garter May 24, 1597, and soon after constable of the Tower ; sat on the trial of the Earls of Essex and Southampton in 1601.

The house of Howard had suffered much on account of their sympathy for Queen Mary, the mother of King James, and King James did not forget the Howards. Lord Howard was sworn of the Privy Council in May, 1603 ; was created Earl of Suffolk July 2, 1603; sat on the trial of Ralegh ; made lord chamberlain; he was a joint commissioner for the office of earl marshal, February 4, 1604; a discoverer of the Gunpowder Plot, and active in the incidents connected therewith, 1605.

"He refused to become a pensioner of Spain, but his wife, Lady Suffolk, fell an easy victim ; " one of those who sent out Henry Hudson to discover a Northwest passage in 1610, and an incorporator of the N. W. P. Co., July 26, 1612 ; Chancellor of Cambridge University, 1613 ; lord high treasurer of England, July 11, 1614; one of the commissioners for executing the office of earl marshal in 1615, and again in 1617; charged with embezzlement and dismissed from office, July 19, 1618 ; accused, with his lady, in the Star Chamber, October 20, 1619; both sent to the Tower, November 20 ; the earl was liberated November 29, 1619, his lady was regarded as really the guilty one. The earl was restored to royal favor in January, 1620; was earl marshal, August 29, 1621. He died May 28, 1626, at his house near Charing Cross, in London, and was buried at Walden in Essex.

Lodge says, "He was singularly unfortunate in his wife and in two of his children, for they were not only culprits of different casts, but their faults were such as made it necessary to expose them by public investigation ; and these domestic calamities fell the heavier on him, because he was a most kind father and husband, and because, perhaps, they might be traced to a monstrous and perverted effect of his own indulgence.

"He was twice married, but by his first lady, Mary, daughter and co-heir of Thomas Lord Dacre of Gillesland, he had no children. His second countess, of whom so much has been said, was Catherine, daughter and co-heir of Sir Henry Knevet, of Charlton in Wilts, and widow of Richard, eldest son of Robert Lord Rich, one of the most celebrated beauties of her time. By her he had a numerous issue." Their oldest son, Theophilus Lord Howard of Walden, was M. C. for Va. One of the daughters, Elizabeth, married, first, William Knollys, Earl of Banbury (an uncle to Lord De la Warr, governor of Virginia), and, secondly, Lord Vaux, " from which marriages arose the long agitated question as to the legitimacy of her reputed issue by the first husband ; " another daughter was Frances, " whose divorce, from Robert Devereux, Earl of Essex, and subsequent marriage to Carr, of Somerset, disfigure the history of the reign in which they occurred."

Howes, Edmund. Of the N. W. P. Co. He published " The Abridgement of the English Chronicles," editions 1607, 1610, 1611, and 1618 ; also " Stow's Annales continued by Edmond Howes," editions 1615 and 1631. Stith, in his " History of Virginia," p. 229, mentions that the company paid him twelve pounds of tobacco, as a pension for the year 1622, for inserting passages concerning Virginia in his book, and adds, "But he either never performed the service, or is at least a writer of that obscurity and insignificancy that I neither know, nor can find anything of him."

Howell — Howle, Richard, 2. Sub. ——; pd. £12 10s.

Hudson — Hodsdon — Hoddeston, etc., **Christopher.** Second son of Simon Hodsdon, of Hodsdon and of Edgeworth in Com. Middlesex, by his wife Joane, daughter of John Etheredge. He was agent and factor of the Merchant Adventurers in Russia for 25 years, from about 1553 to 1576. In 1578 he was a leading citizen and haberdasher of London ; interested in Frobisher's Northwest voyages ; with others he sent a trading vessel to Brazil in 1580 ; consulted about the colony to the southwest of Cape Breton in 1583 ; interested in Davys's Northwest voyages ; governor of Merchant Adventurers of Antwerp, 1582 to 1601. The date of his death is not known to me. I take him to be the Christopher Hodson who was knighted at Whitehall July 23, 1603, before the coronation of the king. He married Alice, daughter of Alexander Carleill, and sister of Capt. Christopher Carleill (see Sir George Barnes, the elder). His "sole daughter and heyre," Ursula, married Sir John Lee, son of Sir Thomas Leigh of Stoneleigh.

Hudson (see Hodgeson), **John,** 2. Sub. ——; pd. £25. Member of E. I. Co. "June 7, 1619, John Hodgson transferred to Francis Whitner two shares in Virginia, which he passed to Mr. Nicholas Ferrar."

Hughes, Rev. Lewis (of Bermudas Islands), married in 1625, Anne, relict of John Smith, citizen and draper of London at St. George, Botolph Lane.

Lowes Hugges.

Humble, Richard, esquire, 2. Sub. ——; pd. £100. Of Southwark, Vintner, and of Goosehayes, County Essex, esquire. A member of the E. I. Co., and an alderman of London. He died in April, 1616, "and lies buried in St. Mary Overy's Church under a fayre monument." His son, Peter Humble, gent., transferred ten shares in Virginia to John Burgh on May 14, 1623. Richard Humble, Esq., was an ancestor of the present Earl of Dudley.

Hungerford, Sir Edward. M. C. for Va., March 9, 1607, at which date there were two knights of the name ; but I think this was the son of Sir Anthony Hungerford, by his wife Sarah, daughter of Giles Crouch, of Cornhill ward, London, because his mother's sister, Jane Crouch, married John Bargrave, of Bifrons, in the Parish of Patricksborn in Kent, who claimed to have been the first person to establish a private plantation in Virginia.

Hungerford, Sir John, 3. Sub. £37 10s. ; pd. ——. Of Down Amprey, Gloucester ; knighted in 1590 ; M. P. County Gloucester, 1597–98 ; and for Cricklade, 1604–11.

Hunsdon, Lord. — Henry Carey or Cary.

Hunt, Rev. Robert. Probably Robert Hunt, A. M., who was appointed to the vicarage of Reculver, Kent, January 18, 1594, and resigned in 1602. (See Richard Bancroft.)

Huntington, Earl of. — Henry Hastings.

Huntley, Sir George, 3. Sub. £75 ; pd. £25. Son of John Huntley, Esq. He was lord of the manor of Woodchester, Gloucestershire ; died in 1622 ; married a daughter of Sir William Wintour of Lydney.

Huntley, John, 2. Sub. ——; pd. £25. Probably the father of Sir George aforesaid.

Hunton. See Hinton.

Hyde. See Hide.

Idiaques, Don Juan de. He was chief secretary of state and of war to Philip II. of Spain, and one of his confidential advisors in the affairs of the great Armada of 1588. Motley, writing of him, under 1607, says, "But Don John of Idiaquez, who had really been the most efficient of the old administration, still remained in the council [of Philip III.]. . . . There was no disposition on the part of the ancient minister to oppose the new order of things. A cautious, caustic, dry old functionary, talking more with his shoulders than with his tongue, determined never to commit himself, or to risk shipwreck by venturing again into deeper waters than those of the harbor in which he now hoped for repose, Idiaquez knew that his day of action was past." (Motley's "United Netherlands," iv. 353, 354.)

Infantado, Duke de. Don Roderic Dias de Vivar de Hurtado de Mendoza Sandoval de la Vega et Luna, seventh Duke of Infantado, who died in 1657 without issue.

Ingram, Arthur, esquire, tallowchandler, 3. Sub. £75; pd. £75. Son of Hugh Ingram, of London, merchant, by his wife, Anne Galthrope. His parents were married in St. Mary Woolnoth Church, London, May 25, 1562, and he was probably born about 1565–70. He became a member of the Tallowchandlers' Guild, and an active man of affairs; comptroller of the customs for London, 1608, and after; M. P. for Stafford, 1609–11; M. C. for Va. Co., 1612; member E. I. Co.; knighted at Theobald's, July 9, 1613. He married, first, Susan, daughter of Richard Brown, of London, by whom, with other issue, he had Arthur (Sir), his heir, of the same name, knighted July 16, 1621, with whom he is frequently confused. His first wife died prior to 1613, and Chamberlaine says he married (secondly), early in September, 1613, " a young widow, Holyday, a proper woman, worth £3,000. She had withstood an army of wooers, and I think now lighted on the worst." Burke gives her maiden name as " Alice Ferrers." She bore her husband one son, and died in October, 1614. Sir Arthur Ingram was chosen sheriff of London, June 27, 1614, but refused to serve; was sworn cofferer to the king's household, February 25, 1615, and displaced in July following. There was some trouble about the office. Chamberlaine wrote July 20, 1615, " He means, they say, to retire to his place at York, and hath contracted to give Sir Edward Greville £22,000 for the best of his lands, *and to marry one of his daughters* and heirs." He had made extensive purchases in the County of York, including the manor of Temple Newsom (from the Duke of Lennox), where Lord Darnley, the king's father, was born; and he was also interested in the alum mines in that county. He married, thirdly, Mary, daughter of Sir Edward Greville. He was sheriff of York, 1619; M. P. for Appleby, 1621–22, and for York, 1624–25, 1625, 1626, and 1628–29. He died in 1642, and was succeeded by his son, Sir Arthur, who died in 1655, whose son, Henry Ingram, was created Viscount Irvine and Baron Ingram, May 23, 1661; an ancestor of the Marquis of Hertford.

Ingram, David. Of Barking, Essex, and aged about fifty in 1582; was put ashore by Hawkins, October 8, 1568, north of the Bay of Tampico, Mexico; traveled northward, and within twelve months reached the Atlantic coast " about 50 leagues from Cape Britton," where he found a French vessel, which carried him and his two comrades (Richard Brown and Richard Twide) to England, " anno 1569." He was examined by Walsingham and others as to America to the southwest of " Cape Britton," in August, 1582, and the same year published "The Relation" of his travels in America; which was afterwards used by Hakluyt in his edition of 1589; but omitted from the edition of 1599, probably because Ingram had evidently drawn, for some of his descriptions, on Sir Thomas More's " Utopia."

Ingram, Captain John. Member of the N. W. P. Co., July 26, 1612. The charter "grants to Thos. Button, captain of the Resolution, and John Ingram, master of the Discovery, and to the mariners and companies of those ships who set to sea in April, 1612, for discovery of the said passage, and to their executors all customs from December 15, 1616, to December 15, 1617." I take him to be John Ingram, of Milborne, County Cornwall, who was granted a pardon for piracy December 13, 1611.

Ipswick, Bailiffes of, 3. Sub. ——; pd. £100.

Irby, Anthony, esquire, 3. Sub. £37 10s.; pd. £37 10s. Of Whaploab, County Lincoln; was bred to the law; M. P. for Boston, 1588–89; " one of the Masters of the Bench of

ANNE
Queen of James I

the Hon. Society of Lincoln's-inn, London, in 32 Eliz. and the following year Autumn Reader to the Society. His arms were depicted in the third window of the chapel, towards the north." (Collins.) He purchased the manors of Moulton, etc., 38 Elizabeth ; was M. P. for Boston, 1597–98, 1601, 1604–11, 1614, and 1621–22. He was also an alderman and the recorder of Boston. May 23, 1620, he transferred two of his shares in Virginia to Sir Nicholas Tufton ; was buried in Whapload Church, October 6, 1625. Richard Bellingham (afterwards governor of Massachusetts) succeeded him as recorder of Boston. His son Anthony, knighted June 2, 1624 (the ancestor of the Lords Boston), married Elizabeth, daughter of Sir John Peyton, Bart., of Iselham, County Cambridge.

Ironsides, Richard, leather-seller, 2. Sub. ——; pd. £75. Member of the Rus., E. I., and N. W. P. companies. He died in 1627, and lies under "A fair monument on the Northside of the chancel of St. Faith's in Faringdon Ward Within, London."

Isaackson, Powell, 3. Sub. ——; pd. ——. Son of William Isaacson, of Sheffield in County Yorke, by Ellen, daughter of Thomas Waplade of Banbury, Com. Oxford.

Isham George, ironmonger, 2. Sub. ——; pd. £37 10s. Also of N. W. P. Co.

Jackson (see Juxon) **Henry**, 2. Sub. ——; pd. £25.

Jacobson, Peter, of Antwerp, merchant, 2. Sub. ——; pd. £50.

Jacobson, Philip, of Antwerp, jeweler, 2. Sub. £37 10s. ; pd. £62 10s. Of St. Margaret's Parish, in Billingsgate ward, London ; one of the king's jewelers ; was the son of Jacob Jacobson de Antwerp. March 18, 1614, he bought the great diamond of the E. I. Co., paying £535 therefore.

Jacques, Gabriel. Pd. £25.

Jadwine, Thomas, cutler. Sub. £37 10s. ; pd. £75. Son of William Jadwyn, of Barwick, esquire; married Lucy, daughter and heir of Sir John Skillicorne, of Preshall, in County Lancaster, knight. I think the above correct ; but when he died, in 1627, his then wife (possibly second wife) was named Elizabeth. (See his Will in "New Eng. Reg.," October, 1888, p. 393.)

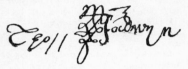

James I. See Stuart.

James, Edward, merchant-tailor, 3. Sub. £37 10s. ; pd. £1. Of E. I. and N. W. P. companies.

James, Thomas, 1. Of Bristol, merchant. William James, from St. John's Brecknock and afterwards of Wollaston and Tidenham, married Margaret Warren. Their son, Thomas James, of whom I write, was " born at Wollaston and married at Almondsbury, to which parish he left a small legacy;" aided in sending out the Maryflowre and other vessels to prey upon the shipping of Spain in 1585 and after. He was sheriff of Bristol in 1591, in which year, on September 14, he wrote a letter to Cecil regarding the discovery of the Island of Ramea near New Foundland. "He was made an alderman of Bristol in 1604, was mayor in 1605 and 1614, and represented the city in three Parliaments, namely, 1597–98, 1604–11, and 1614." M. C. for Va., November 20, 1606; had a dispute with John Whitson in 1616–17. " He died in January, 1619, possessed of considerable property, and was carried to his tomb in St. Mark's Chapel by the four mayor's serjeants. His effigy, kneeling in prayer with an open Bible upon his desk, may yet be seen in the south end of the aisle of the Church of St. Mark."

He left four sons and five daughters. The eldest son, Thomas James, chose the legal profession, and "became a rich barrister at law of the Inner Temple, possessed of all that was calculated to make life easy and happy ; was interested in the supposed North West Passage, left the quietude of his chambers, and adventured his substance and his life in a noble attempt to solve that problem." He made his voyage in the Henrietta Maria, of 70 tons, from May 2, 1631, to October 22, 1632; saw sea service before and after this; died in 1665.

Capt. Thomas James wrote an account of his "Strange and Dangerous Voyage in his intended Discovery of the Northwest Passage into the South Sea," which was published in 1633. "His Map is a singularly correct delineation of the high latitudes for that time."

James, William, Lord Byshopp of Duresme, 3. Sub.——; pd.——. He was chaplain to Robert Dudley, Earl of Leicester, and was the last of his coat that was with him in his sickness. Dean of Durham, 1596 ; bishop, 1606; died May 12, 1617.

Jermyn, Sir Thomas, 3. Sub. £37 10s.; pd. £12 10s. Of Rushbrooke in Suffolk; M. P. Sudbury, 1588–89; knighted by the Earl of Essex before Rouen in 1591; M. P. Andover, 1604–11; Bury St. Edmunds, 1621–22, 1624–25, 1625, 1626, 1628–29, 1640, etc.; was comptroller of the household to King Charles I., and father of the first Earl of St. Albans.

Jewell, James. Pd. £25.

Jobson, Humfrey, gent., 3. Sub. ——; pd. £12 10s.

Jobson, Walter. Pd. £25.

Jobson, William. Pd. £25.

Johnson, Edward, esquire. Of the Inner Temple ; an eminent lawyer ; patented lands in Virginia in 1622 ; one of the commissioners for the Caribbee Islands in 1637; still living in 1642.

Johnson, Humfrey, gent. Sub. £37 10s.; pd. ——.

Johnson, Robert, merchant-tailor. Pd. £60.

Johnson, Robert, grocer, 2. Sub. £60; pd. £241. He was a brother to John Johnson, of Abbot's Anne in Hampshire, Archdeacon of Worcester; sworn a free brother of the Grocers, January 15, 1586, an incorporator of the E. I. Co. in 1600 ; a director of that company in 1606, and frequently thereafter; an incorporator of the N. W. P. Co., and one of the purchasers of the Bermudas Islands in 1612. On the Court of Assistants of the Grocers' Company, 1613; an incorporator of the B. I. Co. in 1615. He was "Director of The Magazine," Deputy Treasurer, and M. C. for Va. Co., and rentor of the Grocers' Company in 1616; sheriff of London, 1617; junior warden of the Grocers and alderman from Cornhill

ward in 1618; a defeated candidate for treasurer and deputy of the Va. Co. in 1619; recommended to that company as a fit person for treasurer by King James in 1620. A witness in Bacon's case, 1621. On October 22, 1622, the New England Council consulted Mr. John Selden and Mr. Robert Johnson, "concerning the heads of ye new Grand Pattent." He was a member of the Smythe faction in 1623; on the commission of July 15, 1624, for the Va. Co. affairs ; governor of the B. I. Co. in 1625, and in 1626 he is mentioned as then "alderman of London, governor of Virginia and Bermudas companies," etc. He had a house at Bow, and Capt. John Bargrave says, "The idea of taking away of the Patent from the Virginia Company was hatched at Alderman Johnson's house at Bow at the King's being there."

He was probably the author of "Nova Britannia" (LXVIII.) and of "New Life of Virginia" (CCX.) and as these show a knowledge of history, he was possibly the Robert Johnson who translated from Botero "An Historical description of the most famous Kingdomes and Common-Weales in the Worlde," which was published in 1601, and again with additions in 1603.

He left an only daughter and sole heir, Martha Johnson, who married Timothy, seventh son of Sir Thomas Middleton, Lord Mayor.

Johnson, Sir Robert, 2. Sub. ——; pd. £56. M. P. Monmouth, 1597 and 1601; clerk of the Deliveries of the Ordnance ; knighted at Whitehall, July 10, 1604; M. P. Monmouth, 1604–11 and 1614.

Johnson, Thomas, fishmonger, 2. Sub. —— ; pd. £62 10s.+£2. A member of N. W. P. Co.

Johnson, Thomas, merchant-tailor. Pd. £1+£25.

Johnson, William, 2. Sub. ——; pd. £37 10s. This name is given as Johnson by Stith; but I take it to be the William Janson or Jonson who paid £37 10s.

Jones, Francis, esquire, haberdasher, 3. Sub. £37 10s.; pd. £37

10s. Son of John Jones, of Claverley in the County of Salop; sheriff of London, 1610–11 ; alderman of Aldgate ward from July 18, 1610; N. W. P. Co., 1612; was a farmer of the customs; knighted March 12, 1617; lord mayor, 1620, and resigned January 22, 1621; resided at Welford and had a town-house in the city in the parish of St. Andrew's Undershaft; died at Welford in 1622.

Jones, Inigo. The great architect; born about 1573; died in 1652.

Jones, Zachary, esquire, 2. Sub. ——; pd. £10.

Jonson (Johnson), Ben. One of the most celebrated English poets ; poet laureate to James I., 1619; M. A., Oxford, July 19, 1620 ; chronologer of London, September 2, 1628; died August 6, 1637, and was buried in Westminster Abbey under a tomb whose only inscription was, " O ! rare Ben Johnson."

Jordan (Jourdan), Samuel, emigrated to Virginia at an early date; was a member of the first Legislature in America " convented att James city in Virginia July ye 30th, 1619," as a representative or Burgess for Charles City, and served on an important committee. His plantation, " Jordan's Jorney," was one of the alliterative names which soon became the fashion in the colony, e. g. : Pace's Pains, Cawsey's Care, Chaplain's Choice, etc., and his residence, ' Beggar's Bush," was possibly the first in the colony to receive a name.

" December 10, 1620, he was granted by patent 450 acres in the Territory of Greate Weyonoke, Charles Cittie." After the massacre of March 21, 1621½, " Master Samuel Jorden gathered together but a few of the stragglers about him at Beggar's Bush, where he fortified and lived in despight of the enemy." Governor Francis Wyatt wrote from Virginia in April, 1622, " that he thought fit to hold a few outlying places including the Plantacion of Mr. Samuel Jourdans; but to abandon others and concentrate the Colonists at Jamestown." July 3, 1622, Mrs. Mary Tue assigned 100 acres of land lying in Diggs his hundred to Samuell Jordan of Charles Hundred, gentleman. He died prior to April, 1623, leaving a wife, Cicely (born in 1600, came to Virginia in the Swan in August, 1611) and at least two children, Mary and Margaret Jordan, both born in Virginia.

Three or four days after Mr. Jordan's death, the Rev. Greville Pooley courted his widow and thought he was accepted ; but some time thereafter she contracted herself to Mr. William Ferrar before the governor and council, and disavowed the former contract. Parson Pooley, however, was not willing to be passed over, and laid his claims before the governor and council, "June 4, 1623, they examined Capt. Isaac and Mary Maddison and Serj. John Harris touching the supposed contract of marriage between Mr. Greville Pooley and Mrs. Cicely Jordan 3 or 4 days after her husband's death." It was too knotty a question for the Virginia court, and they referred it to the Council in London, and on April 24, 1624, the depositions in the case were laid on their table, and after reading same, the court " entreated the Rev. Samuel Purchas to confer with some civilians, and advise what answer was fit to be returned in such a case." I suppose this was the first breach of promise case in our annals.

I am greatly tempted to discourse on the old founder, Samuel Jordan ; but brevity is the rule, and I must resist this temptation. He was probably married more than once, and many very good people, now upholding the country in letters and affairs, claim descent from him.

Joseph, Captain Benjamin. He was killed in a fight with the Portuguese in the East Indies in March, 1617, while captain of the Globe in the service of the E. I. Co. He is spoken of as a man of extraordinary note and respect.

Joshua, John, gent., 2. Sub. ——; pd. £12 10s.

Joy, M. " Afterwards gentleman of the King's chappel."

Juxon, Thomas, Sr., merchant-tailor, 2. Sub. —— ; pd. £25. Son of John Juxon, of London, and uncle of William Juxon, Bishop of London. He was of the N. Fld., E. I., and N. W. P. companies ; died in 1620. (See Will in " N. E. Register," July, 1889, p. 304.) Bishop Juxon attended

Charles I. on the scaffold, and to him the king addressed his last mysterious word, "Remember."

Keile, Sir John, 3. Sub. ——; pd. £25.

Kelke, Sir Charles, 2. Sub. ——; pd. £25. Of Lincolnshire ; knighted at Whitehall, July 23, 1603.

Kendall, Master Abraham. Was on Drake's voyage to America, 1585–86 ; proposal to leave him at Roanoke, June 8, 1586 ; on Dudley's voyage to the West Indies, 1594–95. He died at Porto Bello in Central America in 1597, leaving the plans and papers of which Sir Robert Dudley made good use. Dudley said that John Davis and Abraham Kendall were the best and most expert mariners that England ever had.

Kendall, Captain George. Went to Virginia in the first expedition of 1606–07, and was executed there in the fall of 1607. I believe that he was a cousin to Sir Edwin Sandys. At a little later date we find Edwin and Miles Kendall, cousins of Sir Edwin Sandys, in the Bermudas, and I believe all these Kendalls to belong to the same family. George, Edwin, and Miles were favorite names in the Sandys family. Sir Edwin Sandys of the Va. Co. had a first cousin of the same name living at Latimers, whose daughter Dorothy married a Mr. Kendall, whose pedigree I have not found ; but I believe Capt. George Kendall to be one of this family.

Keneridgebury, Richard, gent., 2. Sub. —— ; pd. £12 10s. (So in Stith ; but the correct name is " Richard Knaresborough.")

Kensington, Lord. — Henry Rich.

Kent, Henry. Pd. £25. Probably Henry Kent, of London, haberdasher, or his son, Henry Kent, Master of Arts and fellow of King's College in Cambridge.

Keth (or Keith), Rev. George. He came to Virginia in 1617 with his wife and son. His wife died in 1624. He held a patent in Elizabeth City in 1626.

Ketley (or Keightley), Thomas, 2. Sub —— ; pd. ——. Was one of the committee of directors of the Va. Co., April 28, 1619 ; an active member of the Sandys party ; had a dif-

ficulty with William Canning in 1623 over the voting on the surrender of the Virginia charter. He married " Rose, daughter of Thomas Evelynge, of Long Ditton in Surrey, Esq."

Kettleby, John, gent., 2. Sub. ——; pd. £25.

Keymis — Kemys, Captain Lawrence. Committed suicide while in Guiana with Ralegh, 1617–18.

Killigrew, Sir Robert, 2. Sub. £75 ; pd. £110. Of Hanworth and Lothburg ; eldest son of Sir William Killigrew, and brother to Elizabeth Killigrew, who married Sir Maurice Berkeley ; M. P. for St. Mawes in 1601 ; knighted at Hanworth, July 23, 1603 ; M. P. for Newport, 1604–11 ; M. C. for Va., 1607 ; M. C. for Va. Co., 1609 ; " committed to the Fleet prison from the council table for having some little speech with Sir Thomas Overbury, who called to him as he passed by his window, as he came from visiting Sir Walter Ralegh in May, 1613 ; " M. P. for Helston in 1614 ; keeper of Pendennis Castle for life, July 7, 1614 ; granted the office of prothonotary of chancery, etc., for life, October 31, 1618 ; M. P. for Newport, 1621–22 ; succeeded to his father's estate in November, 1622 ; a member of the commission for winding up the affairs of the Va. Co. of London, July 15, 1624. According to the " Life of Mr. Nicholas Ferrar," written by his brother, John Ferrar, and edited by Dr. Peckard in 1790, the attested copies of the MSS. Records of the Va. Co. of London (1619–24), now preserved in the library of Congress at Washington, were copied for Mr. Nicholas Ferrar, and by him presented to the Earl of Southampton, " who was afterwards advised not to keep them in his own house, lest search should be made there for them ; but rather to place them in the hands, and entrust them to the care, of some particular friend. Which advice, as the times then stood, he thought proper to follow. He therefore delivered them into the custody of Sir Robert Killigrew, who kept them safely till he died. He left and recommended them to the care of Sir Edward Sackville, late Earl of Dorset, who died in May, 1652." The latter part of this statement must be an error, because Killigrew was really a member of the commission from which these copies were to be especially concealed, and because, it seems, they were really bought by Colonel Byrd directly from the Southampton estate.

In June, 1625, Sir Robert Killigrew was one of "the special commissioners for the affairs of Virginia." M. P. for Penryn, 1624–25; for Cornwall, 1625; for Tregony, 1626; and for Bodmin, 1627–28; "a member of the special commission appointed June 27, 1631, for the better plantation of Virginia." He died in May, 1633, and left by his wife Mary, daughter of Sir Henry Wodehouse of Norfolk, quite a large family, amongst whom, Henry, Thomas, and Sir William Killigrew, the authors. His wife was a niece to Lord Bacon, and he was an uncle to Sir William Berkeley, who was so long the governor of Virginia.

Killultagh, Viscount. — Edward Conway.

King, John, Bishop of London. Was born about 1559; was chaplain to Queen Elizabeth; Archdeacon of Nottingham and Dean of Christ Church; consecrated Bishop of London, September 8, 1611; entertained Pocahontas in 1616; collected £1,000 towards the proposed college at Henrico, Va.; was admitted to the Va. Co., May 17, 1620, and chosen one of His Majesty's Council for Va. Co. Died March 30, 1621, and was buried in St. Paul's.

King, Captain John, 3. Sub. £37 10s.; pd. ——. Master of Prince Henry's ship about 1610. (Possibly one of the Captains King of the Va. Co. went with Ralegh to Guiana in 1617. The only one of his officers who remained faithful to the last, assisting Ralegh in his attempt to escape.)

King, Ralph, 2. Sub. £37 10s.; pd. £62 10s. There were two leading merchants of this name in London at this time. One, a vintner, was churchwarden of St. Mary Woolnoth, and related to John King, Bishop of London. The other, a grocer, who got himself into trouble with the English East India Company by making an adventure to the East Indies in a ship of Brest.

Kingslynne, Towne of, 3. Sub. ——; pd. £75.

Kirkham, Walter, esquire, 3. Sub. ——; pd. £16.

Kirrill. See Carvil.

Kirrill, Richard, 2. Sub. ——; pd. £37 10s. (Kirrell, Kerell, Carril, Carryll, Caryll, etc. The correct spelling is probably Caryll.)

Knaresborough. See Keneridgebury.

Knightley, Richard, esquire. Eldest son of Thomas Knightley, Esq., of Burghall, Stafford; born about 1593; acquired Fawsley on death of his relative, Sir Valentine (next), in 1618; was M. P. Northamptonshire, 1621–22, 1624–25, 1625, and 1627–28; sheriff of that shire in 1626. Died November 1, 1639.

Knightley, Sir Valentine, 3. Sub. £37 10s.; pd. £37 10s. Son of Richard Knightley of Northampton; was M. P. for Tavistock, 1584–85, 1586–87; for Northampton, 1593, and for County of Northampton, 1604–11; knighted May 11, 1603; N. W. P. Co., 1612. Died December 9, 1618.

Knollys, Captain Francis. Afterwards knighted in Holland; was the elder brother of William Lord Knollys; was M. P. for city of Oxford, 1575 to 1589, and for Berkshire, 1597 and 1606–11.

Knollys, William Lord, 3. Sub. ——; pd. ——. Second son of Sir Francis Knollys by his wife, Catharine Cary (first cousin to Queen Elizabeth). He was M. P. for Tregony, 1572–83; County Oxford, 1584–85, 1593, 1597–98, and 1601; was knighted about 1590–92; created Baron Knollys, May 13, 1603, Viscount Wallingford, 1616, and Earl of Banbury, 1626; was successively comptroller of the household, 1590; treasurer of the household, 1601; master of wards, 1616; Knight of the Garter, 1615. Died May 25, 1632, aged 88. (*Vide* Burke, "Extinct Peerage.") He was an uncle to Lord De la Warr, the first lord governor of Virginia.

Lake, Sir Thomas. He was first employed by Sir Francis Walsingham as an amanuensis. By his recommendation Queen Elizabeth appointed him clerk of the signet. He was knighted by King James at Greenwich, May 20, 1603 ; of N. W. P. Co., 1612 ; made a privy councilor in 1614, and joined principal secretary of state with Sir Ralph Winwood in January, 1616, at which time he was a pensioner of Spain. His daughter married William Cecil, Lord Roos, and he became involved in the family troubles with the Countess of Exeter of 1618–19, which resulted in the loss of his secretaryship. He died September 17, 1630, and was buried October 19, following at Stanmore Parva, Middlesex. He is one of Fuller's Worthies of Hampshire.

Lancaster, Sir James. Of the E. I. and N. W. P. companies ; the celebrated navigator ; a native of Bishopstoke in Hampshire ; sailed on a voyage to the East Indies in 1591 ; returning, was wrecked on the island of Mona in the West Indies, 1592; was an incorporator and director of the first E. I. Co., December 31, 1600 ; sailed for the East Indies on the first voyage of the E. I. Co. in 1601, and after his return was knighted at Winchester in October, 1603 ; "possessed of some wealth, lived in his house in St. Mary Axe, and actively promoted all voyages of discovery. He died in 1618."

Landman, Christopher. Sub. £37 10s.; pd. £50. Clerk of the robes and wardrobe to Henry, Prince of Wales. He was one of the bookkeepers of the E. I. Co. in 1614, when he was applauded as one of the most perfect and sufficient accountants in London.

Landman, John. Pd. £25.

Lane, Captain Ralph. "Second son of Sir Ralph Lane, of Orlingbury, and his wife Maud, daughter of William Lord Parr, uncle of Queen Katherine Parr. He was born in Northamptonshire about 1530; entered the queen's service in 1563 ; was an equerry in her court ; served with credit against the rebellion of 1569. Stow describes him as "a projecting man," "a great projector in those times;" in 1574–75 he had a project for raising troops in England to serve against the Turks; in 1576 he "would have monopolized to himself the commission for the restoration of archery," etc., and had several other projects ; was interested in Frobisher's voyages,

1576–78 ; proposed sundry projects against the Spaniards, the kings of Fez and Algiers, etc., 1577–82 ; in 1584 he proposed to the lord treasurer to execute certain laws against "the strangers" forced to England "by reason of the civil wars in the Parts beyond seas;" in 1584 he has certain schemes for Ireland ; February 8, 1585, the queen relieved him from his government of Kerry and Clan Morris, "in consideration of his ready undertaking the Voyage to Virginia for Sir Walter Ralegh at her Majesty's commandment." On the expedition to Roanoke, 1585–86 ; member of the council of war, preparing the defense of England against the Spaniard, November, 1587 ; February 14, 1588, he presented Burleigh with a project for raising troops of horse ; in 1589 he was a colonel in the expedition of Drake and Norris to Portugal. Late in 1589 he had a project about a silver mine at Penrhyn (Penduis ?) "disclosed to him by a mineral man named Hugo Cant of Prague."

He was evidently a "projecting man," and continued to present Burleigh with projects and proposals of various kinds as long as he lived. " He was made muster-master general in Ireland, where he was dangerously wounded ; was knighted by Lord Deputy Fitzwilliam in 1593, and died in 1604 or 1605.

Langham — Langam, Captaine George. " Of London, merchant, one of the Captaines of the city of London." Was still living at the Herald's Visitation of London, 1634, when he records his pedigree.

Langton — Laughton, Thomas, fishmonger, 2. Sub. —— ; pd. £62 10s. "Son of Thomas Langton, of London, who came out of Lincolnshire." Churchwarden of St. Stephen's in Wallbrooke, London, in 1613.

(The names Langton, Langston, Longton, Longston, Langhton, etc., all seem to be used for the same person.)

Latham, Peter, gent., 2. Sub. —— ; pd. £12 10s.

Lawrence, William. Pd. £12 10s. He was probably a brother of Mr. John Lawrence, who bought a share in Virginia from Sir Thomas Gates June 23, 1620.

Lawson, Captain Thomas, 2. Sub. ——; pd. £12 10s. Came to Virginia.

Lawson. See Lewson.

Leate (or **Leake**), **Nicholas,** ironmonger, 3. Sub. £37 10s.; pd. £25. In 1583 he was on the committee of the Mus. Co. appointed to confer with Mr. Carleill upon his intended discovery, etc., in North America. In 1597, Gerarde says, " He was greatly in love with rare and fair flowers, for which he doth carefully send into Syria, and many other countries." An incorporator of the E. I. Co. in 1600 ; a director in 1607, and frequently thereafter ; a member of the committee concerning the plantation in Ulster, January 28, 1609 ; one of those who sent out Hudson to the Northwest in 1610 ; an incorporator and director of the N. W. P. Co. in 1612 ; master of the Ironmongers in 1616. " On the 24th March, 1616, a commission was granted to him and John Dike, to fit out a ship to take pirates and sea-rovers ; his services were very valuable in securing the redemption of captives from the Turks, the Dey of Algiers, &c." He was recommended to the Va. Co. by the king in 1622, as a fit person for deputy ; on the Virginia Commission of July 15, 1624 ; master of the Ironmongers in 1626 and 1627. He died June 10, 1631, and his portrait (supposed to be by Daniel Mytens), was presented to the company by his sons and executors, Richard and Huet Leate, and it is now in the Ironmongers' Hall. He was captain of one of the city trained bands, " a very grave, wise, and well-affected citizen ; who toke very great paynes " in many public improvements about London, as well as in horticultural pursuits.

Leavet. See Lever.

Lee (**Leigh,** etc.), **Sir Francis,** 3. Sub. £37 10s.; pd. £33 6s. 8d. He was the grandson of Sir Thomas Lee, the Lord Mayor of London in 1558, and the son of Sir William, of King's Newenham in County Warwick, by his wife Frances, daughter of Sir James Harington, of Exton. He was made a Knight of the Bath at the coronation of James I.; was M. P. for Oxford, 1601 and 1604–11.

He married the Hon. Mary Egerton,

daughter of Thomas Lord Ellesmere, lord chancellor of England. Their son, Francis Leigh, was created Earl of Chichester.

Lee (or **Leigh**), **Henry,** gent., 2. Sub. ——; pd. £12 10s. Came to Virginia in 1608, and died there in 1609.

Lee, Hugh. " November 8, 1611, grant to Hugh Lee of the office of consul for the merchants trading to Lisbon and Portugal."

Leedes, Sir Thomas, 3. Sub. £37 10s.; pd. ——. Of Suffolk ; made a Knight of the Bath at the coronation of James I., July 25, 1603.

Legate, John, gent., 3. Sub. £37 10s.; pd. ——. " Clerk of the check at Chatham."

Leicester, Earl of. — Robert Dudley and Robert Sidney.

Leigh — Lee, Captain Charles. " Son of John Leigh, Esq., of Addington in Surrey, by his wife Joane, daughter and heir of John Oliph, of Foxgrave in Kent, gentleman, and alderman of London." Charles Leigh's grandmother, Ann Carew, was sister to Sir Nicholas Carew, the grandfather of Sir Walter Ralegh's wife. He was on a voyage to Ramea, in the Gulf of St. Lawrence, in 1597 ; on the West India voyage of the Earl of Cumberland in 1598, " on the 4th of May he left the fleet, and in his owne Barke, called the Blacke Lee, runne himselfe alone for the River of Orenoque." He sailed to plant a colony in Guiana on March 21, 1604 ; died there March 20, 1605, and the colony was abandoned.

Leigh — Lee, Sir Olive (or **Oliph**). Of Addington; born November 24, 1559 ; the elder brother of Capt. Charles Leigh. The vessel which he sent (April 14, 1605) to the relief of his brother's colony never reached there. Sir Oliph Leigh died March 14, 1612. (Sir Thomas Leigh (1639–77), a great-grandson of Sir Oliph Leigh, married Hannah Rolfe, who is said to have been a descendant from John Rolfe and Pocahontas of Virginia.)

Lemos, Count. " Pedro Juan, Count de Lemos, born 1564; president of Council of the Indies, 1603 ; distinguishes himself at siege of Ostend, 1604 ; captain-general, 1604 ; viceroy of Naples, 1612 ; died at Valladolid December, 1634." (Cates.)

Lennard, Sir Samuel, 3. Sub. £37 10s.; pd. £62 10s. Of West Wickham in Kent; born in 1553 ; knighted July 23, 1603 ; benefactor of Hayes ; buried April 15, 1618. He married Elizabeth, daughter of Sir Stephen Slany, alderman of London.

Lenox, Duke of.— Ludovic Stuart.

Leppington, Lord.— Robert Carey or Cary.

Lerma, Duke of. Francisco de Roxas de Sandoval, Duke of Lerma, born about 1545-50. As Marquis of Denia he was the chamberlain to Don Philip, who, when he succeeded to the Spanish throne, in 1598, as Philip III., created his faithful chamberlain, Duke of Lerma, prime minister of Spain, etc. He became the wealthiest and most powerful man in Spain, "the power behind the throne, greater than the throne itself." In 1599 he equipped a fleet against England ; 1602, sent a fleet to assistance of the Irish, which was dispersed by a storm ; 1604, concluded peace with England. He engaged Cervantes to write an account of the festivities and bull-fights with which the Earl of Nottingham, ambassador of King James of England, was received at Valladolid in 1605, when the treaty of August 18, 1604, was ratified on June 15, 1605; in 1608 negotiated a truce with the Dutch; September 11, 1609, procured decree for proscription of the Moors. November, 1616, Carew wrote, " The Duke of Lerma holds his greatness : yet [it is] somewhat diminished by reason of a distraction betweene him and his son the Duke of Uzeda." January, 1617, welcomed Lord Roos as English ambassador to Spain ; 1618, supplanted by his son, the Duke of Uzeda, and, apprehending a storm, took shelter under a cardinal's hat ; created a cardinal by Paul V., he retired to Valladolid, where he took part in the services of the church, passing his old age in devotion and exercises of piety. He died in 1625.

Lever, Thomas, 2. Sub. £37 10s.; pd. £62 10s. (This name occurs as Lever, Leavat, and Leverat.) He was a member of the E. I. and N. W. P. companies also.

Leveson, Sir John, 3. Sub. £37

10s.; pd. £37 10s. Of Haling, Kent, and Lilleshull, Salop ; M. P. for Bossiney, 1584 ; knighted before 1597 ; M. P. for Maidstone, 1597-98 and 1601, and for Kent, 1604-11. He died about December, 1613.

Leveson, Richard, esquire. Second son of the foregoing Sir John Leveson. M. P. for Newcastle-under-Lyne, 1624-25; made a Knight of the Bath at the coronation of Charles I.; M. P. for Salop in 1626, and for Newcastle-under-Lyne, 1640-44 ; Eventually inherited the Lilleshull estate. Died in 1661, without issue, the last male of the Levesons of Lilleshull.

Levett, John, merchant, 2. Sub. ——; pd. £25. (The names, Lever, Leavat, Leverat, Levet, Levette, Leverette, etc., are very confusing in the old records.) Mr. Christopher Levette patented lands in Virginia, and was a member of the New England Council.

Lewellin, Morris, 2. Sub. ——; pd. £37 10s. Of the E. I. Co.

Lewis, Edward, grocer, 2. Sub. —— ; pd. £37 10s. Sworn to the freedom in June, 1593 ; still on the Grocers' books in 1620.

Lewson (or **Lawson**), **William,** mercer, 2. Sub. —— ; pd. £37 10s. Admitted to the Mercers by patrimony in 1605.

Lichfield, Nicholas, esquire, 3. Sub. ——; pd. £6 5s. (See John Middleton.)

Lincoln, Earl of. — Henry Clinton.

Lindesey, Captain Richard, 2. Sub. ——; pd. £25.

Lisle, Viscount. — Robert Sidney.

Litton (or **Lytton**), **William,** esquire, 3. Sub. ——; pd. £37 10s. Of Knebworth, Herts ; eldest son of Sir Rowland Lytton; November 13, 1620, he transferred his three shares in Virginia to Captain Harvey. He was knighted July 23, 1624; was M. P. for County Herts, 1624-25, 1628-29, 1640, and 1640, till secluded in 1648; married Anne, daughter of Stephen Slaney, Esq.; died August 14, 1660, aged 71, and was buried at Knebworth. Ancestor of Lord Lytton.

Lodge, Francis. Pd. £25.

Lodge, Luke, 2. Sub. —— ; pd. £25.

Lodge, Peter. Pd. " in stockins," £12 10s.

Lodge, Sir Thomas, grocer. Alderman of London, 1554; sheriff, 1559; lord mayor and knight, 1562; a leading man in the Merchant Adventurers, traded to Russia, etc.; was interested in the Hawkins voyages, 1562–69. During his mayoralty (1562) he had a terrible scrape with Queen Elizabeth over half a dozen capons; died in 1583; was the father of the poet.

Lodge, Thomas. The poet; son of Sir Thomas Lodge; "a servitor of Trinity College, Oxford;" "studied law at Lincoln's Inn; but afterwards practised medicine;" took the degree of M. D. at. Avignon; first appeared as an author in 1579, as "T. Lodge;" from 1584 to 1595, inclusive, as "T. Lodge of Lincolne's Inne, gentleman;" and during this period most of his poetical works appeared. In 1602 "Tho. Lodge, Doctor in Physicke" translated Josephus. In 1603, under the same address, he published "A Treatise of the Plague," and although he gives certain cures for the same, he died of the plague in September, 1605.

Lok or Lock, Michael. Son of Sir William Lock, alderman, etc.; was born in 1532; left school, 1545; "traveled 32 years (1545–77) through almost all the countries of Christianity;" was captain of a ship for three years in divers voyages in the Levant; had knowledge in languages and in all matters appertaining to the traffic of merchants. Hakluyt used some of his MSS. and maps; a Merchant Adventurer; interested in Frobisher's voyages, 1576–78; still living in 1612, when he published his English translation of Peter Martyr's "Eight Decades of the History of the West Indies," dedicated to his son-in-law, Sir Julius Cæsar. He married, first, Joane Wilkinson, and, secondly, the widow of Dr. Cæsar, the mother of Sir Julius. John Locke, the philosopher, descended from him. (In Queen Mary's reign his sister Rose and her husband Anthony Hickman "sheltred manie of the godlie Preachers (Fox, Hooper, Knox, etc.) in theire house.")

Londonderry, Earl of. — Thomas Ridgeway.

Lore. See Van Lore.

Lorkin, Rev. Thomas. He seems to have been a traveling tutor to Thomas Puckering about 1611, and after to a son of the Earl of Monmouth. He was secretary to the embassy at Paris at the end of the reign of King James and the beginning of King Charles, and is thought to have perished in a storm at sea in November, 1625, when bringing dispatches from Paris to England.

Love, Thomas. Of Plymouth; member of the African Company in 1618. I take him to be the Capt. Thomas Love, afterwards of the New England Company and Council. In the Algiers voyage of 1620 (see Mansell). Knighted at Plymouth, September 23, 1625.

Lovelace, Sir Richard, 3. Sub. ——; pd. £25. Seated at Hurley, Berks; knighted August 5, 1599; M. P. Berks, 1601, Abingdon, 1604–11, Windsor, 1614, and Berks again, 1621–22; sheriff of Berkshire in 1611; created Lord Lovelace of Hurley, May 30, 1627; died in 1634. Fuller says, "He had the success to light on the King of Spain's West Indian fleet; where with he and his posterity are the warmer to this day." ("Worthies of Berkshire.")

Lovelace, Captain William, 2. Sub. ——; pd. ——.

Lovelace, Sir William, 3. Sub. ——; pd. ——. Sir William Lovelace, of Bethersden in Kent, who, I think, was knighted in Ireland in 1599; married Elizabeth, sister of Anthony Aucher, Esq., and died in 1629, leaving with other issue a son, Sir William Lovelace, of Woolwich, Kent (whom I take to be the Capt. William of the Virginia charter, May, 1609). He was knighted at Theobald's, September 20, 1609; M. P. for Canterbury, 1614. "February 12, 1617, Captain Argall and his associates, here under named, allowed several Bills of Adventure for transport of 24 persons, at their charge to Va. viz.: Sir William Lovelace, 1 Bill of £25; Sir Antho. Aucher, 1 Bill of £50; Mabell Lady Cullamore, 1 Bill of £50; John Argall, Esq., 1 Bill of £50; John Tredescant, 1 Bill of £25; Capt. Sam. Argall, 1 Bill of £100." (Va. Records.) Sir William of Woolwich married Anne, daughter of Sir William Barnes, and was the father,

I think, of Mabell Lady Cullamore and of Richard Lovelace, the poet. He was of an elder branch of the Barons Lovelace. Col. Francis Lovelace, probably a brother to the poet, came to Virginia about 1650.

Lower, Sir William, 3. Sub. £37 10s.; pd. £37 10s. Was of Treventy, County Carmarthen, son of Thomas Lower, Esq., of St. Winnow, Cornwall; sheriff of Cornwall, 1578; M, P. Bodmin, 1601, and for Lostwithiel, 1604–11; knighted March 11, 1603; married Penelope, daughter of Sir Thomas Parrott, and died in Wales, April 12, 1615. His widow, in 1619, married Sir Robert Naunton.

Lukin (Lewkin, etc.), Mr. Edward, gent. Sub. £37 10s.; pd. £87 10s. "December 23, 1618. Mr. Edward Lukin renouncing his Prizes in ye Lotteries is to have a Bill of Adventure of £25." (Va. Records.)

Lulls, Arnold, goldsmith or jeweler, 2. Sub. ——; pd. £50. Also of the E. I. and N. W. P. companies. (Mr. Stith has this name as "Hulls.")

Maddison, Captain Isaac. He came to Virginia in 1608, where he was employed in discovering the country, probably in making maps of the rivers, etc., which possibly accounts for the fact that his name is not given in the Smith lists of arrivals for that year. He went to England on business in 1620, and while there, in recognition of his services in Virginia, on July 10, 1621, he was granted two shares of land. He was a leading man in Virginia, and after the massacre of March, 1622, was actively employed against the Indians. In February, 1624, himself and his wife were living at West and Sherley Hundred; but he died before January, 1625, leaving 250 acres of land, planted in the corporation of Charles City. President James Madison is said to have been a member of the same family.

Maddox, Thomas. Pd. £25. He sold his two shares in Virginia to Mr. Stubbs, November 13, 1620.

Maguel, Francis. Probably the same person mentioned in the following abstract from "English State Papers, Domestic," vol. viii. No. 79: —

"December 16, 1610. Examination of Francis Maguer, sailor of Ratcliffe, near London. His meeting with Father Patrick, who tried to persuade him to join some troops to be sent by the King of Spain, to persuade the Irish to rebel. Plots to seize Dublin Castle and to send the Irish regiment from Flanders to Ireland. Met the Earl of Tyrone and Sir William Stanley at the Spanish court."

Francis Maguel, Maguer, or Maguire (?) was probably an adventurer or a spy. Tyrone and Stanley were both regarded in England as traitors (one Irish, the other English) to England at the court of Spain, and both were kept informed regarding affairs in England by correspondents.

Maile (or Moyle), Thomas, gent., 2. Sub. ——; pd. £37 10s.

Mainwaring. See Mannering.

Mallet, Sir John. Of Enmore, County Somerset; married Mary, daughter of Sir John Popham, chief justice of the King's Bench; was made a Knight of the Bath at the coronation of King James, July 25, 1603; M. C. for Va., March 9, 1607; was living in 1614, but probably died before 1620.

Mallory, Sir John, 2. Sub. ——; pd. ——. Of Studley, County York, son of Sir William Mallory, by Ursula, daughter of George Gale; M. P. for Thirsk, 1601, and Ripon, 1604–11; knighted April 17, 1603; married Anne, daughter of William Lord Eure.

Manchester, Earl of. — Henry Montague.

Mandeville, Viscount. — Henry Montague.

Manhood. See Manwood.

Mannering — Mainwaring, Sir Arthur, 3. Sub. £75; pd. £25. Knighted at Charterhouse May 11, 1603; was the carver to Prince Charles, with whom Mrs. Anne Turner (executed for the poisoning of Overbury) fell in love; of the N. W. P. Co., 1612; M. P. for Huntingdon, 1624–25, 1625, and 1626.

Mannering — Mainwaring, Sir Henry. June 10, 1611, granted the office of captain of St. Andrew's Castle, after the surrender of Robert Gosnold. He was a famous sea captain; ranged our coast from the West Indies to Newfoundland; sometime

CHARLES STUART

Prince of Wales, afterwards Charles I.

called "Maynwaring the Pirate;" was pardoned by the king; became lieutenant of Dover Castle; received Gondomar, when he landed there March 5, 1616, with compliments, to which the ambassador "replied by telling him that he would repay him for his courtesy by forgiving him twelve crowns out of the million which he had taken from the subjects of the King of Spain, if only he would promise to make good the rest." He composed and presented to Buckingham, then lord high admiral of England, about 1619, "The Seaman's Dictionary : or An Exposition and Demonstration of all the Parts and Things belonging to a Shippe : Together with an Explanation of all the Termes and Phrases used in the Practique of Navigation." (Captain Smith goes over much the same ground in his "Accidence" of 1626.)

He was knighted at Wolling, March 20, 1618, at which time he was preparing to enter the service of Venice. May 15, 1620, the Earl of Dorset transferred to him ten shares in Virginia; and on the 23d following he transferred five shares to Sir Edward Sackville. His brother Thomas and himself both held lands in Virginia. Early in 1630 Sir Arthur Mannering, Capt. Will. King, and himself petitioned Charles I. for a grant of the uninhabited island, Fernando de Noronha, in about 4° south latitude, and the king was pleased to grant the request of the petitioners.

Mansell—Mansfield, Sir Robert, 3. Sub. £75; pd. £97 10s. The third son of Sir Edward Mansell, by his wife, Lady Jane Somerset, youngest daughter of Henry, Earl of Worcester; was born about 1565. He was probably the "Capt. Mansfield" who was ranging the seas for Spanish prizes as early as 1592. He was knighted by the Earl of Essex for gallantry at the taking of Calais, in 1596; and was captain of the admiral's ship in the fleet under the said earl, sent to the Azores in 1597; vice-admiral of Norfolk in Elizabeth's reign; M. P. for King's Lynn in 1601. In 1602 he destroyed, near Dover, several Spanish ships from Cezimbra, and soon after published "A True Report of the Service done upon certaine Gallies passing through the Narrow Seas." In 1603 he took a carrack freighted with pepper, etc.; in December, 1603, carried a letter from Ralegh to Cecil; in April or May, 1604, he was appointed treasurer of the navy for life, succeeding Sir Fulke Greville; M. P. for Carmarthen County, 1604–11; January 11, 1606, Sir John Trevor and himself recommended Capt. Christopher Newport to Lord Admiral Nottingham for the reversion of the office of one of the principal masters of the navy. August 12, 1606, Mr. John Pory wrote to Sir Robert Cotton, "to attend the King of Denmark on his way homeward Sir Robert Mansell is appointed with the Vanguard and the Moon." M. C. for Va., March 9, 1607; M. C. for Va. Co., May 23, 1609. The court of the E. I. Co. resolve to admit him "as a free brother, without any fine," October 6, 1609; for many years he was one of the directors of the E. I. Co. As treasurer of the navy he was a constant assistant in advancing the interest of the E. I., the Mus. and other companies. He was one of those who sent out Henry Hudson to the Northwest in April, 1610, and also one of those who especially aided in sending out Sir Thomas Gates to Virginia in June, 1611. His ship, the John and Francis, made several voyages to Virginia. He was an incorporator and one of the first directors of the N. W. P. Co., July 26, 1612; M. P. for Carmarthen County in 1614; member of the S. I. or B. I. Co., June 29, 1615; and in the division of the islands one of the tribes was named for him, Mansell's Tribe; but he sold out his interest in the island, and his division was afterwards called Warwick's Tribe. March 15, 1617, Chamberlain wrote to Carleton : "On Tuesday Sir Robert Mansell married his old Mistress Roper, one of the queen's ancient maids of honour; the wedding was kept at Denmark House at the Queen's charge, who gave them a fair cupboard of Plate, besides many good and rich presents from other friends."

As early as June 1, 1615, he was interested in the glass business, and some time prior to May, 1618, the Earl of Pembroke, himself, and some others "had got the sole patent of making all sorts of glass with pit-coal." Just prior to May, 1618, "Sir Wm. Russell bought the treasurership of the navy from Sir Robert Mansell, who is to be made vice-admiral of England;" "May 14, 1618, grant to Sir Robert Mansell of the Lieutenancy of the Admiralty, &c. for life." Member of the Guinea and Binney Company, November 16, 1618. "July 20, 1620, he was appointed vice-admiral [admiral?] for the repression of pirates." The fleet under his command sailed from Plymouth October 12, 1620 ; there is some doubt about the date of its return to England from the Mediterranean. Sir George Calvert, writing to Lord Cranfield, September 12, 1621, says, "The king had been about to recall Mansell from the Straits, but all is set right, and two of the king's ships and ten of the merchants' ships are to stay there," etc. However, he returned some time before March 25, 1622, and J. B. published an account of the "Algiers Voyage in A Journall ; . . . the fleet consisting of 18 sayle, viz., sixe of his Maiesties Ships, Ten Marchants' ships, Two Pinnaces, Under the Command of Sir Robert Mansel Knight, Vice-Admirall of England, and Admirall of that fleet : and a Councell of Warre appointed by his Majestie," etc. The "Councell of Warre" were Sir Robert Mansell, Sir Richard Hawkins, Sir Thomas Button, Sir Henry Palmer, Capt. Arthur Manwaring, Capt. Thomas Love, Capt. Samuel Argall, and Edward Clerke, esquire and secretary.

November 3, 1620, Sir Robert was appointed M. C. for N. E. Co., being then a member of each one of his majesty's colonial councils. In 1622 we find him attending the meetings of the N. E. Council, and some time in this year "Capt. Squibb took possession of Mount Mansell [Mount Desert], in New England, for Sir Robert's use," and in the proposed division of that colony on "Sondaie," June 29, 1623, Sir Samuel Argall drew for Sir Robert lot 15, being the next lot to the northward of Sagadahock. M. P. for Glamorgan in 1624–25, and in 1625 ; for Lostwithiel in 1626, and for Glamorgan again in 1627–28.

April 25, 1635, he was one of those who voted to resign the Great Char-

ter of the N. E. Co. to the crown. In 1638, although advanced in age, he was present at the launching of a ship. "He was continued as vice-admiral of England by Charles I., lived to a very old age, much esteemed for his great integrity, personal courage, and experience in maritime affairs." The date of his death is not known to me ; but he was living and defending his glass monopoly in May, 1642. He is one of the heroes of Scot's "Duellum Britannicum."

Mansell, Sir Thomas, 3. Sub. £75 ; pd. £50. Of Margam in Glamorganshire, was the eldest son of Sir Edward Mansell, and brother of Sir Robert aforesaid. He married, first, on July 30, 1582, Mary, daughter of Lewis Lord Mordant ; she bore him three sons ; after her death he married, secondly, Jane, daughter of Thomas Pole, Esq. M. P. Glamorgan, 1614. He was created a baronet May 22, 1611. Died December 20, 1631.

Manwood—Manhood, Sir Peter, 2. Sub. £37 10s. ; pd. £50. "Eldest son of the most Reverend, excellent, and Learned Judge, Sir Roger Manwood, Lord Chief Baron of the Exchequer." He was M. P. for Sandwich, 1588–89, 1592–93, 1597–98, and 1601 ; made a Knight of the Bath at the coronation of King James I., July 25, 1603 ; M. P. for Saltash, 1604–11 ; M. C. for Va. Co., May 23, 1609 ; M. P. for the County of Kent, 1614, and for New Romney, 1621–22. He was living in October, 1622. The date of his death is not known to me.

Mapes, Francis, 2. Sub. —— ; pd. £12 10s.

Maplesden, Richard, grocer, 2. Sub. £37 10s. ; pd. £50. Of St. Bartholomew, near the Exchange, London ; married in 1593, Frances, relict of Edmund Dawson, of St. Benet Fink, London ; also of E. I. and N. W. P. companies.

March. See Marsh.

Marler, Walter. Son of Walter Marler, the elder, and his wife, Mary Date (or Dale). His mother was a "very good friend to Rev. John Bradford, the martyr, and made him a clean shirt for his burning, which he alluded to in his last prayer as his wedding garment." Walter Marler, the younger, salter, married in 1584, Anne, daughter of Sir George Barnes.

Martin, Christopher. Pd. £25. " Of Billerike in Essex ; " was a partner in Ralph Hamor's plantation, January 15, 1617 ; purchased four shares in Virginia of Capt. George Percy, May 15, 1620 ; sailed for Virginia in the Mayflower in the summer of 1620; landed in New England, " where he and all his dyed in the first infection not long after the arrival." The Mayflower was sent out by the Va. Co. of London. The patent must have been for lands along James River, as no other lands were then being taken up. This company had no right to convey lands north of 40° north latitude.

Martin, Captain John, 2. Sub. ——— ; pd. £95. Son of Sir Richard Martin ; was born about 1560–65. In 1584–85 the Court of Aldermen of London granted him the next reversion of several places, on condition that he should apply himself to the study of the common law. Before he took his degree in law he betook himself to martial affairs. He commanded the Benjamin in Drake's voyage of 1585–86, which passed along our coast. He continued in " martial affairs ; " but I have few particulars of him until he engaged in the Virginia enterprise, to which he devoted his life from 1606 to his death. His biography during this period is embraced in our history, and it will only be necessary to give a brief outline here. His first voyage to Virginia, 1606–08 ; returned to England in July, 1608 ; but went back to Virginia in May, 1609, and remained there until late in 1615, or probably until 1616, when he was in England for a time, and while there he attempted to obtain (under his grant of reversion of 1584–85) the office of " Reader of the Middle Temple," which had become vacant during his absence in Virginia ; but, on the ground that he had devoted himself " to martial affairs," instead of to the law, as he had been required to do, he failed to secure the office, although King James himself, on November 23, 1616, wrote an urgent and flattering letter to the lord mayor (Sir John Lemon) in his behalf.

November 8, 1616, the Va. Co. " allowed Captain Martin in reward ten shares of land in Virginia." He left England in April, 1617, in a pinnace (the Edwin, Capt. George Bargrave ?), and after a five weeks' passage arrived in Virginia about the 20th of May, probably the quickest passage then on record. He located his grant at Martin's Brandon, on the James ; his patent was very broad: " he was to enjoye his landes in as lardge and ample manner, to all intentes and purposes, as any Lord of any Manours in England dothe holde his grounde," etc. This patent was complained of, and was the cause of the first contest in America on charter-rights between " The First House of Burgesses " (July 30, 1619) and their " very loving friend, Captain John Martin, Esquire, Master of the Ordinance." It was for some years " a bone of contention " in the colony and in the company, and forced him to make several trips to England. In January, 1622, William Herbert, Earl of Pembroke, Robert Rich, Earl of Warwick, Robert Sydney, Earl of Leicester, Philip Herbert, Earl of Montgomery, Edmund Lord Sheffield, Sir Robert Mansell, Sir Thomas Smythe, Francis West, William St. John, Robert Johnson, Samuel Argall, and William Canning gave him a very strong certificate in support of his patent ; among other things they certify that " John Martin had been a long and faithful servant of the Colony in Virginia ; a member of the First Council of Virginia ; appointed Master of the Ordinance, fairly in open court ; that he had endured all the miseries and calamities of forepast Times, with the loss of his Blood, the death of his only son . . . [in the undertaking ; in consideration of which things] . . . The Company and Council for his Majesty resident in England had formerly by charter under their Greate Seale granted him special priviledges in his patent, and asking that said Patent should remain in force," etc.

Martin was not a member of the party then in control of affairs, and notwithstanding this strong certificate they took his old patent from him ; offering him a new one, abridging his priviledges, etc., which he refused at first ; but, at last, finding he could do no better, he took the new patent; "which favour he accordingly requited," says Stith, "by propagating and spreading through the Country all the Falshoods and Calumnies against them [the then officers of the company] that he could invent or utter." Very few people would regard an abridgment of their privileges and of their property as a "favour."

October 20, 1623, he was one of those who voted to surrender the charter of the Va. Co. to the crown. The old members who voted generally cast their votes in favor of the surrender; the new members voted against it. The differences between the company and Martin were finally composed, and on February 2, 1624, the council gave him a very favorable letter to the governor of Virginia, which was signed by William Herbert, Earl of Pembroke, Philip Herbert, Earl of Montgomery, William Lord Padgett, William Lord Cavend'sh, Sir Robert Killigrew, Sir John J'anvers, Sir Humphrey May, John White, and Nicholas Farrar, deputy. He returned to Virginia in the Swan, in 1624; was appointed to the council there by royal commission, August 26, 1624. He was residing in Elizabeth City, and owned Martin's Brandon "by Patent out of England (planted)" in 1625.

The date of his death is not known to me; he was living in Virginia March 8, 162⁹⁄₉, on which day he wrote to his brother-in-law, Sir Julius Cæsar; he was then over sixty years old.

The accounts of him, like the accounts of many of our founders, have been based on unfriendly evidence; but justice does not permit us to condemn him without giving him a hearing, and although we have nothing that he wrote in his own defense, we know that he devoted his life to the colony, and this fact speaks much better for him than if he had devoted this time to untrustworthy volumes of self-praise. Captain Smith has given us his opinion of Martin, and we can very well imagine what Martin thought of Smith.

He fills an unknown grave, probably at Brandon, on the James. His dust aids in making the soil of the Old Dominion sacred, and we will not forget that he was the only man to protest against the abandonment of Virginia on the memorable morning of June 7, 1610.

Martin, John, gent., 2. Sub. ——; pd. £25. Was the only son of Capt. John Martin, aforesaid. He died at Jamestown, in Virginia, August 18, 1607.

Martin, Richard, goldsmith. Son of Thomas Martin, of Saffron Walden, in Essex; was born early in the sixteenth century. The churchwardens of St. Mary Woolchurch Hawe, London, bought a "Communyon Cuppe" from him in 1560. Queen Elizabeth farmed out her mint to him early in her reign; warden of the mint before 1572; interested in Frobisher's voyages, 1576–78; alderman of Farringdon Within, 1578; sheriff of London, 1581–82; lord mayor, 1589, "when he gave up to the lord treasurer an account of the debts owing to him," etc. : —

Due by the Jewel-House	£1,300
By Pearls for her Majesty	50
The Lady Leicester	2,500
Lent to the Earl of Leicester upon the Manor of Denbigh	550
Due from Mr. Huddleston	1,826
Due by the Earl of Derby and his Son	1,200
For The Adventure with Sir Francis Drake in his 1st voyage when he went about the world	2,000
Ventured also with Sir Francis, since that, to Carthagena (1585–86), also with Fenton and Wm. Hawkins, together with Divers other Sums	16,600

Making a total of over £26,000, a very large sum at that time; president of Christ's Hospital, 1593 to 1602; again lord mayor, 1594; advised Essex to submit himself to the queen, February 8, 1601; displaced from his offices August 31, 1602, the reasons assigned were his poverty and debt; the real reasons were the debts due him by the court party. In November, 1604, James I. made him master of the mint again; was the oldest alderman then living in 1605. On September 11, 1610, a warrant was issued to pay him £410 due to him by the late queen; December 10, 1611, he was paid £160 for sundry models, tools, and engines for improvement of the coin. He was buried in Tottenham Church, July 30, 1617. Chamberlain says, "He was held near a hundred years old." His wife Dorcas was buried in the same church, September 2, 1599, and his son Richard, May 28, 1616. His daughter

Dorcas, the wife of Sir Julius Cæsar, died June 15, 1595, and was buried in the Temple Church, London. His son, Capt. John Martin, fills an unknown grave in Virginia.

Martin, Richard, esquire, 2. Sub. £37 10s. ; pd. £75. Granger says he was "born at Otterton, in Devonshire [others say 'son and heir of William Martin of Exeter']; studied at Oxford, and afterwards at the Temple [admitted to the Middle Temple, November 7, 1587]. His learning, politeness, and wit were the delight and admiration of all his acquaintance. He understood and practiced the grace of conversation, and was equally esteemed and caressed by Selden and Ben Jonson. His person and manners qualified him to adorn the court, and his eloquence to influence the senate." He was a member of the celebrated club of intellectual men who met the first Friday of every month, at the Mermaid in Bread Street, "an association certainly unrivaled in any preceding time, unequaled by any subsequent assemblage, and in all probability not likely to be witnessed in our own days." Old Fuller says, "He had an excellent pen," and "was accounted one of the highest wits of our age and his nation." John Davies (afterwards Sir John, attorney-general for Ireland, author of "Nosce Teipsum," etc.) dedicated "Orchestra" to him in 1594 or 1596 ; but soon after fell out with him, and was expelled the Temple in February, 1598, "for thrashing his friend, another roysterer of the day, Mr. Richard Martin, in the Middle Temple Hall. . . . Martin (whose monument is now hoarded up in the Triforium of the Temple) also became a learned lawyer and a friend of Selden, and was the person to whom Ben Jonson dedicated his bitter play, 'The Poetaster' [1602]. In the dedication the poet says, 'For whose innocence as for the author's you were once a noble and kindly undertaker : signed, your true lover, Ben Jonson.' " (Thornbury's " Old and New London.")

He was frequently a member of Parliament, and in the Parliament of 1601 spoke most eloquently against the monopolists ; M. P. for Barnstaple, 1601. On May 7, 1603, he was selected to welcome King James to London, and in the name of the sheriffs of London and Middlesex made a most learned and eloquent oration before the king ; M. P. for Christ Church, 1604–11 ; M. C. for Va. Co., 1612. From 1611 he took an active interest in the Bermudas Islands, and in 1615 was an incorporator of the B. I. Co.

In May, 1614, he made his noted speech in behalf of the Virginia Colony, before Parliament ; was Lent Reader at the Middle Temple in 1615. On the death of Sir Anthony Benn, September 29, 1618, King James recommended Martin to the city of London for their recorder, and he was chosen to the position, but died about a month after, of the small-pox, on Sunday morning (November 2 ?), 1618, and was buried in the Temple Church, London.

" Anglorum alumnus, præco Virginiæ ac parens." Martin's Hundred, containing some 80,000 acres, about seven miles below Jamestown, on the north side of James River, was named for him.

Martin, Thomas, gent., 3. Sub. —— ; pd. £37 10s. M. P. 1614.

Mason, Captain, 2. Sub. ——; pd. ——. (I believe this to be Capt. John Mason, of King's Lynn, the founder of New Hampshire, in New England, who died in London in 1635.)

Mason, George. Pd. £12 10s.

Masse, Father Ennemond. Came to America with Father Biard in 1611; went to Canada in 1633, and died there at the house of Saint Joseph de Sillery in 1646, aged 72.

Matthew, Tobias, Archbishop of York. Son of John Matthew, a merchant of Bristol ; was successively Archdeacon of Bath, Prebendary of Sarum, Dean of Christ Church, Dean and Bishop of Durham, whence he was translated to York, September 11, 1606. Died March 29, 1628, and was buried in York Cathedral. He married Frances, daughter of William Barlow, Bishop of Chichester, who brought him three sons, one of whom, named for his father, went over to the Church of Rome.

Maude (or Mande), Josias, 2. Sub. —— ; pd. £12 10s.

Maunsell, Peter, 2. Sub. £37

10s. ; pd. £75. Born in Dorset ; entered Brasenose College, Oxford, 1587; B. A., 1591 ; M. A., 1594 ; pursued the study of physic, 1595–99 ; traveled abroad at Paris, Padua, etc., 1600–04 ; afterwards followed his studies at Oxford and Gresham College in England ; made a second tour abroad, visiting the universities of Basil and Strasburg ; was at Leyden in 1607, prior to which time he took the degree of Doctor of Physic ; chosen to succeed Dr. Gwynne in his professorship in Gresham College in September, 1607 ; remained there until his death. He was buried in St. Helen's, Bishopsgate, October 18, 1615. "Reader of the Phisick Lecture in Gresham College."

Maurice, Count. Of Nassau ; Prince of Orange ; born 1567 ; died 1625.

Mawdet, Otho, merchant - tailor, 2. Sub. —— ; pd. £62 10s. Married Elizabeth, daughter of William Downes by his wife, Elizabeth Rolfe ; left a sum of money to pay a fee to the preacher at St. Dunstan's in the West, London, for a sermon to be delivered on the 28th of October annually.

May, Humfrey, esquire, 3. Sub. —— ; pd. £37 10s. Fourth son of Richard May, of Rawmere, County Sussex ; M. P. for Beeralston, 1604–11 ; knighted at New Market in January, 1613 ; M. P. for Westminster, 1614 ; chancellor of the Duchy of Lancaster, 1618 ; treasurer, 1618–22 ; M. P. for Lancaster, 1621–22 and 1625 ; and for Leicester, 1624–25, 1626 and 1628–29 ; elected to the Virginia council in May, 1623 ; on the commission for Virginia, July 15, 1624 ; one of the executors of Bacon's will ; on the Canada commission about the goods taken by Captain Kirke, 1630 ; master of the rolls, and sworn a privy councilor in 1629; died June 9, 1630.

Maycott, Sir Cavaliero, 2. Sub. £175 ; pd. £175. Knighted at the Tower, March 14, 1604; granted license to travel for three years, May 18, 1604 ; M. C. for Va. Co., 1612; living in 1624. The date of his death is not known to me. He was probably of the same family as Capt. Samuel Macock, Esq., a Cambridge scholar, a gentleman of birth, virtue, and industry, and a member of the governor's council in Virginia, who was killed by the Indians, March 21, 1622, at Master Macock's Dividend in the Territory of Great Weyonoke.

Maynard, Sir William, 3. Sub. —— ; pd. £37 10s. Of Estains, Essex ; was knighted March 7, 1609 ; M. P. for Penryn, 1610–11 ; created a baronet, June 29, 1611 ; N. W. P. Co., 1612 ; M. P. for Chippenham, 1614 ; created Baron Maynard in Ireland, May 30, 1620, and in England, March 14, 1628 ; elected to the Council of Virginia, February 5, 1623. March 17, 1638, he wrote to Archbishop Laud about the exodus to New England : "Hears daily of incredible number of persons of very good abilities, who have sold their lands and are upon their departure thence." He died December 18, 1639.

Meadows — Meddus — Medhurst — Medust, Dr. James, 2. Sub. —— ; pd. £15. Chaplain to King James ; also interested in the Bermudas and Newfoundland.

Mease (or Mays), Rev. Mr. William. He was in England in 1623, at which time he had lived ten years in Virginia. Whether he returned to Virginia or not, I know not.

Medici, Mary de, queen of France. Born 1573; married Henry IV., 1600; crowned May 13, 1610, and left a widow the next day; regent of France to October, 1614 ; died in 1642.

Menendez de Avilés, Pedro. A native of Avilés in Asturias ; was born about 1519. His adventures began when he was only eight years of age. Before he reached the age of manhood, he had distinguished himself in cruises against the Barbary corsairs and the French, and soon thereafter he made a successful voyage to the New World. In 1557 he was captain-general of the fleet which conveyed Spanish troops to St. Quentin, where he shared in the honors of the victory of August 10. In 1559 he commanded the Armada which carried Philip II. back to Spain. In 1560 he was general of the fleet to New Spain, and was instructed by his king to examine, on his return voyage, the Atlantic coast north of Port Royal (South Carolina); and the royal order of September 23, 1561, cites that he had done so, and had made his report thereon to the king. About this time charges were brought against him, and he was imprisoned and fined. Returning from one of his voyages to the West Indies, about May, 1563 (see Froude's " England," vol. viii. pp. 450, 451), he found five brigs from Bristol and Barnstable, at the Azores, which he took and carried to Spain, because they not only neglected to salute the Spanish flag, but continued to carry the cross of St. George at the main.

In 1564 " he was required to make a thorough coast-survey of Spanish Florida so as to prepare charts that would prevent the wrecks which had arisen from ignorance of the real character of the sea line." He wished to conquer and to settle Florida, and on March 20, 1565, Philip II. granted him a patent for that purpose, with the title of governor and captain-general of Florida. He reached that coast August 28, and massacred the Huguenots at Fort Caroline September 21–23, 1565. On October 15, following, he wrote Philip II., proposing to colonize and hold the country by means of a series of forts, at the Chesapeake Bay, Port Royal, the Martyrs, and the Bay of Juan Ponce de Leon. He went to the West Indies in December, 1565, but returned to St. Augustine in March, 1566 ; in Spain in 1567; sailed from San Lucar, March 13, 1568 ; arrived in Florida to find that his colony had been recently destroyed by Dominic de Gourges, and from CCCLX. it seems that he was in command of the Spanish fleet which made the attack on Hawkins in the bay of Mexico on September 23, 1568, just three years after his massacre of the Huguenots, and less than five months after the massacre of the Spaniards by De Gourges. Thus one

event begets another : the murder of the Huguenots, — the murder of the Spaniards, — the betrayal of the English, — the Drakes, the Hawkinses, the avengers, and the final wresting from Spain of a large part of her American possessions.

Menendez had been appointed governor of Cuba, and he was variously engaged in the West Indies and in Florida during 1568–70. In 1570 he had a mission established at Axacan in the Chesapeake Bay, probably on the Rappahannock River, where the party was massacred by the Indians February 8, 1571. He was in Spain in 1571, returned to Florida in 1572, and sailed to the Chesapeake Bay himself, where he captured eight Indians known to have taken part in the murder of the Jesuits (February 8, 1571), and hanged them at the yard-arm of his vessel. On his return to Spain he was appointed to command the great Armada which Philip II. was collecting for an expedition against England and Flanders ; but before it was ready to sail Menendez died quite suddenly at Santander, September 17, 1574, aged 55.

Parkman says, " It was he who crushed French Protestantism in America." And yet it seems that he took part in kindling the spark at the City of the True Cross (September, 1568) which had a wonderful influence on the final plantation of English Protestant colonies in this country.

He was a celebrated admiral, a commander of the order of Santiago, and was styled " conqueror of Florida." The Spaniards regarded him as " a great hero, and the greatest mariner known in his time." He had much of the country which now is Virginia, North and South Carolina, Georgia, and Florida explored, and is said to have made " more than fifty exploring voyages to and in the West Indies by which he facilitated the navigation of the Atlantic, which before him was very difficult and dangerous."

Dr. Shea gives an account of Menendez in the " Nar. and Crit. Hist. of America," vol. ii., and Dr. Parkman gives his portrait and a sketch of his life in " Pioneers of France in the New World."

His only son was lost at sea near

the Bermudas in 1561, and he was succeeded as governor and captain-general of Florida by his nephew, Pedro Menendez de Avilés, son of his brother, Gen. Alvaro Sanches de Avilés. It was this nephew, I suppose, who made the survey, took the soundings, and wrote the "exact description" of the Chesapeake Bay in 1573. The exact date of his death is not known ; but it seems from CCCLX. that he was living when Drake made his attack on St. Augustine in 1586. He was slain by the Indians, probably soon after.

I infer from the will of his son (of the same name) dated at Valladolid, December 18, 1618, that there had been a long lawsuit about the title of governor, and "the capitulations of Florida." I am not certain who was really in authority there during the time of which we write (1605–16) ; but it is important to keep Florida in mind, while making a study of the early history of Virginia.

Merrett (or **Marriott, Maryot,** etc.), **Humfrey,** 3. Sub. £37 10s.; pd. £12 10s. A Huguenot.

Merrick, John, merchant, 2. Sub. £37 10s.; pd. £75. Son of William Merrick, of Gloucester ; a member of the Rus. Co., he was for many years the agent of that company in Muscovia, where he obtained many trading privileges for the English merchants. He was also of the E. I. Co. In 1610 he aided in sending out Hudson; an incorporator of the N. W. P. Co. in 1612; knighted at Greenwich June 13, 1614, and sent ambassador from King James to the Emperor of Russia. June 30, 1614, Chamberlain writes : "Sir John Merricke, my brother George's wife's uncle, is gone ambassador into Muscovy. He was knighted and made a gentleman of the privy chamber, and well graced by the king before his going. He carries about thirty men in liveries, besides seven or eight gentlemen, whereof Becher [afterwards Sir William Becher], that was with the Lord Clifford, is one put to him by Mr. Secretary, for that there is some business to be done betwixt the Muscovite and the King of Sweden, by his Majesty's mediation, wherein he may serve as secretary." Sir John was instrumental in negoti-

ating the treaty between the Emperor of Russia and Gustavus Adolphus of Sweden, which was signed at Stolbova February 27, 1617. He returned to London in November, 1617, bringing with him a Russian ambassador, who brought the king presents of white hawks, live sables, etc.; again ambassador to Russia, 1620–22 ; afterwards governor of the Mus. Co.; M. P. for Newcastle-under-Lyme, 1640, and 1640 till secluded in 1648 ; sergeant-major in parliamentary army, and president of the council of war in 1642, and afterwards general of the ordnance. He married, first, Frances, daughter of Sir Francis Cherry, of London, for whom Cherry Island was named; and, secondly, Dame Jane Witch, at Putney, on May 1, 1647, when he must have been very old.

Merry, Thomas, esquire, 3. Sub. ——; pd. ——. "Clerk compt'ler." knighted at Auckland in Durham in 1617. He was the cousin and executor of John Puntis, vice-admiral of Virginia, who died in 1624.

Meteren, Emanuel Van. Flemish historian, born 1535 ; died 1612.

Mewtis, Captain Thomas, 2. Sub. ——; pd. ——. Lost a limb in the service; probably served under Sir Francis Vere in the Low Countries ; on August 16, 1608, Vere wrote to the Earl of Salisbury that Captain Mewtys had slandered him; knighted at Whitehall, February 10, 1611. Still living in 1614. His sister Frances was the second wife to Robert, Earl of Essex ; his sister Jane Meautis married, first, Sir William Cornwallis, secondly, Sir Nicholas Bacon, K. B. His first cousin, Thomas Mewtis or Meautis, of Westham in Essex, was the father of Frances Meautis, who married Sir John Thorogood, the brother of Capt. Adam Thorogood of Virginia, whose widow, Sarah, or Susan (Offley), married, secondly, Capt. John Gookin, and, thirdly, Col. Francis Yeardley, son of Sir George.

Michelborne, Sir Edward, 2. Sub. —— ; pd. £12 10s. M. P. for Bramber, 1592–93; captain in the fleet at the Azores under Essex in 1597 ; knighted by Essex at Dublin August 5, 1599 ; "a citizen and alderman of London and an incorporator of the East India Company in December,

1600; but before the company was incorporated, on October 3, 1600, the lord treasurer wrote a letter to the company, trying to persuade them "to accept of the employment of Sir Edward Michelborne on the proposed voyage to the East Indies, as a principal commander;" but they resolved not to employ any gentleman in any place of charge or command in the voyage, and begged the lord treasurer "to give them leave to sort their business with men of their own quality." Sir Edward evidently did not submit gracefully to this decision, and on July 6, 1601, he was "disfranchised out of the freedom and priviledges of this fellowship, and utterly disabled from taking any benefit or profit thereby," by order of the court of the E. I. Co. However, Sir Edward was determined to make a voyage to the East Indies, and on June 18 or 25, 1604, he obtained "license to discover the countries of Cathaia, China, Japan, Corea, and Cambaia, &c., and to trade with the people there, *notwithstanding any grant or charter to the contrary.*" He sailed from the Cowes December 1, 1604, in the Tiger, a ship of 240 tons, "with a Pinnasse called the Tigres whelpe." On December 27, 1605, Capt. John Davis, his second in command, was killed in a fight with the Japanese. Returning to England, he came to an anchor in "Portsmouth Roade" July 9, 1606. On August 12, 1606, Mr. John Pory wrote to Sir Robert Cotton that "Sir Edward Michelbourne hath cleared himself with great honour."

M. C. for Va., March 9, 1607. On January 26, 1608, he was consulted by the E. I. Co. regarding the fittest places for trade in India, etc., and among other places he called their attention to Mocha, since so famous for its coffee. He was buried the 4th day of May, 1609, at Hackney, near London.

Middlesex, Earl of. — Lionell Cranfield.

Middleton, John, esquire, 3. Sub. ——; pd. £6 5s. Nicholas Lichfield and himself, as partners, invested in a single share (£12 10s.) in the Virginia enterprise, and the auditors, in auditing the accounts, divided it, assigning a half to each. (He was probably the M. P. for Horsham, 1614–29, and of a distinct family from Robert.)

Middleton, Robert, skinner, 2. Sub. ——; pd. £37 10s. Also of E. I. and N. W. P. companies; M. P. Melcombe, 1604–11, and for London, 1614. Maurice Abbott and himself represented the English E. I. Co. in their negotiations with the Dutch E. I. Co. in 1614–15. He was a brother to Sir Hugh Middleton, founder of the New River, London, and of the next.

Middleton, Sir Thomas, grocer, 2. Sub. £37 10s.; pd. £62 10s. Son of Richard Middleton, Esq., governor of Denbigh Castle, times Edward VI., Mary, and Elizabeth ; apprenticed to Ferdinando Pointz of the Grocers' Company, London ; admitted to freedom, January 14, 1582, and to the livery, March 21, 1592; M. P. for Merioneth, 1597–98 ; paid £20 as his share of the loan to Queen Elizabeth in 1598 ; an adventurer in the East India voyage of 1599, and an incorporator of the E. I. Co. in 1600; elected alderman for Queenhithe ward, May 24, 1603; chosen sheriff, June 24, 1603; knighted at Whitehall, July 26, 1603; alderman for Queenhithe ward, 1603 to 1613 ; he removed to Coleman Street ward, March 22, 1613, and was alderman for that ward until his death in 1631 ; Lord Mayor of London, 1613–14. The New River Head was opened by his celebrated brother Hugh, with great pomp, on the day of his election to the mayoralty on Michaelmas Day (September 29), 1613. On August 1, 1621, "yt pleased the Right Worshipful Knight, Sir Thomas Middleton, to make a very religious speach and exhortation to the whole assemblie of the Misterie of the Grocerie of London." M. P. for London 1624–25, 1625, and 1626; died August 12, 1631 ; a benefactor of the Grocers' Company. "Purchased the manor of Stansted Montfichet, in Essex, where he lyes buried with a long Epitaph." A merchant father of the city ; had four wives. His first wife was Hester, daughter of Sir Richard Saltonstall.

Mildmay, Sir Henry. Sub. ——; pd. ——. There were three knights of this name at this time. Two (and probably all three) of them were interested in the American enterprise.

In reading the records of the time it is frequently impossible to tell the one from the other ; but the following extract from the Mildmay pedigree will give their relationship to each other : Thomas Mildmay, of Chelmsford in Essex (living 1521), left four sons: 1. Thomas, 2. William, 3. Walter, and 4. John.

1. Thomas married Avise, sister of Benjamin Gonson, and their son, Sir Thomas, was the father of Sir Thomas (baronet) and of Sir Henry (the first) of Woodham Walter ; knighted June 19, 1607.

2. William married Elizabeth Pascall, and their son, Sir Thomas, married a daughter of Adam Winthrop of Groton (grandfather of Gov. John Winthrop of Massachusetts), and were the parents of William (who married Margaret Hervey, the cousin of Capt. Edward Maria Wingfield) and of Sir Henry (the second), knighted at Dublin Castle May 25, 1605, who married Alice, daughter of Sir William Harris and niece of Sir Thomas Smythe.

3. Walter, the privy councilor and founder of Emmanuel College, Cambridge, married Mary, sister to Sir Francis Walsingham, and their son, Sir Humphrey, of Danbury Place, Essex (where Capt. John Smith sometime found a sanctuary, and where he " writ," as he tells us, his " Advertisements for the unexperienced Planters of New England or any where "), was the father of Sir Henry (the third), knighted at Kendall, August 9, 1617. Master of the jewel office, 1618; married, in April, 1619, Ann, daughter of Alderman Halliday (who died in 1623, and his widow Susanna, afterwards married Robert Rich, Earl of Warwick). He sat on the trial of Charles I. in January, 1649, and was a member of the Privy Council under the commonwealth.

4. John, of Cretingham in Suffolk, was the father of Robert Mildmay, grocer, of London.

Mildmay, Robert, grocer, 2. Sub. £37 10s. ; pd. £37 10s. Of Lomber Streete, London, and Tarling in Essex; was apprenticed to Henry Stryckeland, grocer ; admitted freeman, 1587 ; paid £10 as his share of loan to Queen Elizabeth in 1598 ; member of the Court of Assistants, October 22,

1613 ; made rentor for the year 1616 with Robert Johnson ; elected alderman of Vintry ward, September 19, 1626, but refused to serve, and was fined £500 ; member of the E. I. and N. W. P. companies. He married, first, . . . daughter to . . . Cranfield, and, secondly, Jane, daughter to Sir Richard Deane, and was still living in 1634.

Mildmay, Thomas, esquire, 3. Sub. £37 10s. ; pd. £12 10s. Son of Sir Thomas, of Moulsham, who was first cousin to Avis Gonson, the wife of Sir John Hawkins ; M. P. for Maldon, 1593; created a baronet, June 29, 1611 ; married twice, but died s. p. February 13, 1626.

Miller, John, 3. Sub. —— ; pd. £37 10s.

Miller, Sir Robert, 3. Sub. £37 10s. ; pd. £37 10s. Of Dorset ; knighted at Whitehall, July 23, 1603.

Millet, William, grocer, 3. Sub. —— ; pd. £37 10s. Of E. I. and N. W. P. companies ; died in 1631 ; a benefactor to the parish of Norwood, etc.

Mitchell (or Michell), Sir Bartholomew. Of Nottinghamshire ; knighted at Whitehall, May 12, 1604 ; M. C. for Va., March 9, 1607. (Related to the Pophams ?)

Mockett, Master Doctor (Richard). Warden of All Souls College, Oxford ; author of " Politia Ecclesiæ Anglicanæ," which was burned in 1616, and Mocket is said to have died from the shock of the humiliation.

Moles, Captain Henry. Pd. £25.

Molina, Diego de. E. I. Co. Records, June 12, 1618 : " Letter read from Henry Bacon, lately returned from Sir W. Ralegh's voyage, stating that Mollina, who was prisoner in Va., incites the king of Spain to send forces to suppress Virginia, by the hopes of a silver mine there, from which he shows a piece to justify the truth thereof."

Monger, James, 2. Sub. —— ; pd. £25. Of St. Michael Basishaw, London, gent. ; married, in 1622, Susan, daughter of William Hammond.

Monmouth, Earl of. — Robert Carey.

Monsell. See Maunsell.

Monson, Sir Thomas, 2. Sub. —— ; pd. ——. Elder brother of Sir

ELIZABETH STUART
Queen of Bohemia

William (the next); born about 1566; knighted in 39 Elizabeth ; created a baronet, 1611; M. P. Crickdale, 1614 ; a great lover of music ; died in May, 1641.

Monson, Sir William. Third surviving son of Sir John Monson ; born about 1569 ; from his youth in the sea service ; became a celebrated admiral. In his naval tracts, he recited the names of the ships in which he served, as follows: " In the Charles, whereof I had no command in 1588 [the year of the Spanish invasion] ; in the Victory, in which voyage I was vice-admiral to my lord of Cumberland, 1589 ; in the Garland, 1591; the Lion, 1593 ; the Rainbow, 1595 ; the Repulse, 1596 [he was knighted by the Earl of Essex at Cadiz in 1596] ; the Rainbow, 1597 [the Island voyage] ; the Defiance, 1599 ; the Garland, 1600 ; the Nonpareille, 1601 ; the Swiftsure, 1602 ; the Mary Rose, 1602 ; the Mere Honour, 1602 [his noted voyage with Sir Richard Levison to the coast of Spain and Portugal in 1602] ; the Mere Honour, 1603 ; the Vengeance, 1604 ; the Rainbow, 1605; the Assurance, 1606 ; the Rainbow, 1607 ; the Vengeance, 1609; the Assurance, 1610; the Rainbow, 1611; the Adventure, 1612 ; the Assurance, 1613 ; the Lion, 1614 ; and the Nonsuch, 1615." He was a pensioner of Spain. Early in 1616 Sir John Digby returned from Spain with evidence, implicating the Earl of Somerset, Sir Robert Cotton, and Sir William Monson, the vice-admiral, in certain clandestine negotiations with Spain. "It was popularly reported that Sir William Monson was under an agreement to carry over the English fleet to the Spaniards." He was committed close prisoner to the Tower, January 13, and " sett at libertye," July 17, 1616. In 1620 he patented lands in Virginia with certain conditions (see Stith, p. 184). In 1635 he was vice-admiral of the fleet sent out to " restore the ancient sovereignty of the narrow seas to the King of England." He was seated at Kinnersley in Surrey ; died in February, 1643, and was buried in St. Martin's in the Fields, London.

Montague, Sir Henry, 2. Sub. —— ; pd. ——. Born at Boughton, Northamptonshire, in 1563. "In his tender years it was foretold of him that he would raise himself above the rest of his family." Educated in Christ's College in Cambridge and in the Middle Temple in London ; called to the bar of the Middle Temple ; M. P. for Higham Ferrers, 1592–93, 1597–98, and 1601 ; recorder of London, May 26, 1603, to November 16, 1616 ; knighted at Whitehall, July 23, 1603 ; M. P. for London, 1604–11 ; M. C. for Va., November 20, 1606 ; M. C. for Va. Co., May 23, 1609 ; sergeant at law, 1611 ; M. P. for London, 1614 ; lent the E. I. Co. £8,000 at 8 per cent. in 1615 ; conducted the prosecution of the Earl and Countess of Somerset, 1616. " Upon his resignation of the Recordership of London he was presented with two hundred double sovereigns by the corporation, as a thankful remembrance for his many careful endeavours for the city." Chief justice of the King's Bench, November 18, 1616, to December, 1620 ; admitted a free brother of the E. I. Co., gratis, December 16, 1617 ; presided on the trial of Sir Walter Ralegh, 1618; lord treasurer, December 14, 1620, to 1621. " He was made lord treasurer by the interest of Buckingham, but was pulled down the next year by the hand that raised him, as he was not sufficiently obsequious to that haughty favorite." Lilly, the astrologer, tells us in the " Memoirs of his Own Life," that " the Lord Chief Justice Montague was on his trial found guilty by a peevish jury ; but petitioning King James by a Greek petition (as indeed he was an excellent Grecian), *By my Saul,* said King James, *this man shall not die, I think he is a better Grecian than any of my Bishops.*" Raised to the peerage as Baron Montague of Kimbolton and Viscount Mandevil, December 19, 1620 ; lord president of the council, October, 1621. In 1623, while investigating the affairs of the Va. Co. of London, he became convinced that they were not well managed. He examined the letters " that make a map of the Colony's misery," and " the business appearing very foul, many at first unwilling were now content to have it ripped up ; " that " relieved they must be, and that presently," and it was determined to annul the charter and take the colony under the protection of the crown. June 24, 1624, the Lord President Mandeville was one of the committee appointed by order of the Privy Council "to resolve upon the Well-settling of the Colony of Virginia and to give order for the Government." July 15, 1624, he was one of the royal commission for winding up the Va. Co. of London ; created Earl of Manchester, February 5, 1626 ; keeper of the privy seal, 1627; "one of the commission for making laws and orders for government of English colonies planted in foreign parts, April 28, 1634."

"He departed this life on November 7, 1642, and had sepulture at Kimbolton, where a noble monument is erected to his memory."

The Kimbolton Manuscripts, Duke of Manchester Records, contain many papers of interest and of value relative to our foundation. I have copies of some of them, which have been of much service to me in compiling this work, although they are generally of a later date than 1616.

Montague, James, Lord Bishop of Bath and Wells, 2. Sub. ——; pd. £75. "Fifth son of Sir Edward Montague, of Boughton, and grandson of the celebrated Sir Edward Montagu (1490–1557), the lord chief justice, times Henry VIII. and Edward VI., and brother to Sir Henry Montague, the lord chief justice, time James I. ; born about 1568; educated at Christ's College in Cambridge ; the first master (in 1598) of Sidney College in that university, to which he was a great benefactor. He may indeed be traced through all his preferments, by his public benefactions and acts of munificence. He was noted for his piety, virtue, and learning. When the university went to meet James I. on his coming from Scotland, his majesty

first took notice of him at Hinchinbroke (the seat of the loyal Sir Oliver Cromwell, uncle to the usurper), and was so pleased with his conversation as a scholar, and his behavior as a gentleman, that he first made him Dean of the royal chapel, and afterwards Dean of Worcester on the 17th of December, 1604 ;" consecrated Bishop of Bath and Wells, April 17, 1608; M. C. for Va. Co., May 23, 1609.

"In 1616 he was translated to the opulent Bishoprick of Winchester. Also for his faithfulness, dexterity, and prudence, King James, who did ken a man of merit as well as any prince in Christendom, chose him to be one of his Privy Council, and, that he might be near him, continued him dean of his chapel, not only when he was Bishop of Bath and Wells, but of Winchester likewise, during which time he translated his majesty's works into Latin. He was a nursing father to Sidney College, and to the University of Cambridge in general no small benefactor, in bringing running water, at a great expense, into King's Ditch, which being at first made for its defence, was become nauseous to it. He laid out large sums in repairing and beautifying the church and episcopal palace at Wells, and in finishing the church at Bath, in which he desired to be buried. He died July 20, 1618, aged fifty, and was interred on August 20 following, on the north side of the church ; and over the grave is an altar-monument erected between two pillars of the same church, with his effigies in full proportion painted to the life, lying thereon."

He was a great admirer of James I., and was a favorite of that king's.

Monteagle, Lord. — William Parker.

Montford. See Mountford.

Montgomery, Earl of. — Philip Herbert.

Montmorencie, Henry de, admiral of France. Son of Henry I., Duke de Montmorency ; was born at Chantilly, April 30, 1595; became the idol of the French court ; grand admiral of France, 1612 ; succeeded his father in the Duchy and as governor of Languedoc, 1614 ; corresponded with Ralegh, 1616–17 ; chevalier, 1620 ; marshal of France, December

11, 1630 ; executed at Toulouse, October 30, 1632. He attempted in vain to resist the rising power of Richelieu.

Moone, Nicholas. Pd. £12 10s. **Moore, Adrian,** 2. Sub. £37 10s.; pd. £100. Of the E. I. Co.; a partner with William and Ralph Freeman and John Eldred in the preëmption and transportation of tin, 1608, and many years after. Howes, writing under the date 1615, says, "In the Tyme of Queene Elizabeth there was a Lecture of the Chiefe Mathematicall Sciences, viz : Geometry, Astronomie, Geographie, Hydrographie, and the Art of Navigation read in the chappell of Leadenhall, but now it is discontinued. But at this daie there is a lecture of Cosmography read in the Blackefryers in the house of Adrianus Marius," [Adrian Moore?].

He was seated at Odyam, Hants; and married Anne, daughter of Sir Nicholas Parker; after his death his widow married Sir John Smith.

More, Sir George, 2. Sub.——; pd. £150. Son and heir of Sir William More, of Loseley, by his first wife, Margaret, daughter and co-heir of Ralph Daniel, Esq., of Swaffham in Norfolk; born November 28, 1553 ; educated at Exeter College, Oxford; M. P. for Guildford, 1584–85, 1586–87, 1588–89, and 1592–93 ; guardian of Edward, afterwards Lord Herbert of Cherbury; knighted at Whitehall on Shrove Tuesday, 1597 ; M. P. for Surrey, 1597–98 ; sheriff of Surrey and Sussex in 1598; succeeded his father, who died July 20, 1600. He had a grant from the crown, 43 Elizabeth, of the lordship and hundred of Godalming; M. P. for Surrey. 1601. In 1600 his daughter Anne (born 1584) was married against his wish to John Donne, afterwards Dean of St. Paul's. (More was not then lieutenant of the Tower as sometimes stated.) M. P. for Guildford again in 1604–1611 ; appointed receiver-general to Henry, Prince of Wales, in 1604. On January 21, 1606, he made a motion in Parliament for more severe laws against popery, "seconded by Sir Francis Hastings, and thirdly by the king's solicitor: the motion prevailed." In 1606 he had the honor of entertaining James I., at Loseley; M. C. for Va., Novem-

ber, 1606. February 14, 1610, in the debate " on the question whether Sir George Somers' seat in Parliament was vacant by his going to Virginia," Sir George More said, " That Sir George Sommers ought not to be removed. That it was no disgrace; but a grace to be Governour in Virginia." In 1610 he was made Chancellor of the Garter. In 1612, an incorporator of the N. W. P. Co.; in 1614, M. P. for Surrey. In November, 1615, he was appointed lieutenant of the Tower of London; received the warrant for Ralegh's release, January 30, 1616; sold the lieutenancy to Sir Allen Apsley for £2,500, and was succeeded by him in that office, March 3, 1617; M. P. for Guildford in 1621–22 and 1624–25, and for Surrey again in 1625; died October 16, 1632.

He married Ann, daughter and co-heir of Sir Adrian Poynings, Knt., and widow of —— Knight, Esq., of St. Denys, Hants, by whom (who died November 19, 1590) he had issue, four sons and five daughters.

More (or Moore), John, esquire, 2. Sub. ——; pd. ——. Recorder of Winchester ; M. P. for Winchester, 1597 and 1604–11.

More (or Moore), John, esquire, 2. Sub. —— ; pd. ——. Recorder of Lymington in 1606; M. P. Lymington, 1624–25, 1625, and 1626.

More, Richard. The first governor of the Bermudas, 1612–1615. He went with Ralegh to Guiana, and died there in 1617.

More, Sir Thomas. Born in London, 1480 ; an envoy to Charles I., at Bruges in October, 1514, and again in May, 1515. While on one of these embassies, he pretended to have gotten the material for his " Utopia " from a Portuguese who had " run the same hazard as Americus Vesputius and bore a share in three of his four voyages that are now published." He may really have met with one of the companions of Vespucius. The " Utopia " was first printed at Louvain in 1516. The " New World " probably made its first appearance on the English stage in " A new interlude and a mery of the nature of the iiii. elements." It has been assigned to various dates from 1510 to 1520, and is thought to have been printed by

More's brother-in-law, John Rastel. One of the characters is one "Experyens" (Experience), who tells of his travels in " . . . this newe lands founde lately, Ben callyd America, by cause only Americus dyd furst them fynde." More was no mean actor, and we are told that when an interlude was being performed he was apt to take a part. Considering the relationship of Rastel and More, and the similar Vespucian idea of the " Interlude " and " Utopia," and More's taste for interludes, it seems probable that he was the author of this one. It also seems certain that in England, as early as 1515, Americus Vespucius was regarded as the discoverer of this continent, by such men as Sir Thomas More, Sir Thomas Eliot, and John Rastel. Possibly America is rightly named after all.

Sir Thomas More was privy councilor about 1519; speaker of the House of Commons, 1523 ; lord chancellor, 1529–32 ; committed to the Tower, April 17, 1534; beheaded before the Tower, July 6, 1535. The " Utopia " should be especially interesting to us, as it is an idea of a perfect republic in the newly discovered America. More's sister Elizabeth married John Rastall the printer, and was the mother of M. Rastel who came to America in 1536, and this fact again illustrates the interest taken in the New World by the family.

Morer (or **Moorer**), **Richard**, grocer, 3. Sub. ——; pd. £25. Of All Hallows Barking ; a leading grocer ; possibly related to the Rev. Richard Hakluyt. He was on the Virginia Commission of July 15, 1624, and on the Tobacco Commission of November 9, 1624. He married, in 1608, "Bridgett Carliell of St. Swithin, spinster, daughter of Lawrence Carliell late citizen and skinner of London, deceased."

Moreton (or **Morton**), **Ralph**, gent., 2. Sub. ——; pd. £30. Came to Virginia in 1607.

Morgan, Sir Charles, 2. Sub. —— ; pd. ——. Of Herefordshire; knighted at Whitehall, July 23, 1603; served in the Thirty Years' War; was a personal friend to William Herbert, Earl of Pembroke.

Morgan, Captain Matthew. Serving in the Netherlands, 1586–87; knighted before Rouen, 1591 ; M. P. Brecknock, 1593; at Cadiz, 1596.

Morris, Thomas, 2. Sub. —— ; pd. £87 10s.

Morrison, Sir Richard, served in the Low Countries and in Ireland; knighted at Dublin, August 5, 1599; died in 1625. His daughter Letitia married Lucius Carey, the great Viscount Falkland.

Morton, Dr. Thomas. Born at York, March 20, 1564 ; chaplain to James I., 1606; Dean of Gloucester, June 22, 1607; Dean of Winchester, November 7, 1609; Bishop of Chester (1615), of Lichfield and Coventry (1618), and Durham (1632); committed to the Tower, April, 1645 ; died in Northamptonshire, September 22, 1659. His daughter Ann married, first, David Yale, and, secondly, Theophilus Eaton, the first governor of the colony of New Haven (Connecticut).

Mountaine (or **Montaigne**), **Dr. George**, 3. Sub. ——; pd. £12 10s. " Deane of Westminster ;" born at Cawood in Yorkshire ; was chaplain to the Earl of Essex, and attended him on his voyage to Cales ; afterwards one of the chaplains to King James; Rector of Cheam, 1609; Dean of Westminster, 1610–17 ; Bishop of Lincoln, 1617–21, and of London, 1621–28. He conferred holy orders on the celebrated Rev. Hugh Peters, and was interested in the plantation of Guiana, South America, 1628. Archbishop of York in June, 1628, and died October 24, 1628. One of Fuller's " Worthies of Yorkshire."

Mountford (or **Momford**), **Thomas**, esquire, 2. Sub. —— ; pd. £20. Came to Virginia in 1607.

Mouse (or **Mowse**), **Arthur**, fishmonger, 2. Sub. £50. ; pd. £37 10s. Second son of Richard Mowse, of Wooborne in Com. Bedford, by his wife Elizabeth, daughter and heir of John Scot, of Northfleete in Com. Kent, esquire, captaine of the Blockhouse at Gravesend. Arthur was living at the Visitation of 1634, and was alderman's deputy for the ward of Walbrooke. Was a benefactor of the Fishmongers.

Mulgrave, Earl of. — Edmund Sheffield.

Muncke, Levinus. "A Dutchman, who came young into England ; one of the secretaries to the Earl of Salisbury ; one of the keepers and registrars of papers and records concerning matters of state and council; one of the clerkes of the signet. January 8, 1619, he was one of the commissioners for settling differences between England and the United Provinces, concerning trade into the East Indies, and was afterwards one of the committee of the English E. I. Co.

John Chamberlain, Esq., wrote to Sir Dudley Carleton from London on June 14, 1623, " Leonus Moncke died lately, very rich for a clerk of the signet; his estate falling out, they say, toward £40,000."

His daughter, Jane Muncke, married Richard Bennett, of London.

Mundy, Jervis, 3. Sub. £37 10s.; pd. £12 10s.

Munks, Lawrence, grocer, 2. Sub. ——; pd. ——. Sworn to freedom March 7, 1597.

Murray, Sir David, 3. Sub. £75; pd. £137 10s. One of the household of Henry, Prince of Wales ; came with him from Scotland, and never quitted him till his last breath ; N. W. P. Co., 1612. He wrote "The Tragicall Death of Sophonisba," published in 1611, and dedicated to Prince Henry. He also wrote " Sonnets to Coelia " (1611), and " A Paraphrase of the CIV. Psalm, 1615." He went in the train of Lord Hay to France in 1616, and was interested in the making of brimstone and Danish copperas in 1617.

Murray, Sir James. A confidential servant to King James.

Mutes (or **Molex**), **Philip.** Pd. £12 10s.

Napier, Sir Robert, knight and baronet. See Robert Sandy, grocer.

Nelson, Master Francis. " Probably the third son of Thomas Nelson, Esq., of Cheddleworth, Berks, by Mary, daughter of Stephen Duckett, Esq., of Colne." He made voyages to Virginia in 1606–07, in 1607–08, and in 1609 ; N. W. P. Co., 1612. In April, 1612, he sailed from England with Capt. Thomas Button, and died in Hudson's Bay in the winter of 1612–13, at " Port Nelson," which was named for him, and he was buried there, near the mouth of Nelson's River

(named for him), which, it was then hoped, would prove to be a ready way to the Great South Sea.

Neville, Sir Henry, of Billingbear, Berkshire, 2. Sub. £37 10s.; pd. £37 10s. Eldest son of Sir Henry Neville, Senr., by his wife Elizabeth, daughter and heir of Sir John Gresham. The celebrated Sir Thomas Gresham left by his will to his nephew, Harry Neville, when he should attain the age of twenty, the sum of one hundred pounds. M. P. for Windsor in 1584–85, 1585–86, and 1592–93 ; sheriff of Berkshire, 1594 ; knighted by Essex for gallantry at Cadiz in 1596 ; M. P. for Liskeard, 1597–98; ambassador to France, April, 1599, and first commissioner for England at the treaty of Boulogne in the summer of 1600. His correspondence with Ralph Winwood, 1599–1600, has been published. He returned to England about October, 1600, and became implicated in " the Essex insurrection," February, 1601, for which he was committed to the Tower. " April 10, 1603, the Earl of Southampton and Sir Henry Neville were this day delivered out of the Tower by a warrant from King James." M. P. for Berkshire, 1604–11 ; M. C. for Va., March 9, 1607. In September, 1607, he obtained license to travel for three years, with his son and William Symondson, fellow of Merton College, Oxford, and while on his travels, in April, 1609, he was " arrested for a pirate by mistake." He then returned to England. M. C. for Va. Co., May 23, 1609.

On the 26th of May, 1609, Dudley Carleton wrote to Sir Thomas Smith, that " his wife was brought to bed on Ascension Day, and begs him to join with Sir Henry Neville as sponsor, in making this young Cockney a Christian."

After the death of the Earl of Salisbury in May, 1612, Sir Henry Neville was an applicant for the secretaryship. June 17, 1612, Chamberlain wrote to Carleton that " Sir Henry Neville has failed of the Secretaryship because of the flocking of Parliament men to him. The king says he will not have a secretary imposed on him by Parliament." However, Sir Henry continued to be an applicant for the place.

M. P. for Berkshire in 1614 ; at the head of the party called "the Undertakers." He favored the project for "drawing the traffic of Persia and the inland parts of the East Indies up the river Hydaspes (Jhylum) into the Oxus that falls into the Caspian Sea, whence the commodities are to be brought up the Volga to a strait of land not above forty miles wide, and so into the Dwina, that comes to St. Nicholas or Archangel, the ordinary stations of English shipping in those parts."

March 31, 1614, he was admitted into the E. I. Co., and adventured £800 in the next voyage. " He published an edition of Chrysostom in 1614 at a great cost." February 9, 1615, "dangerously ill ; " died July 10, 1615. Lord Carew wrote to Sir Thomas Roe, " Sir Henry Neville, who would have been Secretary with a good will, is dead."

He married Anne, daughter of Sir Henry Killigrew, of Cornwall, and had issue, three sons and six daughters. The eldest son, Sir Henry Neville, the younger, married Elizabeth, daughter of Sir John Smith, and niece of Sir Thomas Smith, the first treasurer of the Va. Co. of London. Of the daughters, Elizabeth married Sir Henry Berkeley, the brother of Sir William Berkeley, governor of Virginia; Catherine married Sir Richard Brooke ; Mary married Sir Edward Lukin or Lewknor ; and Frances married Sir Richard Worsley, who patented lands in Virginia in 1620.

Neville, Sir Henry, of Kent, 3. Sub. £75 ; pd. ——. Possibly son of the foregoing who married Elizabeth Smith ; was knighted at Whitehall, March 30, 1609 ; a member of the African Company in 1618 ; died June 29, 1629.

Neville, Sir Henry, of Abergavenny, 3. Sub. ——; pd. ——. Succeeded as seventh Baron Abergavenny in 1622.

Newbridge, Joseph, smith, 2. Sub. —— ; pd. £20.

Newce—Newse—Nuce, George, gent., 2, Sub. —— ; pd. £12 10s. Came to Virginia, and was living at Elizabeth City in 1624.

Newce — Newse, Henry, 2. Sub. —— ; pd. ——. (The origin of the name " Newport News " in Virginia

is a mooted question. It was named about the same time as Nieuw Port Mey, which was named for Cornelis Jacobsen Mey, and was possibly named New Port Newse, for one of the Newce (or Newse, or Nuce) family. In addition to the foregoing, two others of this family emigrated at an early day, namely : Capt. Thomas Newse, deputy for the company's land and member of the council, arrived in the winter of 1620–21, and died about the 1st of April, 1623, leaving a widow and child, and Capt. William Newse, who had served in Ireland at the siege of Kinsale ; in May, 1605, led a company of Irish to enter the Spanish service, and, in 1606, was implicated in a scheme to deliver Sluys, Flushing, and other towns to the Archduke (see Gardiner's " Hist. of England," vol. i. pp. 344–47). From these charges he seems to have cleared himself, and was soon after again in Ireland. He was the first mayor of Bandon; laid out a town opposite called Newce's Town; offered to transport a colony to Virginia, April 12, 1621; patented lands there; chosen marshal of Virginia, May 2, 1621; knighted at Theobald's, May 31, 1621; added to the Virginia Council, June 13, 1621 ; went over with Wyatt ; arrived there early in October, 1621, and died about two months after. The family was seated at Great Hadham, Herts, and intermarried with the Washingtons, Fanshawes, etc.)

Newgate, Christopher, fishmonger. Pd. £25 + £6 5s. Of St. Lawrence, Pountney, London. Married, in 1608, Elizabeth, daughter of William Tapp, of St. Nicholas Olave, fishmonger.

Newport, Captain Christopher, 2. Sub. —— ; pd. ——. He was probably born between 1560 and 1570, and possibly entered the sea service at an early age. He is said to have made several voyages to the West Indies before going to Virginia, but I have found memoranda of only two of them. January 25, 1592, he sailed in command of four vessels; July 28, 1592, contracted with Sir John Boroughs, and September 7, 1592, brought the celebrated Spanish " Caract," the Madre de Dios, into Dartmouth Harbor.

The other voyage was made in 1604–

05. January 11, 1606, Sir Robert Mansell, Sir John Trevor, and others, recommended Captain Newport to Lord Admiral Nottingham for the reversion of the office of one of the principal masters of the navy.

"January 13, 1606, the Lord Admiral wrote to Sir Rob. Mansell, Sir Henry Palmer, Sir John Trevor, and Sir Peter Buck, the principal officers of the Royal Navy, that he granted to Capt. Chris. Newport the reversion solicited, after the placing of Capt. John King."

December 10, 1606, he was commissioned and given by the Council for Virginia the "*sole* charge and command of all the captains, soldiers, and mariners, and other persons, that shall go in any the said ships and pinnace in the said voyage from the day of the date hereof until such time as they shall fortune to land upon the said coast of Virginia." Thus he was in the "*sole* charge and command" of the first expedition of Englishmen that landed in James River. (The name Christopher is worthy of remark. Columbus bore the same name. It means " bearing Christ." This was one of the ideas of the expedition.)

December 19, 1606, to July 29, 1607, his first voyage to Virginia; October 8, 1607, to May 20, 1608, his second voyage to Virginia ; July, 1608, to January, 1609, his third voyage to Virginia; June 2, 1609, to September, 1610, his fourth voyage to Virginia ; March 17, 1611, to December, 1611, his fifth voyage to Virginia.

In 1612 he was appointed one of the six masters of the royal navy, and employed by the E. I. Co. to carry Sir Robert Sherley to Persia. January 7, 1613, to July 10, 1614, his first voyage to the East Indies in command of the good ship "the Expedition of London of about 260 tunnes burthen." He landed the ambassador's party in " the River of Sinde, India, September 26, 1613," and returning well ladened anchored in "The Downes," July 10, 1614. Sir Robert Sherley wrote a letter to the E. I. Co., " highly commending the deserts of Captain Newport." Capt. Walter Peyton's account of the voyage, in Purchas, i., speaks highly of Newport, and "he was much commended by the East India Company for his good services, delivering his charge safely, discovering unknown places (in the Persian Gulf and elsewhere) bringing home his ship well laden, his men in health, and dispatching the voyage in so short a time, and they resolved to gratify him with a present of fifty Jacobuses."

September 20, 1614, the E. I. Co. resolved "to entertain Captain Newport as Admiral," and he entered into the service of that great company ; January 24, 1615, to about September, 1616, on his second voyage to the East Indies, in which he commanded the Lion in the fleet accompanying " Sir Thomas Roe, Embassadour from the King of England (James I.) to the Great Mogoll of India" (Shah Jehan).

Early in 1617 he sailed from England on this third voyage to India in command of the Hope, with the Hound as consort. August 15, 1617, the Hope arrived at Bantam on the isle of Java, "commander Captain Newport, who reported that seven ships were sent this year from England to Surat." A few days after (prior to September 1) "there dyed out of the Hope, Captaine Newport that worthy Seaman and Commander." The Hope was loaded at Bantam, and on Tuesday, January 20, 1618, sailed thence for England, arriving there September 1, 1618, bringing (I suppose) the first account of Newport's death.

From 1592 to his death in 1617, we find Capt. Christopher Newport commanding in active services at sea of special confidence and trust. He brought the first English colonists to Virginia, and supplied them for years. He carried back the first Persian ambassador (to England) to Persia. He was a commander in the expedition which conveyed the first English ambassador to the Great Mogul. He was one of the first Englishmen to explore the Chesapeake Bay and the James River, "the Persian Gulf, and the river of Sinde." He ranged the Atlantic and the Pacific oceans ; "he sailed the wide seas over." We find him commanding in the waters of the West Indies ; we leave him as he sinks to rest beneath the far-off waters of the East Indies. He was one of the founders of English colonies and English commerce ; and he was not the least among those who laid the groundwork of Great Britain's present greatness. The admiral of Virginia lived on the ocean ; he died on the ocean; the ocean is his tomb, and his admirable monument, and the city of Newport News, whether named for him or not, will be his memorial in America. November 17, 1619, the following minute was made at a meeting of the Va. Co. of London : " Whereas the company hath formerly granted to Captain Newport a bill of Adventure for four hundred pounds, and his son now desiring order from court for the laying out of some part of same, Mr. Treasurer, was authorized to write to Sir George Yeardley and the Counsell of State for the effecting thereof."

These lands are supposed to have been located at Newport News on James River.

July 10, 1621, the Va. Co. of London, as a further acknowledgment of Captain Newport's services in the enterprise, gave his widow thirty-five shares of land (3,500 acres) in Virginia. Mr. Christopher Newport was one of the patentees of land in Virginia in 1622–23. Edward Newport, gent., and Richard Newport, gent., both died in Northampton County, Virginia, in 1642, "of a contagious disease called the plague."

Nicholas (Nichols, Nicols, etc.).

Nicholls, Christopher, 2. Sub. —— ; pd. £62 10s. Also of E. I. Co.

Nicholls, Oliver, esquire, 3. Sub. —— ; pd. ——. Also of the African Company of 1618.

Nicholls, Thomas, merchant, 2. Sub. —— ; pd. £62 10s. Also of E. I. Co.

Nicholls, William, clothworker. Sub. £37 10s. ; pd. £50.

Nornicott, Thomas, clothworker, 2. Sub. £37 10s. ; pd. £37 10s. July 24, 1618, he passed his three shares in Virginia to Mr. Francis Meverell. He was master of the Clothworkers in 1625.

Norris, Francis Lord, 3. Sub. —— ; pd. £50. Son of William Norris, marshal of Berwick, who was one of the celebrated brothers, William, John, Edward, Henry, Thomas, and Maximilian, so distinguished in the wars, times of Queen Elizabeth. He succeeded his grandfather in 1600 as second Lord Norreys of Rycote ; summoned to Parliament from October 17, 1601, to April 5, 1614 ; Knight of the Bath at the creation of Prince Charles as Duke of York, January 12, 1606 ; created Viscount Thane and Earl of Berkshire, January 28, 1620 ; died in 1623. He was of impetuous temperament, and was at one time committed to the Fleet prison for an assault on the Lord Scrope in the House of Lords and in the presence of the prince.

North, Dudley Lord, 3. Sub. —— ; pd. £13 6s. 8d. Son of Sir John North by his wife Dorothy, daughter of Sir Valentine Dale, doctor of the civil law, and master of the requests ; born about 1581; succeeded his grandfather as third Lord North. His brothers, Sir John, Roger (who was a sea commander of note, and engaged in making new discoveries for the honor of his country), and Gilbert, and himself were all interested in a plantation of Guiana under a charter to the Earl of Warwick (Robert Rich), and many others of April 30, 1619. Lord North lived to be very old, and died January 16, 1666.

Northampton, Earl of. — William Lord Compton and Henry Howard.

Northumberland, Earl of. — Henry Percy.

Norton, John, stationer. Pd. £10. " Queen's printer in Latin, Greek, and Hebrew ; " an alderman of London in the reign of James I. ; thrice master of the Stationers, and a very great benefactor of that company.

Norton, Thomas. Pd. £13 6s. 8d.

Norwich, Earl of. — Edward Lord Denny and George Goring.

Norwood, Richard. Having been sent out by the B. I. Co. for the purpose, he made a map of the Bermudas in 1616, which was licensed for publication, January 19, 1622, by the Stationers' Company of London ; married at St. Andrew Hubbard, London, in May, 1622, Rachel, daughter of Francis Boughton, of Sandwich, County Kent. In May, 1621, he desired to go to Virginia to survey lands ; but William Clayborne was sent. February 3, 1623, he bought a share in Virginia of Francis Carter, and the same year patented lands in that colony, but, it seems, continued to live in the Bermudas (where he was a schoolmaster) until his death in October, 1675, at the age of about 85. He was one of the first who measured a degree of the meridian with approximate accuracy; made a second survey of the Bermudas in 1662–63, and was the author of several books on "Trigonometry," "The Seaman's Practice on Fortifications," etc.

Nottingham, Earl of. — Charles Howard.

Nuttall, Jonathan, gent., 3. Sub. ——; pd. £12 10s.

Offley, Robert, merchant, 2. Sub. £37 10s.; pd. £112 10s. A leading merchant of London, and of the E. I., N. W. P., B. I., and Va. companies. One of the purchasers of the Bermudas, November 25, 1612; added to the King's Council for the Va. Co. between 1616 and 1620, and recommended by the king as a candidate for deputy treasurer of the company, May 22, 1622. There were two leading merchants of the name, namely, the son of William Offley, of London, merchant-tailor, by Anne, daughter of William Beswicke, of London, alderman (she married, secondly, Sir Henry Bromley, of Holt): which Robert Offley, born about 1582, married in October, 1601, Mary, daughter of Sir Thomas Lowe; and was knighted January 22, 161$\frac{5}{6}$. But the Virginian adventurer was not a knight. He lies buried in the parish church of St. Mary Aldermanbury, Cripplegate ward, London, under a fair monument, with this inscription: "Here lyeth the body of Master Robert Offley, gent., son of Hugh Offley, alderman of this city. Who took to wife Elizabeth the daughter of Humfrey Street; by whom he had issue seven sons and six daughters. He dyed at the age of 64 years, on the 4 day of November, 1631."

Ogle, Sir John, 2. Sub. ——; pd. ——.

Ogle, Sir John, 3. Sub. ——; pd. ——. These names probably belong to the same man, "Colonel Sir John Ogle," who had served under Sir Francis Vere in the Low Countries, and who was still in the service of the States. Greatly distinguished himself at the battle of Nieuport, 1600; at the recovery of Sluys, 1604; resigned his command at Utrecht in 1618 rather than act against Barnevelt. On February 3, 1623, he was again admitted into the Va. Co.; on February 5 he was chosen to be of the council, and on the 19th of April following, Chamberlain wrote of him as being one of the leaders of the Sandys faction in the Va. Co. On June 9, 1623, Henry Lord De La Warr transferred to him three shares in Virginia. He was the author of the "Account of the last Charge at Newport Battle, and of the Parley at the Siege of Ostend," subjoined to the "Commentaries," of Sir Francis Vere. "April 12, 1624. Draft of an Act for the naturalizing of the wife, three sons, and seven daughters of Sir John Ogle, who were born in the United Provinces." (Calendars, House of Lords. See also "The Fighting Veres.")

Oldenbarneveld, Helias. Knighted by King James at Whitehall May 14, 1610.

Oldenbarneveld, John Van (see Barnevelt.) Grand Pensionary of Holland; born 1547 or 1549; ambassador to James I., 1603; concluded truce with Spain, March 30, 1609; arrested with Grotius and others, by States General, February 21, 1618; trial commenced, November 19, 1618; beheaded at The Hague, May 14, 1619.

Oliver, Francis. Pd. £25.

Ortelius, Abraham, geographer. Born at Antwerp, April, 4, 1527; geographer to Philip II. of Spain, 1575; died at Antwerp, January 28, 1598.

Osmotherly, Richard, merchant-tailor. Pd. £25. Of E. I. Co.

O'Toole, Arthurus Severus None-such. A character of the time. John Taylor, the Water Poet, wrote an account of him in 1622, which is dedicated "To the unlimited memory of Arthur O'Toole, or O'Toole the Great, being the son and heir of Brian O'Toole, lord of Poore's Court and

Faire Collen, in the county of Dublin,
in the Kingdom of Ireland, the Mars
and Mercury, the Agamemnon and
Ulysses, both for wisdom and valour,
in the Kingdoms of Great Britaine and
Ireland."

> " Englands, Scotlands, Irelands Mirror,
> Mars his fellow, Rebels Terror :
> These lines doe gallop for their pleasure
> Writ with neither feet or measure ;
> Because Prose, Verse, or Anticke Story,
> Cannot blaze O'Toole's great glory."

There is a portrait of O'Toole (æt.
80, 1618) prefixed, with the following
lines printed thereunder : —

> " Great Mogul's landlord, both Indies King,
> Whose self-admiring fame doth loudly ring ;
> Writes fourscore years, more Kingdoms he hath
>   right to,
> The stars say so, and for them he will fight too.
> And though this worthless age, will not believe
>   him,
> But clatter, spatter, slander, scoff to grieve him ;
> Yet he and all the world in this agree,
> That such another Toole will never be."

Oxenbridge, William, esquire, 2.
Sub. ——; pd. £112 10s.

Paget, William Lord, 3.   Sub.
——; pd. £60. His father, Thomas
Paget, third Baron, a zealous Roman
Catholic, was attainted, "as being a
well-wisher to the Queen of Scotts,"
and died at Brussels in 1587, leaving
an only son, " William Paget, who was
with the Earl of Essex in the memorable attack upon Cadiz in 1596, and
being restored to the lands and honours of his father, by King James, was
summoned to Parliament as [4th]
Baron Paget, from November 5, 1605,
to March 7, 1628." M. C. for Va. Co.,
1612.   Interested in the Bermudas
Islands, and June 29, 1615, was one of
the incorporators named in the Bermudas charter.   In 1623 he was
friendly to the Southampton administration ; June 24, 1624, on " a committee to resolve upon the well-settling of the Colony of Virginia, and to
give order for the government," etc.
July 15, 1624, he was one of the commissioners for winding up the Va. Co.;
buried at Drayton, August 30, 1628.
He married Lettice, daughter of Henry
Knollys, Esq., and first cousin to Lord
De La Warr, the governor of Virginia.   His daughter Anne married,
first, Sir Simon Harcourt, Knight, of
Stanton Harcourt, and secondly, Sir
William Waller, Knight, the celebrated parliamentary general.

Palatyne, Frederick Prince (the
Palgrave). His grandson was crowned
King of Great Britain, October 20,
1714, as George I., the first British
monarch of the House of Guelph, which
still rules Great Britain.

Palmer, Sir Anthony. Son of
John Palmer, of Clerkenwell, esquire
(who died in February, 1586), by his
wife Paulina, daughter of Anthony
Sondes, of Kent, esquire (and sister to
Elizabeth, second wife of Sir Maurice
Berkeley, standard bearer to Henry
VIII., Edward VI., and Elizabeth) ; a
Knight of the Bath at the coronation
of James, July 25, 1603 ; a member of
the E. I. Co ; M. C. for Va., March
9, 1607 ; married, first, Katherine,
daughter of William Kingsmill, Esq.,
who died in 1613 and lies buried in the
church at Putney, " on the south side
of the chancel, under a handsome monument, supported by Corinthian col-
umns of black marble ;" married, secondly, Margaret, daughter of Thomas
Digges, Esq., and sister to Sir Dudley
Digges ; she died in 1619, leaving a
son and heir, Dudley Palmer, who died
in 1666.

Palmer, Miles, 2.   Sub. ——; pd.
£12 10s.

Palmer, William, haberdasher, 2.
Sub. £37 10s.; pd. £62 10s.   A leading member of the E. I., N. W. P.,
B. I., and Va. companies ; one of the
directors of the Va. Co. ; governor of
St. Bartholomew's Hospital ; on the
Va. Commission of July 15, 1624 ;
married Barbara, daughter of Sir
Thomas Archdale, of London. He
died in September, 1636. (See his
will in " N. E. Register," January,
1889, p. 83.)

Palmes, Sir Guy. 3.   Sub. ——;
pd. ——. Of Lindley, County York,
and of Ashwell, County Rutland ;
knighted at the Charterhouse, May 11,
1603 ; M. P. Rutland, 1614, 1621–22,
1624–25, 1625, 1628–29, 1640, and
1640 till disabled in 1644 ; sheriff,
York, 20 James I.   Died (?).

Panton, Sir Thomas, 2.   Sub.
——; pd. ——. Of Denbigh; knighted
at Whitehall, March 2, 1607 ; ap-

HENRY STUART

Prince of Wales

pointed gentleman extraordinary of
the privy chamber to Prince Henry in
1610.

Parker, Sir Nicholas, 3. Sub.
——; pd. £12 10s. Son of Thomas
Parker, Esq., of Ratton in Sussex, by
Eleanor, daughter of William Waller;
was born in 1547 ; captain in Fenton's voyage, 1582 ; knighted by Lord
Willoughby, in the Low Countries, in
1588 ; M. P. Sussex, 1593 ; in the
voyage to the Azores, 1597 ; a deputy lieutenant of Cornwall, 1598; commanded at Plymouth, in the place of
Gorges, in 1603; died March 9, 1619,
aged 73.

Parker, William, Lord Monteagle, 2. Sub. ——; pd. £50. Edward Parker, Lord Morley, married
Elizabeth Stanley (granddaughter of
Edward Stanley, Lord Monteagle, who
so greatly distinguished himself at
Flodden) and was the father, among
others, of William (of whom I write)
and of Mary, who married Thomas
Habington of Hinlip, Esq., and became the mother of William Habington (1605–1645), the poet. William
Parker, in right of his mother, Elizabeth Stanley, was summoned to Parliament as Lord Monteagle, during his
father's life. He was knighted by Essex at Dublin, Ireland, July 12, 1599,
and was imprisoned for a while in
the Tower, in February, 1601, on account of some connection with the
"Essex rising." On October 26, 1605,
he received that memorable anony-
mous letter which led to the detection
of the Gunpowder Plot, and King
James made him a substantial grant
for having thus saved the country from
the most summary convulsion ever
attempted ; M. C. for Va. Co., May
23, 1609 ; also a member of the E. I.
and N. W. P. companies. He went
with Sir Walter Ralegh on his fatal
voyage to Guiana, South America, in
1617–18.

In 1618, at the death of his father,
he succeeded as Lord Morley, and was
summoned to Parliament as "Lord
Morley and Monteagle," from January 30, 1621, to November 4 in the
same year. He died in 1622. He
married Elizabeth, daughter of Sir
Thomas Tresham, and sister to Francis
Tresham, one of the Gunpowder conspirators.

Parker, William, of Plymouth. I
suppose this was Capt. William Parker
of Plymouth, who sailed from that
city in November, 1601, in command
of several vessels for the West Indies,
where he took Saint Vincent and
Puerto Bello, in February, 1602. At
the latter place he took Pedro Melendez, the chief governor of that
town, prisoner ; using him and his far
otherwise than Pedro Melendez, his
great-uncle, used the Huguenots in
Florida. He returned safely to Plymouth, May 6, 1602.

On September 24, 1618, Ralegh
wrote to King James, "If Parker
and Mutton [Mutam ?] took Campeach
and other places in the Honduras
seated in the hart of the Spanish
Indies ; burnt towns, killed the Spaniards ; and had nothing sayed to them
at their returne ; and that myselfe for-
bore to looke into the Indies because I
would not offend I may as justly say,
O miserable Sir Walter Ralegh." On
the very day that Ralegh wrote this
letter, Parker, who was vice-admiral
of the East Indian fleet, under Sir
Thomas Dale, died on the voyage. He
was then old and corpulent.

Parker, William, merchant-tailor.
Pd. £5. Still remembered in London
for his great charities.

Parkhurst, Robert, clothworker,
2. Sub. £37 10s.; pd. £100. Fourth
son of Henry Parkhurst, of Guildford
in Com. Surrey ; sheriff of London and
master of the Clothworkers in 1624;
alderman from Portsoken ward, 1624
to 1634, and from Bread Street ward,
August 28, 1634, to his death in 1636;
M. P. for Guildford, 1626 and 1628–
29 ; gave money to purchase books
for Sion College Library, 1632; Lord
Mayor of London, 1634–35; knighted
at Greenwich May 24, 1635; died in
1636, and was buried in the church of
the Holy Trinity, Guildford, where a
monument was erected to his memory.

Parkins. See Perkins.

Parrett. See Perrott.

Parry, Henry, Bishop of Worces-
ter, 3. Sub. ——; pd. £13 6s. 8d.
Chaplain to Queen Elizabeth; was of
Corpus Christi College, Oxford, and
Greek reader there ; made Dean of
Chester in 1605; Bishop of Gloucester
in 1607, and translated to the see of

Worcester in 1610. He died December 12, 1616.

Parslow, Giles, grocer, 2. Sub. —— ; pd. ——. Having served his apprenticeship, was admitted a freeman of the Grocers' Company in 1581; to the livery, March 21, 1592 ; paid £15 as his part of the £20,000 levied on London by Queen Elizabeth in 1598; was warden of the company in 1606; but came to poverty in 1616; and it was granted and agreed by the Court of Assistants, held December 12, 1616, "that the yearly pension of xxˡⁱ. [£20] per an. shall be by Mr. Rentors of this company payd unto Giles Parsloe, grocer, by quarterly payments as of the common goodes of this house. The first payment to beginn at the feast of the birth of our Lord God next comyng and to continue during his good behaviour and the pleasure of this Court." (Grocers' Records.) Also of E. I. Co.

Partridge, Richard, 2. Sub.—— ; pd. £25.

Pashall — Pascoll — Peashall — Piershall — Pershall — Peshall, etc., **Edmond,** grocer, 2. Sub.—— ; pd. £25. Admitted to livery, May 24, 1596 ; paid £15 as his share of the levy of 1598; warden, 1609, when he had to pay the default of his brother warden, Timothy Bathurst, to the amount of £368 ; was senior warden in 1616. "Westminster. March 29, 1615. Grant to Edmond Peshall and Edw. White of London, of the late imposition of 2s. per lb. on tobacco imported for ten years, paying to the King £3,500 the first year and £7,000 per ann. afterwards, with sole power to import tobacco and to name persons for selling the same, with a proviso of determination at six months' notice, if found prejudicial to the State." ("Sign. Man." vol. v. Nos. 3 and 4.)

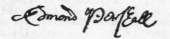

Pass (or **De Passe**), **Simon,** engraver. Born at Utrecht, 1591. He followed his business in England from about 1613 to about 1623.

Paulson, Richard, merchant. Pd. £37 10s. July 22, 1618, he sold four shares in Virginia to Robert Hudson; July 18, 1620, he sold two shares to Mr. Andrews and Mr. Greene. He was long a leading member of the S. I. Co.

Pawlet, John, esquire, 3. Sub. £75 ; pd. £12 10s. M. P. for Somerset, 1614; he "was elevated to the peerage, June 23, 1627, by the title of Baron Poulett of Hinton·St. George; and was knighted with his eldest son, John, by the Earl of Lindsey, on board his majesty's ship, the 'Mary-Honor,' September 27, 1635. This nobleman took up arms in the royal cause, and was an active commander during the civil war. He died March 20, 1649," and was succeeded by his son, Sir John, second Lord Poulett of Hinton St. George, who married a daughter of Horace Lord Vere.

Capt. Thomas Paulett, brother to the first Lord Paulett, born about 1585, came to Virginia in the Neptune in 1618 ; represented Argall's Guifte in our first Legislature, July 30, 1619; and was living at West and Sherley Hundred in 1625; on the commission for Charles City in 1632 and after ; Burgess for Westover and Flowerdieu Hundred in 1633 ; patented 2,000 acres, including Westover, January 15, 163⅞; was a member of the council in 1641–44 ; died in January, 164⅜; and left his possessions in Virginia to his brother, the first Lord Paulett, whose son, the second lord, on April 17, 1665, sold the Westover property of 1,200 acres for £170 to Theodrick, son of John Bland.

Capt. Thomas Paulett is sometimes confused with Robert Paulett, with whom the adventurers for Berkeley Hundred entered into an agreement on September 15, 1620, to go as preacher, physician, and surgeon to Berkeley in Virginia. He sailed in the Supply in September, 1620, and arrived in Virginia in January, 1621. He was appointed to the Council in Virginia by the court of the Virginia Company of London in July, 1621 ; and probably died in Virginia before April, 1623.

Payne, John, gent. Pd. £12 10s.

He sold his share to Dr. Theodore Gulston, December 15, 1619.

Payne (or **Paine**), **Sir Robert**, 2. Sub.——; pd. £25. M. P. Huntingdonshire, 1614, 1621–22, 1626, and 1628–29; knighted at Greenwich, May 22, 1605. Either Robert of St. Neots, who married Elizabeth, daughter of Dr. John Beilby, or his cousin Robert of Medloe, who married Elizabeth, daughter of George Rotherham, of Somery, Bedford. Both living in 1613.

Payne, William, esquire, 2. Sub. £37 10s.; pd. £100. Of the E. I. and N. W. P. companies. Probably the William Payne, Esq., of Highgate, who died in 1628.

Peckham, Sir George. Son of Sir Edmund Peckham, who died in 1564, and brother of Sir Robert Peckham, who, dying abroad in 1569, caused his heart to be sent into England and buried in his family vault at Denham. George Peckham was knighted in 1570; wished to discover new lands in 1574; had an assignment from Gilbert's patent for colonization in 1580; a prisoner for debts to the queen in December, 1580, probably contracted by his father and brother, who had served the late Queen Mary, and the family estates were seized by Elizabeth; still interested in America in 1582; a partner in Gilbert's voyage in 1583, of which he wrote "A True Reporte" in November, 1583, at which time he proposed to make another voyage under Gilbert's patent. The exact date of his death is not known to me; but the inquisition on his estate was held June 21, 1608: "heir, his son George."

Peirscy (Persy — Percy, etc.), Abraham. Pd. £12 10s. Cape merchant; he went to Virginia in the Susan in 1616; had 200 acres given him in Virginia by the company, November 15, 1619; was a Burgess in 1622. His daughters, by his first wife, came to Virginia in 1623. He was appointed on the commission with John Pory, John Harvey, John Jefferson, and Samuel Matthews to look into the state of Virginia, October 24, 1623. This commission inspected Virginia in February, 1624. The report, written by Harvey, is printed in "Mass. Hist. Col." 4th series, vol. ix. pp. 60–73. The "Lists of the livinge and dead in

Virginia," at the time is given in "Colonial Records of Virginia," Richmond, 1874, pp. 37–60. Abraham Peirsey was member of the Council in Virginia, 1624–28. Some time after January, 1625, he married, secondly, Frances, the widow of Capt. Nathaniel West, the brother of Lord De la Warr. In 1626 he held 1150 acres "uppon Apmatucke river." Not long before Governor Yeardley's death, Peirsey bought of him the lands of Flowerdieu Hundred, being 1,000 acres, and of Weanoake on the opposite side of the water, being 2,200 acres, and the sale was confirmed by widow Yeardley and the court, November 16, 1627. Peirsey's will (given in Neill's "Virginia Carolorum," pp. 404–406), is dated March 1, 1627. He died before March, 1634. His daughter Elizabeth married, first, Capt. Richard Stephens, and, secondly, Gov. John Harvey. Her son, by her first husband, Samuel Stephens, married Frances Culpeper, and died s. p. His widow Frances, married, secondly, Gov. William Berkeley, and, thirdly, Col. Philip Ludwell.

Pelham, Thomas, esquire, 3. Sub. ——; pd. £65. Son of Herbert Pelham, Sr., by his wife, Elizabeth West. (See West pedigree.)

Pembroke, Earl of. — Philip, William, and William Herbert.

Pennington, Robert, 2. Sub. ——; pd. £25. (Robert Pennington, grocer and citizen of London, brother of Isaac Pennington (lord mayor in 1643), died in 1645, s. p.)

Percivall, Richard, esquire, 2. Sub. £37 10s.; pd. £62 10s Burke says, "The life of this ultimately successful person was chequered and eventful in no ordinary degree;" but to go into the particulars at all would require much space, and I must, as usual, confine myself to the briefest outline. Of a very ancient family in Somersetshire; born in 1550; educated at St. Paul's School and Lincoln's Inn; married against his father's consent and was cast off; went to Spain and, after the death of his wife, returned to England. In 1586 he deciphered letters in cipher which had been captured and which conveyed to Elizabeth the first certain intelligence of the proposed Spanish Armada to be sent to take England. Secretary, remembrancer, and one of the commissioners for the office of receiver-general of the Court of Wards in England; register of the same court in Ireland, and M. P. for the borough of Richmond, in the county of York, in 1604–11. He died in 1620. He was ancestor to the Earl of Egmont, Lord Lovel, etc. His portrait was engraved for the "History of the House of Yvery," etc., 1742, now a rare work.

Percy, Allen. Pd. £12 10s.

Percy, George, esquire, 2. Sub. ——; pd. £20. Eighth son of Henry, eighth Earl of Northumberland, by his wife Catherine, eldest daughter and co-heir of John Neville, Lord Latimer; was born September 4, 1580 ; served for a time in the Low Countries ; sailed for Virginia in the first expedition, December, 1606; governor during the terrible time from September, 1609, to the arrival of Gates in May, 1610. When Lord De la Warr left in March, 1611, in recognition of his former services as governor, he was again appointed until the arrival of Dale in May following. He left Virginia April 22, 1612, and reached England in the following summer. He probably never returned to Virginia again. On May 15, 1620, he transferred to Christopher Martin four of his shares in Virginia.

After the appearance of Smith's "General History" with his very unjust account of the affairs in Virginia during the time of Percy's government, Captain Percy wrote "A Trewe Relacyon of the procedeinges and ocurentes of momente which have happened in Virginia, from the Tyme Sir Thomas Gates was shipwrackte upon the Bermudas An°, 1609, untill my departure out of the Country which was in Anno. 1612." This "True Relation" he sent to his brother Henry, Earl of Northumberland, with the following letter: —

"My Lorde, This relacyon I have here sente your Lord-shipp, is for two respecks, the one, to showe howe mutche I honor you, and desyre to doe you service, the other, in regard that many untruthes concerninge theis proceedings have bene formerly published, wherein the Author hathe not spared to apropriate many deserts to himselfe

which he never performed, and stuffed his relacyons with so many falseties, and malycyous detractyons not onely of this p'ts and tyme, which I have selected to treate of, Butt of former occurrentes also: so that I could not conteine myselfe, but express the Truth unto your Lordshipp concerninge theise affayres, and all which I ayme att is to manyfeste myselfe in all my actyons both now and alwayes to be your Lordshipps humble and faithfull servante. G. P."

(Mr. Neill has given some extracts from this Relation in the preface to his "Virginia Vetusta," 1885.)

Percy again went to the Low Countries some time after war was declared with Spain, probably in 1625, where, Collins says, "he distinguished himself; had one of his fingers shot off, was captain of a company, A. D. 1627, and died unmarried in 1632."

George Percy

Percy, Henry, ninth Earl of Northumberland. It has been truly written that "the Percys are almost without a peer even in the peerage of Great Britain ; their nobility dates as remotely as the sovereignty of Normandy and their renown, coeval with their nobility, has flourished in every age, and coexisted with every generation since. Not more famous in arms than distinguished for its alliances, the family banner bears a galaxy of heraldic honors altogether unparalleled."

Henry, the ninth earl, of whom I write, was born in April, 1564. He was the oldest brother of Capt. George Percy aforesaid; succeeded his father, 1585; followed Leicester to the Netherlands, December, 1585; joined the fleet against the Armada, 1588 ; K. C. G., 1593 ; at siege of Ostend, 1601 ; challenged Sir Francis Vere, 1602 ; privy councilor by James I., 1603 ; M. A. Oxford, August 30, 1605 ; suspected of being privy to Gunpowder Plot, and committed to the Tower, November, 1605 ; convicted by Star Chamber, fined, and sentenced to imprisonment for life, June 27, 1606. He corresponded with, and was a good friend to, his brother, Capt. George, in

Virginia, 1606–12. He was the patron of Hariot, Hues, and Warner; liberated from the Tower, July 18, 1621.

His brother George sent him a true account of affairs in Virginia (1609–12) in reply to the false account in Smith's "History" of 1624; died at Petworth November 5, 1632; married Dorothy Devereux (sister to the Earl of Essex who was beheaded in 1601), and had two sons and two daughters. Algernon Fort in Virginia and Algernon Sidney, the patriot, were named for his eldest son Algernon, tenth earl. Dorothy, the eldest daughter, married Robert Sidney, second Earl of Leicester, and Lucy, the youngest, married James Hay, Earl of Carlisle.

Perez, Marco Antonio, statesman. Born in Aragon, 1541 ; secretary of state to Philip II., 1567 ; arrests, trials, convictions, etc., 1581–91 ; visited England about 1593–95 ; died at Paris, November 3, 1611.

Perkins (Parkins etc.), **Aden**, grocer, 2. Sub. ——; pd. £25. Apprenticed to Edmond Peshall ; sworn to freedom, March 8, 1608; admitted to the livery, 1617. He was also of the E. I. and N. W. P. companies.

Perkins (or Parkins), Sir Christopher, 2. Sub. £37 10s.; pd. £50. During 1590–94 he was sent several times as an ambassador from Queen Elizabeth to the rulers in the East, Christian, King of Denmark, Sigismund III., King of Poland, and Rudolph II., the emperor of the Romans; M. P. for Ripon, 1597–98 and 1601; knighted at Whitehall, July 23, 1603; M. P. for Morpeth, 1604–11, being then " Dean of Carlisle." In 1617 he married " Mrs. Anne Brett, relict of —— Brett, of Hobie, County Leicester, deceased," an aunt of Buckingham's, when he said he was " about 60 years of age ;" but Chamberlain says he was 77. He succeeded Sir Daniel Dun as master of requests, and died about the last of August, 1622. " His widow, Lady Perkins, is sister to the Countess of Buckingham, and mother to the Countess of Middlesex. He was said to be a papist or Jesuit, a doctor, a dean, a master of requests, a knight, and what not." (Chamberlain.) He was buried in Westminster Abbey, September 1, 1622.

Perkins, Edward, 2. Sub. ——;

pd. £37 10s. He died some time before 1620, at which time his widow held an additional share in Virginia.

Perkins, Francis. Came to Virginia with his son in 1608. Smith gives in his list of this supply only two of the name, " Francis Perkins, gent., and Francis Perkins, labourer." Smith's gentleman and labourer were probably father and son.

Perkins (or Perkin), Thomas, cooper, 2. Sub. ——; pd. £12 10s.

Perrott, Sir James, 3. Sub. £37 10s.; pd. £12 10s. Of Harroldston, County Pembroke. Youngest son, and eventually heir, of Sir John Perrott (natural son of Henry VIII.), by his second wife, Jane Pollard ; M. P. for Haverfordwest, 1597–88 ; knighted at Sir William Fleetwood's, July 9, 1603; M. P. for Haverfordwest, 1604–11, 1614, and 1621–22, and for County Pembroke, 1624–25 ; died, *s. p.*, in 1641.

Petre, John Lord, 2. Sub. ——; pd. £95. Son of "Sir William Petre, Knt., LL. D., a person of great learning, and one of the principal secretaries of state in the reigns of Henry VIII., Edward VI., Mary, and Elizabeth." He was knighted in 1576; M. P. for Essex in 1584–85 ; created Baron Petre, of Writtle, County Essex, July 21, 1603. He died October 11, 1613, at West Hornden in Essex, " of a long, languishing consumption." His sister Dorothy and her husband, Nicholas Wadham, "founded, finished, and endowed Wadham College, Oxford."

Pett, Arthur, 2. Sub. ——; pd. ——. (The same who made the voyage with Jackman in 1580 ?)

Pett (see Peate), Peter, 2. Sub. ——; pd. £12 10s. Lived " on the other side of Depeford in Kent." Son of Peter and brother of the following Phineas. (See Le Neve's "Knights.")

Pett, Phenice (Phineas), 2. Sub. £37 10s.; pd. £37 10s. Of Chatham, Kent. Second son of Mr. Peter Pett, of Deptford-strand in Kent, one of the shipwrights of Queen Elizabeth, who was the son of Peter Pett, masterbuilder of the royal navy to Queen Mary. Born on the 1st of November (and baptized on the 8th), 1570, at Deptford ; educated at Emanuel College in the University of Cambridge, 1586–90. On the death of his father in 1590, he apprenticed himself to Mr. Richard Chapman, a shipwright at Deptford, and was afterwards made one of the shipwrights to King James; a great favorite of Henry, Prince of Wales; succeeded his elder brother Joseph in 1606, as one of the master-shipwrights in the navy. "He is said to have been the first scientific naval architect, remodeled the navy, abolishing the lofty forecastles and poop, which had made earlier ships resemble Chinese junks." (Chambers.) In 1610 he laid down the Prince-Royal, a two-decker, carrying 64 large guns. He was the first master of the Shipwrights' Company, after their new charter of incorporation in 1612.

He fitted out the fleet which carried over the Princess Elizabeth and her husband, the Palsgrave, in 1613, and went in the voyage ; fitted out the fleet and sailed with Prince Charles to Spain in 1623 ; and likewise the fleet which brought over Henrietta Maria in 1625. It was a safe idea to make the shipwright sail in his own vessel on these voyages. In 1637 he launched at Woolwich the celebrated Sovereign of the Seas, the first three-decker, and the largest ship hitherto constructed on modern principles.

Pett, Captaine Phineas, 3. Sub. ——; pd. ——. Second son of Phineas aforesaid, by his wife Anne, daughter of —— Nicholls ; in the expedition, under Sir R. Mansell, against the pirates of Algiers in 1620; captaine of the Tyger man-of-war ; stationed at Chatham in 1642 ; and was, I take it, the "Phineas Pette, Esq., and Captaine," who was buried at Chatham, August 21, 1647.

Pett, Master. "Lamentable Newes, Shewing the wonderfull deliverance of Maister Edmond Pet, Sayler, and Maister of a Ship, dwelling in Seething Lane in London, neere Barking Church. With other strange things lately hapned concerning these great windes and tempestuous weather, both at Sea and Lande. Imprinted at London by T. C. for William Barley, dwelling over against Grace Church, neere Algate, 1613."

Pettus, Sir John, 3. Sub. —— ; pd. £25. Of Norwich ; M. P. for

Norwich, 1601 and 1604–11; died April 9, 1613. A benefactor of Norwich Cathedral.

Peyton, Sir Henry, 2. Sub. £37 10s.; pd. £25. Son of Thomas, of St. Edmondsbury, customer of Plymouth, by his wife, Lady Cecilia Bourchier, daughter of John, second Earl of Bath. Sir Henry followed long the wars in the Low Countries; was knighted by King James at Royston in May, 1606; was of the household of Henry, Prince of Wales. He entered the service of the Venetian Republic in 1618.

Phellipps (Philips, etc.), Sir Edward, 3. Sub. ——; pd. ——. Of Montacute in Somerset ; M. P. Beeralston, 1584–85 ; Melcombe, 1586–87 ; Penryn, 1593 ; Andover, 1597–98; Somerset, 1601 and 1604–11; speaker, 1604; called to the bar of Middle Temple ; serjeant, 1603 ; king's serjeant, May, 1603, when knighted; chief justice of Lancashire, 1604; master of the rolls, 1611 ; N. W. P. Co., 1612; died September 11, 1614.

Phellipps (Philips) Sir Robert. Of Montacute, Somerset ; son of Sir Edward, aforesaid; knighted at Whitehall, July 23, 1603; added to his Majesty's Council for the Va. Co. about 1614 ; M. P. for Saltash, 1614, and for Bath, 1621–22; committed to the Tower for a time in January, 1622 ; a distinguished and active member of the popular party after the dissolution of Parliament, February 8, 1622; friendly to the Sandys party in the factions of the Va. Co., 1622–24; M. P. for Somerset, 1624–25, 1625, and 1628–29 ; married Bridget, daughter of Sir Thomas Gorges, by Helena, his wife, widow of the Marquis of Northampton ; died in 1638, leaving two sons, both afterwards distinguished cavalier commanders.

Phettiplace (or Fettiplace), Michael, gent., 2. Sub. —— ; pd. £12 10s. Came to Virginia in 1607. Probably returned to England.

Phettiplace (or Fettiplace), William, gent., 2. Sub. —— ; pd. £10. Came to Virginia in 1607. Probably returned to England.

Philip II., of Spain. Born 1527; King of Naples, 1554; married Mary, Queen of England, July 25, 1554; his father, Charles V., abdicated to him the crown of Spain and the Spanish possessions in America, February 5, 1556; the council of the Indies advised him to confide the conquest of Florida to Don Luis de Velasco, who sailed for that purpose in September, 1558; Queen Mary died November 17, 1558, and Philip proposed to Elizabeth in January, 1559, but was refused; revolt of the Netherlands, 1565; October 15, 1565, Menendez wrote to him, "unfolding his plan for colonizing and holding Florida by means of a series of forts at the Chesapeake Bay, Port Royal, the Martyrs, and the Bay of Juan Ponce de Leon." His treasure stayed in England on account of the Hawkins trouble in 1568 ; King of Portugal, 1580; at open war with England, 1585; sent the Armada against England, 1588 ; intrigued in France against Henry of Navarre, 1585–93 ; his ministers attempt assassination of Queen Elizabeth, 1593–94; died at the Escurial, September 13, 1598, and was succeeded by his son as Philip III.

Philip III., of Spain. Son of Philip II. by his fourth wife, Anna of Austria, whose mother was sister to Philip II. Born at Madrid, April 14, 1578 ; succeeded his father, September 13, 1598; made Duke of Lerma his first minister ; married Margaret of Austria, April 18, 1599; continued war in the Netherlands ; sent embassy to James I. of England in 1603; concluded treaty of peace with England, August 18, 1604, and signed the same at Valladolid, June 15, 1605 ; concluded truce for 12 years, and recognized independence of the United Provinces, April 9, 1609 (N. S.); expelled all Moors from Spain, January 10, 1610 ; lost his queen, October 3, 1611 ; proposed marriage to the Princess Elizabeth of England, 1612 ; dismissed Lerma, October 20, 1618; ministry of the Duke of Uzeda (Lerma's son); died at Madrid, March 31, 1621. He was timid, indolent, and incapable, and abandoned the direction of affairs to his favorite, the Duke of Lerma.

Phillips. See Phellipps, etc.

Phillips, Thomas. Pd. £12 10s.

Philpot, Henry. Pd. £25.

Pigot, Captain (John), 2. Sub. ——; pd. ——. (Taken prisoner at Mulheim in 1605. Went with Ralegh to Guiana in 1617, and died there.)

Pit, George, 2. Sub. £37 10s.; pd. £112 10s. Also of the E. I. and N. W. P. companies. Probably George Pitt, of Harrow on the Hill in County Middlesex, whose daughter Elizabeth married, first, Sir Henry Hatton, and, secondly, Peter Pett.

Plummer (or Plomer), Edward, merchant, 3. Sub. ——; pd. ——. Probably Edmund Plomer, of London, who was buried in St. Swithin's, London, August 31, 1624.

Plummer — Plumer — Plomer, Thomas, merchant-tailor. Sub. ——; pd. ——. Who bought Sir Walter Ralegh's house and lands at Mitcham in 1616 ; son of Walter Plomer, merchant-tailor, of London. In January, 1637, he was chosen sheriff of London, and King Charles wrote to the lord mayor and court of aldermen, asking them to excuse him from serving, "considering his infirmity in his hearing, and for some other respects best known to ourself, we hold him no way fit to undertake that charge, especially in these times of action." The lord mayor and aldermen were slow in consenting, and on the 17th October, 1637, the king wrote, "commanding that, without further delay, Mr. Plummer's bond should be delivered up to him," etc. He was buried in St. Swithin's Church, London, July 4, 1639. His son, Sir Walter, was made a baronet.

Pocahontas. Strachey says this name means "little wanton" — a name which the settlers would be apt to give to any little Indian girl. Powhatan was the father of more than one "little Indian wanton," and it does seem certain to me that the Po[...] tas (aged ten) seen by Smith 1608; the Pocahontas, *ali[...]* whom Strachey say[...] private captaine c[...] 1610 ; and the P[...] toaka (aged [...] Rolfe in A[...] the sam[...] ence[...] I[...]

was [...] oner [...] In the [...] very inte[...] in Virginia[...] Spanish spie[...]

mainly collected by "that piratical ship called the Treasurer," which, six years later, brought the first negroes to Virginia. In the spring of 1616, Sir Thomas Dale sailed to England in the Treasurer, taking with him the Princess Pocahontas and several other Indians. She was "the lion" of the day; was wined, and dined, and taken to the play. Lord and Lady De la Warr introduced her at court. She was entertained by the Bishop of London as the first fruit of the English Church among the Virginians. She died at Gravesend in March, 1617, and Smith says that Sir Lewis Stukely took charge of her child, Thomas Rolfe. Other accounts make it appear that the child was left with his uncle, Henry Rolfe. Stukely was the vice-admiral of Devon, before whom the whitewashing report of Smith's misadventure was made in December, 1615. In the summer of 1618 he betrayed his cousin, Sir Walter Ralegh. In January, 1619, it was found out that he "had been for many years engaged in the nefarious occupation of clipping coin;" and Gardiner says, "He fled away to hide his shame in the lonely Isle of Lundy, and in less than two years after Ralegh's execution, he died a raving madman, amidst the howling of the Atlantic storms."

Poe, Dr. (Leonard), 2. Sub. ——; pd. ——. One of the king's physicians; chosen a fellow of the College of Physicians, July 7, 1609. He attended Salisbury in his last illness.

Pole — Powle. See Powell.

Poole (see **Powell**), **Jonas,** mariner. He had made several voyages to the northern oceans before coming to Virginia; went to the falls of James River in May, 1607. Purchas says he was paid a certain stipend by Sir Thomas Smythe and the Mus. Co., and that he made annual voyages to the North Sea; that "he was the first namer of Greenland in the voyage of May, 1610 [the land was really Spitzbergen]; that he brought home, on ne of his voyages, the horne of a sea corn, which was good against poi- ; and that soon after his return his voyage of 1612 he was "mis- and basely murthered betwixt e and London."

(or **Pole**), **Sir William,** 3.

Sub. ——; pd. £37 10s. Of Shute, County Devon. The celebrated antiquary; barrister of the Inner Temple and treasurer of the same; sheriff of Devon, 1602–03; knighted at Whitehall, February 15, 1607; died February 9, 1635, aged 74.

Popham Pedigree. (Extract.) Alexander Popham, of Huntworth, County Somerset, married Jane, daughter of Sir Edward Stradling, of St. Donat's Castle, County Glamorgan, and had issue, with others, two sons, Edward and John (of whom hereafter).

The eldest son, Edward Popham, Esq., of Huntworth, married Jane, daughter of Richard Norton, of Abbot's Lee, and had, with others, two sons, Alexander and George (of whom hereafter).

Popham, Alexander. Eldest son of Edward Popham, Esq. (see pedigree); married Dulcibella, daughter of John Barley. He was buried in the Temple, London.

Popham, Sir Francis. Son and heir of Sir John Popham, Lord Chief Justice. "Lived chiefly at Haindstreet Marksbury, near Bath." Knighted by Essex for gallantry at Cadiz, 1596; M. P. for Somerset, 1597–98, and for Wiltshire, 1604–11; M. C. for Va., November 20, 1606; joined the South Va. Co. prior to 1619; M. P. for Marlborough, 1614; M. C. for N. E. Co., November 3, 1620; M. P. for Bedwin (Bodmin?) 1621–22; for Chippenham, 1624–25, 1625, and 1626; for Minehead, 1640 till decease. "He was a strong Parliamentarian, and was excepted out of the general pardon by the king." He was first buried at Stoke-Newington, near London, August 15, 1644; but it seems his body was removed and reburied at Bristol, March 16, 1647. He married Anne (born February 12, 1575), daughter of John Dudley, Esq., of Stoke-Newington (he died in 1581, and his widow married Thomas Sutton, founder of the Charterhouse), son of Hon. Thomas Dudley, by his wife Sarah, daughter and co-heir of Lancelot Thirkeld (was this the same person who aided in sending vessels to America in the first of the sixteenth century?). Sir Francis and Anne Popham were the parents of five sons and eight daughters. The eldest son, John, married, June 21, 1621,

Mary, daughter of Sir Sebastian Harvey. (Harvey died in April before the marriage, and his widow afterwards married Sir Thomas Hinton, whose daughter, by a former wife, married the celebrated Col. Samuel Matthews, of James City, Virginia.)

Popham, Captain George. Second son of Edward Popham, Esq. (see pedigree) ; was probably born about 1553–55; captured from a Spanish vessel at sea, in 1594, documents concerning Guiana, which were used by Ralegh (see his Life by Edwards, vol. i. p. 176). He was a captain in Robert Dudley's voyage to Guiana, November, 1594, to May, 1595. Gorges says, "He was well stricken in years before he went to America [in 1607], and had long been an infirm man." He died February 5, 1608, and was buried, I suppose, near the old fort of St. George.

Popham, Sir John. Second son of Alexander Popham, of Huntworth (see pedigree) ; was born at Wellington, Somersetshire, about 1531 ; educated at Baliol College, Oxford ; M. P. for Lyme Regis, 1557–58 ; reader at the Middle Temple, 1568 ; recorder of Bristol ; M. P. for Bristol, 1571, and 1572–83; serjeant at law, January 28, 1578 ; solicitor-general, June 26, 1579; attorney-general, June 1, 1581; speaker of Elizabeth's fourth Parliament, 1581–83; chief justice of the Queen's Bench, June 2, 1592, when he was knighted and made a privy councilor; summoned Essex to surrender, and was arrested by Essex, February 8, 1601 ; a witness against Essex on his trial. He presided at the trial of Sir Walter Ralegh in 1603.

In 1604 and 1605 there was a " great controversy between the Lord Zouch and the Lord Chief Justice." Carleton, writing to Winwood, says, " There hath a great cause troubled the council often and long, between the Lord Zouch and the Lord Chief Justice ; the one standing for his privileges of the bench, the other for his Court of Presidency, which do sometimes cross one another. The prerogative finds more friends among the lords, but the judges and attorney plead hard for the law; the king stands indifferent; *ad-huc sub judice lis est.*" I believe this quarrel had an effect on our destiny.

On the 30th of October, 1605, Sir John Zouche and Capt. George Waymouth entered into an agreement for settling a private plantation in Virginia ; but, *per contra*, there was a strong movement, with Sir John Popham as leader, against private plantations, "which had always failed," and in favor of public plantations, managed by large incorporated companies, and the Popham idea prevailed. He presided at the trials of Guy Fawkes and his associates in 1606. " March 30, 1607, he was commissioned to supply the place of the lord chancellor in Parliament during his absence." " June 10, 1607, Sir John Popham died suddenly." June 23, 1607, licensed to William Blackwall and William Ferbrand. " A Dyttie of the Commons complaint for the Death of the right honorable Sir John Popham, Lord Chief Justice of England." " His remains repose under a magnificent tomb in the church at Wellington, Somerset, surrounded by a palisade of wood and iron." " He acquired the estate of Littlecote, Wiltshire, and founded the Pophams of that place." He married, about 1560, Amy, daughter and heir of Robert Games, Esq., of Caselton, County Glamorgan, and had issue by her : — 1. Sir Francis Popham, son and heir ; 2. Penelope Popham, married Thomas Hanham, serjeant at law, and they were the parents of Sir John and Thomas Hanham ; 3. Jane Popham, married Thomas Horner, Esq. ; 4. Eleanor Popham, married Roger Warre, Esq.; 5. Elizabeth Popham, married Sir Richard Champernon ; •6. Mary Popham, married Sir John Mallet ; 7. Katherine Popham, married Edward Rogers, Esq.

Pory, John, gen
pd. ——. Born abo
Gonvil and Caius Col

1587 ; about 1597 became a disciple of Hakluyt in "Cosmographie and foreign histories." In 1600 he translated, collected, and published, "A Geographical Historie of Africa, written in Arabicke and Italian, by John Leo, a More, borne in Granada, and brought up in Barbarie." It is dedicated to Sir Robert Cecil. Pory has added a good deal of original matter, which had been collected by him. It contains a good account of Abyssinia, and a map of Africa, tracing the Nile from an inland lake.

M. P. for Bridgewater, 1605–11 ; Master of Arts at Cambridge, April 19, 1610; licensed to travel for three years, May 21, 1611; carried to France a treatise of the Bishop of Ely and Casaubon's to the Cardinal Perron, in answer of a certain letter of his sent to King James, and a present to De Thou, the French historian, of material for Queen Elizabeth's life, collected by Cotton and written out by Camden, defending Mary Queen of Scots ; visiting Turin, with purpose to see those parts in July, 1613 ; became attached to the embassy of Paul Pindar at Constantinople, and when Pindar was recalled in November, 1616, the loss of his place "came ill to pass for poor Master Pory." "It had been long reported in England," says Carew to Roe, "that he had died in Constantinople ;" arrived in England in January, 1617, bringing letters from Sir Thomas Roe, dated at Asmore, East India, in February, 1616, and sent overland to Aleppo, and then to Constantinople, there opened by the ambassador, and delivered to Mr. Pory, who brought them into England ; at The Hague in September, 1617 ; returned to England in October following ; employed with others by the Privy Council to bring back Lord Roos from Rome in the winter of 1617–18 ; returned to England in February, 1618, "saying he had only been to Turin, and south parts of France." On November 28, 1618, he wrote to Carleton, "is offered the secretaryship for Virginia by means of Sir George Yardley, the newly elected governor ; but will not accept it without outfit as well as allowance." He did accept ; sailed from England January 19, 1619, and arrived in Virginia April

19. He was added to the council in Virginia, and on July 30, 1619, he was the first speaker of the first House of Burgesses in America. He remained in Virginia, making voyages of discovery, writing letters, and making himself generally useful until about August, 1622, when he sailed from Virginia in the Discovery, Capt. Thomas Jones, via New England, to discover all the harbors and the shoals off Cape Cod, and to trade along the coast where they could. July 26, 1623, Chamberlain wrote to Carleton, "Our old acquaintance, Mr. Pory, is in poor case, and in prison at the Terceras, whither he was driven, by contrary winds, from the north coast of Virginia, where he had been upon some discovery, and upon his arrival [at the Azores] was arraigned, and in danger to be hanged for a pirate." He probably reached England soon after. On the 20th of October, 1623, the Privy Council chose him to carry over and to publish throughout Virginia, the orders of July 4, 1623 (concerning the relief for Virginia), of October 8, 1623 (declaring the king's resolution in re Virginia), and of October 20, 1623 (explaining the king's position). On the 24th of October he was appointed on the commission to inquire into the real state of the plantation in Virginia. They arrived in Virginia in January, 1624, and performed their commission. In their report, drawn up in February, 1624, they assert that the general desire of the colony is to be immediately under the government and protection of the king, "only some few, employed by the company, fear, by the change of government, their loss of employment, and so desire to be still under the company." Pory was on the Virginia Commission of July 15, 1624, and was a member in England of the council for Virginia ; but, it seems, never returned to America again. He remained in London as a news letter-writer, intelligencer, or reporter, until about 1631, when he retired to his home at Sutton St. Edmonds, where he died in 1635–36, and in April, 1636, administration on his estate was granted by the Prerogative Court of Canterbury to "Anne Ellis, wife of Robert Ellis, and sister of John Pory, late of Sutton St. Ed-

GILBERT TALBOT

Seventh Earl of Shrewsbury

monds, Lincolnshire, bachelor, deceased, intestate."

Pory, Robert. Pd. £25.

Potts, Richard. Clerk of the Council in Virginia, 1608–09; returned to England.

Powell, Sergeant - Major Anthony. Killed at St. Augustine, Florida, by Spaniards, August 8, 1586.

Powell, Captain Nathaniel. One of the first planters; left England in December, 1606, and arrived in Virginia in April, 1607. In the winter of 1608, with Newport, exploring the York River. From July 24 to September 7, 1608, with Captain Smith, exploring the Chesapeake Bay. He was probably the author of the "Diarie of the second voyage in discovering the Bay," which was sent to England by Newport in December, 1608; and the sixth chapter of Smith's "History" was probably partially compiled from this "Diarie," as it bears Powell's signature, and it was probably "Captain Powell's Map" of the bay and rivers which accompanied "The Relation of the Countries and Nations," said to have been sent to England by Smith in December, 1608. He was deputy-governor of Virginia for a short time in 1619, and member of the council there, 1619–22. Himself and wife were killed by the Indians, March 22, 1622. His wife was a daughter of Master William Tracy, and he was interested in the Tracy - Berkeley - Smith of Nibley - Thorpe plantation at Berkeley in Virginia.

Powell — Powle — Poole — Pole — Sir Stephen, 2. Sub. £37 10s.; pd. £100. Son of Thomas Powle, Esq., one of the six clerks of the chancery, by his wife, Jane Tate, which Thomas died in 1601, aged 88, and was buried in St. Dunstan's in the West, London, and "his son, Stephen Powle, Esq., the only survivor of five sons, succeeded him in the office of one of the six clerks of the chancery." He was knighted at Theobald's, July 21, 1604,

as of Essex; M. C. for Va. Co., May 23, 1609; still living in 1619.

Powell, William, gent., 2. Sub. ——; pd. £25. Came to Virginia with Gates in 1611; was the gunner of James City; member of the first House of Burgesses, July 30, 1619. Pace first told him of the plot revealed by Chanco for murdering the colonists, March 21, 1622. He was afterwards employed in taking revenge on the Indians, and was probably killed by them on the Chicahominy, between January 20 and 24, 1623.

Powhatan. "Emperor of the Indians in Virginia;" died in April, 1618. The father of Pocahontas. Hamor says, "Powhatan's father was driven from the West Indies by the Spaniards." Beverley says, "Opechancanough was said to have been a prince of a foreign nation and came to Virginia a great way from the southwest, and by their (the Indians) account we suppose him to have come from the Spanish Indians, somewhere near Mexico, or the mines of St. Barbe." Smith says, "Opechancanough was a brother to Powhatan," which Beverley doubts. However, when we consider the above accounts, with the habits of exploring Spaniards (especially those under De Soto) and the superiority of Powhatan and Pocahontas to the Indians generally, we may enable their descendants to build for their ancestors "castles in Spain."

Poyntell, Richard, fishmonger. Sub. ——; pd. £62 10s. Of the E. I. and N. W. P. companies; will dated in January, 1621; a benefactor of the Fishmongers.

Pratt, John, 2. Sub. ——; pd. £12 10s. Came to Virginia in 1608.

Prescott, Jeffrey, merchant-tailor. Pd. £1. Son of William Prescott, of Copul in the parish of Standish, and of Eccleston, both in County Lancaster.

Preston, Sir Amias ——; pd. £100. " ᴵ ancient family at Cricket, nigh setshire; a valia seaman. He g himself in the bat Armada in 1588, was dangerously w Made a voyage w

Somers to the West Indies in 1595 ; knighted by Essex for gallantry at Cadiz in 1596 ; commanded the Defiance in the fleet sent to the Azores under Essex in 1597. After the Essex rising, early in 1601, it seems Sir Walter Ralegh became involved in a quarrel with Sir Ferdinando Gorges and Sir Amias Preston, and Preston challenged Ralegh for a duel, "but the parties were afterwards reconciled;" appointed by James I. "keeper of the naval stores and ordnance in the Tower," May 17, 1603.

M. C. for Va. Co., May 23, 1609. He is said to have died early in the reign of King James, but the date of his death is unknown to me. The records of the Va. Co. show that he died before 1619. (Amyas Preston, gent., and Julian Burye, widow, of the city of London, were married at Stepney in May, 1581.)

Pretty, George, gent., 2. Sub. ——; pd. £12 10s. Came to Virginia in 1607. (Francis Pretty was one of the very few Englishmen who went twice around the world in the sixteenth century.)

Price, Rev. Daniel. Son of Thomas Price, Vicar of Shrewsbury ; born in 1578 ; M. A. Oxford, and a chaplain to Henry, Prince of Wales, in 1609 ; published several sermons on the death of the prince, also anniversary sermons on that event in 1613 and 1614. He was afterwards chaplain to Charles, Prince of Wales, and in July, 1621, was imprisoned for a few days for a sermon "wherein he was too busy with Rochelle, the Palatinate, and the Spaniard." Dean of Hereford in 1625 ; died in 1631, and was buried in the chancel of the church of Worthy's, near Caus Castle, Shropshire.

Price, Henry, 2. Sub. ——; pd. £12 10s.

Pring, Captain Martin. Born in 1580, probaby near Awliscombe Devon. His will, which was recorded in Bristol in 1626, mentions his father, John Pring, as then living, and his sister Margaret. Charles Kingsley, in his "Westward Ho !" says, "It was to the men of Devon, the Drakes and Hawkins, Gilberts and Raleighs, Grenvilles and Oxenhams, and a host more of 'forgotten worthies,' whom we shall learn one day to honor as

they deserve, to whom England owes her commerce, her colonies, and her very existence." The naval heroes of Elizabeth's warlike reign, who fought battles, are comparatively well-known. The "forgotten worthies" generally belong to the peaceful reign of James I., who established colonies and commerce. They were not confined to Devonshire, although many of them were from that county. I hope "we shall now learn to honor them as they deserve."

In the voyage to our New England coast, March 20 to October 2, 1603, Martin Pring was master of the Speedwell, and chief commander in the voyage ; and as he was then regarded (in his 23d year) as "a man very sufficient for the place," he had probably been bred to the sea, and was familiar with the Atlantic Ocean. The map (CLVIII.) will throw some light on this voyage. Pring named Whitson's Bay, for Master John Whitson, then mayor of Bristol, and one of the chief adventurers in the voyage. He was the founder of the Red Maid's School, Bristol. The bay is now called Cape Cod Bay. "Pring carried to England an Indian canoe, and reported the land he had visited to be full of God's good blessings."

March 21, 1604, he sailed as master of the Phœnix for Guiana ; arrived at Wiapoco in May, but having some misunderstanding, he left the Phœnix; and returned to England in a ship of Amsterdam.

In October, 1606, he was again sent to our northern coast by the North Virginia Company, of which voyage Sir Ferdinando Gorges wrote, "After he [Pring] had made a perfect discovery of all those rivers and harbors he was informed of by his instructions (the season of the year requiring his return), he brought with him the most exact discovery of that coast that ever came to my hand since ; and, indeed, he was the best able to perform it of any I met withal to this present." And on his report an expedition was at once fitted out to establish an English colony on that coast. Where he was in 1608-13, I do not know, but probably in the East India service. On the 1st of March, 1614, he sailed to the East Indies as master of the New Year's

Gift, and, returning, reached England June 25, 1616.

On the 4th of February, 1617, he again sailed to the East Indies as general of the fleet ; arrived at Bantam, July 21, 1617; took Lord Rich's two roving ships, near the river of Surat, in September, 1617; late in 1618, joined his fleet to Sir Thomas Dale's fleet, the whole being under Dale's chief command, and on the 23d of December, 1618, these combined fleets made an attack on the Dutch fleet, off the island of Java. On the 9th of August, 1619, Dale died at Masulipatam, and Pring succeeded him in command of the English East India fleet. He remained in the waters of the East Indies, Japan, etc., until 1621, when he sailed for England, and arrived in The Downs, September 18, 1621. While his ship, the Royal James, was at the Cape of Good Hope, on the return voyage, her chaplain, the Rev. Patrick Copland (whom Dale had interested in Virginia while they were serving together in the East Indies) gathered from the gentlemen and mariners in the said ship the sum of £70 8s. 6d. towards the building of a free school in Virginia. "The highest amount is £6 13s. 4d. by Capt. Martin Pring, and so decreasing to 1s." This money was paid to Henry, Earl of Southampton, for the Va. Co. at their great and general quarter court, held the 21st of November, 1621; and the court added 1,000 acres of land to the said free school, to be at Charles City, and to be called "the East India school." "Towards the furtherance of the East Indie Schoole, an unknowne person" had already added the sum of £30, and at the Quarter Court held the 30th of January, 1622, a "person, not willing as yet to be knowne," sent £25 in gold "to helpe forward the East Indie Schoole ;" and "the gentlemen and mariners that came lately [early in 1622] home from the East Indies in the two ships called the Hart and Roe-Bucke, being at the Cape of Bona Speranza [Good Hope], homeward bound, gave towards the building of the aforesaid Free-Schoole in Virginia the summe of £66 13s. 4d.," making a total of £192 1s. 10d. = about $4,800.

"On the 3d of July, 1622, the Quarter Court of the Virginia Company thought fitt to make Capt. Martin Pring a freeman of the Companie, and to give him two shares of land in Virginia in regard of the large contribution which the gentlemen and marriners of his ship had given towards good works in Virginia, whereof he was an especiall furtherer."

Captain Pring died in 1626, aged 46. His monument still exists in St. Stephen's Church, Bristol, England, with the following inscription: "To the Pious Memorie of Martin Pringe, Merchaunt, Sometyme Generall to the East Indies, and one of ye Fraternity of the Trinity House.

" The living worth of this dead man was such,
That this fayr Touch can give you but A Touch
Of his admired guifts ; Theise quarter'd Arts,
Enrich'd his knowledge and ye spheare imparts ;
His heart's true embleme where pure thoughts did move,
By A most sacred Influence from above.
Prudence and Fortitude ore topp this toombe,
Which in brave PRINGE tooke up ye chiefest roome ;
Hope-Time supporters showe that he did clyme
The highest pitch of Hope though not of Tyne.
His painefull, skillfull travayles reacht as farre,
As from the Artick to th' Antartick starre ;
Hee made himselfe A Shipp. Religion
His onely compass, and the truth alone
His guiding Cynosure ; Faith was his sailes,
His anchour Hope, A hope that never failes ;
His freighte was Charitie, and his returne
A fruitfull practice. In this fatal urne
His Shipp's fayr Bulck is lodg'd, but ye ritch ladinge
Is hous'd in heaven, A haven never fadinge.

Hic terris multum jactatus et undis.

Obit Anno { Salutis } 1626. { Ætatis } 46.

"This Monument was Beautified by Mrs. Hannah Oliver, widdow, 1733."

Captain Pring's daughter, Alice, married Andrews, son of William Burwell. The name is frequently spelled Prynn, and I am quite sure that Mr. John Prynn, who patented lands in Virginia in 1623, was of the same family, and as it seems certain fr⸳ the will of Miles Prickett (s⸳ England Register," Ja⸳ 62), that "the ⸳ Pryn" himself to Virginia in N⸳ be that the pate⸳ who was still livi⸳ seems probable fr⸳ death, and of Prick⸳ either died on his v⸳

or very soon after his return to England.

Pringham. See Springham.

Proctor, Rev. George, 2. Sub. ——; pd. £25. One of the king's chaplains; rector of Holme Spalding-upon-Moor and Barwick-in-Elmett, both in County York.

Proctor, Rev. John, 3. Sub. ——; pd. ——. Possibly came to Virginia in 1609.

Proude, Captain William, 2. Sub. ——; pd. £25.

Prusey (see **Brewsey**), **Ambrose,** gent., 2. Sub.——; pd. £12 10s.

Pruson. See Spruson.

Puckering, Sir Thomas, baronet. Son of Sir John Puckering, an eminent lawyer of the reign of Queen Elizabeth. He was of the N. W. P. Co., July 26, 1612; created a baronet November 25, 1612; resided at the Priory, near Warwick; died March 20, 1636.

Puleston, Roger, esquire, 3. Sub. ——; pd. ——. Of Emral in Flint; M. P. Bodmin, 1584–85 and 1586–87; for County of Flint, 1588–89; for County of Denbigh, 1593, and for County of Flint again, 1604–11. He was knighted August 28, 1617.

Purchas, Rev. Samuel. Son of George Purchas, of the parish of Thaxted in Essex; born about 1574; educated at St. John's College, Cambridge. His license to marry, recorded in the Bishop of London's office, was issued December 2, 1601, and is as follows: "Samuel Purcas, clerk, curate of Purleigh Essex, bachelor, 27, and Jane Lease, of same, maiden, 26, daughter of Vincent Lease, of Westhall, Co. Suffolk, yeoman, her parents both consent, as attested by her brother, Thomas Lease, Mr. D. Freake, parson of Purleigh, whose household servants the said Samuel Purchas and Jane Lease now are, and the said Jane hath lived with said D. Freake these three years, desires licence — at Purleigh aforesaid." (Purleigh is of peculiar interest to Americans. The Rev. Lawrence Washington was rector there, 1633–43. See Sir Warham St. Leger.) Rev. Samuel Purchas was vicar of Eastwood in Essex, 1604–13. His "Pilgrimage," entered for publication at Stationers' Hall, August 7, 1612, issued from the press soon after November 5, 1612. The second edition appeared in 1614, in which year he was collated to the rectory of St. Martin's, Ludgate, London (where he continued to his death), and appointed chaplain to George Abbot, Archbishop of Canterbury.

The Rev. Richard Hakluyt died in November, 1616, and many of his papers coming into the hands of Purchas, he used them in compiling a third edition of his "Pilgrimage," "much enlarged with Additions through the whole worke," which was published in 1617. "Purchas his Pilgrim-Microcosmus, or the Historie of Man" was published in 1619. On the 11th of December, 1621, "Purchas his Pilgrimes" was entered at Stationers' Hall for publication. The imprint begun in August, 1621. The work issued from the press in 1625. May 22, 1622, Purchas was admitted into the Va. Co. of London. May 5, 1623, "The King's Tower and Triumphant Arch of London, written by Samuell Purchas," was licensed to W. Stansby.

Purchas died in 1626, aged 51 years. His will was written May 31, 1625, and proved October 21, 1626. In this instrument he mentions his "father, George Purchas, of pious memory;" his brother William and his sons Daniel and Samuel; his brother George and his son John; his brother Thomas and his son Samuel; his brother-in-law, William Perkins, who had married his sister Mary; his own wife Jane, his own son Samuel, and his own daughter Martha. (An abstract of his will is given in the "New England Hist. and Gen. Register," July, 1884, pp. 319–20.) It is said that he had also a brother Daniel and a sister, who married William Predimore.

There is a difference of opinion as to the qualification of Purchas as an editor of historical matter. Chambers says, "He is excessive full of his own notions, and of mean quibbling and playing upon words. . . . Among his peculiarities is that of interlarding theological reflections and discussions with his narratives." To me it seems that the bent of his mind is shown in his "Pilgrimage." When he edited his "Pilgrimes," his hobby continued to be the traveler's tales of the religions, customs, and privities of foreign countries. Many of the narratives from which he compiled still remain, and it seems evident that he constantly omitted important, practical matter, while retaining the most wonderful, and sometimes fabulous, accounts of people, their religions, and privities. He was probably not well informed as to Virginia, as it was against the interest of the enterprise that he should be. He evidently had no access to the early records of the company. He did not even know the dates of the arrival of the Spaniards in Virginia (1611), and of Argall's voyage to New England (1613) ; events which agitated the courts of half of Europe at the time. Until Hakluyt's death, he was obliged to rely on Smith ; then Hakluyt's papers furnished some other material down to 1616 ; but, unfortunately, before receiving these papers, Purchas had " covered the ground" with Smith's story, and he did not hesitate to mutilate and to sacrifice Hakluyt's valuable papers to his own previously expressed opinions, as influenced by the said story. After 1616, he had again to rely on Smith's and other publications, as the Virginia records were not accessible to him. He acknowledged that Captain Smith was " no reputed favourite or favourer of the Virginia Company and their actions." He joined Smith in ridiculing the cultivation of tobacco as a staple, and grew eloquent in describing " how rich might Virginia become if the colonists would only turn their attention to ginger and hides."

I believe Purchas was at heart a real friend to the Virginian enterprise ; but I am sure that his works display more learning than accurate information or practical knowledge in the premises ; and I feel certain that the managers of the enterprise understood their business much better than their critics did.

" Mr. D. Freake, parson of Purleigh, whose household servant " Purchas was in 1601, I take to be Mr. Dr. Freake, or Rev. Mr. Freake, D. D., the son, I suppose, of Edmund Freake, Bishop of Worcester ; probably his eldest son, John, archdeacon of Norwich and rector of Purleigh, who died in 1604, the year that Purchas removed to Eastwood in Essex, as vicar there.

Purefoy, Nicholas. Sub. ——; pd. £12 10s. This name is given in the Kimbolton MS. as " Sir Nich: Pewrifie."

Pyott (Piggott, etc.), **Richard,** grocer, 3. Sub. £37 10s. ; pd. £25. Of L. I. Co. ; elected alderman of Bridge Without ward, May 3, 1610, and chosen sheriff of London the same year. He died January 19, 1620, and was buried under a very fair monument on the south side of the chancel in the parish church of St. Lawrence, Jewry, London.

Quarles, John, draper, 2. Sub. ——; pd. ——. Son of John Quarles, of London, gentleman and draper, who married three wives, and was the father of twenty-three children. He was probably of the same family as Francis Quarles, the poet, who was the father of eighteen children.

Quicke, William, grocer and apothecary, 2. Sub. £37 10s. ; pd. £62 10s. Served his apprenticeship to " Andrew Juxe ; " admitted a freeman, 1592; mentioned in court minutes, June 22, 1614, as " a Brother of this company [Grocers'] practising in the Arte of misterie of Appothecaries, who refused to take up the Livery of the Grocers to which he had been nominated." He was one of eleven apothecaries interrogated by the court as to their conduct respecting a movement towards founding a distinct corporation of their own. The movement was carried to a successful issue, and the Apothecaries were incorporated as a separate company ; but Quicke did not live to see that day. He died in January, 1615, leaving his adventures in Virginia and the Bermudas to his three daughters. (See his will in " N. E. Hist. Gen. Register," 1884, p. 60.)

Quniga. See Zuñiga.

Rainsford, Sir Henry. Pd. £37 10s. Son of Hercules Rainsford, Esq., of Clifford, County Gloucester, by Elizabeth, daughter of Robert Parry ; was knighted at Whitehall, July 23, 1603 ; M. C. for Va. Co. ; allowed a bill of adventure for three shares in Virginia, June 17, 1618 ; bought three shares from Sir Thomas Gates, May 31, 1620, and two from Francis Carter, April 30, 1621. He married Anne, daughter of Sir Henry Goodere, of Polsworth, County Warwick ; died January 27, 1622, leaving issue.

Rainton, Nicholas, haberdasher. Pd. £25. Son of Robert Rainton, of Highinton, Lincolnshire ; elected alderman of Tower ward, June 22, and chosen sheriff of London, June 25, 1621; Lord Mayor of London, 1632–33; knighted at Whitehall, May 5, 1633 ; alderman for Aldgate ward in 1633, and removed to Cornhill ward, April 29, 1634. President of St. Bartholomew's Hospital, 1634 to his death in 1646 ; imprisoned, May 7 to 15, 1640. He died August 24, 1646, and was buried in the parish church at Enfield. His portrait was at Forty Hall, in Enfield, Middlesex. His granddaughter and heir, Mary Rainton, married Sir John Wolstenholme, the grandson of Sir John Wolstenholme, the younger (who died in 1669), of the Va. Co.

Sir Nicholas Rainton, by his will, dated May 2, 1646, left his residence in Lombard Street, and adjoining property to the Haberdashers' Company for certain charitable purposes, payable annually, namely : to 25 poor of the Company 26s. each = £32 10s. ; Master and Wardens, 20s. each = £5 ; Clerk, £1 ; Beadle, 10s. ; Porter, 13s. To St. Bartholomew's Hospital, £12 ; the City of Lincoln, £10 ; the Parish of Enfield, £10; the Parishes of Washingborough and Heighington, Lincolnshire, £11 8s.; of St. Edmund the King, London, £2 ; and of St. Mary Woolchurch, London, £2. The surplus income was given to the Haberdashers' Company.

Ralegh, Sir Carew, 3. Sub. £37 10s. ; pd. ——. Elder brother of Sir Walter ; seated at Downton in Wilts ; M. P. for Wilts, 1584–85 and 1586–87 ; for Ludgershall, 1588–89 ; and for Fowey, 1601; knighted in 1601 ; M. P. for Downton, 1604–11, 1614, and 1621–22. He married Dorothy, sister of Thomas Wroughton, and relict of Sir John Thynne of Longleat, and was living in 1623. (His wife's son, Sir Henry Thynne, first planned a voyage to Guiana, then, in April, 1612, a voyage to Persia, and in 1614, to the E. I. ; and the E. I. Co. was charged with hindering his voyages in December, 1614).

Ralegh, Sir Walter. Born at Hayes Barton, in Devon, in 1552 ; en-

tered Oriel College, at Oxford, about 1568 ; served with the Huguenots in France, 1569–75; under Sir John Norris in the Low Countries, 1576–78 ; interested with his half-brother, Sir Humphrey Gilbert, in his American schemes, 1578; sailed with Gilbert for America in the fall of 1578, in command of the Falcon ; Gilbert was forced to return, but Ralegh determined to make a raid on Spanish vessels, had a dangerous sea-fight near the Cape Verde Islands, and returned to Plymouth, May 28, 1579 ; was recruiting soldiers for Ireland in July, 1580 ; landed at Dingle, Ireland, in October, 1580 ; took part in suppressing the insurrection in Ireland, and received a grant of 12,000 acres of Desmond's lands, in Cork and Waterford; in favor with Queen Elizabeth, April, 1582 ; furnished a ship, the Ralegh, for Gilbert's voyage to America in 1583; interested in Adrian Gilbert's patent of the North West Passage, February 6, 1584 ; his own letters patent for planting of the New Lands in America, March 25, 1584; aided in sending Amadas and Barlow to America, April 27, 1584 ; Hakluyt wrote for him " A particular discourse concerning the great necessitie and manifold Comodyties that are like to grow to this Realme of England by the Westerne discoveries," etc. ; M. P. for Devon, November 23, 1584, to September 14, 1585 ; the House of Commons took action on his patent, December 14–18, and the House of Lords, December 19, 1584 ; knighted at Greenwich, January 6, 1585 ; Greenville's voyage, taking the first colony to Roanoke, April 9, 1585 ; warden of the Stannaries, July, 1585 ; ventured vessels in the voyages of the Earl of Cumberland ; M. P. Devon, October 15, 1586, to March 23, 1587 ; letter from Hakluyt at Paris, December 30, 1586, telling him that he had dedicated his " Peter Martyr " to him (Ralegh), and advising him to make his plantation in Chesapeake Bay. His colony had returned from Roanoke with Drake, in July, 1586, his indenture to White and others, January 7, 1587. In this year he received a grant of Babington's forfeited estates, March 17 ; White's voyage sailed for Roanoke, May 8 ; Hakluyt's translation of the " Narratives of the

Huguenots in Florida" dedicated to him, May 1 ; he published "The voyage which Antonio de Espeio made in the yeere 1583, of the dyscoverye of Newe Mexico," in May (probably the first book published by Ralegh) ; was captain of the queen's guard and member of the council of war. In 1588 he served against the Armada, and Hariot dedicated his "Briefe and true report of the new found land of Virginia" to him. In 1589 he transferred his American grants to Thomas Smith and others, reserving to himself the fifth part of all the ore of gold and silver only, March 7 ; his vessels were constantly found on the Atlantic in search of Spanish prizes ; he served in the Portugal expedition under Drake, and visited Spenser at Kilcolman Castle. Returned to court ; wrote the report of Sir Richard Grenville's seafight in 1591 ; was a partner in Sir John Watts' voyage to America, March to October, 1591 ; planned a voyage against Panama, 1592 ; married Elizabeth Throgmorton, and was imprisoned in the Tower, 1592 ; M. P. for St. Michael's, February 19 to April 10, 1593 ; Whiddon's voyage to Guiana, 1594 ; his own voyage to Guiana, February to August, 1595 ; at the taking of Cadiz, June, 1596 ; published an account of his voyage of 1595 to Guiana, in 1596, and sent a voyage there under Keymis. January to June, 1596 ; and another under Berry (or Birnie) December 27, 1596, to June 28, 1597. In 1597 he reappeared at court in May, and sailed on the celebrated voyage to the Azores in August; M. P. for Dorset, October 24, 1597, to February 9, 1598; planning another expedition to Guiana, under Sir John Gilbert, in November, 1598 ; governor and captain of Jersey, etc., August 26, 1600 ; M. P. Cornwall, October 27 to December 19, 1601 ; Mace's voyage and Ralegh's letter to Cecil in regard to Gilbert's voyage, 1602 ; his permission for Pring's voyage of 1603 ; met King James on his way to London ; committed to the Tower on charge of implication in the Main conspiracy ; was tried and convicted November 17, 1603 ; Sir John Popham presided at his trial. He remained in the Tower until January 30, 1616. Count Scarnafissi proposed to Ralegh to divert his expedition from Guiana, and to join the forces of the Great Duke of Savoy in making an attack on Genoa. Ralegh was anxious to enter this service, thereby causing a delay in the preparations for the American voyage; but in January, 1617, England refused to aid the duke in his war with Spain, and on March 28 following Ralegh sailed for Guiana, where he made an attack on the Spaniards. He returned to England (sailing past our whole coast, *via* Newfoundland), arriving there in June, 1618 ; was arrested soon after ; beheaded October 29, and buried in St. Margaret's, Westminster. His only surviving son, Carew Ralegh, was admitted into the Va. Co. of London, April 2, 1623.

The story of the second Roanoke colony is the tragedy of American colonization.

Ramirez, Captain Diego. The islands near Cape Horn were named for him.

Ramsden, Millicent, widow, 2. Sub. —— ; pd. £37 10s. On the 24th of June, 1619, she transferred her three shares of land in Virginia to Oliver St. John. She was the widow of Samuel Ramsden, of St. Sepulchre, London, brewer, whom she married in 1604. He was her second husband. Her first husband was John Worsley, brewer.

Ratcliffe, Sir John, 2. Sub. —— ; pd. £50. Son of Sir John Radcliffe, of Ordsall, County Lancaster ; was baptized February 24, 1581 ; knighted in Ireland on "the Sands," September 24, 1599 ; heir to his elder brother, Sir Alexander Radclyffe, slain in Ireland in 1599 ; M. P. for Tewkesbury, 1614, Lancashire, 1621–22, 1624–25, and 1625, and for Tavistock, 1626. He married Alice, eldest daughter of Sir John Byron of Newstead, and was slain in the Isle of Ré, October 29, 1627. His father had five sons, all slain in battle : Alexander and William in Ireland, and Edmond and Thomas in Flanders, all about 1599 ; Margaret, their sister and favorite maid of honor to Queen Elizabeth, died of grief for the loss of these four brothers, and the fifth brother, Sir John, as we have seen, fell at Ré in 1627.

Ratcliffe, Captain John, 2. Sub. —— ; pd. £50. I believe him to be the Captain Ratcliffe who was taken prisoner with Sir Henry Cary and Captain Pigott at Mulheim in the Low Countries in October, 1605.

There is some confusion about his name, and hence it is hard to locate him ; but Smith's allusion to him as " a poor counterfeited imposture " was an unpardonable reflection on a dead man. There was no imposture. He signed his name " John Radclyffe comenly called," and in the list of incorporators of the Va. Co. of London his name is recorded as " Captain John Sicklemore *alias* Ratcliffe."

In these biographies I have generally avoided going into the details of the history of the colony in Virginia, but I believe Ratcliffe served his full term of one year in the presidency from September 10, 1607, to September 10, 1608. Under the laws then ruling he could legally serve no longer in that place, and was succeeded by Capt. John Smith, "as by course it did belong," the only other councilor, Captain Scrivener, having but recently arrived in Virginia. Ratcliffe went to England in January, and returned to Virginia in June, 1609, where he was "betrayed and murthered " by Powhatan in the winter of 1609-10.

It has been unjustly and erroneously stated that Raphe Hamor wrote his epitaph in a few pithy words : " He was not worth remembering but to his dishonor." These words of Hamor were applied to Powhatan's treachery in betraying Ratcliffe, not to Ratcliffe.

(The amount of his payment (£50) is not given in the printed account of 1620. He was then long since dead ; but it is given in the Kimbolton MS.) "George Warburton, gent., of St. Dunstan-in-the-West, on February 19, 161½, was licensed to marry Dorothy Ratcliffe of All Hallows Stayning, 33, widow of John Ratcliffe, late of St. Andrew, Halborn, deceased two years ago" [1609 – 10]. Was this our captain ?

Ravenscrofte, William, esquire,

3. Sub. £37 10s. ; pd. ——.   Of Bretton, County Flint ; M. P. for Flintshire, 1586–87, 1597–98, 1601; Old Sarum, 1604–11 and 1614 ; and for Flint Town, 1621–22, 1624–25, 1625, 1626, and 1628–29.

Ravis, Thomas, Lord Bishop of London. Born at Maulden in Surrey; educated in Christ Church, Oxford, whereof he was dean ; twice vicechancellor of Oxford University ; Bishop of Gloucester ; Bishop of London in 1607, where he died December 14, 1609.

Reynolds, Henry, esquire, 2. Sub. £37 10s. ; pd. £87 10s. November 6, 1622, transferred two shares in Virginia to William Vesy.

Reynolds (or Reynell), Humphrey. Pd. £12 10s.

Reighnolds, John, 3. Sub. £37 10s.; pd. £12 10s. (Master gunner to Henry, Prince of Wales ?)

Reynolds (etc.), **Richard,** 2. Sub. —— ; pd. £50.

Reynell, William, merchant-tailor. Pd. 10s. (This name is particularly hard to locate. I find it spelled Reighnolds, Reynolds, Reynells, Reynell, Renell, and Revell ; then Raighnolds, Raynolds, etc.).

Ribault, Captain Jean. Massacred by Menendez, in Florida, September 23, 1565.

Rich Pedigree. (Extract.) Richard [1] Rich of the Middle Temple attorney at law, the witness against Sir Thomas More, was created Baron Rich, February 16, and lord chancellor of England, October 23, 1547, and died in 1568, leaving, with others, a son and successor, Robert,[2] second Baron Rich, who was the father of several legitimate sons, viz. : of Richard [3] (who married Katherine, daughter of Sir Henry Knevitt, and died *s. p.*,*v. p.*), of (1) Robert,[3] his successor (of whom hereafter), and of others. The second baron was also the father of an illegitimate son, Richard [3] Rich, who married a daughter of John Machell, sheriff of London, and was the father of (2) Sir Nathaniel [4] (hereafter), of (3) Robert [4] (hereafter), of Margery [4] who married Sir Thomas Wroth, of Jane [4] who married Thomas Grimsditch, a nephew to Secretary Sir John Coke, of another daughter [4] who married a Mr. Browne, and another [4] married to a Mr. Morgan. (1) Robert,[3] third Baron Rich, successor to his father, was created Earl of Warwick, August 6, 1618. He married, first, Penelope Devereux, sister to the Earl of Essex (Sir Philip Sidney's "Stella") and had issue by her : (4) i. Robert[4]; (5) ii. Henry[4]; iii. Charles[4]; i. Lettice[4] (or Lucy) married, first, Sir George Cary, and, secondly, Sir Arthur Lake ; ii. Penelope[4] married Sir Gervase Clifton, Baronet of Clifton ; iii. Essex[4] married Sir Thomas Cheeke of Pirgo ; and iv. Isabel[4] married Sir John, son of Sir Thomas Smythe. The third Baron Rich married, secondly, in 1616, Frances, daughter of Sir Christopher Wray, and widow of Sir George Saint Paule (she was the patroness of the Rev. Richard Bernard), but by her had no issue.

Rich, Sir Henry, 3. Sub. ——; pd. ——. (See pedigree, 5.) The second son of the third Lord Rich ; was baptized at Stratford-Bow, August 19, 1590 ; licensed to travel for three years, November 13, 1607 ; made a Knight of the Bath at the creation of Henry, Prince of Wales, June 4, 1610. He married, in 1612, Isabella, daughter of Sir Walter Cope ; M. P. Leicester, 1614; captain of the king's guard in November, 1617. On the 26th of September, 1622, his lady and himself transferred their two shares in the Bermudas Islands to Henry Percy and Marie, his wife (the same being the earliest deed of sale recorded in that island), and on November 6 they transferred four shares of their lands in Virginia to the same Henry Percy ; created Baron Kensington, March 8, 1623 ; employed with the Earl of Carlisle in negotiating the match between Prince Charles of England and Henrietta Maria of France, February to September, 1624 ; created Earl of Holland, September 24, 1624 ; chosen Knight of the Garter, 1625 ; governor of the Providence Islands or Bahamas Company from 1630 to 1639 and probably after ; challenged Lord Weston, 1633. Lord Baltimore's deserted Newfoundland plantation was regranted to him and others, November 13, 1637. In 1638 Will Claybourne of Virginia discovered an island within the limits of the Providence Islands' patent, which Claybourne proposed to call Rich Island in honor of the Earl of Holland ; opposed Stafford, 1640 ; member of committee sent to Scotland to watch proceedings of Charles I. in the fall of 1640. He became wavering in his politics; was appointed captain-general of the army in the north, April 16, 1641 ; attempted to manage the intercourse between the king and Parliament, 1642 ; deprived of his office of groom of the stole ; again joined the Parliament, 1642 ; attempted to regain favor of the king ; fought on his side at Newbury ; published "A Declaration made to the Kingdome," 1643 ; afterwards in the Parliament interest. In July, 1648, appeared in arms for the king ; was taken prisoner by the Roundheads at Neots, July 10, and beheaded March 9, 1649. He appeared on the scaffold, dressed in white satin trimmed with silver, which made Bishop Warburton say that he "lived like a knave and died like a fool." He lived in the celebrated Holland House at Kensington, one apartment in which is now said to be tenanted by the solitary ghost of its first lord, who issues forth at midnight from behind a secret door, and walks slowly through the scenes of former triumphs with his head in his hand. His character has been differently drawn.

Rich, Sir Nathaniel. Sub. ——; pd. £37 10s. (See pedigree, 2.) Eldest son of Richard, illegitimate son of Robert, second Lord Rich; M. P. for Totness in 1614 ; interested in the Bermudas in 1616 ; knighted at Hatton House, November 8, 1617. March 4, 1619, Mr. Joseph Man assigned to him three shares in Virginia, and he was soon after added to the King's Council for the Va. Co.; was on the council for New England, November 3, 1620 ; M. P. for Retford, 1621–22 ; sent to Ireland on the famous commission of March, 1622. He was a leading member of the Warwick party in the factions of the Va. Co. of 1622–24, and many drafts of papers, petitions, charges, and replies, drawn by himself in those disputes, are still preserved among the Kimbolton MS., Duke of Manchester records. (I have copies of them.) M. P. for Harwich, 1624–25 ; on the Virginia Commission of July 15, 1624 ;

M. P. for Newport (I. W.), 1625 ; and for Harwich, 1626 and 1628–29 ; aided in fitting out a voyage for the discovery of the Bahamas in 1629 ; member of the Bahamas Company in 1630 ; deputy governor of that company in 1635.   He died in 1636.   Mr. Stith inaccurately calls him the brother of the second Earl of Warwick. (See Governor Winthrop's letter to him in " Proc. Mass. Hist. Soc.," 1st series, xx. pp. 42–45.   See also Rich's letter in " N. E. Hist. Gen. Register," January, 1883, p. 60.)

Rich, Robert, 2. Sub. ——— ; pd. £12 10s. (See pedigree, 3.) Brother of Sir Nathaniel ; wrecked on the Bermudas, 1609 ; came to Virginia, 1610, and returned to England.   He bought ten shares in the Bermudas of Mr. Raph Hamor in Southampton Tribe, and afterwards sold three of them : one to Sir Thomas Wroth, one to Sir Thomas Cheeke, and one to Mr. Cough.   He was living in the Bermudas in 1617, and died there in 1620.

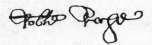

Rich, Sir Robert, 3. Sub. ——— ; pd. £75. (See pedigree, 4.) Eldest son of Robert, third Lord Rich ; born in May or June, 1587 ; made a Knight of the Bath at the coronation of King James, July 25, 1603 ; married Frances, daughter of Sir William Newport *alias* Hatton on February 12, 1605 ; licensed to travel for three years, January 9, 1610 ; M. P. Essex, 1614; member Bermudas Company, 1615.   In 1616 the Count Scarnafissi was sent to England as an ambassador from Charles Emmanuel I., surnamed " The Great Duke of Savoy," to negotiate for English aid against Spain in the war then waging between Savoy and that country.   Scarnafissi granted sundry commissions for ships, under the protection of which they proposed to make prizes of Spanish vessels.   Sir Robert Rich and others, late in 1616, sent two ships with these commissions to rove in the East Indies, where they became involved with the English East India fleet, thereby causing a bitter controversy between Rich and that company.   In April, 1618, before the news from his East India venture had reached England, Sir Robert Rich and others sent the Treasurer (Capt. Daniel Elfrith) to Virginia with one of these commissions " from the Duke of Savoy to take Spaniards as lawfull prize." Himself and associates had applied for a charter for the sole trade in Guinea and Binney prior to October, 1618, when the news of the trouble incident to this East Indian venture reached England, and stayed the progress of this charter for a time, but it was finally granted November 16, 1618, to Robert Lord Rich, Sir Robert Mansell, Sir Ferdinando Gorges, Sir Warwick Heale, Sir Allen Appesley, Sir Richard Hawkins, Sir Henry Nevill, Sir William St. John, Sir Thomas Tracy, Sir Richard Bingley, Sir Giles Mompesson, Sir Thomas Button, Sir John Bingley, Oliver St. John, and twenty-two others.

His father had been created Earl of Warwick, August 6, 1618, at which time he became fourth Lord Rich. His father died in April, 1619, when he succeeded as the second Earl of Warwick.   (Stith confuses the second with the first earl.)   In the fall of 1618, the Treasurer went from Virginia to rove in the West Indies under the Savoy commission, where she took certain negroes from the Spaniards, a part of them, in consortship with a man-of-war of Flushing, she brought to Virginia ; the rest she carried to the Earl of Warwick's plantation in the Bermudas.   He was added to the King's Council for the Va. Co. in 1619.

His controversy with the E. I. Co. and the bad feeling created by the marriage of his sister to Sir Thomas Smythe's son, were influential in causing him to aid the Sandys party in gaining control of the Va. Co. ; this combination afterwards split up among themselves, the Earl of Southampton leading one party and the Earl of Warwick the other.   He was interested in the plantation of Lord North

HORACE VERE

First Baron Vere

and others in Guiana in 1619-20 ; member of New England Council, November 3, 1620 ; signed the first Plymouth patent, June 1, 1621 ; active in the factions in the Va. Co., 1622-24.

The African Company had made voyages to Guinea and the river Gambia in 1618, 1619, and 1620, and after. Sir Edwin Sandys fought against Warwick in this matter, also, and on May 24, 1624, Nethersole wrote to Carleton that "this African Company was condemned as a grievance."

He was on the council in England for Virginia after the dissolution of the Va. Co. of London in 1624, and was governor of the Bermudas Company most of the time between 1627 and 1654. In 1629 he was one of the chief undertakers in the first voyage of discovery to the Bahamas ; signed the patent for the Old Colony of Plymouth, January 13, and the Lincoln Grant, March 13, 1630, at which time he was president of the New England Council, and so continued until 1632. He was an incorporator of the Bahamas Company, December 4, 1630. In 1630 the Plymouth Council granted him the land extending from Narragansett River for the space of forty leagues towards the southwest (120 miles — to 40° N. L. ?) and within that breadth from the Atlantic to the South Sea, and March 19, 1632, he made over this grant to his son, Robert Rich, the Hon. Charles Fiennes, Sir Nathaniel Rich, Sir Richard Saltonstall, Richard Knightley, Esq., John Pymm, Esq., John Hampden, Esq., John Humphreys, Esq., and Herbert Pelhem, Esq., their heirs and assigns, etc., only reserving to himself a fifth part of the gold and silver ore. He retained his interest in the Bermudas and the Bahamas, and continued to supply his plantations with negroes.

Warwick River, one of the first shires in Virginia, was named for him in 1634. "The World Encompassed by Sir Francis Drake" was dedicated to him by Sir Francis Drake the Younger in 1635 ; proposed to go to the West Indies in 1636 ; power granted him to equip ships of war for service in the West Indies, February 7, 1638. In May, 1640, the Earl of Warwick, John Pym, John Hampden, and other Parliament men had all their papers taken from them. July 8, 1640, the Spanish ambassador complained of breaches of the peace by Warwick and others in the West Indies under pretense of letters of marque. Lieutenant of the fleet under the Earl of Northumberland, 1642.

The Lords and Commons in Parliament assembled made him governor in chief and lord high admiral of all those islands and plantations, belonging to any of his majesty's subjects, within the bounds and upon the coasts of America, November 2, 1643. In this year Warwick River, Va., took its present name of Warwick County.

In 1643, 1644, etc., himself and associates made sundry grants of lands in New England ; liberty of conscience granted in the Bermudas, 1645; deprived of his office of lord high admiral in April, 1645. In May, 1648, he was made lord high admiral by Parliament. From August 29 to December 25, 1648, his expedition with the Parliament's navy for reducing the revolted ships, commanded by his Highness Charles, Prince of Wales. His commission as lord high admiral revoked by the Parliament, February 21, 1649. (They beheaded his brother Henry, March 9 following.)

When Cromwell disbanded Parliament, he betook himself to the protection of the protector, and Lodge says, "left his estate more improved and repaired than any man who trafficked in that desperate commodity of rebellion." In 1657 the Rev. Samuel Purchas (the son of the author of the "Pilgrimes") dedicated to him "A Theatre of Politicall Flying-Insects," etc.

Heath, in his chronicle, says, "The old Earl of Warwick (presently after the espousals of his grandson, with Frances, the youngest daughter of the Protector) died April 18, 1658."

The Earl of Warwick's first wife died in August, 1634 ; he married, secondly, Susanna (daughter of Sir Henry Rowe the Elder, and sister of Sir Henry Rowe the Younger, of Shakelwell in Middlesex), relict of Alderman William Halliday, she died January 21, 1645, and the earl married, thirdly, March 30, 1646, Eleanor,

Countess of Sussex, daughter of Sir Richard Wortley, and relict successively of Sir Henry Lee and of the Earl of Sussex. Her grandchild, by her first husband, married Anne, daughter of Sir John Danvers the regicide. After the death of Warwick his widow married, fourthly, Edward Montague, second Earl of Manchester. She died, and was buried at Kimbolton on the 31st of January, $166\frac{6}{7}$.

Mr. Stith says (History, p. 187) that the Warwick faction was composed of only twenty-six persons, when it was strongest. The following is a list of "the Names of Adventurers that dislike ye present proceedings of business in ye Virginia and Somers Islands Companyes." Compiled in April, 1623 (Kimbolton MS. No. 327) : —
"The Earle of Warwick.
Sir Nathaniel Rich.
Sir Henry Mildmay.
Sir Humphrey Hansford.
Sir Samuel Argall.
Sir Thomas Wroth.
Sir Robert Mansfield.
Sir Thomas Smith.
Sir Thomas Button.
Sir John Culpeper.
Sir Thomas Cheeke.
Sir Thomas Hewit.
Sir Philip Cary.
Sir Ferdinando Gorge.
Sir John Worstenholme.
Mr. Alderman Johnson.
Mr. Doctor Medust.
Mr. Morris Abot.
Mr. Robert Bateman.
Mr. William Gibs.
Mr. Nicholas Leate.
Mr. Wiseman.
Mr. Harris and Mr. Harris.
Mr. Goughe.
Mr. Binge.
Mr. Maye.
Mr. Covell.
Mr. Gore.
Mr. Wilkinson.
Mr. Barnard.
Mr. Moore.

Mr. Man (or Mun).
Mr. Lukin.
Mr. Abraham Chamberlin.
Mr. West.
Mr. Paulston.
Mr. Roberts.
Mr. Mould (or Mole).
Mr. Penniston.
Mr. George Tucker.
Capt. Daniel Tucker.
Mr. Darrell.
Mr. Butler and his brother.
Mr. Lewellin.
Mr. Bell.
Mr. Stiles.
Mr. William Palmer.
Mr. Edwards.
Mr. Moorer.
Mr. Dike.
Mr. George Smith, grocer.
Mr. Robert Smith, underchamberlin.
Mr. Canninge.
Mr. Humphrey Slany.
Mr. Thaier [Thayer].
Mr. Edward Bennit.
Mr. Phesant.
Mr. Wrote.
Mr. Stewart.
Mr. John Wrothe.
Mr. Palavicine.
Mr. Christopher Barron.
Mr. Jonson.
Mr. Ticknor.
Mr. Edward Palmer.
Mr. Baynham (or Barham ?)
Mr. Willmore.
Mr. Jadwin.
Mr. Newell (or Nevell).
Mr. Rogers, junior.
Mr. John Woodall.
Mr. Stephen Sparrow.
Mr. Man, junior (or Mun).
Mr. Roberts, junior.
Mr. John West.
Mr. Pearce.
Mr. Cason.
Mr. Robins.
Mr. Wale.
Mr. Hawes.
Mr. Townsend.
Mr. Essington.
Mr. Ditchfield."
There are eighty-five names in the list. The Christian names of many are not given ; but they can generally be identified. Some of them joined the company after the time of which I write ; but enough of them will be found in these biographies to enable

the reader to form a just idea of the Warwick party.

Mr. Stith says, "On the other hand appeared the whole body of Adventurers, to the full amount of a thousand persons in all." This is not correct; it is a natural consequence of following the evidence for one side only. In fact, there were not over three hundred men then taking an active part in the affairs of the company, and not more than one hundred of these were old members. I have given this statement as an act of justice to the Warwick party; but I cannot here attempt to discuss the various reasons which caused the old members to cease their attendance on the Virginia courts, or the motives which are said to have influenced the Sandys party in admitting so many new members. See also CCCLXIV., and I have other lists of the same character giving many additional names.

Richmond, Earl and Duke of. — Ludovic Stuart.

Ridgeway (Ridgwine, etc.), Sir Thomas, 2. Sub. —— ; pd. ——. Of Tor Abbey, Devonshire ; in the voyage to the Azores, 1597 ; sheriff of Devon and knighted in 1600 ; M. P. for Devon, 1604–07 ; vice-treasurer and treasurer at wars, and treasurer of Ireland at various times for sundry years ; was a large undertaker in the first Protestant colony in Ireland. (In 1609 he brought over the beautiful surveys and maps of the escheated lands in Ulster, which lay hidden from that time until 1860.) He was created a baronet, November 25, 1612 ; Baron Gallen-Ridgeway, May 25, 1616, and Earl of Londonderry in Ireland, August 23, 1622.

Ridlesdon, Sir Steven, 2. Sub. —— ; pd. £56. Of York ; knighted at Chatham, July 4, 1604 ; one of the officers of the navy, being clerk of the ordnance.

Rivers, Captain John. Son of Sir John Rivers by his wife, Elizabeth Barnes. (See Sir George Barnes the elder.) His sister, Anne Rivers, married Sir Matthew Carew, and became the mother of Thomas Carew, the poet.

Roberts, Elias, merchant-tailor, 3. Sub. £37 10s. ; pd. £37 10s. Of

E. I. Co.; January 15, 1617, sent one man to Virginia, under Capt. Raphe Hamor. In 1618, himself and his son Elias, Jr., owned four shares in the Bermudas; May 22, 1622, he gave his son 100 acres in Virginia. Will dated January, 1624, proved February 20, 1626. (See "N. E. Register," October, 1888, p. 396.)

Roberts, George. Sub. £37 10s. (See George Robins.)

Roberts, Tedder, Tudor, or **Theodore,** 2. Sub. —— ; pd. £37 10s. Of E. I. Co.

Robins, George, vintner, 2. Sub. £37 10s.; pd. £62 10s. Also of E. I. and N. W. P. companies.

He was at Brest in 1615, and I suppose was the Mr. George Robins who was buried in the parish of St. Mary Woolchurch Haw, London, on August 27, 1646.

Robins, Richard. Pd. £12 10s. Of Longbuckbye in Northampton County, England. His brothers, Obedience and Edward, settled in Northampton County, Virginia.

Robinson, Arthur, 2. Sub. —— ; pd. £25. Of St. Peter, Cornhill, London, mercer; brother to Robert; was a member of the E. I. Co. in 1609 and N. W. P. Co. in 1612. He married, in 1603, Elizabeth, daughter of William Walthall.

Robinson, Henry, esquire, 2. Sub. —— ; pd. £87 10s. Of St. Michael Basishaw, London; born in 1587; son of Henry Robinson, Sr., by his wife Alice, daughter of Thomas Wilkes; married, in 1611, Mary, the daughter of Sir William Glover, knight and alderman of London ; an incorporator of, and a director in, the E. I. Co.; afterwards knighted; buried at Islington, December 21, 1637, in the vault with his mother. His mother was thrice married : first to Henry Robinson, Sr. ; secondly to William Elkin, alderman of London, and thirdly to Thomas Owen, one of the justices of the Common Pleas. Mrs. Alice Owen died in 1613 ; she founded the almshouse for ten widows, and the free-school for 30 boys, at Islington.

Robinson, Jehu (or John), gent., 2. Sub. —— ; pd. ——. He was killed by the Indians in Virginia, December, 1609.

Robinson John, gent., 3. Sub.

£37 10s.; pd. £75. Probably son of John and Martha Robinson (whom see).

Robinson, John, merchant-tailor. Pd. 6s. Married, in 1597, Elizabeth, daughter of Sir Richard Rogers.

Robinson, John, 2. Sub. —— ; pd. ——. Chief searcher of customs ; was buried at St. Olave's, London, December 13, 1609. His widow, Mary, deserves especial mention. She was the daughter of William Ramsey, of London, grocer ; her first husband, John Wanton, of London, gent., a searcher of the customs, died in August, 1592, and she married, secondly, February 26, 1593, John Robinson, aforesaid. Mrs. Mary Robinson was buried with her two husbands at St. Olave's, Hart Street, London, October 13, 1618. The following is an extract from her will : " I give and bequeth towardes the helpe of the poore people in Virginia, towardes the buildinge of a churche, and reducing them to the knowledge of God's worde, the some of two hundred poundes to be bestowed at the discreaĉon of my cozen, Sir John Wolstenholme, knight, with the advise and consulte of four others of the chiefest of the Virginia Company, within two yeares nexte after my decease."

She was a niece of Sir Thomas Ramsey, Lord Mayor of London, who with his wife (Mary, daughter of William Dale, merchant of Bristol) were the great benefactors of the Grocers' Company, of Christ's Hospital, London, and of Queen Elizabeth's Hospital, Bristol.

In the summer of 1619 "a person unknowne " gave for Mistris Mary Robinson's church in Virginia a communion-cup, which precious relic, inscribed " The Communion Cupp for St. Mary's Church in Smith's Hundred in Virginia," is still preserved in the Old Dominion.

Mrs. Mary was John Robinson's second wife ; she bore him no child. Martha Cruxtone was his first wife and the mother of his children. Their daughter Jane married Thomas Smythe, of London (whose daughter, Martha Smythe, married Archdale, son of William Palmer). Another daughter, Susanna Robinson, married William Jordan, of Surrey. The sons ·

of John Robinson were William, Henry, John, and Robert. I believe his son John to be the John, gent., of the Va. Co. He was born about 1578; lived at Gravesend; married, in April, 1612, Bridget, daughter of Robert Jenkinson, of London ; died January 18, 167¾, aged 96, and was buried in Gravesend church.

Robinson, Robert, 2. Sub. —— ; pd. £25. Brother to Arthur; also of E. I. and N. W. P. companies. (I believe that I have identified these Robinsons correctly; but so many men of affairs bore the name, at the time, that I cannot always be certain.)

Rochester, Earl of. — Robert Carr.

Roe — Rowe, Henry, mercer, 2. Sub. —— ; pd. ——. Second son of Sir Thomas Rowe, lord mayor in 1568. He was born in 1544; apprenticed to Matthew Field, mercer ; admitted to freedom in Mercers' Company, 1571; warden of the company, 1591; sheriff of London, 1597, and lord mayor in 1608; died in 1612 and was buried at Hackney, December 22.

His brother, William Roe, Esq. (whose widow married Sir Reginald, the brother of Sir Samuel Argall). is described as a very learned man, who, when in Germany, lived upon terms of intimacy with Immanuel Tremellius and Theodore Beza.

Roe, Sir Thomas, 2. Sub. —— ; pd. £60. Son of Robert Roe (son of Sir Thomas Roe, Lord Mayor of London in 1568), esquire of the body to Queen Elizabeth, by his wife Elizabeth, daughter of Robert Jermy, of Antingham; born about 1580, at Low Leyton in Essex ; entered Magdalen College, Oxford, in 1593; knighted at Greenwich, March 23, 1605 ; M. C. for Va., March 9, 1607; M. C. for Va. Co., May 23, 1609. " This worthy young knight and right valiant Gentleman in 1609–10, at his and his friends charge, builded a shippe, and a pinace for the discovery of Guyana, hee set sayle from Plimmouth, February 24, (1610), and in the end of Aprill (1610) fell with the great river of the Amazons." He spent 13 months in discovering the Amazon, the Wyapoco, and the Orinoco rivers and adjacent regions, and returning " arrived at the Wight, in July, 1611;" between which date and 1615, "he sent twice thither to make farther discoveries and to maintayne twenty men in the River of Amazones, for the good of his countrey, who are yet (1615) remayning there and supplied." (Henry, Prince of Wales, was interested in this enterprise.) M. P. for Tamworth in 1614. On September 7, 1614, Sir Thomas Smith, the governor, proposed to the E. I. Co. that "they should employ Sir Thomas Roe at Agra, he being a gentleman of pregnant understanding, well spoken, learned, industrious, of a comely personage and one of whom there are great hopes that he may work much good for the company." Soon after this, King James I., at the E. I. Co.'s request and expense, appointed Sir Thomas Roe his ambassador to the Great Mogul, Shah Jehan.[1] This was the first royal embassy from England to that remote country. He sailed from Gravesend January 24, 1615, and landed at Surat in September, 1615; resided at the court of the Great Mogul till 1618, whence he proceeded to that of Shah Abbas in Persia; left the East Indies early in 1619, and arrived at Plymouth, England, late in August, 1619. He wrote an account of his embassy, and made a map of the Great Mogul's empire. Bourne, in his "Famous London Merchants," says, "Sir Thomas Roe did much good work. He formed an alliance with the great Mohammedan Emperor of the East, one of the race of mighty potentates who ruled all the north of India, and the vast districts on the other side of the Himalayas, and thus surely laid the foundations of that intercourse between England and India which was to end, after two centuries of trading and fighting, in India becoming the property of England. For all this, not a little of the praise belongs to Sir Thomas Smythe." His sister Mary married Richard Berkeley (whom see), and he was interested in the plantation of Berkeley on James River (see John Smith, of Nibley). On May 17, 1620, James I. recommended him to the Va. Co. as a proper person for governor of that company. July 6, 1620, "Sir Thomas Roe and his partners" procured a pat-

[1] The Emperor Jehanghir, the Selim of Moore's poem, who built the mausoleum Taj Mahal at Agra to his favorite wife, Nourmahal, the Light of the Harem of Moore's *Lalla Rookh*.

ent for the monopoly of the tobacco trade of England. July 7, 1620, Sir John Davers and Sir Thomas Roe were appointed by the South Virginia Company to draw up a letter to the king, asking him to preserve the fishing at Cape Cod free to both Virginia companies. November 3, 1620, Roe is one of the first council and incorporators of the N. E. Co. November 4, 1620, he was desired by the Va. Co. to present their petition, regarding the Cape Cod fisheries, to his majesty, and on November 13 Roe presented a favorable reply to this petition from his majesty. M. P. for Cirencester, 1621–22. From 1622 to 1628, Sir Thomas Roe was the ambassador from England to the court of the Sublime Porte at Constantinople. While there, in 1623, he concluded a truce for the English merchants with the pirates of Algiers and Tunis, and, "by his prudence and sagacity, succeeded in obtaining the most valuable results, not only for the extension of trade, but even for the Christian religion itself." In 1629 he was sent as "ambassador to the King of Poland, and other princes and states in the eastern parts;" and June 11 in that year he was commissioned by the King of England to negotiate a peace between the kings of Poland and Sweden. (On his way he treated with the King of Denmark, as also on his return.) Gustavus Adolphus the Great, King of Sweden, concluded a truce of six years with Sigismund, King of Poland, September 15, 1629. "As usual Roe obtained great advantages to English trade and commerce through his negotiations on this embassy. He also took advantage of this occasion to endeavor the reconciliation of the Lutherans and Calvinists, and to unite them all in conformity with the Church of England." He continued to try for many years to make a peace between the Lutheran and Calvinist, and many letters of his on this subject to Archbishop Laud and others are still preserved.

Sir Thomas Roe was brother-in-law to John Tomlinson (the mayor of Bristol in 1630), and aided both Capt. Thomas James and Luke Fox in their preparations for their voyages to the ·Northwest in 1630 and 1631. In June,

1631, he was one of the special commission for the better plantation of Virginia. In 1637 he was interested in a proposition for an English West India Company. He says "there was no more advantageous way for making war upon the King of Spain than in the West Indies." "May 5, 1638. Commission to Sir Thomas Roe, Chancellor of the Order of the Garter, to treat with the French King, the Queen of Sweden and the States of Belgium, for general peace, and the restoration of the King of England's nephews." "January 30, 1639. Power for Sir Thomas Roe, Chancellor of the Order of the Garter, to conclude a treaty with Christian IV., King of Denmark." M. P. for Oxford University from 1640 to his death. In 1640 he made a celebrated speech in Parliament, which was printed in 1641, "Wherein He sheweth the cause of the decay of Coyne and Trade in this Land, especially of Merchants Trade. And also propounded a way to the House, how they may be increased." "In 1641 he was sent ambassador to the Emperor and the Princes of Germany to be present at the Diet of Ratisbon, and there to mediate on behalf of the Prince Elector Palatine. The Emperor was so pleased with his conduct and his great abilities that he several times said in public : ' I have met with many gallant persons of many nations, but I scarce ever met with an ambassador till now.' " "On his return from Germany he was made a privy councilor, but lived not long to enjoy the honor. He died November 6, 1644, and was buried (November 8) in the chancel of the Woodford church. He was lord of the manor of Woodford."

"During his embassy at Constantinople he collected many valuable Greek and Oriental manuscripts, which he presented to the Bodleian Library, to which he left his valuable collection of coins. The fine Alexandrian MS. of the Greek Bible, which Cyrill, the Patriarch of Constantinople presented to Charles I., was procured by his means."

The historian Carte, speaking of his letters and papers, says, "I have read them with great pleasure, and cannot sufficiently admire his rare abilities, judgment, and integrity, his extraordinary sagacity in discovering the views and designs of those with whom he treated, and his admirable dexterity in guarding against their measures and bringing them over to his purpose. Wise, experienced, penetrating and knowing, he was never to be surprised or deceived, and though no minister ever had greater difficulties to struggle with, or was employed by a court that had less power to support him, yet he supported all his employments with dignity, and came out of them with reputation and honor. In all the honest arts of negotiation he had few equals (I dare say), no superiors. His letters and papers are a treasure that ought to be communicated to the world."

Rogers, Edward, esquire. Of Cannington, County Somerset ; M. P. for Minehead, 1584–85 ; married Katherine, daughter of Sir John Popham, chief justice of England ; M. C. for Va., March 9, 1607 ; also a member of the South Va. Co. He died in 1627.

Rogers, Richard, gent., 2. Sub. £37 10s. ; pd. £75. Comptroller of the king's mint ; N. W. P. Co., 1612. He was living at the Visitation in 1633, aged 84 years, but died soon after. A benefactor of Edmonton.

Rolfe, Henry. Pd. £12 10s. Son of John Rolfe and his wife, Dorothea Mason, of Heacham Hall in Norfolk, England, and brother of John Rolfe of Virginia. He "brought up the child his said brother had by Powhatan's daughter." I believe this Henry Rolfe to be the father of Francis Rolfe, who was town clerk of Lynn in 1622, and was buried in the chapel of St. Nicholas in that town in 1678.

Rolfe, John. Eustacius Rolfe was married to Joanna Jener in the parish church at Heacham in Norfolk, England, May 27, 1560. Their son, John

Rolfe, was baptized there, October 17, 1562. He married there, September 24, 1582, Dorothea Mason, and their twin sons, Eustacius and John, were baptized there, May 6, 1585. Eustacius soon died ; his twin brother, John Rolfe, married in England, possibly in 1608, and sailed for Virginia in June, 1609 ; was wrecked on the Bermudas, and while there a daughter was born to him; she was christened by the Rev. Mr. Bucke, February 11, 1610, Captain Newport, William Strachey, and Mrs. Horton being sponsors ; the child soon died. The parents reached Virginia in May, 1610, where the mother died. In 1612 John Rolfe was the first Englishman to introduce the cultivation of tobacco in Virginia. He was married about the 5th of April, 1614, in the church at Jamestown, to Pocahontas, the daughter of Powhatan. I suppose he was certainly married by Mr. Buck, the minister at Jamestown, and not by Mr. Whitaker, who was the minister at Henrico. He was in England with his Indian bride in 1616–17, and while there, he sent a description of Virginia to King James and to Sir Robert Rich. His wife died in England, March 21, 1617, and he returned to Virginia ; a member of the council in Virginia in 1619 ; married, thirdly, Jane, daughter of William Pierce ; died in Virginia in 1622, leaving a widow and children. His will, dated March 10, 1621, was witnessed by his old friend and pastor, the Rev. Richard Buck, and others. (An abstract of his will is given in the " New England Historical and Genealogical Register," January, 1884, p. 68.) His widow afterwards married Capt. Roger Smith, and his daughter Elizabeth (aged four years, born in Virginia), was living with Capt. Roger Smith at James City, January 24, 1625. Thomas Rolfe, the child of Pocahontas, was then in England.

In January, 1625, Rolfe's father-in-law, Capt. William Pierce, owned Angelo, a negro woman, one of the first negroes brought to Virginia in the Earl of Warwick's ship, the Treasurer, in August, 1619.

Romney, Sir William, haberdasher, 2. Sub. £75 ; pd. £170. Son of William Romney of Tedbury in Gloucestershire ; was a leading merchant of London, a member of the Haberdashers' Company, a Merchant Adventurer, and sometime governor of the Merchants Adventurers. September 22, 1599, he ventured £200 in the intended voyage to the East Indies; September 24, appointed one of the treasurers for that voyage ; October 30, selected for one of the first directors of the proposed E. I. Co.; December 31, 1600, an incorporator and one of the first directors of the E. I. Co. ; January 9, 1601, chosen deputy-governor of that company ; November 5, 1601, urged the E. I. Co. to send an expedition to discover the Northwest passage, either in conjunction with the Mus. Co. or, if possible, alone; December 22, 1601, the Mus. Co. consented to join in the enterprise of which Romney was to be treasurer ; elected alderman of Portsoken ward, London, December 18, 1602 ; elected one of the sheriffs of London, 1603; knighted at Whitehall, July 26, 1603. In 1606 he was governor of the E. I. Co. ; M. C. for Va., November 20, 1606 ; M. C. for Va. Co., May 23, 1609 ; one of those who sent out Henry Hudson for the Northwest in April, 1610. His will was dated April 18. Died April 25, and was placed in his sepulchre, May 24, 1611. He gave liberally to the hospitals ; to forty poor scholars in Cambridge he gave the sum of £20; to the Haberdashers' Company he gave £50 to be lent to a young freeman gratis for two years, etc.

He married Rebecca, only heir of Robert Taylor, late alderman of London, and had issue by her six sons and two daughters.

(Col. Joseph Ball, who afterwards came to Virginia, married, in England, Miss Elizabeth Romney, probably a granddaughter of the above, and from them descended the Travers, Daniels, Conways, etc., of Virginia. "The mother of Washington" was Col. Joseph Ball's daughter bv a second marriage.)

Roscarrocke (or Roscowe), William, esquire, 3. Sub. —— ; pd. £37 10s.

Rosier, James. On the Gosnold voyage to our New England coast, March to July, 1602, and on the Weymouth voyage of March to July, 1605, of which latter voyage he published "A True Reporte" in 1605.

Rotheram, Edward, draper. Pd. £25. He was elected alderman of Bread Street ward, December 3, 1611; chosen sheriff, June 24, 1612. Buried at St. Mary's Aldermary, November 2, 1620.

Roydon, Captain Marmaduke. This was evidently Capt. Marmaduke Rawdon, son of Ralph Rawdon, of Brandsby in Yorkshire; baptized there, March 20, 158$\frac{2}{3}$; went to London at the age of sixteen; apprenticed to Daniel Hall, a merchant, who sent him as his factor to Bordeaux; returned to London about 1610; elected a common councilman; free of the company of Clothworkers; captain of the city militia; treasurer for the French merchants; rigged out a ship for the discovery of the Northwest passage; one of the first that planted in Barbadoes, where he buried above £10,000; a great adventurer to Spain, France, the Canary Isles, and Turkey, to the West Indies, and several other parts of the world, etc.; M. P. for Alborough, 1628–29; defended Basinghouse in 1643; knighted December 28, 1643; died April 18, 1646. In 1611, when he married Elizabeth, daughter of Thomas Thorowgood, of Hodsden, Herts, gent., he was a clothworker of Allhallows Barking, London.

Rumney. See Romney.

Russell, Edward, Earl of Bedford, 3. Sub. —— ; pd. £120. On the death of his grandfather Francis, second Earl (the godfather to Sir Francis Drake), on the 28th of July, 1585, he succeeded as third earl. He married Lucy Harrington at Stepney on the 12th of December, 1594; assigned to Sir Edward Harwood four shares in Virginia on the 9th of December, 1618; died May 1, 1627, without issue.

Russell, John, 2. Sub. —— ; pd. £12 10s. Came to Virginia in 1608.

Russell - Clifford, Margaret, Countess of Cumberland, 3. Sub. —— ; pd. ——. Youngest daughter of Francis, second Earl of Bedford. She married, June 24, 1577, the cele-brated George Clifford, seventeenth Baron Clifford, and third Earl of Cumberland. He died in 1605, and she died in May, 1616, leaving an only daughter, Anne, sole heir to the baronies of Clifford, Westmoreland, and Vesey. She married, first, Richard Sackville, Earl of Dorset, and secondly, Philip Herbert, Earl of Pembroke and Montgomery, and became Countess of Dorset, Pembroke, and Montgomery.

Russell, Dr. Walter. Came to Virginia in 1607. Died prior to September, 1609.

Russell, William, gent. Came to Virginia in September, 1608.

Russell, William, merchant, 2. Sub. £37 10s.; pd. £50. Son of William Russell, Esq., of Surrey; was "sometime agent for the Dutch;" was a member of the Rus. or Mus. Co., and was with Sir Thomas Smythe in Russia in April, 1605. In 1606 he sent the Godspeed and the Discovery to Cherry Island, and these vessels, after their return, went to Virginia with the first expedition sent by the first Colony of Virginia; a member of the E. I. Co.; aided in sending Henry Hudson to the Northwest in 1610, and was an incorporator and one of the first directors of the N. W. P. Co., chartered July 26, 1612; knighted at Theobald's, April 29, 1618.

May 5, 1618, Chamberlain wrote to Carleton, "Sir William Russell, the Muscovy Merchant has bought the Treasurership of the Navy from Sir Robert Mansell, who is to be Vice-Admiral." "May 10, 1618. Grant to Sir William Russell of the Treasurership of Marine Causes for life." James I. suggested him as a suitable person for treasurer of the Va. Co., May 22, 1622. He continued treasurer of the navy under James I. and Charles I.; the latter king made him a commissioner of the navy also, and created him a baronet, January 19, 1629. One of the commissioners "concerning tobacco," June 10, 1634; living, April 2, 1637, when he wrote a letter to the admiralty concerning Governor Harvey of Virginia. The date of his death is not known to me. Two of his grandchildren married members of Lord Protector Cromwell's family.

Sackville, Edward, esquire, 3. Sub.——; pd.——. Born in 1590; educated at Christ Church, Oxford, 1605–09; killed Lord Bruce in the celebrated duel, September, 1613; made a Knight of the Bath at the creation of Charles, Prince of Wales, November 3, 1616; commands troops sent to the Elector Palatine, and fought at Prague in 1620; M. P. for Sussex, 1621–22; sent on an embassy to France in 1621; member of the Privy Council; member of the Southampton party in the factions of the Va. Co., 1622–24; governor of the B. I. Co. in 1623. When his brother Richard, third Earl of Dorset, died (March 28, 1624) he was at Florence in Italy, from whence he returned through France, the latter end of May, 1624, and succeeded his brother as fourth Earl of Dorset. He was on the commission for the better plantation of Virginia, June 27, 1631, and on the commission for plantations of April, 1634. His party were constantly striving to reestablish the Va. Co. of London, making special appeals to King Charles for that purpose in 1625, 1631, 1638, and 1642 (see George Sandys); but they were as constantly met by petitions of the planters against it. The Earl of Dorset was a distinguished cavalier. He died at Witham, Sussex, July 27, 1652.

Sackvill, Richard, third Earl of Dorset, 2. Sub.——; pd. £120. Grandson of Thomas, first Earl of Dorset; was born March 28, 1589, in the Chartreuse in London (now called the Charterhouse); married, February 27, 1609, the very celebrated Lady Anne, daughter and heir of George Clifford, Earl of Cumberland, in her mother's chambers, in Augustine-Friers house, in London, two days after his father's decease, whom he succeeded as third Earl of Dorset. In 1611–12 he was traveling in France and the Low Countries; May 15, 1620, he transferred to Mr. Henry Manwaring ten shares of land in Virginia,

which it seems was all of his stock. He died in Great Dorset-House, London, March 28, 1624, and was buried, April 7, with his ancestors in Witham Church in Sussex; leaving no surviving male issue, he was succeeded by his brother, Sir Edward, as fourth Earl of Dorset.

Sackville, Thomas, first Earl of Dorset. Born in Sussex, 1536; M. P. about 1557; with Thomas Norton, wrote the first regular English tragedy in 1562; imprisoned at Rome 1566; knighted June 8, 1567, and the same day created Baron of Buckhurst; ambassador to Paris, 1570; to the Netherlands, 1587; Knight of the Garter, 1589; Chancellor of Oxford University, 1589; lord high treasurer, 1599; Earl of Dorset by James I. in 1603; died at Whitehall, April 19, 1608. He was the grandfather of the foregoing Sir Edward Sackville and Richard, third Earl of Dorset.

Sad, Stephen. Pd. £12 10s.

Saint Albans, Viscount. — Francis Bacon.

Saint Aldegonde, Marnix de. Philippe de Marnix, Baron of St. Aldegonde; born at Brussels, 1538; attached to the Prince of Orange, 1565; attended Assembly of Dort, 1572; plenipotentiary of republic at Diet of Worms, 1577; in England for a time; defended Antwerp, 1584–85; died at Leyden, 1598.

Saint John, Sir John, 3. Sub. £75; pd. £37 10s. Of Lydiard Tregose, County Wilts, and of Battersea and Wandsworth; knighted at Whitehall, February 2, 1609; created a baronet, May 11, 1611; M. P.——, Wilts, in 1624–25; zealously attached to the royal cause, and had three sons slain fighting under the royal standard; ancestor of the Viscounts Bolingbroke. His daughter, Anne St. John, married, first, Sir Francis Henry Lee, baronet, and, secondly, Henry Wilmot (son of Sir Charles, whom see), first Earl of Rochester. She was grandaunt of the celebrated statesman and author, Viscount Bolingbroke.

Saint John, Sir William, 2. Sub. £75; pd. £50. "Of Heighley, in the County of Glamorgan, Knight;" knighted at Dublin Castle, December 21, 1607, by Sir Arthur Chichester, the lord deputy of Ireland. He was "a distinguished naval officer;" July 3, 1609, the Earl of Nottingham sent by him to Salisbury "a letter of commendations of the bearer, Sir William St. John, who has taken Harris, the pirate, on the Irish coast, and done good service off the West Islands of Scotland." February 6, 1610, John Hopkins, alderman of Bristol, wrote "to Lord Admiral Nottingham, that Sir William St. John has taken a fly boat of 100 tons."

M. C. for Va. Co., 1612. In 1616 Sir Walter Ralegh is said to have paid Sir William St. John and Sir Edward Villiers the sum of £1,500 for their influence in securing his release from prison, and Sir William is said to have afterwards proposed to effect his pardon also, for the additional sum of £1,500 ; " but, upon the counsels of Lord Bacon, the ill-fated Ralegh rejected this overture " (but see Gardiner's "Hist. of England," ii. p. 381, note 1) ; a member of the African Company in 1618. In 1620 Sir William St. John and others sent out an expedition for the discovery of Senegambia, on the coast of Africa, which claimed to have passed 960 miles up the River Gambia into the continent. (See Humfrey Slany.)

Saint Leger Pedigree. (Ex-tract.) Sir Warham [1] St. Leger, chief governor of Munster, 1565 ; knight marshal of Munster, 1579; killed by Hugh Maguire, Lord Fermanagh, 1599 ; married, first, Ursula, daughter of George Neville, Earl of Abergavenny, and had by her, with other issue, Anne,[2] and Anthony.[2] Anne [2] St. Leger married Thomas Digges of Barham, by whom she was the mother of Sir Dudley Digges (whom see) and others. Anthony [2] St. Leger, of Ulcombe, married Mary, daughter of Sir Thomas Scott (see Scott pedigree), by whom he was the father of Sir Warham St. Leger (whom see) and others. Mrs. Mary Scott-St. Leger married, secondly, Alexander Culpeper, of Wigsell, Sussex.

Saint Leger (Sentleger, Sellenger), Sir Warham, 3. Sub. —— ; pd. ——. Of Ulcombe, County Kent; an officer in Ralegh's expedition to Guiana, in 1617-18; was, on his return, one of the witnesses against Ralegh. He married Mary, daughter of Sir Rowland Hayward (whom see). His daughter, Ursula St. Leger, a cousin to Sir Dudley Digges, married Rev. Daniel Horsmanden, rector of Ulcombe, Kent. Their son, Col. Warham Horsmanden, of Purleigh in Essex, went to Virginia, and was the father of Mary, the wife of the first Col. William Byrd, from whom the Byrds of Virginia descend. I believe that Jane Horsmanden, who granted the benefice of Purleigh in Essex to the Rev. Lawrence Washington in March, 1633, was the widow of Rev. Thomas Horsmanden, the brother, I think, of Rev. Daniel aforesaid. But however this may be, there is certainly a very interesting parallel in the lives of Rev. Daniel Horsmanden and Rev. Lawrence Washington; both were royalists, both were removed by Parliament in 1643, both died about 1654, and the sons of both went to Virginia in the cavalier emigration of 1649-58. The advowson of the rectory of Purleigh was granted to Sir Henry Fowke and his heirs, May 6, 1610. I suppose that Gerard Fowke who came to Va. about the same time as the Washingtons, and settled near them, was of the same family as Sir Henry.

Col. Warham Horsmanden returned to Purleigh after the Restoration ; but his descendants still flourish in America. John and Lawrence Washington remained ; and John's great-grandson was "the father of his country." (See "The Ancestry of Washington," by Henry F. Waters, A. M., Boston, 1889.) Sir Warham St. Leger and his wife, Mary Hayward, left "numerous issue," but I have the names of only three : 1. Ursula, born 1600 ; died 1672 ; married Rev. Daniel Horsmanden. 2. John, born 1606 ; married, 1632, Rebecca, daughter of Rev. Richard Horsmanden, "late of Ulchum, deceased." 3. Mary, born 1613 ; married, 1632, William Codd of Pelicans in Kent, esquire. Dame Mary St. Leger was living at Lenham, Kent, in November, 1632 ; her husband, Sir Warham, was then dead.

Salinas, Marques de. " President of the Indies." Had been viceroy of Peru.

Salisbury, Earl of. — Robert and William Cecil.

Salter, Edward, esquire, 3. Sub.

SIR WILLIAM WAAD

——; pd. ——. Knighted at Ampt Hall, July 21, 1621. First cousin to Sir Nicholas Salter (next).

Salter, Nicholas, clothworker, 2. Sub. £37 10s.; pd. £137 10s. Of Enfield in Middlesex; also of the E. I. and N. W. P. companies. A leading merchant of London ; one of the prime farmers of the customs, etc.; knighted at Whitehall, March 12, 1617. His daughter Anne was second wife to Sir Arthur Harris.

Saltonstall, Sir Samuel, 3. Sub. ——; pd. ——. Of London; knighted at Whitehall, July 23, 1603 ; collector of the customs ; March 4, 1618, a bill of adventure was granted him for three shares in the Va. Co. of London. He befriended Capt. John Smith, and is mentioned in Smith's will.

Sambache, William, 2. Sub. ——; pd. £10. Came to Virginia in 1608.

Samms, George, gent., 3. Sub. ——; pd. ——. Of Tolshunt Major in Com. Essex.

Samms, Sir John, 3. Sub. £150; pd. £50. Son of John Samms, Esq., of Lanckford Hall, Essex, by the daughter of Bartholomew Averell ; knighted at Dublin by the Earl of Essex in August, 1599 ; M. P. for Malden in Essex, 1610–11 ; M. C. for Va. Co., 1612 ; an incorporator of the N. W. P. Co. in 1612 ; M. P. for Malden in Essex in 1614. Chamberlain wrote to Carleton, October 14, 1620 : " Sir John Samms is stept aside and gone for Bohemia, as is pretended, being overladen and ready to sink under the burthen of his debts." Married, in 1595, Isabella, daughter of Alderman Sir John Garrard of London ; died in Flanders, where he was governor of Isondike, leaving an only son, Sir Gerard Samms, who married Ursula, daughter of Gawen Champernowne, Esq., and widow of Auditor Saxsey.

Sanderson, William. Married Margaret, daughter of Hugh Snedale, of Hilling in Cornwall, esquire, by his wife, Mary Ralegh, a half-sister to Sir Walter Ralegh. He was interested in the Amidas voyage of 1584 ; in the voyages of John Davys to the North-west, June to September, 1585, May to October, 1586, and May to September, 1587. One of those to whom

Ralegh granted an indenture for colonization, March 7, 1589. He was " the worshipful merchant " whose purse supported Mr. Emmeric Mollineux of Lambeth, while he was making his globes and maps, 1592–98.

Sandy, Robert, grocer. " Alexander Napier (called for distinction Sandy), son of Sir Alexander Napier, and brother of Sir Archibald, came into England *temp.* Henry VIII., and settled at Exeter." His second son, Robert Sandy, of whom I write, became a grocer of London in St. Martin Outwich parish. He was knighted, July 21, 1612, as " Sir Robert Sandie, *alias* Napper," and created a baronet November 25 following. He was of the E. I. and N. W. P. companies. Died in April, 1637.

Sandys Pedigree (Extract.) " The Rev. Edwin [1] Sandys, ' one of the first who conformed to the Protestant Religion,' was born in Lancashire in 1519 ; educated at Cambridge ; supported the claims of Lady Jane Grey to the crown ; refused to proclaim Queen Mary, and was imprisoned July 25, 1553; liberated and escaped to the continent in May, 1554 ; returned to England on the succession of Queen Elizabeth in 1558 ; made Bishop of Worcester, December 21, 1559 ; assisted in new translation of the Bible, 1565; Bishop of London, 1570; Archbishop of York in 1577; died at Southwell, July 10, 1588. By his first wife, Miss Sandys, a relative, it seems, he had no issue. He married, secondly, about 1559, Cicely, the sister to Sir Thomas Wilford (of the same family as the grandmother of Sir Dudley Digges), and by her had seven sons and two daughters. Before a great Bible, printed by Richard Jugge, Queen's printer, 1574, in the Archbishop's own hand, are the names and birthdays of his children, which he had by his said wife Cicely, and were all living October 1, 1576, viz. : —

1. " i. Samuel [2] Sandes was born on December 28, at three of the clock in the morning in the year of our Lord God, 1560. His godfathers, Clement Throckmorton, Esq., John Pedder, Dean of Worcester ; his godmother, Mrs. Anne Berrow.

2. " ii. Edwin [2] Sandes was born [in Worcestershire] on December 9, at

six of the clock in the morning, in the year of our Lord God, 1561. His godfathers, Sir Thomas Russel, Knt., Thomas Blount, Esq.; his godmother: Mrs. Margaret Sheldon, widow.

"iii. Miles [2] Sandes was born on March 29, at twelve of the clock in the morning, in the year of our Lord God, 1563. His godfathers, Miles Sandes, Esq., Thomas Fleet, Esq.; his godmother, Mrs. Pedder.

"iv. William [2] Sandes was born on September 13, at four of the clock in the afternoon, in the year of our Lord 1565. His godfathers, William Ligon, John Littleton, Esq.; his godmother, Mrs. Joan Perry.

"v. Margaret [2] Sandes was born on December 22, at three of the clock in the afternoon, in the year of our Lord God, 1566. Her godfather, John Folliot, Esq.; her godmothers, Lady Margaret Russell, Mrs. Anne Daston. [She married Anthony Aucher, Esq.]

3. "vi. Thomas [2] Sandes was born on December 3, at three of the clock in the afternoon in 1568. His godfathers: Sir Thomas Lucy, Knt., Walter Blount, Esq.; his godmother, Mrs. Elizabeth Packington. [Sir Thomas Lucy is Shakespeare's "Mr. Justice Shallow."]

"vii. Anne [2] Sandes was born on June 21, at eight of the clock in the morning, 1570. Her godfather, John Packington, Esq. ; her godmothers, Mrs. Anne Washbourne, Mrs. Anne Colles. [She married William Barnes, Esq.]

4. "viii. Henry [2] Sandes was born the last day of September, between eight and nine of the clock at night in 1572. His godfathers, Henry, Earl of Huntingdon, William Lord Sandes; his godmother, Lady Margaret Tailboies. *Ita est Edwinus, London.*

5. "ix. George [2] Sandes, born the second day of March at six of the clock in the morning in 1577 [*i. e.*, 1578, N. S]. His godfathers, George Clifford, Earl of Cumberland, William Lord Ewer; his godmother, Catharine, Countess of Huntingdon."

Sandys, Sir Edwin, 2. Sub. £75 ; pd. £287 10s. (See pedigree, 2.) Born December 9, 1561 ; admitted a scholar of Corpus Christi College in Oxford under the tuition of Richard Hooker in September, 1577 ; B. A., October 16, 1579 ; probationer fellow

of that college, January 23, 1580 ; collated to the prebend of Wetwang in the Cathedral of York, March 17, 1582; M. A., June 5, 1583. An Edwin Sandys (either his first cousin of that name, or himself) was M. P. for Andover, 1586, and for Plympton in 1588–89 and 1592–93. He afterwards traveled into foreign countries with his old friend and college-mate, George Cranmer (grandnephew of the great archbishop.) George Cranmer was killed in Ireland in 1600. His brother, William Cranmer, deputy-governor of the Hamburgh Company at Rotterdam, joined the Va. Co. some time after 1616.

While Sandys was at Paris in 1599, he drew up a tract, which was afterwards published under the title of "Europæ Speculum." Returned to England, 1599 ; resigned his prebend, May, 1602 ; entered the service of King James in Scotland, it seems, and came to England with him, by whom he was knighted at the Charterhouse, May 11, 1603, "and was afterwards employed by his majesty in several affairs of great trust and importance." M. P. for Stockbridge, 1604–11 ; at the head of the committee for investigating the complaints against the trading companies, April, 1604. His tract "Europæ Speculum, A Relation of the State of Religion . . . in the Severall States of these Western Parts of the World" was entered for publication at Stationers' Hall, June 21, 1605, and on November 2, 1605, "Sir Edwin Sandys's books were burned in Paul's Church Yard by order of the High Commission." M. C. for Va., March 9, 1607. "July 3, 1607, on the motion of Sir Edwin Sandys, a member of great authority, the House of Commons entered for the first time an order for the regular keeping of their journals." M. C. for Va. Co., May 23, 1609.

Hume says : " At that time men of genius and enlarged minds had adopted the principles of liberty which were, as yet, pretty much unknown to the generality of the people. Sir Matthew Hales has published a remonstrance against the king's conduct towards the Parliament during this session [1604–11]. The remonstrance is drawn with great force of reasoning and spirit of liberty, and was the production of Sir Francis Bacon and Sir Edwin Sandys, two men of the greatest parts and knowledge in England."

The king granted him the Manor of Northbourne and others in Kent, March 12, 1614. M. P. for Rochester, 1614 ; of the E. I. Co. prior to 1614. "Dr. Goulston, at the request of Sir Edwin Sandys, whose life he had saved," was admitted *gratis* into the E. I. Co., August 4, 1614. Of the S. I. Co., June 29, 1615, and Sandys Tribe in that island was named for him. "In regard of Sir Thomas Smythe's sicknes and other imployments, Sir Edwin was chosen as his Assistant in the management of the affairs of the Va. Co., and he did in a manner wholie supplie Smythe's place" from early in 1617 to April 28, 1619. During this time the Puritans of Leyden, about September, 1617, sent two messengers to consult him regarding the settlement in Virginia of the members of that church. "They found the Va. Co. in general well disposed thereto, and gained an active friend in Sir Edwin Sandys, whose brother, Sir Samuel Sandys, the lessee of Scrooby Manor, was a firm advocate of toleration" (see "Narrative and Critical History of America," vol. iii. pp. 264, 265). He succeeded Sir Thomas Smythe (whom see) as treasurer of the Va. Co., April 28, 1619, and was himself succeeded in that office by the Earl of Southampton, June 28, 1620. Late in 1620 Sir Edwin Sandys was chosen to represent Sandwich in the Parliament of 1621–22, after a "tumultuous election." This borough had been represented by Sir Thomas Smythe, and Sandys made the E. I. Co. an issue in the canvass ; he told the voters that "the East Indies Company was a pernicious matter to them and to the whole kingdom, and that he was against it." The Parliament met January 30, 16?9, and Sir Edwin took a noted part in its celebrated acts. He had drafted two of the former Virginia charters, and on February 22, 162?, he notified the company that he was preparing a new patent, making some changes. It seems that John Selden was his counsel in preparing this patent. The Va. Co. gave him twenty shares in Vir-

ginia, May 2, 1621. June 16, 1621, Selden and himself were committed to the custody of the sheriffs of London, and not released until the 18th of July following. This happened during a recess ; and when the House of Commons assembled again in November, 1621, many were indignant at the confinement of the members ; but Pym and the other committeemen were told that "neither Sandys nor Selden had been imprisoned for any Parliament matter." Peckard's Ferrar says that "the matter was the Virginia business." Wodenoth, in his "Short Collection," says, "In the conclusion of a broken Parliament by King James, both the Earl of Southampton and Sir Edwin Sandys were committed close prisoners upon private assumed suggestions, which struck some terrour into most undertakers for Virginia." In "a note which Sir Nathaniel Rich presently took of Capt. Bargrave's discourse concerning Sir E. Sandys." "The purport is that Sandys was opposed to monarchical government in general : had moved the Archbishop of Canterbury to give leave to the Brownists and Separatists to go to Virginia, and designed to make a free popular state there, and himself and his assured friends to be leaders." These matters, whatever they were, were kept strictly private, and therefore but little is really known about them ; but it seems from the proposed new charter of February, the imprisonment of June, and from these passages, that something was in the air. Were "speculative reasoners, already beginning to foretell that these remote colonies, after draining their mother-country of inhabitants, would shake off her yoke ?" Was the seed of our Revolution planted with the colonies ?

The discussion of the factions in the Va. Co. would be too long for these biographies ; but as the matter cannot be entirely overlooked, I shall say something of these troubles in the sketch of Sir Thomas Smythe.

The election for members of Parliament, held in Kent in January, 1624, was another "tumultuous election." Sandys defeated Sir Dudley Digges. The cry of his party was "that Sir Nicholas Tufton was a papist, and Digges a royalist, and it was thought this would incense the king more toward Sandys than ever." He was M. P. for Kent, February, 1624, to March, 1625. Coke and Sandys laid the charges against Middlesex before the Peers, April 15, 1624. The Virginia charter was declared void June 16, 1624. M. P. for Penryn, 1625 and 1626. He died. in October, 1629, and was interred in the church of Northbourne in Kent, " where he had a seat and estate granted to him by King James for some service which he had done his majesty upon his accession to the crown of England." He bequeathed £1,500 to the University of Oxford for the endowment of a metaphysical lecture. He married four times : first, to Margaret, daughter of John Eveleigh, Esq., of Devonshire (issue, a daughter); secondly, to Anne Southcott (issue, a daughter); thirdly, to Elizabeth Nevinson (no issue) ; fourthly, to Catharine, daughter of Sir Richard Bulkeley, and by her (who died in 1640) had, with other issue, five sons, all of whom, save one, adhered to the Parliament interest during the civil wars. (See the sketches of his sons, Edwin, Henry, and Richard, in this Dictionary.)

Edwyn Sandys

Sandys, Edwin, son of Sir Edwin, 3. Sub. ——— ; pd. ———. Of Northbourne Court in Kent ; was a colonel in the Parliament's army ; received a mortal wound at the battle of Worcester, and died in 1642. He married Catherine, daughter of Richard Champneys, Esq., of Hall Place, Kent, and his daughter, Catherine Sandys, married, in 1677, Thomas Bland, son of John Bland (whom see), and elder brother to Col. Theodorick Bland of Virginia.

Sandys, George, gent., 2. Sub. ——— ; pd. ———. Probably the Sir George Sandys, who was hanged at Wapping in March, 1618, for taking purses on the highway, having been formerly pardoned for like offenses. In August, 1616, he (with others) had been convicted for highway robberies

at Kensington, of twelve or thirteen persons in an evening. A real " knight of the road."

Sandys, George, esquire, 3. Sub. ——— ; pd. £12 10s. Youngest son of the Archbishop (see pedigree, 5); entered Oxford University, 1589 ; traveled through parts of Europe, Asia, and Africa, May, 1610, to the autumn of 1611 ; joined the Va. Co. ; published the account of his travels, dedicated to Prince Charles, 1615, and lived to see several editions issue from the press ; a candidate for governor of the Bermudas, but was defeated by Capt. Nathaniel Butler, 1619, after which he assigned his two shares in those islands to others. January 29, 1621, he transferred two shares in Virginia to Sir Francis Weyneman. He had published a first edition of the first five books of Ovid some time prior to 1621 ; in that year a second edition was issued. In April, 1621, he was chosen treasurer of the colony in Virginia, and afterwards appointed to be of the council there. He arrived in Virginia in the fall of 1621, and remained (possibly not continuously) until 1628, and probably after. After the dissolution of the Va. Co., he was appointed to the Council in Virginia by James I. on August 26, 1624, and by Charles I on March 4, 1626, and March 22, 1628. King Charles granted him special license to publish his translation into English verse of the fifteen books of Ovid's " Metamorphoses," " the better to encourage him and others to employ their labors and studies in good literature," on April 24, 1626. The first edition of these fifteen books (the first five books having been twice printed), dedicated to King Charles, appeared in 1626, and was followed by other editions in 1627, 1632, 1640, etc.

On the special commission for the better plantation of Virginia, June 27, 1631, and " having spent the ripest of his years in the public employment in Virginia," understanding that his majesty resolved to govern Virginia by a commission, he petitioned for the appointment of secretary to the commission. The date of this petition is uncertain ; but Mr. Sainsbury assigns it to " 1631 ? ".

King Charles granted him a special license to print and sell his paraphrase of the Psalms of David and other hymns dispersed through the Old and New Testaments, on December 4, 1635. Published " At the Bell in St. Paul's Churchyard, 1636. Cum Privilegio Regiæ Majestatis." Dedicated to the king and queen ; with a complimentary poem, prefixed from Lucius Cary, Viscount Falkland, " To my Noble Frend, Mr. George Sandys, upon his excellent Paraphrase of the Psalms." Under the different title of " A Paraphrase upon the Divine Poems," a second edition, with additions, was issued in 1638, and a third edition in 1648.

"Christs Passion [by Grotius]. A Tragedy. With Annotations. By George Sandys. London, printed . . . 1640."

"A Paraphrase upon the Song of Solomon. Written by G[eorge]. S[andys]. and Dedicated to the Queenes Majesty. Oxford, 1641." Ditto; "London, Printed by John Legatt, 1641." Ditto; "London, printed for H. S. and W. L., 1642."

After his return from Virginia he was appointed a gentleman of the king's privy chamber ; but I do not know the date of his return. In 1638 there was another determined effort made to reëstablish the old Virginia Company, and when this became known in Virginia, the Assembly there, in 1639, appointed George Sandys their agent in England, with particular instructions to oppose the reëstablishment of the company and to give the Assembly in Virginia the earliest intelligence of their machinations, etc.; but whether he was sent from Virginia at this time for this purpose, or whether he, being already in England, was so selected, I do not know. However, he mistook "his advice and instructions from the said Assembly," and presented a petition to the House of Commons, in the name of the Adventurers and Planters in Virginia, for restoring the letters patent to the company. When the Assembly heard of this, on April 1, 1642, they met and passed a solemn declaration against the company, etc. (See "Va. Hist. Register," vol. i. No. IV. pp. 153–161; Hening's "Va. Statutes at Large," vol. i. pp. 230–236.) On July 5, 1642, the king answered this decla-

ration, giving every assurance to the colony against the company. Sandys died in the beginning of March, 1644, at Bexley Abbey in Kent, the seat of his niece, the widow of Governor Wyatt of Virginia, and was interred in the chancel of the church of Bexley, March 7, 1644.

Sandys, Henry, esquire, 2. Sub. ——; pd. £25. The sixth son of the archbishop (see pedigree, 4).

Sandys, Henry, son of Sir Edwin, 3. Sub. —— ; pd. ——. March 7, 1623, Sir Edwin Sandys transferred to Mr. Henry Sandys, his son, five shares in the Virginia enterprise.

Sandys, Richard, esquire, 2. Sub. —— ; pd. ——. Son of Sir Edwin; he purchased Downehall in Kent ; was deputy governor of the B. I. Co. in 1647 ; was a colonel in the Parliament's army. He married Hester, daughter of Edwin Aucher, second son of Anthony Aucher, Esq., of Bourne.

Sandys, Sir Samuel, 2. Sub. £37 10s.; pd. £87 10. Eldest son of the archbishop (see pedigree, 1); born December 28, 1560; inherited from his father the manor of Ombersley, in the county of Worcester; M. P. for Ripon, 1586–87; knighted at Whitehall, July 23, 1603 ; M. P. for Worcestershire, 1609–1611; M. C. for Va. Co., 1612; member S. I. Co., 1615 ; sheriff of Worcestershire in 1618, and M. P. for that county in 1614, and 1621–22; in the latter Parliament he was involved in the same troubles as his brother, Sir Edwin. In May, 1622, he gave his son, Sir Edwin, a share of land in Virginia. March 30, 1623, his brother George wrote him a long letter from Virginia. He died August 18, 1623, and lies buried at Wickhamford, on the north side of the chancel, under a monument of alabaster, supported by five pillars of touchstone.

He married, about 1586, Mercy, daughter of Martin Culpeper, Esq., and had issue four sons and seven daughters; one of the daughters married Sir Francis Wyatt, sometime governor of Virginia, and another married (so it is said) Sir Ferdinando Wenman, who died in Virginia. Sir Edwin, the eldest son, who was afterwards of the Va. Co., was the father of Samuel Sandys, Esq., who married Elizabeth, daughter of Sir John Packington, and widow of Col. Henry Washington, the first cousin to John, the emigrant ancestor of Gen. George Washington.

Sandys, Thomas, esquire, 2. Sub. ——; pd. £25. Fifth son of the archbishop (see pedigree, 3). He was of London, where he was still living at the Herald's Visitation of 1633–34, when he recorded his pedigree. He married "Margaret, daughter of Robert Tyas of the Wardrob Clarke Comptroller there." His eldest son, Robert Sandys, married Alice, daughter of Mr. Lawrence Washington of Sulgrave, and aunt to Col. John Washington, the emigrant ancestor of General George.

It is very interesting to note this relationship between the Washingtons and the son of "Mr. Justice Shallow's" godson.

Sarmiento. See Gondomar.

Savage, Thomas. Born about 1594; arrived in Virginia January 2, 1608, and was soon after exchanged with Powhatan for Namontack; remained with the Indians about three years; with Hamor as interpreter in May, 1614. He traded with the Indians and was long an interpreter for the colony. In 1620 he sent a relation to the Va. Co. of a great trade in furs by Frenchmen to the northward. In 1625 he was living on his "dividient" on the Eastern Shore of Virginia with his wife Ann and two servants. The date of his death is not known to me. The Indians called him "Thomas Newport." At April court, 1668, Northampton County, Va., "the deposition of William Jones, aged 59, sayeth that being at Colonel Robins, deceased about four or five and thirty years since (when Laughing King came annually to visit said Robins in the spring), was desired by Colonel Robins to ask the said King, whose land such a neck of land was? and the King replied that he had given the south side of Wessaponson to his son, Thomas Newport." Savage evidently lived in favor with the Indians, being called son both by Powhatan and the Laughing King. He left two sons: Thomas, who was alive in 1652, but seems to have died without issue, and a younger son, John Savage (a Burgess in 1666, died in

1678), who married, first, Ann Elkington, and had by her two daughters: Susanna (married first to John Kendall and secondly to Henry Warren) and Grace (married George Corbin). John Savage married, secondly, Mary Robins, by whom three sons and two daughters. Nathaniel Littleton Savage of the revolutionary conventions was a descendant of " Ancient Thomas Savage."

Scarpe, John, gent., 2. Sub. ——; pd. £12 10s. Went to Virginia; was lieutenant of Jamestown in 1614.

Scott Pedigree. (Extract.) Sir Reginald [1] Scott of Scot's Hall, Kent; captain of the castles of Calais and Sangatte ; high sheriff of Kent, 1541–42 ; was principally engaged abroad in military service ; died December 16, 1554. He married, first, Emmeline, daughter of Sir William Kempe, of Ollantigh, Kent and had by her Sir Thomas [2] (see hereafter), and two daughters. He married, secondly, Mary, daughter to Sir Bryan Tuke, of Layer Marney in Essex, secretary to Cardinal Wolsey, and had by her Mary, who married Richard Argall (see Argall pedigree), and three other daughters, and Charles [2] and four other sons. Charles [2] was of Egerton in Godmersham ; he married Jane, daughter of Sir Thomas Wyatt, of Allington Castle, Kent (minister *temp.* Henry VIII.; beheaded, second Mary), by Jane, daughter of Sir William Hawte, of Kent. Mrs. Jane Scott was sister to George Wyatt of Bexley (see Sir Moyle Finch).

Sir Thomas [2] Scott, eldest son of Sir Reginald, was a distinguished man; sheriff of Kent, 1576 ; knight of the shire in Parliaments of 1571 and 1586; commander-in-chief of the Kentish forces assembled on Northbourne Downs in 1588, to repeal the threatened Spanish invasion ; died December 30, 1594. He married, first, Elizabeth, daughter of Sir John Baker, by whom he had a very large family; according to some accounts, 17 children. It will only be necessary to mention a few of them.

1. Thomas Scott, eldest son, married, first, Mary Knatchbull; secondly, Elizabeth Honywood.

2. Sir John Scott, of Nettlested, second son.

3. Richard Scott, who married Catherine, daughter of Sir Rowland Hayward.

4. Elizabeth Scott, married, first, John Knatchbull; secondly, Sir Richard Smythe.

5. Emeline Scott, married Robert Edolpe.

6. Mary Scott, married, first, Anthony St. Leger (see Sir Warham St. Leger), and, secondly, Alexander Culpeper, of Wigsell.

7. Anthony Scott, who may be Ensign Anthony Scott.

Sir John Baker (the father of Elizabeth, who married, Sir Thomas [2] Scott) was the speaker of the first Parliament of Edward VI. (1547–1552), which was the first thoroughly Protestant Parliament. His second son, John Baker, married Catherine Scott (the sister of Sir Thomas Scott, aforesaid), and they were the parent of Sir Richard Baker, the chronicler.

Scott, Anthony. Ensign; possibly son of Sir Thomas (see pedigree, 7).

Scott, Edmund, 3. Sub.——; pd. £25. Fifth son of Thomas Scot, of Sevenock, by his wife Margery, daughter of Thomas Clerke, of Ford, County Kent; was in the East Indies, February 2, 1603, to October 6, 1605, and in 1606 published an account of what he saw there; of the E. I. and N. W. P. companies.

Scott, Elizabeth, widow, 3. Sub. £37 10s. ; pd.——. Widow of Thomas Scott, gent. (whom see) ; lived at Sene in Newington, near Hythe, and died there, without issue, aged 60, in 1627 ; and was buried in Brabourne Church where her tomb remains.

Scott, George, of London, grocer, Sub. £37 10s.; pd. £125. Of St. Mary Woolchurch; fourth son of Thomas of Sevenock, and brother of Edmund. He married, in 1602, Elizabeth, daughter of Sir Thomas Campbell, lord mayor, and sister of Sir James Campbell; was of the E. I. and N. W. P. companies. In 1616 he gave to St. Mary Woolchurch Haw "the clock to strike on the great bell, and with two dyales, one towards the streate, the other within the church." He was elected M. C. for Va. Co. in June, 1623.

Scott, Sir John, 2. Sub. £75; pd.——. (See Scott pedigree, 2.) Of

Nettlested Place, Kent, second son of Sir Thomas Scott, knight, of Scot's Hall, by his first wife, Elizabeth, daughter of Sir John Baker (attorney-general to Henry VIII.), and heir of his elder brother, Thomas Scott, gent. He was knighted in the Low Countries in 1588 by Lord Willoughby, under whom he served as captain of a band of lancers; captain in the voyage to the Azores in 1597; implicated in the rising of Essex, 1601; M. P. for Kent, 1604–11; M. C. for Va., March 9, 1607; M. C. for Va. Co., May 23, 1609.

In 1609 Decker dedicated the Phœnix to Sarah, wife of Sir Thomas Smith, and to Catharine, wife to Sir John Scott, signing himself " Humbly devoted to your Ladyships, Thos Dekker." M. P. Maidstone, 1614. Sir John Scott died September 24, 1616, and was buried in Brabourne Church, Kent. He was twice married, but died without issue. His first wife was Elizabeth, widow of Sir William Drury, and daughter of Sir William Stafford by his wife, Lady Dorothy, who was the daughter of Henry Lord Stafford, only son of Edward, last Duke of Buckingham of that line, who was beheaded in 1521. Lady Elizabeth Stafford, born in 1544, was lady of the bedchamber to Queen Elizabeth; by her first husband she was mother of Sir Robert, Sir Drue, and William Drury, and four daughters; by her second husband, whom she married about 1578, she left no issue; she died February 6, 1598, and Sir John Scott married, secondly, prior to September 17, 1599, Catharine, daughter of Mr. Customer Smythe, and widow of Sir Rowland Hayward. She survived Sir John about six months, and died early in 1617, aged fifty-six.

Scott, Thomas, gent., 2. Sub. £37 10s. ; pd. £50. Eldest son of Sir Thomas Scott (see pedigree, 1); captain of a troop of lancers in the Kentish forces in 1588 and 1589; sheriff of Kent, 43 Elizabeth ; a commissioner for the survey of crown lands in Kent, 1608 ; died prior to 1611 ; heir, his brother, Sir John (aforesaid). His widow, Elizabeth (whom see), was daughter of Thomas Honywood, of Sene, by his wife, Margaret Bedingfield, of Bellaview, Kent.

Scrivener, Matthew, 2. Sub. ———; pd. £100. Arrived in Virginia with Newport in January, 1608; a member of the Council in Virginia; in the expedition up York River in February, 1608; possibly acting president of the council, July to September, 1608, and in January, 1609, at which time he was drowned in James River.

(He must have been a man of means, as he contributed a sum about equal to $2,500 of our money to the enterprise. The Rev. Richard Hakluyt mentions in his will, "Mr. John Scrivener, late of Barbican in the suburbs of the cittie of London." Scrivener is not a very common family name, and I infer that the aforesaid Matthew and John were members of the same family, and that they were probably related to the Rev. Richard Hakluyt.)

Scudamore, Sir James, 3. Sub. £37; pd. ———. Of Holme Lacy, Hereford; son of Sir John Scudamore, the "Sir Scudamore" of Spenser's "Faerie Queene;" M. P. for County Hereford, 1604–11 and 1614; probably died soon after; married, in 1599, Mary, daughter of Sir Thomas Throckmorton, and widow of Sir Thomas Baskerville (see Throckmorton pedigree), by whom he was the father of Sir John Scudamore.

Scudamore, Sir John. Sub. ———; pd. ———. Son of Sir James, aforesaid; created a baronet June 1, 1620; M. P. County Hereford, 1621–22 and 1624–25, and for Hereford, 1625 and 1628; created Viscount Scudamore, July 5, 1628. His aunt, the widow of Sir Thomas Dale, gave him by will, in 1640, a ring valued at £60. "He died universally lamented, in the seventy-first year of his age, June 8, 1671."

Sebright (or Seabright), William, esquire, 2. Sub. ———; pd. £12 10s. Of the Inner Temple; eldest son of Edward Sebright of Blakeshall, in the county of Worcester, by his wife Joyce, daughter to William Grosvenor, Esq.; town clerk of London, May 25, 1574, to April 27, 1613; twice married, but left no issue. His second wife, Elizabeth, daughter of James Morley, was the widow of Thomas Bourcher, and by him mother of Sir James Bourcher, the father of Elizabeth, wife of Oliver Cromwell, the Protector. William Sebright died at his house in Lombard Street, October 27, 1620 (or October 28, 1629), and was buried in the Church of St. Edmund the King. He left property for the foundation of a free grammar school at Wolverley, and to sundry other charities. His niece Sara married Sir Thomas Coventry.

Seckford, Sir Henry, 2. Sub. ———; pd. ———. Of Suffolk; knighted at the Charterhouse May 11, 1603; "Master of Tents and Toils." Died before March, 1611.

Seely, Captain Thomas. Probably Capt. Thomas Ceelye of Bideford, second son of Christopher Ceely of Plymouth; but see Froude's "History of England," vol. viii. pp. 452–455.

Selden, John. Sub. ———; pd. ———. The celebrated lawyer and antiquary; author of "History of Tithes," etc. He served on several committees for revising the laws, etc., of the Va. Co. of London. October 22, 1622, the N. E. Council consulted Mr. Robert Johnson and himself concerning the heads of "ye new Grand Pattent."

M. P. Lancaster, 1624–25; Great Bedwin, 1625 and 1626; Ludgershall, 1628–29, and Oxford University, 1640–53; died in London, November 30, 1654, aged 72; buried in the Temple Church.

Seyer — Sayer, Thomas, gent., 2. Sub. ———; pd. £12 10s. Probably Thomas Sayer, of Bowton in Suffolk, a younger brother of Sir George Sayer, who received the honor of knighthood June 4, 1607.

This family name also occurs as Sears.

Seymour, Edward, esquire. Of Berry Pomeroy, County Devon; grandson of the first Duke of Somerset; M. P. for Devonshire, 1592–93, 1601, and 1604–11; M. C. for Va., March 9, 1607; created a baronet, June 29, 1611; died April 11, 1613. He married, in 1576, Elizabeth, daughter of Sir Arthur Champernoune, knight, of Dartington, in Devonshire, and was succeeded by his eldest son.

Sir Edward Seymour, second baronet; knighted at Greenwich, May 22, 1603; returned to two Parliaments by the county of Devon, in the reign of James I.; member of the N. E. Council in 1620; married Dorothy, daughter of Sir Henry Killigrew, of Laroch in Cornwall, and, dying in 1659, left a large family.

Seymour, Rev. Richard. He was the youngest son of Sir Edward Seymour who died in 1613, and brother of Sir Edward Seymour, second baronet.

Shacley (Sheckley, etc.), William, haberdasher, 2. Sub. ——; pd. £25. June 24, 1619, he transferred his two shares in Virginia to Oliver St. John.

Shakespeare, William, poet. Baptized at Stratford - upon - Avon, April 26, 1564; married Anne Hathaway about November, 1582 ; went to London about 1586 ; retired to Stratford probably about 1604 ; died at Stratford, April 23, 1616.

Shanois. See Chanoyes.

Sharp, William, 2. Sub. —— ; pd. £25. Went to Virginia in 1611; still living there in 1625.

Sheffield, Edmund Lord, 2. Sub. —— ; pd. £140. John Sheffield, second Baron Sheffield (who died in 1569), married Douglas, daughter of William Lord Howard of Effingham, by whom (who married, secondly, Robert Dudley, Earl of Leicester) he had, with other issue, Edmund Sheffield, born in 1564 ; succeeded, at the death of his father, in 1569, as third Lord Sheffield ; went to the Low Country wars with the Earl of Leicester in December, 1585. "This nobleman distinguished himself in arms in the reign of Queen Elizabeth, particularly in the celebrated defeat of the formidable Spanish Armada, when he was knighted at sea by the lord admiral, July 26, 1588." "After that he served her Majesty in the Irish Warres, where God so blessed him, that he gained much honor." By King James he was made, in 1603, president of the council for the northern parts of the realm, where he governed many years with such integrity that injustice was never laid to his charge. M. C. Va. Co., May 23, 1609. He was one of the lords who accompanied Richard Martin to the House of Commons in May, 1614, in the interest of the Va. Co., and we find him constantly interested in the success of the Virginia Colony ; one of the first members of the first council for the N. E. Co., November 3, 1620, and one of the signers of the first Plymouth patent, June 1, 1621. He granted a patent of Cape Ann, New England, on January 1, 1624 ; created Earl of Mulgrave by Charles I., February 7, 1626 ; married, first, Ursula, daughter of Sir Robert Tirwhit, of Ketilby, County Lincoln, and had by her no less than fifteen children. His domestic losses were severe; four of his sons were drowned, and the fifth, Sir John Sheffield (grandfather of the celebrated Duke of Buckingham), was killed by a fall from his horse. Of his daughters, by first wife, Mary married (in November, 1608) Sir Ferdinando Fairfax; Frances married Sir Philip Fairfax, and Elizabeth married Sir John Bourchier.

Lord Sheffield married, secondly, Mariana, daughter of Sir William Urwyn, knight, and had by her no less than five children.

Rev. Thomas Lorkin, writing to Sir Thomas Puckering, March 16, 1619, says, "My Lord Sheffield, upon Thursday fortnight last, married a fair young gentlewoman of some sixteen years of age, Sir William Irwin's daughter, and is (for the country's sake, I suppose) highly applauded by the King for his choice. And surely, if it be true, ' Blessed is the wooing that is not long adoing,' we must give him for a happy man, since less than three days concluded wooing, wedding, and bedding."

He lies buried under a black and white altar tomb in the Church of Hammersmith, on the south side of the chancel, with the following inscription : —

"To the lasting memory of Edmond Lord Sheffield, Earl of Mulgrave, Baron of Butterwick and Knight of the most noble order of the Garter. . . . He was a good patron to his country, endevoringe to advance the Church and common weale. He was truly pious, open-handed to feed the poore, and cloathe the naked. As he lived the life, so he died the death, of the righteous, in Oct', 1646, in the 83rd year of his age."

Shelley, Henry, 2. Sub. —— ; pd. £25. Probably Henry Shelley of Warminghurst, Sussex ; M. P. for Steyning, 1586–87 ; Bramber, 1604–11 ; died December, 1623. Or Henry Shelley of Parham, Sussex, whose daughters, Mary and Judeth, married nephews of John and Gregory Bland. He was shipwrecked on the Bermudas in 1609 ; came to Virginia in 1610, but returned to England.

Shelley, Walter. Sub. —— ; pd. £12 10s. Member of the first House of Burgesses in the New World, for Smythe's Hundred, July 30, 1619, and died during the session, August 1.

Shelton, Sir Ralphe, 3. Sub. £37 10s. ; pd. £12 10s. Of Shelton Hall, Norfolk ; knighted at Theobald's, November 30, 1607.

Shepard, Matthew, grocer, 2. Sub. £37 10s. ; pd. £50. Apprentice to Thomas Juxon ; was sworn to the freedom of the Grocers' Company, January 18, 1579 ; married Sara, daughter of John Hawkins of Rugby, Com. Warwick, and widow of Raphe Juxon (the uncle of William Juxon, Bishop of London). His son and late apprentice, Matthew Sheppard, was sworn to freedom, July 3, 1616, and both father and son (senior and junior) were on the Grocers' books in 1620. At the Visitation of London in 1634, the father was dead, and the son was one of the "Leiftenants of the City."

Shepard, Richard, preacher, 2. Sub. —— ; pd. £25.

Sherley (or Shirley), Sir Anthony. The second son of Sir Thomas Sherley, the elder, of Wiston ; was born about 1565 ; B. A. Oxford, 1581 ; serving in the Low Country wars, 1588 ; knighted 1591 ; made a knight of St. Michael's by Henry IV. of France ; but Queen Elizabeth made him return the insignia ; made a voyage to the West Indies and thence along our whole coast, *via* Newfoundland, May 21, 1596, to June 15, 1597 ; in the voyage of 1597 to the Azores ; induced by the Earl of Essex to proceed to the Court of Persia ; set out with his younger brother Robert and twenty-six followers in 1598–99 ; sailed from Venice for Aleppo, May 24, 1599 ; arrived in Persia after many adventures by land and sea in 1599 ; per-

suaded Shah Abbas to make war against the Turk. In 1600 the Shah sent him on an embassy to the Christian princes of Europe to induce them to form a league with him against Mahomet III., and after traveling over Europe on this embassy, he landed at Dover, England, "in the midst of the moneth of September," 1601. Licensed by James I. to remain beyond seas, and recommended to foreign courts, February 8, 1604 ; ambassador from Rudolph II. of Germany to the King of Morocco, Africa, in 1604–05. His brother Robert, who had gone with him to Persia, and who remained there, wrote to him on September 10, 1606, from Casbin, reproaching him for not returning to Persia. He afterwards entered the service of Spain, and was pensioned by Philip III. "The habit of St. Iago " was conferred upon him in 1611. He was afterwards created admiral of the Levant Seas, and made a member of the Spanish Council. Died in Spain after 1630.

Sherley (or Shirley), Sir Robert. The youngest brother of Sir Anthony aforesaid ; born about 1570 ; entered the service of Shah Abbas, 1599 ; drilled his troops, and served with distinction in his army against the Turks. In December, 1608, he was sent ambassador to Christian princes by the Shah. Rudolph II., in token of his great service against the Turk, created him a Count and Knight of the Sacred Roman Empire, June 2, 1609 ; reached Spain early in 1610, and remained there until June, 1611, when he went to England. While in Persia, he married Teresa, daughter of Ismael Khan, who bore him a child there, for whom the Mohammedan king stood godfather, and on November 4, 1611, she bore him a son in England, for whom the Prince of Wales and the Queen were sponsors. Left England for Persia in January, 1613, in the ship of Capt. Christopher Newport ; remained in Persia until 1616 ; represented the Shah in Spain, 1616–20 ; in England in 1624 ; died at Casbin in Persia, July 13, 1628.

Sherley (or Shirley), Sir Thomas. The elder of Wiston ; born May 9, 1549 ; M. P. Sussex, 1572 ; knighted by Queen Elizabeth, at Rye

SIR FRANCIS WALSINGHAM

in Kent, August 12, 1573 ; treasurer at war, 1586–97 ; served in the Low Countries ; died in December, 1612 ; had issue, by Anne, daughter of Sir Thomas Kempe of Ollantigh, seven daughters and five sons. One of the daughters, Cecilia, married Sir Thomas West, Lord De la Warr, the first captain-general and lord governor of Virginia. Three of the sons, Thomas, Anthony, and Robert, are known as " the three celebrated brother travelers."

Sherley (or **Shirley**), **Sir Thomas**. Sub. £37 10s. ; pd. ——. Eldest son of Sir Thomas, the elder, aforesaid; born in 1564; M. P. Steyning, 1584–85; served in the Low Country wars; knighted in Ireland in 1589; M. P. Steyning, 1593; engaged in taking Spanish prizes on the Atlantic Ocean; M. P. Hasting, 1601, and for Steyning, 1604–11 ; became involved in debt, was arrested and lodged in the Fleet from March 15 to May 15, 1604, furnishing the grounds for a celebrated "case of privilege ;" went to Turkey, and was a prisoner there, 1604–1607; released and returned to England; sent to the Tower "for turning Turk," for a short time in September, 1607; while before the King's Bench for debt in June, 1612, he took poison, but recovered; M. P. for Steyning, 1614; was again in the Fleet for debt in January, 1617 ; M. P. for Steyning, 1621–22. His debts forced him to sell the ancestral estate of Wiston. (Sir Robert Sherley, first Earl of Ferrers, who married, for his first wife, Elizabeth, daughter of Lawrence Washington of Garesdon, Wiltshire, was of another branch of this family.)

Sherwell, Nicholas. Pd. £12 10s.

Sherwell, Thomas. Sub. —— ; pd. £12 10s. Merchant of Plymouth; M. P. Plymouth, 1614, 1621–22, 1624–25, 1625, 1626, and 1627–28. This name is sometimes found in the old Virginia records as Sherwin, and I suppose this person to be either the same, or one of the same family, as the Master Thomas Sherwin who was interested in the whale fisheries, and who made voyages to Spitzbergen during 1612–18, and possibly before and after.

Shipley, Hugh, gent., 2. Sub. —— ; pd. £12 10s.

Shipton, Thomas, 2. Sub. —— ; pd. £62 10s. Of the E. I. Co.

Shrewsbury, Earl of. — George and Gilbert Talbot.

Sicklemore, Master Michael, gent. In Virginia, 1608–09.

Sidney Pedigree. (Extract.) Sir William Sidney married Anne Pagenham, and had issue, with others, Lucy and Sir Henry. Lucy Sidney married Sir James Harington, and had issue, with others, Sir John Harrington (father of Sir John and Lucy Harrington) and Elizabeth Harington (mother, by her husband, Sir Edward Montague, of Sir Henry and Bishop James Montague).

Sir Henry Sidney married Mary, daughter of John Dudley, Earl of Northumberland. " Her father, her grandfather, her brother, and her sister-in-law, the Lady Jane Grey, all died on the scaffold in the time of Queen Mary ; and this was the Dudley blood of which her son, the celebrated Sir Philip Sidney, was so proud." By her husband, Sir Henry Sidney, she was the mother of three sons and a daughter, namely : 1. Sir Philip Sidney ; 2. Sir Robert Sidney ; 3. Sir Thomas Sidney, who died a young man ; 4. Mary Sidney.

Sidney, Madame Mary. Daughter of John Dudley (see pedigree). Patron of Le Moyne. Her husband, Sir Henry, and herself were both interested in Frobisher's voyages, 1576–78. She was sister to Robert Dudley, Earl of Leicester.

Sidney, "**Mary,** Countesse of Pembroke," 3. Sub. —— ; pd. ——. Daughter of Sir Henry Sidney and his wife, Mary Dudley (see pedigree); born about 1550 ; married Henry Herbert, Earl of Pembroke, about 1576 ; interested in Frobisher's voyages of 1576–78, and in Fenton's, 1582–83 ; member of the Va. Co., 1612 ; a poetess and authoress. She died at her house in Aldersgate Street. London, September 25, 1621, and Ben Jonson wrote her epitaph : —

> " Under neath this marble hearse
> Lies the subject of all verse :
> Sidney's sister, Pembroke's mother :
> Death, ere thou hast slain another,
> Wise, and fair, and good as she,
> Time shall throw a dart at thee."

She left two sons, Philip and William Herbert (whom see).

Sidney, Sir Philip (see pedigree). Born at Penshurst in Kent, November 29, 1554, and named for Philip II. of Spain, who had recently married Mary, Queen of England. In May, 1564, when not ten years of age, " Philip Sydney, Scholar," was instituted by Thomas, Bishop of St. Asaph, to the rectory and church of Whyteford, as Philip Sydney, clerk, etc. He was then at school in Shrewsbury, and his church preferment was filled by his proctor. From this school he went, about 1568, to Christ Church, Oxford, and from Oxford he is said to have "passed to Cambridge, which he left with a high reputation for scholarship and general ability." In August, 1569, "terms of settlement for a proposed marriage of Philip Sidney and Ann, daughter of Sir William Cecil," were drawn up by Cecil.

Sidney sailed for France with Edward Clinton, Earl of Lincoln, May 26, 1572 ; in Paris at the massacre of St. Bartholomew, August 22, 1572 ; sheltered himself in the house of Walsingham ; quitted Paris as soon as the storm had subsided; at Frankfort, late in 1572 and early in 1573, where he became acquainted with the celebrated Hubert Languet ; in Hungary, September, 1573 ; in Italy, winter 1573–74, to summer, 1574 ; then in Germany ; returned to England about the last of May, 1575.

" He is said to have been invited to enrol himself among the candidates for the crown of Poland vacant, in 1585, by the death of Stephen Bathori." But Bathori did not die until after Sir Philip, in December, 1586. It may be, however, that Sidney was invited in 1574 to enrol himself as the candidate of the Christians against Bathori, who was supported by the Turks.

At the entertainment given Queen Elizabeth by Leicester at Kenilworth, in July, 1575; met his " Stella," Lady Penelope Devereux, in 1575 and 1576. About November, 1576, sent by Elizabeth to condole with Rudolph II. on the death of his father, and with secret instructions to other German princes, to negotiate a union of the Protestant states against the Pope and Philip II.; and the subsequent success of the measure has been ascribed to his arguments and address.

He returned to England in 1577 ; was interested in Frobisher's voyage of 1578. Edmund Spenser dedicated "The Shepheard's Calendar" to him in 1579. It was probably in October, 1579, that he had his noted difficulty with the Earl of Oxford. In 1580 he lived quietly at Wilton, the seat of his brother-in-law, where he began to write his " Countess of Pembroke's Arcadia." M. P. for Kent in 1581 ; sat on a most select committee for devising new laws against the Pope and his adherents ; Hakluyt dedicated his " Divers Voyages " to Sidney in 1582.

His " Stella " had married Lord Rich prior to September 9, 1582, on which day the Lady Penelope Rich, the old Lady Chandose, Mr. Philip Sidney, and Mr. Fulke Greville stood sponsors for the infant Penelope West, sister of Thomas West, afterwards governor of Virginia, and mother of Herbert Pelham, first treasurer of Harvard College, New England.

January 13, 1583, Sidney was knighted at " Windesore, and was on that day lykewise installed for Duke John Cazimir, Conte Palatine, and Duke of Bavier." He married Frances, daughter of Sir Francis Walsingham, about March, 1583; was interested in colonizing America as early as July, 1584 ; M. P. for Kent, 1584–85, and was on the committee for confirming Ralegh's patent, December, 1584. His own colonization schemes had taken definite shape prior to April, 1585 ; interested in the Roanoke colony, and Lane wrote to him from Virginia on the 12th of August, 1585, which letter he probably received in November, just before sailing for Flushing. He went aboard his fleet to sail for America in July, 1585; but the queen ordered him to return to court.

November 7, 1585, appointed governor of Flushing, and on the 18th arrived there ; took Axel, July, 1586; saved the army at Gravelines; wounded at Zutphen, September 22, 1586 ; died at Arnheim, October 17, 1586 ; buried in St. Paul's, London, February 16, 1587.

" England, Netherland, the Heavens and the Arts,
The Souldiers, and the World have made sixe parts
Of the Noble Sidney.
. . . .

His Body hath England, for she it bred :
Netherland his Bloud, in her defence shed,
The Heavens have his Soule, the Arts have his
   Fame :
All Souldiers the Griefe; the World his good
   Name."

Sidney, Sir Robert, Viscount Lisle, etc., 2. Sub. —— ; pd. £90. The second son of Sir Henry Sidney (see Sidney pedigree); born about 1555–56; received his education largely under the direction of his celebrated uncle, Robert Dudley, Earl of Leicester, whom he accompanied to his government of the Low Countries in December, 1585, and continued to serve under him there until 1587 ; a volunteer at Doesbury in 1586, in which year he was knighted by " Roberte, Erle of Lecester in Hollande."

In 1588 he was sent by Queen Elizabeth as ambassador to King James VI. of Scotland (afterwards James I. of England), to discover that prince's intentions with regard to the great schemes of Spain, and to secure the coöperation of that king against the Spanish Armada ; " by whom the King returned answer to the Queen of his faithful friendship and love to her, and to the Religion, and that he hoped for no other benefit from the Spaniard than that which Polyphemus had promised Ulysses, namely, that when the rest were devoured, he should be swallowed last."

About 1589 he was appointed governor of Flushing, "and Elizabeth kept him there several years sorely against his will; because she could not find a more efficient person to send in his place." Sent ambassador to Henry IV. of France, December, 1593, to April, 1594; served in the Netherlands with Sir Francis Vere, and shared honors with him in the victory achieved at Turnholt, in Brabant in 1597, where his gallant conduct was highly praised by Prince Maurice.

James I. granted him many favors. April 22, 1603, he was granted the offices of governor and captain of Flushing during pleasure ; and at the first creation of peers by the king, he was elevated to the peerage as Baron Sydney of Penshurst, County Kent, by letters patent dated May 13, 1603.

In June, 1603, Lord Sidney and Lord Southampton met the French ambassador, Marquis de Rosni, afterwards Duke de Sully, at Canterbury, and attended him to London, and on July 24 in the same year, Lord Sidney was appointed lord chamberlain to Queen Anne. May 4, 1605, he was created Viscount Lisle. M. C. for Va. Co., May 23, 1609.

In 1610 Robert Dowland published " A Musical Banquett, furnished with varietie of delicious Ayres collected out of the best authors, etc.," and dedicated to Sir Robert Sydney of Penshurst, Viscount Lisle, who, with Sir Henry Lee, wrote the greater part of the poetry in the book.

He was a member of the E. I. and N. W. P. companies. The following receipt, of which I give an abstract, is still preserved : " March 20, 1612. Receipt by Thomas Smythe from Viscount Lisle of £100, his adventure on the 2d voyage to the North West Passage and his freedom of the same company."

In 1616 he was installed a Knight of the Garter, and was raised, August 2, 1618, to the earldom of Leicester, the ceremony of creation being performed in the hall of the bishop's palace at Salisbury ; died July 13, 1626.

His lordship married, first, Barbara, daughter of John Gamage, Esq., of Coyty, Glamorganshire, and had issue by her three sons and eight daughters. Of the sons, William and Henry died unmarried. Sir Robert, who succeeded his father as second Earl of Leicester, married, in 1615, Lady Dorothy Percy, daughter of Henry, ninth Earl of Northumberland, and niece of Capt. George Percy of Virginia, and had issue by her, four sons and four daughters, among whom : —

1. Philip Sidney, Viscount L'Isle.

2. Algernon Sidney, the celebrated patriot.

3. Robert Sidney, who died in 1674.

4. Henry Sidney, created Earl of Romney.

5. Dorothy Sidney, baptized at Isleworth, October 5, 1617. (Waller's " Sacharissa " married, first, July 20, 1639, Henry, Earl of Sunderland, who was killed at the first battle of Newbury in 1643. She married, secondly, Robert Smythe, of Bounds in Kent, esquire, the grandson of Sir Thomas Smythe, and from them descended Sir Sidney Stafford Smythe, who died in

1777, the last of the male line of the first treasurer of the Va. Co. of London. "Sacharissa's" youngest sister married Philip Smythe, Viscount Strangford, a grandnephew of Sir Thomas Smythe's.)

Of the eight daughters of Robert Sidney, first Earl of Leicester :

Mary married Sir Robert Wroth of Durance in Middlesex.

Catharine married Sir Lewis Mansel, son of Sir Thomas Mansel.

Phillippa married Sir John Hobart, son of Sir Henry Hobart ; and

Barbara married, first, Thomas Smythe, Viscount Strangford, nephew of Sir Thomas Smythe, and, secondly, Sir Thomas Colepepper.

The first Earl of Leicester married, secondly, Lady Smythe, the widow of Sir Thomas Smythe, the first treasurer of the Va. Co. of London. It is interesting to note this blending of the names Sidney and Smith, and the connection of the Virginia enterprise therewith.

Singleton, Robert, 2. Sub. £37 10s.; pd. £75.

Slany, Humfrey, N. Fld. Co. Of London, merchant. March 2, 1620, Mr. Humfrey Reynolds transferred to Mr. Humfrey Slany five shares in Virginia. He was a merchant of London; traded to Guinea under the Warwick charter of November 16, 1618 (see Robert Rich, second Earl of Warwick), until November 22, 1631, when King Charles annulled the former letters patent granted by King James, and granted the trade to Guinea, Binney, and Angola for 31 years to Sir Richard Young, Sir Kenelm Digby, George Kirke, Humfrey Slany, Nicholas Crispe, and William Clobery. Slany died before May 25, 1650, when his company, in answer to Samuel Vassal and Company, asserted that the first factory on that coast was by Sir William St. John and Company about 35 years since in Gambia River. Humfrey Slany married Joane, daughter of John Weld, of London, haberdasher, and had issue sons and daughters. His daughter Dorothy married, in 1621, William Clobery, of London, merchant, a partner with Claiborne in Virginia.

Slaney, John. N. Fld. Co. ; governor of that company in 1610–28.

He dwelt in Cornhill, London, and entertained for some time there Squanto, one of the twenty Indians captured by Hunt on our New England coast. He sent Squanto to Newfoundland, and from there he was taken back to New England by Mr. Dermer.

Slany, Stephen. Son of John Slany of Staffordshire ; he was born in 1524. In one of his trading voyages to the East was taken by the Turks, and his estate had to be sold to redeem him ; an alderman of London, 1584 ; sheriff, 1584; lord mayor, 1595; president of Bridewell Hospital, 1599, and of Christ's Hospital, 1602, to his death, December 27, 1608.

Smalman, Francis, gent., 3. Sub. ——; pd. £12 10s. M. P. for Leominster, 1621–22.

Smith (Smythe, etc.), Cleophas, draper, 2. Sub. ——; pd. £87 10s.

Smith, Edmund, 2. Sub. ——; pd. £12 10s.

Smith (Smythe, etc.), Edward, haberdasher, 2. Sub.——; pd. £12 10s.

Smith, George, grocer. Of St. Bennet, Grace Church, London ; born 1576; of the B. I. Co. ; married, in 1604, Elizabeth, daughter of Anthony Pennyston, gent., of Saffron Walden, Essex.

Smith, Humfrey, grocer, 3. Sub. £37 10s. ; pd. £37 10s. Also of E. I. and N. W. P. companies ; elected alderman of Farringdon Within ward, February 3, 1628 ; chosen sheriff of London, 1629 ; removed to Cheap ward, February 25, 1633 ; died in August, 1638. He married Anne, daughter of Sir George Bolles.

Smith, John, son of Sir Thomas, 3. Sub. ——; pd. ——. (See sketch of Sir Thomas Smythe, the treasurer.) Hazlitt, in his "Collections and Notes" (1st series, p. 462), mentions a certain copy of "A Preparation to the Psalter [by George Wither], London. Imprinted by Nicholas Okes, 1619," which was dedicated to Sir John Smith, "onely sonne to Sir Thomas Smith, governor of the E. I. Co.," etc., as containing "a long MS. paper in the autograph of Lord Strangford respecting his collateral ancestor," the said Sir John Smith. He was knighted at Whitehall, September 22, 1618.

Smith, Sir John, 2. Sub. —— ; £26 13s. 4d. Of Ostenhanger, Kent ;

eldest brother of Sir Thomas Smith (see the Smith pedigree) ; born about 1554–56 ; married, about 1576–78, to Elizabeth, daughter and heir of Sir John Fineaux, of Herne, Kent (son of Sir John Fineaux, chief justice of the King's Bench) ; sheriff of Kent in 1600 ; knighted at the Charterhouse, May 11, 1603 ; died in 1609, leaving one son and two daughters. The son, Sir Thomas Smith, was created Viscount Strangford, July 17, 1628 ; one of the daughters married Sir Henry Neville, and one of Neville's daughters married Sir Thomas Lunsford, who went to Virginia and died there.

Smith (Smythe, etc.), John, gent., 3. Sub. £75; pd. £37 10s. Of Nibley, the historian of the Berkeleys; born in 1567; educated at the Free School of Derby, whence he came in 1584 to attend upon Thomas, the son and heir of Henry, seventeenth Lord Berkeley, at Callowden, near Coventry ; pursued his studies, with young Berkeley, under the tuition of Mr. Edward Cowper, of Trinity College, Oxford ; February, 1589, they entered Magdalen College, Oxford, where they remained three years, after which Smyth removed to the Middle Temple as a student of common law. On the completion of his studies at the Temple, Smith returned to the Berkeleys, and in 1596 became steward of the household ; was steward of the hundred and liberty of Berkeley in 1597, in which year he married the well-dowered widow of John Drew, Esq., and settled at North Nibley, four miles from Berkeley. In 1607 he built a new house, with the following letters engraved on a stone over the front entrance : —

N. M.   M. H.
S. P.   N. C.

Which are the initials of the Latin couplet : —

Nunc Mei,   Mox Hujus,
Sed Postea   Nescio Cujus.

Which may be paraphrased thus : —

'Tis mine to-day ; tomorrow (perhaps) my heir's ; But after, whose ? Let him reply who dares !

In 1609 his first wife died without issue, and he soon after married Mary, elder daughter of John Browning, of Coaley, who bore him five sons and four daughters.

Besides the stewardship before mentioned, Smyth held many other positions requiring a knowledge of the law: as steward of the borough and manor of Tetbury, of the manor and hundred of Bosham in Sussex, etc., and other properties of the Berkeleys, whom he served faithfully. In 1612 he invested fifty shillings in the lottery for Virginia, and some time after he subscribed sixpence towards a college to be erected there. In 1618 he thought of making a plantation in Virginia, and for that purpose formed a partnership with Sir W. Throckmorton, Sir George Yardley, Richard Berkeley, and George Thorpe. On February 18, 1619, the remaining partners wrote to Sir George Yardley, governor of Virginia, " Since your departure, we have procured our patent for plantation in Virginia (a copy whereof we herewith send unto you, written by the Virginian boy of me, George Thorpe)." This indenture is dated February 3, 1618–19. In reading the company records, 1619–24, " Mr. John Smith " has been mistaken for " Captaine John Smith ; " but they were different men. Throckmorton, Berkeley, Thorpe, and Smith sent the Margaret, of Bristol, loaded with emigrants and supplies to their plantation, " Berkeley Town and hundred," September 16, 1619. On January 10, 1620, Yardley wrote from Virginia, declining to act as co-adventurer, lest it should interfere with his public employment. He says, " The place assigned for the new Berkeley is not on Lord De la Warr's land, as asserted by Capt. West." It was some five miles from Charles City (" City Point "); it was afterwards a seat of the Harrisons, and President William H. Harrison was born there. February 20, 1620, the Virginia Council sent an order to " ye Governor in Virginia to sett out 400 acres for Capt. Powle [Wm. Tracy's son-in-law] and Mr. John Smith ; " and on May 7, 1620, Sir William Throckmorton assigned to William Tracy his interest in the plantation ; August 28, 1620, quadrupartite articles of agreement were entered into by the four adventurers of Berkeley Hundred, namely, Richard Berkeley, George Thorpe, William Tracy, and John Smith, of Nibley; Smith was an active member, and a regular attendant on the courts of the Va. Co.,

1621–1623. He was member of Parliament for Midhurst, January 30, 1621 to February 8, 1622 ; April 12, 1621, at a Virginia court, he proposed "to have a fair and perspicuous history compiled of that country from her first discovery to this day." He does not mention Capt. John Smith in his list of worthies. April 30 following he bought three shares of land in Virginia from Mr. Downes.

February 4, 1623, " Mr. John Smith said, that having spent upon Virginia a very great matter he did by God's blessing hope to receive this year a great quantity of tobacco." He had spent a great deal upon Virginia, as his papers show. These papers are now advertised for sale by Mr. Quaritch, 15 Piccadilly, London, England, in his Catalogue No. 87, as " Virginia Papers : . . . originally collected by one of the early Adventurers, John Smyth of Nibley (the author of the 'Lives of the Berkeleys ') . . . from the Cholmondeley collection, at Condover Hall, Shropshire. £150." Among these papers are several which were sent to John Smith, in England, by Ben Harryson, the clerk of the court in Virginia, about 1634. He evidently retained interests in Virginia. Fosbroke says that " Smith became a violent Puritan ; " but Mr. James Herbert Cooke, F. S. A., says, " There is not the slightest evidence of this in his writings, and there are many expressions and allusions in his works which exhibit an entirely different feeling." He died in 1641, and was buried in Nibley Church.

Among his manuscript works were " Lives of the Berkeleys," in three volumes, folio, containing 933 closely-written pages ; " Description of the Hundred of Berkeley," in one folio volume of 426 pages; " History of the Borough and Manor of Tetbury ; " " History of the Manor and Hundred of Bosham in Sussex ; " a folio volume of the " Tenures by Knight's service under the Berkeleys; " the " Virginia Papers," aforesaid, etc.

The other founders of the famous Berkeley on James River were all related to each other. (See Throckmorton pedigree.)

Smith, Captain John, 2. Sub. —— ; pd. £9. Dozens of biographies have been written of Capt. John Smith ; but they are generally based on the accounts furnished by himself. The world has been searching for data regarding him for two hundred years, but has found little beside what he tells us in his own works, and unfortunately his own story of his life cannot be relied on. It is true that the accuracy of all of his statements cannot be tested ; but enough can be, to make it evident that all must be, before they can be safely taken for use in accurate history or biography. He was the eldest son of George and Alice Smith, poor tenants of Peregrine Bertie, Lord Willoughby ; was baptized at Willoughby, January 6, 1579 (O. S.). His father died in April, 1596, when his mother was still living ; yet he tells us that " his parents died when he was about thirteen yeeres of age." Peregrine Bertie left England to travel abroad after June 26, 1599, and Stuhl Weissenburg was stormed early in September, 1601. In this period of a little over two years, he tells that he first went abroad to attend Master Peregrine Barty into France. From Paris to the Low Countries, where he served " three or foure yeeres ; " then to Scotland, was " ship-wracked," etc. ; then returned to Willoughby, where he studied Marcus Aurelius and " Machiavills Art of Warre," etc. ; then to the Low Countries again ; then to France, Italy, etc., having wonderful adventures everywhere ; was throwne into the sea to appease a storm as a " Hugonoit " and a " Pyrat ; " but rode the storm - tossed waves, and " gat safe to shoree ; " took part in " a desperate seafight in the straights." Then to the distant wars against the Turks, where he said he " releeved Olumpagh by a stratagem of Lights " (which " strange invention " of Smith's will be found in William Bourne's " Inventions " of 1578), and some time thereafter distinguished himself at the siege of " Stowlle Wesenburg." Caniza was taken October 22, 1600, and Smith says Olumpagh was besieged immediately after. Thus within about eighteen months of time he pretended to have had at least five years of adventure. After Stuhl Weissenburg was taken, in September, 1601, the troops with whom Smith says he was were sent to Gen. George Basti in Transylvania, where they soon revolted, not as Smith says, because they preferred " to serve Sigismundus against the Turke, rather than Busca against Sigismund," for Sigismund was not fighting against the Turke ; but because they understood that Sigismund had rallied " beyond all beleefe of men," since his defeat at Moitin, and was coming against the imperial army under Basti with a great army of Polonians, Turks, and Tartars." Under these circumstances, says Knolles, they revolted, " saying their first oath was to their natural Prince (for most of these men were Transilvanian borne) rather than to the Emperor a foreign Prince." Smith also tells us that Sigismund rewarded him for killing three Turks in a series of most remarkable single combats at a time when Sigismund and the Turks were allies. It is useless to follow him farther in the wars of Transylvania. I have found no mention of him in the accounts of those wars, save in the narrative furnished by himself, and according to this narrative it seems certain that he really served for a time with troops who were the allies of the Turk against the Christian. While Smith's narrative is not trustworthy, it is very curious, and it will be found interesting to take his story, and supply it with the correct names and dates. His " Duke Mercury " is the Duke de Mercœur ; " Georgio Busca " is the celebrated Albanian general, George Basti ; " Zachel Moyses " is Moses Tzekely.

The three Bathori brothers are sometimes classed as Turkish adventurers, but they were probably Transylvanians. (See the sketch of Sir Philip Sidney for some reference to the elder brother, Stephen Bathori.)

I do not know when Captain Smith returned to England, neither do I know where he returned from, whether from Ireland or Africa. He does not mention being in Ireland, but he must have been there before he came to Virginia, for Wingfield says, " It was proved to Smith's face that he had begged in Ireland like a rogue, without a lycence ; to such I would not my name should be a companyon." The law at that time required beggars to be licensed, and of course it was considered " like a rogue " to beg, illegally, without one.

Smith tells us that he was interested in the Virginia enterprise for two years before they sailed in December, 1606. He also says he would have been a party in Charles Leigh's South American colony, " but hee dyed," etc. Leigh's death was first known in England in the summer of 1605.

Smith was sent to Virginia by the company in their first expedition, which left The Downs in January, 1607. He was implicated in " Galthorpe's open and confessed mutiny," and was restrained as a prisoner from February to June 10, 1607, having in the mean time arrived in Virginia. He was admitted to the council and sworn on the 10th of June, 1607. On September 10, 1607, " the Triumvirate," Ratcliffe, Martin, and Smith, deposed Wingfield, not only from the presidency, but from the council also ; and Martin and Smith elected Ratcliffe. Smith was acting as Cape Merchant from September to about the 16th of December, 1607, when he was taken prisoner by the Indians, " and by the means of his guide, his lief was saved." I suppose this guide was the " stout young man called Ocanindge " (CCXLV. p. 83), who in 1609 reminded Smith of the " paines he tooke to save his life, when he was a prisoner." After a captivity of sixteen to nineteen days Smith was returned to Jamestown on the morning of January 2, 1607, when the council, under the lead of Archer, condemned him to be hanged as being the cause of the death of Emry and Robinson ; but Captain Newport arriving that night, he was released. He brought wonderful accounts of a ready way to the great South Sea, of mines, and of Ralegh's lost colony. Knowing the Indian character as we now do, it seems very probable that Smith was really spared to be used as a decoy. By these tales the Indians hoped to induce the colonists to make long expeditions into the wilds where they could be easily cut off and destroyed.

Smith and Scrivener (the only other members of the council), it seems from his account, deposed Ratcliffe either about the 22d of July or on the 10th of September (Smith gives both dates), 1608, and elected Smith to the presidency, who had given the colonists "the good hope that our Bay had stretched into the South Sea." He remained president until he was arrested in September, 1609, and was soon after sent to England "to answer some misdemeanors."

Captain Smith did not carry the first colonists to Virginia ; he landed there himself "as a prisoner." He did not support the colony there by his exertions ; the colonists were dependent on England for supplies ; they were succored by every vessel that arrived during his stay in Virginia, and at no time were they found to be more in need than when Argall arrived in July, 1609, during Smith's own presidency. So long as he stayed, the colony was rent by factions, in which he was an active instrument. Instead of making Jamestown a relief station and plantation, as it was intended to be, he was constantly taking off the men from their duties there, going on voyages to discover mines, the South Sea, etc., all of which, I am sure, can be easily proven. He not only failed to give satisfaction to his employers, but he gave great dissatisfaction, and was never employed by the Council of the Va. Co. again. He was in England from December, 1609, to March, 1614. The troubles and misfortunes of the dark days of 1611–12 caused many (who were evidently ignorant of the true state of affairs) to place confidence in Smith's claims, and under their patronage his reason for the cause of "the defailement" (CCXLV.) was published, which work proves that he did not even know the real causes which produced the troubles ; but the generality in England knew no better, and this tract probably gained for him the favor of four London merchants, not members of the Va. Co., who sent him on a voyage with Captain Hunt to our New England coast, March to August, 1614. Some members of the North Va. Co. gave him ample opportunity to prove his assertions of his proficiency, and from June to November, 1615, he was on his so-called "second voyage for New England ; " but

this rival (in his own imagination) of "Sampson, Hercules, and Alexander the Great," was taken prisoner at sea by a French vessel, while his own vessel and crew escaped. After this remarkable event, his self-assertions failed to have any value with business men, and he was never sent from England again, although he seems to have constantly sought employment abroad. For the remainder of his life he was "a paper tiger " at home in Old England.

His "Description of New England" was published in 1616 ; "New England's Trials" in 1620, and a second edition in 1622. In May, 1621, when the company of Virginia was under a different management from that under which Smith served, and probably encouraged thereto by the fact that it was not friendly to the former administration, Smith presented a petition for a reward for services rendered, "as he allegeth," in Virginia, which was referred "to the committees appointed for rewarding of men upon merits." He tells us himself that he failed to get anything. (This petition, it seems, is the only appearance of Capt. John Smith in the Virginia records of 1619–24. See John Smith, of Nibley). "The History of Virginia, the Summer Islands, and Newe England" was published in 1624 (see hereafter). He was never knighted, although it has been so stated. His arms were not granted for his services in America. William Segar, the king of arms of England, in August, 1625 (nearly a generation after the services are "alleged " to have been rendered, in a distant land), certified that he had seen Sigismund's patent, and had had a copy thereof recorded in the Herald's Office. I believe Segar did see it ; but I have no idea that Sigismund ever did. Segar must have been imposed upon as he was when he granted "the royal arms of Arragon with a canton of Brabant to Brandon, the common hangman of London," for, as I have said, the Turks were Sigismund's allies when Smith claimed to have killed them, and Sigismund had no legal right to sign an instrument as "Duke of Transilvania, Wallachia," etc., in December, 1603.

"Smith published "An Accidence or pathwaye of Experience, etc.," in 1626; "The True Travels, Adventures . . . from 1593 to 1629, with a continuation of the General History from 1624 to 1629," in 1630; "Advertisements for the unexperienced planters of New England or anywhere," in 1631, in which he tells us that he had "lived neere 37 yeares in the midst of wars, pestilence and famine." He was then about 50 years old, and had evidently lived over forty years quietly in Old England. He died June 21, 1631. By his will "he required Thomas Packer to disburse about his funerall, the somme of twentie poundes" (which was about one fourth of his estate); and he was buried in "Saint Sepulcher's" Church, London, "on the South Side of the Quire" where a table (i. e., a wooden tablet) was hung containing an inscription very suitable to his character.

Thomas Packer was a clerk of the privy seal and of the Court of Requests, an ancient court of equity in England for the recovery of small debts between citizens and freemen. Captain Smith gave Packer, by will, his interests in the county of Lincoln, in consideration of eighty pounds ; payable, £20 in his lifetime, and the balance after his death. It seems probable that the £20 was to pay some debt for which Smith was then being sued before the Court of Requests.

While the vain character of Captain Smith is amply shown in his own compilations, it can be readily understood why he must have been for many years an object of especial interest in England, and why this interest in him should increase to a sympathy which would in the hearts of some get the better of their judgment. The planting of the colonies in America was an all-absorbing topic of the time; their perils and misfortunes were tragedies of the period; and Smith imagined that these colonies were all "pigs of his sow." He tells us himself, in 1630, that "scarce five of those who first went with me to Virginia remain alive." For many years he was probably the only one of those first sent to Virginia under Newport, in December, 1606, living in England; under these circumstances, Smith must have been

an object of the greatest interest, and a welcome guest by the hearth of many of the gentry of Old England, where "his twice told tales " afforded amusement and interest, or aroused sympathy; and we can easily forgive him for compiling a romance, with himself as his hero, without accepting his story as a trustworthy history of the founding of the first English Protestant colony in America. "The History of Virginia, The Summer Ilands and newe England by John Smith," was entered at Stationers' Hall for publication, July 12, 1624, and probably issued from the press soon after. The publishers seem to have found it hard to work off this book; a fresh title-page is given to it in 1626, another in 1627, and two others in 1632 ; but the text remains the same. It was for about 225 years almost the only source of information regarding our beginning.

The first Book relates to America before 1606, and is compiled from the works of Hakluyt, Hariot, Brereton, Rosier, and others, and by collating these with Smith, his style of compiling will be apparent. The tortuous method which obtains in all of his works has constantly led the historians who have attempted to follow him into errors.

The second Book, is a description of the country, etc., nearly as in CCXLIV. The third Book is based on CCXLV.

That part of the fourth Book which relates to the period of which I am writing is compiled from the last part of CCXLV., and from CXL., CLXXI., CCCXXVII., and CCCXLII., and also from the narrative of William Box, which I have not found. Smith certainly did not compile from, or have access to, the records of the Va. Co. His History is perfectly described by Capt. George Percy in a letter to the Earl of Northumberland, in which Percy says : "The author hathe not spared to apropriate many deserts to himselfe which he never performed, and stuffed his relacyons with many falsities and malycyous detractyons." The truth of these charges can be easily proven. Even when compiling from a published narrative he does not hesitate to insert his own name, or a favorable reference to himself, where there was none. For his own purposes, he takes events of several years and bunches them all together, or an event of one year and assigns it to another year. He evidently appropriated to himself incidents in several publications and in the lives of many other men. However, I do not attribute all of his errors to selfish motives. I believe that many are attributable to his lack of knowledge of the facts. He was certainly incapable of writing correct history where he was personally interested, and after he left Virginia he evidently knew no more of the facts than the generality in England.

He was really in no way properly qualified, or properly equipped, for writing a disinterested and accurate history of the great movement.

We are told that Smith was not the author of his History, that it consisted of narratives written by others. All histories must be largely compiled from the narratives written by others; but when a man sets to work to collect and publish matter to prove that he is one of the greatest men of his time, and that his peers were mere marplots, and calls his compilation a history, his evidence must be presented in the most straightforward, clear, and distinct way, it must be of the highest character and of the most undoubted accuracy, for a tortuous, vainglorious, and prevaricating compilation must be really the strongest possible evidence against that man ; and this is a case in point. Smith's so-called History of Virginia is not a history at all; but chiefly an eulogy of Smith and a lampoon of his peers. And it is seldom, indeed, that we can safely turn a man loose in the field of his own biography.

Smith's position in our early history is a remarkable illustration of the maxim, "I care not who fights the battles, so I write the dispatches."

The establishing of an English colony in America was a vast work, requiring the constant support of the king, the purse of the people, and the careful management of the greatest business men of that period for ten long years of "constant and patient resolution." On the other hand, Smith was a mere adventurer; one of the very

smallest contributors; an agent of the company in Virginia less than two and a half years ; in command there about one year ; failed to give satisfaction; sent home to answer for his misdemeanors, and was never again even employed by the South Va. Company.

The managers of the enterprise had for their own use ample maps, descriptions, and accounts; but it was against the interest of the colonies to make public their affairs, and no history was compiled from their records. No one who had ever taken the official oath could reveal or publish anything regarding the colonies in Virginia, without authority from the council, unless he broke his oath and betrayed his trust, and Capt. John Smith was probably the only official, or ex-official, who did this. He published "the dispatches ; " took possession of the history which others made and turned it to his own service; and it came to pass that for over 200 years these "dispatches " were "almost the only source from which we derived any knowledge of the infancy of our country." I acknowledge that I am anxious to enable the reader to do justice to the real founders of this country, because, as the result of a remarkable chain of circumstances, great injustice has been done them; yet I certainly do not wish to be unjust to Smith. I have weighed well every scrap of evidence within my reach before arriving at the opinions herein given of him and of his so-called "General History." The counter-evidence now available makes it perfectly certain that the true history of our foundation is really grand.

Jo: Smith.

Smith, **Jonathan**. Pd. £12 10s.
Smith, **Othowell**, fishmonger, 2. Sub. £62 10s.; pd. £42 6s. 8d.
Smith, **Richard**, 2. Sub. ——; pd. £25.
Smith, **Sir Richard**, 3. Sub. ——; pd. £37 10s. Of Leeds Castle; brother of Sir Thomas Smythe, treasurer, etc. (see pedigree); knighted at Whitehall, July 23, 1603; receiver of the Duchy

THOMAS WEST
Third Baron Delaware

of Cornwall ; M. P. Hythe, 1614; surveyor-general to Prince Charles; member of the Privy Council ; purchased the estate of Leeds Castle from Sir Warham St. Leger. "He married three wives who were widows:" first, Elizabeth, daughter of Sir Thomas Scott of Scot's Hall, and widow of John Knatchbull, Esq. (see Scott pedigree) ; secondly, Jane, daughter of John White, Esq., of London, and widow of Samuel Thornhill, Esq. The name of his third wife, who survived him, is not known to me. By his first wife he had a son, John, and two daughters ; by his second, an only child, Mary, and by his third wife an only child, Margaret. "In 1627 he gave in stock for provision of Sea-Coals for the Poor of the Parish of St. Stephen, Coleman Street, London, £100 every year, to be returned for the use of the poor forever. And another £100 afterwards for the relief of the poor also." He died July 21, 1628, in his 63d year leaving behind him "£4,500 a year in land, and £6,000 in money, plate, and goods; he hath given a little dwarf daughter of his £2,500, and £300 a year in land." (D'Ewes' Journal.) His son John, knighted at Whitehall, February 28, 1617, was seated at Leeds Castle.

Smith, Robert, merchant - tailor, 2. Sub. ——; pd. £37 10s. "Born at Market Harborough in Leicestershire; became controller of the chamber of London, and one of the four attorneys in the Mayor's Court." He is spoken of as the "under chamberlain" in the records of the Va. Co. In June, 1622, bought two additional shares in Virginia from Francis Carter ; gave £750, to purchase lands for the maintenance of a lecturer in the town of his nativity; one of Fuller's Worthies of Leicestershire ; but Fuller errs in placing his death in 1618, as he was an active member of the Va. Co. for several years after that date.

Robert Smyth

Smith — Smyth, Captain Roger. He was captain of an infantry company under Sir Francis Vere in the Netherlands in 1592 ; "served for 12 or 13 years in the wars in the Low Countries ; " first went to Virginia probably in 1616, and after remaining there "about some three years " sailed for England on the George in November, 1619 ; complained of Governor Yeardley to the court of the Va. Co., March 15, 1620 ; signed the petition to have some man of quality sent governor to Virginia; "recommended to be a gentleman very sufficient for imployment in Virginia; " was employed by the company, and again sailed for Virginia on board the Abigail in February, 1621 ; was appointed to be of the Council in Virginia, July 24, 1621. The Indians killed five men near his plantation in Charles City, in the massacre of March 22, 1622; in April, 1623, he was engaged in building a strong block - house ; married the widow of John Rolfe ; was living with his wife in James City in January, 1625 ; still living and still a member of the Council in Virginia, November 30, 1629.

Smythe Pedigree.—John [1] Smythe of Corsham, County Wilts, esquire, married Joan, daughter of Robert Brouncker, of Melksham, esquire, and died in 1538, leaving five sons and three daughters.

Elizabeth [2] Smythe, the youngest daughter, married Symon Horspoole, citizen and draper of London, and of the ancient Wool Staple ; Merchant Adventurer of the Old Hanse and Mus. companies ; sheriff of London, 1591 ; died January 14, 1601, aged 75. Their son, William Horspoole, married, in May, 1602, Mary, daughter of Laurence Washington, Esq., by his first wife, Martha, daughter of Clement Newce, of Great Hadham, Herts ; which Laurence married, secondly, Mary, the mother of Sir Samuel Argall, with whom Sir Thomas Smythe was thus connected through the Washingtons. But it is the line of Thomas [2], second son of John [1] Smythe, aforesaid, in which we are chiefly interested.

Smythe or Smith, Thomas [2]. Was born about 1520 ; "Collector of the Queen's Majesties Subsidy for tonage and poundage, and farmer for the Custome and Subsidy inwards ; " commonly called " Mr. Customer Smythe."

A man of large wealth, seated at Ostenhanger in Kent, at the coming of the Spanish Armada in 1588, he lent the queen £1,000.

He married Alice, daughter and heiress of Sir Andrew Judde, Lord Mayor of London, by whom he acquired the manors of Ashford and Westure ; died June 7, 1591, and was buried in the church at Ashford, having had issue seven sons and six daughters, namely : —

1. Andrew Smythe, died young.
2. Sir John Smythe.
3. Sir Thomas Smythe.
4. Henry Smythe, died before 1591.
5. Sir Richard Smythe.
6. Robert Smythe.
7. Simon Smythe, slain at Cadiz in 1596.

- 1. Mary Smythe, married "Robert Davys, Esq., Receiver for Wales." (Were they the parents of Captains Robert and James Davies ?)
2. Ursula Smythe, married Simon Harding, of London, gent.
3. Jane Smythe, married Thomas Fanshawe, Esq., of Ware Park (his second wife), which Thomas was remembrancer of the exchequer to Queen Elizabeth from 1568 to his death, February 19, 1601. By his first wife, Mary, daughter of Anthony Bourchier, he was the father of Henry Fanshawe, who married his second wife's youngest sister.
4. Catherine Smythe, married, first, Sir Rowland Hayward ; secondly, Sir John Scott.
5. Alice Smythe, married Sir William Harris.
6. Elizabeth Smythe, married Sir Henry Fanshawe. One of the sisters died before October 12, 1616, on which day Chamberlain wrote to Carleton, "Lady Fanshawe and her four sisters are all widows together."

Smith (or **Smythe**), **Sir Thomas,** skinner, 2. Sub. £75 ; pd. £165. Third son of "Mr. Customer Smythe" (see pedigree). He was the first treasurer of the Va. Co. of London. Was born about 1558 ; was educated at Oxford ; at an early age became a prominent man; so much so that from 1580 to the death of his father in 1591, it is sometimes very hard to distinguish between father and son, each being a leading man of affairs, and

each having the same name ; but it was probably the son who was an incorporator of the Turkey Company in 1581 ; "a principal member of the Russia Company in 1587 ; " at whose house Hood lectured in 1588 ; and the first on the list of those to whom Ralegh assigned (on March 7, 1589) his interest in Virginia, "saving only the fifth part of gold and silver ore." In 1591 he is said to have succeeded his father as master of the customs, and the same year he aided in sending ships to the East Indies ; at Cadiz in 1596, his brother Simon was killed, and he was knighted by Essex for gallantry ; 1599, Hood's lecture dedicated to him ; aided in organizing an expedition to the East Indies ; 1600, "Alderman Sir Thomas Smith," an incorporator and first governor of the East India Company ; sheriff of London, 1600–01 ; February 8, 1601, at the "Insurrection of Essex," the earl drank at his house ; he was a captain of the trained bands of London and a friend of Essex, who, it is said, expected Smith to join him with a thousand trained men, and he was afterwards placed in prison on suspicion ; released from the Tower about September, 1602. On the 13th of May, 1603, knighted at the Tower by King James, who regarded the friends of Essex as his friends. March 19, 1604, appointed ambassador to Russia, and entered on his journey there, June 12, 1604 ; in Russia at the time of the death of Boris Godunof, "The great Lord and Cæsar" (Czar), and at the arrival of the celebrated Demetrius, the pretender, in 1605, "who was very favourable to the English." Returning he sailed from "Archangell" in the White Sea in August, and arrived in England about the 20th of September, 1605. "An account of his voyage and entertainement in Russia" was published in London, probably without his consent, in 1605 and 1607. M. P. for Dunwich from 1604 to 1611; M. C. for Virginia, November 20, 1606.

In 1607 John Nicholl dedicated to him "An Houre Glasse of Indian Newes." In 1609 William Philip dedicated "to Sir Thomas Smith, Knight," the translation of the three voyages of Gerald De Veer. In the same year the Phœnix was dedicated to Sarah, wife to Sir Thomas Smith, knight, and Catherine, wife to Sir John Scott, knight, and signed, "Humbly devoted to your Ladyships, Tho. Dekker;" and the Dove was inscribed to Sir Thomas Smith, and signed, "Ever bounden to your worship, Tho. Dekker."

M. C. for Va. Co., May 23, 1609. He subscribed £75 to the enterprise ; but was one of those who paid even beyond their proportion, in order to uphold that plantation ; he paid £165 ($4,125). His services, in establishing a colony in Virginia, and thus securing a foothold for England in America, cannot be overestimated. The enterprise rested largely upon his shoulders through the darkest hours. And yet, most unfortunately, the history of his administration has been based almost entirely on the unfriendly evidence of his opponents.

July 4, 1609, Sir Thomas Smythe was again elected governor of the E. I. Co., " who for his pains in serving as governor for five years, and in procuring the first (December 31, 1600) and second (May 11, 1609) patents is gratified with £500, besides £150, lately paid by his order to Mr. Farrington ; but he utterly refused to take the oath of governor until the company took back £250, the residue his worship kindly yielded to take."

"December 30, 1609, the King, Queen, and Prince Henry went this morning to the launch of the great Indian ship of above 1,200 ton, newly built by our East Indian merchants, and had a bountiful banquet; at which the king graced Sir Thomas Smythe, the governor, with a very faire chaine of gold, in manner of a collar, better than £200, with a jewell wherein was the King's picture hanging at it, and the king put it about his neck with his own hands, naming the ship The Trade's Increase." " Delicates " were served in fine china dishes, and the dishes were freely permitted to be carried away by all the guests.

March 19, 1610, by order of a court marshal, he was given precedency over certain knights more ancient than he, because he had had the honor to stand covered in the presence of a king (the Emperor of Russia). In 1610, himself and others set forth

Henry Hudson to discover the Northwest passage, and Jonas Poole to Cherry Island.

In 1611 they set forth Jonas Poole on a voyage of discovery to Greenland. In 1612 they set forth Capt. Thomas Button, Master Francis Nelson, etc., to discover a Northwest passage. July 26, 1612, he was an incorporator and the first governor of the N. W. P. Co. He was the treasurer for the Bermudas Islands from the time they were taken in hand by the Va. Co. of London until November 25, 1612, when the island was sold to Sir William Wade and others. Smith's Islands, near Cape Charles, Virginia, generally supposed to be named for Capt. John Smith, were really named for Sir Thomas, as were many other capes, sounds, forelands, etc., on the face of the earth. His name was justly engrafted on land and water in the highest latitudes reached by man in his day.

In 1613 he and others set forth seven good ships for Greenland (Spitzbergen), and on the map which accompanies the account of the voyage, we find Sir Tho : Smith's Bay and Prince Charles I., in 79° N. Lat., and Sir Tho⁸ Smith's Inlet about 80° N. Lat. In this year he was governor of the Mus. Co., as he was many years before and many years after ; but, for exactly what years, I cannot say, as the records of that company have been destroyed.

M. P. for Sandwich in 1614, in which Parliament he protected the interests of the E. I. and the Va. companies. " The courts, consultations, etc., for the East Indies, Virginia, Summer Islands, North and Northwest discoveries, Muscovia, etc., were kept at his house." He was then the head of every one (and a founder of most of them) of the English companies directly interested in foreign colonies and commerce, which have ever since been the chief sources of the wealth and power of Great Britain. July 5, 1614, he asked to be excused from being chosen governor of the E. I. Co., " on account of his long service, his age and health;" but the company insisted on electing him again.

June 29, 1615, one of the incorporators, and the first governor, of the

B. I. Co. ; again chosen governor of the E. I. Co., and gratified with 1,000 marks for his extraordinary care and pains during the past year. He was sick during this year, and Dr. Atkins, who attended him, was admitted into the E. I. Co. *gratis*, on account of his attention to the governor. Sir Dudley Digges addressed his "Defence of Trade" to Sir Thomas Smith, knight, etc., and alluded to him as "his kinsman." He aided in sending Robert Fotherbie to the northwards, who named an island in the Northern sea for him. About 1613 he sent, among other things, his picture to the Great Mogul of India, by William Edwardes, and in 1615 Sir Thomas Roe found this picture hanging in the Great Mogul's court, "who esteemed it for a jewel." His engraved portrait "was originally prefixed," so Granger says, "to the dedication of Woodall's 'Surgeon's Mate,' which is addressed to Sir Thomas Smith" (see John Woodall).

In 1616 he aided in sending Robert Bileth, master, and William Baffin, pilot, on the fifth voyage for a discovery of the Northwest passage ; in this voyage they discovered Sir Thomas Smith's Sound to the north of 78°, which is "admirable in one respect, because in it is the greatest variation of the compass of any part of the world known." While he was the constant patron of the celebrated voyagers of the period, it must not be forgotten that he was also, from early manhood to his death, a constant patron of men of science, as Hood, Wright, etc. "July 16, 1616, Warrant to pay to Sir Thos. Smythe and the East India Company the usual bounty for building three large ships."

March 12, 1617, he assembled the merchant trading companies together at the wish of the king, to see what could be done to fit out a fleet against the Turkish pirates. "They think £20,000 a year for two years might be raised from merchants, but leave the directions to the Council."

June 23, 1618, he was appointed one of the commissioners of the navy, and held that office (in which, as usual, he performed valuable service for his country) to his death in 1625. About the middle of November, his son John married the Lady Isabella Rich, a sister of the second Earl of Warwick. On November 28, 1618, Chamberlain wrote to Carleton, "It falles out true that I wrote the last weeke that Sr Thomas Smith's sonne had maried the Lady Isabella Rich, without his father's consent or privitie, and the affront is the more, beeing don in so goode companie, as the Countesse of Bedford, with divers other Ladies and persons of account, whereof the Lord Chamberlain (William Herbert, third Earl of Pembroke) gave the bride ; but not one of his frends or kindred present or made acquainted withall ; which is thought a straunge thing that so great a man and a counsaillor shold geve countenance to such an action as the robbing a man of his only child, a youth of 18 yeares old (for he is no more) and sure I have seen the time that such a matter could not have ben so caried." The Rev. Thomas Lorkin wrote to Sir Thomas Puckering, that the "Lord Chamberlain sent for his own chaplain, to Barnard Castle, to marry them." "So they were presently married ; and from thence conducted to my Lord of Southampton's to dinner, and to my Lady Bedford's to bed, where all was consummate. But the father is a heavy man to see his son bestowed without his privity and consent." It often happens that some private transaction like this has a direct bearing on public affairs, and this had a direct bearing on the bitter factions which afterwards obtained in the Va. Co.

On the 1st of January, 1619, the trouble began between Lord Rich and the E. I. Co. regarding the taking of two of the said lord's ships by Captain Pring in the Indian Ocean, and this suit also bred ill-will for a time between the Lord Rich (soon after, second Earl of Warwick), and his party, and the officers of the E. I. Co.

"On Saturday, January 30, Sir Thomas Smythe's house at Deptford was burnt down to the ground, and nothing saved that was in it, except the people, who escaped narrowly ;" but in the same year the Marquis Tremonille, ambassador extraordinary from France, with a train of one hundred and twenty persons, was lodged in his house in Philpot Lane, London.

April 28 he declined to stand as a candidate for treasurer of the Va. Co.; he said, "For these twelve yeares he hath willingly spent his labors and endeavors for the support thereof," and asked "the court to showe him so much favor as now to dispence with him, and to elect some worthy man in his place for he had resolved to relinquish it." The Va. Co. was now divided into three chief parties : first, the lords and most of the gentlemen, under the lead of Robert Rich, Earl of Warwick ; second, many of the merchants, especially those of the E. I. Co., with Sir Thomas Smith at the head; and third, "the faction of the auditors," under Sir Edwin Sandys. There was a strong opposition (or jealousy) developing in certain quarters to the merchants of the E. I. Co. (probably because they were growing so rich), and the first and third parties had agreed to concentrate their strength on one man, Sir Edwin Sandys, while the second party, not suspecting such political strategy, putting up two candidates (Alderman Johnson and Sir John Wolstenholme), were taken by surprise and easily defeated, Sandys receiving fifty-nine balls, Wolstenholme twenty-three, and Johnson eighteen.

The same plan was carried out in the election of deputy, the first and third parties uniting on John Ferrar, while the second divided on Johnson and Cletheroe.

Early in May, Smythe was again chosen governor of the S. I. Co. Chamberlain wrote to Carleton on May 8, "The Virginian Company have displaced Sir Thomas Smith, and made Sir Edwin Sandys their governor. But the matter is little amended, when at the next court, they confirmed Sir Thomas Smith in his presidentship of the Bermudas or Summer Islands ; for I could hardly tell how to resolve, if it were put to my choice."

May 28 the Va. Co. gratified Smythe with a gift of 2,000 acres of land in Virginia. July 2 he was again chosen governor of the E. I. Co. In December, 1618, he had agreed to give his son and "his new daughter-in-law" an annuity of £1,600 ; but the affair continued to grate, and in July, 1619, for some reason, "young Sir John Smythe stepped aside, and went over secretly into France." In this year William Philip dedicated to Sir T. Smith "The Relation of a wonderfull voiage made by William Cornelison Schouten."

May 17, 1620, he was one of those recommended by James I. to the Va. Co. for their treasurer. On the same day the name of "Smythe's hundred" in Virginia, which had been named for him, was changed to "Southampton hundred." The Earl of Warwick, who formerly opposed him, saw his error, and became friendly to him ; but the first party under Southampton and the third under Sandys remained united and controlled the Va. Co., and on June 28 the Earl of Southampton was chosen treasurer. Smythe was again chosen governor of the E. I. and S. I. companies in 1620.

He was M. P. for Saltash, 1621–22. In May, 1621, the Earl of Southampton succeeded him as governor of the S. I. Co. July 4, at the election for governor of the E. I. Co., "expressing his own weakness of body, he begged the company would spare him, that they should see he could as well obey as command, and was an adventurer of almost £20,000." Notwithstanding this request, some of his friends gave him a very complimentary vote, and while Alderman Hallidaie was chosen governor for the year ensuing, "Smythe was entreated to assist at consultations, and authorized to have a voice in the courts." He was now grown old in the most remarkable business career that ever fell to the lot of man. He had been in bad health for many years, especially since 1615, and had long wished to relieve himself of several of his many cares. He continued his interest in Virginia, and the committees frequently met at his house ; but affairs were very discouraging, the dissensions in the company continued, and the breach grew wider, until no hands clasped across the chasm. Very similiar "disturbances" were agitating the E. I. Co. at the same time from nearly the same causes, created by some of the same men. The old merchants said they were produced by "gentlemen who, having been taken into the companies by courtesy, do aim to get all the government into their hands, which is a business proper only for merchants," while the other party thought that "Noblemen and gentlemen were fittest for the management of such undertakings."

Chamberlain wrote to Carleton on April 19, 1623, "There is a great faction fallen out in the Virginia Company. The heads on the one side are, the Earl of Southampton, the Lord Cavendish, Sir Edward Sackville, Sir John Ogle, Sir Edwin Sandys, with divers others of meaner quality. On the other side are, the Earl of Warwick, Sir Thomas Smith, Sir Nathaniel Rich, Sir Henry Mildmay, Alderman Johnson, and many more." On July 26, he wrote : "The factions in the Va. and S. I. companies are grown so violent, as Guelfs and Gebellines were not more animated one against another ; and they seldom meet upon the Exchange, or in the streets, but they brabble and quarrel : so that, if that society be not dissolved the sooner, or cast in a new mould, worse effects may follow than the whole business is worth." It was also asserted "that all their meetings and consultations seemed rather cockpits than courts." These men were evidently in no condition to furnish material for disinterested and accurate history. Such evidence as the Sandys faction wished to present to the public is still preserved in the two volumes of Va. Co. Records (1619–24) now in the library of Congress at Washington, and on the faith of this evidence the progress of the colony under the management of that faction has been drawn in the brightest contrast to the dark days of the foundation period ; but our founders are certainly entitled to a hearing, also, before we can have any just right to condemn them.

The Smythe faction said that Sandys and Ferrar, who were managing affairs, were men "of discourse and contemplation and not of reason and judgement." Sandys justly prided himself on his eloquence (he was a noted speaker), and Ferrar on his diction ; but the old merchants were able to present their case in a plain business way, which to King James seemed unanswerable. I can give only a sin-

gle illustration ; but that will be sufficient. The Sandys faction gave glowing accounts of the great numbers of people sent to Virginia under their management. They said "that on the 18. Dec. 1618, there were only 600 people remaining alive in Virginia of near 2,000 that had been sent there, and that between the 18. Dec", 1618, and 28. June, 1623, about 5,000 were sent," etc. The old founder faction replied "that it was true, they were sending a multitude of his Majesties subjects to Virginia to starve and to die there, before they had made any adequate provision for receiving so many. They claimed that instead of only 600 living in Va. December 18, 1618, there were at least 1,200. That in addition to the said 5,000, there were sent between June and December, 1623, about 300 more ; and yet in Feby, 162⁴₃, there were, by the census, then only 1,277 people remaining alive in Virginia, of whom some were born there," and then they make the crushing inquiry, "What has become of the 5,000 missing subjects of his Majesty ? "

These figures are terrible, for even if only 600 persons were living in Virginia in December, 1618 ; evidently over 4,500 were missing out of less than 6,000 within about five years. The rate of mortality was greatest in those years which have been pictured to us as most prosperous. There were two sides to the controversy, much could be said on each side, and it may be that neither side was entirely in the right. Both parties probably did their best "according to the best of their knowledge and belief ; " but we have no right to condemn the old merchant founder party — who had continued to labor at a very great expense to themselves, without any prospect of a present profit, "with a constant and patient resolution, until by the mercies of God," they had established the colony — on the evidence of their adversaries.

I shall not attempt to discuss the matter here ; but it seems certain to me that another issue than the management of the Va. Co. was an important factor in causing, if not really at the bottom of all this bitterness. In the Parliament of 1621–22, the strong movement, under the leadership of Sir Edwin Sandys, against the incorporated companies, which began in 1604, was pushed forward vigorously. The Sandys party were sometimes called Free-traders, and the other party, Protectionists or Monopolists. Both parties were represented in the Va. Co. The question was largely a "matter of life or death" with the members of these companies, and it was natural that the feeling between them and those who wished to destroy their business should become very bitter.

Early in 1624, the Lords of the Privy Council appointed Sir Thomas Smythe governor of the S. I. Co., and he was afterwards regularly elected to that office by the company. He was a member of the Royal Commission for Virginia affairs, July 15, 1624, and continued governor of the S. I. Co. and member of the Virginia Council until his death.

He died September 4, 1625, at his house at Tunbridge, and "was buried under a most superb monument in Hone Church, Kent, having his effigies at full length recumbent thereon." The inscription is a summary of his history : —

"To the glory of God, and to the pious memorie of the honorable Sir Thomas Smith, knt. (late governour of the East Indian, Muscovia, French, and Sommer Island companies ; treasurer for the Virginia plantation ; prime undertaker (in the year 1612) for that noble designe, the discoverie of the North-West passage ; principall commissioner for the London expedition against the pirates, and for a voiage to the ryver Senega, upon the coast of Africa ; one of the chief commissioners for the navie-roial, and sometime ambassador from His majestie of Great Britain to the emperour and great duke of Russia and Muscovia, etc.), *who, havinge judiciously, conscionably, and with admirable facility, managed many difficult and weighty affairs to the honor and profit of this nation,* rested from his labors the 4th day of Septem., 1625."

"Besides many charities in London and elsewhere, he endowed Tunbridge school, which had been founded by his grandfather, Sir Andrew Judd.

Among his numerous bequests, he left funds for providing a four-penny loaf apiece every week to thirty-six of the poorest and honestest persons, in five parishes, and the same number of pieces of cloth, worth twenty shillings each, to be made into winter garments for the recipients of his charity."

His numerous bequests are still annually distributed by the Skinners' Company, of which guild he was a member. His arms were on the north window of Old Temple Hall, Faringdon Ward Without. "Az. a chevron engrailed between three Lions passant gardant, Or." This was the hall of the Knights Templars, and afterwards of the Hospitallers.

Sir Thomas Smythe was nearly related to the Cromwells, and was descended from Sir Robert Chicheley, Lord Mayor of London, eldest brother of Henry Chicheley, Archbishop of Canterbury, founder of All Souls, Oxford.

He was thrice married, first, to Judith, daughter and heir of Richard Culverwell, Esq. (no issue) (see under Dr. William Whitaker), secondly (name unknown to me), and, thirdly, to Sarah, daughter to William Blount, Esq. (and sister to Judith Blount, who married Sir Thomas Chaloner), by whom he had two sons, John and Thomas, both of whom were members of the Va. Co. in 1612 ; but Thomas died before November, 1618. After the death of Sir Thomas, his widow, the Lady Sarah Smythe, married, April 25, 1626, Robert Sidney, first Earl of Leicester (being his second wife).

"Young Sir John Smythe, whose marriage in November, 1618, gave so much trouble, left a son, Robert Smythe, who married, July 8, 1652, Lady Dorothy Sydney (the poet Waller's 'Sacharissa'), daughter of Robert, second Earl of Leicester, widow of Henry, first Earl of Sunderland, and by that earl mother of Robert, second Earl, lineal ancestor of the present Duke of Marlborough." This branch of the family terminated with Sir Sydney-Stafford Smythe, chief baron of the Exchequer in 1772, who died in 1777, *s. p.* "The line of the senior branch of the family became extinct with that accomplished geographer, the eighth Viscount Strangford, who was vice-president of the Royal Geographical Society, and died in 1869."

[signature: Tho: Smythe]

Smith, Thomas, son of Sir Thomas (the treasurer), 3. The second son; he died young, before 1618.

Smith, Sir Thomas. "Clerk of our privy Council;" "born in Abingdon, and bred in the University of Oxford;" "secretary to Robert, Earl of Essex, and afterwards one of the Clerks of the Lord's Council;" knighted at Greenwich, May 20, 1603; appointed the king's Latin secretary, June 8, 1603; "Secretary and Keeper of the Signet to the Council of the North;" "Clerk to the Upper House of Parliament;" "Master of the Requests." M. C. for Va., March 9, 1607, "and was on the road to higher preferment," when he died, November 28, 1609, at his house at Parson's Green, and was buried at Fulham, where his lady erected a monument to perpetuate his memory. He married Frances, daughter of William Brydges, fourth Lord Chandos; she married, secondly, Thomas Cecil, first Earl of Exeter.

Writing of this Sir Thomas Smith, Dr. Fuller says: "God and himself raised him to the eminency he attained unto, unbefriended with any extraction." His only child, Margaret, married the Hon. Thomas Carey, the second son of Robert Carey, Earl of Monmouth; after Carey's death she married, secondly, Sir Edward Herbert.

"This Sir Thomas Smith left a considerable sum of money to the library at Oxford, founded by his friend and neighbor, Sir Thomas Bodley."

Smith, Sir William, of Essex, 3. Sub. £37 10s; pd. £50. Of Hill Hall; nephew and, finally, heir to the celebrated Sir Thomas Smith, secretary of state to Edward VI. and Elizabeth, who died without issue in 1577.

This Sir William was a colonel in the army in Ireland; married, in 1590, Bridget, daughter of Thomas Fleetwood, Esq., of The Vache, County Bucks; knighted at Theobald's, May 7, 1603; M. P. for Aylesbury, 1604–11; died December 12, 1626, aged 76. The family name is now spelled Smijth.

Smith, Sir William, of London. Sub. ——; pd. £45. March 7, 1619, he transferred to Mr. Nicholas Ferrar, the younger, two shares of land in Virginia.

Soame (or Soane), Joseph, 2. Sub. ——; pd. £25.

Soame, Sir Steven, grocer, 2. Sub. ——; pd. £25. Second son of Thomas Soame, of Boteley, *alias* Betely, in the County of Norfolk; born about 1544; alderman of Cheap ward, and sheriff in 1598; mayor of the staple in London for almost twenty years; Lord Mayor of London, 1598–99; knighted April 25, 1599; M. P. for London, 1601; on the committee to meet King James, 1603; master of the Grocers; senior alderman in 1618; died May 23, 1619, aged 75, and was buried at Little Thurlow in Suffolk, where his monument records his good deeds.

Soda, Anthony, grocer. He was a churchwarden of St. Michael's, Cornhill, in 1588, and for many years after.

Somers, Sir George, 1. Sub. ——; pd. ——. Of Dorsetshire; but he bore the same arms, and tradition assigns him to the Somers family of White Ladies, County Worcester, ancestors of Earl Somers. Sil. Jourdan, writing in 1610, says he was then "three score yeares at the least." General Lefroy, in his "Memorials of the Bermudas," says, "Summers, as his name is spelt in the parish register, was born of respectable parents, in or near Lyme Regis (Dorsetshire) in 1554. He commanded naval expeditions in 1595–1600, and in the two following years." In 1596 Capt. Amias Preston and himself made their victorious voyage to the West Indies. October 29, 1597, Sir Walter Ralegh, Lord Thomas Howard, and the Lord Montjoy wrote to Essex: "Wee have this Saterday night receved the cumfortabell newse of George Summers' arivall, whose letter we have here withall sent your Lordshipp." He was knighted at Whitehall, July 23, 1603.

Thomas Winter, M. A., wrote a sonnet to him in 1604 ; M. P. for Lyme Regis in Dorsetshire, March 19, 1604, to February, 1610, when his seat was declared vacant, on account of his absence in Virginia; June, 1609, sailed for Virginia ; July 28, wrecked on the Bermudas or Somers Islands ; May 10, 1610, sailed from there for Virginia; May 23 arrived in Va. ; June 7, abandoning the colony, was met by Lord De la Warr, and turned back ; June 19 sailed for the Bermudas to obtain a supply of pork for Virginia. Was carried by the current to our New England coast ; but finally reached the Somers Islands, and died there November 9, 1610, " of a surfeit in eating of a pig." His heart was buried in the island, and "his cedar ship at last with his dead body arrived at Whitchurch in Dorsetshire, where by his friends he was honourably buried, with many vollies of shot, and the rites of a souldier, and upon his tombe was bestowed this epitaph : —

" ' Alas Virginia's Summer so soone past,
Autumne succeeds and stormy winter's blast,
Yet England's joyfull Spring with joyfull showers,
O Florida, shall bring thy sweetest Flowers.' "

His remains reached England after February 28, 1611, probably about July 26, 1611, on which day the inquest was held.

" From the Record Office, London. Inquisitio post mortem. Inquest taken at Dorchester, July 26 (9th James) before George Estmont, gent., escheator of the King : — Sir George Somers, Knight, was seized before his death in demesne & in fee of the Manor of Upwey *alias* Waybay House, with its members and appurtenances, in Co. Dorset, &c. &c. Of one Messuage or Mansion house, called the manor of Orchard, in the parish of Whitechurche [canonicorum] Dorset, &c. &c. Of a Capital Messuage or Mansion house and farm of the Manor of Berne [in Whitechurch] Dorset, &c. &c. Of a capital messuage or tenement in Marsh wood [in Whitechurch] Dorset, &c. &c. Of three messuages in Lyme Regis, held by Sir George Somers and Johanna his wife of the Mayor & Burgesses of Lyme Regis."

Extract from Sir George Somer's will : " I, the said Geo. Somers do give and bequeath to Mathew Somers and his heirs all that capital messuage

or farm called Waybay House in the parish of Upwaye, all lands &c. called Orcherd in the parish of Whitechurch, a messuage or tenement called Harper's tenement, in the parish of Mershwood and the ground or common at the hill, purchased from Richard Mallack gent, adjoining other lands called Berne in the parish of Whitechurch, and all other lands not bequeath, to Mathew Somers and his heirs forever."

" Sir Geo. Somers died 9th of November last. Nicholas Somers, gent, his cousin and heir. Lady Johanna his wife is still living at Whitechurch."

This document is headed " *Libat fuit in Cur. xxiiij die Novr. anno R. Jacobi, Anglie &c decimo, p. manus Rici Warman.*" I suppose *Libat* stands for *Liberatum*, i. e., " *It was delivered in court 24 Nov. in the 10th year of James, &c.* (1612) *by the hands of Richard Warman.*"

It will be noted that Matthew not Nicholas is mentioned in the extract from the will incorporated in the inquisition, and that the enrollment of the document was delayed from July, 1611, to November 24, 1612. There was probably a dispute over the will between Nicholas, the heir-at-law, and Matthew Somers, who was with Sir George when he died, and he may have been accused of using some illegal means to obtain a will in his favor.

Somers, Master (Matthew). He arrived in England, as before said, with the body of Sir George Somers, in 1611. In 1622 he has a dispute with the Va. and S. I. companies, regarding the estate of Sir George Somers. (See Neill's " Va. Co. of London," pp. 55–61.)

Somerset, Earl of. — Robert Carr.

Somerset, Edward, Earl of Worcester. Fourth Earl, succeeded his father William, third Earl, on February 21, 1589; N. W. P. Co., 1612; died March 3, 1628 ; married Elizabeth, daughter of Francis, Earl of Huntingdon, and had several children. Ancestor of the Duke of Beaufort.

Sondes, Sir Michael, 2. Sub. ——; pd. ——. (Ancestor of Sir George Sondes, Bart., of Lees Court, County Kent, created Earl of Feversham in 1676.) He was M. P. for Queenborough in 1588–89 ; knighted at Greenwich, June 18, 1598 ; M. P. for Queenborough again in 1597–98, in 1601, and in 1604–11 ; M. C. for Va. Co., May 23, 1609, and possibly died soon after. The records of the Va. Co. show that he died before 1619.

In 1594 "the present state of Spaine, translated out of French," was dedicated to his son, Richard Sondes, which Richard was afterwards knighted, and married Catherine, daughter of Sir Rowland Hayward.

The family names Sandys and Sondes are often confused.

Soto, Fernando De. Born about 1500 ; served with distinction under Pizarro in Peru. The Va. Co. made a study of his expedition to Florida (see LXXXIV.). He reached Espiritu Santo Bay, Florida, May 25, 1539, with 570 men and 223 horses, well equipped ; was so fortunate as to find an interpreter in " Juan Ortiz, a Spaniard, who had lived twelve years among the Floridians ;" his life having been twice saved by a favorite daughter of the Indian chief. Wintered at Apalache, Florida ; left March 3, 1540, going northeastward ; reached "Cutisachiqui" [Coosawhatchie], some two days' journey from St. Helena, late in April ; on the 3d of May, marched northward to the golden country of "Yupaha" [Unaka or Smoky Mountains]; reached "Chalaque" [Cherokee] about the 10th of May, and continuing northward, passed near the celebrated Ducktown Coppermines, crossed the mineral belt of the Appalachian Range, and about the last of May came to " Canasaqua " [Canasaga, Polk County, Tenn. ?]; June 5, they arrived at "the island city of Chiaha " [the Chica-maugatown on the island in the Tennessee River, below Chattanooga], "which was subject to the Lord of Cosa," whose country was along the headwaters of the Coosa River of Alabama. Soto remained at "the island city " thirty days, and then went southward to winter down the Tennessee River ; thence through the Coosa country ; " the provinces of Tallise " [Tallassee], and " Tascaluca " [Tuscaloosa, Alabama] to " Mavilla ;" but I only wish to give an outline of his route through the eastern part of our country ; it is not to my purpose to follow him farther in his westward way. He died in Louisiana near the mouth of the Red River, May 21, 1542. About 300 survivors under Moscoso sailed from the mouth of the Mississippi, July 18, 1543. Having spent over four years in exploring the Southern, Middle, and Western States, they left a few horses, a few hogs, many Indian children who could speak the Spanish tongue, and several of their own men, who remained behind having Indian wives.

When we consider the habits of these 570 men during these four years, we may be assured that our forefathers met many an Indian " on the dark and bloody ground," who might count among his ancestors some grandee of Spain.

Southampton, Earl of. — Henry Wriothesley.

Southwicke, John, 2. Sub.——; pd. £12 10s.

Sparrow, Steven, merchant-tailor, 2. Sub. £37 10s. ; pd. £75. January 31, 1620, Steven Sparrow transferred one share in Virginia to John Hope.

Speckart, Abraham, 3. Sub. ——; pd. £25.

Spelman, Henry. Third son of Sir Henry Spelman of Congham, Norfolk, England (1562–1641); the distinguished antiquary and historian; treasurer of the Guiana Company, and one of the Council for New England. Henry, the son, was baptized in 1595; landed in Virginia in August, 1609 ; was sold to the Indians soon after, and lived with them until December, 1610. He returned to England with Lord De la Warr in March, 1611; but afterwards went back to Virginia, where he was employed as interpreter to the colony in 1616. In 1618 he was again in England, but returned to

JOHN WHITSON
Mayor of Bristol

Virginia on board the Treasurer in that year. He "knew most of the kings of that country, and spake their Languages very understandingly." (Howes' Abridgment.) In August, 1619, he was tried by the House of Burgesses for speaking disparagingly of Governor Yardly to Opocancano, and degraded from his office as interpreter, etc. He was trading with the Indians along the Potomac at the time of the massacre in March, 1622 ; and about one year after, on March 23, 1623, he was killed by the Anacostan Indians, probably near the present site of Washington, D. C.

Spencer, Edward, esquire. Fourth son of Robert Lord Spencer. He was seated at Boston in Middlesex ; M. P. for Brackley, 1621–22, 1624–25, and 1625, and for Middlesex, 1626 ; knighted at Hampton Court, December 27, 1625; died February 11, 1655, aged 61.

Spencer, John, clothworker. A native of Waldingfield, Suffolk. Queen Elizabeth gave him the Manor of Canonbury, and visited him there in 1581 ; sheriff of London, 1583 ; on the committee to consult with Carliell about planting a colony to the southwest of Cape Breton in America, 1583 ; alderman of Langbourn ward, 1587 ; lord mayor, 1594–95; knighted 1595 ; a leading member of the Russia and Turkey companies ; an incorporator of the E. I. Co., 1600 ; president of St. Bartholomew's Hospital, 1603–10 ; died March 3, 160,⁹⁄₁₀, and was buried in St. Helen's Bishopsgate, where a tomb is erected to his memory. He was known as "Rich Spencer." His only daughter and heir married, in 1594, William Lord Compton.

Spencer, Sir Richard, 3. Sub. £75 ; pd. ———. Of Hertfordshire ; fourth son of Sir John Spencer of Althorp, and uncle of Robert Lord Spencer ; knighted at Theobald's, May 7, 1603 ; ambassador to Holland ; M. P. for Brackley, 1604–11; died in November, 1624.

Spencer, Robert Lord, 3. Sub. ——— ; pd. £33 6s. 8d. Sheriff of Northamptonshire in the forty-third year of Elizabeth, before which time he had received the honor of knighthood, and when King James ascended the throne, was reputed to have by him the most money of any person in England. Ben Jonson alludes to him in the lines, —

"Who since Thamyra did die,
Hath not brook'd a lady's eye,
Nor allow'd about his place
Any of the female race."

The grief of Sir Robert Spencer, for the loss of his beloved consort, Margaret, daughter of Sir Francis Willoughby, thus beautifully alluded to, was no poetic fiction. He lost her in August, 1597 ; but though he survived her thirty years, he never made a second choice. He was created Baron Spencer of Wormleighton, July 21, 1603. The records of the times gave him a very high character, being spoken of as "The old Roman chosen Dictator," seldom leaving his farm save when called to the Senate. During the debates in Parliament, 1621, relating to the king's power and prerogative, this Lord Spencer, standing up boldly for the public liberty (with the Earls of Oxford, Southampton, Essex, and Warwick), made some allusion to the past, and the Earl of Arundel replying thereto, said, "My lord, when these things were doing, your ancestors were keeping sheep," to which the Lord Spencer, with a spirit and quickness of thought peculiar to him, immediately answered, "When my ancestors were keeping sheep (as you say), your ancestors were plotting treason." So says Wilson's "Hist. of Great Britain," London, 1653, p. 163 ; but see the more correct account given at length in Gardner's "Hist. of England," London, 1886, vol. iv. pp. 114–116. Lord Spencer died October 25, 1627, and was buried in great splendor with his ancestors at Brington. His son William married Penelope, daughter of Henry Wriothesley, Earl of Southampton. "Lord Spencer was the great friend of the Washingtons of Sulgrave," ancestors of Gen. George Washington.

Spencer, Varion, 2. Sub. ——— ; pd. £12 10s.

Spert (or Perte), Thomas. Of an old Bristol family ; master of the Mary Rose ; founded the Trinity House in 1512, and it was incorporated in 1514 (the disputed voyage with Cabot, 1517) ; master of the Harry Grace de Dieu in which great ship Henry VIII. sailed to Calais in May, 1520, on his way to the Field of the Cloth of Gold ; knighted by Henry VIII. at York Place in 1529 ; died September 8, 1541, and was buried in the chancel of Stepney Church. His first memorial having been lost, the Trinity House erected another in 1622.

Spinola, Benedict. Second son of Baptist Spinola, an eminent merchant of Genoa, who in 1556 refused the dukedom of his native city. Benedict came to London, where his friend, Horatio Pallavicino, and himself were sometime known as Queen Elizabeth's bankers.

The Society of Antiquaries, London, have a very curious broadside: " An Epitaph upon the death of the Worshipfull Maister Benedict Spinola, Merchant of Genoa and free Denizon of England, who dyed on Tuesday the 12. of Julie, 1580."

Spranger, Henry, 2. Sub. —— ; pd. £12 10s.

Springham, Matthias, merchant-tailor, 2. Sub. —— ; pd. £25. He was one of those selected by the lord mayor and citizens of London in 1613 to go over and examine the Irish plantation. He died in 1620, and was buried at Richmond, England.

Sprint, Gregory, esquire, 3. Sub. —— ; pd. £37 10s.

Spruson (see Pruson), Hildebrand, 2. Sub. £37 10s. ; pd. £59 9s. 9d. " November 3, 1610, grant to Hildebrand Prosen of the office of Merchant in the East for furnishing the King's ships, for life." The Calendar of State Papers, Domestic, 1611–1618, p. 613, mention some trouble incurred by two of his ships, in the West Indies, with the Spaniards ; but the date of the paper is uncertain. February 27, 1622, he transferred one of his shares in Virginia to Thomas Pemble.

Stacy, Thomas. Pd. £25.

Stafford. See Stratford.

Stallenge, William, gent., 2. Sub. —— ; pd. ——. Merchant of Plymouth ; M. P. for Plymouth in 1597–98 and 1601 ; January 5, 1607, licensed for twenty-one years to print a book called " Instructions for the planting and increase of Mulberry trees, breeding of Silkworms, and making of Silk ; " January 23, 1608, licensed to import mulberry seeds, and to set the same in any part of the realm, for increase and better breeding of silkworms.

Howes, in his Chronicle, writing under 1609, says, " Albeit this is the first publique notice of keeping wormes and making silke in England, yet true it is that many years past there were divers industrious gentlemen that kept wormes and made good silke, amongst which of late years, William Staledge, Comptroller of the Custome house, hath taken ingenious paynes in breeding wormes and making of fine silk for all uses ; he had a patent for seven years to bring mulberry seed, and this year he and Monsieur Verton by order from the king planted Mulberry trees in most shires of England." The state papers contain several warrants to pay him several sums for planting mulberry trees for the king near Westminster Palace and elsewhere.

Stanhope, John, Lord, 2. Sub. —— ; pd. £50. Third son of Sir Michael Stanhope, who was beheaded on Tower Hill, February 25, 1553 ; married, first, Joan, daughter and heir of William Knollys, but by her had no issue. On February 13, 1589, he was one of the sponsors of Ann West (see pedigree). May 6, 1589, he married, secondly, Margaret, daughter of Henry McWilliams, Esq., one of the queen's gentlemen pensioners. June 20, 1590, he was appointed master of the posts, succeeding Thomas Randolph, who had held that office from about 1566, and who is said to have been the first postmaster-general (then called " master of the posts ") of England. He was knighted in 1596, and the same year was constituted treasurer of the chamber for life, and in 1600, constable of the Castle of Colchester for life ; M. P. for the County of Northampton in 1601. On the accession of King James, he was continued vice-chamberlain, sworn of his Privy Council, and appointed by act of Parliament, in the first year of his reign (1603) one of the commissioners to treat of a union with Scotland ; and afterwards by letters patent, May 4, 1605, was advanced to the dignity of a baron of the realm as Lord Stanhope of Harrington. July 26, 1607, grant to John Lord Stanhope, and Charles, his son, of the office of postmaster in England, for life ; M. C. for Va. Co., May 23, 1609.

He continued in his office of vice-chamberlain till 1616, when he resigned it to Sir John Digby. He died March 9, 1620.

Stanley. See Vere-Stanley.

Stannard, William, innholder, 2. Sub. ——; pd. £25. Son of Thomas Stannard, of Bourne in the County of Cambridge. He married Martha Gardner, of Jeningses Bery, Com. Hartford.

Stapers (Staples), Hewet, clothworker, 3. Sub. £60 ; pd. £77 10s. Second son of Richard Stapers or Staples (next); was a member of the E. I. and N. W. P. companies, etc.

Stapers (Staples), Richard, merchant, 2. Sub. ——; pd. £37 10s. A native of Plymouth ; came to London, married Dionise, daughter of Thomas Hewett, of London, gent.; entered into a partnership with Edward Osborne ; they were leading members of the Rus. or Mus. Co., and trafficked over Europe, Asia, and Africa. In 1581 they were the leading incorporators and directors of the Turkey Company. In February, 1583, they sent out the first overland expedition from England to the East Indies, and in the same year Stapers was one of the committee appointed by the Rus. Co. to consult with Capt. Christopher Carlisle in regard to the proposed colony to the southwest of Cape Breton, on our coast. Osborne died in 1591 ; but Stapers continued his interest in commercial affairs, and was one of the incorporators and directors of the E. I. Co., December 31, 1600. He lies in "a very goodly Tomb," says Stow, "erected in the wall on the South side of the Church of St. Martin's Outwich, Broadstreet ward, London, having this inscription : —

" 'Here resteth the Body of the Worshipful Mr. Rich. Staper, elected Alderman of this city, 1594. He was the greatest Merchant in his time ; the chiefest Actor in discovery of the Trades of Turkey and East India : A Man humble in prosperity, painful and ever ready in the Affairs publick, and discreetly careful of his private. A liberal House-Keeper, bountiful to the Poor : an upright Dealer in the World, and a devout Aspirer after the World to Come. Much blest in his Posterity, and happy in his and their Alliances. He dyed the last day of June, An. Dom. 1608. Intravit ut exiret.' "

Sterling, Earl of. — William Alexander.

Stevens, Thomas, esquire, 3. Sub. £37 10s. ; pd. £37 10s. Attorney to Henry, Prince of Wales ; of the Middle Temple, esquire ; N. W. P. Co., 1612.

Steward, Augustine, esquire, 3. Sub. £37 10s. ; pd. £37 10s. Married Anne, aunt of Sir Samuel Argall (see Argall pedigree). December 15, 1619, he assigned to Sir Henry Jones his three shares in Virginia ; owned the site of the monastery, Barking Abbey, granted to him by King James in 1605 ; died in 1628.

Stewkley (Stukely, etc.), **Sir Thomas,** 3. Sub. ——; pd. £37 10s. (Of Sussex ; knighted at the Charterhouse, May 11, 1603 ?) Son of Hugh Stewkley, of Marsh in Somersetshire, and his wife Elizabeth, daughter of Richard Chamberlain. Sir Thomas married Elizabeth, daughter of John Goodwin, Esq., and was living in 1627 ; a nephew of John Chamberlain's, and mentioned in his will.

Stewkley (or Stuckley, etc.), **Captain Thomas.** A younger son of Sir Lewis Stukely, of Ilfracombe in Devonshire, and a most noted character of the age in which he lived; went to London early in life ; visited the court of Henry II. of France in 1551 with Robert Dudley, afterwards Earl of Leicester ; was, perhaps, in Wyatt's insurrection, 1553 – 54 ; buccaneering on the coast of Ireland about 1555 ; determined to be a prince before he died ; resolved to settle a province in Florida in 1563 ; but he made "the sea his Florida," and turned the enterprise into a buccaneering expedition against French and Spanish vessels ; went to Ireland and fought by the side of Shane O'Neill against the Scots at Bally Castle; from Ireland to

Spain ; from Spain to Rome ; commanded a ship in the great naval battle of Lepanto, October 7, 1571 ; sailed on an expedition to conquer Ireland for the Pope ; but joined King Sebastian, and fell fighting by his side at Alcazarquivir, September 22, 1578.

Stile (Style), Humphrey, grocer, 2. Sub. ——; pd. ——. Son of Nicholas Style ; was baptized at St. Mary Woolnoth, November 1, 1581; sworn a free brother by patrimony to the Grocers, November 13, 1605, and admitted to the livery in 1609.

Stile (or Style), Nicholas, grocer. Father of the above Humphrey; was the son of Sir Humfrey Style, of Langley, Kent ; baptized there, January 12, 1545–46 ; a churchwarden of St. Mary Woolnoth in 1588 ; an alderman of London ; died November 16, 1615, and was buried in St. Margaret, Lothbury, London. He was a benefactor of the Grocers' company.

Stile (or Style), Thomas. Sub. £75 ; pd. £62 10s. Of the E. I. Co.; on the Virginia Commission, July 15, 1624 ; of Lincoln's Inn ; one of the captains of the city of London in 1633. He married Martha, fourth daughter of Sir Maurice Abbott.

Stockley (or Stokeley), John, merchant-tailor, 2. Sub. £37 10s. ; pd. £50. Of the E. I. Co.

Stoddard, Sir Nicholas, 3. Sub. ——; pd. ——. Of Kent ; knighted at Whitehall, July 23, 1603.

Stokes, John, fishmonger, 2. Sub. ——; pd. £62 10s.

Stokes, Thomas. Pd. £12 10s.

Stone, George. Pd. £12 10s.

Stone, William. Of the E. I. and N. W. P. companies.

"As the Earth the Earth doth cover,
So under this Stone lyes another," etc.

Extract from his monument.

Stowe, John. Antiquary and historian ; born 1525 ; died 1605.

Strachey, William, gent., 2. Sub. ——; pd. £25. "One of The Graies-Inne Societe." Sailed from England in June, and was wrecked on the Bermudas in July, 1609 ; reached Virginia in May, 1610; was secretary and recorder there ; left in the summer of 1611, reaching England about the last of October in that year; edited CXC.,

December, 1611; wrote CCXVI., 1612; still living in 1618. I believe him to be the William Strachey, of Saffron Walden, who was married in 1588, and was alive in 1620, whose son or grandson, of the same name, came to Virginia in the Temperance in 1620, and was living in 1625, on Hog Island, aged 17. In CXXXV. Strachey mentions having been "on the coast of Barbary and Algiers, in the Levant," etc.

William Strachey.

Stradling, Sir John, 3. Sub. ——; pd. £12 10s. Related to the Pophams; son of Francis Stradling, who resided at St. George's, near Bristol, by his wife Mary, daughter of Bartholomew Mitchel, Esq. ; educated at Oxford, and took his degree in arts as a member of Magdalen Hall in 1583, "being then accounted a Miracle for his forwardness in Learning and Pregnancy of Parts ;" author of "De Vita et Morte Contemnenda," 1597 ; "Epigrammata," 1607 ; knighted May 15, 1608 ; created a baronet, May 21, 1611 ; sheriff of Glamorgan, 1620 ; published "Beatifici Pacifici: a Divine Poem," in 1623 ; M. P. for St. Germans, 1624–25 ; published "Divine Poems : in seven several Classes," 1625 ; M. P. for Glamorgan, 1626 ; died September 9, 1637.

Stratford, Earl of.—Thomas Wentworth.

Stratford (see Stafford), Richard, 2. Sub. £37 10s. ; pd. £75. "Receiver in the principality of North Wales."

Strode, Sir William, 3. Sub. ——; pd. ——. Of Newnham, Devon; M. P. for Devon, 1597 ; for Plympton, 1601, 1604–11, and 1621–22; for Plymouth, 1614 ; and for Devon again, 1624–25 ; will proved February 20, 1638. He was the father of William Strode, one of "the famous five members."

Strongarm — Strongtharm — Strong - in - Arm — Armstrong, Richard, ironmonger, 2. Sub. ——; pd. £100. Of E. I. Co.

Stuart, Queen Anne. Daughter of Frederick II., King of Denmark, and wife of James I. of England ;

died March 2, 1619. The Rappahannock River is named for her, in CLVIII. (map) and Cape Ann, Massachusetts.

Stuart, Prince Charles. The second son of James I.; afterwards Charles I.; born November 19, 1600; crowned February 2, 1625; beheaded January 30, 1649. Cape Charles was named for him; also Charles City (now "City Point"), and the present Charles City County in Virginia, and Charles City River in Massachusetts. He gave the English names on Smith's map of New England (CCCLIV.).

Stuart, Princess Elizabeth. The eldest daughter of James I.; born August 19, 1596; married February 14, 1613; Queen of Bohemia, 1619; exile after the battle of Prague, November 9, 1620; widow, 1632; settled in England, 1660, and died in London February 13, 1662. From whom the present royal line of England. The Potomac is named for her, in CLVIII. (map) "Elizabeth River." On May 17, 1620, the Virginia Council published a broadside to be sent to America, from which I extract: "First, we ordaine and require, that in convenient time, after the sight and publication hereof, the foure ancient generall Burroughs, called James City, Henrico, Charles City, and Kicowtan (which hereafter shall be called Elizabeth City, by the name of his Maiesties most vertuous and renowned daughter), as also the other severall particular Plantations," etc. I suppose that "Cape Elizabeth," on Smith's map of New England was also named for her.

Stuart, Prince Henry, merchant-tailor. Eldest son of James I.; born at Stirling Castle, February 19, 1594; baptized August 30, 1594, with the first Protestant baptismal rites ever administered to a prince in Great Britain; created Prince of Wales, May 30, 1610. Interested in ships and naval affairs, commerce, and discoveries, and especially in the colonization of America by the English; made a study of the West Indies, and Sir Charles Cornwallis says, "It was his expressed desire, if the King his father should on any occasion think proper to break with Spain, that he would himselfe, if his Majesty would permit, undertake the execution of the

attempt against the Spanish possessions in America." Among his servants were the celebrated mathematician, Edward Wright, Phineas Pett, the shipbuilder, and Solomon de Caus, whom Arago regarded as the inventor of the "machine à feu" (steam-engine). The prince was a friend to Ralegh, who wrote for him, "Of the Art of War by Sea," "Of a Maritime Voyage, with the Passages and Incidents therein," and his "General History of the World." He had a little quiet humor, and, in 1611, was the patron of Coryat's "Crudities, Hastily gobled up in five Moneths travells in France, Savoy," etc.; with engravings by W. Hole, and poems by many, in a high panegyric style; and I am not at all sure but that some of the same ideas obtained in the bringing forth of Smith's "New England" in 1616, to which his brother, Prince Charles, was the patron.

Henry, Prince of Wales died of typhoid fever, to the great grief of the whole nation "on Friday, November 6, 1612, between 7 and 8 a clocke at night," and was buried in Westminster Abbey. The prince's chaplain, Dr. Daniel Price, preached a sermon in the chapel December 6, and George Abbot, Archbishop of Canterbury, preached his funeral sermon in the Abbey December 7, 1612. Cape Henry was named for him in 1607; the York River was named for him in 1607 or 1608; the city of Henricus or Henricopolis (in the bend of James River at Dutch Gap) was named for him in 1611, and the old county of Henrico at a later day.

The sorrow at the death of this prince was very great. At the University of Oxford, Dr. William Goodwin preached a funeral sermon; Richard Corbet delivered a funeral oration, and the university afterwards published a collection of Memorial Verses. At the University of Cambridge, the sermon was preached by Dr. Valentine Cary; the oration delivered by Francis Nethersole, and another collection of Memorial Verses was published by this university; and still another by Magdalen College in Oxford; and Dr. Leonel Sharpe published likewise a funeral oration in Latin. The following poets wrote elegies: Sir William Alexander, Robert Allyne, Lord Bacon, Dominic Baudius, of Leyden, Christopher Brooke, William Browne, George Chapman, Alexander Craig, John Donne, William Drummond, Thomas Heyward, Hugh Holland, James Maxwell, Walter Quinn, Joshua Sylvester, William Rowley, John Taylor, Cyril Tourneur, John Warde, John Webster, George Wither, etc.

Stuart, King James, clothworker. The first of the Stuart line of the kings of England, was born in Edinburgh Castle, June 19, 1566 ; succeeded his mother, Mary Queen of Scots, as King of Scotland, July 24, 1567, and was crowned at Stirling, July 29. Married Anne of Denmark, November 24, 1589 ; endeavored to restore peace in Europe in 1590 ; proclaimed King of England on the death of Queen Elizabeth, March 24, and was crowned at Westminster, July 25, 1603; Hampton Court conference, January 14–17, 1604, which resulted in a new translation of the Bible. He favored merchants, and enlarged the privileges of the East India, the Muscovy, the Turkey, and the Merchant Adventurers companies in 1604; granted first charter to the Va. companies, April 10, 1606 ; articles, orders, etc., for the Va. colonies, November 20, 1606; an ordinance and constitution, etc., for said colonies, March 9, 1607 ; Jamestown and James River were rightly named for him, 1607 ; in 1609, on April 11, opened the new exchange; May 3, ordered merchandise, etc., for Virginia to go duty free ; May 11, granted a more ample charter to the E. I. Co. ; May 23, granted a more ample charter to the South Va. Co., and in October encouraged the formation of a company to trade with France ; May 2, 1610, granted a charter to the N. Fld. Co. In 1611 the new translation of the Bible was dedicated to him (read "The Epistle Dedicatory"). March 12, 1612, granted a third charter with increased privileges to the Va. Co. ; July 26, 1612, granted a charter to the N. W. P. Co.; March 29, 1613, granted a charter to the Irish Society of London for settling plantations at Londonderry, etc.; March 30, 1613, granted a more ample charter to the Rus. Co. ; August 28, 1613, granted a charter for an English plantation in Guiana, South America ; June 29, 1615, granted a charter to the B. I. Co. ; August 26, 1616, license to Sir Walter Ralegh to make a voyage to South America; November 16, 1618, granted a charter for trading to Africa ; November 3, 1620, granted a charter to the New England Colony ; December 31, 1622, granted a charter for a plantation in Avalon (Newfoundland). In the factions of the Va. Co. of London, he favored the merchant party, as "he conceived merchants to be fittest, for the management of such undertakings, because of their experience and skill in staple commodities," etc. I believe that he showed good judgment in this opinion, as well as in the selection of the men whom he proposed to the company for the offices of treasurer and deputy. He was a constant friend to the colonies. He agreed to the treaty for the Spanish marriage in July, 1623 ; broke off the treaty in December following, and declared war on Spain, March 10, 1624 ; June 16, 1624, the "charter of the company of English Merchants trading to Virginia" was declared by Chief Justice Lee to be null and void, and the colony was taken immediately under the protection of the crown. He died at Theobald's March 27, 1625, and was buried in Westminster Abbey.

King James was a human being; he had faults. It is said that he swore like a trooper, hunted with hounds, hated war, and did many things which he ought not to have done; but he had some good qualities also, he loved books, literature, arts, and peace. I believe that he loved his country, and to the best of his ability and judgment tried to maintain the English Church, to preserve peace, and to advance the English nation by increasing trades and traffics, by encouraging merchants, commerce, colonization, and discoveries. But the king of England was of "the bare-legged Scottish nation from over the border," and this was "the bitter pill" to many Englishmen.

War had been almost the only profession of princes, and it still had advocates, but under his peaceful policy the colonies in America and the commerce of East India were established. The corner-stone of the present prosperity of the united kingdom of Great Britain and Ireland was laid. The onward march of the English-speaking people over the face of the earth began. It may be that he has found but few friends among the historians of America, yet I am sure that America has more cause to bless him than to blame him.

He has been condemned for the part taken by him in the annual elections of the Va. Co. of London during 1620-24; and for the character of the men recommended by him as suitable for officers of that company ; yet his active interest in these affairs make evident his especial and personal interest in the success of the movement, and those recommended by him as suitable for officers were certainly thoroughly qualified business men, as their sketches in this Dictionary will prove. He is also condemned for appointing the commissions of May 9, 1623, and of June 24, 1624, and for the tasks assigned to them ; but it must now be conceded that these acts were necessary. Both commissions are given in Hazard's "Historical Collections," vol. i. pp. 155-159 and 183-188. At the head of the first was Sir William Jones, one of the justices of the Court of Common Pleas, a distinguished lawyer, author of first Jones's Reports, 18 James I. to 17 Charles I. ; and under him were Sir Nicholas Fortescue, Sir Francis Gofton, Sir Richard Sutton, Sir William Pitt, Sir Henry Bouchier, and Sir Henry Spiller, all either auditors or officers of the exchequer, especially qualified for the work in hand, and all of them disinterested ; none of them were members of the Va. Co., or of either faction thereof. After examining the case thoroughly they made their report, which justified Chief Justice James Ley (or Lee) (afterwards Earl of Marlborough) in declaring the charter, on June 16, 1624, thenceforth null and void. And every man, appointed by the Privy Council on the commission of June 14 (and July 15) 1624, "for the well-settling of the colony of Virginia," was an earnest friend of the object in view, as their sketches in this Dictionary amply demonstrate.

With our present knowledge of the case, the constant care of James I. for his American colonies is evident. It is proven by the records, by the royal charters, orders, commissions, etc., as well as by the remaining contemporary evidence compiled by the different factions in the company. It is true, the Sandys party did not agree with him in thinking merchants (especially those of the E. I. Co.) the best managers for such an enterprise, and that they differed with him in several other particulars ; but I cannot find that even this faction ever called in question, during his life, his good will for the enterprise, or his honesty of purpose, and in their discourse to the Privy Council, after his death, in the spring of 1625, they wrote, "Amongst the many glorious workes of the late Kinge, there was none more eminent, than his gracious inclination, together with ye propagation of Christian Religion, to advance and sett forward a New Plantation in the New World, which purpose of his continued till the last."

His race is probably extinct in the male line ; but continues to rule a great part of the world in the female lines. Among his descendants are to be found the names of almost all the reigning princes of Europe: the Queen of England ; the Czar of Russia ; the emperors of Germany and Austria ; the kings of Spain, Italy, Denmark, etc. (See London "Notes and Queries," 6 ser. xii. pp. 251, 252.)

Stuart, Ludovic, Duke of Lennox. Born September 29, 1574; succeeded, on the death of his father, May 28, 1583, as second Duke of Lennox, in Scotland ; held the high office of great chamberlain of Scotland, as well as high admiral, and went as ambassador from James VI. of Scotland to Henry IV. of France ; attended King James to England in 1603 ; N. W. P. Co., 1612 ; made Earl of Richmond October 6, 1613. The petition of the second colony of Virginia was referred to the Earl of Arundel and himself, March 3, 1620. He was the leading incorporator of, and one of his Majesty's first council for, the N. E. Co., November 3, 1620 ; the first signer of the first Plymouth patent, first of June, 1621; an attendant on the meetings of the New England Council, and a contributor to the enterprise, 1620-24 ; created Duke of Richmond May 17,

1623 ; drew lot number six on the Massachusetts Bay, June 29, 1623 ; died February 16, 1624, and was buried in Westminster Abbey, April 19 following. His widow (she was his third wife, and he was her third husband) was Frances, daughter of Thomas Howard, Viscount Bindon. She was the patroness of Capt. John Smith's "General History " (1624), and in his dedication to her, after telling her how the ladies had rescued and protected the unconquerable warrior ("a Julius Cæsar ") in Europe, Asia, and America, he writes, "And so verily these my adventures have tasted the same influence from your *Gratious hand*, which hath given birth to the publication of this *Narration*. If therefore your *Grace* shall daigne to cast your eye on this poore Booke, view I pray you rather your owne *Bountie* (without which it had dyed in the wombe) then my *imperfections*, which have no helpe but the shrine of your *glorious Name* to be sheltered from censorious condemnation."

Frances Howard was born about 1578 ; married, first, Henry Prannel, who died in 1599 ; secondly, Edward Seymour, Earl of Hertford, who died in 1621, and, thirdly, the Earl of Richmond. She had no children by either of her husbands, and was perhaps the richest dowager in England ; she died October 8, 1639. They moved in different circles ; but Captain Smith and herself were characters of the times. He was perhaps the vainest man and she the vainest woman in England. One of her greatest desires was to be famous for her bounty, which, it is said, was sometimes only "an airy paper-greatness." She was known as " the double duchess " (Lennox and Richmond), and some wags called her the "duchess cut upon duchess." She vowed, after having been the wife of so great a prince as Richmond, never to be blown with the kisses of a subject, and aspired to the hand of King James. The Duke of Brunswick went to see her ; but was only admitted with the proviso, that he must not offer to kiss her ; "but what was wanting in herself," says Chamberlain, "was supplied in her attendants and followers, who were all kissed over twice in less than a quarter

of an hour." Chamberlain, writing to Carleton in December, 1624, says, " I cannot forget one good passage of the Duchess of Richmond, that in discourse of the Lady of Southampton's loss, and how grievously she took it, she used this argument, to prove her own grief was the greater, 'for,' quoth she, 'I blasphemed;' a witty speech forsooth, and worthy to be put into the collection of the Lord of St. Alban's ' Apothegms,' newly set out this week."

Traces of this lady will be found in Smith's map of Ould Virginia, as " Lenox rocks," " Howard's Mountaynes," " Stuard's reach," " Hertford's Ile," etc. And in his list of the adventurers for Virginia, 1620, he inserts the name of " Edward Semer, Earle of Hartford " (her second husband) which is not found in any other list that I have seen. I cannot find that either of her husbands or herself were interested in South Virginia.

Studley, Thomas. The first Cape merchant ; died in Virginia, August 28, 1607.

Stuteville, Sir Martin. Sub. ——; pd. £40. Of Debenham Dalham, Suffolk ; M. P. Aldborough, 1601 ; knighted July 21, 1604 ; a relative and correspondent of the Rev. Joseph Mead.

Suffolke, Earl of. — Thomas Howard.

Suffolke, The Ladie. The wife of Thomas Howard, Earl of Suffolk; a pensioner of Spain. Bayley says, "Members of the council attend mass, and tell their masters' secrets to their wives, by whom they were betrayed to the Jesuits." None of the pensioners were members of the Virginia councils; but this lady's son, Lord Theophilus Howard, was of that council.

Surry, Earl of. — Thomas Howard.

Sutcliffe, Dr. Matthew, of Exeter, 2. Sub. ——; pd. £20. Educated at Trinity College, Cambridge ; Archdeacon of Taunton, 1586 ; prebendary of Exeter, 1588 ; Dean of Exeter, October 22, 1588. His " Treatise of Ecclesiastical Discipline," 1590, and 1591 ; " Disputatio de Presbyterio," 1591 ; " De Catholica et Orthodoxa Christi Ecclesia," 1592. Prebendary of Wells, 1592. His " An Answere to a Certaine Libel Supplicatorie," etc., 1593 ; " The Practice, Proceedings, and Lawes of Armes, described out of the doings of most valiant and expert Captaines, and confirmed both by ancient, and moderne examples, and precedents, . . . 1593." Dedicated to the Earl of Essex. Another of his controversial tracts appeared in 1596; three in 1599; one in 1600; one in 1603; two in 1606, etc.

M. C. for Va., March 9, 1607. "He is best known for the attempt he made to found at Chelsea a College of Polemical Divines, to be employed in opposing the doctrines of Papists and Sectaries." Two of the nineteen fellows were to be employed in recording the chief historical events of the era, "The first stone was laid by King James, May 8, 1609, and the charter of incorporation is dated May 8, 1610. The king, by act of Parliament, in 1609, gave the power of bringing water by means of engines from Hackney Marsh to supply the city of London with water, the profits to go to this college." "Prince Henry was a zealous friend to it and King James, a Learned Prince and firm Protestant, liked well of this Purpose and encouraged it. And when the building began he laid the first stone himself; and moreover gave all the Timber requisite thereto, which was to be fetched from Windsor Forest."

November 3, 1620, Dr. Sutcliffe was made a member of His Majesty's Council for New England. We find him attending the meetings of this council, and in the proposed division of the colony "on Sondaie," June 29, 1623, Dr. Goche drew for him lot 4, near the present site of Boston, Massachusetts.

July 15, 1624, he was one of the commission for winding up the affairs of the Va. Co. of London. He died in 1629. By his will, dated November 1, 1628, he left a large sum of money to complete his college; but after his death the project fell into decay, and his estates were restored to his heirs by decree of chancery, in 1631.

Sutton, Sir Thomas, 2. Sub. ——; pd. ——. This was probably the founder of the Charterhouse; yet, although I find a great deal about him, I cannot find that he was ever knighted, neither can I find any knight of the name (Thomas Sutton) in 1609. He

was born at Knaith, Lincolnshire, in 1532; educated at Eton and Cambridge, and became a student in Lincoln's Inn, and soon after traveled in those countries as a gentleman, to which he afterwards traded as a merchant; master of the ordnance at Berwick, during the rebellion of Northumberland; master-general of ordinance in the north for life in 1569; at the capture of Edinburgh Castle, 1573; aided in having the Spanish bills of exchange (for defraying the Armada expenses) protested in 1587, thereby causing a year's delay. He married (about 1581) the widow of John Dudley, Esq. (whose daughter, Anne Dudley, married Sir Francis Popham), and died December 12, 1611, without issue, leaving to charitable use a fortune superior to that of any private gentleman of his time.

Swift, James, 2. Sub. ——; pd. £25. Ensign; came to Virginia in 1609. Early in 1620 he signed the "Peticion of Sundry Antient adventurers to have some man of qualitye sent Governor unto Virginia." About the same time, in February, 1620, a grant of lands in Virginia was issued to Doctor Bohun, James Swift, and their associates for transportation of 300 persons to Virginia.

Swinhow, George, 3. Sub. £37 10s.; pd. £62 10s. Of N. W. P. Co.

Swinhow, John, stationer, 2. Sub. ——; pd. £25.

Symonds, Rev. William. Born in Oxfordshire, about 1557; at Magdalen College, Oxford, in 1573, and six years later was a fellow thereof. About 1579 he received a curacy, the gift of the Lord Willoughby, at Hatton Holgate, Dioc. Lincoln, where he remained, it is said, until 1605 or 1606. He published "Pisgah Evangelica" in 1605. He preached a sermon at Paul's Cross, January 12, 1606 (1607?) which was published in 1607, at which time he was probably the preacher at St. Saviour's, Southwark. As he was the "preacher at Saint Saviour's in Southwarke," he probably baptized John Harvard (the founder of Harvard College, Mass.) there, on November 29, 1607. He preached the first sermon before the Va. Co. of London, April 25, 1609 (LXXXVI.). In 1612, at the suggestion, it seems, of the Rev. Mr. Crashaw, he seems to have acted a friendly part by his fellow-servant Captain Smith (both of them had been servants to Lord Willoughby) in looking over his collections, and probably aided in having them published at Oxford. Symonds was not a member of the Va. Co., and the exact part taken by him in the transaction is not clear; but it seems evident that Smith and certain members of his faction, who returned to England, taking advantage of the troubles in Virginia, succeeded in making a favorable impression on the good clergymen, Crashaw, Purchas, and Symonds, and in securing their patronage.

I suppose Chamberlain refers to him in his letter of August 1, 1613, where he writes that " old Simons of Oxfordshire is dead." If so, he could have had nothing to do with revising the narrative (as Smith leads us to suppose), as given in the "General History."

It was a comfort to him that no "sonnes of Anak" [Numbers 13: 33] were found in America.

Talbot, George, sixth Earl of Shrewsbury. Had charge of Mary Queen of Scots, 1568–84 ; interested in Fenton's and Carleill's voyages, 1582–84; died November 18, 1590; married, first, Gertrude, daughter of Thomas Manners, Earl of Rutland, by whom four sons and three daughters; secondly, " Besse of Hardwick" (see William Lord Cavendish), by whom no issue.

Talbot, Gilbert, seventh Earl of Shrewsbury, 3. Sub.——; pd.——. Succeeded his father in 1590 ; married Mary Cavendish, daughter of his step-mother ; of the N. W. P. Co., 1612; died in May, 1616, leaving three

daughters, namely, Mary, married to William Herbert, Earl of Pembroke;

Elizabeth, married to Henry Grey, Earl of Kent (see Gray—Grey); Alathea, married to Thomas Howard, Earl of Arundel.

Tanfield, Sir Laurence. N. Fld. Co.; of the Inner Temple, 1569 ; reader, 1595 ; created serjeant at law, January 28, 1603 ; M. P. Oxfordshire, 1604–11 ; justice of the King's Bench, January 13, 1606 ; chief baron of the Exchequer, June 25, 1607; died April 30, 1625, buried at Burford, Oxfordshire, June 9.

Tanner, John, grocer, 2. Sub. ——; pd. ——. " Late apprentice to Henry Dodd, entered and sworn, November 24, 1602 ; still found on the warden's book of the Grocers' Company, 1612."

Tate, Francis, esquire, 3. Sub. £37 10s. ; pd. £25. Second son of Bartholomew Tate, Esq., of De la Pré Abbey ; born in 1560 ; barrister of the Middle Temple ; M. P. for Northampton, 1601, and for Shrewsbury, 1604–11; was a famous lawyer and antiquary; died 1617, *s. p.*

Tate, Lewis, 3. Sub. £37 10s. pd. £25.

Taverner, John, gent., 2. Sub. ——; pd. £37 10s. Probably went to Virginia in 1606. " January 7, 1618, Mr. John Taverner, surrendered to Mr. David Wiffin, a bill of Adventure of £37 10s.; three shares." " March 17, 1619, Mr. John Taverner, allowed a personal share of 100 acres " (showing that he had been to Virginia at his own charge). " June 7, 1619, John Taverner to Thomas Sheppard, three shares in Va." (From Va. Co. Records.)

Taylor, William, haberdasher, 2. Sub. ——; pd. £12 10s. Died 1651; see Will in " N. E. Register," April, 1888, pp. 177, 178. His second wife was sister to Rev. John Wilson, the first minister of Boston, Mass.

Thane, Viscount. — Francis Lord Norris.

Thanet, Earl of. — Nicholas Tufton.

Thesham. See Tresham.

Thorne, Robert, merchant-tailor. Son of Nicholas; was born in Bristol, and removed to London, where he became a prosperous merchant. In 1527 he wrote his exhortation to Henry VIII., and discourse to Doctor

SIR RALPH WINWOOD

Lee in favor of American Discoveries, etc. In 1531 he united with Lord de la Warr in founding the Bristol Grammar School. He died a bachelor in 1532, in the fortieth year of his age, and was buried in St. Christopher's, London, under "a very fair Tomb of pure touch in the South side of the Quire." (The Bank of England now occupies the site of this church.) Thorne gave over £4,445 to pious uses; £5,142 to his poor kindred; and he gave those who owed him their indebtedness. Hakluyt, referring to Thorne's book and map of 1527, says they were "preserved by one Master Emmanuel Lucar, the executor of Master Robert Thorne, and was friendly imparted unto me by Master Cyprian Lucar his sonne." This is not exactly correct.

Emmanuel Lucar, of London, esquire, married, first, Elizabeth, daughter of Paul Withipole, of Walthamstow, who was Thorne's executor; secondly, Joane Turnbull, and she was Cyprian Lucar's mother.

In 1535 Paul Withipole built a chapel at Walthamstow in Robert Thorne's memory. In 1600 Edmund Withipole sold the Rectory of Walthamstow to Sir Reginald Argall. The manor had been granted to Thomas Argall in 1563, and his grandson, Sir Samuel Argall, sometime governor of Virginia, resided there in his old age (see Argall pedigree).

Thornton, Robert, 2. Sub. ——; pd. £25.

Thorpe, George, esquire, 3. Sub. ——; pd. £25. Son of Nicholas Thorpe, of Wanswell Court, by his first wife, Mary Wikes, *alias* Mason, niece of Sir John Mason, a counselor of state; was baptized January 1, 1576 (see Throckmorton pedigree); a captain; a gentleman pensioner; a gentleman of the king's privy chamber; M. P. Portsmouth, 1614; M. C. for Va. Co. He sold his lands in England, and in 1618 formed a partnership for making a private plantation in Virginia with Sir W. Throckmorton, John Smith, of Nibley, Richard Berkeley (whom see), and others. Thorpe was much interested in converting the Indians; had taken an Indian boy and taught him to write (see John Smith, of Nibley); went to Virginia himself in March,

1620, where he was manager of the college lands and a member of the council; took especial interest in the Indians, making a study of their views of Religion and Astronomy; became convinced that "all the past ill success was owing to the not seeking of God's glory in converting the Natives, which are peaceable and wanted but meanes;" was massacred by the Indians March 21, 1622. Capt. George Thorpe was twice married; first to Margaret, daughter of Sir Thomas Porter, who died *s. p.*; and secondly to Margaret, daughter of David Harris; she died in 1629. Their son, William Thorpe, was also twice married, his first wife (married in 1636) being Ursula, daughter of John Smith, of Nibley, the antiquary.

Throckmorton, Sir William, 3. Sub. ——; pd. £75. Of Totworth in Gloucestershire; son and heir of Sir Thomas [3] Throckmorton (see pedigree). For some account of his plantation in Virginia, see George Thorpe and John Smith, of Nibley; created a baronet by King James, June 29, 1611; was thrice married and left issue.

Throckmorton Pedigree. William[1] Throckmorton, sheriff of Gloucestershire, 21 Henry VIII., was the father of Margaret[2] and Sir Thomas[2]. Margaret[2] Throckmorton (who died in 1566) married Thomas Thorpe; they were the parents of Nicholas[3], the father of Capt. George[4] Thorpe.

Sir Thomas[2] Throckmorton, who died in 1586, was the father of Sir Thomas[3] and Anne[3].

Sir Thomas[3] Throckmorton married Elizabeth Berkeley, aunt of Richard Berkeley, Esq., and had issue: —

i. Sir William[4] Throckmorton.

ii. Elizabeth[4], wife of Sir Thomas Dale.

iii. Mary[4] married, first Sir Thomas Baskerville, and, secondly, Sir James Scudamore.

Anne[3], daughter of Sir Thomas[2], married Sir John Tracey and had issue: —

i. Sir John[4] Tracey, married Mary, daughter of Sir Thomas Shirley.

ii. William[4] Tracey, married Mary Conway.

iii. Dorothy[4] (or Anne[4]) Tracey, married, first, Edmond Bray, of Barington; secondly, Sir Edward Conway.

iv. Mary [4] Tracey, married, first, Hoby, and, secondly, Sir Horace Vere.

Timberlake, Henry, 3. Sub. ——; pd. £37 10s. Also of the E. I. and N. W. P. companies. He had traveled in the East, and in 1603 he published "A True and strange discourse of the travailes of two English Pilgrimes: what admirable accidents befell them in their Journey to Jerusalem, Gaza, Grand Cayro, Alexandria and other places. Also, what Antiquities, Monuments, and notable memories, they sawe in Terra Sancta. . . . Written by one of them; on the behalfe of himselfe, and his fellowe Pilgrime. Imprinted at London, for Thomas Archer, . . . 1603." Followed by other editions in 1608, 1609, 1611, etc. These two Pilgrimes, may have suggested to Purchas his Pilgrimages, his Pilgrimes, and his Pilgrim.

Tindall. See Tyndall.

Todkill, Anas, went to Virginia in 1606, as a servant to Capt. John Martin; probably returned to England.

Tomlins, Richard, esquire, 3. Sub. £37 10s.; pd. £37 10s. Probably Richard Tomlins, of Westminster, who was M. P. for Ludlow, 1621–22; 1624–25, 1625, 1626, and 1628–29. He was elected M. C. for Va. Co. in May, 1623.

Totness, Earl of. — George Lord Carew.

Towerson, William. Of Tower Street; made a voyage to the coast of Guinea about 1555; was a Merchant Adventurer; interested in the voyages of Fenton and John Davis. He married the widow of Richard Atkinson, Sr.

Towler, Charles, 2. Sub. ——; pd. £12 10s.

Townsend, Sir John, 2. Sub. £37 10s.; pd. ——. Of Salop; knighted at Sir John Fortescue's in 1603; M. P. Wycombe, 1604–11. I suppose he was a brother to Anne Townsend, who married John Spelman, Esq., the elder brother of Henry Spelman, of Virginia.

Townson (see **Thomson**), **Leonard,** fishmonger. Sub. ——; pd. £25.

Tracy, Sir Thomas, 3. Sub. ——; pd. £37 10s. Knighted at Salisbury in July, 1609; M. P. for Corse Castle, 1614, and for Wilton in 1621, in which year he died.

Tracy, William. Sub. ——; pd. ——. I take this to be the man who married Mary Conway (see Throckmorton pedigree). He sailed from Bristol in September, 1620, in the Supply, with emigrants and provisions for Berkeley Hundred in Virginia. One of his daughters, the wife of Capt. Nathaniel Powell, was massacred by the Indians in Virginia in March, 1622.

Tradescant, John. Pd. £25. Said to have been of Flemish origin. After traveling through Europe and in the East, he settled in England; one of the first collectors of natural curiosities; a partner in Argall's Virginia plantation in February, 1617; with Sir Dudley Digges to Russia in 1618; went on the expedition of Mansell and Argall against the Algerine corsairs, in order to obtain the Algier apricot, 1620; George Sandys wrote to him from Virginia in 1623. He was in the service of George Villiers, Duke of Buckingham, and July 31, 1625, he wrote to Edward Nicholas that it was the duke's pleasure for him to deal with all merchants from all places; but especially from Virginia, Bermudas, Newfoundland, Guinea, Binney, the Amazon, East Indies, etc., for all manner of rare beasts, fowls and birds, shells, stones, etc.; afterwards in the service of Charles I.; died in 1638; his son John in 1642, and his grandson John in 1652. The widow of the last erected, in 1662, a tomb at Lambeth to "John Tradescant, grandsire, father, and son." They are much confused in their biographies. In 1631 Capt. John Smith left a part of his books to "Master John Tradeskyn." In 1637 John Tradescant (the son, I believe) was in Virginia gathering all varieties of flowers, plants, shells, etc.

Tragabigzanda. See Charatza Tragabigzanda.

Tresham (see **Thesam**), **Sir Lewis,** 3. Sub. ——; pd. ——. Second son of Sir Thomas Tresham, by his wife Muriel, daughter of Sir Robert Throckmorton.

The elder brother, Sir Francis Tresham, was involved in the Gunpowder Plot; was attainted of high treason, and succeeded by his younger brother, Lewis, of whom I write.

"Lewis Tresham, of the Inner

Temple, gent., bachelor, aged 25, son of Sir Thomas Tresame, knight, was married in March, 1603, to Mary Perrye, maiden, aged 23, daughter of Mrs. Moore, wife of Alderman John Moore, at St. Bartholomew, Exchange, London." He was created a baronet, June 29, 1611; knighted at Whitehall, April 9, 1612 ; died in 1639.

Trevor, Sir John, 2. Sub. ——; pd. £70. Second son of John Trevor, Esq. (who died July 15, 1589), of Trevallyn, County Denbigh, by his wife Mary, daughter of Sir George Bruges, knight, of London.

"He was of Plas Teg, which he built ; " married, May 24, 1592, Margaret, daughter of Hugh Trevannon, Esq.; M. P. Reigate, 1592–93, 1597–98, and 1601; secretary to Earl of Nottingham (the lord admiral), and surveyor of the royal navy to Elizabeth and James I. ; knighted at the Tower, May 13, 1603 ; made steward and receiver of Windsor Castle for life, June 6, 1603 ; made keeper of the house and park at Oatlands, for life, November 4, 1603; M. P. for Bletchingley, 1604–11; M. C. for Va., 1606 ; M. C. for Va. Co., 1609 ; M. P. for Bletchingley, 1614, and for Bodmin in 1621–22. "February 22, 162⅔, Sir John Trevor ye father transfers to *Sir John ye Sonne* 2 shares of land in Virginia." In 1625 he was M. P. for East Looe. He died in 1630, leaving (with other issue) "Sir John ye sonne," who was knighted in 1619, and died in 1673. The father is generally omitted in the peerages, where "ye sonne" of the same name has taken his place. Sir John Trevor, the son, was M. P. for County Denbigh, 1621–22, Flint, 1624–25, 1625, Great Bedwin, 1628–29, and for Grampound in the Long Parliament, 1640-53.

Trevor, Sir Richard, 3. Sub. ——; pd. ——. Of Allington and Trevallyn, County Denbigh ; eldest son of John Trevor, Esq., and brother of Sir John aforesaid ; knighted by Lord Deputy Sir William Russell in the Glynes, Ireland, May 8, 1597 ; M. P. Bletchingley (Surrey), 1597–98; married Catherine, daughter of Roger Puleston, Esq. He was living in 1612, but the date of his death is not known to me. He left four daughters, his co-heirs.

Trinity House, 3. Sub. ——; pd. £150. "The Ends and Intents of the Foundation of the ancient Corporation of Mariners, the Guild of the most glorious and undivideable Trinity, were for the Encrease and Encouragement of Navigation, for the good government and training of Pilots and seamen for the better security of ships at Sea."

Troughton (Throughton), Andrew, 3. Sub. £37 ; pd. £25.

Tucker, Daniel, 2. Sub. ——; pd. £31 5s. Son of George Tucker, of Milton in Kent, by his wife Mary, daughter of John Hunter, of Gaunte. He was nearly related to " Mr. Tucker, the searcher at Gravesend " in 1619.

He sailed for North Va. with Challons, in 1606 ; was a leading man in South Va., for five years, 1608–13 ; commissioned governor of the Bermudas, February 15, 161⅚; in that island from May, 1616, to about January, 161⅞. He was one of those who signed the petition to the council, in 1619–20, "to have some man of qualitye sent Governor unto Virginia ; " patented lands in Virginia in 1621; was living in the Bermudas in 1623, and died there, at Port Royal, February 10, 162⅘, leaving children there. Many of his descendants are now distinguished citizens of the United States.

Darnell Tucker.

Tucker, George, gent., 3. Sub. ——; pd. £12 10s. Eldest brother of Daniel ; was of Milton in Kent ; married, first, Elizabeth, daughter of Francis Staughton, and, secondly, Mary, daughter of John Darrell, of Cadehill, esquire ; by his first wife he had a son, George (aged 25 in 1619), and by his second three sons (John, Robert, and Henry) and six daughters. He was of the N. W. P. Co.; held ten shares of land in the Bermudas, and was a leading member of the Warwick party in the Va. Co. His daughter Elizabeth married Thomas Legat, half-brother to Capt. John Legat.

His son, Henry Tucker (born in 1611), and probably other sons also,

went to the Bermudas. Their descendants are also in the United States.

George Tucker.

Tucker, John. Probably son of
William Tucker, of Throuley in Devonshire. If so, he was uncle to Daniel
and George Tucker.

Tucker, Lieutenant Thomas.
(Probably brother to John. His granddaughter, Mary Starkey, married
Thomas Young, portreeve of Gravesend and Milton in 1619.)

Tucker, William, gent., 3. Sub.
£37 10s.; pd. £25. (See Capt. James
Erizo.) He sent over two men with
Ralph Hamor in January, 1617, and
either went over at this time, or soon
after, himself ; a member of the First
House of Burgesses for the borough of
" Kiccowtan " (afterwards Elizabeth
City) on July 30, 1619. After the
massacre of March, 1622, he was active in taking revenge upon the Indians. In January, 1623, he was fighting them along the River of Rapahan-
ock, " they being confederates with
Apochankeno ; " a member of the
Council in Virginia prior to March 30,
1623, and continued in that office until
1633, or later. On July 23, 1623,
" Captain William Tucker, commander
of Kicquotan and those lower parts of
the country, fell upon the Nandsa-
monds and Warrasqueakes, with vast
spoil to their corn and habitations, and
no small slaughter." In February,
1625, he was living at Elizabeth City
(aged 36), with his wife Mary (aged
26) and their daughter Elizabeth
(born in Virginia the preceding
August), fourteen white servants,
" William Crawshaw, an Indian Baptised," Anthoney and Isabell, negroes,
and " William theire child, Baptised ; "
of the twenty negroes then in the colony he owned three. He had 150
acres of land in " Elizabeth Cittie and
650 acres on ye south side of the main
River over against Elizabeth Cittie."
He made several voyages to England ;
sailed from Virginia for England in the
spring of 1630, 1632, and 1633, and
possibly made annual voyages. He
was a merchant, a trader, and a protec-
tionist ; in August, 1633, he was in
England, asking the Privy Council to
prevent the Dutch from trading to
Virginia, " praying for a renewal of
their ancient charter, and that their
trade may be carried on wholly by the
English, and the returns made into
England only."

He married Mary, daughter of Robert Thomson, of Watton in Hertfordshire ; she was a sister to the wife of
Elias Roberts, who was interested with
Tucker in the Hamor plantation of
January, 1617. Her brothers, Morris,
George, Paul, and William Thomson,
lived in Virginia for a time, and her
brother Robert owned property in
New England ; they became distinguished men in England, in the time of
the Commonwealth. Morris Thomson
was the father of John, first Baron
Haversham.

Tudor, Elizabeth (Queen). " The
namer of Virginia."

" Spain's Rod, Rome's Ruin, Netherland's Relief,
Heaven's Jem, Earth's Joy, World's Wonder,
  Nature's Chief.
Britain's Blessing, England's Splendor,
Religion's Nurse, the Faith's Defender.
Many Daughters have done vertuously, but thou
  excellest them all.
If Royal Vertues ever crown'd a crown,
If ever Mildness shin'd in Majesty,
If ever Honour honour'd true Renown,
If ever Courage dwelt with Clemency,
If ever Princess put all Princes down,
For Temperance, Prowess, Prudence, Equity,
This, this was she, that in despight of Death,
Lives still admir'd, ador'd, Elizabeth."
  [*From her monument in several London
    churches.*]

Tufton, Sir Nicholas. Sub. ——;
pd. £80. M. P. for Peterborough in
1601 ; knighted at Newcastle-upon-
Tyne, April 13, 1603 ; admitted into
the Va. Co. of London, June 10, 1618,
and added to his Majesty's Council
for that company ; May 17, 1620, one
of those appointed to represent the
company before the king ; May 23,
1620, Anthony Irby transferred to him
two shares of land in Virginia ; M. P.
for Kent, 1624–25 ; elevated to the
peerage, November 1, 1626, as Baron
Tufton of Tufton, County Sussex, and
created Earl of Thanet, August 5,
1628. His lordship married Lady
Frances Cecil, daughter of Thomas,
first Earl of Exeter. He died July 1,
1632, and was buried at Raynham.
His younger brother, Sir William Tufton, was governor of the Barbadoes,
where he was shot in 1650.

Turner, Richard, 2. Sub.——;

pd. £37 10s. Probably the master of tents and toils.

Turner, Richard, merchant-tailor. Pd. £60.

Turner, Dr. (Peter), 2. Sub. ——; pd. £25. Dr. Peter Turner was the son of Dr. William Turner (1510 ?– 1568) one of the first English herbal-ists. He was physician to Ralegh, and made a report in 1606 on the decline of Ralegh's health in the Tower. He died May 27, 1614, aged 72, and was buried in St. Olave's, Tower Street ward, London.

His son, William Turner, who was afterwards interested in Virginia, went, in 1605, to Charles Lee's colony in Guiana, and wrote an account of his voyage, which is given in part by Purchas, vol. iv. pp. 1265–1267.

Turville (or **Turberville**), **Sir Am-brose,** 3. Sub. ——; pd. ——. Of Lincolnshire; knighted at the Charter-house, May 11, 1603 ; M. P. Minehead, 1604–11.

Twide, Richard. Crossed the pres-ent United States in 1568–69 ; died at Ratcliff, England, in John Shere-wood's house there, about 1579.

Twisden, Sir William, 3. Sub. £37 10s. ; pd. £37 10s. Eldest son of Roger Twysden, Esq., of Roydon Hall, Kent, by his wife Anne, daughter of Sir Thomas Wyatt, of Allington Castle, beheaded in 1553 ; M. P. for Helston in 1601; knighted at the Charterhouse, May 11, 1603 ; M. P. Thetford, 1606– 11 and 1614 ; created a baronet, June 29, 1611 ; transferred his three shares in Virginia to his son, Sir Roger Twisden (the antiquary), February 3, 1623; died January 8, 162⅜. He mar-ried Anne, daughter of Sir Moyle Finch, baronet, by whom five sons and two daughters.

Tyndall (or **Tindall**), **Robert,** 3. Sub. ——; pd. ——. First voyage to Virginia, December 19, 1606, possibly to January, 1609 ; second voyage, May to November, 1609 ; third voyage, April, 1610, to June, 1611. It seems certain that Maguel was mistaken about his being a Roman Catholic, as at the time Maguel was writing (July, 1610) Tindall was still actively em-ployed in Virginia.

Tyrone. Hugh O'Neill, Earl of Tyrone, "The Arch Rebel," gave the English much trouble in their attempts

to subdue Ireland. After the flight of the Earls of Tyrone and Tyrconnel, in 1607, their vast estates were forfeited to the crown, as well as those of Sir Cahir O'Dogherty, and other persons of inferior position. These estates, which comprised almost the whole six northern counties of Cavan, Ferman-agh, Armagh, Derry, Tyrone, and Tyr-connel (now called Donegal), were the lands soon after allotted to the Prot-estant and Presbyterian colonists from England and Scotland. Many descendants of these colonists have since emigrated to America.

The Earl of Tyrone died at Rome, blind and old, on July 20, 1616, and was buried with great pomp in the Church of San Pietro Montorio, under a tomb, which no longer exists, bearing the following brief inscription : —

"D.   O.   M.
Hic Quiescunt Ossa
Hugonis Principis O'Neill."

Tyrrel, Francis, grocer, 2. Sub. —— ; pd. ——. Will was dated Au-gust 30, 1609. Buried September 1, 1609, at Croydon, and his funeral was kept at London, the 13th of the same month. He gave £200 to the parish-ioners of Croydon, to build a new mar-ket-house; £40 to repair their church, and forty shillings a year to the poor of Croydon for eighteen years; twenty-six chaldrons of coals yearly, to be paid by the Grocers' Company to the poor of the parishes of St. Mary Mag-dalen Bermondsey ; St. Giles Crip-plegate ; St. Sepulchre Without New-gate ; St. Olave Southwark, and St. Botolph Aldgate ; and also fourteen chaldrons of sea coals to the poor of the Grocers' Company.

Van Lore, Peter. Pd. £112 10s. A native of Utrecht ; traded in Lon-don, and became an opulent merchant, jeweler, and money-lender of that city. In 1595 he tested for Ralegh some stones brought from Guiana. In 1603 Ralegh owed him some £600. Edwards preserved Ralegh's letter to him of July 1, 1616 (in his " Life of Ralegh," vol. ii. pp. 342, 343); knighted November 5, 1621, and soon after lent King James £20,000 on eight per cent. interest which was repaid by an ex-chequer warrant, July 31, 1625 ; died prior to August, 1628, leaving a son of the same name, who was created a baronet in that year, whose daughter Mary married Henry Alexander, third son of William, first Earl of Stirling.

Van Medkerk, Alfonsus. Pd. £25. He was a captain and a Dutchman. Probably a son of Adolphus Van Meetkerke, president of Flanders, who died in London, October 6, 1591, aged 63.

Vane (see **Fane**), **Henry**, esquire, 3. Sub. £75 ; pd. £12 10s. Of Hadlow, Kent ; born February 18, 1589 ; knighted at Whitehall, March 28, 1611 ; M. P. for Lostwithiel, 1614 ; cofferer to Charles, Prince of Wales, March, 1617 ; M. P. for Carlisle, 1621–22, 1624–25, 1625, and 1626 ; was elected for Lostwithiel also in Parliaments of 1621–22 and 1625, but probably selected to sit for Carlisle ; was M. P. for Retford, 1628–29 ; ambassador to Holland, Denmark, and Sweden, 1631 and 1632 ; received Charles I. at Raby Castle, May, 1633; was on the commission for plantations of April, 1634, at which time he was comptroller of the royal household ; treasurer of the household, 1639; postmaster-general, 1640 ; M. P. for Wilton, 1640 and 1640–53 ; principal secretary of state and lord treasurer, and sworn of the Privy Council in 1641, and subsequently dismissed from these offices, it is said, on account of the active part which he took against Strafford ; M. P. for Kent in 1654 ; died at Raby Castle near the close of 1654 (March, 1655 ?). Ancestor of the Dukes of Cleveland. When his son Henry went to New England in 1635, G. Garrard wrote to Lord Conway : "Sir Henry Vane has as good as lost his eldest son, who is gone to New England for conscience sake ; he likes not the discipline of the church of England, none of our ministers will give him the sacrament standing, and no persuasions of the Bishops nor authority of his parents will prevail with him ; let him go." He was elected governor of Massachusetts in 1636, but returned to England in 1637. He was the celebrated Sir Harry Vane of Cromwell's day, who was beheaded on Tower Hill in 1662 (see his Life by Prof. James K. Hosmer).

Vassall, John, gent., 2. Sub. ——; pd. £25. "His father, John Vassall, a Frenchman (Huguenot) of Rinart by Cane in Normandy, was sent into England by his father by reason of the troubles then." He died in England, leaving a son, John (of whom I write) of Cockseyhurst in Com. Essex, who in 1588 equipped and commanded two ships of war, the Samuel and the Little Toby, against the Spanish Armada. He was an alderman of London, and at his death a benefactor of the Trinity House ; buried at Stepney, September 13, 1625. He married three times and had a numerous issue. His sons, Samuel and William, were among the incorporators of the first Massachusetts Company, 1628. Samuel was baptized at Stepney, June 5, 1586 ; married Frances, daughter of Abraham Cartwright of the Va. Co. ; was interested with George Lord Berkeley and others in the settlement of Carolina, 1630 ; traded to New England, Virginia, the West Indies, and Guinea ; M. P. for London in the Long Parliament ; on the parliament commissions for plantations, November 24, 1643 ; "it is all but certain that he died somewhere in America in 1667." There is, or was, a monument to him in King's Chapel, Boston, Mass. His son John died in London in 1664, without issue. William (Samuel's brother) was born in 1592 ; married, in May, 1613, Anne, daughter of George King, of Cold Norton, Essex ; sailed with his family from London in June, 1635, on board the Blessing, for New England, and settled in Scituate within the colony of Plymouth ; went to the Barbadoes about 1650, and died there in 1655. "It is now quite certain that it was he, and not his brother Samuel, who founded the Vassalls of Jamaica, whence sprang the late Lord Holland." He has many descendants in the United States.

Vaughan, Edward, 2. Sub. ——; pd. ——. Probably Edward Vaughn, Esq., of Little Ealing, county of Middlesex, who died in 1612. (Vaughans were numerous.) An Edward Vaughan was the author of "Divine Discovery of Death" in 1612, and other works. An Edward Vaughan was M. P. for Merioneth in 1626.

Vaughan, John, esquire, 3. Sub. £75; pd. ——. Probably John Vaughan, son and heir to Owen Vaughan of

Llwydiarth, which John married, November 3, 1606, Margaret Herbert, sister of George Herbert, the poet; or, John Vaughan, the brother of "Sir William Vaughan of Terracoyd, County Carmarthen, who had also lands in Newfoundland and America," which John (born 1573) married, in 1598, Margaret, daughter of Sir Gilly Meyrick, was knighted in Ireland, February 2, 1617; created Lord Vaughan, July 29, 1621, and Earl of Carbery, August 5, 1628.

Vaughan, Sir Walter, 3. Sub. £37 10s.; pd. £37 10s. Of Fulston, County Wilts; son of Thomas Vaughan, Esq., of Broadwardine, County Hereford; knighted at Sir George Farmers in July, 1603; M. P. for Wiltshire, February, 1606, to 1611. He married three times, and was still living in 1623.

Velasco, Don Alonso de. Ambassador from Spain to the court of London, 1610–13. August 3, 1612, George Abbot, Archbishop of Canterbury, wrote from Croydon to King James: "Zuñiga has removed to the house of the Lieger Ambassador, Alonzo de Velasquez, in the Barbican, that he may more freely transact his secret business. Velasquez (Velasco) has been more free with his masses, having a bell rung and holding several in the day. He sends scandalous reports of English affairs to Spain and Italy. The King of Spain has an advantage in England, because he can avail himself of discontented Catholics. The proffered courtesies of the Queen of France should be received with suspicion, as she is guided by Villeroy and Sillery, both under Spanish influence."

Velasco, Juan Ferdinand de. "Condestable of Castile, Duke of Frias;" was Spanish ambassador extraordinary to England in 1604. Reports reached London in November and December, 1603, that he was coming to treat of peace. He was in London early in August, 1604, and on the 10th Henry Howard, Earl of Northampton, wrote to King James: "The Constable of Castile is delighted with his reception, and praises his Majesty's learning, sweetness, frankness, and faithfulness." On the 18th of August the treaty of peace and mercantile intercourse with Philip III., King of Spain, and Albert and Isabel, archduke and archduchess of Burgundy, was ratified by King James of England, and soon after, Velasco returned to Spain with many rich presents from the King and Queen of England.

He had served in the Low Country wars. Motley says he was "one of Spain's richest grandees and poorest generals."

Venn, Richard, haberdasher, 2. Sub. ——; pd. £12 10s. Son of Hugh Fenn, *alias* Venn, of Wotton-under-Edge, Gloucestershire. October 13, 1616, half of the late Raphe Hamor the elder's adventure of £1,600 in the joint stock of the E. I. Co. was set over to Richard Venne, at the request of Susan Hamor, the executrix of her deceased husband. On the committee of the E. I. Co. in 1619; an alderman of London, 1626–34, for Castle Baynard ward, and 1634–39 for Tower ward; sheriff of London, 1626–27; lord mayor, 1637–38; knighted at Whitehall, May 27, 1638; died August 18, 1639.

Vere, Sir Horatio, 2. Sub. ——; pd. £121. Youngest son of Geoffrey De Vere, third son of John, fifteenth Earl of Oxford; was born in Essex in 1565; accompanied his brother, Sir Francis Vere, to Holland in 1585, and to Cadiz in 1596, where he was knighted for gallantry by the Earl of Essex. He distinguished himself at Nieuport in 1600 and at Ostend in 1601–02, where he was wounded. He was one of the governors of the Brill, 1608 to May 30, 1616. M. C. for Va. Co., May 23, 1609. He served at the siege of Juliers in 1610; in the Low Countries, 1614; commanded the English contingent, aiding the Prince of Orange against the Arminians of Utrecht in 1618. In 1620 he was consulted about certain projected fortifications in Virginia, and was in the same year in command of the auxiliaries sent to Elector Palatine. Chamberlain writing to Carleton from London, July 8, 1620, said: "I am sorry Sir Horace Vere should go so slenderly accompanied as to command but two thousand men, which gives the Spanish ambassador occasion to break jests, and say, he must needs confess we are a very brave nation, that dare adventure with two thousand men to encounter ten thousand." He continued in that service, and "on February 16, 1622, Sir Horatio Vere was appointed captain-general of 8,000 foot and 1,600 horse for the defence of the Palatinate." There was some clash of authority, and on June 3, 1622, King James wrote to him, commanding him "to withdraw his troops, if his son-in-law persisted in following his own courses."

He was forced to surrender Mannheim to Tilly, according to some accounts, in the end of September, 1622; to others in January, 1623.

In 1622 the poet George Chapman wrote : "Pro Vere Autumni Lachrymae. Inscribed to the Immortal Memorie of the most Pious and Incomparable Souldier Sir Horatio Vere, Knight ; besieged and distrest in Mainhem."

He was created Baron Vere of Tilbury, July 25, 1625 ; master of the ordnance for life in March, 1629 ; died in London, May 2, 1635, and was interred in Westminster Abbey.

"The exploits of this gallant personage form a brilliant page in British history, and it would be in vain to attempt even to epitomize them here. He was so great a military officer that the first generals were proud of having served under him."

Fuller says : "Horace Lord Vere had more meekness and as much valour as his brother Sir Francis ; of an excellent temper : it being true of him what is said of the Caspian Sea, that it doth never ebb, nor flow, observing a constant tenor, neither elated with success or depressed with misfortune. Both lived in war much honoured, and died in peace much lamented."

Lord Vere married, in November, 1607, Mary, daughter of Sir John Tracy of Toddington, County Gloucester, and relict of William (or John) Hoby, Esq., and had five daughters, his co-heirs (see Throckmorton pedigree.)

His widow survived him many years. "Upon the death of the Countess of Dorset, the Parliament committed to her care the Duke of York, the Duke of Gloucester, and the Princess Elizabeth, a charge of which she was by no means ambitious. She was a woman of exemplary conduct as a wife and mother, and seems to have been as eminent for her piety as her husband was for his valour." Archbishop Usher, in a letter to her in 1628, speaks of it in a very elevated strain : "If I have any insight," says that prelate, "in things of this nature, or have any judgment to discern of spirits, I have clearly beheld engraven in your soul *the image and superscription of my God.*" She died the 25th of December, 1671, in the 91st year of her age.

Her five daughters were : Elizabeth Vere, married John, son of John Hollis, first Earl of Clare ; Mary Vere, married, first, Sir Roger Townshend, secondly, Lord Mildmay Fane ; Catherine Vere, married, first, Oliver, son of Sir John St. John, and, secondly, John Lord Paulett ;[1] Anne Vere, married the celebrated Thomas Lord Fairfax, "the parliamentary general"; Dorothy Vere, married John, son of Sir John Wolstenholme. (See "The Fighting Veres," by Clements R. Markham.)

Vere-Stanley, "Elizabeth, Countess of Derby," 3. Sub. —— ; pd. ——. Eldest daughter of Edward De Vere, seventeenth Earl of Oxford, by his first wife, Anne, daughter of William Cecil, the celebrated Lord (Treasurer) Burghley. She married, June 26, 1594, William Stanley, sixth Earl of Derby, and had four daughters and two sons.

Vertue, Christopher, vintner, 2. Sub. —— ; pd. £12 10s. Of St. Botolph, Aldgate, London ; married, in 1583, Margaret, daughter of William Joanes of Kyvell, County Wilts, clothier.

Villa Flores. See Zuñiga.

Villeroy, Mons de. Nicolas de Neufville ; born 1542 ; secretary of state, November, 1567; deprived September, 1588 ; reinstated 1594 ; died at Rouen, November 22, 1617.

Villiers, George, Viscount. Born at Brookesby, Leicestershire, August 20, 1592 ; in France, 1610-13 (his half-sister, Anne Villiers, married,

---

[1] The marriage license of Sir John Paulett, dated March 6, 1640-1, does not give the name of the bride as Catherine, but as "Mrs. Mary St. John about 22. daughter of the Right Hon. the Lord Vere."

about 1614, William Washington, uncle to the emigrant ancestor of Gen. George Washington); introduced at court in the autumn of 1614; knighted at Somerset House, April 24, 1615; favored by Somerset's enemies; advocated Ralegh's going to Guiana; made master of the horse in January, and K. G. in April, 1616; Baron Whaddon ("Blechly"?) and Viscount Villiers, August 27, 1616; the royal favorite; Bacon's advice to him; made Earl of Buckingham, January 5, 1617, marquess, January 1, 1618, and lord high admiral, January, 28, 1619. Sir Edwin Sandys wrote to him June 7, 1620, justifying his (Sandys') management of Virginia affairs, and imploring him " by the many great graces wherewith God had furnished him, to protect and repatriate the long exiled (Sandys) in His Majesties favour." He was an incorporator of the New England Charter, November 3, 1620, and M. C. for N. E. Co.; signed the first Plymouth patent, June 1, 1621; went with Prince Charles to Spain, February 17, 1623; created Duke of Buckingham, May 18, 1623 (there had been no dukes in England since Norfolk's execution, June 2, 1572); was interested in Virginia affairs, tobacco, etc., 1624; sent to Paris to marry Henrietta Maria as proxy for King Charles, May, 1625; John Tradescant was employed by him in procuring "all manner of rare beasts, fowls and birds, shells and stones, etc," "especially those from Virginia, Bermudas, Newfoundland, Guinea, Binney, the Amazon, and the East Indies," in July, 1625, and after; impeached March, 1626; chancellor of the University of Cambridge, June 1, 1626; still interested in the colonies; an incorporator of the Guiana Company, May 19, and chosen governor of that company in June, 1627; commanded in the expeditions to Rochelle and Isle of Ré, July to October, 1627; murdered at Portsmouth August 23, 1628. Two days after this (25), Lord Baltimore wrote a long letter to him from Ferryland, Newfoundland. He was a great patron of learning, and of the fine arts; collected American rarities, Arabic manuscripts, Italian paintings, etc.

Vincent, Henry, 2. Sub. £37

10s.; pd. £37 10s. Of London, merchant; was living at the Visitation, 1634, aged 80 years.

Vines, Richard. A trusted agent and friend of Sir Ferdinando Gorges. I am unable to add anything to the incomplete accounts of him previously published in this country. He probably visited the New England coast as early as 1609, and probably spent the winter of 1616–17 at the mouth of Saco River, where he afterwards settled; had a grant of land there, and became the founder of Biddeford, Maine. He removed to Barbadoes in 1645, and died there in 1651.

Wade — Waad, Armigil, "The British Columbus." Of an ancient family of Yorkshire; went to America in 1536; clerk of the Privy Council of Kings Henry VIII. and Edward VI.; M. P. for Wycombe, 1547–53; died at Belsize, June 20, 1568; buried in the parish church at Hampstead. "He was most completely furnished with the knowledge of the greatest arts, skilled in many languages, discharged most honourable embassies, and among the Britons was the first explorer of the American Indies. He married two wives, Alice Paten and Anne Marbury, and begot 20 children."

Wade (or Waad), Nathaniel, 2. Sub. ——; pd. £25. Of the E. I. Co.

Wade, Sir William, 2. Sub. £75; pd. £144 10s. "Son of Armigell Wade, the British Columbus;" clerk of the Privy Council (from about 1583); successively ambassador to Spain, France, and Scotland. "An active enemy to the Jesuits;" "about 1584 Creighton, a Scottish Jesuit, being taken by Dutch Pirates, tore up certain papers and attempted to throw them into the sea; but the wind brought them back to the ship; which being delivered to Sir William Wade, were joyned again, and revealed new plots of the Pope, the Spaniard, and Guisians to invade England," etc. In Bishop Carleton's "Thankful Remembrance of God's Mercy" is a small picture of Wade, represented in the act of putting the fragments of these treasonable papers together.

M. P. for Aldborough in 1585; for Thetford in 1597; and Preston in

1601 ; knighted at Greenwich, May 20, 1603 ; one of the judges on Ralegh's trial in November, 1603 ; M. P. for West Looe, 1604–11 ; lieutenant of the Tower from August 15, 1605, to May, 1613, when he was removed by the Somerset influence. In 1605–06 he was very active in prosecuting the Gunpowder Plot conspirators. M. C. for Va., 1606 ; M. C. for Va. Co., 1609.

In 1612 John Taylor, the water poet, dedicated his earliest publication, "The Sculler," etc., "To the Right Worshipfull and worthy favourer of learning, my singular good Maister, Sir William Waad, knight," etc. He was one of those who bought the Bermudas Islands from the Va. Co. November 25, 1612, and resigned them to the crown, November 23, 1614.

After his removal from the lieutenancy of the Tower, he seems to have lived quietly at his seat, Belsize House ; died October 25, 1623, and lies buried with his father at Hampstead.

Granger says he was "a man of great learning, generosity, and benevolence, who had been employed by Queen Elizabeth in several embassies, was removed from the lieutenancy of the Tower, to make way for Sir Gervase Elways, a man of a prostitute character, who was the chief instrument in poisoning Sir Thomas Overbury."

"Lloyd tells us that to his directions we owe ' Rider's Dictionary ; ' to his encouragement, ' Hooker's Polity ; ' and to his charge, ' Gruter's Inscriptions.' "

"This excellent man employed a faithful and judicious friend to admonish him of everything that he saw amiss in his conduct."

His first wife (married in 1586), Anne, daughter of Owen Waller, of St. Alban, Wood Street, London, "conspicuous in disposition, genius, and family," died in 1589, in her 19th year, in childbirth, and is buried under a "Fair Marble Monument in Oval" in the parish church of St. Alban's, Wood Street, in Cripplegate ward, London. There is some confusion as to his second wife. Walford says, " He married as his second wife a daughter of Sir Thomas Wotton, who surviving as his widow . . . left Bel-

size to her son, Charles Henry de Kirkhaven, by her first husband." Burke says, "Katherine, daughter of Thomas Lord Wotton, married, first, Henry Lord Stanhope, secondly, John Poliander Kirckhoven (and had a son, Charles Henry Kirckhoven), and, thirdly, Colonel Daniel O'Neile."

The life of Thomas Bushell (Lord Bacon's servant) states that he married " Anne, widow of Sir William Waad, lieutenant of the Tower."

Waiman. See Weymouth.

Waldo, Captain Richard, 2. Sub. —— ; pd. ——. Came to Virginia in 1608 ; was drowned in James River in January, 1609.

Wale, Thomas, 3. Sub. £37 10s.; pd. £75. Of Bradfield, County Essex, and of Gray's Inn. Eldest son of Thomas Wale, of Radwinter, Essex, by Jane, daughter of Richard Westley ; died in 1659.

Walker, George, sadler, 2. Sub. —— ; pd. £25.

Walker, John. "John Walker and his company, in the service of Sir H. Gilbert, discovered a silver mine within the river of Norumbega (the Penobscot, Maine ?) in 1580." Gilbert had a conference with him as to America to the southwest of Cape Breton prior to August, 1582. It may be that he was the chaplain to Robert Dudley, Earl of Leicester, who sailed with Fenton and died at sea February 5, 158⅔.

Walker, Thomas, esquire, 2. Sub. —— ; pd. £25. Of Westminster, hereditary chief usher of the court of Exchequer, and marshal proclamator and barrier of the court of Common

SIR HENRY WOTTON

Pleas, and to the justices in eyre; died October 12, 1613.

Waller (see **Wooler**), **John,** esquire, 2. Sub. ——; pd. £5. Went to Virginia in 1606. (John Waller and John Walter are sometimes mistaken for each other in reading the Virginia Records. I suppose that Waller was of the same family as the poet.)

Wallingford, Viscount. — William Knollys.

Walsingham, Sir Francis. "The third and youngest son of William Walsingham of Scadbury in the parish of Chislehurst, by Joyce, daughter of Edmund Denny of Cheshurst, in Hertfordshire; born about 1536; bred in his father's house under a private tutor, and afterwards studied for a time in King's College in Cambridge, from whence he went, very young, to seek a more enlarged education on the continent. The persecution raised by Mary induced him to remain abroad till her death, for his family were zealous Protestants, and he was earnestly attached to that persuasion. He returned soon after the accession of Elizabeth, a self-made statesman, with a perfect knowledge of most of the European languages, for he had always the reputation of being the first linguist of his time." M. P. for Banbury, 1559; ambassador to France in 1561, "where he served, from time to time, many years with the most refined diplomatic skill, during the dreadful civil war." M. P. for Lyme Regis, 1563; ambassador to France from August, 1570, to April, 1573 (in which time the fearful massacre of St. Bartholomew, August, 1572); principal secretary of state and privy councilor, 1573; subscriber to Frobisher's voyages, 1576–78; knighted at Windsor in November, 1577, and in the same month consulted Dr. Dee regarding Queen Elizabeth's titles to the new lands; ambassador to the Netherlands in 1578, in which year Thomas Nicholas dedicated "The Pleasant Historie of the Conquest of the West Indies" to him; took an interest in the schemes for colonizing America, 1579–80; ambassador to France, 1581; subscriber to Fenton's voyage, 1582–83; took a very active part in the colonization movement from August,

1582, to April, 1583; ambassador to Scotland, 1583; sent the Rev. Richard Hakluyt to Paris (with Stafford), with special instructions to occupy himself chiefly in collecting information of the Spanish and French movements, "making diligent inquirie of such things as might yield any light unto our Western discoverie in America," etc., in October, 1583. In November of the same year Sir George Peckham dedicated his "True Reporte . . . of the Newfoundlands" to him; one of the commission for confirming Ralegh's patent, December 14, 1584; Hakluyt wrote to him from Paris in 1584 and 1585 regarding western discoveries, colonization, etc.; Lane wrote letters and discourses to him from Virginia in August and September, 1585, and Sir Richard Greenville reported to him on his return from Virginia, October 29, 1585; discovered Babington's plot, 1586; a commissioner at the trial of Mary Queen of Scots, October, 1586; made chancellor of the Duchy of Lancaster in 1587, and afterwards a Knight of the Garter. Hakluyt dedicated his "Principal Navigations," etc., to him in 1589. He died April 6, 1590, and was buried in St. Paul's. "One of the chief pillars of the throne of Elizabeth and of the Protestant cause." A leader in the schemes for colonizing Protestantism in the New World. He married, first, about 1563, Anne Barnes (see Sir George Barnes the elder), and, secondly, about 1569, Ursula, daughter of Henry St. Barbe, and widow of Richard Worsley, who bore him two daughters, Mary and Frances. Mary married Capt. Christopher Carleill. Frances was thrice splendidly wedded: first, to Sir Philip Sidney; secondly, to Robert Devereux, Earl of Essex, and, thirdly, to Richard Bourke, Earl of Clanricarde.

Walsingham, Sir Thomas, 3. Sub. £37 10s.; pd. £37 10s. Of Scadbury, Kent; grandson of Sir Edmund Walsingham, lieutenant of the Tower of London, who died February 9, 15$\frac{48}{50}$. He was born in 1570; M. P. Rochester, 1597–98, 1601, and 1604–11; Kent 1614; died August 11, 1630.

Walter, John, esquire, 3. Sub. £37 10s.; pd. £37 10s. Eldest son of Edward Walter of Ludlow in the county of Salop, by his wife Mary, daughter of Thomas Hackluit, Esq., of Eyton (the eldest brother of the Rev. Richard Hakluyt, I suppose). He was born in 1563 ; educated at Brasenose College, Oxford ; afterwards of the Inner Temple ; called to the bar, 1590 ; counselor for the University of Oxford ; attorney-general to Prince Charles, 1613–25 ; knighted May 18, 1619 ; M. P. for East Looe in 1621–22 and 1624–25 ; serjeant at law, 1625 ; chief baron of the Exchequer, May 12, 1625 ; died at his house in the Savoy, November 18, 1630, and was buried at Wolvercote, Oxon. One of Fuller's Worthies of Shropshire.

Ward, William. Pd. £37 10s. "Marshal of the Admiralty court of the Cinque Ports." The Wards and Pophams were related.

Warner, Mr. Probably Walter Warner, the mathematician.

Warner, Richard, 3. Sub. £37 10s. ; pd. ——. Probably "Richard Warner, of London, grocer, son of John Warner, of Bucknall in County Oxon." (*Vide* Visitation, 1634.)

Warr, Thomas, esquire, 3. Sub. £37 10s.; pd. £25. Of Hestercombe, Somerset. Third son of Roger Warr by Eleanor, daughter of Sir John Popham. M. C. for Va., 1606 ; M. P. Bridgewater, 1614.

Chamberlain, writing to Carleton from London, April 19, 1617, says, " One Warre, a towardly lawyer, was drowned coming from an island he had purchased in the Severn ; " and Carew, writing to Roe, under April, 1617, says, " Mr. Thomas Warre, a counciler-att-Law, who, I think, was well knowne unto you, is lately drowned in Severne in Walles." He was recorder of Bridgewater, and was buried there, April 30, 1617.

Warwick, Earl of. — Robert Rich.

Waterhouse (see **Woodhouse**), **David,** esquire, 2. Sub. £37 10s. ; pd. £37 10s. M. P. for Aldborough (York), 1588–89, and for Berwick, 1601 ; clerk of the crown in the King's Bench ; lord of the Manor of the town of Halifax. September 16, 1618, he passed a Bill of Adventure of £50 in the Va. Co. to Mr. Bland.

Waterhouse, Sir Edward, 2. Sub. —— ; pd. £25. Of Leith, County York ; son of Robert Water house of Halifax, and nephew of David Waterhouse, Esq., aforesaid. He was knighted at Charterhouse, May 11, 1603 ; died without issue.

Waterhouse, Edward. Probably son of Thomas Waterhouse of Barkhamsted, County Hertford. If so, he was nephew of the celebrated Sir Edward Waterhouse (1535–91), and uncle of Edward Waterhouse (1619–70), an author of some note.

He was a secretary of the Va. Co., and June 11, 1621, he was recommended by Sir John Danvers for secretary of state for the colony of Virginia, but in the election was defeated by Mr. Christopher Davison. November 21, 1621, the council gave him two shares of land in Virginia. August 21, 1622, there was entered for publication at Stationers' Hall " A Booke called A Declaration of the State of the Colony of Virginia with the relation of the Massacre of the English by the Native Infidells with the names of those that were then massacred." This book was written by Waterhouse, " Published by Authoritie," and " Imprinted at London by G. Eld, for Robert Mylbourne, and are to be sold at his shop, at the great South doore of Pauls, 1622."

January 28, 1624, Waterhouse was one of those who examined, compared, and signed the first volume of the Virginia Company's Records now preserved in the library of Congress at Washington.

Waters, Edward. Born about 1585 ; in the service of Sir George Somers ; with him in the shipwreck at the Bermudas in 1609; went with him in the Patience to Virginia in 1610, and in the same year returned with him to the Bermudas. When Matthew Somers sailed for England, he was one of the three who remained to keep possession of the island, and who found the historic piece of " Amber Greece." He remained in the Bermudas until about November, 1615, at which time he was a member of the council, and went to the West Indies for supplies. The badly mixed-up and unfriendly account of this voyage given in Smith's History is the only account that I have seen. He left the Bermudas for Virginia in 1618 or 1619 ;

married, probably about 1620, Grace O'Niel, and at the great massacre of March, 1622, himself and wife were taken prisoners by the Nansemund Indians, but finally made their escape. In January, 1625, he was living, aged forty, with his wife, aged twenty-one, and two children, William and Margaret, both born in Virginia, at Blount Point, Elizabeth City. He was a captain, a burgess, and a justice of Elizabeth City, and was still living in March, 1629, but died soon after. His wife, who survived him nearly fifty-three years, married, secondly, Col. Obedience Robins.

The descendants of Capt. Edward Waters are numerous and respectable (some of them highly honorable) citizens of this country, and it gives me pleasure to be able to clear their ancestor of the crime of murder, which Capt. John Smith fastened on him. The real murderer was a sailor, named Robert Waters; he it was who remained in the Bermudas with Christopher Carter when Gates sailed to Virginia in May, 1610. He returned to England with Capt. Matthew Somers; entered the service of the E. I. Co., and died at sea on the voyage to East India, August 6, 1614, "a man long diseased in bodie, disturbed in minde by torment of conscience, for a man by him killed in Virginia."

Watson, Thomas, esquire, 2. Sub. £75; pd. £112 10s. September 28, 1601, Sir George Carey wrote to the Mayor of Totness and his brethren, "begging them to confer a burgesshipp [M. P.] upon Mr. Thomas Watson." He was a teller of the exchequer; M. C. for Va. Co., 1612; of the N. W. P. Co., 1612; M. P. Rye, 1614; knighted at Halstead, June 25, 1618, as of Kent.

Wattey, William, 2. Sub. ——; pd. £25.

Watts, Sir John, clothworker, 2. Sub. £37 10s.; pd. £162 10s. "Son to Thomas Watts of Buntingford in Hertfordshire"; married, probably before 1568, Margaret, daughter of Sir James Hawes, Lord Mayor of London in 1574–75. On the 20th of March, 1591, three ships, furnished "at the special charges of Mr. John Wattes, of London, merchant," sailed for the relief of Ralegh's colony. In

1593 his fleet was before Havana (Cuba), "wayting for purchase." In a cause between Sir M. Morgan and himself, he was designated as "Alderman Watts," May 17, 1593. "He was elected alderman of Aldersgate ward, October 26, 1594; chosen sheriff, June 24, 1596." In 1598 Capt. John Watts (probably the alderman's son) commanded the Prosperous in the Earl of Cumberland's voyage to Saint John de Porto Rico. November 1, 1600, the Court of Adventurers to the East Indies resolved that "Alderman Watts, on account of his great experience in shipping and other directions in voyages to be used as a committee in all things concerning the business." An incorporator of the E. I. Co., December 31, 1600; governor of the company from April 11, 1601, to July, 1602 (Sir Thomas Smythe having been implicated in the Essex insurrection); removed to Tower ward, April 21, 1601; knighted at Whitehall, July 26, 1603; removed to Aldersgate, May 29, 1605; and to Langbourn, January 28, 160⅚; Lord Mayor of London, 1606–07; a member of the Clothworkers' Company, and on June 12, 1607, he entertained King James I. at his house, adjoining Clothworkers' Hall, "on which occasion the King was made a free Brother of the Clothworkers' Company, to whose Hall they adjourned for the purpose."

M. C. for Va. Co., 1609; member of the Bermudas Company, 1615. "He died in September, 1616, and was buried at Ware, Hertfordshire, September 7, 1616." Chamberlain wrote to Carleton in his gazette letter of October 12, 1616, "Sir John Watts, our neighbour at Ware, died likewise upon two days' warning, being as lusty a man of his years as I know any." In his will "he left a sum of £4 per annum for the relief of the poor of Buntingford, Herts, his native place; £10 to Christ's Hospital, and £20 to St. Thomas's Hospital in Southwark, London."

His eldest son, also Sir John Watts, was knighted at Plymouth, September 23, 1625. About 1626 he wrote "A Discourse upon Trade." In 1629 he was consulted as "a seaman of great note" regarding the differences between Lords Carlisle and Montgomery concerning their possessions in the West Indies. About 1637 he wrote a treatise, setting forth a design for the taking of Hispaniola, entitled "This relation is for future times," etc.

Waynam. See Weynman.

Webbe, Edward, 2. Sub. ——; pd. £100. Probably the author of "The Rare and most Wonderful Things which Edward Webbe, an Englishman borne, hath seene and passed in his troublesome Travailes, in the cities of Jerusalem, Dammaske, Bethlem, and Galely; and in the Landes of Jewrie, Egipt, Grecia, Russia, and in the Land of Prester John, etc., London, 1590." The women were not so kind to Webbe as they were to Capt. John Smith.

Webbe, Captain George. Captain of the Lion; was living in Virginia in 1616.

Webbe, Richard, haberdasher, 2. Sub. £37 10s.; pd. £62 10s.

Webbe, Sandys, esquire, 2. Sub. ——; pd. £12 10s.

Webbe, Thomas, esquire, 2. Sub. ——; pd. £12 10s.

Webbe, Thomas, 2. Sub. ——; pd. ——. One of these, Thomas Webbes, went to Virginia in 1606, and was still living July 10, 1621, when the company allowed him three shares of land on account of his services in Virginia, and one of them was probably a member of the Massachusetts Company.

Webster, William, 2. Sub. ——; pd. £37 10s. Probably related to John Webster, the dramatist.

Weeks, Thomas, clothworker. Pd. £12 10s.

Welby, William, stationer, 2. Sub. £37 10s.; pd. £87 10s. He sold five shares of land in the Bermudas to Robert Rich, second Earl of Warwick.

Welch, Edward, 2. Sub. ——; pd. £25.

Weld, Sir Humphrey, grocer, 2. Sub. ——; pd. £37 10s. Fourth son of John Weld, of Eaton in Cheshire, by his wife Joanna, daughter of John FitzHugh of Congleton; born about 1546; admitted as a member of the Court of Assistants of the Grocers' Company, May 3, 1596; assessed at £60 for his share of the Grocers' Company's contribution towards loan levied on the city of London by the queen in 1598; an alderman of London for Farringdon ward; sheriff of London in 1599; a member of the Rus. Co.; knighted by King James, July 26, 1603; Lord Mayor of London, 1608–09; M. C. for Va. Co., 1609. He took an active part in advancing the interest of the Virginia colony during the term of his mayoralty.

He gave £100 to be distributed among the several hospitals; died November 29, 1610, aged 64, and is buried in St. Olave's, London; married Mary Ann, daughter of Nicholas Wheeler, Esq., and left a son and successor, John Weld, afterwards knighted, who was also interested in Virginia.

In the Warden's Accounts of the Grocers' Company, A. D. 1610–11, is the following: "Item, Received of the Right Worshipful Dame Mary Weld wydowe and John Weld Esqre Executors of the Right worshipful Sir Humfrey Weld knight deceased the the some of £20 by him given to make a dynner for the Livery of this Company attending his corps to Church on the day of his funeral."

Weld, John, esquire, 3. Sub. £37 10s.; pd. £37 10s. Of Arnolds, County Middlesex; son of Sir Humfrey aforesaid; founder of Southgate Chapel, Edmonton parish, Middlesex, which was consecrated by Bishop King in 1615. I take him to be the Sir John Wilde who was knighted at Theobald's, November 11, 1617. He died in 1622, and was buried in the chapel, Edmonton, where there is a monument to his memory. He married Frances, daughter of William Whitmore, Esq., and was the ancestor of the Welds of Lulworth, Dorset.

Weld, John, gentleman. N. Fld. Co. Son of John Weld, of London; was a first cousin to John Weld, esquire and knight, aforesaid. He was "of London Towne Clarke and of Willey Com. Sallop Esqr," and was living in 1633 (see Visitation, ii. 336); admitted to the office of town clerk, April 27, 1613; discharged by Common Council, October 27, 1642; knighted in 1642; readmitted town clerk, September 21, 1660, and died in 1666; married Elizabeth, eldest daughter of Sir William Romney of London, knight and alderman.

Welles, Thomas, grocer, 2. Sub. ——; pd. £25. There was a William Wells, grocer, at this time; but no Thomas. However, there was a Thomas Wells of London, mercer. I suppose this to be either William Welles, grocer, or Thomas Welles, mercer. There must be a mistake either as to his Christian name, or as to his occupation.

Wentworth, Sir John. Sub. £37 10s.; pd. £12 10s. Of Gosfield, County Essex; licensed to travel for three years, February 20, 1604; again licensed to travel for three years, July 25, 1609; created a baronet, June 29, 1611; married a daughter of Sir Moyle Finch; died in October, 1631. He was probably M. P. for Wotton Basset in 1601.

Wentworth, Thomas, esquire, 3. Sub.——; pd. ——. This was either Thomas Wentworth, Esq., of North Elmsal, Yorkshire, born about 1590, and died in 1650, who married, first, Mary, daughter of Sir William Bamborough, and, secondly, Martha, daughter of Sir Thomas Hayes, Lord Mayor of London; or Thomas Wentworth, Esq., of Wentworth Woodhouse in Yorkshire, born April 13, 1593; the unfortunate statesman, so well known in history as the Earl of Strafford; beheaded on Tower Hill, May 12, 1641. He married, first, Lady Margaret Clifford, daughter of Francis, Earl of Cumberland, and, secondly, Lady Arabella Holles, daughter of John, Earl of Clare.

West Pedigree. (Extract.) Sir Thomas West[1], second Lord De la Warr, of the new creation, married, November 19, 1571, Anne, daughter of Sir Francis Knollys, by his wife, Katherine Cary (first cousin to Queen Elizabeth, and sister to Henry Cary, first Lord Hunsdon), and had issue, thirteen children, as follows:—

i. Elizabeth, born September 11, 1573; sponsors in baptism, Queen Elizabeth, the Countess of Lincoln[2], and the Earl of Leicester[3]. (She married, in 1594, Herbert Pelham, Sr., and had issue, Thomas Pelham, Esq., of the Va. Co)

ii. Robert, born January 3, 1575; sponsors, the Earl of Leicester[3], Sir

Francis Knollys[4], and the Countess of Warwick[5]. (He married, but died without issue in June, 1594.)

iii. Thomas, born July 9, 1577; sponsors, Sir Thomas Sherley[6], Mr. West[7] of Testwood, and the Lady Anne Askin[8]. (See hereafter.)

iv. Walsingham, born November 13, 1578; sponsors, Sir Francis Walsingham[9], the Lord De la Warr[10], and the Countess of Pembroke[11]. (He died young.)

v. Lettice (or Letitia), born November 24, 1579; sponsors, the Countess of Essex[12], the Lady Leyghton[13], and the Lord Hunsdon[14].

vi. Anne, born May 21, 1581; sponsors, the Lady Anne Askin,[8] the Lady Cary[15], and Sir Christopher Hatton[16].

vii. Penelope, born September 9, 1582; sponsors, the Lady Penelope Rich[17], the old Lady Chandose[18], Mr. Philip Sidney[19], and Mr. Folke Grevell[20]. (She married, in 1599, Herbert Pelham, Jr., and had issue, sixteen children, of whom the following went to New England, viz.: Herbert (first treasurer of Harvard College), William, John, Elizabeth, and Penelope, who married Gov. Richard Bellingham.)

viii. Katherine, born December 27, 1583; sponsors, Catherine, Countess of Huntingdon[21], the Lady Catherine Howard[22], and William Knollys[23]. (Said to have died young.)

ix. Francis, born October 28, 1586; sponsors, Sir Francis Knollys[4], Mr. Francis Hastings[24], and the Countess of Hartford[25]. (Went to Virginia (see hereafter).)

x. Helena, born December 15, 1587; sponsors, the Lady Helena, Marques of Northampton[26], the Lady Sidney[27], and the Earl of Essex[28]. (She married Sir William Savage of Winchester, recorder.)

xi. Anne, born February 13, 1589; sponsors, the Lady Hennige[29], Mrs. Edmonds[30], and Mr. John Stanhope[31]. (She married John, son of Sir Benjamin Pellet.)

xii. John, born December 14, 1590; sponsors, Sir John Norris[32], Mr. John Foskir[33], Mrs. Scudamore[34], and Mrs. Ratcliffe[35]. (Went to Virginia (see hereafter).)

xiii. Nathaniel, born November 30, 1592; sponsors, Sir Francis Knollys,

Jr. [36], Mr. Tasburgh [37], and the Lady Robert Knollys [38]. (Went to Virginia, and died there (see hereafter).)

The second Lord De la Warr died at Wherwell, Southampton, on the 24th of March, 1602, and was succeeded by his second, but eldest surviving son, Sir Thomas West, of whom hereafter.

Notes on the West Pedigree.

1. He was a great-grandson of Sir Thomas West, eighth Lord De la Warr, who was installed a Knight of the Garter in the second year of King Henry VIII. He was of an ancient and honorable family. Old Gerard Legh, in his " Accedens of Armorie " (1568), says, " This noble Knight of worthy fame did beare twelve severall cotes [of arms]. The first whereof is Argent, a fesse dansé, Sable, by the name of West. The second Geules, crusulé botoné fytché, a Lion rampande Argent, by the name of Lawarre. The third is Azure, three Leopardes Heads jessant Flowers Or, by the name of Cantelupe. The fowerth [giving the arms] Mortimer." Fifth Peverell ; sixth Tregose ; seventh Forte ; eighth Fitzperse ; ninth Verst. " The tenth, Argent, on a bende betweene two bendelets geules, three mullettes Or, persed, by the name of Hakelet " [Hakluyt]. Eleventh Grisley, and twelfth Thorley. This old baron and Knight of the Garter married twice, and by his wives left five sons and four daughters who married into the leading families of England.

2. Elizabeth, third wife of Edward Clinton, Earl of Lincoln. She is known as Surry's " Fair Geraldine." Her nephew, Gerald Fitzgerald, Lord Ophely, married Catherine Knollys, the child's aunt. The Wests and Clintons were also nearly related.

3. Robert Dudley, Earl of Leicester, the child's cousin.

4. The child's grandfather.

5. Lady Anne Russell, wife of Ambrose Dudley, Earl of Warwick.

6. The child afterwards married his daughter.

7. The child's great-uncle.

8. Probably Anne, daughter of the Earl of Lincoln, who married Sir Francis Ascough.

9. Patron of American colonization by the English.

10. The child's grandfather, distinguished at St. Quintin ; the first Lord De la Warr of the new creation.

11. Mary Sidney, the child's cousin.

12. The child's aunt ; and then really the wife of 3.

13. The child's aunt.

14. The patron of Cavendish, and great-uncle to the child.

15. Anne, daughter of Sir Thomas Morgan and wife of 14.

16. Patron of Sir Francis Drake.

17. Penelope Devereux, sister to the Earl of Essex, and first cousin to the child. " The Stella " of Sir Philip Sidney. She was then the wife of Lord Rich, and became the mother of the second Earl of Warwick.

18. She married, secondly, William Knollys, the child's uncle.

19. The celebrated Sir Philip Sidney, and (20) his friend Foulke Grevell.

21. Daughter of John Dudley, Duke of Northumberland.

22. Daughter of 14.

23. The child's uncle.

24. The father of George, fourth Earl of Huntingdon.

25. Frances, sister of Charles Howard, and second wife of Edward Seymour, Earl of Hertford.

26. She married, secondly, Sir Thomas Gorges.

27. Frances, daughter of Sir Francis (9) Walsingham, and widow of Sir Philip Sidney (19).

28. Robert Devereux, Earl of Essex, whom 27 afterwards married.

29. Anne, daughter of Sir Nicholas Poyntz, and wife of Sir Thomas Heneage. (She was a friend to the Rev. John Fox.)

30. ?

31. Afterwards Lord Stanhope.

32. He commanded the joint expedition with Drake to Portugal.

33, 34, 35. I cannot identify these with any certainty.

36. The child's uncle. He commanded a ship in Drake's voyage to America in 1585-86.

37. Married the child's aunt.

38. Married the child's uncle.

West, Captain Francis, esquire, 2. Sub. ——; pd. 25. Born October 28, 1586 (see West pedigree) ; went to

Virginia with Newport about July, 1608; elected a member of the council there in August, 1609, and soon after, while at "The Falles" (Richmond) an "unkindness" arose between Captain Smith and him. Spelman says, "Capt. Smith at that time replied litell, but afterward conspired with the Powhatan to kill Capt. Weste, which plott took but small effect, for in ye meantime Capt. Smith was aprehended, and sent abord for England."

About January, 1610, Captain West returned to England in the Swallow, arriving there in May. He probably returned to Virginia the same year (1610) in June or December. After Percy left in 1612, West succeeded him as commander at Jamestown, in which office he continued for many years, being, I am quite sure, a member of the council also. He was certainly a member of the Council in Virginia from April, 1619, to February, 1633. He was one of those who, in 1620, petitioned to have "some man of qualitye sent Governor unto Virginia."

In January, 1622, he was one of the signers of the certificate indorsing Capt. John Martin; March 22, 1622, in the great massacre, the Indians killed two men on his plantation "at Westover, about a mile from Berkley Hundred." In November, 1622, he was commissioned by the New England Council to be admiral of New England; his instructions having been drawn up by Sir Ferdinando Gorges. He was in Virginia in March, 1623; went to New England in May or June; returned to Virginia; again in New England in August, and was still there when the governor, Robert Gorges, arrived "about ye middle of September." "Captaine Francis West, ye aforesaid admirall," had also been appointed a member of the Governor's Council. He left New England soon after, and had arrived in Virginia some time prior to February 16, 1624, when he was living "at West and Sherley hundred Iland." "Westover" and "Sherley," the original plantations of his brothers and himself, are now historic seats on the James. In 1625 he was living, for some reason, on the company's land in "Elizabeth Cittie," and his brother Nathaniel's widow,

Mrs. Frances West, and her infant son Nathaniel were living with him.

About November 14, 1627, he was elected governor of Virginia, and continued in that office until March 5, 1629, when Dr. John Pott was elected in his place, as he had been chosen to go to England to settle some disputes. He arrived in England in the same year, and while there he resisted the planting of Lord Baltimore's proposed colony within the limits of Virginia. He returned to Virginia prior to December, 1631, when I find him attending a meeting of the council here; again in February and September, 1632, and in February, 1633. After the last date I have found no mention of him in our records. "There is a tradition in the Earl of De la Warr's family that he was drowned."

May 2, 1645, on the recommenda-. tion of the Lord Mayor, Aldermen, and Common Council of London the House of Lords appointed a Colonel Francis West to be lieutenant of the Tower of London. He died August 11, 1652. The members of the Virginia Council are always styled "Colonel" in our old records, and this may be our Virginia colonel; but the name is a hard one to trace. There were at least three "armigers" of this name living in or about London at this time.

West, John, esquire. Twelfth child of the second lord (see West pedigree). At the time of the massacre, March, 162½, Capt. Francis West, Master John West, and Capt. Nathaniel West, each had a plantation "at Westover, about a mile from Berkley Hundred," and the Indians killed two men at each plantation. I do not know when he first came to Virginia; he was a burgess 1629–30; member of the council, 1630 to his death; governor of the colony from May, 1635, to January, 1637; marshal and muster master-general, 1641. He died about 1659, leaving, by his wife Anne, a son John, many of whose descendants have been distinguished in the annals of this country.

West, John, grocer, 2. Sub. £37 10s.; pd. £50. The name of his first wife, who was the mother of his children, is not known to me. He married, secondly, Catharine, daughter of Giles Hambler, of Ghent in Flanders (see Katharine West), and died about 1614, leaving a son, John West, Jr. (next), and a daughter Mary, who married William Harrison.

West, John, Jr., grocer. Of the B. I. Co., son of the above.

West (Fust), Katharine, 2. Sub. ——; pd. £25. She married, first, Richard Fust, of Hill, Gloucester (said to have been of the family of John Fust, of Mentz in Germany, who, about the year 1430, invented the art of printing); he died in December, 1613; she then married John West, grocer; and then Sir Edward Conway. Her will is dated March 29, 1637. She left a large sum for charity in the care of the Grocers, with Mary Harrison (the daughter of John West, grocer, aforesaid) as an executrix.

West, Nathaniel, esquire. Thirteenth child of second lord. (See West pedigree and the sketches of his brothers.) He died in Virginia between April, 1623, and February, 1624.

West, Thomas, 2. Sub. ——; pd. £500. Third Lord De la Warr (see West pedigree); born July 9, 1577; educated at Oxford, and was a master of arts of that university; knighted by Essex at Dublin, Ireland, July 12, 1599. I have few particulars of his early life; but he served with distinction in the Low Countries, and probably this fact, or the fact that he was a very strong Church of England man, will account for the evident bitterness of Zuñiga towards him. He was implicated in the Essex rebellion, February 8, 1601, and was imprisoned "at Wood Street counter." On February 19, Essex "asked pardon of his father for bringing his son into danger, who was unacquainted with the whole matter." His father, the second lord, died March 24, 1602, and he succeeded as third Lord De la Warr, and also as a member of the Privy Council of Queen Elizabeth, and, on her death, became a privy councilor to James I. He took the most active interest in the American enterprise, and from about 1608 to his death he devoted his life to the movement for establishing English Protestant colonies in the New World; M. C. for Va. Co., 1609; first governor and captain-general for life, February 28, 1610. On his first voyage, and in Virginia, from March, 1610,

to June, 1611. He died while on his way to Virginia, June 7, 1618, and the news of his death reached England October 5 following. John Pory says "he died in Canada." Baker, in his Chronicles, says "he arrived and died in Virginia." (The Virginia of that day extended to 45° north latitude.) Smith says "his ship stood in for the coast of New England." It seems quite certain that he died on our northern shore. Stith says, "And I think I have somewhere seen that he died about the mouth of the Delaware Bay;" but this idea must have been purely imaginary, for I have searched in vain for any evidence of it.

He was married, on November 25, 1596, in the old church of St. Dunstan in the West, Fleet Street, London, to "Cesellye, daughter of Sir Thomas Sherley," and sister of the three celebrated brother travelers. The ceremony was performed by the Rev. Thomas White, D. D., prebendary of St. Paul's Cathedral, vicar of St. Dunstan's from 1575 to 1624, and founder of the celebrated Sion College, London.

The third lord's son and successor, Henry, fourth Lord De la Warre, married Isabella, daughter of Sir Thomas Edmonds. He was elected M. C. for Va. Co. February 5, 162⅔. During 1619-23, his mother, the Lady De la Warre, and himself transferred to others many shares of land in Virginia.

Soon after the death of the third lord, James I. granted his widow Cecily a pension of £500 per annum for thirty-one years, to be paid out of the customs of the plantation, and in 1634, the said grant being more than half expired, she petitioned Charles I. for a renewal of the same "for thirty-one years from the present time," on the ground "that the great profits and advantages accruing from thence are due to the large sums of money expended by her late husband out of her jointure, while he was settling the plantation, where he died and left her burdened with many debts, and only £10 per annum to maintain herself and seven children." We find the great services rendered by the third Lord De la Warr, in the matter of founding the colony, officially acknowledged at various times by the crown, by the company, and by the colony ; and if any one man can be called the founder of Virginia (*i. e.*, this country) I believe that he is that man. The late representative of Great Britain in the United States, the Hon. Sackville-West, descends from him in the direct male line.

West, Captain William. Lord De la Warr's nephew. He was killed by the Indians at the falls of James River, Virginia, in 1611.

Weston, Garret. Pd. £12 10s.

Westrow, John, 2. Sub. ——; pd. £37 10s.

Westwood, Humfrey, goldsmith, 2. Sub. ——; pd. £62 10s. The gold ore which Ralegh brought from Guiana, in 1595, was first assayed by Master Westwood, a refiner, dwelling in Wood Street. He was on the "jury of sixteen of the most honest, skillfullest, and best reputed gouldsmiths," who tried the money in the mint, May 9, 1611 ; died in 1622, and was buried at Tottenham.

Wetwood (Welwood ?), Randall, 2. Sub. ——; pd. £25.

Weymouth, Captain George. Made a voyage to discover a Northwest passage in 1593 ; another, May to September, 1602 ; to our New England coast, March to July, 1605 ; pensioned in 1607 ; employed at Woolwich in 1609.

Weynman — Wenman — Weyman — Wayneman — Wayman — Waynam, etc., **Sir Ferdinando,** 2. Sub. —— ; pd. ——. Master of the ordnance in Virginia, 1610. " June 28, 1620, Sir Ferdinando Weynman allowed upon account to his daughter, for £100, adventured with ye Lord La Warr, 4 shares in Virginia." "More allowed his said daughter for adventure of his person, 4 shares in Virginia " (from Va. Co. Records).

Thomas Wayneman, esquire, married, June 9, 1572, Jane West, an aunt of the third Lord De la Warr. Sir Ferdinando was their son. Mr. Neill, in

" Virginia Vetusta " (p. 75, note), says he " married Ann, daughter of Sir Samuel Sandys, and her sister became the wife of Sir Francis Wyatt, afterwards governor of Virginia."

Weynman (etc.), Sir Thomas, 2. Sub. ——; pd. ——. Of Oxford; knighted at the Charterhouse, May 11, 1603. Sir Robert and Sir Francis Wenman were also members of the Va. Co. at a later period.

Wharton, Sir George, 2. Sub. ——; pd. ——. Eldest son of the third Lord Wharton. M. P. for Westmoreland in 1601 ; made a Knight of the Bath at the coronation of King James, July 25, 1603 ; fell in a duel with his friend, Sir James Stuart, son of Lord Blantyre, November 8, 1609 ; both combatants were slain, and both interred in one grave at Islington, by the king's command, on November 10, 1609.

Wheatley — Whitley — Whitney, Thomas, grocer, 2. Sub. £37 10s. ; pd. £87 10s. Of the E. I. and N. W. P. companies ; one of the committee of directors of the Va. Co. of London, April 28, 1619; active in the affairs of that company and of the S. I. Co. during 1619–24 ; elected to his Majesty's Council of the Va. Co. in June, 1623.

He was quite certainly the " well disposed gentleman that desires not to be named," who gave eight sermons yearly to the parish of St. Mildred, Poultry ; one to be delivered at the beginning of August in commemoration of God's great mercy in delivering the nation from the Invincible Armada of Spain in 1588 ; another on the 17th of November, in commemoration of God's great mercy in delivering us from under the more than Egyptian bondage of Popish slavery, and restoring true religion to this nation. The other six sermons to be preached in their several seasons upon the doctrines of the nativity, passion, resurrection, ascension of our Lord Jesus, upon the coming down of the Holy Ghost, and the Trinity. He gave the minister fifteen shillings for preaching each sermon, and he gave ten shillings to the poor on the day of each sermon. By his will, in 1653, he increased the minister's fee to twenty shillings, and the gift to the poor to the same amount. He was also a benefactor of the Grocers' Company.

Wheeler, Nicholas. Sub. £12 10s.; pd. £12 10s.

Wheeler, Thomas, draper, 2. Sub. ——; pd. £12 10s. Of the E. I. Co.

Whistler, Francis, gent., 2. Sub. ——; pd. £25.

Whitaker, Rev. Alexander, 3. Sub. ——; pd. ——. Son of Rev. William Whitaker; born at Cambridge in 1585; M. A. Cambridge about 1604; had a good parish in the northern part of England, but determined to go as a missionary to Virginia; went with Dale in March, 1611, with purpose to stay three years; preacher to the colony at Henrico in 1612 and after; living at Rock Hall, his parsonage, on the church land opposite Henrico in 1614; minister at Bermuda Nether Hundred in the spring of 1616; drowned before June, 1617.

It has been claimed that he married Rolfe to Pocahontas; but I have not seen the evidence of it, circumstantial or otherwise. The only evidence that I have seen is circumstantial, and it points quite conclusively to the Rev. Mr. Bucke, the minister at Jamestown, — where it is said the ceremony was performed, — the friend of Rolfe, and a witness to his will.

Whitaker, Dr. (William). The father of Alexander Whitaker; a celebrated Puritan divine; born in 1547; became the head of St. John's College, Cambridge, and died in 1595. Nicholas Culverwell (a relative to Judith Culverwell, the first wife of Sir Thomas Smythe), a citizen of London, and Queen Elizabeth's merchant for wines, was the father of the famous Puritan divines, Ezekiel and Samuel Culverwell, and of three daughters, who married respectively Dr. Laurence Chaderton, Dr. Thomas Gouge, the father of Dr. William Gouge, and Dr. William Whitaker. Miss Culverwell was Dr. Whitaker's first wife, and the mother of Rev. Alexander Whitaker, and others. The doctor married, secondly, April 8, 1591, Joan, widow of Rev. Dudley Fenner, who, it is said, bore him eight children; but this seems unreasonable, as the doctor died December 4, 1595, having survived his marriage only about four years and eight months. Many in America claim descent from him.

Whitbourne, Captain Richard. Of Exmouth, Devonshire; a traveler and adventurer into foreign countries at 15 years of age; often in France, Spain, Italy, Portugal, Savoy, Denmark, Norway, Spruceland, the Canaries and Soris Islands; and Newfoundland was almost as well known to him as his own country. He made his first voyage thither about 1579; was there in 1583, when Sir Humfrey Gilbert took possession and sailed from thence towards Virginia; was again there in 1585, when Sir Bernard Drake came with a commission, and took many Portugal ships laden with fish and carried them to England as prizes. He served in a ship of his own against the Spanish Armada in 1588, and afterwards made frequent voyages to Newfoundland. On one of these voyages in 1610, he saw something which he supposed was a "Maremaide," but "whether it were a Maremaid or no," he wisely left "for others to judge." While on that coast he fell into the hands of the arch-pirate, Peter Easton, in 1612, and of Sir Henry Manwaring in 1614. He returned to Newfoundland with a commission out of the High Court of Admiralty in 1615; a ship of his was taken by a "French Pyrate of Rochell" in 1616; was again sent over with a commission (this time from Henry Viscount Falkland) in 1618. He published "A Discourse and Discovery of Newfoundland" in 1620, which the king and council indorsed by letter of June 30, 1621. He published as a sequel to this in 1622 "A Discourse Containing A Loving Invitation . . . for the advancement of his Maiesties most hopefull Plantation in the New-Fovnd-Land." Dedicated to Henry Viscount Falkland. By letter of April 12, 1622, the king gave Whitbourne the sole benefit of printing his book for one and twenty years;

HENRY WRIOTHESLEY

Third Earl of Southampton

commended the book to the Archbishops of Canterbury and York ; had it distributed in the several parishes " for the incouragement of Adventurers unto the plantation there " and ordered collections to be made in all the parishes " towards the charge of printing and distributing these bookes, and the said Captaine Whitbourne's good endeavours, and service with expence of his time and meanes in the advancing of the said Plantation ; and his severall great losses received at Sea by Pyrats and otherwise, of which his Maiesty hath beene credibly certified . . . which will be both a good incouragement unto others in the like indeavours for the service of their country, and some reward to him for his great charge."

He was still living November 10, 1626, when he wrote a letter calendared as " Sir Rich. Whitbourne to the Duke of Buckingham ;" but I cannot find that he was ever knighted. From this letter and an accompanying certificate signed by Sir Edward Seymour, John Drake, and eight others, he seems to be intending to settle himself and others in Newfoundland. He was then over sixty, I suppose. I find nothing more of him.

Capt. John Smith, in his " General History," gives some extracts from Whitbourne's publications, but calls him incorrectly " Captaine Charles Whitbourne." It is highly probable that Smith desired just such a letter (in his behalf and in the behalf of his books) as that from the king, of April 12, 1622, to the archbishops.

White, James, gent., 2. Sub. ——; pd. £25.

White, Captain John. Went with Lane to Roanoke in 1585, and remained there until taken off by Drake in 1586. He was an artist ; made maps of the country, and drawings of the inhabitants and of all curious things. Many of these paintings are now in the Sloane collection and in the Grenville Library in the British Museum. One of those to whom Ralegh assigned, January 7, 1587 ; sailed with the unfortunate colony to Roanoke, May 18 ; returned to England for supplies, November 8, 1587. Again sailed, April 25 ; but returned in May, 1588, without reaching the colony ;

one of those in the Indenture, March 7, 1589; some of his maps, drawings, etc., were engraved by De Bry in Hariot's Report of the Newfoundland of Virginia in 1590 ; again sailed to Roanoke on the voyage of March–October, 1591. He wrote to Ralegh " from my house at Newtowne in Kylmore, February 4, 1594." (Several of the De Bry engravings were used in Smith's " General History.")

White, John. Son of Henry White of Henllan, Pembroke, esquire, and his wife Jane, daughter of Thomas Fletcher ; was born June 29, 1590; at Oxford, 1607–1611; " afterwards studied law and became a barrister and counselor of eminence, and one of the masters of the bench in the Middle Temple ;" elected M. C. for Va. Co. in May, 1623; counselor of the Massachusetts Company, and is supposed to have drawn up their charter, 1628; M. P. for Southwark, from 1640 till his decease in January, 164⅘. At the time of his death he was one of the lay members of the Westminster Assembly. While a member of the Long Parliament, he served on the committee " to inquire into the scandalous immoralities of the clergy," and " The First Century of Scandalous, Malignant Priests Made and admitted into Benefices by the Prelates," was published by him, by order of Parliament, November 17, 1643. Among the " Malignant Priests " we find Rev. Lawrence Washington, the father of Colonel John, the Virginia emigrant.

(John White, the Puritan, must not be confused with John White, the Royalist, who was M. P. for Rye, April–May, 1640, and of the Long Parliament from November 3, 1640, till disabled as a Royalist, February 5, 164¾.)

White, Leonard, gent., 2. Sub. ——; pd. £25. Of the E. I. Co.; on January 9, 1610, his adventure and freedom in the E. I. Co. were made over to Sir Richard Lovelace.

White, Thomas, grocer, 2. Sub. —— ; pd. £62 10s. Of the E. I. Co.

White, William. He had formerly lived with the Indians. There was a William White among the Roanoke colonists of 1585–86; a Capt. William

White was exploring Guiana in South America about 1609 ; and William White of London, linen-draper, who died about June, 1627, had interests in Virginia (see his will in " N. E. Register," January, 1887, p. 63). I have a presentiment that the life of William White was very interesting, and I do not forgive Purchas for suppressing his description of Virginia.

Whitley. See Wheatley.

Whitmore, George, haberdasher, 2. Sub. ——; pd. ——. Son of William Whitmore by his wife, Anne Bond (sister of Capt. Martin Bond); an incorporator of the E. I. Co.; sheriff of London, 1621–22 ; alderman of Farringdon Within ward, June 2, 1621, to November 7, 1626, then of Langbourne ward to May, 1643 ; on the Virginia Commission, July 15, 1624 ; Lord Mayor of London, 1631–32 ; knighted May 27, 1632 ; seated at Balmes, in Hackney Parish, Middlesex; a devoted Royalist, assisted the king with money to the extent of £15,000, and was imprisoned because he would contribute nothing for the service of Parliament ; died December, 1654 ; a great benefactor to St. Paul's Cathedral and to the Haberdashers. Three of his sisters married persons named in this Dictionary, namely: Margaret, Sir Richard Grobham, Elizabeth, Sir William Craven, and Frances, Sir John Weld.

Whitson, Master John. Born at Clearwell, in the parish of Newland, in the County of Gloucester, about 1575 ; went to Bristol about 1575 ; was servant to Mr. Trenchard, a winecooper in Nicholas Street, who fitted out ships for the sea in that line, and probably had some share in their cargoes ; became first clerk in his master's counting-house, and when his master died he married his widow and carried on the business. When the King of Spain laid the embargo of 1585 on English ships, he was one of the Bristol merchants who sent out the " Mary-flowre," a ship of war to take " Spaniardes goods at sea;" the venture was successful; but Whitson, not liking the business, sold out to Mr. Thomas James, and never after held any part in " any prizall goods." He gave many instances of his charity in times of scarcity and sickness. He

served the office of mayor of Bristol in 1603, in his house in St. Nicholas Street ; in which year he aided in sending Capt. Martin Pring to our New England coast, on which voyage Whitson's Head (now Cape Cod) and Whitson's Bay (now Cape Cod Bay) were named for him. We find him repeatedly representing Bristol, in sundry cases, before the courts at London; M. P. for Bristol, 1605–11 and 1614; mayor of Bristol, 1615. " There was a great question for precedencie between M^r. Whitson and M^r. James, in the yeares 1616, and 1617 ; but in the end M^r. James yeelded and M^r. Whitson and M^r. James were made good freends." M. P. for Bristol, 1621–22, in which Parliament he voted with the " free traders." Admitted into the Va. Co. of London, May 22, 1622 ; again M. P. for Bristol, 1625. " November 7, 1626, he was violently assaulted by one Christopher Callowhill, who having a naked knife in his hand stabbed him therewith, through the nose and lip into his mouth, thinking to have killed him; the occasion was a matter of debt, referred to him (Whitson) to settle as arbitrator." " Alderman Whitson died with a fall from his horse, and was buried on Mounday, March 9, 162$\frac{8}{9}$, in the Crowd of St. Nicholas Church, in Bristol ;" where there is a monument, " In Memory of that great Benefactor, to This City, John Whitson, merchant, twice Mayor and Alderman, and four times member in Parliament for this city; who died in the seventy-second year of his age, A. D. 1629. A worthy Pattern to all that come after him!" In his will, dated March 27, 1627, we find, among others, the following bequests: —

	"Per annum.		
	£	s.	d.
To fifty-two child Bed women,	52.	0.	0.
To The Red Maid's Hospital,	120.	0.	0.
To the Redcliff Free School,	8.	10.	6.
To the Merchant's Almshouse,	26.	0.	0.
To Poor Scholars of Oxford,	20.	0.	0.
To Poor Housekeepers,	52.	0.	0.
To Poor Widows,	26.	0.	0.
To St. Nicholas Church,	3.	0.	0.
	307.	10.	6.

£500. to the use of Merchants and poor Tradesmen, interest free."

He wrote " The Aged Christian's final farewell to the world and its vanities," which was first published in 1729, one hundred years after his death.

He married three times; one of his wives was grandmother of John Aubrey, the antiquary and naturalist.

Whittingham, John, grocer, 2. Sub. ——; pd. £12 10s. " Late apprentice to M^r. Alderman Welde ; sworn to Freedom, January 10, 1598; *nihil quia* Aldermannuo (no fee); admitted to the livery, May 22, 1613." (Grocers' Records.)

Whittingham, Thomas, 2. Sub. ——; pd. ——. In September, 1609, master's mate, Henry Ravens and the Cape Merchant, Thomas Whittingham sailed in the long boat from the Bermudas for Virginia, and were never heard of again.

Wickham, Rev. William. He was still serving at Henrico in 1619, and possibly until 1621 a member of the council in Virginia in 1619; several members of this family were in the East India service, and it is said that the first reference to tea, by a native of Britain, is found in a letter written in the East Indies by a Mr. Wickham, June 27, 1615.

Widowes, Richard, goldsmith, 2. Sub. ——; pd. £25.

Wiffin, David. Pd. £12 10s.

Wiffin, Richard, 2. Sub. ——; pd. £12 10s. Went to Virginia in 1607.

Wigmore, Sir Richard, 2. Sub. ——; pd. ——. Of Herefordshire ; knighted at Newark, April 22, 1603. In 1604 and 1605 he was licensed to import 16,000 lasts of cod and ling fish for twenty years.

Wilde. (See **Weld.**)

Wilkes, Edward, 2. Sub. ——; pd. £25.

Willeston — Wollaston, Hugh, 2. Sub. ——; pd. £12 10s. I believe this to be the son of William Wollaston, of Trescott Grange, by his wife, " Miss Jordaine of Dunsley." He was born in 1553 ; came to Virginia in 1608, and died there in 1609. His nephew, John Wollaston, who received a grant of New Hampshire, April 18,

1635, which he transferred to his brother-in-law, Capt. John Mason, June 11, 1635, was Lord Mayor of London, 1644–45, and active under Cromwell.

Willeston — Wollaston, William, 3. Sub. ——; pd. £37 10s. Probably the first cousin to John Wollaston, the Lord Mayor of London, 1644–45. He was born in 1580; sheriff of Leicestershire, 1629, and of Staffordshire, 1630 ; died December 10, 1666, aged 86.

(The Captain Wollaston who went with Ralegh to Guiana, in 1617, was probably the same who went to Massachusetts about 1625.)

Willet (or Willest), John, clothworker, 3. Sub. £37 10s.; pd. 37 10s.

Willet (or Willest), William. Pd. £12 10s.

Williamson, Sir Richard, 2. Sub. ——; pd. £25. Son of John Williamson, Esq., of Gainsborough, Lincolnshire, by his second wife, Jane, daughter of Christopher Dobson, Esq.; knighted at Whitehall, May 30, 1604; in some service on the borders in 1607–08; M. C. for Va. Co., 1609. He was master of requests in 1612, and high steward of the borough of East Relford, Notts ; M. P. for Richmond in 1614. The records of the Va. Co. show that he died before 1620 ; but I cannot find when or where.

Williamson, William. Pd. £50. Of the E. I. Co.

Willoughby, Sir Percival, 3. Sub. £75; pd. £50. Knighted April 21, 1603 ; M. P. for Nottinghamshire, 1604–11 ; for Tamworth, 1614 ; died about the beginning of the civil war.

Wilmer, Andrew, 2. Sub. ——; pd. £25.

Wilmer, Clement, gent., 2. Sub. ——; pd. £25. May 8, 1622, he transferred to George Wilmer two shares of land in Virginia.

Wilmer, George, esquire, 2. Sub. ——; pd. £25. Seated at Stratford le Bow, County Middlesex ; married Margaret, daughter of Marmaduke Tweng, Esq., of Yorkshire ; May 8, 1622, purchased two shares in Virginia of Clement Wilmer ; on the Virginia Commission of July 15, 1624 ; died in 1626, and was buried in the church at Westham.

Wilmot, Sir Charles, 2. Sub.

£37 10s. ; pd. £52 10s. A distinguished soldier in Ireland ; knighted by Essex at Dublin, August 5, 1599 ; constable of Castlemain, 1600–05 ; M. P. Launceston, 1614 ; president of Connaught, 1616 to his death in 1644; member of the Privy Council ; raised to the peerage of Ireland as Viscount Wilmot of Athlone, January 4, 1620. His son was created Earl of Rochester in 1652.

Wilsford, Sir Thomas, 3. Sub. £37 10s. ; pd. £50. Of Ildinge, County Kent ; knighted at Whitehall, November 20, 1607; M. P. for Canterbury, 1625; married Elizabeth, daughter of Sir Edwyn Sandys, of Northbourne.

Wilson, Felix, 2. Sub.——; pd. £25.

Wilson, Thomas, esquire, 2. Sub. £37 10s.; pd. £37 10s. About the year 1603 he was employed by Salisbury, on secret service in Spain, and was awarded a pension for the same. He became a secretary to Salisbury, and keeper of the state papers ; M. P. Newton, 1605–11; was much interested in new discoveries, foreign commerce, etc., and had many correspondents abroad (see Purchas, i. pp. 408–413, and the East India papers); lived "at his house at the Britaine Burse at the Strand;" knighted at Whitehall, July 20, 1618; keeper of Sir Walter Ralegh from September 9 to his execution, October 29, 1618.

On July 14, 1622, he wrote that "the Indians have killed in Virginia at least 300 or 400 English, and but for an accident, that gave warning, man, mother, and child had all been slain."

Wimarke. (See **Wymarke**.)

Wimbleton, Viscount. — Edward Cecil.

Winch—Wynche, Daniel, grocer, 2. Sub. ——; pd. ——. Admitted a freeman of the Grocers by patrimony in 1591; paid £10 as his share of £20,000 levied on London by Queen Elizabeth in 1598; married Sibbell Shortis,

of London; resided in the parish of St. Mildred, Poultry. He was buried in that church, January 20, 162⅘, and his

widow, who bequeathed money to the church, was buried therein, November 2, 1631 (see Wyche). One of the same name was a member of the Massachusetts Company.

Wingfield Pedigree. (Extract.) Sir John Wingfield, of Letheringham, of a family famous for their knighthood and ancient nobility, dying in 1481, left by his wife, Elizabeth Lewis, three daughters and twelve sons. The eleventh son, "Sir Richard Wingfield, of Kimbolton Castle, one of the most distinguished soldiers of the era in which he lived, was chancellor of the Duchie of Lancaster ; lord deputy of Callis; and made Knight of the Garter by Henry VIII. ;" married, first, Katherine, Duchess of Bedford and Buckingham (daughter of Richard Woodville, Earl Rivers, sister of Elizabeth, queen consort of Edward IV., aunt of Elizabeth, queen consort of Henry VII., and widow, first, of Henry Stafford, Duke of Buckingham, and, secondly, of Jasper Tudor of Hatfield, Duke of Bedford), by whom Sir Richard had no issue. He married, secondly, Bridget, daughter of Sir John Wiltshire, and had all his children by her. He died July 22, 1525, while "ambassadour in Spain, and was buried at Toledo." He had, with other children, 1. Charles ; 2. Thomas-Maria ; and 3. James.

1. Charles, his heir, of Kimbolton, married Jane, sister to Sir Francis Knollys (see West pedigree); and his great-grandson sold Kimbolton to Sir Henry Montague. (The references to Edward Wingfield, quoted in Neill's "Virginia Vetusta," pp. 7–8, evidently apply to a member of the Kimbolton branch of the family; which Edward, I think, was afterwards knighted.)

3. James, the third son of Sir Richard, was in service in Ireland as early as 1574 (see George Lord Carew); was master of the ordnance there ; fought at Glenmalure, etc.

2. Thomas-Maria, apparently the second son of Sir Richard, was so christened by Queen Mary and Cardinal Pole (his sponsors in baptism). He was probably born about 1520; was M. P. for Huntingdonshire, 7 Edward VI., and in two Parliaments of Mary, and in 2 and 3 Philip and Mary. He married a daughter of Kerry or Kaye,

of Yorkshire, who bore him several children, among whom were Edward-Maria (of whom hereafter) and Thomas-Maria, who commanded a company in Leicester's army in the Low Countries in 1585, and was knighted in Ireland, in the Glynes, by Sir William Russell, May 8, 1597.

Sir Richard Wingfield's widow, the Lady Bridget, married, secondly, Sir Nicholas Hervey, gentleman of the privy chamber to Henry VIII., and bore him several children. Among her Hervey grandchildren (first cousins to Capt. Edward-Maria Wingfield) were George Lord Carew, William Lord Hervey (whose first wife, Mary, was widow of Henry, second Earl of Southampton and mother of Henry, the third earl), and Margaret Hervey, who married William Mildmay, first cousin to Governor Winthrop, of Massachusetts (see Sir Henry Mildmay).

Lady Bridget Wingfield married, thirdly, Sir Robert Tyrwhytt.

Wingfield, Captain Edward-Maria, esquire, 1, 2. Sub. ——; pd. £88. "Of Stoneley Priorye" in Huntingdonshire; born about 1560, probably before that date; a soldier, as his forefathers were; served in Ireland; then in the Low Countries, where he was a prisoner of war at Lisle, with Ferdinando Gorges and others, in 1588; and afterwards served in Ireland. The only member of the first colony mentioned in the first charter who came with the first planters to Virginia. He was elected, May 14, 1607, the first president of the first council in the first English colony in America. "There were never Englishman left in a forreigne Countrye in such miserie as wee were in this new-discovered Virginia." They were assailed by pestilence and famine. Wingfield was blamed for what he could not prevent, and was made a scapegoat by the other members of the council, who deposed him, not only from the presidency, but from the council also, September 10, 1607. He left Virginia April 10, and arrived in England May 21, 1608. I cannot find that he ever returned to Virginia again. He was still living, and unmarried, in 1613. When he died I do not know.

He was a man of age (probably near fifty) and long experience in the wars when he went to Virginia, and was presumably thought to be better qualified for the position to which he was elected than any other one of the colonists (see XLIX. for his defense of his services in Virginia); but in the midst of the terrible misfortunes which assailed the colonists, the serious charges were brought against him by his opponents: that he was a Catholic, that he did not bring a Bible with him, that he conspired with the Spaniards to destroy Virginia, etc. He was of a Catholic family — Cardinal Pole and Queen Mary were sponsors for his father — and such charges brought against him under such circumstances necessarily destroyed every prospect of his usefulness in a colony being established especially in the interests of Protestantism, directly antagonistic to Romanism.

During his absence in Virginia, in 1608, a relative named an infant son for him, which Edward-Maria was knighted; died in 1670, and was buried at Richmond in Surrey.

Mr. Richard and Sir Robert Wingfield also had interests in Virginia soon after 1616, and possibly before that date.

Winne (Wynne), Edmund, merchant-tailor, 2. Sub. £37 10s.; pd. 62 10s. Son of George; he patented lands in Virginia in 1621.

Winne (Gwinn), Captain Owen, esquire, 3. Sub. £37 10s.; pd. £50. Son of Sir John Wynn (1553–1626), the author of the "History of the Gwydyr Family," by his wife Sidney, daughter of Sir William Gerrard. At the death of his elder brother, Sir Richard Wynne, baronet of Gwydyr, in 1649, Captain Owen (who, it seems, had been knighted) succeeded him in the baronetcy. He married Grace, daughter of Hugh Williams, and died about 1660.

Winne (etc.), Captain Peter, 2. Sub. ——; pd. ——. Died in Virginia in the spring of 1609. Not knowing of his death, and reposing especial confidence in him, Sir Thomas Gates, having been wrecked on the Bermudas, selected him from the members of the council in Virginia to be his lieutenant-governor there, and sent to him, by a bark of Aviso, a particular commission.

Winne—Wynne, Capt. Thomas, 2. Sub. —— ; pd. £25.

Winston, Dr. Thomas. Son of Thomas Wynston, of Panswick in Com. Gloucester, by his wife Judith, daughter of Roger Lancaster, of Hertfordshire, was born in 1575 ; educated at Clare Hall, Cambridge ; studied medicine at Aquapendente, Padua, and Basil; professor of physic at Gresham College from 1615 to 1642; was a constant attendant on the meetings of the Va. Co. of London until October, 1621; was interested with Dr. Bohune in his Virginia plantation in 1619; was one of the editors (appointed December 15, 1619) of "A Declaration of the state of the Colonie and Affaires in Virginia," etc., published in 1620. William Capps, of Virginia, corresponded with him; was "Doctor in Phisick to our Dread Soveraigne Lord King Charles." He went abroad in 1642, and stayed about ten years in France; died October 24, 1655. His "Anatomy Lectures at Gresham College, London," were published in 1659.

Winter, Captain Edward. Son of Admiral Sir William Winter; with the Drake expedition to America, 1585–86; M. P. for Newport, 1586–87; served as captain of a ship against the Armada, 1588; M. P. Gloucestershire, 1588–89 ; knighted in 1595 ; M. P. Gloucestershire, 1601; was still living in January, 1608. He married a sister of Henry, first Marquis of Worcester, whose eldest son became famous for the part which he took towards discovering the steam-engine. Two of Capt. Edward Winter's sons, Frederick and Edward, came to Maryland in 1633.

Winter, Master Nicholas. Son of Admiral Sir William Winter.

Winter, Captain William. Commanded the English fleet in the north, on the coast of Scotland; partner in the Hawkins voyage, 1562–63 ; in charge of the ships at sea before New Haven (Havre) in August, 1563; interested in the Hawkins voyage, 1564–65; sent with Sir Thomas Smith to demand of the King of France the restitution of Calais in 1567; interested in the Hawkins voyage of 1567–69, and the subsequent events; conducted a great treasure of the Genoan merchants safely into the Netherlands in 1569 ; knighted in 1573. Richard Eden dedicated "A very necessarie and profitable Booke concerning Navigation " to " Sir Wm. Wynter, Master of the Ordnance," in 1574. On November 4, 1575, his wife, the Lady Mary Winter, died at his house in Seething Lane, London, and was buried at Lidney in the Forest of Dean, Gloucestershire. With Robert Beale, clerk of the council, he was employed into Zealand, to demand the restitution of English ships in 1576. "A booke called the 'Treasure for Traveilers,'" was dedicated to "Sir William Winter, Master of the Quenes Maiesties Ordinance by Sea, Survaior of her highnesses marine causes," in 1578 ; commanded the ships before Fort-del-Ore in 1580; vice-admiral of England; distinguished himself in the fight with the Armada in 1588; founded the navy office in Seething Lane. The date of his death is not known to me. The names of three of his sons will be found in this work, Edward, Nicholas, and William. A great-grandson of Vice-admiral Winter was the celebrated Sir Edward Wynter, who lived at Yorkhouse, Battersea, and died there in 1686. His epitaph quite casts that of Capt. John Smith into the shade.

" Alone unarm'd a tyger he oppressed
And crush'd to death the monster of a beast.
Twice twenty mounted Moors he overthrew
Singly on foot, some wounded, some he slew,
Dispersed the rest — what more could Samson
   do ? —
True to his friends, a terror to his foes. —
Here now in peace his honor'd bones repose."

Winter, Captain William, 2. Sub. ——; pd. ——. Son of Vice-admiral Sir William Winter. He was stationed at Portsmouth in 1609, and was then the oldest captain in the navy, and had served well for many years.

Winwood, Sir Ralph, 3. Sub. ——; pd. £75. Born at Aynhoe in Northamptonshire about 1565 ; fellow Magdalene College, Oxford, 1582 ; M. A. June, 1587 ; bachelor of civil law, 1590, and proctor in 1592. He was secretary to Sir Henry Neville, ambassador to France, in 1599 ; appointed by King James as resident counselor to the States General, June 24, 1603; knighted at Richmond, June 28, 1607; joint-ambassador to Holland, August, 1607 ; ambassador to the Hague 1608 to 1613; M. P. for Buckingham, 1614 ; made a secretary of state in March, 1614 ; member S. I. Co., June 29, 1615. He was bitterly opposed to Spain, and is said to have urged Ralegh, on his voyage to Guiana in 1617, "to break the peace at all hazards, and to fall upon the Mexico fleet as the best means of bringing James I. to a rupture with Spain;" but he died before Ralegh's return, at his house in the Great Bartholomew's, London, October 27 or 28, 1617, and was buried in the church of St. Bartholomew the Less.

Wirrall, Sir Hugh, 2. Sub. ——; pd. £25. Knighted at Whitehall, July 23, 1603. He settled a plantation in Ireland called "Monaghan."

Withers, John, esquire, 3. Sub. ——; pd. ——. Of Manydown, Hants, who married Joane, daughter of John Love, Esq., of Basing. He died in 1620, and was buried at Wotton June 2, in that year. George Wither, the celebrated poet, was the son of his half-brother George. Anthony Withers, Esq. (baptized July 19, 1585), the son of John Withers (aforesaid), was admitted into the Va. Co. of London, July 24, 1621, and became a very active member.

Wodenoth, Arthur. Author of "A Short Collection of the most Remarkable Passages from the Originall to the dissolution of the Virginia Company. London Printed by Richard Cotes for Edward Husband, at the Golden Dragon in Fleet Street, 1651." He was not a member of the Va. Co. of London until some time after 1612. He was a goldsmith in Foster Lane, London ; was related to Nicholas Ferrar, through Ferrar's mother (who was Mary Wodenoth), and, like Ferrar, he was a constant friend to the poet, George Herbert, whose eyes he closed at death, and whose executor he was. He was deputy governor of the S. I. Co. in 1644; but was dead at the time of the publication of his aforesaid tract in 1651.

Wollaston. See Willeston.

Wolley, Sir Francis, 2. Sub. ——; pd. ——. Knighted at Charterhouse, May 11, 1603, as of Lincolnshire ; "clerk of the pipe of the exchequer ; " died about 1610, and was buried in St. Paul's, Faringdon Ward Within, London. He was probably the M. P. for Haslemere in 1601.

Wolstenholme, Henry, gent., 3. Sub. —— ; pd. ——. Son of Sir John (whom see) ; of N. W. P. Co. ; died in the wars in the Palatinate while serving under Sir Horatio Vere.

Wolstenholme, John, esquire, 3. Sub. ——; pd. ——. Son of Sir John (whom see); of N. W. P. Co. also ; M. P. for West Looe, 1625 and 1626 ; knighted in 1633 ; created a baronet 1665 ; died September 12, 1669, and was buried at Stanmore ; suffered great losses on account of his loyalty to the king in the civil wars ; married Dorothy, youngest daughter of Horace Lord Vere, but died childless.

Wolstenholme, John, merchant, 2. Sub. £75; pd. £137 10s. His father, John Wolstenholme, younger son of an ancient Derbyshire family, came to London in the time of Edward VI., and obtained an office in the custom-house. He died at Stanmore, in Middlesex, where he lies buried, leaving by his wife, whose maiden name was Larkin, a daughter and three sons: Henry, who died unmarried ; John, of whom I write; and Thomas who died a commander in Muscovy.

The second son, Sir John Wolstenholme, knighted by James I., was a farmer of the customs, and, acquiring great wealth, purchased Nostell Abbey in Yorkshire. Born about 1562; one of the incorporators of the E. I. Co. in December, 1600 ; one of the farmers of the customs in February, 1608 ; M. C. for Va. Co., 1609 ; one of those who sent Henry Hudson to the Northwest in April, 1610, when Hudson named Cape Wolstenholme for him ; one of the incorporators of the N. W. P. Co., July 26, 1612, and one of its first directors. One of those who purchased the Bermudas Islands from the Va. Co., November 25, 1612. Sir Thomas Smythe and himself employed and paid the celebrated Edward Wright to deliver courses of lectures to mariners and others. The purchasers of the Bermudas resigned the island to the crown, November 23, 1614.

One of those who sent Bileth and Baffin to the Northwest Passage in 1615, in which voyage Wolstenholme's Sound was named for him. He had previously aided in sending three voyages to the Northwest, namely, Hudson (1610), Button (1612), and Gibbons, and he again aided in sending Bileth and Baffin in 1616.

He was a member of the S. I. Co., June 29, 1615; advancing the Virginia enterprise constantly; knighted at Whitehall, March 12, 1617. His faith was strong in a Northwest passage, and he was ever ready to try, try again. January 20, 1618, he urged the E. I. Co. to aid in another attempt, and said that he himself intended "a good round adventure in his own particular."

I have some reason for thinking that he was related to Rev. John Robinson. The English dissenters at Leyden had been in correspondence with him in regard to their removal to Virginia prior to 1618, and a few of their letters, written in January and February, 1618, on that subject, have been preserved. On the 28th of April, 1619, he was one of the candidates for the treasurership of the Va. Co. of London; but was defeated by Sir Edwin Sandys. In 1619 he was one of the committee of the Va. Co. on the proposed college in Virginia.

He was a leading director of the E. I. Co. In December, 1619, "he was by the king's command committed for a time to his house, for muttering against a patent and newly erected office in the custom house." We find him constantly interested in the Virginia affairs. May 22, 1622, he was one of those recommended by the king to the Va. Co. as a most suitable person to be treasurer of that company. He was a member of the commission for winding up the Va. Co., appointed July 15, 1624, and remained for years after a member of his Majesty's Council for Virginia, taking special interest in the college, etc. On the 6th of April, 1627, "The Planters and Adventurers of Virginia and the Company of Somer Islands," held a meeting at his house regarding tobacco. June 27, 1631, one of commissioners appointed for advising upon some course for the better plantation of Virginia. He still retained his interest in the Northwest Passage, and in 1631 he aided in sending out the celebrated Luke Fox, afterwards known as the Northwest Fox. "The present church of Stanmore Magna parish, near Lon-

don (dedicated to St. John), was built at the sole expence of Sir John Wolstenholme, knight, on a piece of ground given by Mrs. Barbara Burnell, Sir Thomas Lake, and Mr. Robinson. It was consecrated by Bishop Laud on the 16th of July, 1632. The building is of brick, and consists of a nave and chancel. At the west end is an embattled tower, almost overgrown with ivy. The porch was designed by Nicholas Stone." (There was probably some connection between the Mr. Robinson, who contributed towards buying the piece of ground for this church to be built upon, and Mrs Mary Robinson (whom see).)

In August, 1633, one of the Virginia commissioners who favored the renewal of the ancient charter to the old Va. Co.; one of those who, "at great charge," aided Capt. Will. Claybourne, in 1631, "in settling an island, by them named the Isle of Kent, within Chesapeake Bay," which, in 1633, was comprehended in Lord Baltimore's patent, and in November, 1633, he joined the other planters in a petition to the Privy Council, praying that they may enjoy that island, and that Lord Baltimore may settle in some other place."

In 1634 he was one of the tobacco commissioners. May 25, 1635, Capt. Sam. Matthews wrote to him from Newport News regarding affairs in Virginia. He evidently always had correspondents in Virginia, and several of their letters to him are still preserved. One of the commissioners for the Caribbee Islands in 1637.

He died, aged 77, on November 25, 1639, and was buried in Stanmore Magna Church, where there is a handsome monument to his memory, by Nicholas Stone, which cost £200.

He married Catherine Fanshaw, and had issue by her two sons, Sir John and Henry, and two daughters, Joan (who married Sir Robert Knollys, first cousin to Thomas West, Lord De la Warr) and Catherine (who married William Fanshaw, nephew of Sir Thomas Smythe).

Wood, Captain Benjamin. Went to Roanoke in 1584; captain and in the West Indies, 1593, 1594–95; perished in his voyage to the East Indies in 1596.

Wood, Thomas, 2. Sub. ——; pd. £25. (June 13, 1621, the council of the Virginia Company granted "to Ambrose Wood, as heir to his brother, Thomas Wood, deceased, 4 shares in Virginia, and one share more for the adventure of his person — total, 5 shares.")

Woodall, John, 2. Sub. £37 10s.; pd. ——. Also of E. I. and S. I. companies ; son of Richard Woodall, of Warwick, by his wife Mary, daughter of Peirse Ithell, of North Wales ; born about 1556; surgeon in the army, and, in 1612, appointed surgeon to St. Bartholomew's Hospital ; published "The Chirurgion's Mate, etc., London," 1612 or 1617, the first edition; general surgeon for the E. I. Co. The auditors of the Va. Co., in their printed report, do not give him credit for having paid his adventure, and July 18, 1620, "report was made unto the Courte that Mr. Woodall had scandalized that book . . . and that he had caste a foule aspercon upon Sir Edwin Sandys ; " for which he was suspended from the court, until the charges should be examined into. He was friendly to Sir Thomas Smith, and the Sandys party speak of him as "surgeon to Sir Thomas Smith." He was early interested in sending cattle to Virginia, milk being considered an essential in the colony. October 20, 1623, he voted to surrender the Virginia charters to the crown. He published in 1628 "Viaticum being the pathway to the surgeon's chest."

June 24, 1636, the Privy Council of England wrote to the governor and council of Virginia, inclosing a petition of John Woodall, "who," they write, "deserves encouragement for his chargeable and constant adventures in that plantation. Direct them to cause speedy justice to be done against those of the petitioner's servants who do not give him a just account of his goods and cattle, and to put his new agent, John Convers, in possession of the petitioner's estate."

March 23, 1639, Governor Sir John Harvey and the council of Virginia wrote from James City to the Privy Council of England : "Have in obedience to orders of 29th November last restored the goods and cattle belonging to the estate of Capt. Samuel Matthews, to the agents of John Woodall, of London, surgeon. Certify the true state of the cause between Woodall, plaintiff, and Matthews, defendant."

"John Woodall, Master in Chirurgery," published a second edition of " The Surgeon's Mate," etc., under the following title, " The Surgeon's Mate, or Military & Domestique Surgery. Discovering faithfully & plainly y⁰ method and order of y⁰ Surgeon's chest. . . . London, Printed by Rob. Young for Nicholas Bourne . . . MDCXXXIX." There is a congratulatory "Epistle to Sir Christopher Clitherow, knight, ancient Alder-Governor of the East India Company, etc.," and a portrait of Woodall by G. Glover in the engraved title. This is the earliest book in which lemon-juice was prescribed in the treatment of scurvy. "Woodall's works," says Watts, "are deservedly much esteemed."

He was probably alive in 1641 (see Argall). The name sometimes appears in the records as Woddall and Waddall.

John woodall

Woodhouse. See Waterhouse.

Woodhouse, Captain Henry, 2. Sub. —— ; pd. ——. (Probably the governor of the Bermudas Islands, 1623 to January, 1627 ; in the expedition to Ré and Rochelle, 1627–28 ; muster - master of Suffolk, England. He said that King Charles promised him in 1631 the place of governor of Virginia, and in 1634 and again in 1635 he petitioned the king to fulfill that promise. In a deed of April 15, 1640, he signed himself as "of Virginia, planter." One of the same name, a Burgess for Lower Norfolk, 1647–52, was of the parish of Linhaven, and made his will in January, 1637.)

Woodliffe, John, gent., 2. Sub. —— ; pd. ——. First went to Virginia about 1608, and remained there eleven years ; interested with John Smith, of Nibley, in Berkeley town and hundred, and September 4, 1619, the four adventurers agreed with him to be the first governor of the proposed settlement, and drew up ordinances, directions, and instructions for him for said government. He sailed with thirty-eight planters in Edward Williams' ship, the Margaret, of Bristol, from Kingroad, September 16, 1619, and landed "at Keeketan" in Virginia in a good harbor on the 30th of November following. On August 28, 1620, the commission to Woodliffe to be governor or agent was revoked, and a commission to George Thorpe and William Tracy to be governors in Virginia was executed. The following extract from a letter ("of June, 1620, about our accompts for the Virginia ship then returned") of John Smith to Richard Berkeley will probably explain this revocation : "I fear the old Virginian trick of surprise of lettres (if not counterfeiting also) is cast upon us by Mr. Woodleefe." In 1626 he owned 550 acres by pattent in "the Territory of great Weyonoke."

Woogan (or **Wogan**), **Devereaux**, 3. Sub. £37 10s. ; pd. £50. Of the E. I. Co.

Wooller, Edward, merchant-tailor, 2. Sub. ——— ; pd. £50. Son of the next. November 19, 1617, sold five shares in Virginia to Gabriel Barber.

Wooller, John, merchant - tailor. Sub. £37 10s. ; pd. £25. By his will, dated March 26, 1617, he gave to the Merchant-Taylors' Company the rents of certain property, called the Cross Keys, in Thames Street, etc., to be bestowed yearly forever in certain charities, including £4 per annum to a poor scholar at St. John's College, Oxford.

This name is sometimes given in the records, and probably correctly, as Waller.

Worcester, Earl of. — Edward Somerset.

Worrell. See Wirrell.

Worsley (**Worley** — **Worsleep**, etc.), **Sir Richard.** He was probably the Richard Worley, gent., who went to Virginia in 1607. The widow of his great uncle (Richard Worsley, governor of the Isle of Wight, who died April 12, 1565), was the second wife of Sir Francis Walsingham, and the mother of his children.

Sir Richard was the son of Thomas Worsley, Esq., of Appuldercombe, "who was brought up under Walsingham ;" born about 1586 ; knighted at Whitehall, February 8, and created a baronet, June 29, 1611; patented lands in Virginia, which patent was "renewed November 3, 1620 ;" died June 27, 1621 ; married Frances, daughter of Sir Henry Neville of Billingbere, and grandniece of Sir Thomas Smythe.

Sir Bowyer Worsley, who was interested in Plowden's patent of New Albion at a later date, also patented lands in Virginia in 1620 or before.

Wortley, Francis, esquire, 3. Sub. £37 10s. ; pd. ———. Of Wortley, County York ; knighted January 15, and created a baronet, June 29, 1611 ; M. P. for East Retford, 1624, 1625, 1626, and 1628–29. Burke says, "At the outbreak of the civil wars Sir Francis, whose devotion to the royal cause shone conspicuous among the most faithful of the cavaliers, fortified his house at Wortley, and raised a troop of horse, with which he maintained a guerilla warfare, extremely harassing to his opponents. In 1644 he was taken prisoner at Walton House, near Wakefield, his estate sequestered, and he himself sent to the Tower, where he remained in captivity for many years, solacing the hours of his long confinement by literary occupations to which he was much attached. He wrote several small tracts principally connected with the occurrences and controversies of the times, and one larger work to prove that episcopacy is pure divine." He died before 1660. His great grandson, Edward Wortley Montague, married the Lady Mary Pierrepont, the celebrated Lady Mary Wortley Montague.

Wotton, Sir Henry, 3. Sub. ——— ; pd. ———. Born at Bocton Hall, Kent, April 9, 1568 ; entered Oxford University, 1584; M. A., 1588; traveled on the continent about 1589–98 (?) ; again went abroad, 1601; knighted in 1603 ; M. P. Appleby, 1614. The English commissioners to treat with the Hollanders concerning differences in E. I. and the fisheries of Greenland in 1614–15 were Sir Henry Wotton, Clement Edmondes

EDWARD ZOUCHE

Eleventh Baron Zouche

(translator of Cæsar's commentaries), Robert Middleton, and Maurice Abbott; the celebrated Hugo Grotius was one of the Dutch commissioners. Provost of Eton, 1625 ; died there in December, 1639.

"He was sent thrice ambassador to Venice, once to the States General, twice to the Court of Savoy, and upon several other equally important diplomatic missions." (See his Life by Izaak Walton.)

Wotton, Thomas Lord (second baron). Sub. —— ; pd. ——. Son of Edward, first Baron Wotton (who was the half-brother of Sir Henry Wotton). He succeeded his father about 1604, and died April 2, 1630, aged forty-two. He became a Roman Catholic.

Wright, Edward, mathematican. He was in Drake's celebrated voyage to our coasts (1585–86) as "Capt. Edward Careless *alias* Wright ; " in the Earl of Cumberland's voyage to the Azores (1589) as "Capt. Edward Wright ; " developed the Mercator idea of projection for charts or maps in 1590 ; formed tables of meridional parts, 1597 ; map in Hakluyt's works, 1598–1600; "The Haven finding Art," etc., and "Certaine Errors in Navigation, etc., 1599." He became tutor to Henry, Prince of Wales, in mathematics and cosmography, and keeper of his library (the wages of the latter office were £30 per annum). He was a member of the N. W. P. Co. in 1612 ; "The Description and Use of the Sphære, etc., 1613 ; " "A short Treatise of Dialling, etc., 1614." March 14, 1614, from court minutes of the E. I. Co. : "Mr. Wright, the mathematician, who has gathered great knowledge in the Universities, and effected many worthy works in rectifying errors formerly smothered ; resolved that for his courses of lectures *hitherto paid for* by Sir Thomas Smythe and Mr. Wolstenholme, the company will allow him £50 per annum ; he to examine their journals and mariners and perfect their plotts " (maps, etc.). Died in London in 1615 ; translated Napier's "Description of the Admirable Table of Logarithmes," which was published by his son, Samuel Wright, in 1616.

Wright, John, mercer, 2. Sub.

—— ; pd. £25. Apprenticed to Edward Barnes; admitted in 1604 (from Mercers' Records) ; also of E. I. Co.

Wright, John, stationer. As a bearing on the discussion about "The Tempest," the following reference to Wright is interesting: "Shake-speares Sonnets never before Imprinted. At London by G. Eld for T. T. and are to be solde by John Wright, dwelling at Christ Church gate. 1609." Dedicated by Thomas Thorpe, the stationer to Mr. W. H. (*Mr.* William *H*ackwell or Hakewill, "of the Right worshipfull Fraternitie of Sirenicall gentlemen, that meete the first Friday of every moneth, at the signe of the Mermaid in Bread-street, in London " ?) Thus it will be seen that R. Rich's account of the tempest and wreck at the "Bermoothawes" (CXXXVIII.) and Shakespeare's Sonnets were sold by the same bookseller. Nathaniel Butter, John Harrison, W. Jaggard, and Matthew Law also were interested in the publication of several of Shakespeare's plays during 1606–16.

Wriothesley, James Lord. Eldest son of the next ; was M. P. for Callington, 1621–22, and for Winchester, 1624–25. He died, *s. p.*, in the Netherlands, and before his father in 1624.

Wriothesley, Henry, 2. Sub. —— ; pd. £350. Third Earl of Southampton, "The Friend of Shakespeare."

Pedigree : Henry [2], second Earl of Southampton (son of Thomas [1], first earl, who was lord chancellor to Henry VIII.), was a friend of Thomas Howard, Duke of Norfolk, and involved himself in trouble by promoting the contemplated marriage of that nobleman with Mary Queen of Scots, "to whom and her religion (says Dugdale) he stood not a little affected." He married Mary, daughter of Anthony Browne, Viscount Montagu (she married, secondly, Capt. Edward-Maria Wingfield's cousin, William Hervey), and had issue, among others, —

Henry [3], of whom I write, and Mary [3], who married Thomas, Lord Arundell of Wardour (whom see).

Henry [3], the second, but only surviving son of the second earl, was born October 6, 1573, and succeeded at the death of his father in 1581, as third

Earl of Southampton; admitted to St. John's College in Cambridge, December 11, 1585; "spent his time at Cambridge in the study of good letters, and afterwards confirmed that study with travel and foreign observation." In 1589 he took the degree of bachelor of arts (Cambridge), "and seems to have left the university in that year, to proceed on his travels." In 1593 Shakespeare dedicated "Venus and Adonis" "to Henry Wriottesley, Earl of Southampton," and, in 1594, the same author dedicated the "Rape of Lucrece" "to the Earl of Southampton."

In 1596 with Essex at Cadiz; 1597, commanded the Garland on the island voyage, and knighted for gallantry by Essex; 1598, married a first cousin of the Earl of Essex, without obtaining the queen's permission, and is attainted; 1599, went to Ireland with Essex, who made him general of the horse, "clean contrary" to the queen's instructions; in 1600, in the Netherlands; February 8, 1601, took part in the Essex rebellion; February 19, 1601, tried and found guilty; his execution was stayed, but he remained a close prisoner in the Tower till the queen died. In 1602, while in prison, he aided in sending Gosnold to America. Rev. P. Peckard, in his "Memoirs of Nicholas Ferrar," says, "the Earl of Southampton had been converted from Popery by Sir Edwyn Sandys."

April 10, 1603, he was discharged out of the Tower by a warrant from the king, sent post-haste from Scotland, April 1; May 16, grant of pardon and restitution; restored to his honors; July 2, Knight of the Garter; July 7, Governor of the Isle of Wight for life; July 21, recreated Earl of Southampton, and afterwards granted many pensions, favors, etc. On July 2, 1603, he had a noted quarrel with Lord Grey, of Wilton, a professed enemy of Essex, and Strickland says, "It is extremely probable that this quarrel was connected with the mysterious plot discovered a few days after, in which Lord Grey, Lord Cobham, Sir Walter Raleigh, and the faction which had brought Essex to the block, were deeply implicated." 1604, "The first bill which was read in the first Parliament of King James was for his restitution in blood." 1605, he aided in sending Weymouth to America; M. C. for Va. Co., 1609, admitted into the E. I. Co. in 1609, and promised to present them with a brace of bucks annually at their elections; April, 1610, he aided in sending out Henry Hudson to the Northwest; July 26, 1612, an incorporator of the N. W. P. Co.; 1614, he subscribed £100 towards Harley's voyage to our present New England coast, and in the same year served at the siege of Rees in the Duchy of Cleves; June 29, 1615, an incorporator of the S. I. Co., and Southampton tribe in that island was afterwards named for him; 1617, he attended the king in his long visit to Scotland. On Friday, April 30, 1619, he was sworn of the king's Privy Council; June 28, 1620, he was chosen treasurer of the Va. Co., without opposition, being "such a one as might at all times and occasions have free accesse unto the King;" November 3, 1620, a member of the New England Council; May 2, 1621, again chosen treasurer of the Va. Co., without opposition. "He had some quarrelling with the Marquis of Buckingham," for which he was under arrest from June 16 to September 1, 1621; again chosen treasurer of the Va. Co., May 22, 1622 (at this election it had pleased the king to suggest several merchants as being better suited to the business) (see Sir Thomas Smythe); he continued treasurer until the charter of the Va. Co. was declared void, June 16, 1624. Soon after which time "Mr. Nicholas Ferrar, late deputy, delivered his copies of the Va. Records to the earl, who, when the commissioners applied for them, replied that he would as soone part with the evidences of his Land as with the said copies; being the evidence of his honour in that service."

It is curious to read the charge that James I. took away the Va. charter in the interest of Spain, at the instance of Gondomar, in 1624, when, in fact, Gondomar left England in 1622; the king had declared war against Spain March 10, 1624, and the earl (then governor of the Va. Co.), since early in June, 1624, had been, under commission from James I., actively engaged in enlisting troops to fight against Spain. About August he went over to the Netherlands in command of a regiment, where his eldest son, James, died at Rosendale, and he, soon after, at Bergen - op - Zoom (November 10, 1624), while on his way to England with his son's body. Father and son were buried at Titchfield, in Hampshire, on December 28, 1624.

Lodge says, " He was a man of no very unusual character, in whom several fine qualities were shadowed by some important defects. His understanding seems to have been lively and acute; and his acquired talents, united to a competent erudition, an extensive and correct taste for polite letters, and the most highly finished manners. His friendships were ardent and lasting; his personal courage almost proverbial; and his honor wholly unsuspected : but his mind was fickle and unsteady ; a violent temper engaged him in frequent quarrels, and in enmities injurious to his best interests ; and he was wholly a stranger to that wary circumspection which is commonly dignified by the name of prudence."

The name of Smythe's Hundred (first named for Sir Thomas Smythe) was changed on May 17, 1620, to Southampton Hundred, being so named for the earl. It lay in the lower part of the present Charles City County, between "Southampton *alias* Chickahomine River " and the James, and contained 100,000 acres of land. Hampton River, near Fortress Monroe, was originally named for him " Southampton River."

He married Elizabeth, daughter of John Vernon, Esq., by Elizabeth, sister of Walter Devereux, first Earl of Essex, and had by her three daughters and two sons : James, aforesaid, and Thomas, his successor, that eminently loyal servant to Charles I., and virtuous lord treasurer to Charles II., at whose death, May 16, 1667, the title became extinct.

Colonel William Byrd, the first of the name in Virginia, is said to have purchased the two volumes of Va. Co. Records, now in the library of Congress, from the executors of this last Earl of Southampton.

Wrote, Samuel, esquire. Son of Robert Wrote, of Gunton in County Suffolk, esquire, by his wife Catherine, daughter of Vincent Randall (Randolph), of London, gent. He was

" cosen Germane " to Lionel Cranfield, Earl of Middlesex; M. C. for Va. Co. Sir Thomas Gates transferred five shares of land in Virginia to him, March 2, 1620. George Sandys wrote to him from Jamestown, Virginia, March 28, 1623. He was a leading opponent of the Sandys party, and was suspended by them from the company; a member of the Virginia Commission of July 15, 1624 ; appointed to the royal council for Virginia, November 16, 1624; mentioned as a late commissioner for Virginia, and as still interested in Virginia affairs, 1629; on the special commission for the better plantation of Virginia, June 27, 1631; was still living 1634. He married Sarah, daughter of William Bussel (Burrel ?). Wrote's cousin, Lionel Cranfield (the " smooth versifier "), was brother to Martha Cranfield who married Sir John Suckling (member of the Privy Council and of the Va. Commission of July, 1624), and became the mother of Sir John Suckling, Jr., the celebrated poet.

Wroth Pedigree. (Extract.) Sir Thomas [1] Wroth (chief gentleman of the bedchamber to Edward VI.), who fled into Germany for conscience' sake in the reign of Queen Mary, married Mary, daughter of Richard, first Lord Rich, and great aunt of Robert Rich, second Earl of Warwick, and was the father, among others, of 1. Sir Robert [2] and 2. Thomas [2] Wroth.

1. Sir Robert [2], known as Sir Robert Wroth, the Elder; M. P. for Middlesex, from 1572 to his death, January 27, 1606 ; married " Susan, daughter of Frauncis Stonard, of Loughton in Essex, Esquier," and was the father, among others, of " John [3] Wrothe a Captayne," and " Sir Robert [3] Wrothe of Durance."

2. Thomas [2] Wroth of the Inner Temple, Esq., married Joan, daughter of Thomas Bullman, of London, and had issue, among others, Sir Thomas Wroth.

Wroth, John [3], esquire. Sub. ——; pd. £87 10s. Second son of Sir Robert Wroth, Sr., of Durance Enfield, Middlesex (see pedigree) ; baptized June 11, 1577 ; M. C. for Va. Co.; one of the auditors of that company, and a member of the Warwick or Smythe party in 1622–24. He strongly protested against the sending of so many people to Virginia, until the colony was prepared to receive them. In 1623 he wrote "that in the yeares 1619, 1620, 1621 there was 3,560 or 3,570 persons sent to Virginia, and Sir Thomas Smith left above 700 persons, which in all make 4,270 persons; whereof the Remainder being about 1240 about the tyme of the massacre, it consequentlie followes, that wee had then lost 3,000 persons within those three yeares. And in the latter end of the yeare 1622, there were sent near upon 1000 persons, whereof manie dyed by the way, and it appeareth by some letters, that by the sword and sickness, there are perished above 500 since the massacre. So that by this accompt, there cannot be above 1700 persons now in the Collonie." He had served in the wars as a captain; married " Mawde dau. to Rich. Flewellen of Wales wydow to Captayne Gregory Lennad brother to Henry Lord Dacre." Died in 1644.

Wroth, Sir Robert [3], 2. Sub. £75; pd. £50. "Of Durance in Enfilde and of Lowghton in Essex." Son of Sir Robert Wroth, Sr., and brother of John Wroth, Esq., aforesaid (see extract from pedigree); M. P. for Newtown, Isle of Wight, in 1601; knighted at Sion House in June, 1603; M. P. for Middlesex, 1607–11; sheriff of Essex, 1613–14; died March 14, 1614. He married Mary, daughter of Robert Sidney, Viscount Lisle, etc. "Ben Jonson dedicated to this distinguished woman his admirable comedy of the Alchemist, and to her husband an excellent moral epistle in commendation of the innocence and felicity of the country life to which Sir Robert devoted himself." "Their residence was the resort and asylum of men of letters; they were the friends of merit, and the patrons of genius in distress."

Wroth, Sir Thomas Sub. ——; pd. ——. Son of Thomas of the Inner Temple (see pedigree).

He resided at Petherton Park, County Somerset; married Margaret, daughter of Richard Rich, of Lee in Essex, and sister (not to the Earl of Warwick as Stith says, page 182, but) to Sir Nathaniel Rich. He was knighted at Theobald's, November 12,

1613. In 1620 he published "The Destruction of Troy, or the Acts of Æneas. Translated ovt of the second Booke of the Æneads of Virgill, that peereless Prince of Latine Poets. . . . As also a Centurie of Epigrams, and a Motto upon the Creede, thereunto annexed." Dedicated to Sir Robert Sidney, Viscount Lisle, and containing an epigram "to his worthy friend Captaine [Nathaniel] Butler."

He was M. C. for New England, November 3, 1620; a leader of the Warwick party in the Va. Co., 1621–24; on the Virginia Commission of July 15, 1624; M. P. for Bridgewater, 1628–29. His wife, Dame Margaret, died of a fever October 14, 1635, and he wrote an account of her life, sickness, and death to her brother Sir Nathaniel Rich (whom see), the greater part of which is printed in "Court and Society from Elizabeth to Anne" (vol. i. p. 343). "His sad Encomiem upon his Dearest Consort" was also published in London, in 1635. M. P. for Bridgewater, in Somerset, from 1645, until the dissolution of 1653; on January 3, 1648, he made the celebrated motion "to lay the King by and to settle the Kingdom without him." He was appointed one of the commissioners on trial of the king, but refused to sit; was on the commission of June 25, 1653, for governing the affairs of the Bermudas Islands. A strong Parliamentarian and confirmed Rumper; he was elected to the Cromwellian Parliaments of 1656–58 and 1659, and to the Convention of 1660. He died, s. p., in 1672, his will being proved August 24, 1672.

Wyche (see **Winche**), **Richard**, skinner. Of the N. W. and E. I. companies; married Elizabeth, daughter of Sir Richard Saltingstall, Lord Mayor of London, and had by her 12 sons and six daughters. Died November 20, 1621, aged 67, and was buried in St. Dunstan's in the East. His sixth son, Sir Peter, was ambassador from Charles I. to Turkey for twelve years.

Wymark (see **Wimark**), **Ned.** Whom Thomas Osborne, in his "Traditional Memoirs of King James," page 7, styles, "The Paul's Walker, and the Witty." In December, 1618, he got himself into serious trouble by "wishing that Raleigh's head was on Secretary Naunton's shoulders."

Wynche. See **Winch.**

Wynne. See **Winne.**

Yaxley, Sir Robert, 3. Sub. ——; pd. ——. Knighted at Dublin in Ireland, September 8, 1599 ; M. P. for Thirsk in 1614.

Yeardley (or **Yardley**), **George,** gent., 2. Sub. ——; pd. £25. Son of Raph Yardley, citizen and merchant-tailor, of Bionshaw Lane, London, who married, first, May 15, 1575, Agnes Abbot ; she died December 18, 1576, and he married, secondly, Rhoda ——. He had four sons, Raphe, George (of whom I write), John, and Thomas, and a daughter, Anne, who married Edward Irby.

George, born (1577–80 ?) ; "a soldier truly bred in that university of Warre, the Lowe Countries ;" sailed for Virginia as "Captain of Sir Thomas Gates his company" in June, 1609 ; wrecked on the Bermudas ; arrived in Virginia in May, 1610 ; acting governor from the departure of Dale in April, 1616, to the arrival of Argall, May 15, 1617 ; went to England in 1618, where he spent very near three thousand pounds in furnishing himself for his return to Virginia ; M. C. for Va. Co. ; chosen governor of Virginia for three years on the 18th of November, 1618 ; granted on the same day twenty great shares for transport of twenty-six persons, and was knighted by the king at Newmarket six days after ; sailed for Virginia in January, and arrived April 19, 1619. Under instructions from Sir Thomas Smith's administration he convened the first legislature in America, July 30, 1619, at Jamestown ; continued governor three years, to November 18, 1621, when he was relieved by Sir Francis Wyatt. He was then a member of the council in Virginia until May, 1626. When Wyatt wished to leave Virginia for a time on business in 1624, King James on the 18th of September, 1624, commissioned Yeardley to act as governor during Wyatt's absence ; but Wyatt did not leave at this time. On the 14th of March, 1626, Charles I. commissioned Sir George Yeardley to be governor of Virginia ; he entered into that office

in May, 1626, and continued to serve until his death in November, 1627. (An abstract of his will is given in the "N. E. Hist. and Gen. Register" for January, 1884.) He married, about 1618 (and took his lady to England with him in that year), Miss Temperance ——, who came to Virginia in the Faulcon in 1609. In January, 1625, they were living at Jamestown with their three children born in Virginia, viz. : Elizabeth, aged six years, 1. Argall[1], aged four years, and 2. Francis, aged one year.

Sir George Yardley was a first cousin to Richard Yerwood, one of the stepfathers of John Harvard, the founder of Harvard College, Massachusetts. [Was this the Richard Yarwood, gent., of Southwark, who was M. P. for Southwark, 1614, 1621–22, 1624–25, 1625, 1626, and 1628–29 ?] He was a prosperous man, and left his children well supplied with worldly goods. His descendants are now scattered over the United States. Of his daughter Elizabeth I know nothing.

1. Argall[1] married, about 1640, Ann, daughter of John Custis, and died in 1655, leaving, at least, three sons (Argall[2], Henry, and Edmond) and two daughters (Rose and Frances). Argall[2] (with whom his father, Argall[1], is nearly always confused) married, in 1670, Sarah, daughter of John Machell, and died in 1682, leaving five children, viz. : John, Argall[3], Elizabeth, Frances, and Sarah.

2. Francis married Sarah, widow of Capt. John Gookin, and before of Capt. Adam Thorogood, and is said to have left no issue.

Yeomans, Simon, fishmonger, 2. Sub. ——; pd. £12 10s. Of St. Botolph, Billingsgate, London ; married, in 1594, Mary, daughter of John Barkeley, of Essex, gent.

Yong (or **Young**), **William,** a tailor, 2. Sub. ——; pd. £12 10s. Came to Virginia in 1607.

Zouch, Sir Edward. Of the North Virginia Company ; was interested in patents for making glass ; a courtier, etc. Strickland, in her "Lives of the Queens of England," says, "In the midst of the mad revelry of Shrovetide (February), 1618,

James I. was taken ill with the gout in his knees ; some rantipol knights of his bedchamber, Sir George Goring, Sir Edward Zouch, and others tried to amuse him by acting some little burlesque plays, called 'Tom-a-Bedlam,' 'The Tinker,' and 'The two Merry Milk Maids.' But the gout and the cold weather pinched the king, and nothing could put him in a good humor. He reproved his knights for ribaldry — not without reason, called their little burlesque plays, mad stuff, and was utterly unmanageable by his masculine attendants."

Sir Edward Zouch was granted the office of knight marshal of the household for life, April 29, 1618; the agent for sending certain dissolute persons to Virginia in November and December, 1619 ; a member of the New England Council in 1620.

Zouch, Edward Lord, 2. Sub. —— ; pd. £60. Son of George, tenth Lord Zouch, whom he succeeded in 1569 as the eleventh Lord Zouch, under which title he was summoned to Parliament from April 2, 1571, to May 17, 1625.

In 1593 he was sent ambassador to James VI., king of Scotland, with instructions to protest against the act of the council of November 26, which was too favorable to the Earls of Angus, Huntley, and Errol, who were in league with Spain; to say that the queen would resist the landing of any Spanish or other foreign forces in Scotland as their purpose was only to invade England ; to form a party for the defense of the religion and of the peace between England and Scotland. He had a conference with James VI. of Scotland concerning Bothwell and his accomplices, February 25 to March 2, 1594. In 1598 he was an ambassador to Denmark, treating of "merchantile affairs," etc. In 1603 James I. of England (his old friend James VI. of Scotland) appointed him to his Privy Council. "April 13, 1603, commission appointing Edward Lord Zouch, lord president of the council in Wales to be the king's lieutenant in Wales." "May 14, 1603, he wrote to the king, thanking him for bestowing on him so great a gift, before it was asked for." During the time he was lord president of Wales, he had a long and bitter controversy with Sir John Popham, lord chief justice of England, about precedency, etc., which came before the Privy Council in December, 1604, but was not at that time settled.

M. C. for Va. Co., 1609. "July 13, 1615, grant to him of the office of Lord Warden of the Cinque Ports and Constable of Dover Castle for life." July 20, 1615, Chamberlain to Carleton: "The Lord Zouch hath his patent signed and sealed for the Wardenship of the Cinque Ports, a place he never sought for nor pretended."

July, 1615, Carew to Roe : "The Lord Zouche is Lord Warden of the Cinque Ports, which is displeasing to the priests." "August 9, 1615, commission to Edward Lord Zouch, Lord Warden of the Cinque Ports, concerning the examining and licensing of passengers, with instructions touching the same."

In December, 1617, he adventured £100 ($2,500) with Lord De la Warr towards a plantation, etc., in Virginia. In 1618 he was interested with John Bargrave in some Virginia enterprise. He sent his pinnace, the Silver Falcon to Virginia in 1619, and evidently took a great interest in the colony. He was also one of the first members of the New England Council, November 3, 1620. He died at Hackney in 1625, and was buried in a small chapel adjoining his house. "Ben Jonson, who was his intimate friend, discovered that there was a hole in the wall affording communication between the last resting-place of Lord Zouch and the wine-cellar, and thereupon vented this impromptu : —

'Wherever I die, let this be my fate
To lye by my good Lord Zouch —
That when I am dry, to the tap I may hye,
And so back again to my couch.'

"Lord Zouch was much interested in experimental gardening and the science of botany, of which he was so great an encourager that he cultivated a physic garden in the parish of Hackney at his own expence, committing the superintendence of it to the celebrated Lobel." He brought many shrubs and seed from abroad. He was also a patron of Dr. John Gerarde. He married Sara, daughter of Sir James Harington of Exton, and widow of Francis Lord Hastings, who died in 1596. After the death of Lord Zouche, his widow, in 1626, became the second wife of Sir Thomas Edmondes.

Zouche, John, esquire (see next). Sub. —— ; pd. £25.

Zouche, Sir John. Mr. Neill, in his "Virginia Vetusta" (p. 2, note), says, "Captain John Zouche and Sir Walter Raleigh were each in command of a company at the siege in 1580 of the Spanish Fort near Tralee, in the southwest part of Ireland, and in August, 1581, Zouche was promoted as Governor of Munster."

John Zouche of Codnor, Derbyshire, was knighted at Beaver Castle, April 23, 1603. His son, John Zouch, Esq., had joined the Virginia enterprise, prior to 1616 ; in 1623 he patented lands in Virginia. In 1631 the father, Sir John Zouche, was one of the "commission for the better plantation of Virginia," and in 1634 he spent some time in Virginia, with his son and daughter, who were then living there. He is said to have been of the Puritan sect.

Zuñiga — Cuñiga — Quñiga. Don Pedro de Zuñiga, Marques de Villa Flores et Avila. He came as ambassador to England in the autumn of 1605, succeeding in that office Juan de Taxis, Count of Villa Mediana, who sailed from Dover, September 1, 1605, with Sir William Monson, for Flanders. The new resident ambassador is said to have found in England seven pensioners of Spain, namely : Henry Howard, Earl of Northampton ; Charles Blount, Earl of Devonshire ; Thomas Sackville, Earl of Dorset; the Lady Suffolke; Robert Cecil, Earl of Salisbury ; Sir William Monson; and Mrs. Drummond, the first lady of Queen Anne's bedchamber.

"On the morning of November 5, 1605, the news of the great deliverance from the Gunpowder Plot ran like wildfire along the streets of London," and it was necessary to take prompt measures to protect Zuñiga from the fury of the people. He seems to have kept very close afterwards ; I do not find his name in the Calendar of State Papers, 1605–10. The celebrated Italian jurist, Alberigo Gentilis, was advocate to the Spanish embassy from the autumn of 1605 to his death, June 19, 1608. Zuñiga was succeeded by Velasco about May, 1610. Some time after his return to Spain he was created "Marques de Villa Flores et Avila." In 1612 he was sent as ambassador extraordinary to James I., with private instructions, if he saw fair prospect of success, to offer the hand of Philip III. (then a widower) to the Princess Elizabeth of England ; but "he found that the marriage with the Elector was irrevocably decided upon." He had his first audience with James I. on July 6, 1612. He was soon dismissed ; but continued to linger in England, which was not much liked. On July 22, 1612, Archbishop Abbot wrote to James I., "The lingering in England of the Spanish ambassador, Zuñiga, is very suspicious. He has secretly dispersed £12,000 or £13,000 already in England, and tampers by night with the Lieger ambassador from France. He was in England at the time of the Powder treason, and God knows what share he had in that business." (See also Abbot's letter of August 3, 1612, in sketch of Velasco.) George Calvert wrote to Sir Thomas Edmondes on August 1 : "Zuñiga is yet here, no man knows why, for he hath taken his leave of the king. But to show that he is unwelcome, as he was riding in his *carrosse* with his six mules over Holborn Bridge the other day, with his great lethugador about his neck and coming upon his elbow, at the side of the *carrosse*, comes a fellow by him on horseback ; and whether *de guetapens* or otherwise, I cannot tell, but he snatches the ambassador's hat off his head, which had a rich jewel in it, and rides away with it up the street as fast as he could, the people going on and laughing at it." Chamberlain says,

"The ambassador, observing a well-dressed cavalier approaching his carriage, pulled off his hat out of the window, which was enriched with a handsome band and Jewel, when the fellow snatched it out of his hand and rode off." James I. instructed Digby to find out the reasons for his stay (see CCXXVIII.). He was still in England in the first part of October, 1612, when he was complaining "of the opening by the custom-house officers of a chest of his." He probably left soon after.

Our histories do not mention him; but it can be safely said that the English would never have succeeded in establishing Protestant colonies in America, if the matter could have been controlled by Don Pedro de Zuñiga.

ADDITIONAL MEMBERS OF PARLIAMENT.

I WISH to give as complete a list as possible of the members of the first Parliament of James I. who were interested in the American enterprise. I think that all of the following were members of the Va. Co.; most of them certainly were. I believe that I have identified nearly all of those who were of the South Virginia Company; but the list is necessarily very deficient of the Northern Company. However, I feel very sure that a majority of the Parliament of 1604–11 was interested in American colonization.

Berkeley, Richard, esquire. Gloucestershire, 1604–11, and 1614.

Bertie, Perigrine. Lincolnshire, 1614.

Bing (or Byng), William, esquire. New Romney, 1610–11 ; Winchelsea, 1614 ; admitted to Gray's Inn 1612; Governor of Deal Castle ; younger brother of George Byng, of Wrotham, Kent, and of the same family as the present Viscount Torrington.

Bingley, John. Chester, 1610–11, and 1614. Probably admitted to Gray's Inn in 1612.

Bowyer, Robert, esquire. Evesham, 1605–11.

Carew, Sir George. St. Germans, 1604–11 ; the lawyer and diplomatist who died in 1612.

Carey, Henry. Sussex, 1609–11.

Cavendish, Sir William. East Retford, 1614.

Cecil, Sir Edward. Stamford, 1609–11.

Cecil, William, Lord Cranborne. Weymouth, 1610–11.

Chute, Sir Walter. East Retford, 1614.

Connock, Richard, esquire. Bodmin, 1593, Liskeard, 1614; auditor of the Duchy of Cornwall, and friend to Ralegh ; will proved February 15, 1620.

Cranfield, Lionell. Hythe, 1614.

Danvers, Sir John. Montgomerytown, 1614.

Earle, Walter. Poole, 1614, 1621–22, 1624–25 ; Dorset, 1625 ; Lyme Regis, 1626; Dorset, 1628–29; Lyme Regis, April, 1640 ; Weymouth and Melcombe Regis, 1640, until secluded in 1648; Dorset, 1654–55, 1659; Poole, 1660. Of Charborough, Dorsetshire ; knighted May 4, 1616 ; bought five shares of land in Virginia from Sir Thomas Gates. He was the well known Parliamentary colonel ; governor of Dorchester, 1643, and master of the ordnance; died in 1665.

Fawcett (or Forcett), Edward, esquire. Wells, 1606–11.

Fearne, John. Boroughbridge, 1604–11.

Goodere, Sir Henry. West Looe, 1604–11.

Harrington, Sir John. Rutlandshire, 1604–11.

Harris, John, esquire. West Looe, 1614.

Herbert, Philip. Glamorganshire, 1604, until peer, 1605.

Holcroft, Sir Thomas. Cheshire, 1604, until decease, 1610.

Hollis, Sir John. Nottinghamshire, 1604–11, and 1614.

Howard, Theophilus. Malden, 1605, until peer.

Ingram, Sir Arthur. Romney, 1614.

Jermain, Sir Thomas. Suffolk, 1614.

Mansell, Sir Thomas. Glamorgan, 1605–11.

Michell, Bernard, gent. Weymouth, 1610–11, 1614, 1625, and 1626.

Miller (or Meller), Sir Robert. Bridport, 1604–11.

Monson, Sir Thomas. Castle Rising, 1604–11; Cricklade, 1614.

Nevill, Sir Henry. Lewes, 1604–11.

Nevill, Sir Henry. Wycombe, 1614 ; Wilton, 1621–22 ; son of Sir Henry Nevill, of Billingbere, Berks.

Pawlett, John, esquire. Somerset, 1610–11, 1614 ; Lyme Regis, 1621–22. He was created Baron Poulett, 1627.

Percy, Alan, esquire. Beverley, 1604–11.

Phellips, Sir Robert. East Looe, 1604–11.

Plomer, Thomas, gent. Romney, 1604–11.

Rich, Henry, esquire. Leicester, 1610–11.

Rich, Sir Robert. Malden, 1610–11.

Smith (or Smythe), Sir John. Hythe, 1604 until decease, 1609 ; brother to Sir Thomas Smythe, the first treasurer of the Va. Co.

Stanhope, Sir John. Newton, 1604, until peer, 1605.

INDEX.

———

I have indexed the historical portion (pp. 1–805) closely. I have indicated all personal references in the brief biographies (807–1070), and all places referred to outside of England and all subjects bearing on discovery, commerce, and colonization; but it was not advisable to cumber the Index with the numerous English places named, or with the various subjects having no bearing on the Genesis of the United States.

I have sometimes found it preferable to use the name instead of the page figures when referring to the biographies.

The names of persons are *all* indexed in alphabetical order, as are places and subjects generally; but foreign localities, when not referred to often, are given under the city, country, etc., to which they belong; and scattered, unfrequent subjects are collected together under proper comprehensive headings, which are arranged alphabetically.

See Africa; America; Ancient names; Asia; Atlantic Ocean; Bays; Bermudas; Brazil; Capes; Chili; Climate; Commodities; Companies; Diseases of Virginia; Distress in Virginia; Doctors and Medical Treatment; East India; Emigrants; England; Europe; Fauna; Firsts; Fish, etc.; Flora; Florida; Fortifications, Forts, etc.; France; French; Houses, Buildings, etc., in Virginia; Islands; Lands, etc., in Virginia; Law, Government, etc.; London; Lotteries; Mexico; Minerals; Ministers; Native Inhabitants; Naval Affairs of England; New England; Newfoundland; New France; New Spain; North America; Pacific Ocean; Pedigrees; Peru; Plays; Poetry; Portugal; Protestantism; Provisions; Ralegh or Roanoke Colony; Rivers; Romanism; Ships; South America; Spain; Spanish; State; Tempest; Trade; United States of Holland and the Netherlands; Virginia; Voyages; West Indies, etc.

The heavy face figures refer to the BIOGRAPHIES. *Port.* = Portrait.

ABANDONMENT of Virginia, 401, 404–407, 414, 415, 417, 418, 617, 618, 648, 649, 680, 681, 802. See Capt. John Martin.

Abbas I. (Shah of Persia, 1582–1628), 985, 1000.

Abbay, Thomas, 601, **811**.

Abbot, Agnes, 1065; George, archbishop of Canterbury, translator of the Bible, etc., 541, 542, 576, 606, 676, 679, 686, 790–795, **811**, 812, 845, 851, 863, 878, 906, 927, 974, 993, 1025, 1037, 1051, 1067, *Port.*, 10; Martha, 1024; Mary, 879; Maurice, the elder, 811; Maurice (or Morris), the younger, merchant, diplomatic commissioner, etc., 469, 574, 770, 797, 803, **811**, **812**, 879, 982, 1024, 1061; Robert, bishop of Salisbury, 811.

Abdey, Anthony, merchant, 548, 770, 812; Roger, 812.

Abergavenny, Lord. — Henry Neville.

Abot, Jeffra, 600, 812.

Ackland, Sir John, 466, 544, **812**.

Acosta, Antonio de, Portuguese merchant in London, 659.

Acquaviva, Rev. Father Claude, Italian general of the Jesuits, 700, **812**.

Acuña. See Gondomar.

Adams, Nicholas, merchant-tailor, 304; Nicholas, vice-admiral of Pembroke, 722; Capt. Robert, 812; Thomas the elder, 812; Thomas, stationer, 292, 748, **812**; William, 138; Capt. ——,

329, 488–490, 492, 497, 639, 653, 663, 689, **812**.

Adelmare. See Dr. Cæsar Adelmare.

Aderley, William, 770.

Adventurers for Va. (Incorporators, Planters, Undertakers, etc), "who contribute their money and do not go in person," 272; ancestors of, founders of first organized English company for discovery, etc., 3; interested in the Northwest Passage, 8; Adventurers in Fifth Parliament of Elizabeth, 13; in the Protestant wars of the United States of Holland, etc., 17; in the Armada fight, 20; roving the Atlantic, 20–27; at Cadiz, 24; at the Azores, 24; interested in proposed voyage to East India, 25; incorporators of first East India charter, 25. [The foregoing references apply to Planters as well as to Adventurers. See Biographies and Emigrants.] 49, 52, 53, 228, 229, 236, 248, 272, 280, 281, 284, 295, 302, 316, 317, 415, 425, 426, 466, 503, 505, 507, 541–548, 574, 579, 582, 587, 588, 625–630, 769, 775–779, 781, 798, 802–805, 808, 982. See Charters, Emigrants, Subscribers, etc.

Advice of the Va. Council, 79–85, 102; of Lord Bacon to Viscount Villiers, 795.

Africa: Abyssinia, 970; Africa, 32, 147, 440, 785, 916, 970, 994, 1000, 1007, 1023,

* These references are to critical sources.

Haselrig, Hazlerigg, Francis, gent., 223, 915.

Hastings, Elizabeth, 1019; Francis, 915, 1067; Francis, 1046; Sir Francis, 953; Francis, Earl of Huntingdon. 1019; George, 915, 1046; Henry, Earl of Huntingdon (1572), 992; Henry, Earl of Huntingdon, 542, **915**, *Port.*, 491; Sara, Lady, 884.

Hatfield House Library, 145.

Hathaway, Anne, 999.

Hatton, Sir Christopher, 13, 823, 881, auto., **915**, 1045, 1046; Sir Christopher, Jr., 889; Dorothy, 915; Frances, 980; Sir Henry, 967; Lady, 819, 851; "Sir Wm. Newport alias Hatton," 851, 980.

Haukinson, George, 228, 915.

Hauterive, Mons. de (French), 622.

Havana (Cuba), 23, 128, 198, 443, 451, 456, 472, 510–513, 518, 521–525, 531, 533, 539, 554, 588, 592, 607, 653, 1043.

Haveland, Anthony, 390; Thomas, stationer, 356.

Haversham, Baron, 1034.

Hawes, Humphrey, clothworker, 277, 915; Sir James, 1043; Lawrence, 915; Margaret, 1043; Mr. ——, 982; Robert, fishmonger, 282.

Hawes, Hames, Himes, Hine, Nicholas, 95–97, 128, 134, 639, 640, 645.

Hawkeridge, Capt. Giles, 467, 546.

Hawkins, Charles, 220, 468, **915**, 918; Sir John, 4–7, 23, 568, 674, 792, 793, 813, 851, 854, 856, 881, 882, 889, 893, 901, **915**, **916**, 918, 922, 926, 930, 939, 947, 950, 967, 1056, *Port.*, 501; John, 216, **916**, 918; John, merchant-tailor, 304; John, the elder, 915; Sir John, the author, 917, 918; John, of Rugby, 1000; Lady Judith, 917; Mary, 919; Sir Richard, author, 16, 94, 771, **916–918**, 942, 980; Sara, 1000; Capt. William (1st), 916, 918; Capt. William (2d), 6, **915**, **916**, **918**, 944; Capt. William (3d), 918; William, Esq., 919; "Hawkins," 972.

Hawks, Rev. F. L., 242.

Hawley (see Harley), Capt. ——, 213.

Hawte, Jane, 996; Sir William, 996.

Hay, James Lord, etc., 542, 797, auto., **918**, 920, 921, 955, 965, 979, 1044, *Port.*, 511.

Hayden, Haydon, Heyden, etc., Jeremy, or Jerome, 468, 594, 748, 770, **918**; Sir John, 918.

Hayes, Hays, Edward, author, 12, **918**; Martha, 887; Sir Thomas, 887.

Hayward. See Haiward.

Hazard's Historical Collections, 1027.

Hazleden. See Haselden.

Hazlerigg. See Haselrig.

Head of the river (see Falls), 504.

Heale, Hele, Sir John, 919; Sir Warwick, 466, **919**, 980.

Heath, Robert, Esq., 797, 803, 879, **919**, *Port.*, 531.

Heath's Chronicle, 981.

Hebrides, 601.

Heiborne, Heyborne, Sir Ferdinando, or Sir Francis, 467, 545, **919**.

Heightley, Peter, 804, 919.

Heiton, Frauncis, gent., 547.

Hellowes, Edward, author, 926.

Helme, John, merchant-tailor, 305.

Helpringham, 359.

Hemp, 268, 317, 398, 482, 492, 493; dressers, 470; planters, 470.

Heneage, Elizabeth, 891; Sir Thomas, 891, 1046.

Hening's Virginia Statues at Large, 65, 91, 201, 995.

Henningham, Abigail, 877; Sir Arthur, 877.

Henrico (town), Va., 581, 583, 584, 611, 614, 649, 652, 660, 744, 751, 782, 795, 823. 1025, 1050, 1053; county, Va., 1025; Henricopolis, 1025; Henries towne, 644; Henricus, 504, 1025; New town in Virginia, 491, 492, 504; New Townes in Virginia, 778.

Henrietta Maria, 966, 879, 1039.

Henry, Cape, 158, 354, 401, 403, 404, 409, 414, 429, 484, 565, 781, 1025, XLVI., CLVIII. See Rivers.

Henry, Prince. See Henry Stuart.

Henry II of France (1551), 1023.

Henry IV. of France and of Navarre (1589–1610), 40, 278, 391, 534, 716, 831, 848, 877, 893, 946, 967, 1000, 1003, 1027, *Port.*, xxxi.

Henry VII. of England (1485–1509), 1, 2, 263, 313, 368, 672, 693, 837, 838, 859, 1054. See Tudor.

Henry VIII. of England (1509–1547), 2, 277, 837–839, 846, 859, 922, 965, 1022, 1030, 1039, 1046, 1061. See Tudor.

Henry VIII. (the play), 637.

Henshaw, Hinshaw, Thomas, merchant-tailor, 222, 306, 307, 469, 829, **919**.

Heralds, College of, 308, 309.

Herbert, Capt. ——, 213; Arthur, 920; Charles, 919; Edward, Lord, author, 874, 927, 953; Edward, Esq., 804, **919**, **920**, 1018; Rev. George, poet, 874, 919, 1037, 1057; Henry, Earl of Pembroke, 920–922, 1001; Margaret, 1037; Mary, Countess of Pembroke (see Sidney), 1045, 1046; Philip, Earl of Montgomery, 209, 231, 379, 384, 465, 548, 549, 681, 855, **920–922**, 943, 944, 988, 1001, 1044, 1069, *Port.*, 541; Richard, Esq., 874; William, Earl of Pembroke, 4, 839, 922; William, Earl of Pembroke, poet, 90, 98, 209, 231, 239, 318, 319, 379, 384, 465, 532, 676, 681, 686, 755, 770, 847, 920, **921**, **922**, 941, 943, 944, 954, 1001, 1002, 1014, 1030, *Port.*, 551.

Herbert's History of the Twelve Great Livery Companies of London, 611, 857.

4, 839, **939**; Dr. Thomas, poet, 21, **939**; Timothy, fishmonger, 281.

Lodge's Life of Sir Julius Cæsar, 813, 840; Illustrations of British History, 12, 321; Portraits, 847, 849, 927, 928, 1063.

London, vi, xiii, 11, 36, 45, 46, 51–54, 85, 88, 97, 102, 106, 110, 116, 118, 126, 141, 147, 152, 172, 175, 197, 208, 209, 240, 241, 250–254, 265, 279, 280, 283, 294, 296, 308, 312, 314–316, 329, 337, 338, 356, 357, 359, 360, 373, 383, 388, 391, 418–420, 439, 440, 445, 455, 469, 473, 474, 494–496, 523, 526, 528, 532, 537, 559, 560, 562, 571, 572, 576, 595, 601, 602, 610–612, 621, 631, 633, 635, 637, 638, 645, 656–659, 667, 675, 676, 678–680, 684–687, 697, 705, 722–725, 735, 737, 746–748, 756, 759, 761, 765–767, 769, 771–774, 780–782, 784, 791, 811–1070, *passim*; Archers of, 924; artillery, 831, 909; Bank of England, 910, 1031; Banquetting House, 678; Bernard's Inn, 26; Billingsgate, 30; Blackfriars, 747; Blewe Anchor Taverne, 30; Booksellers (see Stationers), 495; "Britaines Burse," 595, 1054; Burbage's Company, 637; Burleigh House, 850; citizens of, 468, 469, 547, 548, 571; Cope Castle, 179, 862, 979; Durham House, 179; Exeter House, 206, 850; Fenchurch Street, 747; Filpot (see Philpot) Lane; fire of 1666, ix, 250, 571 (see under Russia Company); Fleet Street, 791; Gate House, 610; Globe Theatre, 637; Gray's Inn, 678; Guilds (see Companies); Herald's College, 308, 309; Holland House (see Cope Castle); Inns of Court, 604; Kensington, 179, 654, 862, 979; Lincoln's Inn, 604; Londoners, 769; London Derry, 611; Lyceum Theatre, 851; Mermaid Club, 945, 1061; Middle Temple, 604; New Bourse, 179; Newgate, 767; Notes and Queries, 916, 1027; Old Jewry, 571; Pageant, 667; Philpot Lane, 248, 439, 445, 465, 764, 1014; Precepts, 254, 277, 324; Public Record Office, 115; Royal Exchange, 767, 860; St. Dunston's churchyard, 791; St. Mary Cole Church, 571, 572; St. Mary Wool Church, 572; St. Saviour's, Southwark, 282, 283, 1029; St. Sepulchre, 319, 767; Temple, 373; Temple Bar, 604; Thames, 82, 251, 583; Tower, 358, 774; Trained Band, 831, 937, 1012; Wellington Street, 851; White Chappel, 282, 283, 287; Wood Street counter, 1048. See British Museum, Companies, Hampton, Highgate, Libraries, London, Aldermen of, Lord Mayors, Lotteries, Merchants, Parliament, Paul's Church, or St. Paul's, Society of Antiquaries, Stationers' Hall, Virginia, Westminster, White Hall.

London, aldermen of, 252, 253. See Abbot, Abdy, Allen, Barkham, Barnes, Bateman, Bolles, Bond, Campbell, Chester, Cletheroe, Cockayne, Cordell, Cotton, Craven, Deane, Freeman, Gerrard, Gore, Hamersley, Hansford, Haydon, Hayward, Heron, Hicks, Hodges, Humble, Johnson, Jones, Lodge, Martin, Middleton, Mildmay, Norton, Parkhurst, Plumer, Pyott, Rainton, Romney, Rotheram, Slany, Smiths, Soame, Spencer, Staplers, Stile, Venn, Watts, Weld, Whitmore, and Wollaston.

London in 1616, drawn by Visscher, frontispiece to vol. ii., showing the bridge with the traitors' heads, Burley House, various churches, Fishmongers' Hall, Guild Hall, Leaden Hall, St. Paul's, The Tower, White Hall, etc.; Southwark, the Globe, the Swan, etc.; and the Thames, with the earliest known representation of a royal procession by water; the notorious floating place of entertainment and resort for the gallants, alluded to by Ben Jonson, called the Galley Fuste; ships, etc.

Londonderry, Earl of.—Thomas Ridgeway.

Long Island, 707, 892.

Longitude, 81.

Longmans & Co., 416.

Longston (see Langton), Thomas, grocer, 558, 591, 686.

Lopez, Franciscus (Spaniard), 18.

Lord Mayors of London, 99, 210, 250, 252–254, 257, 306, 324, 326, 667, 688, 690, 740, 773; Pageant, 667, precepts, 254, 277, 324. See Abbott, Barkham, Barnes, Bolles, Campbell, Cletheroe, Cockayne, Cotton, Craven, Deane, Freeman, Garway, Gore, Hamersly, Jones, Lee, Lemon, Middleton, Parkhurst, Rainton, Rowe, Soame, Venn, Watts, Weld and Whitmore.

Lords. See Parliament, and Peers.

Lorkin, Rev. Thomas, 637, 697, 734, 736, 900, 906, **939**, 999, 1014.

Lotteries for sustaining the colony of Virginia, 537, 538, 551–553, 555, 558, 560, 561, 568, 570–572, 575, 591, 592, 594, 608, 633, 634, 661, 681, 684, 685, 687, 690, 691, 760–765, 768, 769, 773, 852, 878, 940, 1005.

Articles for the second Lottery, 571; blanks, 764, 765; "Booke called ye Lotterie," 571; "A booke or thinge called the Publicacon of the Lottery for Virginia," 538, 555; books, broadsides, etc., in behalf of, 538, 555, 558, 571, 608, 684, 761–766; crownes, 764, 765; differing of, 558; drawings of, 568, 570, 571, 773; letters in behalf of, 555, 685, 686, 688, 760, 761; lots, 769;

Spenser, Edmund, poet, 881, 977, 998, 1002.

Spert, or Pert, Sir Thomas, 2, **1022**.

Spies, employed by Spain, 44, 117, 476, 495, 497, 538, 554, 560, 745 ; by England, 607. See, also, Prisoners, Spain, and Spanish, etc.

Spiller, Sir Henry, 1027.

Spinola, Baptist (Genoese), 1022 ; Benedict, 6, **1022**.

Spitzbergen, 610, 822, 878, 968, 1001, 1013.

Spofford, Hon. A. R., xvi.

Spranger, Henry, 226, 1022.

Springham, Matthew, merchant - tailor, 219, 306, **1022**.

Sprint, Gregory, Esq., 546, 1022.

Sprott, George, 811 ; Roger, merchant-tailor, 305 ; William, 305.

Spruson, Pruson, etc., Hildebrand, 216, 468, 771, **1022**.

Spry, Capt. Henry, 212.

Squanto (an Indian), 1004.

Squibb, Capt. ——, 942.

Stab, Edmund, fishmonger, 281.

Stacy, Thomas, 804, 1022.

Stafford, Lady Dorothy, 997 ; Edward, 14 ; Sir Edward, 864, 1041 ; Edward, Duke of Buckingham, 997 ; Elizabeth, 997 ; Henry, Lord, 997 ; Henry, Duke of Buckingham, 1054 ; Richard, 221 ; Sir William, 997 ; (Wentworth) 979.

Stallenge, Staledge, William, gent , author, 216, 320, **1022**.

Stalls, Book, See Stationers Company.

Standish, Mr. ——, stationer, 292.

Staneries, the, 239.

Stanhope, Cordelia, 818 ; Charles, 1023 ; Edward, 914 ; Henry, Lord, 1040 ; Jane, 914 ; John, Lord, 209, 231, 677, 679, 686, 818, 877, **1022, 1023**, 1045, 1046, 1070 ; Sir Michael, 1022.

Stanley, Anne, 835 ; Edward, Lord Monteagle, 961 ; Elizabeth, 961 ; Ferdinando, 835 ; William. sixth Earl of Derby, 1038 ; Sir William, 940 ; William, merchant-tailor, 304. See Vere-Stanley.

Stannard, Thomas, 1023 ; William, innholder, 225, **1023**.

Stansby, W., stationer, 576, 621, 767, 891, 974.

Stanton, Capt. Richard, 16.

Stanwell, 120.

Stapers, Staper, Staples, Alice, 925 ; Hewet, merchant, 388, 468, 547, 574, **1023** ; Richard, 11, 179, 215, **1023**.

Stapleton, Thomas, merchant-tailor, 304.

Starkey, Lieut. Alexander, 16 ; Mary, 1034.

Starrington, Sir John (?), 549.

State, or government, of England : commonwealth, xiv, 268, 464, 775 ; courts of, 111, 138 ; crown of, 32, 689, 672 ; Great Seal of England, vii, 731, 733 ; kingdom of England, 255, 507, 798,

1027 ; political government, 301 ; politicians, 289, 314 ; remarks on, 255 ; royal arms, 309 ; royal assent, 41, 42 ; royal colonies, v–viii, xiv, xv, 32, 42, 117 ; the state, 775. See Charters, His Majesties Council for Virginia, His Majesties Council for the Virginia Company of London, the Privy Council, Oaths, Objects, Parliament, State Papers, Treaties, Wars, and Westminster.

State Papers and Documents issued by the government, 400, 413, 501, 669, 760, 783, 789 ; Articles and Instructions, 64–75 ; Ordinance and Constitution, 91–95 ; Salisbury to Customs Officers, 307 ; Privy Council to the Heralds, 308, 309 ; Orders of, 676, 677, 679, 680 ; to city companies of London, 685, 686 ; to cities and towns of England, 760, 761 ; to France, 733, 734 ; minute, 760 ; James I. to States-General, 735. See, also, all Charters, Letters, or Communications between Government and Officials, Ambassadors, etc., the Parliament Journals, etc.

States General of the United States of Holland and the Netherlands, 446–451, 735, 737, 745, 1056, 1061 ; President of, 449. See United States of Holland, etc.

Stationers' Company of London, 24, 227, 250, 292, 293, 309, 333, 495, 597, 756, 757, 812, 813, 818, 824, 828, 829, 832, 837. **858, 859**, 891, 913, 958, 1029, 1044, 1061.

Stationers' Hall, 29, 242, 282, 293, 321, 337, 360, 373, 427, 471, 477, 495, 528, 538, 558, 571, 576, 611, 684, 746, 781, 1009, 1042.

Stationers' Records, 292, 293, 309, 310, 757 ; Register, 295, 571.

Stationers' stalls, or shops : " at Christ-Church dore," 420, 495 ; " at Christ-Church gate," 1061 ; " at S. Magnus Corner," 676 ; " at the three cranes in the Vin-tree," 748 ; " shop over against Saint Sepulchres Church without Newgate," 767 ; " shop at the south entry of the Royal Exchange," 767 ; " at his House called the Lodge in Chancery Lane, over against Lincolnes Inne," 781 ; " shop in Saint Dunston's churchyard in Fleet Street," 791 ; " at the golden Dragon in Fleet Street, 1057 ; " " at the great South doore of Pauls," 595, 1042 ; in " Pauls churchyard at the signe of the Bishops head," 279, 280 ; in " Pauls churchyard at the signe of the blacke Beare," 428 ; in " Pauls churchyard at the signe of the Bul-head," 241 ; in " Pauls churchyard at the signe of the crane," 338 ; in " Pauls churchyard at the signe of the Foxe," 312 ; in " Pauls churchyard

Freake, J. Gilbert, F. Gorges, B. Grenville, F. Greville, R. Hawkins, T. Holecroft, E. Hungerford, T. James, R. Killigrew, J. Mallet, R. Mansell, E. Michelborne, B. Michell, H. Montague, G. Moore, H. Neville, A. Palmer, F. Popham, E. Rogers, T. Roe, W. Romney, E. Sandys, J. Scott, E. Seymour, T. Smith, T. Smith clerk of the Privy Council, M. Sutcliffe, J. Trevor, W. Wade, and T. Warr. The work began under the guidance of these men. See, also, His Majesties Council for the London Company of Virginia.

Virginia, North (40° to 45° N. Lat.), the second colony, Company and Council of. See under New England.

Virginia, South (34° to 40° N. Lat.), the London Company for the first colony of (p. 54), afterwards received by their special charter the name of "The Treasurer and Company of Adventurers and Planters of the city of London for the Colony in Virginia" (p. 229) : general mentions, *passim*, see pp. v–xv, xvii, 1, 3, 8, 13, 17, 20, 24, 52–54, 58, 73, 177, 178, 181, 184, 199, 228, 229, 249, 252–254, 276, 277, 283, 284, 286, 295, 296, 313, 316, 317, 332, 402–413, 458, 542, 593, 594, 597, 665, 680, 681, 689, 722–724, 730–733, 735, 751, 752, 760, 766, 780, 798, 802–805, 807, 808, **859, 860**, 1013, 1017.

Incorporation of, see Adventurers, Incorporators, Planters, Subscribers, and Undertakers ; also, Captains, Cities, Citizens, City Companies, Corporations, Countesses, Doctors, Esquires, Gentlemen, Knights, Ladies, Lawyers, Lord-Mayors, Merchants, Ministers, Noblemen, Parliament, Peers, Widows, and Yeoman.

Organization of, see Auditor, Beadle, Bookkeeper, Cashier, Clerks, Committees, Council, Courts, Deputy-Treasurer, Husband, Secretary, and Treasurer.

Records of, vi–x, 64, 428, 460, 464, 466, 807, 808, 874, 890, 934, 935, 1008, 1016, 1041, 1042, 1062, 1063 ; mostly missing, but the originals of the following were probably filed away "in the companies chest of evidences": V, VI., VII., VIII., XII., XIX., XXI., XXII., XXIII., XLIX., LXVI., LXVII, LXXII., C., CII., CXXI., CXXII., CXXXIII., CLV¹., CLV²., CLIX., CLXI., CLXII., CLXIII., CLXXIII¹., CLXXIII²., CXCIV., CC., CCIII., CCLXXIV., CCCXXI., CCCLXI., CCCLXIV. See Documents (not found).

Sundry references : Business of Virginia, 655–657 ; charge of transportation, 252 ; crucial test, 599 ; directions, 75–79 ; ends of, 339 ; enterprise of charge, 503 ; feasible, 339, 340 ;

friends, 367, 619 ; generalitie, 456 ; honour, 352, 798 ; inconvenience, 342 ; instruments, 77 ; means, 463 ; money, may coin, 58 ; new adventurers, 779 ; noble, 339, 340 ; officers of, 233, 273 ; old adventurers, 779 ; piety, 352 ; rumors (false), 354 ; "trewe relation," Percy, 570 ; unmasking of Virginia, 836 ; varnishing reports, 752 ; ways, 339, 341. See Advice, American enterprises, Articles, Bills, Broadsides, Charters, Colonies, Commissions, Companies, Councils, Darkest hour, Declarations, Dedications, Diplomacy, Discouragements, Discourses, Discoveries, Documents, Emigrants, Encouragements, "Epistles Dedicatorie," Evidence, Factions, Founders, France, Instructions, Laws, Letters, Lists, Lottery, Managers, Maps, Narratives, Objections, Objects, Orders, Parliament, Patrons, Peace, Protestantism, Relations, Remarks, Reports, Romanism, Seal, Sermons, Spain, State, Subscribers, Tracts, Trades, United Provinces, Virginia Colony, Voyages, etc.

Virginia, South (34° to 40° N. Lat.), the London Company, etc., His Majesties Council for: viii, x, xii–xiv, 205, 207, 231–240, 247, 249, 250, 252–254, 272, 277, 279, 302, 307, 308, 314, 316, 324, 330, 331, 336–358, 368, 369, 373, 376–384, 392, 428, 439, 445, 461–470, 477, 488–497, 530, 532, 533, 548, 549, 551, 555, 558, 559, 596, 608, 611, 616, 637, 661, 677, 679, 685, 687, 730–733, 752, 761, 775–779, 796–799 (801), 1025, 1028.

Their authority began with the company's first special charter, LXVI., and they were the authors of : LXVII., LXX., LXXII., C., CXIV., CXV., CXXI., CXXII., CXL., CXLII., CXLVIII., CLXI., CLXIII., CCX., CCLIII., CCCXVII., CCCXLII., CCCLIII., CCCLXII.— CCCLXIII. and CCCLXIII. were written by members of this council, and I think that LXVIII., LXXX., and CCXCIV. were also. Nearly all of their prints have been collected together in this work, but their written records are still very largely wanting. See Documents (not found).

Members of (see their biographies). The following were managers from the first (231, 232) : F. Bacon, M. Berkeley, G. Bridges, C. Brooke, G. Carew, H. Carey, E. Cecil, T. Cecil, T. Challoner, H. Clinton, E. Conway, W. Cope, G. Coppin, O. Cromwell, D. Digges. R. Drury, J. Eldred, H. Fanshawe, T. Gates, W. Godolphin, W. Herbert, B. Hicks, H. Hobart, Theo. Howard, R. Killigrew, R. Mansell, P. Manwood, H.